Communications
in Computer and Information Science   1834

Rationale

The CCIS series is devoted to the publication of proceedings of computer science conferences. Its aim is to efficiently disseminate original research results in informatics in printed and electronic form. While the focus is on publication of peer-reviewed full papers presenting mature work, inclusion of reviewed short papers reporting on work in progress is welcome, too. Besides globally relevant meetings with internationally representative program committees guaranteeing a strict peer-reviewing and paper selection process, conferences run by societies or of high regional or national relevance are also considered for publication.

Topics

The topical scope of CCIS spans the entire spectrum of informatics ranging from foundational topics in the theory of computing to information and communications science and technology and a broad variety of interdisciplinary application fields.

Information for Volume Editors and Authors

Publication in CCIS is free of charge. No royalties are paid, however, we offer registered conference participants temporary free access to the online version of the conference proceedings on SpringerLink (http://link.springer.com) by means of an http referrer from the conference website and/or a number of complimentary printed copies, as specified in the official acceptance email of the event.

CCIS proceedings can be published in time for distribution at conferences or as post-proceedings, and delivered in the form of printed books and/or electronically as USBs and/or e-content licenses for accessing proceedings at SpringerLink. Furthermore, CCIS proceedings are included in the CCIS electronic book series hosted in the SpringerLink digital library at http://link.springer.com/bookseries/7899. Conferences publishing in CCIS are allowed to use Online Conference Service (OCS) for managing the whole proceedings lifecycle (from submission and reviewing to preparing for publication) free of charge.

Publication process

The language of publication is exclusively English. Authors publishing in CCIS have to sign the Springer CCIS copyright transfer form, however, they are free to use their material published in CCIS for substantially changed, more elaborate subsequent publications elsewhere. For the preparation of the camera-ready papers/files, authors have to strictly adhere to the Springer CCIS Authors' Instructions and are strongly encouraged to use the CCIS LaTeX style files or templates.

Abstracting/Indexing

CCIS is abstracted/indexed in DBLP, Google Scholar, EI-Compendex, Mathematical Reviews, SCImago, Scopus. CCIS volumes are also submitted for the inclusion in ISI Proceedings.

How to start

To start the evaluation of your proposal for inclusion in the CCIS series, please send an e-mail to ccis@springer.com.

Constantine Stephanidis · Margherita Antona ·
Stavroula Ntoa · Gavriel Salvendy
Editors

HCI International 2023 Posters

25th International Conference
on Human-Computer Interaction, HCII 2023
Copenhagen, Denmark, July 23–28, 2023
Proceedings, Part III

Editors
Constantine Stephanidis
University of Crete and Foundation for
Research and Technology - Hellas (FORTH)
Heraklion, Crete, Greece

Margherita Antona
Foundation for Research and Technology -
Hellas (FORTH)
Heraklion, Crete, Greece

Stavroula Ntoa
Foundation for Research and Technology -
Hellas (FORTH)
Heraklion, Crete, Greece

Gavriel Salvendy
University of Central Florida
Orlando, FL, USA

ISSN 1865-0929   ISSN 1865-0937 (electronic)
Communications in Computer and Information Science
ISBN 978-3-031-35997-2   ISBN 978-3-031-35998-9 (eBook)
https://doi.org/10.1007/978-3-031-35998-9

This Springer imprint is published by the registered company Springer Nature Switzerland AG
The registered company address is: Gewerbestrasse 11, 6330 Cham, Switzerland

Foreword

Human-computer interaction (HCI) is acquiring an ever-increasing scientific and industrial importance, as well as having more impact on people's everyday lives, as an ever-growing number of human activities are progressively moving from the physical to the digital world. This process, which has been ongoing for some time now, was further accelerated during the acute period of the COVID-19 pandemic. The HCI International (HCII) conference series, held annually, aims to respond to the compelling need to advance the exchange of knowledge and research and development efforts on the human aspects of design and use of computing systems.

The 25th International Conference on Human-Computer Interaction, HCI International 2023 (HCII 2023), was held in the emerging post-pandemic era as a 'hybrid' event at the AC Bella Sky Hotel and Bella Center, Copenhagen, Denmark, during July 23–28, 2023. It incorporated the 21 thematic areas and affiliated conferences listed below.

A total of 7472 individuals from academia, research institutes, industry, and government agencies from 85 countries submitted contributions, and 1578 papers and 396 posters were included in the volumes of the proceedings that were published just before the start of the conference, these are listed below. The contributions thoroughly cover the entire field of human-computer interaction, addressing major advances in knowledge and effective use of computers in a variety of application areas. These papers provide academics, researchers, engineers, scientists, practitioners and students with state-of-the-art information on the most recent advances in HCI.

The HCI International (HCII) conference also offers the option of presenting 'Late Breaking Work', and this applies both for papers and posters, with corresponding volumes of proceedings that will be published after the conference. Full papers will be included in the 'HCII 2023 - Late Breaking Work - Papers' volumes of the proceedings to be published in the Springer LNCS series, while 'Poster Extended Abstracts' will be included as short research papers in the 'HCII 2023 - Late Breaking Work - Posters' volumes to be published in the Springer CCIS series.

I would like to thank the Program Board Chairs and the members of the Program Boards of all thematic areas and affiliated conferences for their contribution towards the high scientific quality and overall success of the HCI International 2023 conference. Their manifold support in terms of paper reviewing (single-blind review process, with a minimum of two reviews per submission), session organization and their willingness to act as goodwill ambassadors for the conference is most highly appreciated.

This conference would not have been possible without the continuous and unwavering support and advice of Gavriel Salvendy, founder, General Chair Emeritus, and Scientific Advisor. For his outstanding efforts, I would like to express my sincere appreciation to Abbas Moallem, Communications Chair and Editor of HCI International News.

July 2023   Constantine Stephanidis

HCI International 2023 Thematic Areas and Affiliated Conferences

Thematic Areas

- HCI: Human-Computer Interaction
- HIMI: Human Interface and the Management of Information

Affiliated Conferences

- EPCE: 20th International Conference on Engineering Psychology and Cognitive Ergonomics
- AC: 17th International Conference on Augmented Cognition
- UAHCI: 17th International Conference on Universal Access in Human-Computer Interaction
- CCD: 15th International Conference on Cross-Cultural Design
- SCSM: 15th International Conference on Social Computing and Social Media
- VAMR: 15th International Conference on Virtual, Augmented and Mixed Reality
- DHM: 14th International Conference on Digital Human Modeling and Applications in Health, Safety, Ergonomics and Risk Management
- DUXU: 12th International Conference on Design, User Experience and Usability
- C&C: 11th International Conference on Culture and Computing
- DAPI: 11th International Conference on Distributed, Ambient and Pervasive Interactions
- HCIBGO: 10th International Conference on HCI in Business, Government and Organizations
- LCT: 10th International Conference on Learning and Collaboration Technologies
- ITAP: 9th International Conference on Human Aspects of IT for the Aged Population
- AIS: 5th International Conference on Adaptive Instructional Systems
- HCI-CPT: 5th International Conference on HCI for Cybersecurity, Privacy and Trust
- HCI-Games: 5th International Conference on HCI in Games
- MobiTAS: 5th International Conference on HCI in Mobility, Transport and Automotive Systems
- AI-HCI: 4th International Conference on Artificial Intelligence in HCI
- MOBILE: 4th International Conference on Design, Operation and Evaluation of Mobile Communications

List of Conference Proceedings Volumes Appearing Before the Conference

1. LNCS 14011, Human-Computer Interaction: Part I, edited by Masaaki Kurosu and Ayako Hashizume
2. LNCS 14012, Human-Computer Interaction: Part II, edited by Masaaki Kurosu and Ayako Hashizume
3. LNCS 14013, Human-Computer Interaction: Part III, edited by Masaaki Kurosu and Ayako Hashizume
4. LNCS 14014, Human-Computer Interaction: Part IV, edited by Masaaki Kurosu and Ayako Hashizume
5. LNCS 14015, Human Interface and the Management of Information: Part I, edited by Hirohiko Mori and Yumi Asahi
6. LNCS 14016, Human Interface and the Management of Information: Part II, edited by Hirohiko Mori and Yumi Asahi
7. LNAI 14017, Engineering Psychology and Cognitive Ergonomics: Part I, edited by Don Harris and Wen-Chin Li
8. LNAI 14018, Engineering Psychology and Cognitive Ergonomics: Part II, edited by Don Harris and Wen-Chin Li
9. LNAI 14019, Augmented Cognition, edited by Dylan D. Schmorrow and Cali M. Fidopiastis
10. LNCS 14020, Universal Access in Human-Computer Interaction: Part I, edited by Margherita Antona and Constantine Stephanidis
11. LNCS 14021, Universal Access in Human-Computer Interaction: Part II, edited by Margherita Antona and Constantine Stephanidis
12. LNCS 14022, Cross-Cultural Design: Part I, edited by Pei-Luen Patrick Rau
13. LNCS 14023, Cross-Cultural Design: Part II, edited by Pei-Luen Patrick Rau
14. LNCS 14024, Cross-Cultural Design: Part III, edited by Pei-Luen Patrick Rau
15. LNCS 14025, Social Computing and Social Media: Part I, edited by Adela Coman and Simona Vasilache
16. LNCS 14026, Social Computing and Social Media: Part II, edited by Adela Coman and Simona Vasilache
17. LNCS 14027, Virtual, Augmented and Mixed Reality, edited by Jessie Y. C. Chen and Gino Fragomeni
18. LNCS 14028, Digital Human Modeling and Applications in Health, Safety, Ergonomics and Risk Management: Part I, edited by Vincent G. Duffy
19. LNCS 14029, Digital Human Modeling and Applications in Health, Safety, Ergonomics and Risk Management: Part II, edited by Vincent G. Duffy
20. LNCS 14030, Design, User Experience, and Usability: Part I, edited by Aaron Marcus, Elizabeth Rosenzweig and Marcelo Soares
21. LNCS 14031, Design, User Experience, and Usability: Part II, edited by Aaron Marcus, Elizabeth Rosenzweig and Marcelo Soares

22. LNCS 14032, Design, User Experience, and Usability: Part III, edited by Aaron Marcus, Elizabeth Rosenzweig and Marcelo Soares
23. LNCS 14033, Design, User Experience, and Usability: Part IV, edited by Aaron Marcus, Elizabeth Rosenzweig and Marcelo Soares
24. LNCS 14034, Design, User Experience, and Usability: Part V, edited by Aaron Marcus, Elizabeth Rosenzweig and Marcelo Soares
25. LNCS 14035, Culture and Computing, edited by Matthias Rauterberg
26. LNCS 14036, Distributed, Ambient and Pervasive Interactions: Part I, edited by Norbert Streitz and Shin'ichi Konomi
27. LNCS 14037, Distributed, Ambient and Pervasive Interactions: Part II, edited by Norbert Streitz and Shin'ichi Konomi
28. LNCS 14038, HCI in Business, Government and Organizations: Part I, edited by Fiona Fui-Hoon Nah and Keng Siau
29. LNCS 14039, HCI in Business, Government and Organizations: Part II, edited by Fiona Fui-Hoon Nah and Keng Siau
30. LNCS 14040, Learning and Collaboration Technologies: Part I, edited by Panayiotis Zaphiris and Andri Ioannou
31. LNCS 14041, Learning and Collaboration Technologies: Part II, edited by Panayiotis Zaphiris and Andri Ioannou
32. LNCS 14042, Human Aspects of IT for the Aged Population: Part I, edited by Qin Gao and Jia Zhou
33. LNCS 14043, Human Aspects of IT for the Aged Population: Part II, edited by Qin Gao and Jia Zhou
34. LNCS 14044, Adaptive Instructional Systems, edited by Robert A. Sottilare and Jessica Schwarz
35. LNCS 14045, HCI for Cybersecurity, Privacy and Trust, edited by Abbas Moallem
36. LNCS 14046, HCI in Games: Part I, edited by Xiaowen Fang
37. LNCS 14047, HCI in Games: Part II, edited by Xiaowen Fang
38. LNCS 14048, HCI in Mobility, Transport and Automotive Systems: Part I, edited by Heidi Krömker
39. LNCS 14049, HCI in Mobility, Transport and Automotive Systems: Part II, edited by Heidi Krömker
40. LNAI 14050, Artificial Intelligence in HCI: Part I, edited by Helmut Degen and Stavroula Ntoa
41. LNAI 14051, Artificial Intelligence in HCI: Part II, edited by Helmut Degen and Stavroula Ntoa
42. LNCS 14052, Design, Operation and Evaluation of Mobile Communications, edited by Gavriel Salvendy and June Wei
43. CCIS 1832, HCI International 2023 Posters - Part I, edited by Constantine Stephanidis, Margherita Antona, Stavroula Ntoa and Gavriel Salvendy
44. CCIS 1833, HCI International 2023 Posters - Part II, edited by Constantine Stephanidis, Margherita Antona, Stavroula Ntoa and Gavriel Salvendy
45. CCIS 1834, HCI International 2023 Posters - Part III, edited by Constantine Stephanidis, Margherita Antona, Stavroula Ntoa and Gavriel Salvendy
46. CCIS 1835, HCI International 2023 Posters - Part IV, edited by Constantine Stephanidis, Margherita Antona, Stavroula Ntoa and Gavriel Salvendy

47. CCIS 1836, HCI International 2023 Posters - Part V, edited by Constantine Stephanidis, Margherita Antona, Stavroula Ntoa and Gavriel Salvendy

https://2023.hci.international/proceedings

Preface

Preliminary scientific results, professional news, or work in progress, described in the form of short research papers (4–8 pages long), constitute a popular submission type among the International Conference on Human-Computer Interaction (HCII) participants. Extended abstracts are particularly suited for reporting ongoing work, which can benefit from a visual presentation, and are presented during the conference in the form of posters. The latter allow a focus on novel ideas and are appropriate for presenting project results in a simple, concise, and visually appealing manner. At the same time, they are also suitable for attracting feedback from an international community of HCI academics, researchers, and practitioners. Poster submissions span the wide range of topics of all HCII thematic areas and affiliated conferences.

Five volumes of the HCII 2023 proceedings are dedicated to this year's poster extended abstracts, in the form of short research papers, focusing on the following topics:

- Volume I: HCI Design - Theoretical Approaches, Methods and Case Studies; Multimodality and Novel Interaction Techniques and Devices; Perception and Cognition in Interaction; Ethics, Transparency and Trust in HCI; User Experience and Technology Acceptance Studies
- Volume II: Supporting Health, Psychological Wellbeing, and Fitness; Design for All, Accessibility and Rehabilitation Technologies; Interactive Technologies for the Aging Population
- Volume III: Interacting with Data, Information and Knowledge; Learning and Training Technologies; Interacting with Cultural Heritage and Art
- Volume IV: Social Media - Design, User Experiences and Content Analysis; Advances in eGovernment Services; eCommerce, Mobile Commerce and Digital Marketing - Design and Customer Behavior; Designing and Developing Intelligent Green Environments; (Smart) Product Design
- Volume V: Driving Support and Experiences in Automated Vehicles; eXtended Reality - Design, Interaction Techniques, User Experience and Novel Applications; Applications of AI Technologies in HCI

Poster extended abstracts are included for publication in these volumes following a minimum of two single-blind reviews from the members of the HCII 2023 international Program Boards. We would like to thank all of them for their invaluable contribution, support, and efforts.

July 2023

Constantine Stephanidis
Margherita Antona
Stavroula Ntoa
Gavriel Salvendy

25th International Conference on Human-Computer Interaction (HCII 2023)

The full list with the Program Board Chairs and the members of the Program Boards of all thematic areas and affiliated conferences of HCII2023 is available online at:

http://www.hci.international/board-members-2023.php

HCI International 2024 Conference

The 26th International Conference on Human-Computer Interaction, HCI International 2024, will be held jointly with the affiliated conferences at the Washington Hilton Hotel, Washington, DC, USA, June 29 – July 4, 2024. It will cover a broad spectrum of themes related to Human-Computer Interaction, including theoretical issues, methods, tools, processes, and case studies in HCI design, as well as novel interaction techniques, interfaces, and applications. The proceedings will be published by Springer. More information will be made available on the conference website: http://2024.hci.international/.

General Chair
Prof. Constantine Stephanidis
University of Crete and ICS-FORTH
Heraklion, Crete, Greece
Email: general_chair@hcii2024.org

https://2024.hci.international/

Contents - Part III

Interacting with Data, Information and Knowledge

Voyaging: Crowdsource Application for Safe Travelling Experience 3
   Richie Ang and Owen Noel Newton Fernando

BingoFit: A Bingo Clothes Presentation System for Utilizing Owned
Clothes 10
   Yukino Aoki, Kouta Yokoyama, and Satoshi Nakamura

Exploring Design Principles for Speech-to-Visualization Data Entry
Interfaces 18
   Tamara Babaian

Crowdsourcing a More Realistic Emotional Lexicon Process 24
   Robert Ball, Joshua Jensen, and Samuel Romine

Exploring Opportunities for Visualization-Based Information Translation
in Environmental Education: Using Taiwan's Chenglong Wetland
as an Example 32
   Wen-Huei Chou, Yao-Fei Huang, Jia-Yin Shih, and Chung-Wen Hung

A Harmonized Multi-lingual Terminology for ICT Devices and Services
with a User-Centric View 40
   Emmanuel Darmois and Martin Boecker

ProtoLife: Enhancing Mobile Multimedia Narratives Through Prototyping
Techniques 46
   Yifan Deng

Development of Interactive Teaching Device for Difficult Teaching
of Collaborative Robot 54
   Jeyoun Dong, Dongyeop Kang, and Seung-Woo Nam

Exchanging Files Securely in a Stationary Telepresence Consultation
System Using Jitsi Meet 60
   *Dennis Eller, Matti Laak, Dominic Becking, Anne-Kathrin Schmitz,
   Udo Seelmeyer, Philipp Waag, and Marc Weinhardt*

Iteration, Iteration, Iteration: How Restructuring Data Can Reveal
Complex Relationships Between Chronic Illnesses and the Apps Intended
to Support Them 68
   Hannah Field, Lisa Thomas, and Emmanuel Tsekleves

Development of Applications that Integrate Information from Diverse
Systems with a Focus on Information Organization 76
   Mayo Fukata and Eiichi Hayakawa

Characterizing the Information Consumer Behavior: An Explorative Case
Study in a Chilean Organization Department 83
   María Paz Godoy, Cristian Rusu, Isidora Azócar, and Noor Yaser

Privacy-Preserving Data Management and Provision System for Personal
Data Store 90
   Kaisei Kajita, Kinji Matsumura, and Go Ohtake

SPOTLink - An Interactive User-Driven Tool to Document and Share
Assembly Knowledge in SME 97
   Christian Kruse and Daniela Becks

Understanding the Relationship Between Behaviours Using Semantic
Technologies 103
   Suvodeep Mazumdar, Fatima Maikore, Vitaveska Lanfranchi,
   Sneha Roychowdhury, Richard Webber, Harriet M. Baird,
   Muhammad Basir, Vyv Huddy, Paul Norman, Richard Rowe,
   Alexander J. Scott, and Thomas L. Webb

Supporting Nail Art Consultation by Automatic Image Selection
and Visual Information Sharing 110
   Yoshino Minakawa and Hiroshi Hosobe

Clarifying Patterns in Team Communication Through Extended
Recurrence Plot with Levenshtein Distance 118
   Saki Namura, Sunichi Tada, Yingting Chen, Taro Kanno,
   Haruka Yoshida, Daisuke Karikawa, Kohei Nonose, and Satoru Inoue

Quantitative Assessment Methods for the Needs of Airline Safety
Management Personnel 124
   Xueyan Peng and Yuan Zhang

Using Automatic and Semi-automatic Methods for Digitizing
the Dictionary of Trinidad and Tobago English/Creole into a Graph
Database 133
   Divindra Ramai and Phaedra S. Mohammed

I Have No Idea What Are These Terms! Exploring Users' Understanding
and Interpretation of Genealogy Results 141
   Lipsarani Sahoo and Mohamed Shehab

Modeling Foraging Behavior in GitHub 149
   Abim Sedhain, Yao Wang, Brett Mckinney, and Sandeep Kaur Kuttal

iWIll: A Real-Time Mobile Application to Expedite First-Aid and Reduce
Casualties 156
   Palaniselvam Shyam Sundar and Owen Noel Newton Fernando

"User Journeys": A Tool to Align Cross-Functional Teams 163
   Jessica Tan

Supporting Presentation Document Creation Using Visualization
of Logical Relationship Between Slides 168
   Hiroka Umetsu, Mitsuhiro Goto, and Akihiro Kashihara

Generation of Instruction Range Map Based on Analysis of Demonstrative
Words and Spatial Domain for Reduction of Miscommunication Among
Chinese, Vietnamese and Japanese in Care Facilities 176
   Binyu Wang, Weiqing Xiang, Masanari Ichikawa, and Yugo Takeuchi

Learning and Training Technologies

Tiktok as a Learning Tool for Elementary School Students 187
   Paulina Magally Amaluisa Rendón, Carlos Alberto Espinosa-Pinos,
   and María Giovanna Núñez-Torres

Automated Content Generation for Intelligent Tutoring Systems 194
   Andrew Emanuel Attard and Alexiei Dingli

E-Newspaper in International Chinese Language Education 202
   Shasha Cai

The iMagic E-Learning System on University Students' Achievement
During the COVID-19 Pandemic: Based on Learner-Centered Instruction 210
   Wei-Ting Chen and Mengping Tsuei

Effect of Online Synchronous Peer-Tutoring Writing on the Writing
Performance and Attitude of Children 216
   Wei-Ting Chen and Mengping Tsuei

Investigation of Chromatic Perception of School Children During HCI
in Computer-Supported Collaborative Learning 225
    Niki Choudhury and Jyoti Kumar

Learning Experience of Students:: A Framework for Individual Differences
Based on Emotions to Design e-Learning Systems 231
    Jelle de Boer and Jos Tolboom

Augmented Reality as a Promoter of Visualization for the Learning
of Mathematics in Ninth-Year of Basic Education 238
    Carlos Alberto Espinosa-Pinos, Paulina Magally Amaluisa Rendón,
    María Giovanna Núñez-Torres, and Juan Quinatoa-Casicana

Wordhyve: A MALL Innovation to Support Incidental Vocabulary Learning ... 246
    Mohammad Nehal Hasnine, Junji Wu, and Hiroshi Ueda

Evaluating Young Children's Computational Thinking Skills Using
a Mixed-Reality Environment 251
    Jaejin Hwang, Sungchul Lee, Yanghee Kim, and Mobasshira Zaman

Exergame to Promote Exercise Outside Physical Education Classes
During a Pandemic 259
    Akari Kanei and Hiroyuki Manabe

Development and Application Study of Coding Learning Game Using
Augmented Reality-Based Tangible Block Chips for Children of Low Age
Groups 267
    Nayoung Kim

Challenges in Cybersecurity Group Interoperability Training 273
    Virgilijus Krinickij and Linas Bukauskas

Research on the Preference of University Students for the Form of Library
Desktop Partition 279
    Jinzhu Li and Zhanying Gao

Exploring the Potential of Augmented Reality in English Language
Learning: Designing an Interactive Pronunciation Training App 288
    Farzin Matin and Eleni Mangina

Integrating 360 Degree, Virtual Reality (VR) Content via Head Mounted
Displays (HMD) into Social Sciences Classes 296
    Brian J. Mihalik, Hyunsu Kim, and Linda Mihalik

Design of BPM Processes in Higher Education in Ecuador 303
Rosa Molina-Izurieta, Jorge Alvarez-Tello, Mireya Zapata,
and Pedro Robledo

Model Educational ReVIso Based on Virtual Reality 311
Jose Ricardo Mondragon Regalado, Alexander Huaman Monteza,
Julio César Montenegro Juárez, Jannier Alberto Montenegro Juárez,
Abelardo Hurtado Villanueva, Nazario Aguirre Baique,
Julio Arévalo Reátegui, and Norma Judit Padilla Suárez

From Physical to Digital Storytelling. A Comparative Case in School
Education 318
María Giovanna Núñez-Torres, Paulina Magally Amaluisa Rendón,
and Carlos Alberto Espinosa-Pinos

Interactive Course Materials in Higher Institute Learning 325
Jabez Ng Yong Xin, Chia Wen Cheng, Trinh Tuan Dung,
and Owen Noel Newton Fernando

Data-Driven Approach for Student Engagement Modelling Based
on Learning Behaviour 334
Fidelia A. Orji, Somayeh Fatahi, and Julita Vassileva

Enhancing First-Generation College Students' Prosocial Motivation
in Human-Computer Interaction Design: A Review of Literature 343
Hye Jeong Park, Yongyeon Cho, and Huiwon Lim

Investigating Factors that Influence Learning Outcomes in K-12 Online
Education: The Role of Teachers' Presence Skill and Students' Grade 351
Lingli Pi, Jiayi Hou, Fei Wang, and Jingyu Zhang

Research on the Personalized Design of Gamification Element in E-learning ... 358
Qiuyue Zhao, Dong Min Cho, and Maoning Li

Interacting with Cultural Heritage and Art

Research on the Design of Building a Personalized Intelligent Art
Interaction System from the Perspective of Scenes 367
Yihui Cai, Yi Ji, Xudong Cai, Yinghe Xiao, Zhenni Li, and Shaolong Zheng

Insights on Metrics' Correlation of Creativity Assessment for Museum
Cultural and Creative Product Design 376
Hui Cheng, Shijian Luo, Bingjian Liu, Liang Xia, Jing Xie, and Xiao Qiu

Research on Folk Belief Space in Fengzhou Ancient Town Based on GIS 385
  Yue Cui, Jie Zhang, Ying Zhang, Chenglin He, and Dashuai Liu

Digital Construction Strategy of Yangtze National Cultural Park Based
on Digital Twinning Technology 393
  Lingjing Duan and Yangshuo Zheng

Research on the Digital Protection and Inheritance of Yao Nationality
Costumes—Take the Yao Nationality in Liannan, Guangdong
as an Example 399
  Yixin Fan and Xiaoping Hu

Connecting Historic Photographs with the Modern Landscape 408
  Michalis Foukarakis, Orestis Faltakas, Giannis Frantzeskakis,
  Emmanouil Ntafotis, Emmanouil Zidianakis, Eirini Kontaki,
  Constantina Manoli, Stavroula Ntoa, Nikolaos Partarakis,
  and Constantine Stephanidis

Artificial Intelligence Painting Interactive Experience Discovers
Possibilities for Emotional Healing in the Post-pandemic Era 415
  Tanhao Gao, Dingwei Zhang, Guanqing Hua, Yue Qiao,
  and Hongtao Zhou

Research on Protection of Village Cultural Heritage Based on Residents'
Perception and Experience—A Case Study of Fengzhou Ancient Town,
Nan'an City, Fujian Province 426
  Chenglin He, Jie Zhang, Dashuai Liu, Yue Cui, and Ying Zhang

The Future of the Performing Arts with Extended Reality 440
  Tanja Kojić, Iva Srnec Hamer, Maurizio Vergari, and Sebastian Möller

Information and Communication Technology in Yogyakarta Heritage
Tourism Marketing 446
  Aromah Udaningrum Kusumadewi and Filosa Gita Sukmono

Use of Semiotics on the Character Development of Choreography 453
  Jui-Hsiang Lee and Shu-Ling Chiu

Interaction Design Practice of Luohua Bird Embroidery Jacket Information
in Mixed Reality Context 461
  Chenlu Li and Songhua Gao

Research on Systematic Design Framework of Subway Public Art Based
on Urban Spirit 470
  Lian Liu and Boyuan Zhang

Newbie Guides for Omnidirectional Guidance
in Head-Mounted-Device-Based Museum Applications 478
  Yu Liu, Yan Huang, and Ulrike Spierling

A Study on Exhibitions of Art Interventions for Environmental
Sustainability in Rural Communities 486
  Li-Shu Lu and Jia-Yi Liu

Digital Information Provision on Gastronomic Tourism 499
  Vassiliki Neroutsou, Michalis Methimakis, Eirini Kontaki,
  Emmanouil Zidianakis, Argiro Petraki, Eirini Sykianaki,
  Stavroula Ntoa, Nikolaos Partarakis, George Kapnas,
  and Constantine Stephanidis

What are the Drivers in Cultural Development 510
  Matthias Rauterberg and Pertti Saariluoma

Study on the Living Inheritance Strategies of Funan Wickerwork
in the Context of Rural Revitalization 518
  Tianxiong Wang, Jiaxin Fu, Liu Yang, and Xian Gao

Study of Development of Library Cultural and Creative Products
from the Perspective of the Metaverse 527
  Mengli Xu and Junnan Ye

A Study on the Decoding of Regional Cultural Genes and the Design
of Cultural and Creative Products 535
  Junnan Ye and Yue Wu

Analysis on the Characteristics of Advocating Business in the Decorative
Art of ShanShaanGan Guild Hall from the Perspective of Image Semiotics 543
  Zhao Yiming

Visualizing Ocean Fragility: Glitch Art and Social Media in Marine
Conservation 554
  Mickey Mengting Zhang, Yu Shen, and Ihab Salah Ali Mohamed

Research on the Design of Digital Experience of Sichuan Opera
Face-Changing Based on Flow Theory 562
  Xiuhui Zheng, Xudong Cai, and Fangfang Huang

Research on the Phygital Innovation Path of the Art Museums Based
on Public Participation 572
  Li Zhuang and Muzi Zheng

Author Index 581

Interacting with Data, Information and Knowledge

Voyaging: Crowdsource Application for Safe Travelling Experience

Richie Ang[✉] and Owen Noel Newton Fernando

Nanyang Technological University, Singapore 639798, Singapore
`richie002@e.ntu.edu.sg, ofernando@ntu.edu.sg`

Abstract. Tourism has always been an important economic sector around the world with millions of tourists travelling every year. With the recent easing of covid restrictions around the world, the tourism industry has been recovering and growing rapidly. While it is a significant contributor to global economy, it is also a source of danger for tourists. Research studies have found that tourists are vulnerable to a variety of dangers and risk, including injury and death, while visiting tourist attractions around the world. Some of the most common causes of tourist fatalities include road traffic accidents, drowning, falls and crimes. It has been found that in a study done in New Zealand, an estimated 20% of overseas visitor injuries and 22% of fatalities are by tourism related activities.

We have developed a mobile application called Voyager is focused to help users be more informed about the dangers and safety culture of their travel destinations. The Voyager aims to help tourists identify safe locations, understand local law and safety culture. By providing this information, the Voyager aims to minimize the risks associated with tourism and enhance the overall travel experience for users.

Keywords: Mobile interaction · Safety mobile app · Human computer interaction

1 Introduction

Tourism has always been an important economic sector around the world with millions of tourists travelling every year. With the recent easing of covid restrictions around the world, the tourism industry has been recovering and resuming its upward climb. In the first quarter of 2022 alone, there has been a 182% increase in international tourists from the previous year, with about 40 million travelers in the first quarter of 2021 to almost 117 million in 2022 [7].

While international tourism is a significant contributor to the global economy, it is also a source of danger for tourists. Foreign travels expose travelers to unfamiliar infectious diseases, as well as dangers brought on by a greater exposure to unfamiliar transportation and leisure activities. The health and safety risks encountered by foreign travelers are substantially different from their original country and can be increased with the lack of traveler familiarity with the new environment. As such, tourists travelling to

C. Stephanidis et al. (Eds.): HCII 2023, CCIS 1834, pp. 3–9, 2023.
https://doi.org/10.1007/978-3-031-35998-9_1

unfamiliar locations are vulnerable to a variety of dangers and risks, including injury and death. Out of millions of tourists travelling globally every year, it is estimated that 30% to 50% are either injured or become ill while overseas. [9] Some of the most common causes of tourist injuries and fatalities include road traffic accidents, drowning, falls, and crimes [1]. According to a study done in New Zealand, an estimated 20% of overseas visitor injuries and 22% of fatalities are caused by tourism-related activities (Reid, 2017). As the tourism industry recovers, the number of incidents resulting in tourist injuries and fatalities will likely increase.

Tourist safety has been tackled by many existing applications, such as the Emergency App by the US Red Cross and Smart Traveller by the US State Department. The scope of these existing apps covers a limited geographical scope and only encompasses a specific functionality that does not provide for all the needs of a general traveler. In contrast, this study selected all the useful components of existing solutions and combined them into a one-stop tourist safety application.

This study advances beyond previous solutions by implementing a new platform for travelers to obtain safe travel information. A mobile application called Voyager is developed to help users be more informed about the dangers and safety culture of their travel destinations. The objective of the app is to help tourists identify locations that are reviewed as safe by other tourists, understand local laws, and culture, and allow for user to choose recommended travel locations so that travelers can minimize the risks associated with tourism and have a better travel experience.

2 Background and Related Works

Given the significance of the problem when it comes to tourist safety, there exist several existing solutions in the market. In this section, existing solutions that aim to tackle or enhance travelers' safety experience in an unfamiliar environment will be reviewed. Specifically, the review will be divided into two areas, namely (a) research into the impact and awareness of tourist safety and (b) the features and functionalities of relevant and popular traveler's safety mobile application. The section ends with a reiteration of the objectives behind the investigation.

2.1 Related Research

The concept of implementing a technology solution for an existing problem is not new, many studies such as technology acceptance modal (TAM) [10] and the information system success modal (ISSM) [11] have been done to identify the key factors that would enable new technology to benefit the users. It has been found that information quality factor is the most important dimension of technology and that it affects user satisfaction the most, with the second most important dimension being system quality [12–14]. Crucial information that is to be presented to the user for their safety should be verifiable or managed by government bodies to ensure that they are unmodified. In recent years, multiple government initiatives around the world have provided east access to open government data that could allow for innovation using credible data [15].

The use of data and technology has brought many opportunities to the tourism industry. Much research has also been done to examine the impacts of smart tourism technology, with multiple sources identifying that accessibility of information, ease of use, and perceived benefits to be positively correlated to travel experience satisfaction [16, 17, 19]. Smart tourism apps that are implemented effectively have been known to significantly reduce safety risks and augment the perceived safety of the users [18]. Smart tourism technology has shown its effectiveness when implemented with proven modals [18, 20]. The implementation of Voyager aims to reduce safety risks of the general traveler in a new environment through accessible and quality data.

2.2 Related Applications

Within the United States of America, there are two mobile applications that are released by the government or state bodies that aim to provide travel safety information to US travelers. They are the Smart Traveler by the US Department of State and the Emergency App by the American Red Cross. Other popular apps used by users around the world include GeoSure, the travel location ratings app, and Trip Lingo which help travelers overcome language and cultural barriers overseas. The Table 1 provides information on existing applications with features aimed to provide more awareness of tourist safety have been compiled to identify features that incorporated in the Voyager mobile application.

Smart Traveler is a mobile application developed to help US citizens traveling abroad stay safe by providing up-to-date travel advisories and warnings for countries around the world, as well as information on the local laws, customs, and visa requirements of the destinations [3]. Emergency App is a mobile application designed to provide users with a range of tools and resources for emergency responses. The app includes features such as real-time weather alerts, information on American Red Cross shelters, and instructions for first aid and CPR procedures. The application is mainly made to be a comprehensive resource for travelers to prepare for and respond to emergency situations within the United States of America [4]. GeoSure is developed to provide user-reviewed safety and security ratings for over 200 countries and territories around the world, which are based on a range of factors such as crime rates, political stability, and environmental hazards [5]. Trip Lingo is mainly used by travelers to overcome language hurdles when it comes to communicating with the locals. The application provides a voice translator, a phrasebook with phrases for a variety of situations, and a cultural guide on local etiquette [6].

Despite the number of existing popular applications that aim to tackle the problem of tourist safety, each of them provides a feature that focuses on one component that a general traveler needs while travelling. The Smart Traveler and Emergency App are useful applications when it comes to travelling to new environments, however their services are mainly catered to use within the United States with most of the solutions being limited to the general American citizens. As for the GeoSure, it provides an innovative social solution that allows users to have an informed travel plan, the application lacks information on safety risks and guides upon reaching the location. Lastly, Trip lingo is mainly a communication application and does not provide much safety information.So far, there has been a considerable amount of research and solution provided worldwide to combat the issue of tourist safety, however, more could have been done to allow for

Table 1. Comparison on different mobile applications

	Smart Traveler [3]	Emergency App [4]	Geo Sure [5]	Trip Lingo [6]	Voyager
Weather Information		✓			✓
Location Review			✓		✓
Map		✓	✓		✓
Local Emergency Contact		✓		✓	✓
Location Safety Rating			✓		✓
Travel Warning & Alerts	✓	✓			✓
Map of shelters		✓			
Medical phrases in different language				✓	✓
Local Do's and Don'ts, Culture Notes				✓	✓
Local Law	✓				✓
Entry, Exit & Visa Requirements	✓				✓
Emergency Responses		✓			✓

a more convenient way to access all the useful safety information for travelers who are on foreign lands. Therefore, the Voyager application in this paper aimed to provide an all-in-one platform with relevant features from existing applications for the user to effectively plan for their travels and be informed of the local laws and safety responses to minimize the risk associated with tourism.

3 Design and Implementation

3.1 System Overview

The information displayed on Voyager must be up-to-date and accurate. With information quality in mind [12], the data and information utilized for Voyager are mostly through public APIs that from government data platforms or organizations that specialized in

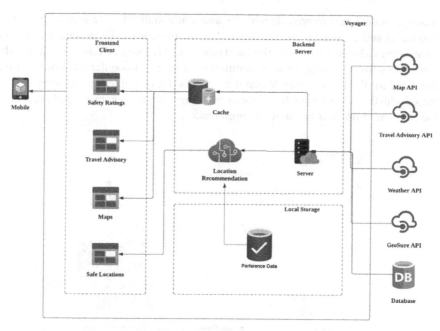

Fig. 1. System Overview

the data we require [15]. Voyager utilizes attraction recommendation algorithm that are based on user's preference data and location to recommend attractions in the user interface. In addition, Voyager acts as a social platform for users to provide additional feedback or insights into the information presented (Fig. 1).

3.2 Features of Voyager

Fig. 2. User Interface for Main Features

Voyager is designed to provide features and functionality for the user who is planning to travel and users who are already at their destinations to be informed about the location safety risks, travel information, and emergency responses. The Fig. 2 shows the user interfaces for browsing through recommended safe and popular locations that are personalized for the current user. When the user first logged in to the app, they will be presented with the safety rating, travel alerts, warnings, and the recommended attractions for the user based on their location and preferences.

Setting Screen   Map / Search Screen   Authentication Screen

Fig. 3. User Interface for Authentication

The Fig. 3 shows the settings page and the login page for the Voyager application. The app includes a page to allow user to search for the location safety information. On every main page, there are built-in responses for a variety of situations, and emergency contacts based on the user's current location and country of origin.

4   Conclusion and Future Work

In this paper, the mobile application called Voyager is presented, it is a novel system that uses preference data to provide safe and popular tourist attractions recommendations. The app also allows users to access relevant safety information and emergency responses for their current location. Unlike other solution that provides a focused safety solution, Voyager provides all the effective component of existing applications into one consolidated platform and is adaptive to the user's location and preferences. There are a few information whereby public APIs does not provide and will be researched upon to enhance the experience for user.

In future work, we plan to improve the user experience of the Voyager client, which is an important factor during emergencies. Since majority of the safety information derives from multiple public APIs, we intend to enhance the system by eliminating such dependencies as much as possible. On top of that, the safety rating on tourist attractions and locations can be further analyzed to identify consistently hazardous locations for user to avoid.

References

1. Reid, C.: The global epidemiology of tourist fatalities 3–4 (2017)
2. Bentley, T., Page, S., Meyer, D.: How safe is adventure tourism in New Zealand? An exploratory analysis. Appl. Ergon. **32**(4), 327–338 (2001)
3. Smart Traveler App. https://2009-2017.state.gov/r/pa/ei/rls/dos/165020.htm. Accessed 2 Feb 2023
4. Emergency App. https://www.redcross.org/about-us/news-and-events/news/2022/check-out-the-new-and-improved-red-cross-emergency-app.html. Accessed 2 Feb 2023
5. GeoSure App Global Homepage. https://geosureglobal.com/. Accessed 2 Feb 2023
6. Trip Lingo App Homepage. http://triplingo.com/. Accessed 2 Feb 2023
7. UNWTO: Tourism Recovery Gains Momentum As Restrictions Ease And Confidence Returns. UNWTO.org. Accessed 22 Feb 2023
8. Leff, A., Rayfield, J.T.: Web-application development using the Model/View/Controller design pattern. In: Proceedings Fifth IEEE International Enterprise Distributed Object Computing Conference, pp. 118–127 (2001)
9. McIntosh, I.B.: The pre-travel health consultation. J. Travel Med. **22**, 143–144 (2015)
10. Marangunić, N., Granić, A.: Technology acceptance model: a literature review from 1986 to 2013. Univ. Access Inf. Soc. **14**, 81–95 (2015)
11. Jeyaraj, A.: DeLone & McLean models of information system success: critical meta-review and research directions. Int. J. Inf. Manage. **54**, 102139 (2020)
12. Alzahrani, A.I., Mahmud, I., Ramayah, T., Alfarraj, O., Alalwan, N.: Modelling digital library success using the DeLone and McLean information system success model. J. Librariansh. Inf. Sci. **51**(2), 291–306 (2019)
13. Zaied, A.N.H.: An integrated success model for evaluating information system in public sectors. J. Emerg. Trends Comput. Inf. Sci. **3**(6), 814–825 (2012)
14. Chiu, P.-S., Chao, I.-C., Kao, C.-C., Pu, Y.-H., Huang, Y.-M.: Implementation and evaluation of mobile e-books in a cloud bookcase using the information system success model. Libr. Hi Tech **34**(2), 207–223 (2016)
15. Chan, C.M.L.: From open data to open innovation strategies: creating e-services using open government data. In: 46th Hawaii International Conference on System Sciences (2013)
16. Pai, C.-K., Liu, Y., Kang, S., Dai, A.: The role of perceived smart tourism technology experience for tourist satisfaction, happiness and revisit intention. Sustainability **12**(16), 6592 (2020)
17. Choi, K., Wang, Y., Sparks, B.: Travel app users' continueduse intentions: it's a matter of value and trust. J. Travel Tour. Mark. **36**(1), 131–143 (2019)
18. Garvey, M., Natraj, M., Das, N., Verma, B., Su, J.: PASSAGE: A Travel Safety Assistant with Safe Path Recommendations for Pedestrians. IUI (2016)
19. Chen, C.-C., Tasi, J.-L.: Determinants of behavioral intention to use the personalized location-based mobile tourism application: an empirical study by integrating TAM with ISSM. Future Gener. Comput. Syst. **96**, 628–638 (2017)
20. Hossain, E., Karim, M.R., Hasan, M., Zaoad, S.A., Tanjim, T., Khan, M.M.: SPaFE: a crowdsourcing and multimodal recommender system to ensure travel safety in a city. IEEE Access **10**, 71221–71232 (2022)

BingoFit: A Bingo Clothes Presentation System for Utilizing Owned Clothes

Yukino Aoki[✉], Kouta Yokoyama, and Satoshi Nakamura

Meiji University, Nakano 4-21-1, Nakano-ku, Tokyo, Japan
yukino.hahaha@gmail.com

Abstract. When we select clothes to wear, various factors such as weather, place, and occasion, in addition to personal preferences, must be considered. It is also essential to view the overall balance of the outfit by properly combining items such as tops, bottoms, and outerwear. However, it is not easy to consider a combination of various clothing items daily. For example, people tend to wear certain clothes frequently, or they might forget clothes in the back of their closet and stop wearing them, resulting in an uneven dressing style. We focus on a bias in the wearing of clothes and research to promote clothing utilization by having people wear all their clothes more regularly. In this study, we propose and implement the "BingoFit" system, which presents a user's clothes using the bingo style. The user uses the BingoFit system by filling in squares showing clothes on a bingo card and then wearing the clothes shown. We conducted experiment tests to use our system during multiple seasons. Then, we found that using BingoFit to select clothes helped them discover new combinations of clothes and encouraged them to wear infrequently worn clothes, thereby promoting their use of the clothes they owned.

Keywords: Clothes · Bingo · Coordination · Fashion

1 Introduction

Clothes are one of the means of expressing individuality, and a person's impression and clothes mutually influence each other [1, 2]. When we select clothes to wear, various factors such as weather, place, and occasion, in addition to personal preferences, must be considered. It is also important to consider the overall balance of the outfit by properly combining items such as tops, bottoms, and outerwear. However, it is not easy to combine various clothing items daily. For example, people tend to have fixed clothes to wear during the week, or they might forget clothes in the back of their closet and stop wearing them, resulting in an uneven dressing style. By choosing clothes unevenly, people cannot utilize all of them, which limits their range of outfits.

To solve this problem, several studies have tried to support fashion coordination by using the user's wearing history [3, 9]. They store the user's past clothing combinations and suggest optimal coordination for the user. In addition, the suGATALOG system [9] compares several combinations by swapping the top and bottom images. However, these methods do not focus on encouraging clothing coordination.

Our work aims to solve this problem of bias in wearing clothes. We focus on enjoying fashion coordination and encouraging the users to wear all their clothes more regularly. In this study, we propose "BingoFit," a clothing presentation system that incorporates the bingo game into fashion coordination and utilizes the fun of combining clothing. In addition, we also implement a prototype system and show its usefulness based on an experiment.

2 Related Work

Several studies have been conducted to provide coordination support based on information about clothing and its past wearing history. Tsujita et al. [3] proposed the "Complete Fashion Coordinator," a system that uses photos of clothes taken in the past and suggests optimal coordination based on the clothing's wearing history and weather data. The system also allows users to receive feedback and evaluations of their coordination from their friends via social networking services. Fukuda et al. [4] proposed "Clothes Recommend Themselves," a system that recommends clothing coordination that the wearer's emotions and reason for wearing based on the garment's characteristics and the wearing history. Evaluation experiments suggest that the system reduces the burden of thinking about daily coordination and allows users to enjoy coordinating their outfits. Cheng et al. [5] classified clothes by impression using neural network learning and automatically found appropriate clothes by inputting the wearing situation into the system. Iwata et al. [6] also recommend suitable coordination for a given garment by learning from photos in fashion magazines.

These studies focus on reducing the time and effort of daily clothing selection based on information about clothing and the past wearing history and do not address the issue of eliminating bias in the number of times certain clothes are worn. In addition, the specific clothing recommendations are intended to encourage passive choice for the user and do not encourage the user to act voluntarily. This research aims to broaden users' coordination options by coordinating their clothes differently from the past and eliminating bias in their clothing selection.

Some research applied bingo games. Tietze [7] led a bingo game for university students in which tasks were presented in bingo squares to advance understanding of the content of a class. The experiment showed that students who completed the bingo task achieved higher grades than the average, suggesting that the application of bingo has a beneficial effect on learning. Kuwamura et al. [8] proposed the Bingo Survey, in which interactive bingo is applied to a survey form to solve the problems of lack of credibility and respondent withdrawal in online surveys. The results of an online survey revealed that the proposed method improves respondents' motivation and increases the number of valid responses. Based on these studies, this research is expected to apply bingo to daily clothing selection to eliminate selection bias without sacrificing the enjoyment of coordination.

3   BingoFit

3.1   Method

In this study, we propose the "BingoFit" system, a clothing presentation system that incorporates elements of bingo, to reduce the bias in the number of times a garment is worn and to expand the range of coordination options of its owner.

The system presents a bingo card with the user's clothes arranged in 25 squares (five rows and five columns) (see Fig. 1). The user selects the clothes to wear, referring to the bingo card. If the user wears clothes on the bingo card, the user can fill their squares.

We expect that users will create new combinations of clothes depending on the arrangement of clothes on the bingo card. For example, combining tops and bottoms in vertical, horizontal, and diagonal lines can make a winning bingo line. Moreover, when clothes are worn, the squares on the bingo card are filled, preventing users from wearing the same clothes in a short period and encouraging them to wear clothes they do not usually wear. We also expect that users will make a wearing plan considering the clothes to be worn in the future and select clothing that suits the weather, place, case, and schedule every day by checking the bingo card.

3.2   Implementation and Usage

We implemented a prototype system of the BingoFit as a system that can be used on the Web using Vue.js, a JavaScript framework. MySQL was used as the database.

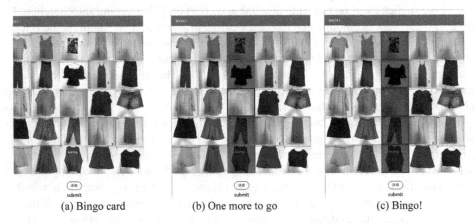

(a) Bingo card   (b) One more to go   (c) Bingo!

Fig. 1. A screen snapshot of the BingoFit system (Color figure online)

In this system, users first take pictures of their clothes and register them in the database. At the beginning of the week, the system extracts 25 pieces of clothing to be displayed on the bingo card from the user's clothes registered in the database. The system randomly selects the garments to be presented. The number of each item presented on the bingo card is determined as equal to the ratio of the total number of tops, bottoms, and all-in-ones owned by each user. The number of tops and bottoms was kept the same not to narrow the range of combinations. Next, the 25 extracted clothes are randomly placed in 25 squares and presented to the user (see Fig. 1(a)). The given clothes and their placement remain unchanged for one week.

When the user clicks on the garment image on the bingo, the system displays a black dotted line around the image. Then the user presses the submit button, and the system records the image in the database as a worn garment. The image is displayed darker than the original image, and the number of days the garment was selected is shown in the upper left corner of the picture. When four squares are selected, either vertically, horizontally, or diagonally, the system displays the red border around the candidate square for bingo (see Fig. 1(b)). When five squares are selected for bingo, all five squares are surrounded by a blue frame (see Fig. 1(c)).

4 Experiment

To clarify the usefulness of our system, we conducted an experimental test to ask participants to use our system. Because the type and number of garments worn varied with the season, we conducted the experiment tests in multiple seasons.

4.1 Experiment Procedure

As a preparation for the experiment, we asked participants to take pictures of all their clothing for each season. We classified the photos into tops, bottoms, and all-in-ones and registered these pictures in our system.

In the experiment, we explained how to use the system and asked the participants to play bingo by wearing the clothes. We also asked them to look at our system when selecting the clothes they would wear daily for one week.

After the one-week experiment, we asked participants to answer a questionnaire about the clothing worn and the bingo plan.

4.2 Results

We recruited nine participants who owned more than 40 pieces of clothing each season. We asked each participant to participate in the experiment in the season in which they could participate. The duration of the experiment and the number of participants were as follows:

- 2021/09/10 – 2021/09/16 (eight participants)
- 2021/09/20 – 2021/09/26 (nine participants)
- 2022/03/05 – 2022/03/11 (five participants)
- 2022/03/12 – 2022/03/18 (five participants)
- 2022/05/02 – 2022/05/08 (six participants)

Five participants participated in all the experiments. Figure 2 shows the results of the bingo cards by three participants who participated in all the experiments.

Through the post-experiment questionnaire, we found that during the experimental period, all participants wore clothes that had not been worn for several years or had used new coordinations of garments. One participant commented, "when I first looked at the bingo card, I identified a row where I would be able to bingo and put on the clothes presented in the row." Thus, some participants commented that they had planned and selected their clothing to reach bingo. On the other hand, some participants commented that it was difficult to bingo in one week, and they had been presented with clothes they could not wear due to the temperature.

Tables 1 and 2 show the average number of squares filled in a week in each season, the probability of "one more to go," and the probability of getting a winning bingo line. Table 1 is for all participants, and Table 2 is for five participants who participated in all the experiments. These results show that the average number of squares of the bingo card filled in a week and the completion rate were relatively high in September. However, the bingo completion rate in September was the lowest and the highest in May. These results show that achieving more bingos with fewer squares increases depending on our system's usage.

Participant A in September   Participant B in March   Participant E in May

Fig. 2. Examples of the bingo card results.

Table 1. Results for all participants.

	Sep	Mar	May	Avg
Squares filled	7.6	6.8	6.8	7.1
One more to go (%)	47.1	40.0	50.0	44.8
Getting Bingo (%)	23.5	30.0	50.0	31.4

Table 2. Results for five participants who participated in all experiments.

	Sep	Mar	May	Avg
Squares filled	7.3	6.8	5.8	6.8
One more to go (%)	50.0	40.0	40.0	44.0
Getting Bingo (%)	20.0	30.0	40.0	28.0

5 Discussion

5.1 Usefulness of the BingoFit System

We found that the BingoFit system creates an opportunity to wear clothes that have not been worn for a long time and helps to eliminate bias in clothing wear. We also found that it could broaden the range coordination range by assisting people in finding new outfits they had not worn before. Based on the above, BingoFit is effective in promoting the utilization of clothing.

On the other hand, some participants commented that winning a bingo line in one week was challenging and presented with clothes they could not wear due to the temperature. To prevent users from being discouraged from filling in the squares, we plan to add a mechanism that allows users to arbitrarily set the clothes presented in the initial stage and the changes to be made.

The experimental results show that more squares can be filled in the high-temperature season than in the low-temperature season. One of the possible reasons for this result is the difference in the degree of freedom in selecting items. In the low-temperature season, the number of items to be worn increases. In addition to tops and bottoms, other garments such as jackets and coats can be worn, and considering combinations of these items becomes more complicated. During warmer temperatures, the number of other items to be considered was relatively small, suggesting the difficulty of selecting clothing on the bingo card was lower.

The results for the participants who participated in all of the experiments showed that they achieved more winning bingo lines with fewer and fewer squares as the experiments progressed. This result may be because the participants learned how to fill in the squares for bingo efficiently and how to coordinate clothing as they used the BingoFit system.

The medium-term experiments found that the BingoFit system was effective for some people but not others. Therefore, we plan to focus our future research on those for whom BingoFit was more effective.

5.2 Relationship Between the Location of Squares and Clothing

In a typical bingo card, the probability of achieving a winning bingo line depends on the position of the filled squares. For example, the square in the center of the bingo card overlaps four columns (one vertical, one horizontal, and two diagonal columns). On the other hand, the square in the center of the top row overlaps only two columns (one vertical and one horizontal). Thus, an effective strategy for winning at bingo is to fill the center of the bingo card.

Table 3 shows the average selection rate for each importance in making a bingo on the cards. The results showed that the selection rate of the square in the center was 35.3%, which was the highest value. The square between the center and the four corners had the lowest selection rate at 23.5%. From these results, we found that participants could choose an effective strategy for winning bingo in the BingoFit system.

To determine whether the clothes in the squares placed close to each other were likely to be combined, the distance between the selected squares on the bingo card was calculated using the Manhattan distance. The expected value of the distance is 3.33, while

Table 3. Selection rate of squares (%).

Classification of squares	Selection rate
Center square	35.3
Corner squares	27.2
Squares between the center and the four corners	23.5
Other squares	28.7

the average value for all participants in the experiment is 3.15. This result indicates that squares were selected that were close to each other were selected. This result may be because it was easier to imagine how the clothes in the squares placed close to each other would look when combined, and it was easier to consider the coordination of the clothes.

These results suggest that it is possible to guide the selection of clothing. Therefore, placing a garment worn less frequently in the central square of the bingo card or placing a garment that has never been combined with a garment in a nearby square may help eliminate bias in the number of times a garment is worn and may promote the discovery of new combinations. We plan to investigate the possibility of guiding selection by such an arrangement.

6 Conclusion

In this study, we proposed and implemented the BingoFit, a bingo-style clothing presentation system that encouraged the discovery of new clothing coordination patterns. To verify the usefulness of our system, we conducted a mid-term clothing coordination experiment using the BingoFit system. The results suggested that coordination using BingoFit supports new fashion coordination and promotes clothing utilization. We also found that the filled squares varied depending on the season and the number of experiments.

Based on these results, we plan to conduct long-term experiments to investigate the possibility of using the number of times the garment is presented and worn and the location of the squares to induce choice.

Acknowledgement. This work was partly supported by JSPS KAKENHI Grant Number JP22K12135.

References

1. Johnson, B.H., Nagasawa, R.H., Peters, K.: Clothing style differences: their effect on the impression of sociability. Home Econ. Res. J. **6**(1), 2–94 (1977)
2. Gibbins, K., Coney, J.R.: Meaning of physical dimensions of women's clothes. Percept. Mot. Skills **53**(3), 720–722 (1981)

3. Tsujita, H., Tsukada, K., Kambara, K., Siio, I.: Complete fashion coordinator: a support system for capturing and selecting daily clothes with social networks. In: AVI 2010, vol. 20, pp. 127–132 (2010)
4. Fukuda, M., Nakatani, Y.: Clothes recommend themselves: a new approach to a fashion coordinate support system. In: WCECS 2011, vol. I (2011)
5. Cheng, C., Liu, D.S.: An intelligent clothes search system based on fashion styles. In: ICMLC, vol. 7, pp. 1592–1597 (2008)
6. Iwata, T., Watanabe, S., Sawada, H.: Fashion coordinates recommender system using photographs from fashion magazines. In: IJCAI 2011, vol. 3, pp. 2262–2267 (2011)
7. Tietze, K.J.: A bingo game motivates students to interact with course material. Am. J. Pharm. Educ. 71(4) (2007)
8. Kuwamura, N., Fuyuno, M., Yoshimura, R.: Application of gamification to online survey forms: development of digital template system "bingo survey" and evaluation. In: 2021 Nicograph International (NicoInt), pp. 62–69 (2021)
9. Sato, A., Watanabe, K., Yasumura, M., Rekimoto, J.: suGATALOG: fashion coordination system that supports users to choose everyday fashion with clothed pictures. In: Kurosu, M. (ed.) HCI 2013. LNCS, vol. 8008, pp. 112–121. Springer, Heidelberg (2013). https://doi.org/10.1007/978-3-642-39342-6_13

Exploring Design Principles for Speech-to-Visualization Data Entry Interfaces

Tamara Babaian[✉]

Bentley University, Waltham, MA 02452, USA
tbabaian@bentley.edu

Abstract. We present an interface for automatic transcription and simultaneous visualization of spoken narratives on a timeline. We discuss the results of initial laboratory testing of the interface and interviews with prospective users of the approach in two different domains. Speech transcription and entity recognition errors inherent in machine-learning-based approaches to natural language processing place special requirements on the system-user interaction. We outline the design principles for this kind of interface based on the results of testing and interviews with potential users. The presented approach differs from other state-of-the-art text-to-visualization systems in that it constructs a visualization from a speech narrative, while automatically identifying data of interest, as opposed to building plot visualization for user-specified data in structured form based on user's spoken instructions.

Keywords: Text-to-visualization · Natural language interfaces · Data visualization · Human-computer interaction

1 Introduction

Advances in Artificial Intelligence (AI) and Natural Language Processing (NLP) have made it much easier for the machines to hear, understand, and respond to us. Voice-based assistants that can handle short commands and answer standalone questions are becoming widely adopted in personal use and as assistants to customers in domains with the cost of making a mistake is not very high [1]. ChatGPT and similar chat-based tools have taken the world by the storm recently, providing useful assistance with many tasks via a chat interface, despite no guarantees of accuracy. Dictation-based data-entry interfaces are used to automate transcription, helping doctors record their notes while being at the patient's side, without a need to go to a computer [2]. In the area of visualizations from speech, novel natural-language-based interfaces can translate spoken instructions to specifications of a variety of plots and charts using ChatGPT-generated Python code [3]. Another, transformer-based deep neural net [4] successfully translates user instructions on building a plot into a language of graphical primitives [5].

Simultaneously with the rapid progress of speech- and NLP-based AI, exciting developments in the field of interactive visualizations help present data and tell stories in ways

C. Stephanidis et al. (Eds.): HCII 2023, CCIS 1834, pp. 18–23, 2023.
https://doi.org/10.1007/978-3-031-35998-9_3

that enable greater insight and in-depth understanding by the readers of newspaper sites and informational portals. Despite these advances, the potential of using these powerful technologies in information systems to support work in business, health, education and so many other domains in transformative ways, remains largely untapped. In this paper, we investigate an approach to creating a timeline visual representation from a narrative, which has broad applicability in a variety of task contexts.

The successes of large language model based chatbots notwithstanding, there are very few examples of state-of-the-art technologies being deployed in workplace information systems. The reasons for this scarcity stem from several associated challenges, which include the complexity of the technology and the high costs of development, as well as the risks associated with potential failures. To create a successful interface that uses built-in AI, requires imagining, designing, implementing, testing and fine-tuning it for the task context and working environment in order to provide clear benefits from the practitioner standpoint [6].

Overcoming the usefulness threshold is a significant challenge for novel interfaces and it often requires the knowledge of the domain practices and task context, for which the interface is developed. General-purpose tools, be that trained language models or user interface libraries, often lack essential specificity. For example, both voice recognition and speech models for natural language processing, developed on corpora consisting of formal, well-structured sentences, typically do not perform well on colloquial and noisy texts, such as those found in social media postings and dialogs. Hence, systems that are supposed to work with unstructured texts require additional development of specialized models combined with support for dealing with the results of imperfect transcription. Similarly, in the domain of user interactions design, the use of generic interface components hinders productivity and is often rejected by users [2]. To create a new interface that provides real advantages to the user in a specific work context, requires careful tailoring based on thorough considerations of the domain, task, and user context, derived from field-based research with potential users and evaluations of prototypes [7, 8]. Careful attention has to be paid to the distribution of labor between the human and a computer, to the interaction affordances and their optimal design rooted in the context of the task context [9, 10].

A new type of system-user interaction involving the use of natural language processing and simultaneous visualization of a spoken narrative is a subject of a design research study presented in this paper. The innovative design described here holds a great potential for broad scope of application domains. The advantage comes from eliminating the need for typing while simultaneously enhancing the process of data entry with a visualization, which aids the user in verifying correctness and completeness of the collected data. Using an implemented prototype interface as an exemplar for an exploratory design investigation, this project addresses the following questions:

1. how to combine speech-based natural language interface for data entry with visualization, specifically, a timeline visualization,
2. what performance issues related to the use of AI were identified during the laboratory assessment of the implemented interface prototype,
3. what design principles were identified and implemented to address those issues,

4. what are the parameters of usability that play a role in different application for the new speech-to-visualization-based interaction model that stem from its application in different domains.

2   The Prototype

Figure 1 presents a snapshot of the interface, implementing the following functionality:

– speech transcription, audio recording, and playback of the recorded audio,
– identification of entities of interest and their highlighting in text,
– an editable summary view of all entities of interest detected in text,
– an interactive, editable timeline view placing entities on a timeline.

Although the prototype was designed to collect contact tracing history for covid patients, it can be reconfigured for other application domains involving retrospective data collection or prospective planning. The prototype works as follows. A user starts recording, simultaneous transcription, entity identification and placement on the timeline by clicking on the recording button in the top left corner of the interface page. While the user speaks, the transcription, in which detected entities of interest are highlighted in color, appears on the page. As entities are detected, they are also placed in a table, which identifies their type and attribution to specific dates, and on a timeline, based on the system's best guess of the date.

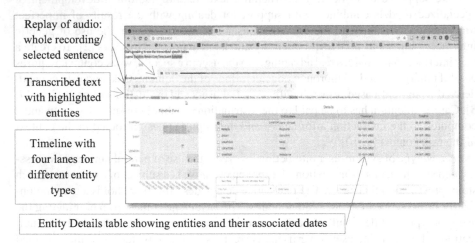

Replay of audio: whole recording/ selected sentence

Transcribed text with highlighted entities

Timeline with four lanes for different entity types

Entity Details table showing entities and their associated dates

Fig. 1. Speech-to-timeline data entry interface run in a browser.

3   Testing

The prototype we tested was implemented using Google Speech-to-Text and Natural Language APIs, Python Dash and Javascript and run in a browser. The application was configured to recognize and highlight references to the following entities: dates and times, events, locations, people, and COVID-19 symptoms. Aside from the symptoms, all other entities were obtained using Google's Natural Language API Entity Recognition functionality. Symptoms were identified via a simple string-matching algorithm.

Laboratory Testing. We have tested the interface in a laboratory setting to capture three different types of input for approximately 5 min:

- a person *reading well-structured text*, like the content of newspaper articles,
- a person narrating a COVID *self-report,* as well as
- a *dialog* between two people conducted over Zoom.

The testing revealed the following initial findings:

a. The performance of automatic transcription, despite a lag in capturing the speech, works sufficiently well in terms of its speed.
b. Number of errors in transcription is lowest when reading an article, and greatest in a dialog.
c. Entity identification rates vary, with significant number of commonly occurring ones such as 'yesterday', 'two days ago' (date/time), 'Tufts University' (location) not being recognized consistently.
d. Names, especially foreign ones, are a problem from both the transcription and entity recognition standpoint.
e. Connecting entities of interest to an associated date based on the meaning of the narrative is the most difficult problem.

User Interviews. To assess attitudes of potential users towards this approach to unobtrusive capture and visualization of temporal information, we conducted two interviews. The interviewees were an IT professional and a college student, both from Northeast of USA and fluent in technology. Each interview started with a demonstration of the prototype capabilities, followed up by the following questions:

1. Would this kind of speech-to-visualization interface be useful for any of your work or personal tasks?
2. If the answer to the first question is yes, for which tasks would you use this interface?
3. Are there specific performance requirements on interface needed for these tasks?
4. What adjustments need to be made to the interface to accommodate these tasks?

The respondents reacted positively to the prospect of using the presented interface, or approach to visualizing a spoken narrative on a timeline, in the work and personal context. The suggested tasks included:

(a) augmenting work Zoom-meeting transcription to capture information about planned deadlines and future meetings (date/time, event entities), people involved (person entity), and topics (which would be a new entity).
(b) using the tool to plan travel, including collaborative trip planning by multiple people, capturing dates, locations, meetings, and people.

The performance observed during the demo was deemed sufficient by both interviewees, provided it is augmented with editing capabilities to make up for the mistakes made by the automation. Even with the need for some corrections, both interviewees saw clear benefits in the automatic capture of the information that otherwise needs to be entered manually from scratch.

In response to questions 3 and 4, one of the participants, observing system's difficulties in recognizing foreign names, suggested the system be pretrained ahead of time to recognize the names of meeting participants. For applications in travel planning, the participant suggested that the interface must allow simultaneous access to editing by multiple collaborators.

4   Design Principles

Based on the findings from laboratory testing and interviews with potential users, we identified the following design principles for speech-to-timeline interfaces:

DP1. Given the presence of transcription errors, the interface must include a mechanism for easy review and editing of the transcription. This requires access to an audio recording, including replay of a part of audio selected by selecting a portion of transcribed text.

DP2. To make up for entity recognition errors, an interface must include an easy way to label entities of interest, as well as to remove such labeling.

DP3. To prevent some recognition errors the interfaces can be pretrained to recognize specific entity instances, for example, locations and names associated with the context of application and specific users.

DP4. The timeline should enable easy adjustment of placement of entities.

DP5. The captured and user-edited information must be easily exportable into different formats and objects, to enable interfacing with calendars and other workplace and personal-use applications.

5   Conclusions and Future Work

We presented findings from a laboratory test of an interface for automated data entry based on transcription of speech and its visualization on a timeline. We described the feedback from potential users, who identified different domains in which the speech-to-timeline approach would be useful. Best on the results of lab testing and interviews, we identified important design principles for these kinds of interfaces. While some of these principles are already implemented, others require further design and evaluation, planned as future work.

References

1. Ilievski, A., Dojchinovski, D., Gusev, M.: Interactive voice assisted home healthcare systems. In: Proceedings of the 9th Balkan Conference on Informatics, Sofia Bulgaria, pp. 1–5. ACM (2019). https://doi.org/10.1145/3351556.3351572
2. Bhatt, V., Li, J., Maharjan, B.: DocPal: a voice-based EHR assistant for health practitioners. In: 2020 IEEE International Conference on E-health Networking, Application & Services (HEALTHCOM), pp. 1–6 (2021). https://doi.org/10.1109/HEALTHCOM49281.2021.9399013

3. Maddigan, P., Susnjak, T.: Chat2VIS: Generating Data Visualisations via Natural Language using ChatGPT, Codex and GPT-3 Large Language Models (2023). http://arxiv.org/abs/2302.02094

4. Luo, Y., Tang, N., Li, G., Tang, J., Chai, C., Qin, X.: Natural language to visualization by neural machine translation. IEEE Trans. Visual Comput. Graphics **28**, 217–226 (2022). https://doi.org/10.1109/TVCG.2021.3114848

5. Tang, J., Luo, Y., Ouzzani, M., Li, G., Chen, H.: Sevi: speech-to-visualization through neural machine translation. In: Proceedings of the 2022 International Conference on Management of Data, pp. 2353–2356. Association for Computing Machinery, New York (2022). https://doi.org/10.1145/3514221.3520150

6. Gil, Y., Selman, B.: A 20-Year Community Roadmap for Artificial Intelligence Research in the US (2019). http://arxiv.org/abs/1908.02624

7. Babaian, T., Lucas, W., Xu, J., Topi, H.: Usability through system-user collaboration. In: Winter, R., Zhao, J.L., Aier, S. (eds.) DESRIST 2010. LNCS, vol. 6105, pp. 394–409. Springer, Heidelberg (2010). https://doi.org/10.1007/978-3-642-13335-0_27

8. Topi, H., Lucas, W., Babaian, T.: Identifying usability issues with an ERP implementation. In: Proceedings of the International Conference on Enterprise Information Systems (ICEIS-2005), pp. 128–133 (2005)

9. Grosz, B.J.: Beyond mice and menus. Proc. Am. Philos. Soc. **149**, 529–523 (2005)

10. Lucas, W., Babaian, T.: The collaborative critique: an inspection method for expert evaluation of user interfaces. Int. J. Hum.-Comput. Interact. **31**, 843–859 (2015)

Crowdsourcing a More Realistic Emotional Lexicon Process

Robert Ball[✉], Joshua Jensen, and Samuel Romine

Weber State University, Ogden, UT 84408, USA
{robertball,joshuajensen1}@weber.edu

Abstract. Even though sentiment analysis and emotion analysis are relatively new subfields of natural language processing, they are increasingly being used by businesses and academics. Their primary objective is to automatically capture the emotions and opinions of people as they wrote their text. Whether the text is from social media, literature, or any other form of text, it is a difficult problem. We present a novel approach by introducing the idea of capturing a range of universal primary emotions (i.e., sadness, happiness, anger, disgust, surprise, and fear). By crowdsourcing the emotion lexicon, it creates a diverse lexicon of emotions. This type of lexicon shows how many people within the same culture and language can have both convergent emotions where everyone universally every agrees that a word has a single emotion behind it (e.g., yummy = happy) and divergent emotions where there is a range of feelings for the same word (e.g., hated = angry, disgusted, and sad). Finally, we empirically prove that emotions are not binary as is often used by modern approaches to this problem (e.g., not sad ≠ happy), showing that people's emotions are complex and nuanced.

Keywords: Sentiment analysis · emotion analysis · natural language processing · emotion · sentiment · opinion mining

1 Introduction

Sentiment analysis is a subset of natural language processing (NLP) that analyzes sentiment, emotion, opinion, and attitudes in text [16]. This subfield of NLP is relatively new and can be traced back to the beginning of the millennium. Sentiment analysis is primarily concerned with polarity, how positive or negative a set of text is [10]. Emotion analysis has the same goal as sentiment analysis but is a newer term that is reserved for analysis that strictly analyzes text for emotions (e.g., sad, happy, etc.) [13].

Sentiment analysis involves various areas of data science, human-computer interaction, and NLP for the purposes of decision making, finding opinions, getting the "feel" of a situation, web scraping, data mining, predicting stock market fluctuations, understanding how much people like or dislike a restaurant, etc. Many modern business decisions are made based on sentiment analysis [8, 10, 11].

However, the previous body of knowledge on this topic makes one faulty assumption – that the relationship between emotion and opinion is consistent across people

C. Stephanidis et al. (Eds.): HCII 2023, CCIS 1834, pp. 24–31, 2023.
https://doi.org/10.1007/978-3-031-35998-9_4

and culture. This assumption is false as explained by Jackson et al., that "emotions can vary systematically in their meaning and experience across culture and language" [9]. In other words, not everyone shares the same opinions nor backgrounds. This creates a fundamental flaw in the current approach to emotion analysis. We propose a new way of doing sentiment analysis and emotion analysis. We account for the realities where people view the world and express themselves differently from one another because individual people have a diversity of thought and emotion from one another that stems from their unique individual differences and experiences in life.

Due to individuality, even with people that agree with the same opinion, they might use different language. Because people are inherently diverse in their backgrounds, word choices, cultures, etc. the same word may evoke different emotions for different people.

2 Related Works

Many scientists through the centuries noted that emotions are directly tied to changes in facial muscles [3]. Perhaps the most influential work surrounding Facial Feedback Theory is Paul Ekman's work where he identified six universal emotions: anger, disgust, fear, happiness, sadness, and surprise. Ekman traveled the world both taking and presenting images of people at different emotional states. He found that in both literate and illiterate societies (where there was no outside exposure of media to confound the study) that people were able to recognize the six universal emotions through facial expressions [15]. Ekman later postulated that there might be more universal emotions than just six that exist [4]. Indeed, work by other scientists found this to be true [1, 2].

Exactly how many emotions are there? Robert Plutchik expanded on Ekman's theory with what is referred to as the wheel of emotions. First, Plutchik added two emotions to Ekman's six: trust and anticipation. Also, each of Plutchik's eight emotions can have a range of strength or intensity. For example, anger can be a range from simple annoyance to extreme rage. In addition, Plutchik suggests that by combining emotions that you get new emotions. [14].

In 2019 Jackson et al. show that aside from the fact that there are primary emotions, "[t]here is a growing recognition, however, that emotions can vary systematically in their meaning and experience across culture and language." In addition, they found that in surveying the emotion theory and linguistics literature that studies that had imposed training phases and forced choice paradigms found more evidence of universal recognition of emotion, but studies that had fewer constraints had more cultural variability [9].

In other words, Jackson et al. found that emotions and words are not universal but have a great deal of cultural and contextual variability. The idea is like what many children ask: "When you see red, do you see the same red as I do?" For emotions, the question would be the following: "When you feel sad, do you feel that same sad that I feel?" The answer is no, which leads to the conclusion that sentiment and emotion lexicons should not have only one sentiment or emotion associate with just one word.

In 2004 Hu and Liu published a seminal work on sentiment analysis. Since then, sentiment analysis is typically performed by comparing a corpus (a set of text of any length) to sets of established words in a lexicon. Hu and Liu's original algorithm counts all the words in the text that are in the positive set and all the negative words that are in the negative set. The remaining words that are not in the positive or negative sets are then considered neutral. If there are more positive words, then the text is considered positive. The same is true for negative and neutral [7].

In 2010 Mohammad and Turney proposed the idea of using emotions instead of polarization (positive/negative) to create a richer lexicon [12]. They later further fleshed out their idea [13]. Their disruptive concept is twofold: First, use crowdsourcing to create the lexicon and second, determining the intensity of each of the emotions for the word along with the typical polarization (e.g., positive/negative/neutral) to words. Their lexicon is called EmoLex. EmoLex is a good step forward, however, recent research from Jackson et al. shows that the more constrained a study with emotion the less varied the result [9].

Our work is heavily based on Mohammad and Turney's work with EmoLex. We will show that the idea of crowdsourcing for emotion is arguably one of the best approaches to getting representative emotions. We also show while sentiment analysis is quite useful that emotion analysis also has a place for richer insight into text.

3   Creating a More Realistic Emotion Lexicon

We created an emotion lexicon that was crowdsourced like EmoLex but with the result that shows the diversity of primary emotions for a given subject.

We got our words to add to the lexicon from two sources: First, we used 3,000 books from Project Gutenberg, a repository of tens of thousands of books in the open domain (either not copyrighted or the copyright has expired). Second, we web scraped over 4.5 million reviews from AllRecipes.com.

Using the NLTK collocations package and the PMI score we used the highest scored adjectives and adverbs unigrams from the Gutenberg books and recipe reviews. We did the same for the highest scored trigrams and quad grams for the recipe reviews to test if phrases would have the same results.

We then set up three surveys that we called "quizzes" for the public. The surveys were loosely patterned after BuzzFeed.com quizzes where participants enjoy finding out how much they know or do not about popular culture facts. We used licensed Pixar *Inside Out* images to appeal to popular culture and entice more people to take our surveys.

We had approximately 35 words or phrases per survey. Our intention was not to create a full emotion lexicon, but to test our theories. Figure 1 shows a screenshot of the choice that volunteers were presented with when they took the survey. The "Food Words" survey was the top unigrams from the AllRecipes.com reviews. The "Words from books" surveys was the top unigrams from the Gutenberg books. The "Cooking Expressions" survey was the top trigrams and quadgrams from the AllRecipes.com reviews.

We also implemented Google's free reCAPTCHA on our website to ensure results were from actual humans. reCAPTCHA is a free service from Google that tests if the current user is a human or not. It helps prevent automatic software from filling out our surveys.

As an added security check, we recorded how long it took volunteers to take the surveys and how long it took assign an emotion to each word. In other words, if someone

After you cooked or baked a recipe and say...

was a huge hit ®

You feel...

Angry | Sad | Happy | Afraid | Surprised
Disgusted | No Emotion

Skip Word

1/48 total words

Instructions

Words produce emotions in people.Pick the first emotion that you feel when you see a word.

If you do not feel that the word that you see has an emotion then click the "No Emotion" button.

If you just can't decide then click the "Skip Word" button.

Fig. 1. Screenshot of the "Cooking Expressions" survey. Note that the emotion buttons were presented in a different order for each volunteer. That order was consistent for the duration of the quiz for that person.

simply clicked as fast as they could without reading the words then we can detect that and disregard those answers.

In addition, to have a good experimental design we randomized the word order for each survey so that each volunteer was given the words in a random order. We also randomized the emotion buttons so that all emotions were presented to different people in different order. When the quiz began the buttons were randomly put in an order. That order was consistent for the duration of the quiz for that person. There were two exceptions: the "No Emotion" button was always last and the "Skip Word" button was on the bottom.

After the volunteer assigned an emotion to all the words or phrases, the person was presented with an optional demographics page that asked for their age, gender, and racial/ethnic background. After selecting the "submit" button they were presented with a colorful and fun results page. The intent of the results page was to share it with their friends who might then take the survey themselves.

4 Results

In this section we present several of our findings. We present examples from our emotion lexicon, show that words do not necessarily have an emotional opposite, and discuss crowdsourcing for emotion lexicon creation.

4.1 Example Words and Their Emotions

We created a proof-of-concept algorithm patterned after the open-source polarity_scores function used with the VADER lexicon in the Sentiment Intensity Analyzer Python NLTK module. Our function takes in any text and reports back the primary emotions associated with it from our emotion lexicon. We do not claim that our proof-of-concept algorithm is as sophisticated as the VADER function in NLTK, but it is used here as a demonstration of using emotions instead of simply using positive, neutral, and negative.

Our function first checks for phrases that match phrases found in our emotion lexicon. For example, if the phrase will make again is found then the functions adds the emotions associated with that phrase. The function then removes all stop words. It then adds all the emotions for unigrams found in the emotion lexicon. Unigrams that are part of phrases that have already been counted are not counted again. Finally, the results are normalized so that they add to 1.0.

Table 1. Results of running the NLTK VADER Sentiment Intensity Analyzer module on All-Recipes.com recipe reviews. This data is provided to show a comparison to our emotion analysis results, which is shown in Table 2.

How many stars the review received	Negative	Neutral	Positive	Compound
1	11%	79%	10%	3
2	7%	80%	13%	24
3	5%	79%	17%	43
4	2%	76%	22%	64
5	2%	71%	27%	72

Table 1 shows the results from the NLTK VADER polarity_scores function on the AllRecipes.com reviews. The reviews were organized from one to five stars with five stars being the most positive reviews. For the 4.5 million reviews that we web scraped, there is not an even distribution of reviews in the dataset, so we randomly selected 90,000 reviews from each star category.

Table 2. Results of running our custom emotion analysis function on the same data from AllRecipes.com as compared to Table 1.

How many stars the review received	Angry	Happy	Disgusted	Afraid	Surprised	Sad
1	19%	20%	19%	2%	4%	36%
2	14%	31%	15%	2%	5%	32%
3	10%	48%	10%	2%	6%	24%
4	3%	81%	3%	1%	6%	6%
5	1%	90%	1%	0%	5%	2%

Considering that the NLTK VADER sentiment analyzer uses a general-purpose lexicon, it did a remarkable job if you consider the trend of negative and positive. There is a clear trend of positive percentage to the number of stars and a clear negative trend to negative percentage to the number of stars. The trend is also clear if you refer to the compound column.

Table 2 shows the results from our custom function using our emotion lexicon. Our results also have positive and negative trends similar to Table 1 except for surprised, which seems to be constant at around 5%.

Interestingly, one can see that happy is very similar to positive from the VADER function. What would be the equivalent of negative? It appears that angry, disgusted, afraid, and sad could all be considered negative. However, Table 2 shows that the different emotions are more nuanced than simply negative and provide a richer and more complete emotion spectrum. This fits the stated goals of emotion analysis much more thoroughly.

How can someone interpret these results? For the VADER results, one possible interpretation is that Table 1 shows how most people would feel in terms of positive and negative sentiment when reading the recipe reviews.

On the other hand, the results from our emotion analysis in Table 2 is that there is a range of emotions that people could feel when reading the lower rated reviews, but for the higher rated reviews there is more of a consensus of a happy feeling. No one person would necessarily feel 19% angry, 20% happy, 19% disgusted, 2% afraid, 4% surprised, and 36% sad when reading the one-star reviews. Our interpretation is that these results are similar to a poll where a wide range of people expressed their feelings.

4.2 Finding that There is no Opposite Emotion

When selecting the words for the surveys we purposely tried to find many words that are opposite in terms of definitions. For example, we used the words *impressive* and *unimpressive* to test how words with opposite meanings correspond to emotions. This is important because modern analysis tools simply negate the resulting emotion when an opposite definition is introduced.

Table 3 shows that most positive words tend to converge on *happy*. On the other hand, negative words have a much larger spectrum of emotion. For instance, even though *awful*, *bad*, and *disappointing* could all be considered negative words, they all differ in the degree of anger, disgust, and sadness. For example, *awful* is 48% anger, 36% disgust, and 16% sad. However, *disappointing* is 26% anger and 74% sad with 0% disgust.

There are many papers that show that sentiment analysis can be improved by using negations such as *not* and *but* (e.g., [5, 6]). The idea is that if a positive word, such as *good* is negated, like *not good*, then the meaning becomes negative. This has been proven to be useful in sentiment analysis many times.

However, we show through our empirical results that simple negation of emotion is insufficient and misleading. Table 3 shows a series of opposite words in sentiment analysis, but that are not automatically opposite in our emotion lexicon. For example, the opposite of *hated* could be *loved*. If *hated* is negative then the opposite, *loved*, should be positive, which it is. However, our results of emotion analysis show that *hated* has an emotion spectrum anger, disgust, and sad, while *loved* has only happy.

One of the reasons that Mohammad and Turney (EmoLex) cited for using Plutchik's emotion theory is that Plutchik's wheel of emotions has opposites [13]. For example, Plutchik's wheel of emotions shows that happy is the opposite of sad.

However, this does not appear to always be the case. For example, the word *loved* is a simplistic word that only has happy associated with it but *hated* is more complex and

Table 3. Example of some words in the emotion lexicon. These examples show a convergence of *happy* with traditionally positive words but show more of an emotion spectrum with traditionally negative words.

	Angry	Happy	Disgusted	Afraid	Surprised	Sad
delicious	0%	100%	0%	0%	0%	0%
wonderful	0%	100%	0%	0%	0%	0%
yummy	0%	100%	0%	0%	0%	0%

	Angry	Happy	Disgusted	Afraid	Surprised	Sad
awful	48%	0%	36%	0%	0%	16%
bad	25%	0%	21%	0%	0%	54%
disappointing	26%	0%	0%	0%	0%	74%

has a range of primary emotions of anger, disgust, and sadness. Looking at the phrases at the bottom of Table 3 shows similar complexities.

We are not prepared to say that Plutchik's wheel of emotions is wrong in terms of opposites, however, we are prepared to say that given our empirical results that the opposite of one emotion is not always simplistically another one. For example, *not sad* does not always equal *happy* for all people, but it does for some people.

Our findings are that there are not universal emotional opposites for all people. Since people come from a broad range of backgrounds and cultures it shows that emotion theory be necessarily as complicated as the people that exhibit the emotions.

5 Discussion

There are now many sentiment lexicons and emotion lexicons. However, each lexicon has a different purpose. For example, Hu and Liu's Lexicon is simple and easy to interpret: Is the given text more positive or negative?

Our proposed approach provides a *range* of primary emotions that different people might feel given a text. In this paper we have provided a novel approach to enrich the field of emotion analysis. We advocate crowdsourcing the original authors of the text or similar authors for statistical sampling. We also show that although negation works well with sentiment analysis that negation does not work in the same way with emotion analysis.

Lastly, we have shown that emotion analysis is not simple. Specifically, we have empirically proved that people are different and that they do not all agree on a single emotion for a single word. Human beings are complex creatures and should be treated thus.

References

1. Cordaro, D.T., Keltner, D., Tshering, S., Wangchuk, D., Flynn, L.M.: The voice conveys emotion in ten globalized cultures and one remote village in Bhutan. Emotion **16**(1), 117–128 (2016)
2. Cordaro, D.T., Sun, R., Keltner, D., Kamble, S., Huddar, N., McNeil, G.: Universals and cultural variations in 22 emotional expressions across five cultures. Emotion **18**(1), 75–93 (2018)
3. Davis, J.I., Senghas, A., Ochsner, K.N.: How does facial feedback modulate emotional experience? J. Res. Pers. **43**(5), 822–829 (2009)
4. Ekman, P., Cordaro, D.: What is meant by calling emotions basic? Emot. Rev. **3**(4), 364–370 (2011)
5. Hatzivassiloglou, V., McKeown, K.: Predicting the semantic orientation of adjectives. In: Proceedings of Annual Meeting of the Association for Computational Linguistics (ACL-1997) (1997)
6. Hiroshi, K., Nasukawa, T.: Fully automatic lexicon expansion for domain-oriented sentiment analysis. In: Proceedings of Conference on Empirical Methods in Natural Language Processing (EMNLP-2006) (2006)
7. Hu, M., Liu, B.: Mining and summarizing customer reviews. In Proceeding of SIGKDD KDM-04 (2004)
8. Hutto, C.J., Gilbert, E.E.: VADER: a parsimonious rule-based model for sentiment analysis of social media text. In: Eighth International Conference on Weblogs and Social Media (ICWSM 2014), Ann Arbor, MI, June 2014 (2014)
9. Jackson, J.C., et al.: Emotion semantics show both cultural variation and universal structure. Science **366**(6472), 1517–1522 (2019)
10. Liu, B.: Sentiment Analysis: Mining Opinions, Sentiments, and Emotions (Studies in Natural Language Processing), 2nd edn. Cambridge University Press, Cambridge (2020)
11. Liu, B.: Sentiment analysis and subjectivity. In: Handbook of Natural Language Processing, vol. 2, pp. 627–666 (2010)
12. Mohammad, S., Turney, P.D.: Emotions evoked by common words and phrases: using mechanical Turk to create an emotion lexicon. In: Proceedings of the NAACL-HLT 2010 Workshop on Computational Approaches to Analysis and Generation of Emotion in Text, Los Angeles, CA, pp. 26–34 (2010)
13. Mohammad, S., Turney, P.D.: Crowdsourcing a word–emotion association lexicon. Comput. Intell. **29**(3), 436–465 (2013)
14. Plutchik, R.: Emotions in the practice of psychotherapy: clinical implications of affect theories. American Psychological Association, Washington, DC (2000)
15. Shiota, M.N.: Ekman's theory of basic emotions. In: Miller, H.L. (ed.) The Sage Encyclopedia of Theory in Psychology, pp. 248–250. Sage Publications, Thousand Oaks (2016)
16. Liu, B.: Sentiment analysis and opinion mining. Synth. Lect. Hum. Lang. Technol. **5**(1), 1–167 (2012)

Exploring Opportunities for Visualization-Based Information Translation in Environmental Education: Using Taiwan's Chenglong Wetland as an Example

Wen-Huei Chou[1], Yao-Fei Huang[2](✉), Jia-Yin Shih[1], and Chung-Wen Hung[3]

[1] Department of Digital Media Design, National Yunlin University of Science and Technology, Yunlin, Taiwan

[2] Department of Graduate School of Design, National Yunlin University of Science and Technology, Yunlin, Taiwan
d11130003@gemail.yuntech.edu.tw

[3] Department of Electrical Engineering, National Yunlin University of Science and Technology, Yunlin, Taiwan

Abstract. Global climate change has caused environmental and ecological anomalies and alterations, including catastrophes caused by climatic variations in the greater environment, the severity of disasters being affected by human factors, changes in ecological species, and transformations of local cultures. The interrelationships between the causal factors behind these phenomena are highly complex. The Chenglong Wetland, located in the Kouhu Township of Taiwan's Yunlin County, is of great local importance but the situations there have been altered by climate change, ranging from wetland formation to the people's livelihoods, economy, and living environment. The general public has a delayed temporal awareness and weak perception of environmental changes. Consequently, local residents find it difficult to form specific ideas and comprehend numerous data and various influencing factors when facing disasters and impending changes. The purpose of this study is to clarify the factors affecting the Chenglong Wetland through a literature review and by holding focus group interviews with local stakeholders. The identified factors then served as the basis for proposing the designs and texts on environmental changes for visualization-based information translation, with the aims of providing users with an in-depth understanding of the issues and stimulating cognitive changes in them, thereby affecting their attitudes and behaviors indirectly.

Keywords: Information Visualization · Environmental Education · ChengLong Wetland

1 Introduction

The global environment and climate are constantly changing. In addition to natural changes, human activities comprise a major source of carbon emissions. Increases in carbon dioxide concentrations [1] and emissions of various greenhouse gases have caused

C. Stephanidis et al. (Eds.): HCII 2023, CCIS 1834, pp. 32–39, 2023.
https://doi.org/10.1007/978-3-031-35998-9_5

sustained increases in average global temperatures, resulting in the phenomenon of global warming. Climate warming affects agricultural and other ecosystems [2] and triggers the occurrence of disasters related to extreme precipitation and temperature levels. Furthermore, rising temperatures cause aquatic death and sea level increases affect the lives and safety of coastal residents [3, 4]. Meanwhile, the Intergovernmental Panel on Climate Change (IPCC) has been consistent in publishing its assessment reports on the global climate, which has prompted countries around the world to pay more attention to the issue of climate change [5].

The Chenglong Wetland, located in the Kouhu Township of Taiwan's Yunlin County, is of great local importance [6]. Typhoons that hit the region in 1986 and 1996 brought vast amounts of wind and precipitation. The region has also been affected by ground subsidence, which has worsened over the years. Consequently, the land was flooded and the surging runoffs did not recede, leading to the formation of wetlands. The process from the occurrence of the disaster to the resultant environmental changes took approximately 24 years. Arising from the severe challenges of climate change, the region's main economic activities have shifted from agriculture to fishery. Considering that the living environment there is beneath the water surface, the residents had either relocated or need to raise the foundations of their houses continuously [7, 8]. The resultant issues that the region faces include population outflow, no successor to take over family undertakings, gaps in passing down its culture and heritage, leasing land to optoelectronic enterprises to ensure livelihood, forced transformation of local industries, wetland preservation, and ecological transformation.

Climate change gradually permeates human lives and is not easily detectable. The issue is often clouded by people's past experiences and memories, and cognitive differences, resulting in their weak perceptions of the issue [9]. The various related data—climate information, sea level rises, precipitation amounts, and severity of ground subsidence—interact with one another and can easily lead to misunderstanding the actual information. It is also difficult for people to gain specific ideas and comprehension of the issue, which indirectly caused them to make cognitive errors during decision-making on issues related to the natural environment and their livelihoods [10]. This is the situation that the Chenglong Wetland faces.

Existing research indicates that enhancements in people's understanding of environmental and climate changes and other related knowledge contribute toward their risk awareness and generate support for their participation in related actions [11]. Environmental education is the starting point to effectively educate more people on environmental issues and attract them to care and be concerned about those issues. However, the recipients of information encompass people in a wide range of age groups and with different levels of ability to understand information. Thus, the challenge is to identify ways to effectively provide information that can be rapidly understood by all users. With more people paying attention to the issue of climate change, information visualization, which is often used to explain data, has become the language of cross-domain communication. Visualization-based designs also provide a means of communicating information to explain complex environmental and natural changes. This method leads to faster comprehension of information and extended learning of knowledge and is also appropriate for facilitating different users' comprehension [12, 13].

Following the above discussion, this study examined ways of clarifying the causal factors affecting the complex issue of environmental changes in the Chenglong Wetland through various historical and current data, including those on the region's environmental ecology, its' narrative of culture and heritage, and hydrological information, as well as focus group interviews with local stakeholders. Various scenarios were then proposed and described using visualization-based information translation (VIT). The stipulated research questions were: (i) how to clarify the factors affecting environmental changes in the Chenglong Wetland through a literature review and focus group interviews with stakeholders, and (ii) what the process and method of designing images is that depicts the main essential factors based on VIT.

2 Research Methods and Process

The research site of this study was the Chenglong Wetland. Data on its culture and heritage, landscape, industries, ecology, and conservation were integrated using the literature review method. The main essential factors were clarified through focus group interviews with local stakeholders before designs and texts were proposed based on VIT. The research process was as follows: (i) data collection and inventorization: the relevant information on the Chenglong Wetland, including its ecology, environment, climate, culture and heritage, and application of green energy were collected; (ii) focus group interviews with stakeholders: the purpose was to clarify the essential factors and the effects of mutual interactions between these factors; and (iii) information visualization: information from the literature review and focus group interviews were summarized for context, textual contents, and designs based on VIT.

3 VIT Process

3.1 Information Collection and Inventorization

The purpose of the literature review and focus group interviews with the stakeholders was to understand and analyze the related issues. Through the collection of literature and materials on the Chenglong Wetland, we achieved this aim. The related information was then categorized into: (i) overview of its culture and heritage, which includes the historical evolution, population composition, cultural landscape, and industrial structure of the Chenglong community; (ii) its narrative, which includes information on wetland hydrology, ecology, climate, and carbon sequestration, and (iii) environmental changes and warming trends, which includes an examination of global temperature and sea level rises, and the dynamics behind the emissions of greenhouse gases.

Under the first category of information, changes to the Chenglong community arising from the two typhoons were identified by understanding the community's geographical location and historical evolution. Massive precipitation amounts and strong surface runoff were retained in the region after the typhoons, forcing the community to adjust its industry structure and lifestyle, which resulted in population outflow and an aging community. The second category of information provided an in-depth understanding of the detailed data on ground subsidence and industrial and environmental changes, and survey data on variations in climate and precipitation over the years, which led to an understanding of the wetland ecology and the functions of its ecosystem. The third category of information focused on climate change and global warming. Emissions of greenhouse gases have caused global temperatures to increase and triggered chain effects such as rising sea levels, which will eventually cause the western coastal areas of Taiwan to be submerged. Finally, an understanding was achieved regarding the current developmental status of green energy in Taiwan. These categories of information led to the compilation of the complex issues affecting the environmental ecology of the Chenglong Wetland, establishment of its critical narrative, and clarification of the related problems, all of which served as references for the follow-up textual and visual designs of contents for environmental education.

3.2 Focus Group Interviews with the Stakeholders

The stakeholders invited to participate in the focus group interviews included Chenglong community residents, representatives of the Kuan Shu Education Foundation, and teachers of the Chenglong Elementary School. There were three interview sessions involving two to three participants per session. In the end, a total of 113 pieces of information were extracted. During the interviews with the community residents, we investigated the cultural environment, industry, cultural evolution, and current situation of the Chenglong Wetland. In the interviews with the Kuan Shu Education Foundation, we learned about its role in and long-term observations of the local community, as well as its experiences in promoting awareness of environmental issues within the community. Local elementary school teachers were invited to share their experiences of the local culture and landscapes during their teaching tenures, and their teaching experiences when introducing local environmental issues and technological devices into the curriculum and teaching process.

At the analysis stage, the interview contents were typed into a verbatim draft for sorting and coding into the following categories to finalize the context: (i) environmental warning signs and backlash, (ii) ecological transformation and impacts, (iii) introduction to environmental education, (iv) community transformation and creation of new livelihoods, and (v) goals for environmental and ecological protection. Information from the literature review in the previous step and that from interviews with the stakeholders were combined to determine the mutually interacting factors affecting the complex environmental issues. Next, the important information was extracted to determine the essential factors to be featured using designs and texts based on VIT.

3.3 Designs for VIT

Data visualization can be used as a method to convey social issues to the public for their understanding. The process of information and data translation lead to the users being inspired by, paying attention to, and changing their views on issues, thereby making them consider the potential advantages and disadvantages of the situation and improving their cognitive attitudes toward events and issues [14]. Images from VIT have been widely used as important tools to supplement explanations, promote understanding of contents, improve learning efficiency, and transmit public information [15, 16]. Following the determination of the complex issues faced by the Chenglong Wetland, which further confirmed the need for and importance of this study's attempts to introduce the contents of environmental education into the community based on VIT.

Naparin and Sadd (2017) stated that data must be analyzed and evaluated prior to information visualization, so that the available information is ascertained before the design stage. The various qualitative data obtained in this study, and related information would have a certain degree of influence on the designs and texts based on VIT. The complex environmental issues faced by the Chenglong Wetland, as summarized, and identified from the data collection, were combined with the aforementioned to arrive at the conclusion that the infiltration and impact of climate change had accumulated over a long period of time. However, human perceptions of the situation were weak and as such, the people's attention to the issue and the necessary preventative preparations were lacking. Therefore, the proposed designs and texts focused on the wetland ecosystem; changes to the climate, environment, industries, and residential types; and policy implementation. The relevant information and data were then integrated to form speculative contents on future environmental changes for VIT. The outputs could provide the people with an understanding of environmental changes and the ability to visualize imaginary situations (Fig. 1).

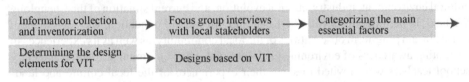

Fig. 1. VIT process

Following information integration and issue clarification to determine the complex issues, five main scenarios were arrived at for the designs and texts based on VIT, namely: (i) climate change: global warming affects sea level rises, (ii) ground subsidence affects residents' livelihoods and living environment, (iii) wetlands are important ecosystems but also ticking time bombs, (iv) extreme climate conditions cause crises in the wetlands, and (v) A circular economy reduces the carbon emissions of products; global efforts will realize the saving of the world. The application of VIT could effectively provide users with a real understanding of the future changes that the Chenglong Wetland might undergo, leading to the proposal of preventative efforts.

Analysis of the system map and information from the overview of the region's culture and heritage revealed that the community predominantly comprised the young and elderly populations. Descriptions derived from the VIT process are not affected by the users' literacy rate and thus, would facilitate the transmission of information to everyone and facilitate their rapid understanding. The comprehensive VIT process and the corresponding design elements are shown in Fig. 2.

The correlations and causal relationships between the complex environmental issues faced by the Chenglong Wetland were determined through analyzing information in the literature. Next, the contents of focus group interviews with stakeholders were used for an in-depth examination to clarify the complex issues. Following that, the design elements

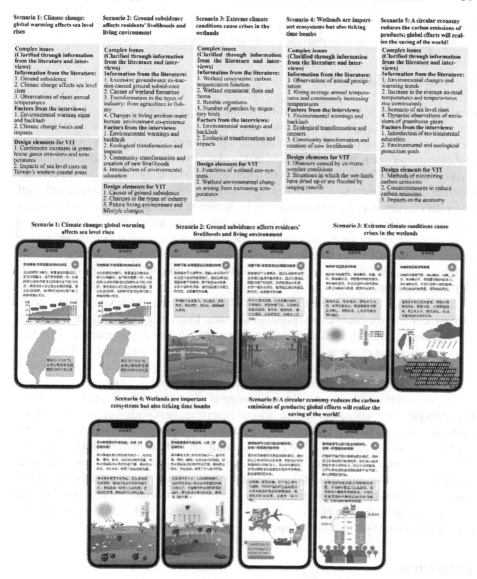

Fig. 2. List of design elements based on VIT.

were comprehensively inventorized, reviewed, and categorized to extract the important information on environmental education for learners. The relevant information were then used to deduce the texts and plan the designs based on possible future changes to the region arising from environmental changes. Plans for the designs and texts based on VIT were proposed to provide users with contents supplemented by visualization that would assist them in understanding the complex environmental information. The visualization designs maintained sufficient contrast between the background and graphics to accommodate the different levels of learners' abilities to recognize information. Additionally, the operational design was intuitive to facilitate clear reading and judgment by users. Audio information was also provided to assist in conveying the information.

4 Results and Conclusion

Climate change is a challenge faced by human beings around the world. The factors affecting climate change and environmental issues cover a wide range of domains. It is necessary to convey information effectively and provide details that are easily understood so that users can grasp the importance of making improvements to their behaviors and the correct decisions. The findings of this research were: (i) the causal relationships between complex environmental issues faced by the Chenglong Wetland were ascertained through a literature review to gather information on its culture and heritage, landscape, industries, ecology, and conservation; this was then combined with information gathered during focus groups interviews with stakeholders; and (ii) the main essential factors, which were determined through a literature review and interview results, were used to establish the design elements for the scripted scenarios, before designing the images based on which VIT was conducted.

The graphics of the proposed images and the accompanying texts facilitate users' understanding of the complex environmental issues. Users could also gain more concrete concepts of the interrelationship between the region's future development and climatic and environmental changes, rather than relying only on their imagination. In doing so, they gain the requisite abilities to respond to the changes and prevent negative outcomes. Based on the aforementioned research findings, we will continue to update and integrate the augmented reality-based app on environmental education of the Chenglong Wetland. Following that, we will gather the operational experiences of Grade 4 users before further evaluating the feasibility of introducing technology into environmental education and verifying its acceptance level. The aim is to equip learners with the ability to interpret and comprehend information. The knowledge that they gain will serve as a reference for future environmental education to solve complex issues; it can effectively enhance human awareness of climate change, and ecological and environmental issues. This will help the general public to put forward and defend their opinions effectively, and raise their level of attention to critical issues.

References

1. Garba, M.D., et al.: CO2 towards fuels: a review of catalytic conversion of carbon dioxide to hydrocarbons. J. Environ. Chem. Eng. **9**(2), 104756 (2021)
2. Yerlikaya, B.A., Ömezli, S., Aydoğan, N.: Climate change forecasting and modeling for the year of 2050. In: Fahad, S., et al. (eds.) Environment, Climate, Plant and Vegetation Growth, pp. 109–122. Springer, Cham (2020). https://doi.org/10.1007/978-3-030-49732-3_5
3. Shukla, J.B., Verma, M., Misra, A.K.: Effect of global warming on sea level rise: a modeling study. Ecol. Complex. **32**, 99–110 (2017)
4. Moomaw, W.R., et al.: Wetlands in a changing climate: science, policy and management. Wetlands **38**(2), 183–205 (2018)
5. Callaghan, M.W., Minx, J.C., Forster, P.M.: A topography of climate change research. Nat. Clim. Chang. **10**, 118–123 (2020). https://doi.org/10.1038/s41558-019-0684-5

6. Urban and Rural Development Branch: Construction and Planning Agency, Ministry of the Interior Chenglong Important Wetland (Local Level) (2017). https://wetland-tw.tcd.gov.tw/tw/GuideContent.php?ID=19&secureChk=ee02ef35d8706e03964b82096e54916e

7. Yunlin County Government: Draft Conservation and Utilization Plans for the Chenglong Important Wetland (Local Level) (2020). https://wetlandfiles.tcd.gov.tw/index.php?id=1636

8. Information of Land Subsidence Prevention in Taiwan: Current Situation of Ground Subsidence in Yunlin (2021). http://www.lsprc.ncku.edu.tw/zh-tw/trend.php?action=view&id=18

9. Fischer, E.M., Knutti, R.: Anthropogenic contribution to global occurrence of heavy-precipitation and high-temperature extremes. Nat. Clim. Chang. 5(6), 560–564 (2015)

10. Li, Y.Y., Liu, S.C.: Examining Taiwanese students' views on climate change and the teaching of climate change in the context of higher education. Res. Sci. Technol. Educ. 40(4), 515–528 (2022)

11. Lee, T.M., Markowitz, E.M., Howe, P.D., Ko, C.Y., Leiserowitz, A.A.: Predictors of public climate change awareness and risk perception around the world. Nat. Clim. Chang. 5(11), 1014–1020 (2015)

12. Naparin, H., Saad, A.B.: Infographics in education: review on infographics design. Int. J. Multimedia Appl. (IJMA) 9(4), 5 (2017). https://doi.org/10.5121/ijma.2017.9602

13. Parveen, A., Husain, N.: Infographics as a promising tool for teaching and learning. J. Emerg. Technol. Innov. Res. 8(8), 554–559 (2021)

14. Markant, D.B., Rogha, M., Karduni, A., Wesslen, R., Dou, W.: Can data visualizations change minds? Identifying mechanisms of elaborative thinking and persuasion. In: 2022 IEEE Workshop on Visualization for Social Good (VIS4Good), pp. 1–5 (2022)

15. Barlow, B., Webb, A., Barlow, A.: Maximizing the visual translation of medical information: a narrative review of the role of infographics in clinical pharmacy practice, education, and research. J. Am. Coll. Clin. Pharm. 4(2), 257–266 (2021)

16. Jaleniauskiene, E., Kasperiuniene, J.: Infographics in higher education: a scoping review. E-Learn. Digit. Media (2022). https://doi.org/10.1177/20427530221107774

A Harmonized Multi-lingual Terminology for ICT Devices and Services with a User-Centric View

Emmanuel Darmois[1]([⊠]) and Martin Boecker[2]

[1] CommLedge, Viroflay, France
emmanuel.darmois@commledge.com
[2] Dr. Böcker & Dr. Schneider GbR, Munich, Germany
boecker@humanfactors.de

Abstract. Information and Communications Technology (ICT) has become central to the life of all citizens in the European Union.

This comes with challenges for users, as different device manufacturers or service providers may use a divergent set of terms to denominate identical devices and service features: a name is therefore a primary means by which a user can recognize and understand them.

This supports the requirement for the user-centered terminology which has been developed to provide a referential for the *end users*, and a structured guideline to support the *ICT actors* (e.g., the industrial stakeholders) in the provision of harmonized services and documentation.

The harmonized terminology is covering commonly used, basic ICT features of current and upcoming ICT devices (4 groups), services and applications (12 groups) focusing on communication in mobile contexts of use. The result is a multilingual terminology supporting over 800 terms.

The work described has been undertaken by the Technical Committee Human Factors (TC HF) of the European Telecommunication Standards Institute (ETSI). Its main deliverable, the ETSI Guide (EG 203 499), has been developed in three steps, incorporating a growing number of supported languages and corresponding EG versions. The last step of the work is currently undertaken with the inclusion of eight languages that will finalize the coverage of all the 27 official languages of EU (the European Union) and EFTA (the European Free Trade Association). This EG is a public and freely available document. Once achieved, this version is expected to be proposed to standardization.

Keywords: Human Factors · ICT Terminology · User-centered Design

C. Stephanidis et al. (Eds.): HCII 2023, CCIS 1834, pp. 40–45, 2023.
https://doi.org/10.1007/978-3-031-35998-9_6

1 Introduction

When interacting with the various information systems they have to deal with, end-users face the challenge of making sure that there is a strong adequation between what on the one hand they believe that the terms used for this interaction are referring to, and on the other hand what was intended by the manufacturers/developers of these information systems (and their user interface). Manufacturers will typically employ a (potentially large) number of terms for the processes and tools in order to identify, store and manage company, customer, or product-specific information that are employed in the development processes, in the user interfaces of products, and in the user documentation, all of which possibly need to be translated into the languages spoken in the target markets (see e.g., Philpotts, 1996).

These potentially large compendiums of terms need to be managed by manufacturers and service developers within well-defined terminologies: harmonized – i.e., agreed-upon – terminologies facilitate comprehension, data exchange, and content production in a wide range of domains. Such state-of-the-art terminologies based on computational and/or artificial intelligence are being used in diverse areas such as medicine, (software) engineering, and public-sector services (Bourigault et al., 2001).

Information and Communications Technologies (ICT) is an area in which users encounter a plethora of terms. The effective access of all users to ICT depends on users being able to understand the features (such as the controls and capabilities) of the products and services that are required to operate them. To discover and understand these features, users must first identify and recognize them. Their names (terms, words, labels) are a primary means by which users can recognize and understand them.

If product and service features are poorly named, or if a familiar feature is named differently to the way that users have previously encountered it (e.g., on the device of a different manufacturer), they are likely to fail to recognize and understand it. If they fail to recognize and understand those features, they may not be able to use them effectively.

At best, terms that have clear and well-understood meanings will support the users with this initial memorization task. On the contrary, if the terms for the same features are different from product to product, users will need to learn multiple terms that refer to the same underlying feature, and will have to understand which name is used in which product (or, even worse, in different parts of the same product). This additional complexity may disproportionally disadvantage elderly users and users with learning or cognitive disabilities who may have impaired memory and comprehension abilities.

While some terms are introduced by manufacturers to designate a new class of features or to promote their own features against those found in competitors' products, most other terms designating device or service features are not necessarily intended for differentiation (e.g., battery). However, in the absence of a harmonized or recommended terminology, the use of those terms may differ considerably both among device manufacturers and service providers.

The alternative to a wide and confusing plethora of terms encountered by end users is a reasonable degree of harmonization among devices, services, and application: a harmonized terminology can help preventing the negative effects of an uncontrolled growth of terms, such as:

- Increased user difficulties in understanding complex, ambiguous, and inconsistently used terms, leading to unnecessary confusion
- Increased efforts in the creation of media for user education (user guides)
- Increased costs for user support (hotline calls and call agent training)
- Limited understanding or uncertainty regarding the expected effect (or undesired consequences) of certain features preventing customers from using them, with some revenue missed as a consequence
- Increase of cognitive complexity and subsequent learning effort
- Abuse in the use of proprietary terms and lack of consistent use of terms across internal and external product documentation

A harmonized terminology of device and service features will better support continuous market evolution (e.g., new players), frequent feature updates (often not carried over in user documentation), or changing business models (e.g., fewer subsidized devices linked to fixed service plans reducing end-user loyalty).

2 An Approach for Harmonizing ICT Terms

The Technical Committee "Human Factors" (TC HF) of the European Telecommunication Standards Institute (ETSI) is conducting work to develop the publicly available ETSI Guide EG 203 499 that addresses the need for harmonized ICT terminologies. This ETSI Guide aims at recommending implementation-oriented terms in major European languages, applicable to product User Interface (UI) and user documentation design, thereby easing knowledge and learning transfer.

Developed in three phases, the ETSI Guide will ultimately cover the 27 official languages of the European Union (EU) and the Free Trade Association (EFTA), namely Bulgarian, Croatian, Czech, Danish, Dutch, Estonian, French, Finnish, German, Greek, Hungarian, Icelandic, Irish, Italian, Latvian, Lithuanian, Maltese, Norwegian, Polish, Portuguese, Raeto-Romance, Romanian, Slovak, Slovene, Spanish, and Swedish.

For this work, a Design-for-All approach was chosen that takes into account functional limitations of elderly users and those with cognitive, physical, or sensory variations. This is done with different potential target people:

- Intended *users* of EG 203 499 are those designing, developing, implementing, and deploying user interfaces for and interaction with mobile ICT devices, services, and applications.
- Intended *end users* of that ETSI Guide are people who use mobile ICT devices, services, and applications ranging from first time users to experienced users.

The method employed for developing harmonized terminologies consisted of three phases as described below.

2.1 Phase 1: Identification of Objects and Activities

In this first phase, the identification of functional areas (e.g., telephony or photography) defines the range of functionalities covered by the EG: those functionalities that are most frequently used by many or most users of mobile ICT devices.

For each functional area, relevant objects and activities (i.e., those that are frequently used, and used by most users) were identified and defined. The principles applied in this process were:

- Objects and activities were selected if they help users identify the functionality (i.e., help the user understand what it does), access the functionality, understand the available options related to a functionality, or understand messages displayed in the context of using a functionality (e.g., error feedback)
- One the other hand, objects and activities were not selected if they cover the content of an application (e.g., "photo"), common terms easily found in a dictionary (e.g., "hotel"), common verbal expressions indicating an action taken on an object (e.g., "take a photo"), or words, acronyms, or abbreviations used in a specific technical sense (e.g., "CCNR").

2.2 Phase 2: Collection of Terms

For each functional area, the relevant providers (ICT device manufacturers, service providers, and application vendors) have been identified, and the terms they use for the objects and activities of the respective functional area have been collected in the languages covered by the EG. Functionalities offered by one provider only were not included in the analysis.

2.3 Phase 3: Analysis and Selection

For all languages, localization experts and/or specialists in the linguistics of the respective languages were consulted to make recommendations regarding the terms to be selected. This included checks for consistency between manufacturers (i.e., prevalence of certain terms), preference of terms that reflect the language of the end users as opposed to the language of developers, and compliance with linguistic requirements from the languages covered.

3 Scope of the Harmonized Terminologies

The recommended terms published in the EG are divided into the following domains or categories:

Device-related terminologies	Service- and application-related terminologies
1. General terms	1. General terms
2. Accessibility terms	2. Messaging services
3. Telephony terms	3. Media services
4. Photography	4. Societal services and communications
	5. Social media services
	6. Banking services
	7. eHealth services
	8. Travel planning
	9. Navigation
	10. Games
	11. Searching and browsing
	12. Tools/Miscellaneous

Figure 1 shows an example of the contents of the second release of EG 203 499. For each entry, an index number, a "Technical term" (expected to be understood by implementers), a detailed description of the functionality, and the recommended terms in the languages covered by the EG.

Table 16e: Telephony services: Voice call handling

Index	Technical term	Functional description	Slovak	Spanish	Swedish
D.230	automatic call answering	Mode in which incoming calls are automatically accepted	automatická odpoveď; automatické prijímanie hovorov	desvío al buzón de voz/contestador automático	svara automatiskt
D.231	call log list	List of previous incoming, outgoing, and missed calls made from the mobile device	denník hovorov, história hovorov	(lista de) llamadas	samtalslogg
D.232	contacts (list)	Allows the user to enter and store names, numbers and other data for easy and fast dialling	zoznam kontaktov	(lista de) contactos	kontakter
D.233	handsfree (speaker-phone)	Mode of using a telecommunications terminal that does not require the terminal to be held against the ear and mouth	reproduktor	altavoz; manos libres	högtalare
D.234	missed calls list	List of previously missed calls	zoznam zmeškaných hovorov	(lista de) llamadas perdidas	missade samtal
D.235	mute (microphone off)	Allowing the user to temporarily turn off the microphone during a call	stlmiť; vypnúť mikrofón	silenciar/desactivar el micrófono	ljud av; stäng av mikrofonen
D.236	redial	Allows the user to dial again a previously dialled number	automatické opätovné vytáčanie	rellamada	återuppringning

Fig. 1. Example contents of EG 203 499

4 Conclusion

Considering that the first version of EG 203 499 was well received, an extension of the ETSI Guide to cover further European languages was encouraged, and undertaken by ETSI Specialist Task Forces (STF 604 and STF 652). The final (third) release of EG 203 499 is expected to be published in the 2nd quarter of 2024 after the ETSI approval process is completed.

Since the second release (October 2022), the corresponding tables of terms have been made available on the ETSI GitLab for free download by the EG users (those who will develop user documentation or services User Interfaces). They will be updated with the publication of the third release.

Once the publication of the ETSI Guide is finalized, it is expected that it will gradually be adopted by the target users (as for previous similar undertakings of ETSI). The possibility that the ETSI Guide be transformed into a standard will be subject to the decision of ETSI Technical Committee Human Factors.

Acknowledgments. This work has been co-funded by the European Commission (EC) of the European Union (EU) and the European Free Trade Association (EFTA). The current (third) phase of the work is funded and conducted by ETSI.

References

Philpotts, M.: An introduction to the concepts, benefits and terminology of product data management. Ind. Manag. Data Syst. **96**(4), 11–17 (1996)

Bourigault, D., Jacquemin, C., L'Homme, M.C.: Recent Advances in Computational Terminology. In: Natural Language Processing, vol. 2. J. Benjamins Publishing Company (2001)

ETSI DEG 203 499 v2.1.2: Human Factors (HF); User-centred terminology for existing and upcoming ICT devices, services and applications (2022)

ProtoLife: Enhancing Mobile Multimedia Narratives Through Prototyping Techniques

Yifan Deng[✉]

School of Design, South China University of Technology, Guangzhou 51000, GD, China
dengyf2002@foxmail.com

Abstract. Social media and digital albums are a popular tool for capturing and preserving memories, but creating a cohesive narrative from these multimedia elements can be a challenge. The lack of connection and logic between content in digital storage makes it difficult to create a meaningful story from captured multimedia. We propose ProtoLife, a mobile solution for recording and creating multimedia stories. It uses the concept of flow and connectivity in prototyping, a common approach to interface design, to enhance the logic and connections between multimedia elements. This approach allows for a more immersive and compelling storytelling experience, as it is key to the media collective and storage tools. The results can also serve as a valuable tool for researchers and practitioners in the field of human-computer interaction, as it provides an example of an approach to enhancing the narrative of multimedia content.

Keywords: Multimedia · Prototyping · User Experience

1 Introduction

The advancement of technology in the mobile device industry has completely changed the way people record and share their memories. Previous studies of have shown that retrieval cues, which are environmental or internal stimuli presented in multimedia forms such as the image of a familiar face, the sound of a particular song, or the smell a specific scent, are essential for the recall of a specific memory [1]. Hence, digital storytelling often uses tools such as podcasts, videos, and blogs for creating a more interactive and engaging experience [2]. Learning that multimedia elements can be used to enhance the storytelling experience and engage the user [3], many mobile applications have been developed to support the creation of multimedia stories, providing users with a more interactive and dynamic way to record their lives [4].

However, social media apps currently available in the market are primarily focused on image editing, video editing, and text creation. They are still adopting traditional and singular storytelling methods. For instance, image editing functions commonly use text, image stickers, and multi-picture collages to create a narrative. Video editing functions use a timeline concept, where material on the same timeline is edited based on duration, and then combined into a complete video file. Text creations are usually provided with

© The Author(s), under exclusive license to Springer Nature Switzerland AG 2023
C. Stephanidis et al. (Eds.): HCII 2023, CCIS 1834, pp. 46–53, 2023.
https://doi.org/10.1007/978-3-031-35998-9_7

a text workspace, where various text editing tools can be used to create text and images can be inserted to enhance its meaning [4].

Unfortunately, the above methods fail to create the most immersive storytelling experiences, as some apps cannot integrate all sensory elements, while others may be time-consuming and lack logical structure, making it difficult to tell a compelling story [5]. Previous studies of Wang and Tan has presented a solution to this using a series of snapshots of a piece of specific memory with the associated context, namely time, location, people, activity, imagery and emotion in digital albums [6]. But the storytelling experience is still lack of usability and logic attachments since it's still adopting a traditional way of a movie-like slide show as a visual form of memory.

ProtoLife aims to meet the growing need for simple and effective tools to capture, store, and share multimedia content. It provides a user-friendly platform for creating multimedia stories by connecting multimedia elements using the principles of prototype design, which lowers the learning curve and enhances the user experience.

Prototype design is a mature method in interface design that helps designers build a quick and viable working model to evaluate and improve the feasibility of each interaction before final implementation [7]. In ProtoLife, this technology is applied to the process of creating multimedia stories, enabling users to quickly organize the story's logic and add more narrative elements to it. An intuitive and easy-to-use interface allows users to effortlessly create dynamic and captivating multimedia stories [7, 8].

2 Design and Implementation

2.1 System Overview

The ProtoLife platform was designed and implemented to provide a fast, user-friendly, and effortless solution for recording and creating multimedia stories. To achieve this goal, we simplified the process of storytelling by studying the narrative concept and combed the process into a system structure where multimedia elements are able to link and dynamically refer to each other (see Fig. 1). We developed the program using SwiftUI and Objective-C and created a MVP (Minimum Viable Product) demo of our application based on iOS platform.

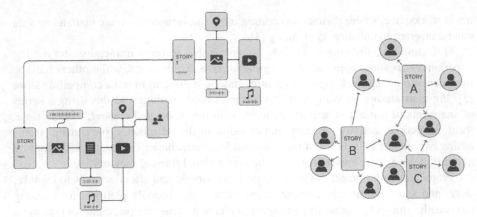

Fig. 1. An example of the functional structure of ProtoLife. Left: ProtoLife simplified the process of storytelling into a systematic structure where multimedia elements are able to link and dynamically refer to each other. Right: ProtoLife is able to link friends and circles to different stories that helps to create a story network.

2.2 Fluid Interface

The fluid storyboard interface is a key feature of ProtoLife. The interface uses the common "canvas" concept in modern prototyping methodologies [9], representing each narrative element in a modular card form (see Fig. 2).

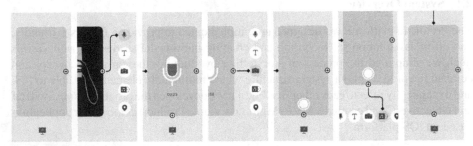

Fig. 2. Modular card-form canvas used in ProtoLife. There are currently six multimedia canvas options available, linked by dynamic arrows represent the logical relationship between them.

There are currently six multimedia canvas options available, including photo, video (share the same portal with Photo Canvas), music, audio, location, and personnel canvas. Dynamic arrows are used to connect these cards, expressing the logical relationship between each element. Each modular canvas card has a specific function in building the story, which is outlined below:

Photo Canvas: the function designed for users to upload pictures from system album, allowing users to capture and record the surrounding visual information when the story occurs.

Video Canvas (share the same portal with Photo Canvas): the function designed for users to upload videos from files, allowing users to capture and record the dynamic environment around the story.

Music Canvas: clicking on the music canvas allows the user to select a music work provided by the system with complete intellectual property rights, enabling users to record the music environment around the story.

Location Canvas: obtains the user's geographic location information and presents it on a small interactive map on the card, allowing users to record the geographic information around the story.

Audio Canvas: a recording function similar to a WeChat voice message or an Instagram voice message. When the user presses and holds the button, the built-in microphone of the phone can be used to record audio, allowing users to record the sound information around the story.

Personnel Canvas: the function to link to nearby friends and strangers or friends already in the user's friend list. The user can choose to add the person to the personnel canvas, allowing users to record the character information around the story.

2.3 Navigation

We use a large "map" to hold all modular cards on the page, but only one card is displayed in the screen display area at a time. This is typically designed to integrate all the multimedia elements to form a consistent storyline [10]. When the user clicks on the overview navigation button at the bottom, the map will be displayed, allowing the user to know the relative position of the card they are editing.

2.4 Interactions

When using the application, users can use simple and natural interactive gestures, such as single tapping, long-pressing, dragging, and sliding, to select and connect elements. This provides users with the ability to seamlessly weave various multimedia elements together to create a unified and strongly logically related story [11].

Users can create or connect two canvas cards in two ways:

I. Start by long-pressing a card on the screen and dragging out a dynamic and changing arrow while holding it, the location where the arrow is released will be the object that the user wants to add or connect to (see Fig. 3-a).

II. By clicking the floating plus button on the right border of the card, users can select a connecting object or create a new card (see Fig. 3-b).

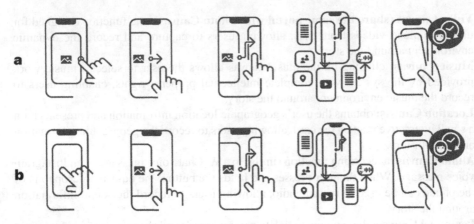

Fig. 3. Interactive options to start with. a: Start by long-pressing a card on the screen and dragging out a dynamic and changing arrow while holding it. b: click the floating plus button on the right border of the card to select a connecting object or create a new card.

2.5 Social Sharing

Along with the storyboarding and commenting feature, users can easily share their stories with friends or the public through social media platforms or by generating a shareable link to their story. Moreover, users can invite friends to collaborate on a story and grant them editing permissions, making it an ideal platform for creative collaboration.

3 Evaluation

The evaluation of ProtoLife was conducted using a mixed-method approach that included both qualitative and quantitative data. This allowed for a comprehensive assessment of the effectiveness of the application in supporting the recording and creation of multimedia stories.

3.1 Usability Test and Data Collection

Data was collected through in-depth interviews with 37 participants who had used the application for at least two weeks. We developed a minimal viable product, which retained the primary storyboard features and allowed users to share their story creations on social media. We sent this minimal viable product to the users for usability testing and conducted follow-up interviews two weeks later (see Fig. 4). The interviews were conducted in a semi-structured format, allowing participants to provide insights into their experience using the application. The interviews were recorded and analyzed using thematic analysis to identify common themes and patterns in the participants' responses.

Fig. 4. User conducting a series of tasks during usability test. Left: User drag to create a new Photo Canvas. Middle: User speaks to the microphone on the Audio Canvas. Right: User taking a picture on the Photo Canvas.

While we want the product to mainly highlight its features on emotional connections, we specifically asked users about their subjective perceptions of the emotional value of the memories our products provide for them. This method is widely recommended in designs with emotional connections taken into consideration [12].

Descriptive statistics were used to analyze the data to determine the mean, median, and mode of each question, and inferential statistics were used to test for statistical significance.

3.2 Data Analysis

The results of the qualitative data analysis showed that the majority (20/23) of participants considered ProtoLife to be a valuable tool for recording and creating multimedia stories. Participants reported that the application was easy to use and its user-friendly interface allowed them to capture and organize their experiences in multimedia format easily. Participants also appreciated the application's ability to enhance their life narratives and memories, with some reporting that they were able to retrieve past memories more vividly, giving them a unique experience.

The results of the quantitative data analysis showed that participants had a high level of satisfaction with the application. On a 5-point Likert scale administered to the 38 respondents, the overall satisfaction score averaged 4.5, indicating that participants were generally very satisfied with their experience using the application. The average score for the application's usability was also high, averaging 4.3, indicating that participants considered it a valuable tool for recording and creating multimedia stories. Participants also reported that the application was effective in enhancing their life narratives, with an average score of 4.1 on the same scale.

Inferential statistical analysis showed that there was no significant difference in participants' satisfaction with the application based on demographic factors such as age, gender, or previous experience with multimedia storytelling. This suggests that the application is effective in supporting diverse user groups in recording and creating multimedia stories. However, this can occur due to the shortfall in the number of testers.

4 Conclusion and Future Work

The evaluation results of ProtoLife demonstrate that this application is a valuable tool for users who want to record and create multimedia stories. The implementation of prototyping methods in storytelling using multimedia is effective and accessible. The participants in the evaluation were highly satisfied with ProtoLife, and they found its interface to be user friendly, which made the process of recording and organizing their experiences in a multimedia format much simpler. In addition, the participants look forward to using ProtoLife to enhanced their narratives about their lives, with a number of them reporting feeling more connected to their experiences because of using the application.

Since the result might occurs due to the shortfall in the number of testers, in the future we are seeking a massive evaluation towards the usability of ProtoLife to further optimize our solution. In addition, future research should continue to explore the potential of ProtoLife to support the recording and creation of multimedia stories in more application scenarios.

References

1. Tulving, E.: Précis of elements of episodic memory. Behav. Brain Sci. 7(2), 223–238 (1984). https://doi.org/10.1017/S0140525X0004440X
2. Clemens, S., Kreider, M.: What's your story? Using digital storytelling to enhance 21st century skills. In: Lowenthal, P.R., Thomas, D., Thai, A., Yuhnke, B., (eds.) The CU Online Handbook, pp. 73–80. University of Colorado, Denver (2011)
3. Tsiviltidou, Z.: Digital storytelling with mobile media for inquiry-based museum learning the student as author of the museum experience. In: 2015 International Conference on Interactive Mobile Communication Technologies and Learning (IMCL), Thessaloniki, Greece, pp. 91–95 (2015). https://doi.org/10.1109/IMCTL.2015.7359562
4. Poulsen, S.V.: Becoming a semiotic technology – a historical study of Instagram's tools for making and sharing photos and videos. Internet Histories 2(1–2), 121–139 (2018). https://doi.org/10.1080/24701475.2018.1459350
5. Herman, D.: Story logic: Problems and possibilities of narrative. U of Nebraska Press (2004)
6. Wang, D., Tan, A.-H.: MyLife: an online personal memory album. In: 2015 IEEE/WIC/ACM International Conference on Web Intelligence and Intelligent Agent Technology (WI-IAT), Singapore, pp. 243–244 (2015). https://doi.org/10.1109/WI-IAT.2015.148
7. Floyd, C.: A systematic look at prototyping. In: Budde, R., Kuhlenkamp, K., Mathiassen, L., Züllighoven, H. (eds.) Approaches to Prototyping, pp. 1–18. Springer Berlin Heidelberg, Berlin, Heidelberg (1984). https://doi.org/10.1007/978-3-642-69796-8_1
8. Amato, F., et al.: Multimedia story creation on social networks. Futur. Gener. Comput. Syst. 86, 412–420 (2018). https://doi.org/10.1016/j.future.2018.04.006
9. D. Baumer, W. Bischofberger, H. Lichter and H. Zullighoven, "User interface prototyping-concepts, tools, and experience," Proceedings of IEEE 18th International Conference on Software Engineering, Berlin, Germany, 1996, pp. 532–541, doi: https://doi.org/10.1109/ICSE.1996.493447
10. Pratt, J.A., Mills, R.J., Kim, Y.: The effects of navigational orientation and user experience on user task efficiency and frustration levels. J. Comput. Inf. Syst. 44(4), 93–100 (2004)

11. ShyamSundar, S., Bellur, S., Jeeyun, O., Qian, X., Jia, H.: User experience of on-screen interaction techniques: an experimental investigation of clicking, sliding, zooming, hovering, dragging and flipping. Human-Comput. Interact. **29**(2), 109–152 (2014). https://doi.org/10.1080/07370024.2013.789347

12. Demirbilek, O., Sener, B.: Product design, semantics and emotional response. Ergonomics **46**(13–14), 1346–1360 (2003). https://doi.org/10.1080/00140130310001610874

Development of Interactive Teaching Device for Difficult Teaching of Collaborative Robot

Jeyoun Dong(✉), Dongyeop Kang, and Seung-Woo Nam

Electronics and Telecommunications Research Institute, Daegu, South Korea
jydong@etri.re.kr

Abstract. As the demand for collaborative robots increases, the manufacturers have come to use touchpad-typed teaching devices, and human-friendly interfaces have played a significant role in robot teaching. Accordingly, the needs for development of a user-friendly intuitive interface is increasing, and several companies are emerging to develop a user-friendly teaching interface.

In addition, even if there is a teaching pendant that provide an intuitive interface, it is basically difficult to teach a high-difficult task such as peg-hole work, pivot work, flat and curved sanding work requiring precise teaching without professional programming.

In this paper, to provide an easy robot teaching method for these high-level hard tasks, we have developed a wizard that provides a step-by-step process without programming for the sophisticated teaching. By teaching robots with unit tasks in the wizard, one main task can be completed. Each hard task is defined by several detailed teaching steps, and one task is completed by following step-by step instructions by manipulating an external device such as hand-held device. The user performs the robot teaching by using the preparation state, guidance information, and task start and finish buttons provided by the wizard. In the next step, the user-created trajectory is automatically corrected. Finally, the user can check the correction result for the teaching trajectory and execute the entire teaching result. In addition, the usability of the developed wizard was evaluated. The success rate of our wizard is 12% higher than that of conventional wizard for teaching the high-level hard tasks.

Keywords: difficult teaching · interactive teaching device · collaborative robot

1 Introduction

In the past, industrial robots and collaborative robots have been mainly used in the manufacturing industry [1]. As automation using a collaborative robot(cobot) is introduced in various industries including service and food and beverage as well as manufacturing industries, the demand for collaborative robots is increasing.

In addition, the importance of a user-friendly teaching interface that even non-expert users can use is being emphasized. A cobot's user interface plays an important role in determining the success of a task, as it acts as an intermediary between the cobot and the user, conveying information about the task [2].

In order to operate the robot, the user's work intention must be implemented so that the robot can understand it, which is called a teaching. Teaching is a skill that allows a human to perform a new task on a robot, or to perform a possible task. Although the user needs to directly teach using a robot, write programming, or input waypoints using a teaching pendant, the difficult task in the actual process tends to be performed by experts. The primary users of cobots may not be robot-experts. It is difficult for an operator who is not a robot expert to use an interface for creating, modifying, and operating a teaching program. Also, it is currently impossible to teach high-difficult tasks (eg, pivot work, combining work, peg-hole work, and etc.) that require precise teaching on the speed, acceleration, and contact force of robot movement without separate programming by experts [3].

Therefore, it is necessary to develop and commercialize a teaching device that allows non-experts as well as experts to easily use the robot. Leading robot manufacturers are recognizing the importance of teaching complex work, and are trying to develop various types of intuitive teaching devices and apply them to robots.

In this paper, an interactive wizard was developed that allows non-experts to easily and quickly teach hard robot tasks. In order to improve usability for non-experts, detailed tutorials on teaching tasks are provided through interactive wizards without separate robot training. By step-by-step process of the form of a template through wizard, even non-experts can perform, sophisticated teaching tasks such as peg-hole work, pivot work, and combination work without separate training and programming. Each challenging task is defined in several detailed steps, and one task is completed by following instructions using hand-held device. After reading the preparation and guidance information provided by the wizard, the user performs teaching by using the start and end buttons. In the next step, the trajectory created by the user is automatically corrected. Finally, the user can check the result of the corrected trajectory and execute the teaching results of the entire process.

In addition, usability evaluation was conducted to find out the usability of the developed wizard. Usability evaluation to improve the developed wizard interface is an important process. By improving the usability of the wizard interface, the level of a teaching device that is safe, easy to use, and error free can be raised in the future. Key metrics used in usability evaluation are success rate, effectiveness, efficiency and satisfaction with which specified users achieve specified tasks in test-bed environments.

A usability evaluation was conducted to check how easy teaching is possible for high-difficult tasks such as pivot work and peg-hole work. A total of 25 participants had a success rate of 75.2%, among which 15 engineering majors had a success rate of 80.3% and 10 non-engineering majors had a success rate of 70%. This result is 12% higher than the teaching success rate of 63.2% using the existing teaching pendant.

This work is structured as follows. Section 2 introduces the design of the interactive wizard. Section 3 describes methods of usability test and results of experiment. Finally, Sect. 4 establishes discussion of the findings of experiments and conclusions.

2 Design of the Interactive Wizard

In this paper, a wizard was developed to facilitate high-difficult teaching work using a hand-held device and a programless template. If an error occurs while the users are performing the entire task, the teaching task must be performed again from the beginning. Therefore, each task was divided into several unit works. Each unit task consists of a user teaching step, a (trajectory) correction step for the user-created teaching task, and a trajectory confirmation step. After completing each unit task, one high-level task is completed, and it can be executed in the wizard's simulation and actual robot.

2.1 Selection Steps of High-Difficult Task

This wizard can be divided into recommended and user defined tasks. The recommendation task in the form of a programless template is composed of several unit tasks.

As shown in Fig. 1, the user can drag and move the selected recommended task to the workspace and start the wizard. Also, user-defined tasks can be composed of user-desired tasks by combining unit tasks.

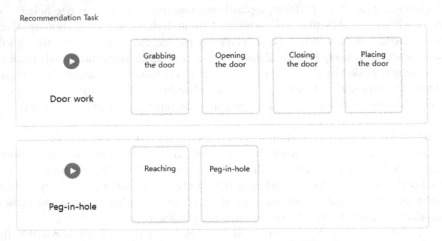

Fig. 1. Recommendation Task Menu in Wizard

2.2 Execution Steps of High-Difficult Task

Each high-difficult task was performed by clicking a button in the wizard without programming, and frequently used functions were made into icons and placed at the top of the screen.

Each hard task is composed of several unit tasks, and each unit task proceeds as follows. First, in the user teaching operation step, teaching is performed using the start/finish button for the provided time. The wizard provides directions so that users can easily perform a task. At this time, you can use a hand-held device such as Vive without programming to move the robot like the animation provided on the wizard screen.

After the user teaching is finished, a trajectory correction step created by the user is performed, and the user checks the corrected trajectory. If the generated trajectory is not satisfactory, the user can perform re-teaching in the user teaching step.

Finally, after performing all tasks consisting of several unit tasks, the teaching results for the high-level tasks can be executed in simulation and actual robots. Since safety is important for robots, it was designed so that the results could be confirmed through simulation. After checking the work in the simulation, the user can also check the high-level work with the actual robot.

3 Methods and Result of Usability Test

When new collaborative robots and teaching pendants are introduced, it is important for operators to adapt, which will affect production. Usability evaluation is an important process because it is important for workers to learn and adapt quickly and easily. In addition, it is necessary to improve the usability of the wizard interface so that it is easy to use safely and error-free in the future.

3.1 The Purpose of the Usability Test

The purpose of usability testing is to measure the wizard's performance in terms of work effectiveness, effectiveness, and satisfaction by performing tasks. So, you can get feedback and problems to improve the wizard.

In particular, the common objective of usability test in this is to evaluate the usability of cobots, wizards, and hand-held devices in terms of how easy and helpful they are when used by the operator. The proposed usability evaluation is based on the international usability standard ISO 9241-11 [4] and considers both objective and subjective metrics. According to this standard, the effectiveness of usability is evaluated through the measurement of task success rate as the percentage of tasks that users complete correctly. In addition to these objective measures, questionnaires using 7-point Likert scale have been developed to assess subjective usability [5].

3.2 Procedure of Experiments

Users performed teaching tasks using Neuromeka's Indy7 cobot and hand-held devices such as Vive and Wizard.

The evaluation consisted of instruction on how to use, wizard usability evaluation, a interview and questionnaire.

A total of 25 participants, consisting of 15 engineering majors and 10 non-engineering majors, performed pivot work (door work) and peg-in-hole task on the provided test bed shown as Fig. 2 and Fig. 3. The door work consists of grabbing, opening, closing, and placing the door, and the peg-in-hole work consists of reaching and peg-in-hole.

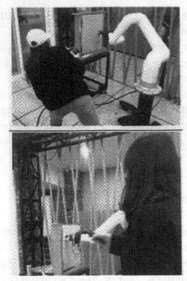

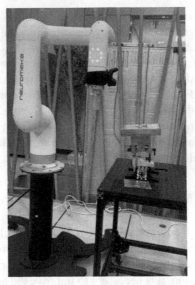

Fig. 2. Door Work (Pivot Work) Usability Test

Fig. 3. Peg-in-hole Testbed

3.3 Results of Experiments

Among a total of 25 participants, effectiveness, or a success rate, was 75.2%, and among them, 11 engineering majors showed a success rate of 80.3%, and 10 non-engineering majors showed a success rate of 70%. This is 12% higher than the existing teaching pendant's success rate. Efficiency using a 7-point Likert scale received 5.8, and satisfaction obtained 5.4. It was found to be above average.

However, we received various feedbacks such as how to solve errors, the number of stored teachings, and the size of the gripper. This will be applied and improved in future works.

4   Conclusions

In this paper, we described an interactive wizard that allows non-experts to quickly and easily teach high-level tasks without training and programming.

Previously, in order to teach, programming was performed using a teaching pendant. However, according to the directions, the hand-held device such as Vive is used to teach the robot in the wizard developed in this study. A high-level task is composed of several unit tasks, and when a user teaches, a trajectory is created, and the trajectory is automatically corrected. The user can select a corrected trajectory or operate teaching again. Completed tasks can be performed in simulations or in real robots.

Usability evaluation was conducted for this wizard so that it could be applied immediately to field workers, and various feedbacks were obtained.

In future works, we plan to improve the wizard by applying feedback obtained through usability evaluation, such as how to solve errors and change the size of the gripper.

Acknowledgments. This work was supported by the Industrial Strategic Technology Development Program (20009396) funded By the Ministry of Trade, Industry & Energy (MOTIE, Korea).

References

Chacón, A., Ponsa, P., Angulo, C.: Usability study through a human-robot collaborative workspace experience. Designs **5**(2), 35 (2021). https://doi.org/10.3390/designs5020035

Sriviboon, Y., Jiamsanguanwong, A.: Usability evaluation and user acceptance of Cobot: case study of universal robots CB series. In: Proceedings of the International Conference on Industrial Engineering and Operations Management, Istanbul, Turkey (2022)

Rossato, C., Pluchino, P., Cellini, N., Jacucci, G., Spagnolli, A., Gamberini, L.: Facing with collaborative robots: the subjective experience in senior and younger workers. Cyberpsychol. Behav. Soc. Netw. **24**(5), 349–356 (2021)

ISO Central Secretary.: Ergonomics of Human-System Interaction. Usability: Definitions and Concepts. Standard ISO 9241–11:2018. International Organization for Standardization, Geneva, CH, Switzerland (2018)

Joshi, A., Kale, S., Chandel, S., Pal, D.K.: Likert scale: explored and explained. Br. J. Appl. Sci. Technol. **7**(4), 396–403 (2015)

Exchanging Files Securely in a Stationary Telepresence Consultation System Using Jitsi Meet

Dennis Eller[1]([envelope])[ORCID], Matti Laak[1], Dominic Becking[1][ORCID], Anne-Kathrin Schmitz[2],
Udo Seelmeyer[1], Philipp Waag[2], and Marc Weinhardt[2]

[1] Bielefeld University of Applied Sciences, 32427 Minden, Germany
dennis.eller@mail.de, mlaak1@fh-bielefeld.de
[2] University of Trier, 54296 Trier, Germany

Abstract. Despite the growing number of online consultations, paper documents are still often used in Germany. It has been observed that the exchange of files between counselor and consultee often takes place via e-mail, which can be cumbersome, and problematic in terms of data protection. STellaR is a stationary telepresence counseling system for collaborative work on paper documents that can be used without computer skills. Previous work has shown that digital telepresence applications can be an alternative to face-to-face meetings if they provide a good user experience. STellaR builds on Jitsi because it is suitable for digital consultations, and it is customizable due to its open-source nature. For STellaR, a file exchange functionality was implemented, which user experience was evaluated using the UEQ and a short version of the meCUE. The new exchange system has a good and above average user experience and is slightly preferred over e-mail and is perceived as more intuitive.

Keywords: Telepresence · Videoconference · Digital counseling

1 Introduction

Telepresence systems played an important role during the corona pandemic and according to current estimates will continue to play an important role [12]. Even before the corona pandemic, there was a need to provide consultations digitally. Because paper documents are often used in consultations in Germany, digitizing them requires the right equipment and expertise. Therefore, online services must be adapted to the needs of those seeking advice. As part of the counseling session, there is a need to exchange files. It has been observed that, this exchange often occurs via e-mail (referred to as current system).

This research and development project is funded by the German Federal Ministry of Education and Research (BMBF) within the funding program "Forschung an Fachhochschulen" (13FH034SX8). The project is in cooperation with Bundesarbeitsgemeinschaft der Freien Wohlfahrtspflege (BAGFW) e.V., Deutscher Caritasverband e.V. and AWO Unterbezirk Hagen-Märkischer Kreis.

STellaR is a stationary telepresence consultation system for collaborative work on paper documents. The system consists of dedicated rooms for video counseling, where a consultee can interact with a remotely located counselor. It is planned that paper documents will be digitized and transferred from the STellaR system to the counselor and that annotations made on the digitized documents are made visible on the paper documents using a projector [9]. Sending confidential data by e-mail is problematic in terms of data protection, as it cannot be ruled out that the e-mail may be read by third parties in transit or on servers of e-mail providers. The contents of e-mails can be protected using encryption (e.g. PGP), however, encryption does not cover meta-data such as sender, recipient or subject [1]. In addition, the setup requires expertise, which, based on our own observations, is not always present among those seeking, receiving, or giving advice. Furthermore, the use of e-mail (with or without PGP) can be perceived as cumbersome. STellaR is based on Jitsi Meet, which currently does not allow file exchange[1]. Therefore, a file exchange functionality with a good user experience should be implemented.

2   Related Work

2.1   Usage of Telepresence Applications

Telepresence applications have been used in a variety of areas, for example for pain management for veterans. Pain management services for veterans in rural areas have similar problems as debt and family counseling with reaching the target audience. One study has shown that the use of telepresence applications can be helpful and is viewed positively by the participants [3,5]. When used in rural elder care facilities, researchers concluded that participants were less lonely with telepresence applications but preferred face-to-face conversations. Lower satisfaction was due in part to problems with technical devices [6,7]. In the psychotherapeutic context, it was found that satisfaction and treatment effectiveness did not differ significantly by using telepresence applications [13].

2.2   Technical Solutions

According to Ushakov et al., video conferencing software can be categorized by the technologies used. These include IP telephony (SIP), Flash or RTMP/RTSP, and browser technologies (e.g. WebRTC) [15]. Open-source solutions include Big-BlueButton[2] and Jitsi Meet[3], which are WebRTC capable. Part of Jitsi's security concept is that conference rooms and associated data such as chat histories or statistics exist only for the duration of a conference. Jitsi tries to establish a P2P connection in a conference with two people. If this is not possible or if there are more people in the conference, communication with the server is done using the

---

[1] https://github.com/jitsi/jitsi-meet/issues/5831.
[2] https://bigbluebutton.org/.
[3] https://jitsi.org/.

Jitsi video bridge (JVB). Jitsi's web application is built with the React library for the interface and Redux for state management.

2.3   Measurement of User Experience

According to DIN EN ISO 9241-210 [4], the term user experience includes user-related (capabilities, behaviors) and product-related (presentation, functionality) factors. As stated by Winter et al. the factors are divided into pragmatic and hedonic quality, and other factors. These factors are mapped into scales by user experience questionnaires [16]. Hassenzahl et al. define pragmatic quality as the ability of an interactive product that is suitable for manipulating the environment and is also perceived as such by its users. Hedonic quality is defined as if an interactive product expands the user's possibilities through new functions, poses new challenges, stimulates through visual design and novel forms of interaction, or communicates a desired identity [8]. According to Thomaschewski et al. [14], products such as messengers have high requirements for all factors of pragmatic quality. These include perspicuity, efficiency, dependability. Hedonic factors such as stimulation and novelty were also rated as important by the subjects. In addition to the user experience factors, it also measures general attractiveness.

There are a number of questionnaires for measuring user experience, each covering different factors and thus suitable for other product groups. Thomaschewski et al. conclude that no questionnaire covers all factors. They recommended combining two questionnaires, using a long version questionnaire in combination with a short version questionnaire to achieve a high response rate [14].

3   Methodology

Related work shows that in order for telepresence applications to be successful, they should be customized to the users, as they may be limited in different ways. To achieve a highly immersive telepresence counceling, attention should be paid to the user experience during implementation.

3.1   Technical Implementation

For the technical implementation, Jitsi Meet is used, as it is suitable with the functions provided. Due to code changes and data protection reasons, an own Jitsi instance is run on the servers of the Bielefeld University of Applied Sciences. Since the communication channel shall be reused in further work and the update to new versions shall be simplified, a new button is added to the already existing toolbar. The button can be used to open a dialog that allows users to exchange files. Already shared files can be requested by the other user. Once the file has been transferred, it can be saved using the browser's save dialog. The current status of the file transfer is displayed to the user. A dialog with different shared files is shown in Fig. 1.

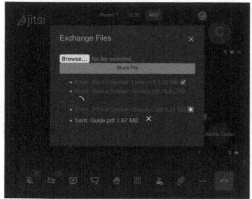

Fig. 1. Exchange File Dialog   **Fig. 2.** Technical Flow

Shared files are displayed in a list in the dialog with sender, file name, size, and transfer status. Entries of files shared by other users are shown in the file list including a downward arrow. Files that have already been downloaded are marked with a check mark. If files are still in transit after being requested, a loading indicator is shown. Users also have the option to remove files from the list. For communication, the `sendEndpointMessage` method of Jitsi is used. With this method, messages can be sent to other users. Depending on the configuration, the transmission is done through WebSockets or the JVB. In both cases, the file to be sent must be converted to Base64 and split into individual packets. On the user side, incoming messages can be processed by a custom reducer via the Redux action `ENDPOINT_MESSAGE_RECEIVED` in the Redux store. The dialog is automatically updated by Redux and the data can be received even if the dialog is closed. The technical flow is shown in Fig. 2. After a file is selected by a user, it can be shared (`ADD_FILE`). The other user can then request the file (`REQUEST_FILE`). This causes the file to be sent in individual packets on one user's side (`CONSUME_FILE_PART`). The last data packet to be sent is an end-of-file (`EOF`) packet. When the `EOF` packet has arrived, the sender receives a `FILE_RECEIVED` message that the file has been successfully transmitted.

3.2   Test Setup

To evaluate the user experience we asked counselors to test the exchange system and fill out a questionnaire. The questionnaires evaluate the following hypotheses. Hypothesis H1: *The exchange system has a good user experience.* Hypothesis H2: *The participants perceive the exchange system as more intuitive than the current system.* Hypothesis H3: *The participants prefer the exchange system over the current system.* In total, the evaluation was conducted with 9 participants. The age of the participants ranged from 22 to 63 years, with a median of 54 and a mean of 46.44. 7 participants were female and 2 were male. 3 of the participants work in family counseling, 4 in general social counseling, and 2 in integration assistance services.

Execution. The evaluation is carried out in the facilities of the counselors with two participants at a time per session. Before the evaluation starts, the procedure is explained to each participant. Participants are given two tasks. The first task is sending a file to another participant. The second task is to receive a file from another participant. Two laptops are prepared with the files to be sent and an active video conference before every test. After the first participant sent a file and the second participant received it, both participants fill out a questionnaire. The second participant then sends a file to the first participant. After these tasks are completed, the questionnaire is filled out again. The assignment of which participant sends his file first is randomized for each pair.

Questionnaire. According to Thomaschewski et al. [14], a combination of UEQ and meCUE covers the widest possible range of important factors for messengers that can be covered by current questionnaires. The UEQ [10] is used because it covers many pragmatic factors. Additionally a shortened version of the meCUE [11] with the modules I (perception of task-related quality), IV (consequences), and V (global) are used. The UEQ and meCUE parts are used to capture the user experience and thus to test H1. To test H2 and H3 the following questions are asked: *I think this system is more intuitive than the current system. I prefer this system over the current system.* They are integrated in a custom questionnaire that builds on the SUS questionnaire [2].

4 Results

With this number of participants, no statistical analysis can be performed. All results should only be seen as tendencies. The UEQ and the meCUE questionnaire provide an evaluation spreadsheet. The results of the UEQ questionnaire are shown in Fig. 3.

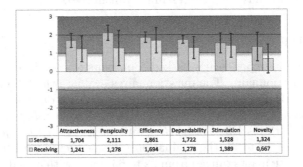

	Attractiveness	Perspicuity	Efficiency	Dependability	Stimulation	Novelty
Sending	1,704	2,111	1,861	1,722	1,528	1,324
Receiving	1,241	1,278	1,694	1,278	1,389	0,667

Fig. 3. UEQ: Measured factors for sending and receiving

Mean values between –0.8 and 0.8 can be considered neutral. Values less than –0.8 are considered negative and values greater than 0.8 are considered positive. All factors were rated as positive for both sending and receiving, whereas *Novelty* was rated neutral when receiving. With the UEQ benchmark (Fig. 4) a relative measure of quality to other products can be drawn.

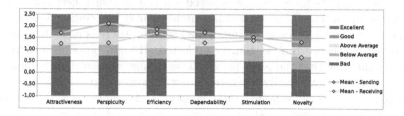

Fig. 4. UEQ: Benchmark

According to the UEQ benchmark, a good to excellent user experience was measured for sending files. When receiving, an above average to good user experience was measured, except for the category *Novelty*, where a value below-average was measured. The results of the meCUE part can be found in Table 1.

Table 1. meCUE: Results of the modules used. Median and mean.

	Sending	Receiving		Sending	Receiving
Module I			**Module IV**		
Usefulness	6.00; 6.00	6.33; 5.96	Intention to use	4.33; 4.15	4.33; 4.44
Usability	6.00; 6.07	5.67; 5.22	Product loyalty	4.00; 4.00	4.67; 4.44
Module V					
Overall evaluation	4.00; 3.50	3.25; 3.10			

The response options for module I and IV range from *disagree completely* (1) to *neither* (4) to *agree completely* (7). For module V the response options range from *as bad* (-5) to *as good* (5). For module I, *usefulness* and *usability* are rated positively. A high value in *usefulness* means that participants were able to fully achieve their task-related goals with the help of the system. For *usability*, a high value shows that participants were able to use the product easily. In Module IV, *intention to use* and *product loyalty* are rated positively. This means that participants are motivated to continue using the system and value the advantages compared to other systems. Module V was rated positive as well. Based on the results, H1 can be confirmed as the exchange system shows a tendency to offer a good user experience. According to the UEQ benchmark, the exchange system also has a good user experience in comparison to other systems.

The Intuitivity of the exchange system is rated via a five-level Likert scale. The corresponding Likert scale ranges from *disagree completely* (1) to *neither* (3) to *agree completely* (5). Here, a median of 3.5 and a mean of 3.63 were measured for sending and a median of 4, and a mean of 3.88 for receiving. H2 can be confirmed because there is a tendency that the users rated the exchange system slightly more intuitively than the current system, especially when receiving. Which system the participants prefer to use is rated via a five-level Likert scale as well. Here, a median of 3 and a mean of 3.5 were measured for sending and a median of 4 and a mean of 3.88 for receiving. When sending there is a small preference, when receiving the current system is preferred. H3 can be confirmed because there is a tendency that the users prefer the exchange system slightly more than the current system, especially when receiving. In general, participants liked the exchange system. Positive points such as *speed* and *simplicity* were mentioned. The negative points mentioned were *small font size* and *unclear language*. The counselors mentioned suggestions such as a *notification when files are received, integration into the chat*, and *more appropriate naming in the user interface.*

5   Conclusion and Outlook

The exchange system has a good user experience (H1), is rated more intuitive than the current system (H2) and is slightly preferred by the participants (H3). Receiving files was rated slightly better than sending them. Positive points such as *speed* and *simplicity* and negative points such as *small font size* and *unclear language* were mentioned. In general, the participants mentioned suggestions such as a *notification when files are received, integration into the chat*, and *more appropriate naming in the user interface*. To reduce the technical obstacles for people seeking and giving advice, the next step could be to send the documents to the advisors using a document camera. For data exchange, the implemented communication channel could be used. Furthermore, data archiving should be implemented, which secures complete documents as well as the changes made. One possibility would be to store the files in a blockchain.

References

1. Blumenthal, M., Clark, D.: Rethinking the design of the internet: end to end arguments vs. the brave new world. ACM Trans. Internet Technol. **1**, 70–109 (2001). https://doi.org/10.1145/383034.383037
2. Brooke, J.: Sus: a quick and dirty usability scale. Usability Eval. Ind. **189** (1995)
3. Cosio, D., HL, E.: Delivery of pain education through picture-telephone videoconferencing for veterans with chronic, non-cancer pain. Clin. Med. Invest. **1**(2) (2016). https://doi.org/10.15761/cmi.1000105
4. DIN EN ISO 9241–210: DIN EN ISO 9241–210:2011–01, ergonomie der mensch-system-interaktion - teil 210: Prozess zur gestaltung gebrauchstauglicher interaktiver systeme (ISO 9241–210:2010); deutsche fassung EN ISO 9241–210:2010 (01 2011). https://doi.org/10.31030/1728173

5. Elliott, J., Chapman, J., Clark, D.J.: Videoconferencing for a veteran's pain management follow-up clinic. Pain Manag. Nurs. **8**(1), 35–46 (2007). https://doi.org/10.1016/j.pmn.2006.12.005

6. Guilfoyle, C., Wootton, R., Hassall, S., Offer, J., Warren, M., Smith, D.: Preliminary experience of allied health assessments delivered face to face and by videoconference to a residential facility for elderly people. J. Telemed. Telecare **9**, 230–233 (2003). https://doi.org/10.1258/135763303322225571

7. Guilfoyle, M.C., et al.: User satisfaction with allied health services delivered to residential facilities via videoconferencing. J. Telemed. Telecare **9**(1), 52–54 (2003). https://doi.org/10.1258/135763303322196349

8. Hassenzahl, M., Burmester, M., Koller, F.: Attrakdiff: Ein fragebogen zur messung wahrgenommener hedonischer und pragmatischer qualität. In: Szwillus, G., Ziegler, J. (eds.) Mensch Comput. 2003: Interaktion in Bewegung, pp. 187–196. B. G. Teubner, Stuttgart (2003)

9. Laak, M., Schmitz, A.K., Becking, D., Seelmeyer, U., Waag, P., Weinhardt, M.: Stellar - a stationary telepresence counselling system for collaborative work on paper documents. In: Stephanidis, C., Antona, M., Ntoa, S. (eds.) HCI International 2021 - Late Breaking Posters, pp. 383–389. Springer International Publishing, Cham (2021)

10. Laugwitz, B., Schrepp, M., Held, T.: Konstruktion eines fragebogens zur messung der user experience von softwareprodukten. In: Heinecke, A.M., Paul, H. (eds.) Mensch und Computer 2006: Mensch und Computer im Strukturwandel, pp. 125–134. Oldenbourg Verlag, München (2006)

11. Minge, M., Riedel, L.: mecue - ein modularer fragebogen zur erfassung des nutzungserlebens. In: Boll, S., Maaß, S., Malaka, R. (eds.) Mensch und Computer 2013: Interaktive Vielfalt, pp. 89–98. Oldenbourg Verlag, München (2013)

12. Standaert, W., Muylle, S., Basu, A.: How shall we meet? understanding the importance of meeting mode capabilities for different meeting objectives. Inf. Manag. **58**(1), 103393 (2021). https://doi.org/10.1016/j.im.2020.103393

13. Stefan, S., David, D.: Face-to-face counseling versus high definition holographic projection system. efficacy and therapeutic alliance. a brief research report. J. Cogn. Behav. Psychother. **13**, 299–307 (2013)

14. Thomaschewski, J., Hinderks, A., Schrepp, M.: Welcher ux-fragebogen passt zu meinem produkt? In: Hess, S., Fischer, H. (eds.) Mensch und Computer 2018 - Usability Professionals. pp. 437–446. Gesellschaft für Informatik e.V. Und German UPA e.V., Bonn (2018). https://doi.org/10.18420/muc2018-up-0150

15. Ushakov, Y.A., Ushakova, M.V., Shukhman, A.E., Polezhaev, P.N., Legashev, L.V.: Webrtc based platform for video conferencing in an educational environment. In: 2019 IEEE 13th International Conference on Application of Information and Communication Technologies (AICT), pp. 1–5 (2019). https://doi.org/10.1109/AICT47866.2019.8981724

16. Winter, D., Hinderks, A., Schrepp, M., Thomaschewski, J.: Welche ux faktoren sind für mein produkt wichtig? In: Hess, S., Fischer, H. (eds.) Mensch und Computer 2017 - Usability Professionals. Gesellschaft für Informatik e.V., Regensburg (2017). https://doi.org/10.18420/muc2017-up-0002

Iteration, Iteration, Iteration: How Restructuring Data Can Reveal Complex Relationships Between Chronic Illnesses and the Apps Intended to Support Them

Hannah Field[(⊠)], Lisa Thomas, and Emmanuel Tsekleves

Lancaster University, Lancaster LA1 4YW, UK
h.field1@lancaster.ac.uk

Abstract. This study intended to gain a broad understanding of how commercial apps may support people with chronic illness management, through the restructuring of data for analysis. The study formed an initial part of a larger PhD project looking into symptom tracking for people with chronic illnesses.

The study included apps designed for people with Rheumatoid Arthritis, Crohn's and Inflammatory Bowel Disease (IBD), Myalgic Encephalomyelitis (ME), and Anxiety conditions (aggregated and including Bi-Polar Disorder, Generalised Anxiety Disorder and Panic Disorder) to give an overview of how apps might engage with different types of chronic illness, all of which feature fatigue as a main symptom.

In this paper, we report on the process of creating and using an iterative process to rearrange the data collected in order to reveal more complex relationships between the chronic illnesses and the apps intended to support them.

Keywords: Symptom tracking apps · iterated analysis

1 Data Collection

Data was collected to provide a holistic overview of four chronic illnesses, Rheumatoid Arthritis, Crohn's and Inflammatory Bowel Disease (IBD), Myalgic Encephalomyelitis (ME), and Anxiety conditions, as well as an impression of various apps designed to support patients.

1.1 Chronic Illness Data Collection

The relevant NHS pages for each condition formed the foundation for data collection: ME [6], Rheumatoid Arthritis [7], Crohn's and IBD [8], and Anxiety [9]. Further data was gathered using charitable websites dedicated to each chronic illness: the *ME Association* [13] for ME, *NRAS* [11, 12] and *Versus Arthritis* [19] for Rheumatoid Arthritis, Crohn's and Colitis [2] for Crohn's and *Anxiety UK* [1] for Anxiety conditions. Combined, the websites provided a working list of symptoms, emotional impacts, lifestyle changes -

both advised and inevitable - and treatments, including complimentary treatments as well as evidence-based interventions. Common comorbidities listed on these sites were also included.

1.2 App Data Collection

An organic search was used to discover apps designed to support patients with each disease. This search replicated the method an ordinary patient might use and therefore took in pages recommending apps including Healthline [5] and the NHS Library [10]. While this is not an exhaustive list of relevant apps, the total of 38 apps selected covered a range of approaches, from games to help non-sufferers understand a condition and its implications better, to pain mapping and diary apps. The app description was used to gain an impression of what the functions and intentions of each app were.

2 Method of Analysis

An iterative process was used to rearrange the data in order to produce different modes of analysis. Iteration of analytical processes embodies the idea that "design action is essential to the knowledge generation." [18] and, rather than stopping at one method of analysis, repeating the process creates further opportunities to uncover greater nuance in relationships between elements and, hopefully, to discover an 'aha!' moment [15].

2.1 First Iteration: Linear Mapping

In the first iteration (Fig. 1) the information regarding each illness was clustered together. The different elements - symptoms, treatments, complementary treatments, lifestyle changes (inevitable), lifestyle changes (recommended), emotional responses - were each written on separate pieces of paper and were colour coded to make each element easier to identify. These clusters are arranged vertically on the left side (Column One) as shown in Fig. 2.

In this iteration, all the data is arranged in a single place and reads naturally from left to right. The data for each app was written on individual sheets of paper, lining up horizontally with the relevant illness. Post-it notes were added to the apps to add further details along with colour-coded stickers (green dots for a diary or tracking feature; blue dots for NHS approval or testing; yellow dots for social network element; red dots for pain mapping; whale stickers for a 4 star rating or higher[1]). The apps are grouped roughly so that those with similar features appear close together. The apps that include tracking as a feature are on the left, with alternative and companion apps, which may not be designed to help manage the condition, on the right. For example, the toilet finder apps are furthest to the right as they don't deal with any symptoms but do offer a practical service. Broadly, the more features, the further to the left the app was arranged.

---

[1] Please note that the type or colour of sticker is not offering any deeper metaphorical meaning. Especially the whales.

Fig. 1. This image is a close-up, showing the arrangement of data for Anxiety Disorders.

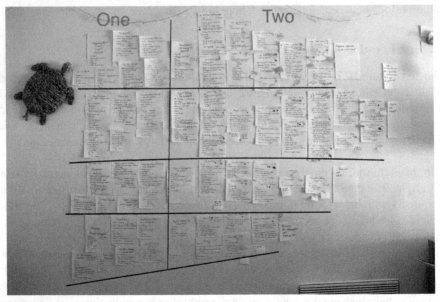

Fig. 2. Image shows data collected during the study, with the chronic illnesses detailed on the left hand side in Column One, followed by the apps on the right in Column Two.

2.2 Second Iteration: Stacked Discs

Chronic illnesses are not linear or static: symptoms may recede and relapse, may be cyclical, and there may be no particular logical progression. This means that while a patient may have a particular set of needs one day, they may have different requirements on another. To reflect this insight, the second iteration asked: *what would happen if the data was rearranged into a circular design that could be manipulated?*

A prototype for ME was made (Fig. 3), placing the disease elements onto a series of stacked discs that could be rotated. Rather than reading left to right, this model encouraged the researcher to move the layers in order to read them, naturally rearranging and reorganising as they did. This afforded a new kind of analysis that grouped different elements together to offer new perspectives. Rather than grouping apps to see how they compared to each other, now the various elements were being grouped to consider their relationships. This new grouping allowed further insight into how different elements of each disease might interact and how an app might be able to support that interaction.

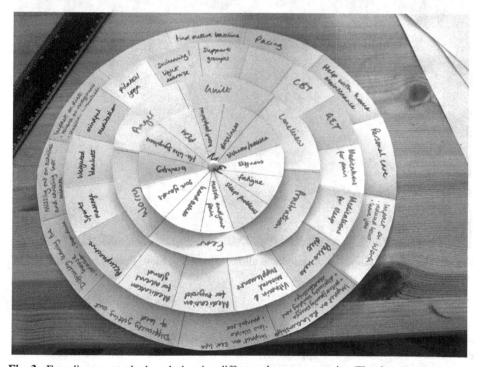

Fig. 3. Four discs are stacked, each showing different element categories. The elements are colour-coded to match the first iteration. The discs can be rotated so that different elements may appear together.

2.3 Third Iteration: Clocks

An immediate problem with the second model was the fixed arrangement of data on the discs: some elements would never appear together. To resolve this problem, the third iteration - inspired by the Weasley family clock in Harry Potter, which offers information including characters' state of being rather than the time [16, 17] - used rotating hands, effectively splitting up the elements and allowing freer movement (Fig. 4). Each 'hand' on the clock had a single element written on it which meant that any of the elements across the categories could be considered together in groups. Crucially, while grouping elements, there were never any elements that weren't visible, retaining the sense of exploring the whole disease, not just the most visible parts. Again, colour-coding was retained.

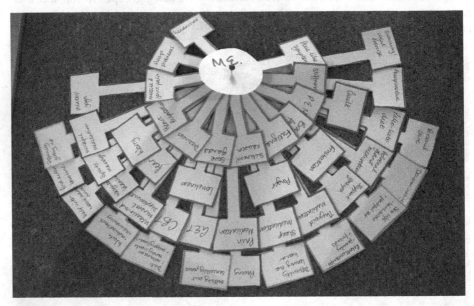

Fig. 4. The clock is pinned in the middle to allow the hands to move freely and for elements to be grouped together.

This third model afforded a more flexible way to rearrange the data but also offered an opportunity to measure how each app could be relevant to the various elements of each disease by placing the app description at the top of the clock and then moving the relevant hands to point toward it. This process was repeated for each app and every configuration of the clocks was photographed for comparison (Fig. 5).

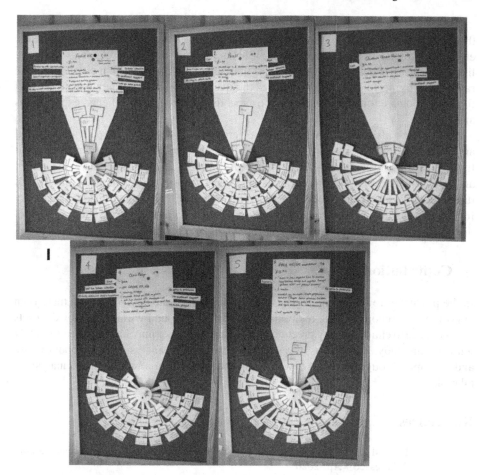

Fig. 5. Five apps are compared to the symptoms of ME.

3 Key Findings

Reiterating the data models encouraged different styles of analysis. The initial map was a commonplace, practical method of gathering a large amount of data but the stacked circles and the clocks challenged assumed linearity and offered a method for reimagining the data by physically moving it around and, in doing so, embraced the complexity of understanding the elements that make up the experience of each chronic illness.

Moving the data to match elements of each chronic illness to apps offering support gave a clear indication of both how elements tend to cluster together and how many simply cannot be supported by an app. For M.E, each examined app interacted with a couple of elements, but it is clear from the pictures just how many other aspects of the chronic illness remain unsupported. Despite different offerings from diary keeping to hypnosis, it is also notable that the same cluster of a few symptoms match up to the aims of the apps.

In a tick-box analysis, it would be easy to conclude that the app that interacts with the most elements would be the most effective for the patient. However, in grouping the elements together in the third iteration, it becomes clear that some elements are more likely to cluster together than others and that apps tend to focus on a single outcome rather than trying to do it all. This raises the question of whether there is a sweet spot for an app doing enough and whether app capabilities match up to patients' expectations and need.

The clocks also showed which apps offered unique kinds of support, not centred around improving the condition per se but still intended to help the patient manage their lifestyle. For example, *Flush - Toilet Finder and Map* [3], an app for people with Crohn's and IBD, isn't relevant to the medical management of most of the elements of the chronic illness but offers a creative solution to needing to find a public toilet quickly, a necessity for many patients. This indicated that even while using a more holistic interpretation of the disease, the framework for analysis could still be refined.

4   Contribution

In the process of reimagining new models for displaying and analysing data, there is an opportunity to reconsider the relationships that may be found within complex data sets and a chance to challenge any preconceptions the researcher may have entered the study with. In this study, the process of reimagining models for analysing data about disease and its impact brought forward new insights and allowed for a more holistic analysis to take place.

References

1. Anxiety UK. n.d.a. Anxiety Information. https://www.anxietyuk.org.uk/get-help/anxiety-inf ormation/. Accessed 7 Apr 2020
2. Crohn's and Colitis UK. Living with Crohn's or Colitis: Your Guide, May 2019. http://s3-eu-west-1.amazonaws.com/files.crohnsandcolitis.org.uk/Publications/Living-with-Crohns-or-Colitis. Accessed 7 Apr 2020
3. Flush - Toilet Finder and Map (5.0.0). iTunes App Store. Accessed 7 Apr 2020
4. Healthline. The Best Rheumatoid Arthritis Apps of 2019, May 2019. https://www.healthline.com/health/best-ra-apps. Accessed 7 Apr 2020
5. Healthline. The Best Crohn's Disease Apps of 2019, May 2019. https://www.healthline.com/health/best-ra-apps
6. NHS. n.d.a Overview: Myalgic encephalomyelitis or chronic fatigue syndrome (ME/CFS). https://www.nhs.uk/conditions/chronic-fatigue-syndrome-cfs/. Accessed 7 Apr 2020
7. NHS. n.d.b. Overview: Rheumatoid arthritis. https://www.nhs.uk/conditions/rheumatoid-art hritis/. Accessed 7 Apr 2020
8. NHS. n.d.c. Overview: Crohn's Disease. https://www.nhs.uk/conditions/crohns-disease/. Accessed 7 Apr 2020
9. NHS. n.d.d. *Overview - Generalised anxiety disorder in adults*. Available at: https://www.nhs.uk/mental-health/conditions/generalised-anxiety-disorder/overview/ [Accessed: 7th April 2020]
10. NHS. n.d.e. Apps Library. https://www.nhs.uk/apps-library/category/mental-health/ [Accessed: 7th April 2020]

11. NRAS. n.d.a Support for living with RA. https://nras.org.uk/. Accessed 7 Apr 2020
12. NRAS. n.d.b Emotions, Relationships and Sexuality. https://www.nras.org.uk/data/files/Pub lications/Emotions,%20Relationships%20&%20Sexuality%20Graphics%20updated%20A pril%202016%20lo%20res%20a-.pdf. Accessed 7 Apr 2020
13. ME Association. n.d.a What is ME? https://meassociation.org.uk/about-what-is-mecfs/. Accessed 7 Apr 2020
14. My Therapy App. n.d.a. Tired of Being Tired? Here's an App to Help You Manage Chronic Fatigue Syndrome. https://www.mytherapyapp.com/how-to-use-apps-for-fighting-chronic-fatigue-syndrome-cfs. Accessed 7 Apr 2020
15. Papanek, V.: Design for the Real World. Thames and Hudson, London (2020)
16. Rowling, J.K.: Harry Potter and the Chamber of Secrets. Bloomsbury, London (1998)
17. Rowling, J.K.: Harry Potter and the Goblet of Fire. Bloomsbury, London (2000)
18. Stappers, P.J., Visser, F.S., Keller, I.: The role of prototypes and frameworks for structuring explorations by research through design. In: Rodgers, P.A., Yee, J. (eds.) The Routledge Companion to Design Research, pp. 163–174. Routledge (2014). https://doi.org/10.4324/978 1315758466-16
19. Versus Arthritis: n.d.a. What is Rheumatoid Arthritis? https://www.versusarthritis.org/about-arthritis/conditions/rheumatoid-arthritis/. Accessed 7 Apr 2020

Development of Applications that Integrate Information from Diverse Systems with a Focus on Information Organization

Mayo Fukata[✉] and Eiichi Hayakawa

Takushoku University, 815-1 Tatemachi, Hachioji-Shi, Tokyo, Japan
23m307@st.takushoku-u.ac.jp, hayakawa@cs.takushoku-u.ac.jp

Abstract. With the COVID-19 craze, remote work and on-demand learning using Microsoft Teams and other tools at home has become popular. The problems with this include the risk of being late for class and start time due to lack of chimes, and the risk of missing assignment deadlines due to increased number of assignments and media and unmanageable workspace. To reduce these risks, the main objective of this study was to provide the ability to integrate information and notify users of assignment due dates.

Developing applications that integrate information from different systems with a focus on information organization. Remote working has increased the risk of delays due to misplaced or misunderstood information. To mitigate this risk, we developed a PC application feature that intermittently notifies users when the due date of an assignment registered in the Google Calendar is approaching and allows users to stop the notification only if they correctly answer a four-choice topic selection question. These specifications were designed to reduce the risk of missing deadlines.

A questionnaire survey of three respondents revealed that two had experienced the usefulness of the notification feature. The results of the survey indicated that the notification feature is effective for remote classes.

Keywords: Notification · student support · assignment and schedule support · Integrated application information systems

1 Introduction

Today, in addition to proprietary systems, collaboration tool like Microsoft Teams or Zoom, organization-issued e-mail, and online storage services are used to share information within organizations such as universities and corporations. This makes it is necessary to access and retrieve information separately.

In addition, with the Corona craze, remote working and on-demand learning using Teams and other services at home has taken off. The current problems are the risk of being late for class and the start of the school day due to the lack of chimes, and the risk of missing assignment deadlines due to an increase in the number of assignments

© The Author(s), under exclusive license to Springer Nature Switzerland AG 2023
C. Stephanidis et al. (Eds.): HCII 2023, CCIS 1834, pp. 76–82, 2023.
https://doi.org/10.1007/978-3-031-35998-9_11

and an unmanageable workspace. The main objective of this study was to implement a notification feature to solve these problems.

Kimura [1] developed to register regularly scraped organizational system information in Google Calendar and to provide notifications via a specially designed smartphone application. Although a smartphone was used in that study, with the introduction of online classes, PCs are being used more frequently. Therefore, this system is designed to run on a PC.

In addition to the previous study, the purpose of this study is to use systems such as Teams and Slack to obtain class and meeting information, and to add a feature to control cloud services to further improve convenience.

Eto [2] was used to log in to all systems with a single ID and password by synchronizing different authentication information for each system. There are two problems with this research: First, it takes time to synchronize when changing passwords, and second, since the systems themselves are separate, logins must be done individually. This system also solves these problems as well.

2   Research Summary

The system configuration diagram is shown in Fig. 1. The term "private" here does not refer to an account provided by an organization, but to an account for personal use.

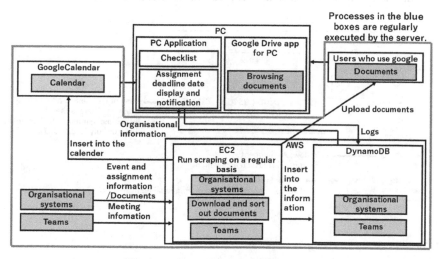

Fig. 1. A system configuration diagram

In this study, we use Amazon Web Service's DynamoDB as the database server, EC2 as the periodic execution server, and Electron as the PC application platform. The periodically collected Teams and Slack data is registered in DynamoDB. The PC application retrieves the data and implements a feature that notifies students before classes start and before assignments are due.

As a result of the proliferation of classes and work styles using Teams and other methods associated with the Corona Vortex, there are many opportunities to use PCs, so this system runs on PCs.

3   Developed Features

The following features were developed in this study,

3.1   Integrated Information Systems of Applications

Information is obtained from systems used by the organization through APIs or scraping and registered in DynamoDB and Google Calendar. Authentication information registered in DynamoDB by the initial setup function is used.

3.2   Assignment Due Date Display

Figure 2 shows the application screen. The schedule can be confirmed by retrieving and displaying the information registered by the "Integrated Information Systems of Applications" via API.

The blue frame on the right side of the screen displays the name of the assignment and the due date, which is used as the basis for the notification function.

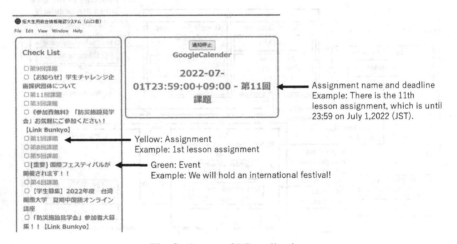

Fig. 2.   Screen of PC application

3.3   Automatic Download and Sorting of Documents

Materials are automatically downloaded from the internal system, automatically sorted by class name, and uploaded to Google Drive.

3.4 Notification

The application screens are shown in Figs. 3 and 4. When a deadline registered by the "Integrated Information Systems from Applications" approaching, a balloon notification as shown in Fig. 4 is sent out every 15 s. When the notification is clicked, the dialog box shown in Fig. 3 appears. The user can select the name of the class for which the deadline is approaching from a list of options and stop the notification only when the answer is correct. The purpose of this is to reduce the risk of unnoticed delays.

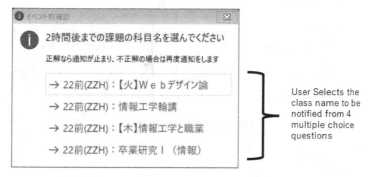

User Selects the class name to be notified from 4 multiple choice questions

Fig. 3. Screen for selecting subjects from 4 options

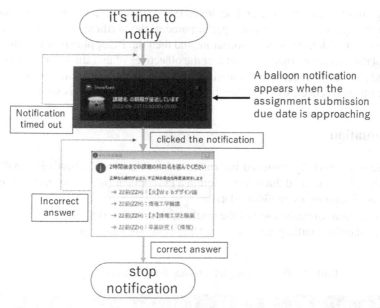

Fig. 4. Notification flow

3.5 Checklist

The checklist portion of the application screen is shown in Fig. 5. The information stored in DynamoDB by the "Integrated Information Systems of Applications" features is displayed in a list format and can be cleared when checked. Event information and issues are color-coded for easy identification.

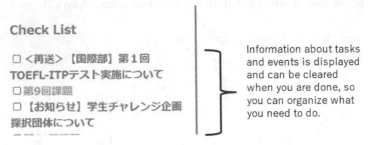

Fig. 5. Screen of checklist.

4 Implementation

The program was implemented and deployed on a Windows server using EC2 and a PC application. Five students in a class participated in the verification. First, the students registered their authentication information, and then the PC application was distributed to each of them to verify that they had met the objectives of this study. First, the students registered their authentication information, and then the PC application was distributed to each of them to check whether they had met the objectives of this study.

5 Evaluation

The system successfully retrieved information from the organization's internal system and displayed and notified the information in a PC application. The system also enabled the review of documents on GoogleDrive.

The time from the activation of the notification features to notification was recorded for five verification participants (A ~ E). The results are shown in Table 1.

Table 1. Time to complete the notification disabling process.

Verifier	A	B	C	D	E
Time (sec)	16.5	6.8	19.2	No data	No data

Table 2. Shows the results of the usage status of the checklist function.

Verifier	A	B	C	D	E
Checked items/total items	36/37	5/43	39/48	37/50	6/49
Check rate (%)	97.3%	11.6%	81.2%	74.0%	12.2%

Table 3. Results of the system questionnaire.

	Was the notification method appropriate?	Was the default setting of the notification time (2 hours before the deadline) appropriate?	Was the notification function actually useful?	Was the design and feel of the screen appropriate?	Were there any bugs or errors in the system?	Was the checklist function actually useful?
A	2	5	1	2	4	3
B	5	3	4	4	5	4
C	2	5	3	5	5	—
Average	3.0	4.3	2.7	3.7	4.7	3.5

At the end of the validation, a questionnaire survey was conducted among the users. The results are shown in Table 3.

An integrated environment of PCs was constructed for remote classes.

Table 1 shows that the user response time was short, ranging from a few seconds to several tens of seconds. This indicates that the balloon notification method was appropriate.

Table 2 shows that the checking rate of the checklist function differs between high and low users. This result indicates that there are those who need this feature and those who do not. The questionnaire results in Table 3 indicate that this feature is useful for those who need it.

The results in Table 3 show that the user interface, checklist function, and system stability of this system were highly rated.

These three results show that this system is effective as a student support system for distance learning.

One problem during the validation phase was that the fourth-year students who participated in the validation took few classes, and the system did not fully demonstrate its effectiveness. In the future, it may be possible to conduct the validation with students in lower grades.

6 Conclusion

In addition to the previous study, this study added support for notifications, team information gathering, material download and sorting, and checklist features to meet the goals of supporting distance learning. As a result of the verification, it was found that this system was effective in supporting students.

Future work will include additional validation and the addition of features to support publication patterns of materials and assignments.

References

1. Kimura, T.: Development of an integrated schedule confirmation system for Takushoku University students, Graduation thesis, Takushoku University (2019)
2. Eto, H., Watanabe, K., Tadaki, S., Watanabe, Y.: Integrated authentication for campus-wide information systems. IPSJ Res. Rep. 2002-DSM-027

Characterizing the Information Consumer Behavior: An Explorative Case Study in a Chilean Organization Department

María Paz Godoy$^{(\boxtimes)}$ (iD), Cristian Rusu (iD), Isidora Azócar, and Noor Yaser

Escuela de Ingeniería en Información Y Control de Gestión, Universidad de Valparaíso, Valparaíso, Chile
mariapaz.godoy@uv.cl, NOOR.YASER@alumnos.uv.cl

Abstract. Data and knowledge management has taken on a fundamental role in decision-making processes into organizations in recent years. The consumption of information within the organization is present in most of the operational and administrative processes of the organization. Therefore, information consumption also takes on importance in the design and application of organizational strategy initiatives. The Information Consumer Experience (ICX) can be considered as a particular case of Customer eXperience (CX), involving expectations, satisfactions and pains of information consumers within the organization. ICX analyzes the interaction between employees or departments and the information provider organization or departments, through their information products, systems and services offered. The main objective of this work is to analyze ICX within an organization by conducting an exploratory analysis in order to make a diagnosis based on three fundamental elements: organizational departments involved, participants (Sample) and information products, systems or services used by information consumers. As results of this analysis, consumers' needs were identified and consumers profiles were generated, which lead us to elaborate a Customer Journey Map that described the different points of contact and the perceptions of consumers. Finally, the greatest pains of consumers can be identified, related to: (1) high complexity for information searching, (2) better-known information systems preference over the more specialized ones, and (3) the isolated Information distribution across departmental unit hides the overview state of the department.

Keywords: Information Consumer Experience · Touchpoints · Customer Experience

1 Introduction

Currently, the consumption of information within organizations is present in most of their operational and administrative processes, which is why data and knowledge management has played a fundamental role in decision-making processes. Therefore, the consumption of information has been relevant for the design and implementation of organizational strategy initiatives.

C. Stephanidis et al. (Eds.): HCII 2023, CCIS 1834, pp. 83–89, 2023.
https://doi.org/10.1007/978-3-031-35998-9_12

Information Consumer eXperience (ICX) is considered a specific instance of the customer experience (CX), as the latter analyzes the multidimensional process that focuses on cognitive, emotional, behavioral, sensory, and social responses [1]. The study of ICX can be approached using analytical methods from the CX domain to understand ICX within an organization, identify different touchpoints, represent ICX through a customer journey map, and evaluate ICX using well-known CX evaluation techniques [2].

This study examines ICX in a department of an organization, identifying information providers, analyzing products, services, and/or information systems to explore information consumer interactions within the organization. In Sect. 2, the concept of ICX is analyzed, followed by a description of touchpoints in Sect. 3. Section 4 describes the practical case, highlighting touchpoints, and finally, Sect. 5 presents the conclusion and future work.

2 Information Consumer Experience (ICX) Systematic Review

The Information Consumer Experience (ICX) is considered a specific case of Customer Experience (CX) involving the expectations, satisfactions, and pains of information consumers within the organization. Although within the literature, can be observed that ICX involves all interactions between employees (consumers) and products, information systems, and services within an organization, including tasks such as information use, generation, management, information exchange between departments, teamwork-based information use, and decision-making. All of these interactions represent touchpoints between information consumer employees or departments and information provider departments within the organization [2].

Within ICX, elements related to people that can influence their experience cannot be dismissed, as they play an important role in interpreting reports, as they contribute to the consumer experience either positively or negatively. In this sense, from an expansive perspective, the customer experience is considered holistic in nature, incorporating cognitive, emotional, sensory, social, and spiritual aspects into all interactions with a company [3].

It is important to consider that consumer satisfaction encompasses both personal and information-related factors. Personal elements that can be identified include beliefs, values, emotional factors, academic degree, cognitive processes, among others. These factors could affect the information consumer's perceptions.

3 Touchpoint

The concept of touchpoints is related to the interaction of a customer with a company or a service, and it is important to note that not all touchpoints have the same level of importance for customers [4]. These touchpoints can occur through different channels, such as social media, email, phone, or in-person, and they are essential because they are the means by which a company can share relevant information with its current and potential customers about its products or services, generating interaction with its customers [5].

Also, it is relevant to consider that during a touchpoint, technological applications play an important role. Digital personalization tools such as intelligence query platforms, option evaluation tools, configurators, concurrent platforms, and co-design, among others, can be used. [6] Therefore, touchpoints are a source or channel of information distribution with which the consumer interacts with different types of information retrieval tools, highlighting that this can be done in different ways, for example, from an information system, spreadsheet, calls, including even from the interaction between two employees.

4   Information Consumer Journey Map Applied in a Practical Case

The Customer Journey Map (CJM) is a strategic tool that allows diagramming a customer's journey, as well as all their interactions with touchpoints, with a specific company [7]. For this reason, the use of the customer journey map is becoming more popular, due to its usefulness in understanding the customer experience of an organization [8], as it helps identify both positive and negative aspects, and critical points where improvements are necessary [9]. Each point present in the diagram reflects the perception at a certain stage, and the classifications include positive experience, which reflects customer satisfaction, whereas dissatisfaction represents a negative experience, causing concern for strategic management. Lastly, a neutral experience is the midpoint between the two experiences.

Figure 1 represents the customer journey map for information within a particular case in a Chilean organization, where the sequential interactions that a group of workers must carry out to obtain the necessary information for their tasks are presented, identifying each of the stages, touchpoints, and perceptions of the ICX, with the latter being classified into three types of ICX: positive, neutral, and negative as mentioned earlier.

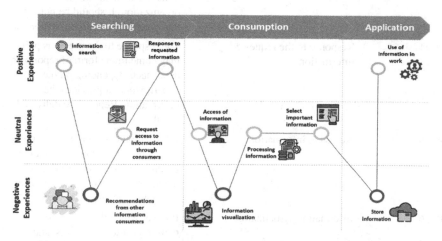

Fig. 1. Map of the information consumer journey in a Chilean organization.

In Table 1, each of the identified touchpoints for obtaining information is described and displayed on the map. The first column assigns an ID to each touchpoint, and the second column provides the name, followed by a description.

Table 1. Touchpoint

ID contact points	Touchpoint	Definition
TP001	Information search	It arises from the need to consume information, so the person searches for information from different access sites for the department's employees
TP002	Recommendations from other information consumers	Optional touchpoint for the information consumer, as they may or may not turn to other consumers to facilitate information search by recommending a system, information product, or service to find the required information
TP003	Requesting access to information through other information consumers	Not all information consumer profiles within the department had access to the same information, so some consumers had to request information from the department coordinator through established protocols. This way, they would be provided with the necessary information or if it is required to request information from other departments of the organization. It should be noted that this touch point can also be optional
TP004	Response to the requested information	The response to the previous points may come in the form of reports or data sheets depending on the department that provides the information. Reports are delivered via email
TP005	Access to information	Information consumption can come from a report or from information products, systems or services where the information consumer has access, and how to access it
TP006	Information visualization	Point at which the information consumer filters, explores, and visualizes information using information tools

(*continued*)

Table 1. (*continued*)

ID contact points	Touchpoint	Definition
TP007	Process information	Within the department, the obtained information needs to be processed to make it more user-friendly for the information consumer and easily understood. This includes formatting changes to help them select the relevant information for their tasks
TP008	Selecting important information	Once the information has been processed and properly formatted, the information consumer selects the information based on their own criteria, choosing what is useful for their work
TP009	Store information	After using the information and/or data, the information consumer must register or store the information they will use in their daily work in order to access it only from the cloud to have integrated information
TP010	Use of information in tasks	Use of information in work tasks by the information consumer, either in the creation of reports, updating spreadsheets, among others, to incorporate it into their work

Table 2 provides a summary where the main findings obtained from this research can be appreciated, such as the perception of the information consumer in each of the points of contact, the interaction components in each of them, and their respective recommendations for managing the perceptions obtained. These recommendations are provided with the aim that all perceptions become positive.

Table 2. Summary table

ID contact points	Components	Appreciation	Recommendation
TP001	Interaction between information consumers and/or products, systems or information services	Positive	Maintain the positive interaction that exists between information consumers and/or information products, systems, or services
TP002	Interaction among information consumers, information provider departments, products, systems, and information services	Negative	Generate a cooperative environment among the programs that integrate the unit Enhance teamwork both at the middle level of the unit and operationally through focus groups
TP003	Interaction between information consumers and information products, systems, and services	Neutral	Transparent monitoring of the status of the request through the protocol established by the unit
TP004	Interaction between information consumers and information products, systems, or services	Positive	To maintain good interaction between information consumers and information products, systems, or services
TP005	Interaction between information consumer and information products, systems or services	Neutral	Establishing a base system that contains integrated, updated, and easily accessible information
TP006	Interaction of technological products	Negative	Train the members of the unit on services acquired by the organization, for example Tableau
TP007	Processing. Interaction between information product, systems and/or services and information consumer	Neutral	Use a base system such as the academic portal, where the largest amount of information is integrated with standardized formats
TP008	Interaction of technological products	Neutral	Create a monitoring record for tracking responses to information requests from other departments
TP009	Interaction between information consumer and information products, systems or services	Negative	Interactive workshop taught by the Information and Communication Technologies department explaining the operation of the systems used by the unit to provide greater confidence in having the information in the future and knowledge of the benefits provided by the implemented technologies
TP010	Communication between information consumers, information products, systems, or services	Positive	Maintaining the good communication that exists among information consumers, information products, systems or services

5   Conclusion and Future Work

The consumption of information by employees in organizations has showed a rapid increase in recent times. It is important to note that the concept of ICX is related to all the interactions that a consumer has in order to obtain information and fulfill assigned tasks to achieve the company's strategic objectives. Therefore, this research aims to analyze various fundamental concepts related to the information consumer experience.

Upon analysis on a Chilean organization study case, it has been observed that many touchpoints need improvement as they directly influence the information consumer experience. Managing some of these touchpoints may even require the implementation or enhancement of information products, systems, or services. As a result, future work proposes to study the information consumer experience comprehensively across the organization, rather than from one specific area. This study aims to incorporate various types of variables and explore beyond the factors that may affect the information consumer experience according to consumer types. By addressing this, organizations can optimize the information consumer experience and thereby contribute to the achievement of the company's strategic goals.

References

1. Temkin, B.D.: Mapping the customer journey. Forrester Res. **3**(1), 20 (2010)
2. Godoy, M., Rusu, C., Ugalde, J.: Information Consumer Experience: A Chilean Case Study (2022)
3. Lemon, K.,Verhoef, P.: Understanding customer experience throughout the customer journey. J. Mark. 70 (2016)
4. Wyner, G.: How do you measure the customer experience. Mark. Res. **15**, 6–7 (2003)
5. Bascur, C., Rusu, C., Quiñones, D.: User as customer: touchpoints and journey map. In: Ahram, T., Karwowski, W., Taiar, R. (eds.) Human Systems Engineering and Design. AISC, vol. 876, pp. 117–122. Springer, Cham (2018). https://doi.org/10.1007/978-3-030-02053-8_19
6. Chatzopoulos, C.G., Weber, M.: Challenges of total customer experience (TCX): measurement beyond touchpoints. Int. J. Indus. Eng. Manage. **9**(4), 187–196 (2018). https://doi.org/10.24867/IJIEM-2018-4-187
7. Matus, N.: Experiencia del Estudiante de la Escuela de Ingeniería Informática de la PUCV (2020)
8. Rosenbaum, M.S., Otalora, M.L., Ramírez, G.C.: How to create a realistic customer journey map
9. Javier Mejías. https://javiermegias.com/blog/2013/04/customer-journey-map-mapa-experiencia-cliente/

Privacy-Preserving Data Management and Provision System for Personal Data Store

Kaisei Kajita[✉], Kinji Matsumura, and Go Ohtake

Japan Broadcasting Corporation, Tokyo, Japan
`kajita.k-bu@nhk.or.jp`

Abstract. In systems that manage and provide personal information, such as personal data stores (PDS), the privacy of the data stored on cloud servers is paramount. Simple adoption of cryptographic primitives such as AES does not allow re-encryption for each destination without decrypting personal data, and users are thus required to maintain different secret keys for each destination. In this paper, we propose a system that utilizes ID-based proxy re-encryption to securely manage and deliver data without sacrificing the convenience of PDS.

Keywords: Personal data store · ID-based proxy re-encryption · Privacy preserving

1 Introduction

1.1 Background

Systems that manage and provide personal information, such as personal data stores (PDS), have attracted attention in recent years. With PDS, users voluntarily provide their personal data to a service provider so that they can enjoy services based on the provided data. When PDS users manage their personal data, e.g., location information or online shopping purchase history, they often utilize cloud servers for convenience. In these cases, the data must be encrypted and only authorized providers can decrypt it to avoid compromised scenarios such as data leakage.

Unfortunately, simple cryptographic primitives such as symmetric key encryption (SKE) and public key encryption (PKE) are not suitable for PDS. In the case of SKE (e.g., AES), users must maintain different keys for each service provider, which increases key management costs. As for PKE, (e.g., RSA), huge data storage costs are necessary because the encrypted data must be created for each service provider. PDS also requires the selectability of data, but it is not possible to select and provide data with SKE and PKE unless it is decrypted once, which causes data leakage in the cloud. We therefore need a method that can encrypt personal data without compromising the convenience of PDS.

© The Author(s), under exclusive license to Springer Nature Switzerland AG 2023
C. Stephanidis et al. (Eds.): HCII 2023, CCIS 1834, pp. 90–96, 2023.
https://doi.org/10.1007/978-3-031-35998-9_13

1.2 Related Works

Security of Current PDS. Data encryption is essential for building a PDS system using a cloud server. In Solid [1], which is discussed in W3C [2], data is protected by encryption over a communication channel (such as TLS) and access control. However, Solid does not encrypt data itself in the cloud, and counter-measures are thus required. Another PDS framework, the Personal Life Repos-itory (PLR) [7], utilizes individual-driven digital rights management (DRM) to encrypt and control access to data. The advantage is that existing DRM can be used, but DRM was originally designed for copyright management and the use charges of license server are high. In addition, DRM is based on a symmetric key cryptosystem that requires users and service providers to maintain symmetric keys that correspond to each other on a one-to-one basis. When selecting from data encrypted by symmetric encryption in a cloud server and providing it to service providers, the data must be decrypted once. Therefore, the data to be provided must be stored for each service provider, which increases storage costs because individual cloud storages need to be prepared.

Encryption Scheme for PDS. Blaze et al. proposed proxy re-encryption (PRE) [3] in 1998, a cryptographic scheme that can re-encrypt encrypted data on the cloud without decrypting data. PRE efficiently converts the ciphertext corresponding to a user's public key into the ciphertext of the other user by means of a semi-trusted proxy (cloud server) without requiring either the par-ticipants' private keys or any plaintext. In 2007, Green and Ateniese introduced the identity-based encryption (IBE) mechanism [4] into the proxy re-encryption scheme and proposed identity-based proxy re-encryption (IB-PRE) [8], where participants' public keys are expressed by a unique identifier, such as a phone number or e-mail address. IB-PRE effectively avoids the complexity of distribut-ing and managing public key certificates. Following IB-PRE, a great number of relevant schemes have been studied [5,9–13], including schemes with security proofs in the standard model [5], schemes secure against quantum computers [9,10], schemes combined with attribute-based cryptography [11,12], schemes with verifiability [12,13], and so on. Returning to our motivation, we are inter-ested in schemes that can be re-encrypted in the cloud with low cost in term of both keys and cloud storage. Therefore, we focus on the original IB-PRE scheme, which is simple and already proven to be secure.

1.3 Contribution

To the best of our knowledge, no prior research has examined the application of IB-PRE into PDS. In this paper, we propose a privacy-preserving data manage-ment and provisioning system that can be applied to PDS using IB-PRE. Our proposed system satisfies three key requirements for PDS: the preservation of privacy, selectability of data and authorization setting, and scalability of secret keys and cloud storage. As such, all data can be managed in encrypted form without decryption on the cloud, and data can be re-encrypted so that only designated service providers possessing an ID specified by the data owner can decrypt it. These functions enable a system configuration that guarantees a high level of security.

2   Service Model

The following data management and provision service model considered in this work includes three entities, as shown in Fig. 1: the data owner (DO), service provider (SP), and cloud (CL). The flow of the service model is as follows.

Step 1. DO stores data in the *encrypted PDS* of CL.
Step 2. DO decides which SP to provide the data to.
Step 3. DO selects the data to be provided to SP from the Eencrypted PDS.
Step 4. CL *re-encrypts* the selected data and provides it to SP.
Step 5. DO receives services from SP according to the provided data.

Note that KGC corresponds to a system manager that generates public parameters and secret keys based on the ID for each entity, and is omitted in Fig. 1. Both SP and the data provided to SP are decided by DO, which is one of the requirements of PDS.

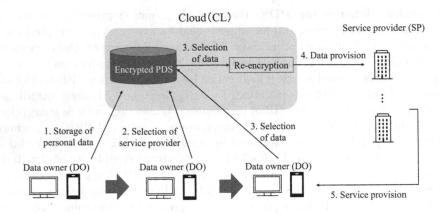

Fig. 1. Service model.

3   Proposed System

Before introducing our proposed system, we define the *non-interactive ID-based proxy re-encryption (IB-PRE)* scheme proposed by Green and Ateniese [8]. Note that we define encryption level as an ciphertext property, where MaxLevels is the highest possible encryption level.

Definition 1. *A non-interactive identity-based proxy re-encryption (IB-PRE) scheme is tuple of algorithms* (Setup, KeyGen, Encrypt, RKGen, Reencrypt, Decrypt):

– Setup(1^κ, MaxLevels) accepts a security parameter κ and a value MaxLevels indicating the maximum number of consecutive re-encryptions permitted by the scheme. The algorithm outputs both the master public parameters (pp), which are distributed to users, and the master secret key (msk), which is kept private.
– KeyGen(pp, msk, id) inputs a public parameter pp, an identity $id \in \{0,1\}^*$, and msk, and then outputs a decryption key sk_{id} corresponding to that identity.
– Encrypt(pp, id, m) inputs a public parameter pp, an identity $id \in \{0,1\}^*$, and a plaintext $m \in \mathcal{M}$, and then outputs c_{id}, the encryption of m under the specified identity.
– RKGen(pp, sk_{id_1}, id_1, id_2) inputs a public parameter pp, a secret key sk_{id_1} (derived via the KeyGen algorithm), and identities $(id_1, id_2) \in \{0,1\}^*$, and then outputs a re-encryption key $rk_{id_1 \to id_2}$.
– Reencrypt(pp, $rk_{id_1 \to id_2}$, c_{id_1}) inputs a public parameter pp, a ciphertext c_{id_1} under identity id_1, and a re-encryption key $rk_{id_1 \to id_2}$ (generated by the RKGen routine), c_{id_1}, and then outputs a re-encrypted ciphertext c_{id_2}.
– Decrypt(pp, sk_{id}, c_{id}) decrypts the ciphertext c_{id} using the secret key sk_{id}, and then outputs m or $\perp$.

Correctness Let Reencrypt$^n(\cdots$, Encrypt(pp, $\cdot$, m)) be an n-level properly generated ciphertext. Then $\forall m \in \mathcal{M}, \forall id_1, id_2 \in \{0,1\}^*, \forall n < \text{MaxLevels} - 1$, where $sk_{id_1} = \text{KeyGen}(\text{msk}, id_1), sk_{id_2} = \text{KeyGen}(\text{msk}, id_2)$, and $rk_{id_1 \to id_2} \leftarrow \text{RKGen}(\text{pp}, sk_{id_1}, id_1, id_2)$. The following propositions then hold:

– Decrypt(pp, sk_{id_1}, c_{id_1}) = m
– Decrypt(pp, sk_{id_2}, Reencrypt(pp, $rk_{id_1 \to id_2}$, c_{id_1})) = m

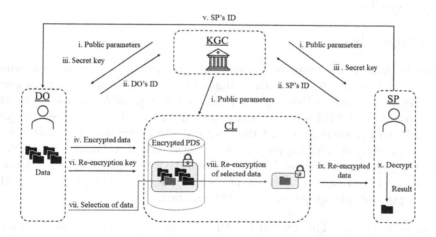

Fig. 2. System architecture

We now employ the IB-PRE scheme and propose an efficient privacy-preserving system (Fig. 2) for the service model described in Sect. 2. Note that subsequent services provided by SP to DO (as described in Step 5) are outside the scope of the proposed system. There is an additional Key Generation Center (KGC) entity that corresponds to a system manager. Here, we define MaxLevels = 2 as an example and set the ID of DO and SP to id_{DO} and id_{SP}, respectively. Concretely, our proposed system works as follows.

i. KGC runs Setup to set up keys including public parameters (pp) and a master secret key (msk). Hereafter, pp are implicitly utilized in all IB-PRE algorithms.

ii. DO and SP send their IDs id_{DO} and id_{SP} to KGC.

iii. KGC runs KeyGen to generate secret keys (sk_{DO}, sk_{SP}) for DO and SP by using their IDs and msk, then sends sk_{DO} and sk_{SP} to DO and SP, respectively.

iv. DO runs Encrypt to encrypt the user's data based on id_{DO} and then sends encrypted data to CL. Encrypted PDS is then created, where all encrypted data have search indices.

v. SP sends the user's ID id_{SP} to DO. Note that although only one SP is described here, there are multiple SPs in the actual system.

vi. DO first selects the SP that DO wants to provide their data to. DO then runs RKGen and generates a re-encryption key ($rk_{id_{DO} \rightarrow id_{SP}}$) by using the id_{DO}, the selected id_{SP}, and sk_{DO}.

vii. DO selects data to provide SP with and sends search indices of encrypted data to CL.

viii. CL searches data by using the indices and re-encrypts them with $rk_{id_{DO} \rightarrow id_{SP}}$ by the Reencrypt algorithm.

ix. CL sends re-encrypted data to SP.

x. SP runs Decrypt to decrypt the re-encrypted data with sk_{SP} and obtains the results.

4   Properties

To our knowledge, the proposed system is the first privacy-preserving data management and provision system satisfying a high level of security and efficiency that can be applied to PDS. Our system makes it possible to re-encrypt the encrypted data of PDS without ay decyprtion on the CL. It also securely provides SP with re-encrypted data that can only be decrypted by an authorized SP. Concretely, the following properties are satisfied and summarized in Table 1. Note that even with SKE and PKE, the selectivity of data and authorization setting can be satisfied by decrypting once in the cloud, but in that case, the most important privacy-preserving is not satisfied.

Privacy-Preserving. The data in the PDS is encrypted and provided data for SP is re-encrypted. Hence, CL cannot know any information related to the DO.

Selectability of Data and Authorization Setting. DO can voluntarily select SPs and the data they provide to SPs. Only the SP selected by the DO can decrypt the re-encrypted data.

Scalability. DO and SP do not need to share secret keys with each other. In addition, CL only requires storage corresponding to the encrypted data and temporary memory for computing the re-encrypted data. The number of keys held by each entity and the amount of data stored in CL are independent of the number of DOs and SPs. Therefore the system is scalable in terms of secret key management and cloud storage.

Table 1. Comparison of properties among encryption schemes applied to PDS.

	SKE	SKE with CL's decryption	PKE	PKE with CL's decryption	IB-PRE
Preservation of privacy	✓	–	✓	–	✓
Selectability of data	–	✓	–	✓	✓
Authorization setting	–	✓	–	✓	✓
Scalability of secret key management	–	–	✓	✓	✓
Scalability of cloud storage	–	–	–	–	✓

5 Conclusion

PDS is an important mechanism for data management and provision, but as yet there is no suitable cryptosystem for it. We therefore developed a system that can securely manage and provide data without compromising the convenience of PDS. Our proposed system satisfies the essential PDS characteristics of preservation of privacy, selectability of data and authorization setting, and scalability.

References

1. https://solidproject.org/TR/
2. https://www.w3.org/
3. Blaze, M., Bleumer, G., Strauss, M.: Divertible protocols and atomic proxy cryptography. In: Nyberg, K. (ed.) EUROCRYPT 1998. LNCS, vol. 1403, pp. 127–144. Springer, Heidelberg (1998). https://doi.org/10.1007/BFb0054122
4. Boneh, D., Franklin, M.: Identity-based encryption from the weil pairing. In: Kilian, J. (ed.) CRYPTO 2001. LNCS, vol. 2139, pp. 213–229. Springer, Heidelberg (2001). https://doi.org/10.1007/3-540-44647-8_13
5. Chu, C.K., Tzeng, W.G.: Identity-based proxy re-encryption without random oracles. In ISC **7**, 189–202 (2007)
6. Dutta, P., Susilo, W., Duong, D.H., Roy, P.S. : Collusion-resistant identity-based proxy re-encryption: lattice-based constructions in standard model. Theoret. Comput. Sci. **871** (2021)
7. Hasida, K.: Personal life repository as a distributed PDS and its dissemination strategy for healthcare services. In: 2014 AAAI Spring Symposium Series (2014)

8. Green, M., Ateniese, G.: Identity-based proxy re-encryption. In: Katz, J., Yung, M. (eds.) ACNS 2007. LNCS, vol. 4521, pp. 288–306. Springer, Heidelberg (2007). https://doi.org/10.1007/978-3-540-72738-5_19

9. Singh, K., Rangan, C.P., Banerjee, A.K.: Lattice based identity based proxy re-encryption scheme. J. Internet Serv. Inf. Secur. $3(3/4)$, 38–51 (2013)

10. Dutta, P., Susilo, W., Duong, D.H., and Roy, P.S. : Collusion-resistant identity-based proxy re-encryption: lattice-based constructions in standard model. Theoret. Comput. Sci. **871**, 16–29 (2021)

11. Luo, S., Hu, J., Chen, Z.: Ciphertext policy attribute-based proxy re-encryption. In: Soriano, M., Qing, S., López, J. (eds.) ICICS 2010. LNCS, vol. 6476, pp. 401–415. Springer, Heidelberg (2010). https://doi.org/10.1007/978-3-642-17650-0_28

12. Ge, C., Susilo, W., Baek, J., Liu, Z., Xia, J., Fang, L.: A verifiable and fair attribute-based proxy re-encryption scheme for data sharing in clouds. In IEEE Trans. Depend. Secur. Comput. **19**(5), 2907–2919 (2021)

13. Li-qiang, W., Xiao-yuan, Y., Min-qing, Z., Xu-an, W.: IB-VPRE: adaptively secure identity-based proxy re-encryption scheme from LWE with re-encryption verifiability. J. Ambient Intell. Hum. Comput. **13**, 469–482 (2021)

SPOTLink - An Interactive User-Driven Tool to Document and Share Assembly Knowledge in SME

Christian Kruse[✉] and Daniela Becks

Westfälische Hochschule Gelsenkirchen, Bocholt, Recklinghausen, Münsterstraße 265,
46397 Bocholt, Germany
{christian.kruse,daniela.becks}@w-hs.de
https://www.w-hs.de

Abstract. The two aspects most succinctly characterizing current trends in knowledge management are the utilization of social and collaborative technologies as well as a good, intuitive user experience. While large enterprises can afford professional knowledge management solutions, small and medium sized enterprises (SME) often lack both adequate financial resources and necessary skills. To stay competitive in times of volatile markets and rapidly changing technologies, SME need to find suitable ways to cope with the challenges of knowledge management.

This paper presents SPOTLink, an intuitive tool that allows to manage the mainly tacit knowledge of a company in an user-friendly way. It was deliberately designed without a fine-grained role concept to encourage each employee to easily use it, collaboratively edit and share valuable expert knowledge. As a particular focus was set on usability and joy of use the tool was extensively evaluated including e.g. various interactive user tests. The results of this iterative evaluation are summarized at the end of this paper.

Keywords: Analytics and visualization · Industry 4.0 · User-centered design · Knowledge management · Assembly priority graph

1 Introduction

In Germany, more than 99 % of all companies belong to the segment of small and medium sized enterprise (SME) [4]. This segment encompasses all enterprises with up to 249 employees and an annual turnover of less than 50 Mio. €. Typically, the SME can be characterized by one or more of the following features:

This research and development project was funded by the European Social Fund (ESF) and the German Federal Ministry of Education and Research (BMBF) within the program "Future of work" (02L18B000) and implemented by the Project Management Agency Karlsruhe (PTKA). The authors are responsible for the content of this publication.

- scarce personnel resources, which usually work in multiple roles
- insufficient financial resources
- lack of specialized IT expertise
- digital transformation still in its infancy

In general, SME often operate in specialized, customer-focused niche markets and are highly dependent on efficient knowledge management. The need for efficient knowledge management is acerbated by the emerging demographic change towards an aging workforce. Hence, SME need to find ways to encourage the knowledge exchange between younger and experienced workers to enable mutual learning processes and to prevent the loss of specialized know-how. Furthermore, the ever increasing complexity of products, machines and manufacturing processes adds to the complexity of knowledge management. Typically, production and assembly processes are very knowledge intensive and require a highly qualified workforce. Hence, on-the-job-learning and knowledge transfer have become integral parts of the daily work routines for blue-collar workers.

This is particularly challenging for SME since they rarely have full fledged knowledge management systems in place. Typically, SME find these commercial systems too complex, too expensive and rarely suitable for their specific needs. As a result, knowledge is commonly handled in manual fashion. The knowledge landscape of many SME is characterized by numerous isolated documentation pools of text or pdf files, unstructured collections of images and personal, sometimes handwritten notes. These are - if at all - stored in the depths of personal file systems and not accessible for or shared by coworkers. Knowledge is not treated as an organizational resources and hence production and assembly workflows are often interrupted due to insufficient information.

2   Knowledge Documentation and Transfer in SME

One objective of the FlexDeMO research project was to develop a knowledge management tool that is specifically tailored to the needs of production and assembly processes of SMEs in the field of mechanical engineering. Based on a comprehensive literature review, a participatory approach [3] was chosen involving a mixed group of assembly workers representing the targeted users. To understand their working environment as well as their information competencies and information demands, interviews were conducted and their daily routines were documented with the help of work shadowing. Soon it became clear that blue-collar workers document and handle knowledge significantly different than office workers. While the latter rely mostly on text-based knowledge representations, which are typically well catered for in existing knowledge management software, assembly workers mainly work in a visually oriented manner using technical drawings or pictures to solve a problem and photos to document their assembly steps. Dealing with text based systems which rely on manual input is considered a waste of time and a major hindrance in a smooth assembly process. In addition, the general level of information literacy - defined as a set of abilities individuals require to recognize when information is needed and to be able to locate, evaluate, and use effectively the needed information [2] was relatively low. The assembly workers nearly exclusively consumed information but did not actively create and share it.

To enhance the information literacy of the assembly workers it was of significant importance to translate the inherently visual information paradigm of the blue-collar workers into a suitable design concept. As a consequence, when developing SPOTLink the focus was on an user friendly but well-structured, graphical interface and the use of pictures instead of editing detailed descriptions enhancing as much user experience as possible.

3 SPOTLink - Document and Share Your Work with Joy

The resulting knowledge management tool [1] consists of a graph-based visualization based on the concept of assembly priority graphs [5] that allows to easily navigate through the steps of the assembly of a machine. It operates both in desktop and tablet mode. Thereby, the latter is extremely suitable for the assembly worker since they can utilize the knowledge management tool for a seamless documentation of the machine assembly tasks on the shop floor. All documents are stored in a central database and can be viewed, modified and annotated by other employees.

3.1 UX-design Driven by the Users

As mentioned in Sect. 2 technical drawings as well as pictures play a vital role in the working context of blue-collar workers. Thus, for the acceptance of the knowledge management tool it was crucial to allow an intuitive integration and retrieval of pictures. Hence, pictures may be uploaded from e.g. a local directory or linked from a file browser. It was important that these are not just displayed but that the assembly workers may be able to interact with the pictures comprising:

Zoom and scroll Users are able to zoom into annotated pictures to fetch technical details relevant for an assembly task.

Arrange pictures Uploaded pictures may be put in line according to the assembly process allowing especially inexperienced workers to easily follow necessary assembly steps.

Effective search and browse During the workshops the assembly workers explained that they would like to be able to browse a list of all pictures relevant for a specific machine. This functionality was realized in two different ways. On the one hand the user may enter a search term (e.g. an assembly part of the machine) and on the other hand there exists the option to view a complete list of all linked pictures documenting the assembly procedure of a machine (see Fig. 1).

In this way, the SPOTLink tool on demand supplies the assembly workers with information relevant to the actual work context avoiding time-consuming search activities and reducing cognitive stress of the employees.

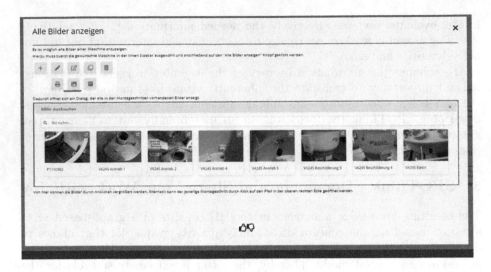

Fig. 1. Context-sensitive provision of pictures

3.2 Collaborate and Share Knowledge

Assembling complex machines requires the cooperation of different teams on the shop floor. In the underlying use case, two specially qualified teams take care of assembling the mechanical resp. electrical components. The provision of parts is addressed by the internal material logistics team while the assembly scheduling team is responsible for the overall coordination. Sharing information is important for smooth operation among the teams. Hence, the SPOTLink tool provides access to the relevant information systems such as the ERP-system for bill-of-material and inventory information or the CAD-system for technical drawings via internal URI-links replacing the hitherto paper-based information flow. This is depicted in Fig. 2. In addition, the intricacies of a particularly difficult assembly task can be annotated by the assembly workers. As a result, with the help of SPOTLink the assembly workers are in a position to share their knowledge e.g. by uploading photos, linking assembly steps to internal information systems or annotating and documenting special assembly procedures. Acceptance of SPOTLink was further boosted by introducing mobile devices such as smart phones and tablets yielding a substantial increase in information literacy on the shop floor.

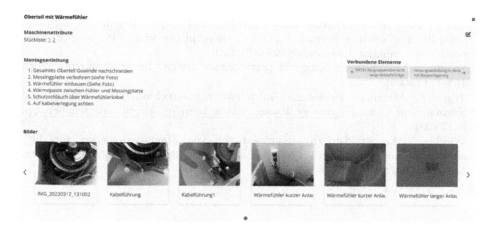

Fig. 2. Enriching and sharing assembly knowledge via SPOTLink

4   Discussion and Outlook

The knowledge management tool SPOTLink was evaluated extensively including both performance tests and interactive user tests particularly focusing usability and integration into the work context. Right from the beginning, the feedback was quite positive and revealed that the chosen bottom-up approach lead to high acceptance of the software. Already during the first interactive tests, it became apparent that the workers could actually start describing even complex assembly procedures without any additional training. In this context the implemented interactive guidance functionality proved to be extremely advantageous. As it assisted the users in describing the assembly of their first machine more and more employees joined the knowledge documentation and soon remarkable efforts were made. As a result, a significant number of highly specialized machines has already been described with the help of SPOTLink and a couple of isolated information pools disposed.

While SPOTLink was exemplary developed and evaluated for the domain of mechanical engineering focusing in particular on assembly knowledge it is not restricted to this use case. In the future, the tool might also be deployed to other departments or used for the documentation of other processes like e.g. onboarding or controlling.

References

1. Kruse, C., Becks, D., Venhuis, S.: User-centered assembly knowledge documentation: a graph-based visualization approach. In: Fui-Hoon Nah, F., Siau, K. (eds.) HCI in Business, Government and Organizations. HCII 2022. Lecture Notes in Computer Science, vol. 13327, pp. 194–207. Springer, Cham (2022). https://doi.org/10.1007/978-3-031-05544-7_15

2. Landøy, A., Popa, D., Repanovici, A., Landøy, A., Popa, D., Repanovici, A.: Basic concepts in information literacy. In: Collaboration in Designing a Pedagogical Approach in Information Literacy, pp. 23–38 (2020)
3. Spinuzzi, C.: The methodology of participatory design. Techn. Commun. **52**(2), 163–174 (2005)
4. Tegel, T.: Merkmale kleiner und mittelgroßer unternehmen. Multidimensionale Konzepte zur Controllingunterstützung in kleinen und mittleren Unternehmen, pp. 5–17 (2005)
5. Wiesbeck, M.: Struktur zur Repräsentation von Montagesequenzen für die situationsorientierte Werkerführung, Forschungsberichte / IWB, vol, vol. 285. Utz, München (2014)

Understanding the Relationship Between Behaviours Using Semantic Technologies

Suvodeep Mazumdar[1]([envelope]) [iD], Fatima Maikore[2] [iD], Vitaveska Lanfranchi[2],
Sneha Roychowdhury[2], Richard Webber[3], Harriet M. Baird[4], Muhammad Basir[4],
Vyv Huddy[4], Paul Norman[4] [iD], Richard Rowe[4], Alexander J. Scott[5],
and Thomas L. Webb[4]

[1] Information School, University of Sheffield, Sheffield, UK
s.mazumdar@sheffield.ac.uk
[2] Department of Computer Science, University of Sheffield, Sheffield, UK
{f.maikore,v.lanfranchi,s.roychowdhury}@sheffield.ac.uk
[3] School of Health and Related Research, University of Sheffield, Sheffield, UK
r.webber@sheffield.ac.uk
[4] Department of Psychology, University of Sheffield, Sheffield, UK
{harriet.baird,m.basir,v.huddy,p.norman,r.rowe,
t.webb}@sheffield.ac.uk
[5] School of Psychology, Keele University, Keele, UK
a.scott@keele.ac.uk

Abstract. While a growing number of studies report on relationships between behaviours (e.g. alcohol consumption, political behaviours, sleep, recycling), there is a need for a shared understanding of behaviour (e.g. how to characterise and differentiate between behaviours) and the ability to integrate insights on the relations between behaviours. Semantic technologies and ontologies can help in formalising the behaviour domain in a structured approach to support sharing, reuse and interoperability in a manner that can allow future researchers to build on activities in this space. In this work-in-progress paper, we describe the semantic technologies (ontology, data capture tool and visualisations) that are currently being developed by the TURBBO (Tools for Understanding the Relationship between Behaviours using Ontologies) project to support researchers in understanding relations between behaviours and reason upon the existent data. In this paper, we also describe our future plans to evaluate the technologies being developed as a part of the project.

Keywords: ontologies · behavioural studies · data visualisation · semantic technologies

1 Introduction

Everyday life is characterised by a range of behaviours such as eating, sleeping, walking etc. Psychologists and behavioural scientists often study these behaviours in isolation, seeking to, for example, improve sleep or increase levels of physical activity. Sometimes,

C. Stephanidis et al. (Eds.): HCII 2023, CCIS 1834, pp. 103–109, 2023.
https://doi.org/10.1007/978-3-031-35998-9_15

these studies will consider the extent to which changes in one behaviour impact another (e.g. increasing physical activity may increase consumption of calories). These analyses are typically only limited to a small number of behaviours, usually within the same domain. There is a growing interest in studying multiple behaviours simultaneously, or how behavioural interventions can impact other behaviours over a range of domains. Much of the evidence needed to understand these relationships already exists in the literature - studies measuring behaviours and reporting correlations between them can be used to estimate relations between the behaviours.

Despite the presence of a large body of research on behaviour correlations, the community currently lacks a shared understanding of behaviour (how we can describe and characterize behaviours, how can we differentiate between them etc.) and the ability to integrate insights on the relations between behaviours across existent data. The TURBBO (Tools for Understanding the Relationship between Behaviours using Ontologies) project aims to address this gap by developing a set of semantic technologies to help behavioural scientists study correlations between behaviours. As a first step in achieving this goal, the project aims to develop a 'collaboratively edited ontology' that user communities can contribute to, beyond the project lifetime.

Ontologies are formal descriptions of concepts, including their attributes and relationships, of which domain experts share a common understanding [1]. Logical rules and constraints [2] are further defined which enable software to reason about the knowledge represented by the ontology, and discover new knowledge [3]. Ontologies provide a standardized representation of the semantics of a domain and so can be used to exchange data and models, encouraging re-use, communication, collaboration and integration [1]. In the TURBBO project, we used a co-design methodology to co-create our ontology with user communities [4], which included researchers, academics and practitioners. In this work-in-progress paper, we provide a brief overview of the ontology, a data capture tool and a set of visualisations that are currently being evaluated with user communities.

The paper is organized as follows: we first discuss some of the ontologies developed for the behavioural science domain, and then discuss various visualizations for studying behaviour correlations (Sect. 2). We then present a high-level overview of our ontology and some of the tools developed in the TURBBO project (Sect. 3). We conclude the paper with some discussions around future research in the project (Sect. 4).

2 Related Work

We discuss related work from two perspectives – (i) an initial discussion presents some of the previous efforts in developing ontologies that are relevant to studying human behaviour, and (ii) a discussion on different approaches taken in visualizing behavioural data. Understanding previous efforts in developing ontologies is important as one of the key considerations to be made is how existing ontologies could be re-used, refined or extended, to avoid duplication and promote interoperability [5]. In the TURBBO project, we conducted a systematic review of the literature using existing databases (Bioportal, Ontology Lookup Service, OBO Foundry) to identify 70 ontologies that could be relevant for our research. While over half of these ontologies considered health behaviours (physical activity, substance use, food consumption appearing most frequently), there is a lack of ontologies that explore the field of behavioural studies and human behaviour more holistically. We also identified domain specific ontologies such as Legal APA ontology [6] (criminal and antisocial behaviours), Education Cluster ontology [7] (learning and education), International Classification for Nursing Practice [8] (behaviours related to religious practices like praying), Physical Activity Ontology [9] (a range of activities), and Neuro Behaviour Ontology [10] (learning, sleeping, substance use). Our review also included a range of taxonomies that have been developed to classify human behaviours into different hierarchies and categories such as [11, 12]. Given the need for capturing existing studies reporting on the correlations between behaviours, we were also interested in understanding existing ontologies that are used to measure empirical data. As such, the Consumer Wearable Devices Ontology [13], Intervention Setting Ontology [11] are ontologies that we identified as relevant to our ontology. Finally, the need to capture details about existing research makes it important to identify ontologies that can capture scholarly and scientific activities such as Documents Components Ontology, ScholOnto[14], Core Information about Scientific Papers [15], Semantic Web Conference Ontology and Core Scientific Concepts [16]. There are also existing generic ontologies which are helpful vocabularies for describing documents, individuals and organisations such as Friend of a Friend (FOAF), Dublin Core Metadata Terms, and SIOC. A longer, separate paper detailing the systematic review of existing ontologies and taxonomies is currently being prepared by the project team.

Given the range and typologies of human behaviour, the need to conduct meta-analysis in order to give greater weight to correlations from studies with larger samples when estimating relations between behaviours, our data involves complex data structures. Furthermore, the interpretation of these data relies on evaluation and integration of a range of statistical information and provokes the need for application of data visualization tools [17]. Beyond the behavioural studies domain, a range of visualisations exist that can represent relationship data. These are predominantly network visualisations, employing different types of configurations and layouts such as force-directed, circular, or hierarchical visualisations, applied within other domains such as social network analysis [e.g. 19], transport and mobility [e.g. 20], bibliometrics [e.g. [20] and so on. Other visualisations such as scatterplot, correlation matrix or even treemaps can provide insights on the strength of relationships between different behaviours. A range of applications exist that allows the creation of network visualisations such as Cytoscape [21], Gephi, and TreeNetViz [22]. Closer to behavioural studies, Rethomics [23] is a framework for the analysis of high-throughput behavioural data, particularly to study circadian and sleep data. ViSiElse [24] can be used to visualize raw behavioral data over time extracted from visually recorded sessions of experimental observations. More specific to the application of visualisations for meta-analysis, a range of visualisations have been proposed, such as the Vitruvian plot [25], forest plot, funnel plot and meta-regression plots [26], or a combination of multiple visualisations such as forest plots, radial plot, network visualisations and so on [27]. The literature highlights a range of possible visualisations that are relevant for studying the relationships between behaviours, and our user studies highlighted existing practices within the user community.

3 Development of Semantic Technologies

As described previously, our starting point for the project was to co-design an ontology that could be used and curated by the community. We conducted a systematic review of ontologies, which identified a set of ontologies that we could extend and re-use. Together with this activity, we organized a set of six workshops, that involved 22 participants in total (academics, practitioners, businesses and charities interested in behaviour). The workshops involved providing a brief overview of what we mean by ontologies and how they are helpful. The sessions then involved the use of Miro, an online whiteboarding software that offers interactive features such as collaborative mind mapping, voting, building workflows, user stories and so on. Participants provided their views on what concepts would be important for describing and modelling behaviour, through a series of tasks. The participants were invited to indicate how the concepts can be potentially connected and describe the type of relationship that exists between the concepts.

A subsequent desk-based activity by the research team then brought together the concepts and relationships identified by the participants in the workshops. This required understanding which concepts were most commonly highlighted as important, identifying similar concepts and how the concepts could be hierarchically arranged. Over several iterations, the team developed the Relationship Between Behaviours Ontology (RBBO). The ontology consists of three independent modules which can be combined to form a complete schema. The TURBBO_Behaviours module provides a hierarchical organization of different behaviours (moving, self-care behaviours, communication etc.) and we re-used the IC-Behaviour taxonomy [11] as a starting point. The TURBBO_Properties_of_behaviour module describes classes of behaviour characteristics (e.g. motivation, effectiveness, goal etc.) and other properties represented as data properties (e.g., whether a behaviour is habitual or not, opportunistic or not etc.). The TURBBO_Properties_of_studies_measuring_behaviour module consists of concepts for describing studies that report on behaviours (e.g., methodological design, participants, context). Figure 1 presents a high-level conceptual view of the main concepts and relationships within the three modules in RBBO.

Following the development of the ontology, we created a knowledge base that can be populated by the behavioural research community to capture data about studies reporting on relations between behaviours. This is, for the time being, a manual task, where researchers in our project team identify a relevant paper and enter the details of the experiments, findings and behaviours reported in the study through an online interface, as can be seen in Fig. 2 (left). The elements in the data collection system directly align with the ontology and therefore, all data inputted from the system gets stored in a knowledge repository, accessible through an API. In the TURBBO project, we are currently evaluating the data collection application with user communities, using a task-based approach. The project is also in the process of developing tools to analyse and visualize the knowledge base. While this is a work in progress, early prototypes are presented in Fig. 2 (right).

The Fig. 2 (right) presents some example visualisations that the TURBBO project is implementing and is currently work in progress, using a synthetic dataset created for the purpose of testing our tools. The aim of this activity is to develop a dashboard that can incorporate multiple visualisations and help researchers answer questions about

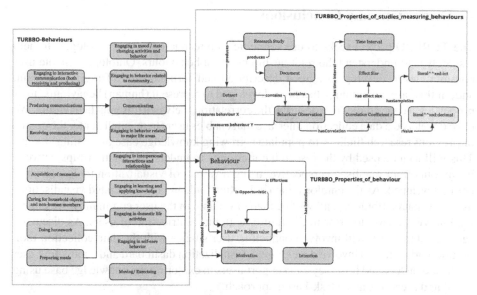

Fig. 1. A fragment of RBBO showing some concepts from the TURBBO_Behaviours, TURBBO_Properties_of_behaviour   and   TURBBO_Properties_of_studies_measuring_ behaviours modules.

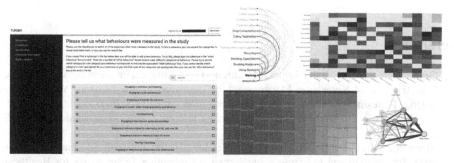

Fig. 2. (left) Data collection application for recording behaviour correlation and associated data. (right) a composite of visualisations (based on synthetic data) currently being developed to support researchers study behaviour correlations

the relationship between behaviours. In the figure, the top left image presents an arc diagram which enables users to hover over a specific behaviour to find other behaviours that are correlated with the behaviour of interest. The image in the top right presents a colour-coded correlation matrix, while the image in the bottom left presents a treemap that presents colour-coded pairs of behaviours. The colour-coding is based on the strength of the correlations, which is calculated as a combination of correlation values reported from multiple studies. The right image presents a force-directed network that allows users to select a specific behaviour to highlight connections with other behaviours.

4   Discussions and Conclusions

The TURBBO project seeks to use semantic web technologies and ontologies to help researchers to understand the relationship between behaviours. Ontologies enable user communities to develop an agreed description and formalization of a given domain, and, in this case, an ontology has been developed to represent (human) behaviours, their properties and the studies that describe the correlations between different behaviours. We have developed a data collection interface that enables users to manually enter the details of previous research findings to populate a growing knowledge base of existing studies. This will then be used by the research community to understand relationships between behaviours from a holistic perspective, using a variety of visualization tools, currently being developed. As the ontology, data collection tool, and the associated visualisations use open source libraries, and will be made available to the user community, we expect the knowledge base to grow in the future, with the contribution of users. As discussed earlier, future work will involve conducting user studies with the data collection tool. Future work will also involve developing a visualization dashboard and conducting user studies to understand how they can support users in exploring the knowledge base using simulated scenarios and a task-based approach.

Acknowledgements. This work is done as part of the TURBBO project which is funded by the ESRC (Award #ES/T009179/1). We would also like to thank our participants for their valuable insights and contributions during the co-design workshops.

References

1. Gómez-Pérez, A., Fernández-López, M., Corcho, O.: Ontological Engineering: with examples from the areas of Knowledge Management, e-Commerce and the Semantic Web. Springer Science & Business Media, London (2006). https://doi.org/10.1007/b97353
2. Bechhofer, S., et al.: OWL web ontology language reference. W3C Recommend. **10**(2), 1–53 (2004)
3. Bleumers, L., et al.: Towards ontology co-creation in institutionalized care settings. In: 2011 5th International Conference on Pervasive Computing Technologies for Healthcare (PervasiveHealth) and Workshops, pp. 559–562. IEEE, May 2011
4. Schuler, D., Namioka, A. (Eds.) Participatory Design: Principles and Practices. CRC Press (1993)
5. Noy, N., McGuinness, D.L.: Ontology Development 101. Stanford University, Knowledge Systems Laboratory (2001)
6. The Legal APA ontology. https://bioportal.bioontology.org/ontologies/LEGALAPA. Accessed 5 May 2022
7. Education Cluster ontology. https://bioportal.bioontology.org/ontologies/
8. APAEDUCLUSTER. Accessed 5 May 2022
9. International Classification for Nursing Practice. https://bioportal.bioontology.org/ontologies/ICNP. Last accessed 5 May 2022
10. Physical Activity Ontology, https://bioportal.bioontology.org/ontologies/PACO. Last accessed 5 May 2022
11. The Neuro Behaviour Ontology. https://bioportal.bioontology.org/ontologies/NBO. Accessed 5 May 2022

12. Nudelman, G., Shiloh, S.: Mapping health behaviors: Constructing and validating a common-sense taxonomy of health behaviors. Soc. Sci. Med. **146**, 1–10 (2015)
13. Consumer Wearable Devices Ontology, https://bioportal.bioontology.org/ontologies/CWD. Accessed 5 May 2022
14. Norris, E., et al.: Development of an intervention setting ontology for behaviour change: specifying where interventions take place. Welcome Open Res. **5**, 124 (2020). https://doi.org/10.12688/wellcomeopenres.15904.1
15. Shum, S.B., Motta, E., Domingue, J.: ScholOnto: an ontology-based digital library server for research documents and discourse. Int. J. Digit. Libr. **3**(3), 237–248 (2000)
16. Liakata, M., Teufel, S., Siddharthan, A., Batchelor, C.R.: Corpora for the conceptualisation and zoning of scientific papers. In: Proceedings of the International Conference on Language Resources and Evaluation. (2010)
17. Liakata, M., Saha, S., Dobnik, S., Batchelor, C., RebholzSchuhmann, D.: Automatic recognition of conceptualization zones in scientific articles and two life science applications. Bioinformatics **28**(7), 991–1000 (2012)
18. Kossmeier, M., Tran, U.S., Voracek, M.: Charting the landscape of graphical displays for meta-analysis and systematic reviews: a comprehensive review, taxonomy, and feature analysis. BMC Med. Res. Methodol. **20**(1), 1–24 (2020)
19. Ahmed, W., VidalAlaball, J., Downing, J., Seguí, F.L.: COVID-19 and the 5G conspiracy theory: social network analysis of Twitter data. J. Med. Internet Res. **22**(5), e19458 (2020)
20. Di Donato, V., Patrignani, M., Squarcella, C.: Netfork: Mapping time to space in network visualization. In: Proceedings of the International Working Conference on Advanced Visual Interfaces, pp. 92–99, June 2016
21. Akinlolu, M., Haupt, T.C., Edwards, D.J., Simpeh, F.: A bibliometric review of the status and emerging research trends in construction safety management technologies. Int. J. Constr. Manag. **22**(14), 2699–2711 (2022)
22. Smoot, M.E., Ono, K., Ruscheinski, J., Wang, P.L., Ideker, T.: Cytoscape 2.8: new features for data integration and network visualization. Bioinformatics **27**(3), 431–432 (2011)
23. Gou, L., Zhang, X.L.: Treenetviz: revealing patterns of networks over tree structures. IEEE Trans. Visual Comput. Graph. **17**(12), 2449–2458 (2011)
24. Geissmann, Q., Garcia Rodriguez, L., Beckwith, E.J., Gilestro, G.F.: Rethomics: an R framework to analyse high-throughput behavioural data. PLoS ONE **14**(1), e0209331 (2019)
25. Garnier, E.M., Fouret, N., Descoins, M.: ViSiElse: an innovative R-package to visualize raw behavioral data over time. PeerJ **8**, e8341 (2020)
26. Ostinelli, E.G., et al.: Vitruvian plot: a visualisation tool for multiple outcomes in network meta-analysis. BMJ Ment. Health **25**(e1), e65–e70 (2022)
27. Kiran, A., Crespillo, A.P., Rahimi, K.: Graphics and statistics for cardiology: data visualisation for meta-analysis. Heart **103**(1), 19–23 (2017)
28. Nevill, C.R., Cooper, N.J., Sutton, A.J.: A multifaceted graphical display, including treatment ranking, was developed to aid interpretation of network meta-analysis. J. Clin. Epidemiol. **157**, 83–91 (2023)

Supporting Nail Art Consultation by Automatic Image Selection and Visual Information Sharing

Yoshino Minakawa and Hiroshi Hosobe(✉) 🄳

Faculty of Computer and Information Sciences, Hosei University, Tokyo, Japan
hosobe@acm.org

Abstract. People are increasingly becoming interested in nail art, and many of them have treatments in nail salons. Nail technicians decide nail art designs according to their understandings of their clients' requests. The results of nail art depend on the preceding consultations. However, there are problems with such consultations: some clients cannot appropriately express their requests; some nail technicians have difficulties in deciding designs because of their clients' unclear requests. In this paper, we present a consultation system that supports both clients and nail technicians. The system consists of two applications: one assists a client in selecting the images of nail art designs and sends them to a nail technician; the other enables the client and the nail technician to visually share their information including the client's requests. The combination of the two applications bridges the gap between the client and the nail technician about the design and treatment of nail art. We show the results of an experiment on the operation of our system in nail salons.

Keywords: Consultation support · Image search · Information sharing

1 Introduction

People are increasingly becoming interested in nail art, and many of them have treatments in nail salons. Nail technicians decide nail art designs according to their understandings of their clients' requests. The results of nail art depend on the preceding consultations. However, there are problems with such consultations: some clients cannot appropriately express their requests; some nail technicians have difficulties in deciding designs because of their clients' unclear requests. However, to the authors' knowledge, no previous research exists on supporting the entire consultations between clients and nail technicians for the decision of nail art designs in nail salons.

In this paper, we present a consultation system that supports both clients and nail technicians. The system consists of the following two applications:

- One application assists a client in selecting the images of nail art designs and sends them to a nail technician;

C. Stephanidis et al. (Eds.): HCII 2023, CCIS 1834, pp. 110–117, 2023.
https://doi.org/10.1007/978-3-031-35998-9_16

- The other application enables the client and the nail technician to visually share their information including the client's requests.

The combination of the two applications bridges the gap between the client and the nail technician about the design and treatment of nail art. We show the results of an experiment on the operation of our system in nail salons. We perform the evaluation of the system based on the interviews with the participants in the experiment including professional nail technicians. Also, we discuss the benefits and limitations of our system.

2   Related Work

There have been studies on supporting nail art design in self-treatment (where nail technicians were not involved). Umezaki et al. [9] proposed a nail recipe retrieval system using words about impressions and difficulties of designs. Odajima and Ito [6] proposed a nail art recommendation system based on user preferences by the machine learning of the features of nail art images on the Web.

There has been research on nail art from other viewpoints than that of supporting nail art design. Fujishima and Hoshino developed a fingernail detection system [1] that used the distributions of pixel colors to distinguish fingernails from palms, and further developed a virtual nail art system [2] that appropriately superimposed nail chips on fingernails. Ishihara [3] studied the color and design factors of impressions on nail art by conducting sensory analysis on 36 nail chips with 9 colors and 4 designs.

Systems have been developed to support nail salons in client management and to support clients in searching for nail art designs and nail salons. Before After [5] is a client management system used in many nail art salons and other kinds of salons. However, some nail technician gave the opinion that its electronic record creation function was difficult to use. Nailbook [8] is a system that allows users to search for nail art designs and nail salons. When the users make requests to nail salons, they need to send nail art images one by one, which imposes the burdens of storing and sending the images.

Apart from nail art, Nakagawa et al. [4] proposed a system for supporting the expansion of variations of makeups. It enabled users to record information about cosmetics and their photographs after the makeups and to share the information and the photographs with other users.

3   Proposed System

In this paper, we propose a system that supports consultations on the design of nail art in nail salons. We particularly tackle the following two problems that the clients and the nail technicians encounter.

- Many clients search and view the images of nail designs before visiting nail salons. They need to store such images if they find interesting designs. Also, it is sometimes difficult for them to appropriately inform technicians about details of designs such as colors and patterns that they prefer.

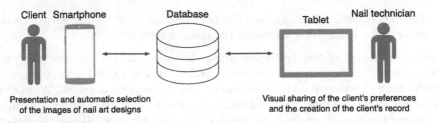

Fig. 1. Architecture of the proposed system for supporting nail art consultation.

- Nail technicians sometimes face the problem of the gap arising between the designs that their clients imagine beforehand and the results of the treatments that the technicians perform according to their understandings, which is due to their verbal communications about the designs in nail salons. Some technicians have difficulty in deciding designs because of the differences of feeling and sense from their clients.

To solve these problems, we compose our system from two applications, one that enables the automatic selection of images for the clients, and the other that allows the nail technicians to share visual information with the clients. As depicted in Fig. 1, the two applications share necessary information via the database connected to them.

The application for clients enables them to inform nail technicians about the designs and preferences of nail art even if these are difficult to verbally express. For this purpose, it provides the following two functions

- Its view and search function allows the clients to view and search nail art designs without interfering with their actions;
- Its automatic image selection function eliminates the need to manually store images. Since it automatically shares the selected images with the application for nail technicians, the clients can inform their preferences without verbal communication.

The application for nail technicians enables visual information sharing as well as the creation of the electronic records of their clients necessary for consultations. By visual information sharing, we mean to allow a technician to visually recognize the requested designs by regarding the images of nail art as the requests of the clients. For this purpose, it provides the following two functions:

- Its function for showing the selected images of nail designs allows the clients and the technicians to view the screen at the same time to clearly share their understandings of the designs;
- Its client record creation function eases the task of the technicians to make the electronic records of their clients.

Fig. 2. Application for clients showing (a) thumbnails, (b) an expanded image, (c) search results, and (d) selection results.

4   Implementation

We implemented the two applications by using Android Studio and Java. We used a smartphone (HUAWEI P30 lite) for the application for clients and a tablet (Lenovo Yoga Tab 11) for the application for nail technicians. We adopted Google Sheets API and Google Apps Script to implement a database for information sharing between the two applications. The images of the nail art designs used in the two applications were contributed by a nail technician [7]. The images were stored in the applications as their resources.

We developed the application for clients as shown in Fig. 2. It provides the view and search function and the automatic image selection function. When a user enters a hashtag, the application displays the set of the images corresponding to the hashtag. Each image is assigned three hashtags that express its characteristics. Hashtags include the characteristics of nail art designs, primary colors, and words expressing related seasons. The automatic image selection function displays images in the order of the time that the client spent to carefully view the images by expanding them. The application sends information about the selected images to the database.

We implemented the application for nail technicians as depicted in Fig. 3. When started, it displays nail art images by obtaining information about the images that were automatically selected by the application for the clients. In addition, it provides the function for the creation of the electronic record of clients based on check boxes for questions about their nails.

5   Experiment

To evaluate the proposed system, we conducted an experiment on its operation in nail salons. We combined expert review and subjective evaluation: the expert review was performed by two professional nail technicians; the subjective evaluation was performed by two participants who played the roles of the clients. The experiment consisted of two cases: case A with an actual treatment; case

Fig. 3. Application for nail technicians showing (a) selected images and (b) a client's electronic record.

B with simulated actions but without a treatment. After the experiment, we conducted interviews about our system as well as questionnaires about their past experiences of nail art design. Table 1 summarizes the characteristics of the participants in this experiment.

Table 1. Participants in the experiment.

Client	Gender	Age	Medium ordinarily used	Ordinary way of presenting designs
A	Female	24	Instagram	Presenting Instagram images at the treatment
B	Female	25	Instagram	Presenting Instagram images at the treatment
Nail technician	Gender	Age	Medium ordinarily used	Ordinary way of creating records
A	Female	26	Financial application with note taking	Application with text entry
B	Female	27	Before After	Application with text entry

5.1 Procedure

In nail salons, we asked the clients and the nail technicians to operate the corresponding applications. We asked the clients to search for nail art images that they preferred and wanted to use for reference. After judging that they searched sufficiently, we asked them to check the results of the automatic image selection.

After the clients' operations were completed, we asked the technicians to view the selected nail art images by using the application for the technicians. Also, we asked them to create the clients' records by using the application.

During consultation and treatment, they discussed nail art designs by viewing the images on the tablet together.

After the experiment, we interviewed the clients and the technicians. The interviews lasted for approximately 1 h in case A and for approximately 40 min in case B.

5.2 Subjective Evaluation by Clients

Concerning the view and search function of the application for clients, we obtained the following comments from clients A and B.

A. A good thing is that it provides easy view and allows the expansion of images. Another good thing is that it allows search with hashtags like Instagram. I want it to provide more kinds of hashtags.
B. Its ability to search with hashtags is the same as the existing one. Its operability does not feel bad. I want it to allow the tapping of hashtags and the expansion of images by pinching out.

Regarding the automatic image selection function, we obtained the following comments.

A. It is easy to use because it does not require the process of sending and presenting images to the nail technician. The images that I particularly liked were displayed at the top of the screen. It would be better than Instagram if I could use it in the salon.
B. It eliminated the task of storing and presenting images to the technician. I want it to allow the removal of the image that I expanded but did not like. I felt that it correctly selected the images that I liked.

Concerning the entire application for clients, we obtained the following comments.

A. I will use Instagram if I search designs at home. However, I would like to use the proposed application if I would be in the treatment of removing the gel for new nail art.
B. Because of the convenience of the search function, I would like to use Instagram rather than the proposed application. The application requires the verbal communication of requests for detailed colors that did not appear in the list of displayed images.

5.3 Expert Review by Nail Technicians

Concerning the showing of automatically selected images, we obtained the following comments from nail technicians A and B.

A. It eases communication with clients about multiple requests, which is useful for deciding designs. Since it is sometimes difficult to verbally communicate, the application's ability to use images as design requests is good.

B. The large screen is good because the client can point it out with a finger during her explanation. I normally use a smartphone to display the image sent from a client, and the tablet is not easy to use in the same way because I need to turn my eyes.

Regarding the client record creation function, we obtained the following comments.

A. Its use of check boxes is good for recording the items about which I always ask clients. I want it to additionally provide text fields. I want it to allow the storing of data specific to clients.
B. I would like to use it as a part of record creation because it is simpler than the existing one. However, it is insufficient since it omits the storing of some basic information in electronic records.

Concerning the entire consultation support system consisting of the two applications, we obtained the following comments from the technicians.

A. The elimination of the need for clients to send nail art images is good. It also is good that I can confirm the request of a client by looking at the tablet during the treatment. The system is useful for deciding designs since it allows the viewing of multiple designs at the same time. It will be useful when I communicate with clients only verbally and when I give treatments to clients who have not decided requests for designs.
B. The automatic sharing of images is convenient. The system enabled me to grasp the client's request, and made me feel that I successfully shared information. There would be a risk of staining nails if a client operated the application after the removal of the gel. I would like to use it if the existing problems could be solved.

6   Discussion

Based on the comments obtained from the clients in Subsect. 5.2, we consider that the automatic image selection function eliminates the troublesome task of manually storing and presenting images and enables the easy communication of the preferences of clients to nail technicians. However, it turned out that the application made the clients feel that it was difficult to view and search images. We consider that this is because the application did not provide basic functions including the tapping of hashtags and the pinch-out operation as well as sufficient numbers of nail art images and hashtags.

Based on the comments obtained from the nail technicians in Subsect. 5.3, we consider that visual information sharing assists interaction between nail technicians and clients in deciding designs. However, it allows the sharing of only images stored in the application for clients. To allow them to appropriately share detailed colors and other designs that do not exist as prepared images, we need to additionally implement necessary functions.

Nail art designs differ among technicians, and preferences for designs differ among clients. Therefore, we need to consider providing functions for adding user-defined images and a wider range of images other than nail art. To treat a larger number of images, we will need to store them in a server.

7   Conclusions and Future Work

In this paper, we proposed a system for supporting clients and nail technicians in nail salons in deciding nail art designs and performing consultations by sharing nail art images and by bridging the gap between their recognitions of designs. The application for the clients eliminated the tasks of the clients by automatically selecting the images that they preferred, and assisted their communications of preferences to technicians. The application for the technicians assisted them in recognizing the requests of the clients by sharing the images that they preferred.

It was found that, in both applications, the insufficiency of data and the lack of the function for avoiding unclearness due to verbal communications caused problems. Therefore, our future work includes the enhancement of nail art images, hashtags, and the client record creation function as well as the visual sharing of information other than nail art images. Also, since we obtained many comments on additional functions from the participants in the experiment, we need to conduct interviews with multiple nail technicians and other involved persons before further enhancing our system.

Acknowledgment. This work was partly supported by JSPS KAKENHI Grant Number JP21K11836.

References

1. Fujishima, N., Hoshino, K.: Fingernail detection system using differences of the distribution of the nail-color pixels. J. Adv. Comput. Intell. Intell. Inform. **17**(5), 739–745 (2013)
2. Fujishima, N., Hoshino, K.: Virtual nail art system. In: Proceedings of IEEE GCCE, pp. 766–770 (2014)
3. Ishihara, H.: The color factor and design factor to be involved in the image of the nail art. Nagoya Univ. Arts Sci. Sch. Media Des. Res. Bull. **6**, 95–102 (2013). (in Japanese)
4. Nakagawa, M., Tsukada, K., Siio, I.: Smart makeup system: supporting makeup using lifelog sharing. In: Proceedings of ACM UbiComp, pp. 483–484 (2011)
5. Naradwa Inc. BEFORE AFTER. https://app.bfaf.jp/. Accessed 16 Mar 16 (2023)
6. Odajima, M., Ito, K.: Proposal of a nail art recommendation method based on user preferences. Proc. DEIM **P1–117**, 1–3 (2019). (in Japanese)
7. ROROnail. RONOHI: Characteristic and stylish nail art. https://www.instagram.com/roro_nail/. Accessed 16 Mar 2023
8. Spika Inc., Nailbook: Nail art designs and nail salons. https://nailbook.jp/. Accessed 16 Mar 2023
9. Umezaki, J., Matsunami, Y., Ueda, M., Nakajima, S.: Proposal of a nail recipe retrieval method considering feelings and situations of users. Proc. DEIM **P8–6**, 1–5 (2017). (in Japanese)

Clarifying Patterns in Team Communication Through Extended Recurrence Plot with Levenshtein Distance

Saki Namura[1], Sunichi Tada[1], Yingting Chen[1], Taro Kanno[1(✉)] ⓘ, Haruka Yoshida[2],
Daisuke Karikawa[3], Kohei Nonose[4], and Satoru Inoue[5]

[1] The University of Tokyo, Bunkyo-Ku, Tokyo 113865, Japan
tkanno@g.ecc.u-tokyo.ac.jp
[2] Nihon University, Narashino 275-875, Chiba, Japan
[3] Tohoku University, Sendai 980-8578, Miyagi, Japan
[4] Central Research Institute of Electric Power Industry, Yokosuka 240-0196, Kanagawa, Japan
[5] Electronic Navigation Research Institute, Chofu, Tokyo 182-0012, Japan

Abstract. In this study, we have analyzed the patterns and quantitative features in the verbal data of team communications and explore an indicator to assess the quality of responses to dynamic changes in task demands. We conducted collaborative-task experiments with three-person teams and collected and analyzed the data from these experiments. A coding scheme with twelve categories representing the contents and functions of the utterances in the communications was used to code the data. Then, a recurrence plot (RP) was used to visualize the sequential patterns with the verbal codes in the team communications. We applied the Levenshtein distance, a quasi-distance between two sequential codes, which converts discrete and categorical data into continuous data. We also applied recurrence quantification analysis (RQA) to quantify and analyze the characteristics of the RP. We compared the analysis results with those obtained using a regular RP for discrete and categorical data. The proposed RP that considered the Levenshtein distance visualized the sequential patterns more clearly and provided more comparable RQA measures—such as recurrence rate (RR) and percentage of determinism (DET)—than the typical RP did. The regular RPs were sparse with many single dots and thereby did not reveal clear patterns. This result suggested that the proposed RP could reveal hidden sequential patterns in qualitative data, such as communication and behavioral data, more efficiently than the existing RP could.

Keywords: Communication Analysis · Qualitative Data Analysis · Categorical Data · Recurrence Plot · Levenshtein Distance

1 Introduction

Verbal communication contains rich information about the cognition behind team collaborations or interpersonal interactions [1]. Thus, the analysis of verbal communication is a major research topic in human factors studies, including human-computer interaction

C. Stephanidis et al. (Eds.): HCII 2023, CCIS 1834, pp. 118–123, 2023.
https://doi.org/10.1007/978-3-031-35998-9_17

(HCI) [2]. Deductive qualitative data analysis [3] is often used for the primary analysis of verbal data to categorize utterances under a coding scheme that provides a structured analytical viewpoint. After completing the primary analysis, the characteristics of the communication can be explored by applying various analytical methods to the coded data and calculating the required statistics [4].

Communication can be analyzed from different analytical perspectives using different coding schemes. However, coded qualitative data are unsuitable for exploring the dynamic nature of communication since they are discrete and categorical. This explains why most qualitative studies have only presented summary statistics and atemporal aspects in their results. One of the few exceptions is the recurrence plot (RP) used for analyzing sequential patterns [5], which is also applicable to discrete and categorical data. However, because the RP was originally designed to analyze continuous and numerical data, directly applying it to discrete and categorical data does not fully exploit its total analytical capabilities. In this study, we present a new RP for discrete and categorical data, (such as coded verbal data), wherein the quasi-distance function is introduced to calculate the proximity between any two plots of coded data.

The next section provides a brief explanation of an RP and its limitations when applied to discrete and categorical data. Section 3 describes our proposed method to extend the standard RP by introducing the quasi-distance function. Section 4 presents the results obtained using the proposed method and the comparison of these results with those obtained using the standard RP. Finally, Section 5 presents the conclusions.

2 Limitations in Standard Recurrence Plot

An RP visualizes patterns in the time series of variables that describe the behavior of a dynamic system [5]. It plots the proximity of system states at different times in a two-dimensional plane, which can be expressed by the binary recurrence matrix $R(i,j)$ shown in Eq. (1):

$$R(i,j) = \begin{cases} 1, & d(x(i),x(j)) < \\ 0, & otherwise \end{cases} \tag{1}$$

where $x(i)$ represents a system state at time i, d is the distance, and ϵ is a recurrence threshold. When an RP is applied to discrete and categorical data such as coded qualitative data, the recurrence matrix is usually modified as shown in Eq. (2):

$$R(i,j) = \begin{cases} 1, & c(i) = c(j) \\ 0, & otherwise \end{cases} \tag{2}$$

where $c(i)$ is a code assigned to the i-th utterance in the communication. Using a recurrence matrix, the characteristics of an RP can be quantified in different ways, including recurrence quantification analysis (RQA) [6]. The typical RQA measures are listed below:

- DET (Determinism): the percentage of the recurrence points that form diagonal lines.
- LAM (Laminarity): the percentage of the recurrence points that form vertical lines.
- RR (Recurrence rate): the density of the recurrence points.
- TT (Trapping time): the average length of the vertical lines.
- Vmax: the maximum length of a vertical line.

2.1 Limitations in the Standard Recurrence Plot

As described in Eq. (2), a standard RP for discrete and categorical data will only include a point if two codes match at different times. Therefore, as the number of codes in a coding scheme increases, the RP becomes sparser, making it difficult to find patterns in it. Furthermore, the exact sequence of the codes appearing in the RP may not be important in real communication, with the set of codes and rough sequences found in the set of utterances being potentially more important. For these reasons, applying the standard RP to discrete and categorical data is not as effective as expected in finding sequential patterns in communication.

3   Proposed Recurrence Plot with Quasi-distance Function

This section describes an extended RP for discrete and categorical data. We applied sliding window analysis and introduced the quasi-distance function to the existing RP to overcome its existing limitations.

3.1 Sliding Window Analysis

We considered an n-sequence of codes, instead of a single code, as the unit of analysis in the extended RP, where n is the size of the window that is moved along the sequence of codes that appear in the entire communication to define the i-th segments. For example, if the sequence of codes appearing in a communication is "ABCDEF," and the window size is three, then the first segment is "ABC," and the second is "BCD."

3.2 Levenshtein Distance

To calculate the similarity between different communication segments in an RP, we introduced the Levenshtein distance. The Levenshtein distance is the minimum number of single-character edits required to change one string into the other and can measure the similarity between any two strings. For example, the distance between "ABC" and "BCD" is three, because all three characters need to be replaced. The extended RP in this study is represented in Eq. (3):

$$R_n(i,j) = \begin{cases} d_{Lev}, & d_{Lev}(seg_n(i), seg_n(j)) < \varepsilon \\ 0, & otherwise \end{cases} \tag{3}$$

where $seg_n(i)$ represents a sequence of codes appearing in the i-th segment with window size n, and d_{Lev} represents the Levenshtein distance between any two segments.

4 Sample Results Under the Proposed Method

We applied the extended RP to the verbal communication data from the experiment conducted in our previous study [7], wherein ten three-person teams prepared light meals according to random orders. First, we analyzed the communication data using a coding scheme with twelve codes [8] and then, we applied the proposed method to visualize the sequential patterns in the communication. We also used the RQA measures to quantify the characteristics of the RP. In the following section, we have compared the results under both the proposed extended and standard RP methods and discussed the advantages of the proposed method.

4.1 Comparison of Visualization Results

The left and right figures in Fig. 1 show the standard and extended RP, respectively, for team 4. Regarding the extended RP, the Levenshtein distance was calculated and included with a threshold value of 4.0. Comparing the two figures, the extended RP has more plots than the standard RP does, and it is easier to visually capture speech patterns in it. Additionally, in the extended RP, several clusters of plots forming a rectangle are observed. This meant that the same utterances were continuous at that point and implied that the proposed method had captured patterns in the communication that the conventional method had not.

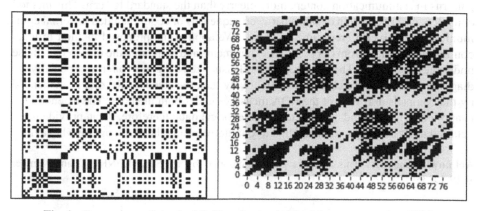

Fig. 1. Comparison of standard (left) and extended (right) recurrence plots (RPs)

4.2 Comparison of Recurrence Quality Analysis Measures

We also compared the RQA measures under the standard and extended RPs. Figure 2 shows the average RQA measures for the 10 teams. During the RQA calculation, we set the threshold value of the Levenshtein distance to 4.0. As shown in Fig. 2, the DET value of the extended RP is much larger than that of the standard RP. This shows that the proposed RP can also reveal patterns more effectively in terms of RQA measures.

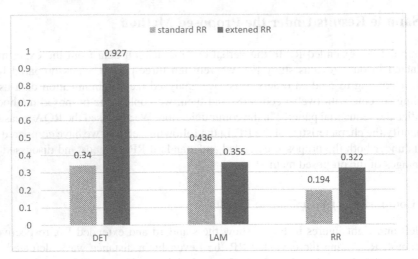

Fig. 2. Comparison of RQA measures. DET: Determinism; LAM: Laminarity; RR: Recurrence rate

5 Conclusions

This study proposes a new RP for discrete and categorical data that can capture sequential patterns in communication content more clearly than the standard RP can. This method considers the Levenshtein distance between sequences of codes included in verbal communication in two different time windows. We applied the proposed method to team communication data from our previous experiments and compared the results with those under the standard RP. The proposed method visualized the given patterns, especially the diagonal patterns, more clearly and effectively than the standard RP did, as evidenced by the comparison results of the RQA measures under both methods. The extended RP is applicable to any kind of discrete and categorical data; therefore, it can provide more detailed analysis results when applied to qualitative data related to cognitive behavior.

Acknowledgments. . This work is partly supported by JSPS KAKENHI (Grant Number JP19H02384).

References

1. Chen, Y., Kanno, T., Furuta, K.: An empirical investigation of the underlying cognitive process in complex problem solving: a proposal of problem-solving discussion performance evaluation methods. Int. J. Cogn. Inf. Nat. Intell. **16**(1), 1–15 (2022). https://doi.org/10.4018/IJCINI. 301204
2. Chen, Y., Kanno, T., Furuta, K.: Cognition-oriented facilitation and guidelines for collaborative problem-solving online and face-to-face, Unpublished paper. In: CHI '23: Proceedings of the 2023 CHI Conference on Human Factors in Computing Systems, pp. 1–15, April 2023. https://doi.org/10.1145/3544548.3581112. Article No. 61

3. Merriam, S.B.: Qualitative Research and Case Study Applications in Education. Jossey-Bass Publishers, San Francisco (1998)
4. Foltz, P.W., Martin, M.J.: Automated communication analysis of teams. In: Salas, E., Goodwin, G. F., Burke, C. S. (eds.), Team effectiveness in complex organizations: cross-disciplinary perspectives and approaches, pp. 411–431. Routledge/Taylor & Francis Group, Oxfordshire, UK (2009)
5. Bakeman, R., Quera, V.: Recurrence analysis and permutation tests. In: Sequential Analysis and Observational Methods for the Behavioral Sciences, pp. 148–162. Cambridge University Press, Cambridge, UK (2011)
6. Marwan, N., Romano, M.C., Thiel, M., Kurths, J.: Recurrence plots for the analysis of complex systems. Phys. Rep. **438**(5–6), 237–329 (2007). https://doi.org/10.1016/j.physrep.2006.11.001
7. Namura, S., Kanno, T., Furuta, K., Chen, Y., Mitsuhashi, D.: Exploring quantitative indicators for monitoring resilient team cognition. In: Ho, A. G. (eds.), Human factors in communication of design. International Conference on Applied Human Factors and Ergonomics (AHFE) 2022, vol. 49, AHFE International, USA (2022). https://doi.org/10.54941/ahfe1002052
8. Mitsuhashi, D., Kanno, T., Inoue, S., Karikawa, D., Nonose, K., Furuta, K.: Prescriptive and descriptive similarity of team contexts. In: Nunes, I.L. (ed.) AHFE 2019. AISC, vol. 959, pp. 185–193. Springer, Cham (2020). https://doi.org/10.1007/978-3-030-20040-4_17

Quantitative Assessment Methods for the Needs of Airline Safety Management Personnel

Xueyan Peng[⊠] and Yuan Zhang

China Academy of Civil Aviation Science and Technology, Beijing 101300, China
{pengxy,zhangyuan}@mail.castc.org.cn

Abstract. Safety managers are responsible for recognizing and controlling safety risks in the operation process, monitoring safety performance and implementing safety training. It is very necessary to evaluate safety manager quantity needed for different parts of the safety management system under the current running state. In this study, a calculation model of airlines' demands for safety managers was constructed. The routine safety management duties were determined and information about unconventional management duties was collected. Moreover, some factors were considered in this model, including leave, fatigue, extra working hours, personnel quality, office automation degree, and so on. Based on this model, an airline company was chosen for case study and data of normal working hours of safety managers was collected. The safety manager demands under the current running conditions were evaluated. Research conclusions provide references for companies to evaluate human resource demands.

Keywords: Safety Managers · Personnel Demand · Workload · Effective Working Hour

1 Purpose and Background

Safety is the bottom line of enterprise production and management. Safety managers are vital to safety of civil aviation and they are responsible for recognizing and controlling safety risks in the operation process, monitoring safety performance and implementing safety training. Determining the at least number of safety managers for the safety management of the company is an important premise for continuous safety operation of airlines. Laws and regulations regulate setting of safety production management organizations and equipments of full-time or part-time safety production managers, but there's no regulation on number of safety managers. In many industrial fields including construction, hazardous chemicals, electric power, road transport, metallurgy, building materials, mechanical engineering and light industry, the equipment proportion of safety managers of relevant enterprises has been refined. In the civil aviation, it only regulates to establish a safety management system and have safety managers to meet needs of safety management. In practical situation, there's no regulation on how to equip safety managers in accordance of enterprise scale and no model of safety manager demands of enterprise has been established. Determining safety manager demands based on experiences might lead to inadequate safety managers and increase safety risks of civil operation. Elen et al. [1] studied correlation among human resource management shrinkage, working worsening, and safety and security risks in business aviation, and concluded that human resource management shrinkage increased safety and security risks through the worsening working environment through a model test. It is pointed out in the evaluation report of expert configuration demands in the aviation system related with facility maintenance of United States Federal Aviation Administration (FAA) that understaffing will affect performance, increase inherent risks in the system and create potential risks within the system through overtime level, pressure accumulation and use of shortcut. For current running conditions, some problems still have no explicit solutions, such as whether personnel workload is over saturated, whether excessive workload may influence safety state of enterprises, whether it is necessary to increase personnel, and how many personnel has to be added.

Hence, to prevent adverse safety influences caused by cost minimization, this study aims to measure safety manager demands of enterprises according to needs and determine the at least quantity of safety managers under the premise of safety running.

2   Current Situation Analysis of Personnel Demand Assessment

2.1   Study on Ordinary Personnel Demands

At present, the efficiency-based personnel allocation method is used the most extensively. Production personnel with explicit production quota calculates workloads according to product yield or task load and norm of working hours per unit product or task. In the field of health human resource allocation, the World Health Organization (WHO) issued the health manpower configuration method (WISN) based on workload index. The key steps include estimation of available working time (AWT), definition of workload, formulation of activity standard, establishing workload standard, and calculation of adjustment factor and personnel demands [2]. Qu Xiangdong [3] used the average trial time for various tasks in a single case as the workload and calculated the quantity of judges according to the ratio between trial tasks and trial working time.

On this basis, many scholars have improved the formula to some extent during application to adapt to their studies. Some scholars calculated working hours of temporary tasks thoroughly. Moreover, the allowance time determined by relaxing ratio was added [4]. According to characteristics of posts, some scholars considered the adjustment coefficient produced by different alpine environment in plateau and allocation of production force [5]. Some scholars weighted physical time for work by using working environment and labor intensity.

2.2 Safety Manager Demands of Civil Aviation

Studies on personnel allocation calculation in civil aviation mainly focus on employees of frontline business departments. Lin Qiang et al. [6] reviewed duties of ground officials and calculated workloads of duties one by one, formulated the airport ground service system. Duan Zhezhe [7] calculated personnel of airport ground service department by using the efficiency-based personnel allocation method through the total production tasks in the planning period and per capita efficiency hours. Dong Ziliang [8] calculated demands of controlling officers by using the post-based personnel allocation method and compared the calculation results based on number of posts and number of personnel per post with the calculation results based on number of needed working hours of a post and working hours per employee on duty. He found that the later calculation of personnel structure was relatively reasonable.

Based on above research status and estimation model of personnel demands, it found that research objects can be divided into two types: one is frontline pure operators who have single structure of job content and high repeatability. The other type is non-pure operators, such as judges and workers in health institutions. Research object of this study chooses safety managers. Compared with judges and workers in health institutions, the job contents of safety managers are more diversified, accompanied with more complicated working structure and lower frequency of occurrence of duplicate tasks. As a common calculation method of personnel quota and allocation, the efficiency-based personnel allocation method can calculate the needed personnel accurately by measuring the workload. For scientific and accurate determination of safety manager quantity of enterprises, the research idea of efficiency-based personnel allocation method was chosen and the quantity of safety managers was determined through labor hours and legal working hours. On this basis, the safety manager allocation of civil aviation was studied.

3 Construction of the Safety Manager Demands Evaluation Model

Personnel allocation was calculated through labor hours and legal working hours in this study. Labor hours refer to the time needed to finish tasks in a period and it is determined by number of task executions and time per unit task. The number of task executions is determined by practical situations. Nevertheless, time per unit task differs significantly and only a statistical analysis on time for various tasks can be carried out. Time per unit task is surveyed or measured through questionnaire survey and field measurement. The statistical analysis results were used as the estimated basic data directly. The data accuracy was higher and the calculation results were closer to situations of the company.

Based on above personnel allocation, the safety manager quantity was calculated by the ratio between time for workload in the period and effective working hours of personnel: $N = P/T$, where N is the number of safety managers, P is the safety management workload, and T is effective working hours of personnel. Since some safety management is carried out by years, the model calculation used years as the calculation period. Specifically, safety management workload can calculate normal working hours of conventional job and temporary job. Combining with studies of various personnel,

personnel demands might be influenced by personnel quality, job content and office conditions. These influencing factors were added into the formula as adjustment coefficient when calculating effective working hours of personnel to calculate personnel demands under different influencing factor levels.

3.1 Safety Manager Demand Evaluation Model

The calculation formula of quantity of safety managers can be expressed as:

$$N = \frac{P}{T} = \frac{\sum_{i=1}^{m} s_i t_i + \sum_{j=1}^{n} f_j h_j}{T_1(1-\alpha)(1-\beta)(1+\gamma)ab} \tag{1}$$

Based on the above model, the safety management workload and effective working time of personnel which are applicable to organization institutions, operation scale, job contents and working atmosphere of research objects can be gained. As a result, the safety manager demands could be calculated specifically. Based on the calculated results, workload can be divided through responsibility-based personnel allocation method, which is conducive to arrange various tasks reasonably.

3.2 Calculation of Safety Manager Workloads

Except for route acts have to be made daily in safety management, there are unconventional jobs like temporary meeting, conferences and administrative responsibilities may occupy working hours. Therefore, the calculation of safety management workload was divided into conventional workload and temporary workload, which were expressed in working hours. The total working hours of this task were calculated by number of work tasks in a period and norm of working hour of this task. Therefore, the calculation formula of safety management workload was:

$$P = \sum_{i=1}^{m} s_i t_i + \sum_{j=1}^{n} f_j h_j \tag{2}$$

where I = 1,2,3, i, ..., m——set of the ith conventional responsibilities of safety managers;

J = 1,2,3,...,n——set of the jth unconventional responsibilities of safety managers, including temporary tasks, conference, working records and other administrative jobs;

s_i——operation frequency of the ith conventional responsibility, i ∈ I;

t_i—— normal time to finish the ith conventional responsibility, i ∈ I;

f_j—— operation frequency of the jth unconventional responsibility, j ∈ J;

h_j——normal time to finish the jth unconventional responsibility, j ∈ J.

3.3 Estimation of Effective Working Time

Except legal working days, absences caused by personal leave, sick leave, annual leave and training all may decrease working time and working days shall be calculated by actual attendance. The daily legal working hours is not equal to effective working hours. Some company may require overtime and not all of working hours are effective working hours. Due to factors like psychology and psychology, working efficiency of employees in a day fluctuates to some extent. Hence, fatigue allowance time shall be considered. Besides, personnel quality level and office conditions of companies also can influence effective working hours of employees. With comprehensive considerations to above factors, the calculation formula of effective working hours of personnel was:

$$T = Tl\,(1 - \alpha)\,(1 - \beta)\,(1 + \gamma)ab \tag{3}$$

where Tl is the annual legal working hours;

α——absence rate, expressed by the ratio between annual absent days for personal leave, sick leave, annual leave and training and annual legal working days;

β—— fatigue allowance, expressed by the ratio between weekly fatigue allowance time and legal working hours;

γ—— overtime rate, expressed by the ratio between weekly overtime and legal working hours.

a——personnel quality level, determined by education background and business-related skills.

b—— office automation degree, determined by the degree that job can be completed by automatic software or system.

4   Implementation Process

With full considerations to the premise that enough safety managers are needed to complete safety management tasks and guarantee operation safety of enterprises, allocation of safety managers in an enterprise can be performed according to following steps. According to efficiency-based personnel allocation method, the above safety manager allocation model was used as the basis and the basic framework to study safety manager allocation was established.

4.1   Determine Safety Management Programs

In this study, job contents of safety managers referred to Safety Management Manual (Doc 9859) of International Civil Aviation Organization and requirements in legal standards, such as requirements of safety management system construction of air operators, airports and air traffic control unit. Besides, working status of real safety management department was surveyed and the basic safety management responsibilities were determined preliminarily from 12 elements, four pillars of the safety management system. On this basis, the safety management task list was adjusted according to expert interview. The final safety management task list is shown in Table 1.

Table 1. Final safety management task list.

Pillars	Elements	Job contents	workloads
Safety policy and objectives	Safety responsibility	Issue rewards and punishment list	18
	Appoint core safety personnel	Materials of Security Commission	120
	Coordinate formulation of emergency plans	Emergency rehearsal, evaluation effect, follow-up of emergency plan rectification	30
	Safety management system document	Revision of safety management system document	60
Safety risk management		Risk source database management, risk evaluation report, implementation of risk measures	432
Security assurance	Safety performance management	Monitor safety performance index, issue the note of rectification, track and verify implementation and effects of measures, review and revise safety performance index	216
	Safety inspection	Formulate inspection plan, formulate inspection list, issue note of rectification, track and verify implementation and effects of measures, identify problems and analyze data in safety inspection	1200
	Event survey	Implement survey, form survey report, issue note of rectification, track and verify implementation and effects of measures	540
	Safety report	Safety information data analysis, issue note of rectification, track and verify implementation and effects of measures	1460

(*continued*)

Table 1. (*continued*)

Pillars	Elements	Job contents	workloads
	SMS review	Formulate review scheme, document review and field review, write review report, issue note of rectification, track and verify implementation and effects of measures	30
	Flight data analysis	Analyze flight data, issue note of rectification, track and verify implementation and effects of measures	576
	Safety information comprehensive analysis and management	Collect external safety information, comprehensive analysis of various safety information, issue note of rectification, track and verify implementation and effects of measures	120
	SMS management review	SMS management review report, SMS management review meeting, track implementation and effect of management review decision	14
Safety promotion	Safety training and education	Formulate safety training plan, implement safety training and evaluate effect, establish and perfect safety training files of workers, carry out safety education activities	40
	Safety information exchange	Carry out safety information communication activities and evaluate effect	72

4.2 Data Acquisition and Processing

Respondents. In civil aviation enterprises and institutions, safety management is characteristic of systematic and diversified. Management structure in enterprises also tends to be flattening. In this study, personnel allocation covered all employees responsible for safety management as much as possible, and their workloads were quantized. This improved accuracy of really needed safety manager quantity which was estimated by the personnel allocation model. Hence, the survey objects of this study were all workers exclusive for safety management in enterprises.

Survey Contents. Based on the above personnel allocation model, information which had to be collected in questionnaire included time of safety managers of a post to complete various safety responsibilities and working frequency; time of leave and return; time of annual leave, personal leave and sick leave; scores of personal quality level and scores of office automation. To calculate consistency of data in computation, time indicators except the ratio indicator all used days as the unit.

Data Acquisition. Before implementation of survey, we communicate with respondents fully to interpret the research goal and investigate meanings of items. During field survey, doubts of respondents to the questionnaire were solved and inappropriate places of the questionnaire were adjusted timely. Moreover, missing times were supplemented and amended timely. The reality, reliability and usability of questionnaire data were improved.

Data Processing. Monthly data and annual data in the questionnaire were surveyed uniformly. The monthly data was adjusted into annual data according to 12 months in a year, which was convenient for the next calculation processing of data. This was also consistent with annual effective working hours. The time and frequency of route job items were multiplied and workloads of all routine jobs of all respondents in the calculation period were organized. Moreover, time of all unconventional jobs of all respondents in the calculation period were organized. Workloads of safety management of an enterprises were calculated according to Eq. (2). The absent days for annual leave, personal leave and sick leave, working hour data for rest adjustment, average overtime, personnel quality level and office automation degree were brought into Eq. (3) to calculate the effective working hours. Combining with Eq. (1), ratios of above results were used as safety manager demands which were calculated according to existing workloads.

5 Case Study

To verify feasibility of the model, Airline A was chosen as the research object. Combining with practical operation conditions and safety managers, safety manager demands were further evaluated by the model. Now, Airline A has 20 employees in the Department of Safety Supervision, including 6 in the safety supervision sector, 8 in the safety management sector and 6 in the flight quality monitoring sector. The annual workload of each safety manager in Airline A was collected through field survey and questionnaire survey, including annual frequency of a task and average time per implementation. Workloads of all employees involved in each job were summarized. It concluded that the total workloads of safety managers were 5005 man-day and the workloads results are shown in Table 1.

According to questionnaire survey, the average weekly fatigue allowance of safety managers in Airline A was 4.85 h, the annual absence time was about 19.15 days, and the weekly average overtime was 4.95 h. The personnel quality level and office automation degree were both industrial average levels, so their adjustment coefficients were both 1. The above data were brought into Eq. (3), thus getting the annual effective working hours per person of about 227.95 days. It calculated from the evaluation model of safety manager demands that the safety manager demands of Airline A were 21.96. Compared with existing personnel, 2 safety managers shall be added to meet existing job contents and strength. This can decrease working pressure of existing safety managers to some extent and guarantee safety operation of flights.

6 Conclusions

Safety managers assume the important safety management responsibilities. They recognize operation risks and control them at an acceptable level through risk management, performance monitoring and control, safety communication, and safety training. To guarantee safety operation of flights, the safety managers in accordance to current development stage and operation scale shall be evaluated. In this study, a quantitative evaluation method of safety manager demands is established to estimate workloads of safety management in a period and effective working hour. The proposed method can get actual demands of safety managers accurately and provide theoretical references to further evaluate existing labor sources in airlines.

References

1. Paraschi, E.P., Georgopoulos, A., Papanikou, M.: Safety and security implications of crisis-driven austerity HRM practices in commercial aviation: a structural equation modelling approach. Saf. Sci. **147**, 105570 (2022)
2. World Health Organization. Workload indicators of staffing need: user's manual. Geneva: World Health Organization (2010)
3. Xiangdong, Q.: Model estimation of case-based personal allocation and judge quota. Modern Law Sci. **38**(03), 160–180 (2016)
4. Yibin, W., Guohua, F., Tao, S., Ming, X., Xianfeng, H.: Research on flexible determination of posts for the pump station project in the Jiangsu section of east route of the south-to-north water transfer project. Water Conservancy Cconomy **36**(03), 39–44+79 (2018)
5. Zeqian, Z., Kexin, Z., An, Y.: Discussion on labor allocation standards for the railway engineering system in high-altitude and complicated dangerous mountainous areas. Railway Energy-saving, Environ. Protect. Saf. Health **11**(04), 37–42 (2021)
6. Qiang, L., Xin, G., Huibin, J.: Application of method study in personnel allocation in airport ground services. J. Tianjin Univ. (Soc. Sci.) **15**(05), 406–410 (2013)
7. Zhezhe, D.: Operator allocation model in ground service department of China's civil aviation and its applications — an empirical study based on ground service department of airport a. J. Nanchang Hangkong Univ. (Soc. Sci.) **18**(01), 60–67 (2016)
8. Ziliang, D.: Calculation methods of controlling officers in civil airport planning and construction. Build. Tech. Dev. **44**(17), 16–17 (2017)

Using Automatic and Semi-automatic Methods for Digitizing the Dictionary of Trinidad and Tobago English/Creole into a Graph Database

Divindra Ramai[✉] and Phaedra S. Mohammed

Department of Computing and Information Technology, The University of the West Indies, St. Augustine Campus, Port of Spain, Trinidad and Tobago
Divindra.Ramai@my.uwi.edu, Phaedra.Mohammed@sta.uwi.edu

Abstract. The Dictionary of Trinidad & Tobago English/Creole (DTTE/C) is the first scholarly dictionary to cover the lexicon of three of the languages of Trinidad & Tobago that are all regarded as low-resourced languages. There have been no successful attempts, prior, to efficiently digitize the dictionary for adoption and use in research communities within the broad field of Artificial Intelligence. As such, this paper presents the work done to produce an efficient DTTE/C digitisation framework using a series of automatic and semi-automatic methods. Through detailed modeling of the dictionary as a graph structure, the research uses graph database technology for the generation of a DTTE/C knowledge graph and lexical semantic layering by referencing upper level concepts in the SUMO ontology. Fauna datasets consisting of entries from Mollusc, Crustacean and Mammal categories were successfully modeled in the graph with F1 scores of 0.929, 0.886, and 0.987 respectively for headwords.

Keywords: Knowledge Graph · Digitisation · Dictionary · Creole · Lexical Semantics

1 Introduction

A low-resource language (LRL) is one that has limited digital resources, including limited online content compared to a high-resource language [1]. These languages are often poorly represented in natural language processing due to lack of data, which presents a significant challenge in developing effective language models [2]. The Dictionary of Trinidad & Tobago English/Creole (DTTE/C), edited by Lise Winer [3] is the first and only scholarly dictionary to comprehensively cover the lexicon of three of the languages of Trinidad & Tobago that are all regarded as low-resourced. These are Trinidad & Tobago English (TTE), Trinidadian English Creole (TrinEC) and Tobagonian English Creole (TobEC). However, the DTTE/C faces the same common challenges as other LRLs which, according to [4], is the lack of electronic resources for speech and language processing which includes software tools such as parsers and taggers, pronunciation dictionaries, vocabulary lexicons, and digital corpora.

C. Stephanidis et al. (Eds.): HCII 2023, CCIS 1834, pp. 133–140, 2023.
https://doi.org/10.1007/978-3-031-35998-9_19

As the result of over 30 years of research, the DTTE/C adds a valuable dataset of both the English language and English Creole languages to research communities and undertaking the digitisation is worthwhile for many reasons. For instance, the dictionary relates common lexical terms within Caribbean English Creoles and across those found in Standard British and North American English. These relationships allow lexical mappings to eventually be created for better understanding of translations across languages. In addition, the dictionary contains detailed information that can enable clustering of lexical entries by temporal aspects (archaic, obsolete, modern) or cultural dimensions (region, ethnicity, religion). This is useful for creating tailored, relevant content for different speech communities using natural language generation techniques. Lastly, multiple-meaning entries, where the use of a particular sense has different social implications, enable disambiguating context and subtle nuances.

One challenge of digitizing the DTTE/C was defining a flexible, general graph schema that provided structure, established existing connections between entries and encoded major characteristics of lexical entries. This design needed to be very flexible since while extracting the data from the source document using automated means gives insight regarding a general format for an entry, there are several outliers which require fringe annotations. The major challenge however was creating a text extractor module that automatically located and compiled the appropriate values for each of the fields of an entry. The final challenge reported in this paper involved verifying the validity and completeness of the automatically extracted data against manually produced benchmarks for critical counts relevant for the entries.

The paper is organized as follows. Section 2 describes the DTTE/C in more detail, highlights major characteristics of the entries and gives statistical details about the data. Section 3 outlines the methodology followed in pre-processing and cleaning the dictionary data, creating a graph schema for structuring the data, and using automatic and semi-automatic text mining techniques to extract and format the data. Section 4 describes how the text extractor performance was evaluated and analyzes the success and limitations so far. The paper concludes in Sect. 5 with future work and conclusion in Sect. 6.

2   The Dictionary of Trinidad and Tobago English/Creole

The DTTE/C is a historical, descriptive dictionary containing 990 pages of entry data, and reportedly over 12,200 full entries; 2,500 related to flora and 2,200 to fauna alone [3].

2.1   Types of Entries and Sample Format

There are three main types of entries: single meaning, multiple-meaning and cross-reference. All three types start with a bold headword which can be a single word, multiple words, or a phrase. Cross-reference entries only contain a reference to a main entry indicated in small capitals. Single and multiple-meaning entries however may consist of alternate spellings, part of speech, usage notes, definition, phonetic symbol pronunciation, etymology, synonyms, and citations. The different senses of a multiple-meaning entry are identified numerically. Figure 1 shows samples of these types of entries annotated with labels that identify the main features described earlier.

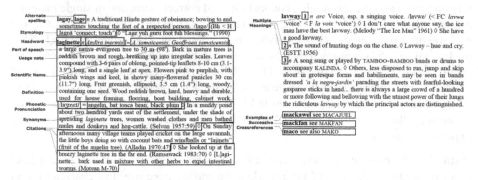

Fig. 1. Samples of Single-Meaning, Multiple-Meaning and Cross-Reference DTTE/C Entries

2.2 Fauna Datasets

According to [3], the original dictionary comprises 4,500 Flora (plant) and Fauna (animal) entries, which account for approximately 36.9% of all dictionary entries. Of these 4,500 entries, Fauna consists of approximately 2,194 or 48.8% of all of the DTTE/C's biological and ecological sections combined, and approximately 18.0% of all dictionary entries. For this research, small sample files, derived from Fauna listing specifically Molluscs, Crustaceans and Mammals entries, each containing 29, 40 and 168 headwords, respectively were manually extracted from a master JSON dataset containing all of the dictionary entries. This represents a combined sampling of 237 Fauna entries or approximately 11% of all Fauna entries and 2% of all dictionary entries. These particular datasets were selected in order to incrementally test the effectiveness of the methodology in preparation for the larger digitisation datasets.

3   Digitisation Methodology

Three main stages were involved in the digitisation process: (1) preprocessing and transformation of the raw DTTE/C data, (2) construction of a knowledge graph with a uniform schema that covers all types of entries, and (3) incremental population of the graph with the Fauna datasets along with verification checks for completeness.

3.1   Data Preprocessing and Transformation

Text Mining. Since the DTTE/C data was only available as a PDF file, it was first converted to an XML format in order to identify a general structure for performing parsing and data extraction. Custom pattern matching rules were built for extracting the key fields of an entry and identifying data errors that were intrinsic due to human and formatting errors in the original PDF document. Human-produced tallies of the single-meaning, multiple-meaning and cross referenced entries revealed that the DTTE/C actually contains 17,299 entries in total. Low relative Percentage Differences (RPD) between manual human counts and the text mining counts indicated correct extraction of single meaning entries (RPD = 0.53%, s.d. = 2.82), cross-references (RPD = 1.08%, s.d. = 11.61) and multiple-meaning entries (RPD = 0.49%, s.d. = 5.29). Low RPD scores overall (RPD = 0.31%, s.d. = 1.52) confirmed that the pattern matching techniques worked adequately for producing a cleaned version of the DTTE/C data. However, there were still errors that limited a fully automated solution from being used for preprocessing the data. These included missing delimiters between fields in entries, inconsistent formatting (which posed a challenge for well-formed XML data), and general limitations in the regular expression criteria.

Data Transformation. Another set of custom repair rules were built to handle special cases of headword errors for Multiple-Meaning entries, page overflow character errors (such as added hyphenation characters within entries), and etymology phrase construction. These filtered and flagged poorly-formed entries for manual review and significantly reduced the manual effort needed during the data preparation steps.

3.2   Graph Generation and Ontology Referencing

Given that the DTTE/C knowledge graph is meant to accommodate a combined dataset of over 17,000 distinct entries with many linkages, query and load performance becomes paramount. The knowledge graph was therefore implemented in Neo4j due the need to store, generate and retrieve highly connected data [5], and facilitate rule-based filtering and disambiguation of polysemic requests as identified by [6]. The graph schema, shown in Fig. 2, was extended natively through the use of concepts from the SUMO ontology [7] in order to accommodate semantic reasoning, as described by [8]. This allowed for expressive semantic modeling of an entry's main fields (as identified in Fig. 1) and lexical mappings for taxonomic consistency which were especially important for the Fauna datasets described earlier. Strict adherence was paid to the linked data principles as described by [9] in leveraging the creation of semantically interoperable structured DTTE/C data.

3.3   Graph Population with Fauna Datasets

A series of 22 Cypher queries [10] were produced which generated nodes representing relevant SUMO concepts (such as the Animal class and relevant subclasses to support Mammal, Fish and Mollusc entries), different types of DTTE/C entries with their native fields, established subsumption relationships and set up other necessary linkages. These queries also loaded the data into the nodes, merged duplicate entries, and generated new knowledge based on expanded linkages especially between cross-referenced and multi-meaning entries.

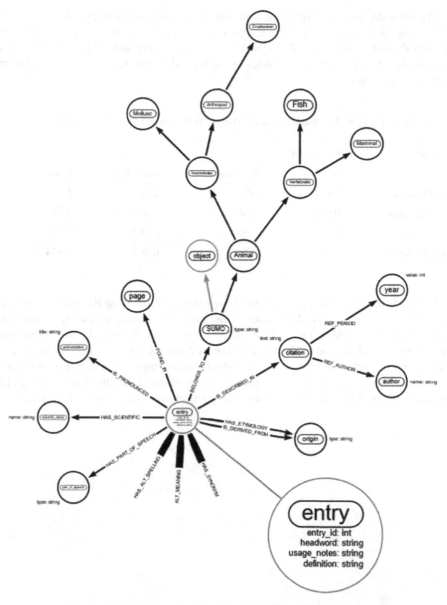

Fig. 2. DTTE/C Data Model with SUMO Semantic Referencing

4   Evaluation

A major goal of this work was to verify whether any data that was automatically extracted from the dictionary was correctly and completely rendered in the knowledge graph. Additionally, it was important to determine whether any new knowledge was generated for the entries as a result of the graph structure.

The three stages of the digitization methodology was applied independently to each of the three Fauna datasets. Table 1 presents the overall precision, recall and F1 scores for each dataset where, overall the performance was acceptable (F1 = 0.934). This confirms that the majority of the entries in the three datasets was correctly rendered in the knowledge graph.

Table 1. DTTE/C Knowledge Graph Classification Performance for Fauna Datasets.

Statistic	Fauna Datasets			
	Mollusc	Crustacean	Mammal	Overall
Total Entries	29	40	168	237
Avg. Precision	0.927	0.900	0.988	0.938
Avg. Recall	0.934	0.884	0.987	0.935
Avg. F1 Score	0.929	0.886	0.987	**0.934**

Figure 3 illustrates the outcomes of the queries performed on the Mollusc dataset when verifying the headword accuracy. This dataset had many entries with multiple meanings, such as "chip-chip", "devil fish", "kochikong", "sea cockroach", and "sea tatu". Consequently, some of the cross-referenced entries were not true Molluscs and were therefore excluded. Discoveries of additional synonyms in the graph dictionary were made for entries, "clam" and "pacro", which showed that the knowledge graph demonstrated an ability to add new knowledge and create meaningful data linkages.

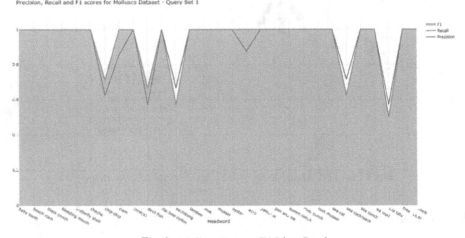

Fig. 3. Mollusc Dataset F1 Line Graph

For the Crustacean dataset, the F1 score dropped for one particular entry ("bush crab") as shown in Fig. 4. This entry deviated from the established etymology standard of the source text and revealed a limitation in the text mining tool's handling of ad-hoc variations for multiple meanings of an entry. However, the knowledge graph created new relationships between entries in the latter half of the dataset and disclosed previously unknown patterns in the data further contributing to dips in the graph. The mammal dataset on the other hand was the most consistently rendered group in the knowledge graph as shown in Fig. 5, owing to least ambiguity with the entry names (more single-meaning entries).

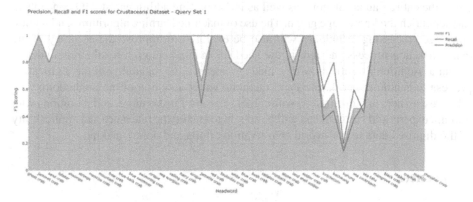

Fig. 4. Crustacean Dataset F1 Line Graph

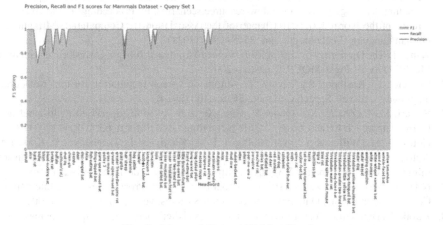

Fig. 5. Mammal Dataset F1 Line Graph

5   Conclusion and Future Work

In conclusion, digitizing LRLs can be challenging but a rewarding endeavor for natural language processing. The Dictionary of Trinidad & Tobago English/Creole (DTTE/C) comprises a valuable language corpus for the research community, enabling lexical mapping and the creation of text tailored to language groups through the use of familiar cultural vocabulary and references. Digitising the DTTE/C involved defining a simple, general knowledge graph schema and along with a text extractor module that parsed and transformed each entry, and populating the knowledge graph with the entry data through Cypher queries. Generating high F1 scores of 0.929, 0.886, and 0.987 respectively for selected Fauna datasets shows the feasibility of this digitisation approach in dealing with similar and increasing datasets.

Future work for digitising the dictionary includes expanding the dataset scope to cover the entire Fauna category, as well as incorporating additional SUMO concepts to further enrich the knowledge graph. The use of machine learning algorithms and natural language processing techniques will also be explored to improve the accuracy of the data extraction process and reduce the need for manual curation for the remainder of the data. Additionally, efforts will be made to improve the scalability of the digitization process to handle larger datasets and facilitate wider adoption of the methodology by other researchers and institutions within LRL regions. Furthermore, collaborations with domain experts and stakeholders will be sought to ensure the relevance and applicability of the digitised data to real-world conservation efforts and policy-making.

References

1. Kamble, S., Gaikwad, M: A survey on natural language processing for low-resource languages. Int. J. Adv. Res. Comput. Sci. **12**(2), 98–105 (2021)
2. Hedderich, M.A., Lange, L., Adel, H., Strötgen, J., Klakow, D.: A survey on recent approaches for natural language processing in low-resource scenarios. In: Proceedings of the 2021 Conference of the North American Chapter of the Association for Computational Linguistics: Human Language Technologies, pp. 2545–2568 (2021)
3. Winer, L: The Dictionary of the English/Creole of Trinidad & Tobago: On historical principles. McGill-Queen's Press-MQUP, Kingston (2009)
4. Besacier, L., Kastberg, S., Schultz, T.: Automatic speech recognition for under-resourced languages: a survey. Speech Commun. **56**, 85–100 (2014)
5. Bukari, M.M., Zhang, X., Abudu, S., Guo, X.: A novel semi-supervised multi-label deep learning approach for automatic wildlife recognition. Eco. Inform. **63**, 101349 (2021)
6. Hettne, K.M., Williams A.J., van Mulligen, E.M., Kleinjans, J., Tkachenko, V., Kors, J.A.: Automatic vs. manual curation of a multi-source chemical dictionary: the impact on text mining. J. Cheminformatics **2**(3)(2010). https://doi.org/10.1186/1758-2946-2-3
7. Niles, I., Pease, A.: Towards a standard upper ontology. In: Proceedings of the International Conference on Formal Ontology in Information Systems, vol. 2, no. 1, pp. 2–9 (2001)
8. Kubik, T.: Digital transformation of the etymological dictionary of geographical names. Appl. Sci. **11**(1), 289 (2020). https://doi.org/10.3390/app11010289
9. Gillis-Webber, F.: Conversion of the English-Xhosa dictionary for nurses to a linguistic linked data framework. Inf. **9**(11) 274 (2018). https://doi.org/10.3390/info9110274
10. Neo4j Cypher Reference Manual. Retrieved 24 March 2023, (2021). https://neo4j.com/docs/cypher-manual/current/

I Have No Idea What Are These Terms! Exploring Users' Understanding and Interpretation of Genealogy Results

Lipsarani Sahoo$^{(\boxtimes)}$ and Mohamed Shehab

University of North Carolina at Charlotte, Charlotte, NC 28223, USA
{lsahoo1,mshehab}@uncc.edu

Abstract. This paper explores users' understanding and interpretation of genealogy results. Furthermore, we analyzed the website's usability and gathered users' suggestions to improve the site. We developed a website imitating the most popular public genealogy site to attain these goals. We conducted a qualitative study where users' performed a few tasks on the mocked platform, then explained the use of different filters present and the result columns. Overall, we found that all users faced difficulty in interpreting the terminologies of filters and result columns.

Keywords: Usability · Genealogy · Public genealogy databases

1 Introduction

Lately, commercial genetic testing has gained immense popularity. Over 26 million people worldwide have taken a commercial DNA test to explore genetic ancestry, health predisposition, or inherited traits [5]. In this genetic openness era, two types of companies are primarily rising: testing companies and public genealogy databases. Testing companies provide genetic kits and results along with the raw DNA data. Most of these testing companies also offer a platform to create a social profile to find their DNA relatives present in their database. The second kind of company is public genealogy sites. These sites do not sell kits or test a person's DNA sample. These sites are primarily free genealogy sites that let users upload their raw DNA data results, irrespective of any testing companies, to compare autosomal DNA data files and find related individuals. GEDmatch is a very popular site of this kind [4]. GEDmatch provides tools to facilitate the goal of family finding. The preparatory starting point is "one-to-many tool." The one-to-many tool is very popular for comparing your genetic profile to all other GEDmatch users. This tool provides a list of members with whom user share chromosome segments and their email addresses for quick contact.

A user-friendly website provides users engaged support in accessing the preferred information efficiently. Nevertheless, the user's interest in a website depends upon the swiftness of the website [1]. A website could be considered unfriendly if users face difficulty understanding or get confused about performing a task. Furthermore, design features influence users' motivational and cognitive

C. Stephanidis et al. (Eds.): HCII 2023, CCIS 1834, pp. 141–148, 2023.
https://doi.org/10.1007/978-3-031-35998-9_20

aspects to use the product or not [3]. Thus, the design quality of websites is crucial for their success [2]. Several authors investigated the implications of design attributes in many sectors, such as retail, mobile banking, etc. These implications provide effective approaches for developing reliable interfaces to satisfy users and keep users' commitment to the website.

As the concept of public genealogy sites is relatively new, there has not been a fair amount of research that looked at users' preferences for these sites. To close this gap, we aimed to investigate the site's usability and discover the problem areas of average users.

More specifically, in our study, we investigate the following research questions:

- RQ1: Is the most popular public genealogy site user-friendly and efficiently caters to users' needs?
- RQ2: How do users perceive the usability of the site?
- RQ3: How could the site be improved for more usability?

We developed a website name "Genealogy Research Site" (GRS). The website had the same filters and results tables using fake data as on the GEDmatch site. We interviewed ten users to perform tasks using one-to-many tool on GRS. All participants confronted huge difficulty understanding the terminologies and using the filters to perform their tasks and stated that the platform was unfriendly and technical for an average person. Therefore, GEDmatch, the most popular public genealogy platform, cannot cater to users' needs and expectations for DNA-relative findings. We gathered and listed users' suggestions to improve the site for better interpretation of results and to facilitate the search for DNA matches. Our findings are valuable for users, UX researchers, UI designers, and developers as public genealogy sites continue to become widely used.

2   User Study

We conducted semi-structured interviews through Zoom [6] with ten users. Interviews lasted, on average, 30 min. We did inductive coding to analyze our data. For our goal, we chose the most popular or the starting point of a relative finding tool, i.e., "one-to-many" search. This tool delivers an index of people that share chromosome segments with the user. Email addresses for matches are provided as well to allow the user to contact their matches quickly. Users can also specify further criteria for the filter, such as screening for top matches, as well as the number of matches that will be displayed. These filters are called "With this offset" and "With this limit." As an example, setting the "with this offset" filter to 1000 and the "with this limit" filter to 100 will display matches starting with the top 1000th match, followed by the next 100 matches. There are various other filter criteria and display options as well. Our target population was 18 or older because this population is likely the most typical or allowed to create a profile and upload their genetic data to these sites.

2.1   Demographics

We recruited 10 participants: eight females and two males, all aged 23 to 60. Participants had various fields, such as teaching professors, administrators, etc. A few (3) participants have already taken at-home DNA testing and used the testing company's platform. However, none of the participants has ever used any public genealogy site. We recruited participants until we felt we reached saturation (i.e., no new information attained) during analysis and thus did not seek additional participants. The study was carried out in May 2022. Our Institutional Review Board approved the study. Each participant was compensated with $5 Amazon gift cards.

2.2   Website Description and Study Process:

We developed a website name "Genealogy Research Site" (GRS). We tried to mimic the GEDmatch site to learn users' understanding of the most popular public genealogy site. We used mock data and followed the same pattern as conferred by GEDmatch. Figure 1 screenshots of filters and results.

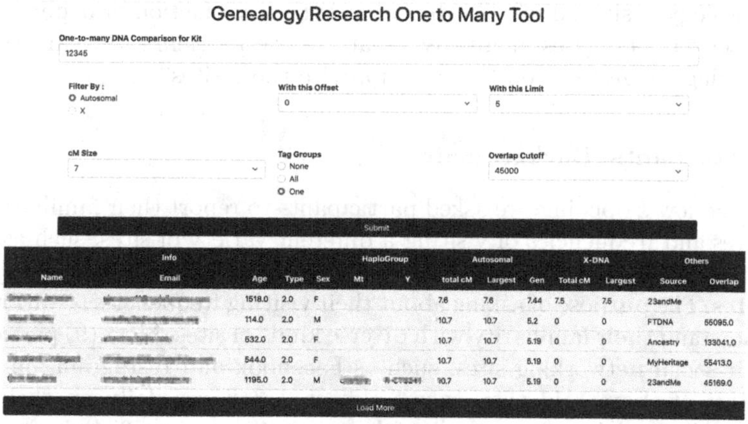

Fig. 1. GRS: One-to-Many tool Result

We started the interview by asking about their regular usage time on the internet and browsing different kinds of websites because we wanted to find out users' abilities to navigate different sites. We also asked about their confidence in using various websites. Participants were then asked to provide background information about their prior genealogy experience and the GEDmatch site or any other public genealogy site. Then, we explained at-home DNA tests and how these sites work. Then, we asked about their interest and confidence in using these kinds of sites. Followingly we showed them the site and asked them general questions about DNA relative findings and how they would use the site to find their relatives. Then the interviewer asked participants to complete only one-to-many searches on GRS. Participants were provided with a random bogus kit number required to perform the search task. A kit number is a number assigned to the user's data (e.g., sample number) by DNA genealogy sites. The participants only entered that kit number in the kit number field and clicked on submit. The outcome of this task showed them a similar result table as shown in GEDmatch some mock data. After the participants completed the search tasks, the interviewer asked participants a series of questions seeking to explain their understanding of each filter and all the columns of the result in their own words. During these questions, participants were allowed to use the filters and site to aid them freely. Additionally, they were asked to rate their overall experience with the genealogy search and site. These questions served the purpose of learning the overall usability experience and analyzing the problem area or difficult areas for the users to understand and interpret the genealogy search results.

3   Results

To find out the user-friendliness, usability, and difficulty areas of public genealogy website, we analyzed the following elements in our exploratory study. First, we assessed participants' foreknowledge about at-home DNA testing and the kinds of reports they provide. Secondly, how does an average user interpret these genealogy task results? Thirdly, what is the satisfaction or experience of a typical user on these sites? Fourthly, what are the barriers a regular user faces and gathering suggestions on how to improvise these sites?

3.1   Participants' Backgrounds

At the interview's opening, we asked participants to report their familiarity with online sites and frequencies of visiting a different variety of sites, such as; social networking, banking site, online retail or shopping sites, blogs, and house/rental search sites. The purpose of asking about their visiting frequencies to various sites is to understand their familiarity with diverse kinds of sites. Most (9) participants visit their social networking sites, such as Facebook and Instagram, on a daily basis. Most of them said they spend almost 2–3 hours daily on their social networks. All participants use online shopping sites nearly 3–4 times a week. Most (8) participants operate their banking applications or sites almost 3–4 times a week. Many (6) participants visit different blogs almost 2–3 times a week. All participants said they had an excellent experience accomplishing their intended goals on these sites. They reported high confidence in using any kind of site. Thus, we can infer most of our participants are tech-savvy.

3.2   Participants' Familiarities, Interests and Confidence

After collecting details about participants' general use of the internet on a daily basis and visiting various websites, we asked participants if they knew about at-home DNA testing or not. All (10) participants were familiar with at-home DNA tests and the reports that these tests provide. But, only 3 participants knew about public genealogy databases. After assessing their foreknowledge about athome

DNA testing, and public genealogy sites, we elaborately discussed at-home DNA tests, public genealogy databases, and the way public genealogy site works. After discussion, we asked participants if they would be interested in using such a site if they had their raw DNA data with them. Most (8) participants were thrilled to use the site. The primary motivation was to find DNA relatives. We asked participants about their confidence in using such sites to attain their goal of finding genetic relatives, and all of them were confident to very confident in using these sites. Comprehensively, we can imply that our participants were highly interested in and confident in using public genealogy sites.

3.3   Tasks Accomplishment

After discussing about public genealogy sites and how these sites work, we provided them with a kit number and asked them to do a "one-to-many" search. We found that all (10) participants were able to put the kit number in the correct query field and hit submit button after that to find their matches in the first time itself. They also correctly comprehended that the names that showed up in the results were people related to the kit number assigned to them. In the next task, they were asked to perform to interpret results or use filters to find their top 10 matches. None of the participants were able to accomplish this task. They were not able to interpret the one-to-many tool results. All of them hovered around the filters present in the query box and tried to use different options to discover a list of the top 10 matches. However, none of them accomplished this task. They said these terminologies and numbers are particularly technical, confusing, and difficult to understand. In this context, (P1) said

> " I just have no idea how I can find top people matching to me; I m trying some options here, it does change something here in the result, but I m not sure who and could someone be related to me. As a normal person, I would not understand overlap cutoff or whatever if you put these kinds of terminologies. So maybe instead of these kinds of terminologies, you can either put simpler ones or user-friendly terms."

3.4   Interpretation of Search Query Filters and Result Columns

To explore how average users apply and interpret the filters present in the search query box, we asked them to play around with all the filters. While playing around, we requested them to think aloud and describe what and how they are deciphering these filters and how they evaluate the way in which these filters function. The participants applied each filter one by one to see changes in the results. Still, most of them could not figure out how these filters work and what these filters exactly mean. Only one participant (P6) explained that "filter by X" means matches would be shown based on your gender or sex. Another participant rightly guessed that more overlap cutoff means more closely related to you though it was not clear. All participants confronted huge difficulty understanding the terminologies and using the filters to perform their tasks; Afterwards, they commented that the platform was unfriendly and technical for an average person. In this context (*P2*) said;

> " I think you need to be a technical biologist to use these kinds of platforms. I do not understand these terms or how it works, this site is very unfriendly, at least for me."

The next step to accomplish our research goal was to investigate how average users interpret the results rendered by one-to-many tool after submitting the search query. We asked participants to explain each column of the result tables. All participants could correctly explain the name and email address column. They also pointed out that the presence of email addresses is to connect with the matched quickly. They were not able to comprehend the age here indicates the days of somebody's data present in the database. Some (2) thought this age displays the ancestral age of the individual in years. Most (7) participants accurately explained the sex column, whereas 3 participants could not explain that. None of the participants were able to illustrate any other terms in the result section; however, some (3) participants figured out the source column rightly. They accurately said that the person must have been tested by this company and uploaded their DNA to GRS. Others believed that GRS had access to these companies' databases and collected these DNA data from these respective companies. (*P10*) said;

> "These are the companies' names from which you have collected your data and uploaded it here."

Overall, we see that respondents' understanding of the one-to-may tool search results is at a reasonably lower level even when the participants are highly educated, and some of them even have already taken a genetic test. Hence, we can infer that the existing GEDmatch platform is not usable and pleasant for average users.

3.5   Overall Usability of the Website

Participants were asked ten five-point Likert scale questions to rate various aspects of the platform. We asked participants to talk about why did they choose the particular option. The first question was *"Rate your overall experience with the platform"*. Many (6) participants were highly dissatisfied, and the remainder (4) of them were moderately dissatisfied. The uttered reason behind dissatisfaction was the terminologies used in the platform were very difficult to understand. The moderate dissatisfaction is that they could still find contact information (email id) of the matches and the span of time users are in the database as that can give them the idea of if the user is a new or old user. Then, we asked *" I found the platform easy to understand, use and perform the task. "*, all participants strongly disagreed. They did not find the platform easy to understand, use or perform the task. Next, we asked them to rate their confidence; nine of them reported being highly incompetent in performing the tasks. They found the platform terminologies are very complex and imagined that most people would not be able to use the platform without an expert's support. To sum up, they did not find the platform user-friendly and interactive. Therefore this platform cannot cater to users' needs and expectations for DNA-relative findings.

3.6   Expectations and Suggestions to Improve the Site

We asked the participants for their expectations, recommendations, and suggestions to improve the platform to make it user-friendly. In this section, we list all the users' recommendations gathered in Table 1. All users highlighted the change in terminologies is a must commenting that average users will face a challenge in understanding it. Most users also suggested adding more filters that would serve the purpose of a better interpretation of results and facilitate the search for DNA matches. We document all the users' suggestions for new filters for search queries, and the results are assembled in Table. 2.

Table 1. Participants' suggestions to improve the platform

Suggestions	Freq.	Description
Simplified terms	10	Terms used on this site need to be simplified
Explanation/Key Table	8	A table should explain each terms used in the search query box and result columns
Keys on hover	5	When the user hovers on a term, they should see the key or definition of the term
User guide	5	Add a user guide to detailing about use of each filters along with the guide to interpret the results
Visuals and Graphics	4	Graphs, charts, visuals should be used in results to make it more explainable

Table 2. Participants' suggestions for the search query and results columns

Suggestions for make search query & results user-friendly (Freq.)	Description
Probable relationships (7)	Options to search for the relationship. Such as; 1st Cousin, 2nd Cousin, etc
Display paternal side or maternal side (5)	The match should be displayed with the probable paternal side match or maternal side match
Percentage of matches (5)	Show % of your DNA matches with the other one
Age (4)	Should indicate the age of the match
Top matches (4)	Should use colors to show the top 20 matches
Geographic region (3)	Option to choose the geographic region of matches (city, state, country)
Generation range (2)	Options to choose which generation matches user wants to see; for example, Generations Range: 4 or more, 3–4, 2–3, 1–2, or Any

4   Discussion and Conclusion

Many commercial DNA testing companies allow comparing their consumers' DNA to those of others who have tested with the same company. That is why genetic genealogists recommend using public genealogy sites where anyone can upload their DNA file, irrespective of the testing companies. By doing so, there is a better chance of finding genetic relatives, such as adoptees who could find their biological family. Our results suggest that the current public genealogy sites have severe and critical usability issues, as even tech-savvy users face difficulty completing the primary essential task and interpreting the results. Most participants could not figure out how the names in the result columns are related to them, how they could understand the top matches, and their relations with them before deciding whether to contact them. As public genealogy sites could play a significant role in family findings, users' involvement in the design and evaluation stages should be applied to build these websites. Additionally, users should be included in the implementation process to align the platform with users' needs also, as these platforms are meant to be used by different categories of users with unique needs (e.g., family finding, family tree making), which leads to the imperative of assessing their needs. Thus, user involvement in all the development stages is vital. Our findings and suggested changes for the platform could serve as a guide for developers to build a usable platform.

References

1. Palmer, J.W.: Web site usability, design, and performance metrics. Inf. Syst. Res. **13**(2), 151–167 (2002)
2. Dedeke, A.N.: Travel web-site design: information task-fit, service quality and purchase intention. Tourism Manag. **54**, 541–554 (2016)
3. Mithas, S., Ramasubbu, N., Krishnan, M.S., Fornell, C.: Designing web sites for customer loyalty across business domains: a multilevel analysis. J. Manag. Inf. Syst. **23**(3), 97–127 (2006)
4. GEDmatch - https://www.gedmatch.com
5. 26 million people. https://www.technologyreview.com/2019/02/11/103446/more-than-26-million-people-have-taken-an-at-home-ancestry-test/
6. Zoom video conferencing - https://www.zoom.us

Modeling Foraging Behavior in GitHub

Abim Sedhain[1], Yao Wang[1]($\boxtimes$), Brett Mckinney[1],
and Sandeep Kaur Kuttal[1,2]

[1] University of Tulsa, Tulsa, OK 74104, USA
[2] North Carolina State University, Raleigh, NC 27695, USA
yaw1549@utulsa.edu
https://engineering.utulsa.edu/computer-science/
https://www.csc.ncsu.edu/

Abstract. We operationalized GitHub using Information Foraging Theory to built a semi-supervised learning model to aid developers in their pursuit for the relevant repository among its variants.

Keywords: GitHub · Modeling · Information Forging Theory ·
Quantitative · Unsupervised learning · Modeling evaluation

1 Introduction

GitHub is the largest code hosting site with 128 million public repositories and supports 73 million users [1]. GitHub developers create code versions (in repositories) or share them with the community. This creation and sharing of open-source code over time increases the number of variants for the same project. Hence, a developer planning to reuse a variant of a project must sift through all variants, then evaluate and select a variant. This process costs both time and cognitive effort [2]. Developers' information-seeking behavior on GitHub can be modeled using Information Foraging Theory (IFT).

IFT was originally used by Pirolli and Card to explain how experts forage information in document collections [3] and information visualization [4]. IFT has been successfully employed in various domains such as the web, user interfaces, and programming [5–18]. IFT states that users try to maximize their rate of information gain by lowering the amount of effort spent.

In this paper, we operationalized developers' behavior on GitHub using IFT and built a semi-supervised machine-learning model to classify high/low cost/value projects. Our model aids developers pursuing relevant projects among their variants.

2 Operationalize: IFT for GitHub

To apply a theory to a new domain, the theory's constructs need to be operationalized. Hence, we used systematic mapping of GitHub information contents to IFT constructs. Table 1 describes foraging variables that developers can utilize on GitHub to evaluate a variant/project. The variables provided by GitHub were utilized for the model, and variables where a developer needs to open the project were not considered. Figure 1 shows the project variants of *'stock visualizer'*. The developer comparing and evaluating projects/repositories among their variants is called *between-variant* foraging.

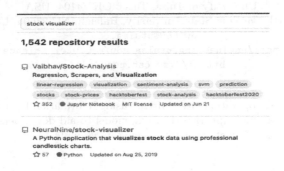

Fig. 1. Snapshot of GitHub repositories for the search term *'stock visualizer'*

3   Computation Models: GitHub Foraging

3.1   Data Processing

GitHub repositories contain various programming languages. We narrowed our data collection to JavaScript language because (1) it is one of the most popular programming languages in GitHub with over 1.4 million repositories [19], and (2) our prior user study (for evaluation) was conducted using JavaScript. To collect the search terms, we scrapped Leetcode[1] to get the question titles, and then we used GitHub API to iterate over those question titles and gather related projects/repositories. We collected 6419 repositories from 865 Leetcode keywords. From the collected repositories, we gathered the variables mentioned

Table 1. GitHub's foraging variables

Variable	Description	Outcome
Repo Name	Number of words in repo title	Value,Cost
Repo Description	Number of words in repo description	Value,Cost
Topics	Number of topics in the repo	Value,Cost
Stars	Number of repo stars	Value
Licenses	Presence or absence of License in the repo	Value
Last updated time	Time the repo was last updated	Value
Issues	Number of open issues in the repo	Value,Cost

---

[1] https://leetcode.com/problemset/all/.

in Table 1. The variables were pre-processed to numeric and categorical as the machine learning model operates on these formats only. All variables were converted to numeric variables. New variable *'time_value'* was derived by subtracting the creation date and the last updated time of the repo. Only *'Licenses'* variable was in the categorical format.

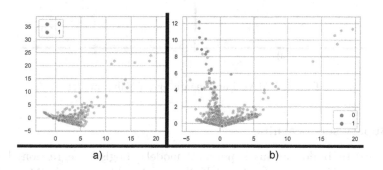

Fig. 2. Hierarchical Clustering of Value(a) and Cost(b) models

3.2 Unsupervised Learning

To build any supervised model, we need labeled data, but no labeled data exists for GitHub. Therefore, we utilized hierarchical clustering to obtain the labels. We were focused on high/low cost and value, so we set the number of clusters to 2 (i.e., binary classification). This gave us two clusters each for the value model and cost models. But, as we can see from Fig. 2, there is no clear distinction between the clusters for the value model, whereas, for the cost model, there is a clear separation of the clusters. To get a clear picture of the value clusters, we used UMAP(Uniform Manifold Approximation and Projection for Dimension Reduction) [20] on the labels we collected from hierarchical clustering. It is a dimension-reduction technique that can be used for better visualization. Figure3(a) shows the new set of clusters. But, a few observations are still in the other cluster. So, we relabeled them to be in the cluster they are closer to. Figure 3(b) shows the final set of clusters and Table 2 shows the cluster distribution for cost and value models.

Table 2. Cluster distribution of Value and Cost models

Clusters	Value	Cost
Low	4,921	6,184
High	1,354	91

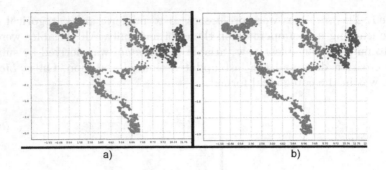

Fig. 3. UMAP implementation of Value model

3.3 Supervised Learning

We decided to build various supervised models: Logistic regression, Decision Tree, Random Forest, Naive Bayes, K-Nearest Neighbor, and SVM, so we can compare their performance and select the best one. Firstly, we split the data into a 70/30 training-testing ratio. But from Table 2, we can see that our cost model dataset is imbalanced. So, we first balanced the training data using SMOTE as the ratio was worse than 1:4 and needed correction [21]. We then performed K-Fold cross-validation on the training data. After the model was fitted and trained, we tested it against the test data. We employed Matthews Correlation Coefficient (MCC) [22] for model evaluation. MCC ranges from −1 to 1, with +1 being the best agreement between the predicted and actual values and 0 being no agreement which means prediction is random according to the actuals. Figure 4 illustrates the MCC of cost and value models respectively. We observed Random Forest has the highest MCC in both cost and value.

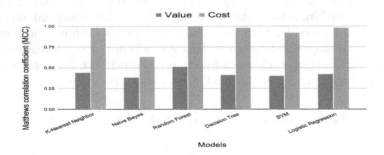

Fig. 4. Value[Blue] and Cost[Orange] Model metrics

4   Evaluation: Lab Study

To evaluate our model's performance, we decided to evaluate it against a prior user study that investigated between-variant foraging behavior in GitHub [2].

In this study, participants searched and selected a repository for reuse. The selected repositories were labeled as high (1) and the others were labeled as low (0). When unsure about a relevant repository, participants selected more than one repository. In total, we collected 143 unique repositories, with 16 repositories labeled high (1) and the rest to be low (0) value.

We tested the Random Forest Model (selected) against the lab data and Table 3 shows the confusion matrix. The model had an accuracy of 27.9% due to its inability to classify low-value repositories. But by analyzing how the model handled the high-value repository, we can see it accurately predicted 75% of them. We conjecture the model is biased to labeling the observations as high. We observed in our lab studies the participants dived deeper into a repository (within-variant foraging) to select a variant while our model was built on the variables visible on the first-page search result. We can add within-variant foraging in the future to make the model robust.

Table 3. Confusion matrix of user study

		Actual Values	
		Low	High
Predicted Values	Low	28	4
	High	99	12

5 Conclusion

Our contribution includes (1) extending IFT to a new domain of GitHub, (2) developing a methodology of obtaining labels using unsupervised learning and then using those labels to build a supervised learning model that can be utilized in other domains such as question-answer websites (Stack Overflow), and (3) sharing evaluation strategy for developed models using test data from lab studies.

Acknowledgments. This material is based upon work supported by the Air Force Office of Scientific Research under award number FA9550-21-1-0108 and National Science Foundation (CAREER) under award number 2046205. Any opinions, findings, and conclusions or recommendations expressed in this material are those of the authors and do not necessarily reflect the view of the NSF and AFOSR.

References

1. The state of the octoverse (2021). https://octoverse.github.com
2. Sedhain, A., Kuttal, S.K.: Information seeking behavior for bugs on github: an information foraging perspective. In: 2022 IEEE Symposium on Visual Languages and Human-Centric Computing (VL/HCC), IEEE, pp. 1–3 (2022)

3. Pirolli, P., Card, S.: Information foraging in information access environments. In: Proceedings of the SIGCHI Conference on Human Factors in Computing Systems, pp. 51–58 (1995)
4. Card, S.K., Mackinlay, J.: The structure of the information visualization design space. In: Proceedings of VIZ'97: Visualization Conference, Information Visualization Symposium and Parallel Rendering Symposium, IEEE, pp. 92–99 (1997)
5. Fu, W.-T., Pirolli, P.: Snif-act: a cognitive model of user navigation on the world wide web. Hum.-Comput. Inter. **22**(4), 355–412 (2007)
6. Pirolli, P., Fu, W.-T.: SNIF-ACT: a model of information foraging on the world wide web. In: Brusilovsky, P., Corbett, A., de Rosis, F. (eds.) UM 2003. LNCS (LNAI), vol. 2702, pp. 45–54. Springer, Heidelberg (2003). https://doi.org/10.1007/3-540-44963-9_8
7. Pirolli, P., Fu, W.-T., Chi, E., Farahat, A.: Information scent and web navigation: theory, models and automated usability evaluation. In: Proceedings of HCI International (2005)
8. Pirolli, P.: Computational models of information scent-following in a very large browsable text collection. In: Proceedings of the ACM SIGCHI Conference on Human factors in computing systems, pp. 3–10 (1997)
9. Larson, K., Czerwinski, M.: Web page design: Implications of memory, structure and scent for information retrieval. In: Proceedings of the SIGCHI Conference on Human Factors in Computing Systems, pp. 25–32 (1998)
10. Spool, J.M., Perfetti, C., Brittan, D.: Designing for the scent of information: the essentials every designer needs to know about how users navigate through large web sites, User Interface Engineering (2004)
11. Lawrance, J., Burnett, M., Bellamy, R., Bogart, C., Swart, C.: Reactive information foraging for evolving goals. In: Proceedings of the SIGCHI Conference on Human Factors in Computing Systems, pp. 25–34 (2010)
12. Henley, A.Z., Singh, A., Fleming, S.D., Luong, M.V.: Helping programmers navigate code faster with patchworks: a simulation study. In: 2014 IEEE Symposium on Visual Languages and Human-Centric Computing (VL/HCC), IEEE, pp. 77–80 (2014)
13. Martos, C., Kim, S.Y., Kuttal, S.K.: Reuse of variants in online repositories: foraging for the fittest. In: 2016 IEEE Symposium on Visual Languages and Human-Centric Computing (VL/HCC), IEEE, pp. 124–128 (2016)
14. Fleming, S.D., Scaffidi, C., Piorkowski, D., Burnett, M., Bellamy, R., Lawrance, J., Kwan, I.: An information foraging theory perspective on tools for debugging, refactoring, and reuse tasks. ACM Trans. Softw. Eng. Methodol. (TOSEM) **22**(2), 1–41 (2013)
15. Piorkowski, D., et al.: Reactive information foraging: an empirical investigation of theory-based recommender systems for programmers. In: Proceedings of the SIGCHI Conference on Human Factors in Computing Systems, pp. 1471–1480 (2012)
16. Kuttal, S.K., Sarma, A., Rothermel, G.: Predator behavior in the wild web world of bugs: an information foraging theory perspective. In: 2013 IEEE Symposium on Visual Languages and Human Centric Computing, pp. 59–66. IEEE (2013)
17. Kuttal, S.K., Sarma, A., Burnett, M., Rothermel, G., Koeppe, I., Shepherd, B.: How end-user programmers debug visual web-based programs: an information foraging theory perspective, Journal of. Comput. Lang. **53**, 22–37 (2019)
18. Kuttal, S.K., Kim, S.Y., Martos, C., Bejarano, A.: How end-user programmers forage in online repositories? an information foraging perspective. J. Comput. Lang. **62**, 101010 (2021)

19. Github api (2021). https://api.github.com/search/repositories?q=javascript
20. McInnes, L., Healy, J., Melville, J.: Umap: uniform manifold approximation and projection for dimension reduction, arXiv preprint arXiv:1802.03426 (2018)
21. Krawczyk, B.: Learning from imbalanced data: open challenges and future directions. Progress in Artif. Intell. **5**(4), 221–232 (2016). https://doi.org/10.1007/s13748-016-0094-0
22. Chicco, D., Jurman, G.: The advantages of the matthews correlation coefficient (mcc) over f1 score and accuracy in binary classification evaluation. BMC Genomics **21**(1), 1–13 (2020)

iWIll: A Real-Time Mobile Application to Expedite First-Aid and Reduce Casualties

Palaniselvam Shyam Sundar[✉] and Owen Noel Newton Fernando[✉]

Nanyang Technological University, 50 Nanyang Ave, Singapore 639798, Singapore
{shyamsun001,ofernando}@e.ntu.edu.sg

Abstract. iWILL is a mobile emergency response application designed to provide prompt and efficient assistance to individuals experiencing emergencies. The application enables users to quickly seek help in times of emergencies, which then creates an alert that is broadcasted to nearby CPR-trained users who are also registered with the application. These trained users can then navigate to the incident location using the application to provide expedited first-aid measures before the professional medical services arrive. In addition, the application displays a map indicating the nearby Automated External Defibrillators (AEDs), which users can navigate to in case of a cardiac emergency. The application aims to expedite emergency response times, potentially saving lives in critical situations.

Keywords: Cardiopulmonary Resuscitation (CPR) · Automated External Defibrillator (AED) · Mobile Interaction

1 Introduction

Several casualties including (but not limited to) out-of-hospital cardiac arrests (OHCAs) could have been addressed [1, 2], provided some form of first aid such as CPR is performed by a bystander, before the arrival of the emergency medical system. With an average global incidence rate of 55 OHCAs per 100,000 person-years, this has been an ongoing problem [3]. The use of AEDs in addition to CPR as opposed to only performing CPR significantly increases the chances of survival [4]. In addition, studies have found that about 60% of the OHCA cases were shockable using an AED but a bystander shock was applied only 18.8% of the time [5]. This is pertaining to the reluctance to perform CPR or defibrillation by a bystander [6].

Over the past decade, the popularity of mobile devices has increased almost 4-fold with the number of smartphone users sitting at over 5.2 billion as of 2023 [7]. Besides trivially owning the device, it has become an integral part of everyday life, serving as the main source of information and communication. With the widespread availability of mobile devices [8], these devices have become the primary way people interact with the digital world.

This poster paper presents a mobile application named iWILL, designed to provide users with a rapid response system for emergency situations. By leveraging the ubiquity and versatility of mobile devices and the expertise of trained responders, the application

C. Stephanidis et al. (Eds.): HCII 2023, CCIS 1834, pp. 156–162, 2023.
https://doi.org/10.1007/978-3-031-35998-9_22

provides users with a quicker response time, potentially saving lives and reducing the severity of injuries in emergency situations.

The application's key features include an alert system that notifies nearby trained individuals, real-time location information, directions to the emergency location (to provide assistance), and a map showing the nearest AEDs. AEDs can be used by non-medical personnel with little to no training [9]. The application is designed to fill a critical gap in emergency response systems by leveraging the power of mobile devices to provide a rapid and effective response in emergency situations. By empowering users with the ability to request assistance quickly and easily, and by providing responders with real-time location information and directions, the application could expedite first aid in time-critical situations.

In the following pages, related work in the field will be discussed. In addition, an overview of the application design and implementation will be highlighted, along with usage scenarios showcasing the application screens. The paper will conclude with a discussion regarding the application's impact and some details regarding future work.

Overall, this poster paper aims to demonstrate the potential of mobile technology to make a significant impact in emergency response systems, providing users with a powerful tool to support and get help when they need it most. We hope that our work will inspire further innovation in this field and ultimately contribute to saving more lives in emergency situations.

2 Related Work

Developing effective emergency response mobile applications requires a thorough understanding of the existing literature and technologies in this field. This review aims to provide insights and inspiration for the design and development of our own emergency response mobile application - iWILL, presented in this paper.

Extensive research has been conducted on various heart-related ailments. The American Heart Association's 2022 report [10] highlights the persistent challenge faced by many Americans in managing the traditional risk factors associated with cardiovascular disease. Furthermore, cardiac arrest is frequently caused by arrhythmias or irregular heartbeats, which can cause heart rates to skyrocket or plummet to dangerously low levels [11]. In cases where such conditions lead to an OHCA, iWILL can prove to be an invaluable tool.

An application that is closely related to iWILL is the myResponderApp by the Singapore Civil Defence Force (SCDF) [12]. While it is a useful tool for connecting patients with emergency response services in Singapore, it relies on the presence of a bystander to report the incident. There would be no means for a case to be broadcasted to the AED-trained specialists if there is no bystander. In time-sensitive situations such as cardiac arrests, iWILL can provide a critical lifeline. With the click of a big red button **'GET HELP'**, the user's location would be broadcasted to trained users who will be alerted, and help will be on its way. Additionally, the application finds the nearest trained users based on a fixed radius. This could potentially be a problem in situations where there is no registered user in that radius. In contrast, iWILL is implemented to broadcast to the nearest 5 trained users.

Now, we highlight a Singaporean study that explores the effectiveness of bystander-focused public health interventions on CPR and survival rates [13]. While bystander CPR can significantly increase a victim's chance of survival [1], many individuals are hesitant to perform CPR due to fear of doing it incorrectly or lack of familiarity. The study found that incorporating CPR and AED training programs and the myResponderApp increased the likelihood of bystander CPR.

iWILL builds upon these efforts with its user-friendly application that addresses some of the limitations of myResponderApp. One such step taken by the application is the inclusion of a visual and audio aid in the form of a guided CPR video. This allows responders to feel better prepared, particularly in situations where they have not performed CPR in the recent past, thereby reducing their reluctance to perform CPR.

3 Design and Implementation

The mobile application was developed using the SOLID design principles [14] and established in the Model-View-Controller (MVC) pattern [15].

The Model layer is responsible for defining the 'user' model class, which instantiates a logged-in user and provides access to their details. The View layer contains the user interface components, including the home screen, user information screen, and alert screen, among others. Lastly, the Controller layer contains the core logic of the application and implements the necessary functions for performing CRUD operations with the 'userData' and 'alerts' databases. It also interacts with the Model layer to retrieve user data and uses it to perform various functions within the application (Fig. 1).

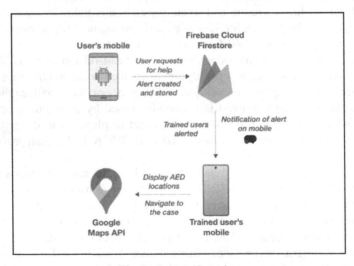

Fig. 1. System Overview

The application's authentication and user management system were implemented using Firebase Authentication. User data and alert information are stored using Cloud Firestore as two different collections, which provides a scalable and secure cloud-based database solution.

One key feature of the application is its ability to quickly identify the nearest 5 CPR-trained registered users to an incident for a selective broadcast. This is achieved using Haversine distance, a mathematical formula used to calculate the distance between two points on a sphere, such as the Earth. When a user requests emergency assistance, the application calculates the Haversine distance between their location and the location of all registered CPR-trained users. The haversine formula is a very accurate way of computing distances between two points on the surface of a sphere using the latitude and longitude of the two points [16]. The application then identifies the 5 nearest trained users and sends them an alert requesting their assistance.

The trained user is then able to use the application to navigate to the incident location with the click of a button. This is possible through its integration with Google Maps (Figs. 2, 3, 4 and 5).

4   iWILL – Application Interfaces

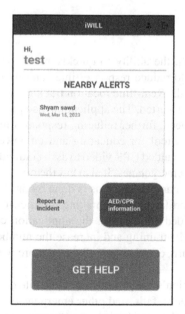

Fig. 2. Home Interface

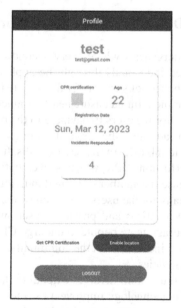

Fig. 3. Profile Interface

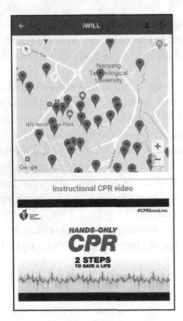

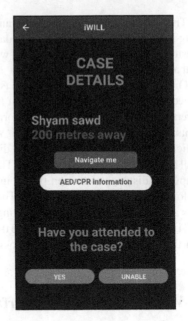

Fig. 4. AED/CPR Interface   **Fig. 5.** Alert Information Interface

5   Discussion and Future Work

In emergencies where every second counts [17], the ability to quickly notify nearby trained individuals through the application could reduce response times and improve the chances of survival for the affected individuals. Real-time location tracking and the haversine formula ensure nearby trained users are alerted. The application also provides a way for the users to navigate to the person in need, further reducing response times.

In addition, the application could serve as a tool for educating and empowering individuals to learn life-saving skills. It provides a guided CPR video to assist individuals in performing CPR, which is an essential skill in emergencies. It also has the potential to increase the number of trained individuals in the community. This is done by providing a means for the users to get/renew their CPR certification. By making it easier to find AED locations and providing users with a guided CPR video, the application could encourage more people to undergo CPR and AED training and increase the number of trained individuals in the community. This, in turn, could potentially save more lives in emergencies.

Future work involves extending the application's use to integrate wearable devices (as the technology improves) to detect heart attacks, falls, and other emergencies. This information can be used to broadcast alerts, further optimizing the response time. In addition, a widget of the application can be created for the home screen of mobile devices to enable easy access to the 'GET HELP' button.

6 Conclusion

This poster paper has demonstrated the key features and development of the iWILL application, which offers an easy and effective method for users to request immediate help during emergency situations and connect with trained individuals in close proximity. By utilizing the widespread accessibility and practicality of mobile devices, the iWILL application has the potential to make a significant impact in emergency response scenarios. It can greatly improve response times and potentially save lives by enabling expedited first-aid before the ambulance arrives. The user-friendly interface and incorporation of features such as a guided CPR video also make it a valuable tool in addressing the shortcomings of existing emergency response applications. Overall, the potential benefits of iWILL in emergency response scenarios are immense, and its development marks a promising step towards enhancing public safety and well-being.

References

1. Liou, F.Y., et al.: The impact of bystander cardiopulmonary resuscitation on patients with out-of-hospital cardiac arrests. J. Chin. Med. Assoc. **84**(12), 1078–1083 (2021). https://doi.org/10.1097/JCMA.0000000000000630
2. Yan, S., et al.: The global survival rate among adult out-of-hospital cardiac arrest patients who received cardiopulmonar resuscitation: a systematic review and meta-analysis. Crit Care **24**, 61 (2020). https://doi.org/10.1186/s13054-020-2773-2
3. Berdowski, J., Berg, R.A., Tissen, J.G., Koster, R.W.: Global incidences of out-of-hospital cardiac arrest and survival rates: systematic review of 67 prospective studies. Resuscitation **81**(11), 1479–1487 (2010)
4. Weisfeldt, M.L., et al.: Survival after application of automatic external defibrillators before arrival of the emergency medical system: evaluation in the resuscitation outcomes consortium population of 21 million. J. Am. College Cardiol. **55**(16), 1713–1720 (2010). https://doi.org/10.1016/j.jacc.2009.11.077. PMID: 20394876, PMCID: PMC3008654
5. Pollack, R.A., et al.: Impact of bystander automated external defibrillator use on survival and functional outcomes in shockable observed public cardiac arrests. Circulation **137**(20), 2104–2113 (2018). https://doi.org/10.1161/CIRCULATIONAHA.117.030700. PMID: 29483086, PMCID: PMC5953778
6. Dobbie, F., MacKintosh, A.M., Clegg, G., Stirzaker, R., Bauld, L.: Attitudes towards bystander cardiopulmonary resuscitation: results from a cross-sectional general population survey. PLoS ONE **13**(3), e0193391 (2018). https://doi.org/10.1371/journal.pone.0193391
7. Degenhard, J.: Smartphone users in the world 2028, Statista (2022). https://www.statista.com/forecasts/1143723/smartphone-users-in-the-world. Accessed 15 Mar 2023
8. Laricchia, F.: Smartphone sales worldwide 2007–2021, Statista (2022). https://www.statista.com/statistics/263437/global-smartphone-sales-to-end-users-since-2007/. Accessed 15 Mar 2023
9. What is an automated external defibrillator? - American heart association (no date). https://www.heart.org/-/media/files/health-topics/answers-by-heart/what-is-an-aed.pdf. Accessed 17 Mar 2023
10. Tsao, C.W., et al.: Heart disease and stroke statistics-2022 update: a report from the American heart association. Circulation. **145**(8), e153-e639 (2022). https://doi.org/10.1161/CIR.0000000000001052. Epub 2022 Jan 26. Erratum in: Circulation. 2022 Sep 6;146(10):e141. PMID: 35078371

11. Sudden cardiac arrest (no date) HealthXchange. https://www.healthxchange.sg/heart-lungs/sudden-cardiac-arrest/arrhythmia-abnormal-heartbeat-sudden-cardiac-arrest. Accessed 17 Mar 2023
12. Community & Volunteers (no date) SCDF. https://www.scdf.gov.sg/home/community-volunteers/mobile-applications. Accessed 15 Mar 2023
13. Blewer, A.L., et al.: Impact of bystander-focused public health interventions on cardiopulmonary resuscitation and survival: a cohort study, The Lancet Public Health. Elsevier (2020). https://www.thelancet.com/journals/lanpub/article/PIIS2468-2667(20)30140-7/fulltext. Accessed 16 Mar 2023
14. Oloruntoba, S.: Solid: The first 5 principles of object oriented design, DigitalOcean. DigitalOcean (2021). https://www.digitalocean.com/community/conceptual-articles/s-o-l-i-d-the-first-five-principles-of-object-oriented-design. Accessed 17 Mar 2023
15. Hernandez, R.D.: The model view controller pattern – MVC architecture and Frameworks explained, freeCodeCamp.org. freeCodeCamp.org. (2021). https://www.freecodecamp.org/news/the-model-view-controller-pattern-mvc-architecture-and-frameworks-explained/. Accessed 17 Mar 2023
16. Distance on a sphere: The Haversine formula (2021) Esri Community. https://community.esri.com/t5/coordinate-reference-systems-blog/distance-on-a-sphere-the-haversine-formula/ba-p/902128. Accessed 15 Mar 2023
17. Huang, L.H., Ho, Y.N., Tsai, M.T., Wu, W.T., Cheng, F.J.: Response time threshold for predicting outcomes of patients with out-of-hospital cardiac arrest. Emerg Med Int. 11(2021), 5564885 (2021). https://doi.org/10.1155/2021/5564885.PMID:33628510;PMCID:PMC7892213

"User Journeys": A Tool to Align Cross-Functional Teams

Jessica Tan[✉]

User Experience Researcher, Google Inc, San Francisco, CA, USA
jessicatan@google.com

Abstract. This paper discusses the challenge of aligning high-level product priorities and key performance indicators for user experience (UX) professionals working with product teams that have a disproportionately high number of other cross-functional partners in the organization. When a UX professional joins an organization with no prior UX support, engineering work is likely prioritized in silos based on the technical lead's and engineering manager's "gut feeling." To implement product user feedback and improve prioritization, the team can adopt the use of "user journeys" for planning short- and long-term engineering work. The adoption of user journeys involves workshops and trainings for the engineering leads to understand and write user journeys related to their area of the product. These journeys are then listed in a shared document, reviewed and prioritized by engineering leads, and validated with live product users through surveying. The top five prioritized user journeys are then used to craft an annual vision and key performance indicators for the product. The method of using user journeys for planning engineering work proves to be successful in giving cross-functional teams a shared language for tackling product improvements together. By involving the entire team in the process and validating decisions with live product users, the team can achieve alignment and visibility into the decision-making process.

Keywords: user journey · user experience (UX) · cross-functional collaboration

1 Introduction

When working as a UX professional in an organization that has no prior experience working with UX and a disproportionate ratio of UX professionals to cross-functional partners, such as engineering, product management and program management, there are specific tools and methods that drive scalability in aligning a product on user needs and goals.

One of these tools are user journeys: user journeys are a great tool to align teams on who their users are and their users' needs and goals. Some benefits of utilizing user journeys as a tool for cross-functional collaboration include aligning teams with a data-driven and -based "story" around the user and promoting a shared vision that can be used to make critical product decisions. User journeys are an efficient way to improve the overall user experience of a product while fostering efficient cross functional collaboration.

C. Stephanidis et al. (Eds.): HCII 2023, CCIS 1834, pp. 163–167, 2023.
https://doi.org/10.1007/978-3-031-35998-9_23

This paper will detail a specific case where user journeys were successfully utilized in an organization that had a disproportionately high number of engineering partners compared to the sole UX professional.

2 Methods

2.1 Choosing the Right Method

There are many different methods and tools a UX professional can use to align a product team on user goals and needs. The very first step in the process is to gather cross-functional stakeholder input and feedback. This step is important for the UX professional to understand the context they are stepping into as it relates to the product. The UX professional will probe cross-functional stakeholders on things that have worked in the past, challenges the organization has faced, and expectations they have for the future of the product. To paint the most comprehensive picture of the product experience, it is best to gather feedback and input from cross-functional stakeholders across many different job functions. Some include but are not limited to: engineering, product management, and program management.

Once this feedback is gathered, the UX professional will have data to inform them in making a decision for the best possible method to align all their cross-functional stakeholders. The UX professional will perform a methods analysis based on the timeline proposed by stakeholders. In the particular case discussed, the organization's leadership desired a methodology that would enable lasting change spanning multiple quarters. Thus, user journeys were chosen as an option for aligning the organization on their user needs and goals.

2.2 User Journey Education

The first step in implementing the user journeys practice to is to educate the cross-functional stakeholders on what user journeys are, their benefits, limitations, and how to write them. In the described case, the engineering leads in the organization partic-ipate in a series of remote workshops and training to teach them basic understanding of user journeys. These workshops and trainings highlighted how other products have successfully used the user journey practice and showed examples of how these journeys are structured and written.

After engineering leads have been exposed to user journeys, they are prompted to start writing user journeys that relate to the area of the product they are working on. Generally, the user journey structure includes a user goal along with the associated user tasks that relate to the specific goal. A single user goal can have multiple tasks; usually, however, there are not multiple goals associated with a single user task. Engineering leads are asked to write their own journeys because they have the most expertise in that specific area of the product. To ask the UX professional to write all these journeys is neither scalable nor comprehensive enough to accurately describe the product user's full experience.

2.3 User Journey Alignment and Validation

Once engineering leads have written journeys to cover their area of the product, these journeys are listed in a shared document, reviewed, and prioritized by the engineering leads collectively. Once the journeys are revised in their final stages, the document is shared to the entire team for feedback. This facilitates organizational alignment on the highest priority user journeys and fosters visibility into how decisions are made.

Finally, the top five prioritized user journeys are validated with live product users through surveying. If the chosen user journeys are indeed what product users prioritize, then the engineering leadership crafts a vision and annual key performance indicators centering these top journeys. The method of using user journeys for planning engineering work gives cross-functional teams a shared language for tackling product improvements together.

2.4 Limitations Due to Biases

Some known limitations to the user journey method include cross-functional stakeholders' and product users' biases. Since stakeholders are asked to write journeys that relate to their product area expertise, they may have biases developed during the time they have worked on the product. Especially in an organization that has limited to no experience working with a UX professional, stakeholders are likely not trained in user-centric thinking and may interpret their experience as the typical product users' experience.

Additionally, in this method, product users are asked to validate the journeys proposed by the organization by responding to a survey, which introduces another kind of bias. It is well known that users are limited in their ability to predict their own behaviors, which can result in inconsistent answers when users try and predict which journeys are highest value to them.

3 Results

The results of implementing user journeys in this specific case were shown through successful alignment on the annual product goals and vision, written by the organization's engineering director. The deliverable was an overarching vision document highlighting the top user journeys the organization would focus on for the next year. Below each journey, the technical leads responsible for the "health" of that specific journey were listed.

In previous years, the organization approached annual planning in product area silos, having each engineering lead write their own annual goals and visions without any input from others or sometimes even awareness of other respective engineering leads' goals and visions. After the successful implementation of user journeys in this organization, the engineering director identified the top priority user journeys to focus on for the year and enabled each engineering lead to write their goals and vision around the high property journeys. Having the engineering director validate the high priority user journeys with their leadership lens further aligned the overall team and organization on the product goals and vision. This process in turn led to the discovery of overlapping engineering work where engineering leads could deduplicate and/or collaborate with other engineering leads on next steps.

4 Discussion

4.1 Implications

These results indicate that user journeys are an effective tool for fostering cross-functional collaboration and alignment. Once cross functional stakeholders are educated and gain experience implementing user journeys to their area of the product, they are more likely to be "bought in" to the methodology and see the benefits of having the shared language when talking about the user. Additionally, having the process incorporate both the "top down" view from leadership and the "bottom up" view from implementing teams ensures all perspectives are reflected in the process.

4.2 Organizations New to UX

The method of implementing user journeys is an effective starting point for organizations that are new to user-centric thinking and want a tool they can continue to build upon. The role of the UX professional in this case is facilitating conversations around the best tool and method for the organization and providing resources to implement the method. Additionally, having a few key user journeys to focus on makes it easier for the UX professional, especially one working as the only UX person, to prioritize their UX work in line with the overall organizational priorities.

4.3 Limitations to User Journeys

User journeys are a great way to align large organizations with individuals in cross-functional roles. There are, however, limitations to what user journeys can answer for a product. Some of these limitations include baked in participant biases, the cost of coordination, lack of agreement on user story prioritization, and/or user questions that need to be answered within a tighter timeline.

4.4 Next Steps

After the initial implementation of user journeys, the next steps might include collaborating with adjacent organizations that may or may not have a more mature user journey program, in order to determine if any user journeys are shared or split across products. In the case discussed, user journeys were implemented to align a single organization and product. This same method could be used to align priorities with other organizations with products that may share the same users. This could facilitate and streamline any experiences that may be duplicated or rated with low satisfaction.

References

1. Caddick, R., Cable, S.: Communicating the user experience: a practical guide for creating useful UX documentation (2011)
2. Cajander, A., Larusdottir, M., Geiser., J.: UX professionals' learning and usage of UX methods in agile. Information and Software Technology, vol. 151(2022)

3. Endmann, A., Keßner, D.: User journey mapping – a method in user experience design. J. Interact. Media **15**, 105–110 (2016)
4. Leachman, L., Scheibenreif, D.: Using technology to create a better customer experience
5. https://hbr.org/2023/03/using-technology-to-create-a-better-customer-experience?ab=hero-subleft-2. Accessed 16 Mar 2023
6. Journey mapping 101 https://www.nngroup.com/articles/journey-mapping-101/. Accessed 16 Mar 2023

Supporting Presentation Document Creation Using Visualization of Logical Relationship Between Slides

Hiroka Umetsu(✉), Mitsuhiro Goto⬤, and Akihiro Kashihara⬤

The University of Electro-Communications, 1-5-1, Chofugaoka, Chofu, Tokyo, Japan
`u2230026@gl.cc.uec.ac.jp`

Abstract. Recently, presentation is conducted in various situations, and researchers have to create presentation documents (P-documents). However, it is not easy for novice researchers as learners to create their own P-documents without logical leap. This paper proposes a visualization of logical flow embedded in P-document called slide map, with which learners are induced to consider the logical relationships between slides. Constructing the map, they could create their own P-document without logical leap. We have conducted a case study whose purpose was to assess effects of constructing a slide map to rearrange the slides in a P-document made by another person. The results suggest that the construction of slide map could allow learners to reconsider the logical structure of the P-document.

Keywords: Presentation Document · Logical Structure · Visualizing

1 Introduction

Presentation documents (called P-documents), which consist of the number of slides describing what presenters want to transmit to the audience, have been used as instructive materials in classroom or presentation materials for conferences and meetings. It is important for presenters to create P-documents that have well-organized and logical structure to appropriately transmit the contents. To create such P-documents, the presenters are required to divide the contents into some segments including several slides, and to sequence the slides according to the role of each slide and the logical relationships between the slides [1]. However, it is hard for novice presenters to precisely and concurrently conduct such segmentation and sequencing by themselves because presentation applications do not have the functions for helping users to consider the segments to sequence the slides in an effective way. These applications display only thumbnails lined up in a row and enlarged one of them according to users' operation. As a result, novice learners tend not to consider the logical structure, and mainly pay attention to make the contents and design of slides during creating P-document.

In order to address this issue, various methods were proposed in terms of supporting creation of P-documents with visualization of logical structure. Kojiri et al. [2] proposed automatic visualization of logical relationships between slides depending on the

C. Stephanidis et al. (Eds.): HCII 2023, CCIS 1834, pp. 168–175, 2023.
https://doi.org/10.1007/978-3-031-35998-9_24

contents. It successfully computes and visualizes the topic flow of slides for text-based P-documents. Hasegawa et al. [3] proposed extraction of typical structure of P-documents accumulated in a research group, with which the novice researchers as learners are allowed to create the slide contents embedding the presentation heuristics maintained in the group. Moreover, it is important not only to create the sophisticated P-document but also to consider the flow of oral script corresponding to the P-document. Kojiri et al. [4] supported novices in creating complementary speech with automatic visualization of the relations between a pair of slides. These studies focused on creating the contents such as slides and oral scripts. On the other hand, there are few studies that induce learners to reconsider the logical structure of their P-documents by themselves.

The main purpose of our work presented in this paper is to help learners construct a logical structure during creating their P-documents. Such logical structure construction allows learners to visualize and become aware of logical relationships between slides, and to create the P-documents that are easy to understand without logical leap. We have developed a system for creating P-document and constructing the logical structure. This paper also reports a case study with the proposed system whose purpose was to evaluate the effectiveness of the system. The results indicate that visualizing the logical structure built by learners contributes to reconsidering and understanding the logical structure.

In Sect. 2, we introduce the overview of P-document creation support with visualization of logical structure. In Sect. 3, we demonstrate the P-document creation support system with the visualization. In Sect. 4, we report the case study to ascertain the effectiveness of the proposed system. Finally, we summarize our work in Sect. 5.

2 P-Document Creation Support

As stated above, novice learners would have difficulties in creating logical P-document with existing presentation applications, which display only a row of slides. In this work, learners are provided with the P-document creation support system, which allows them to construct and visualize the logical relationships using a format of visualization expression called Slide Map originally designed by Goto et al. [1].

2.1 Slide Map

Slide map visualizes the logical relationships between slides in a P-document so that learners can overview each slide without confirming the contents as shown in Fig. 1(a). This map represents the structure of the P-document with slides' thumbnail images as nodes and the logical relationships among the corresponding nodes as links, which includes a logical sequence from top to bottom.

This map consists of three sequence areas: main-sequence, support-sequence and rebuttal-sequence area. The main-sequence area includes the main topic slides, which describe the main topic of the P-document. The support-sequence includes slides, which supplement the slide contents in the main sequence, and which are not always necessary to describe the main topic. The rebuttal-sequence area includes slides, which rebut the main-sequence contents. Each node is placed in the corresponding sequence area according to the role of the slide which could be decided with the link category. There

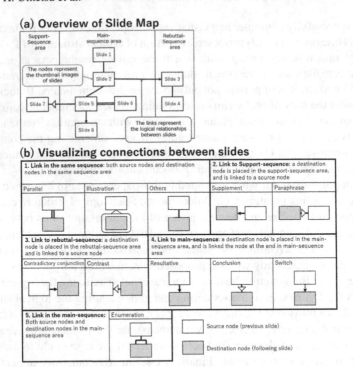

Fig. 1. Overview of Slide Map and Examples of Visualizing Logical Relationships.

are five link categories, and there are 10 link types in all for representing logical relationships, which are defined based on Japanese conjunctions classified by Ishiguro [5], and which could be applied to the oral research presentation. Figure 1(b) shows examples of visual representation for each logical relationship. The "others" link is used to express a connection relationship that do not fit any of the 10 types.

2.2 P-Document Creation Model

In this work, we also propose a model of creating a P-document that involves constructing the slide map as shown in Fig. 2. This model consists of three phases, which are the slide contents creation phase, the slide map creation phase, and the refinement phase.

In the first phase, learners are expected to create the contents of slides from what they want to present. In the second phase, they are expected to construct the slide map by themselves while considering the relationships between the slides created in the previous phase. In the slide map construction, they are expected to choose the type of link between slides, which would allow them to become aware of the logical structure embedded in their P-document and the slide contents. For example, when they could not find an appropriate conjunction as link type, they would have chances to reflect on whether the contents of the slides are appropriate and adequate.

In the third phase, they are expected to refine the contents and the order of the slides with reference to the slide map. The learners repeat these three phases until they finish creating both their P-document and the slide map.

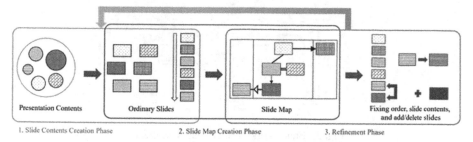

Fig. 2. Model of P-document Creation with Slide Map

The previous work done by Goto et al. [6] has suggested that a slide map is helpful to find out the structure of a P-document in a short time. According to this suggestion, the slide map has been used to promote understanding P-documents created by others.

In this work, learners create slide maps by themselves. They would accordingly have a heavier burden in comparison to usual creation of P-document. However, the slide map greatly reduces the burden of reviewing the P-document creation process. Learners could gradually get a logical structure of P-document in constructing the slide map. This allows them to more easily notice unbalanced usage of conjunction and sequence area, which contributes to refining their P-document.

This work aims to support the creation of easy-to-understand P-documents with fewer logical leaps through constructing a slide map.

3 Slide Map Visualizer

3.1 Framework of Proposed System

The P-document creation support system called slide map visualizer was developed as an add-in of Microsoft PowerPoint. It enables seamless connection between creating slides and a slide map. The framework of the system is shown in Fig. 3. Learners input a P-document file to the system, and then the thumbnail image files of slides are automatically generated. Subsequently, the slide map is displayed with the P-document and these thumbnail data. The learners can create and modify their P-document, and construct the slide map in parallel using the generated data. They can also review the visualized logical relationships of the P-document with the slide map.

3.2 User Interface of Proposed System

The user interface of the system is shown in Fig. 4, which consists of three parts, 1) Ribbon area, 2) Slide map construction area and 3) Slide contents creation area.

1) **Ribbon Area.** Ribbon Area is located at the top of the PowerPoint user interface (upper part of Fig. 4). This area has "SLIDEMAP" as additional tab. There are some

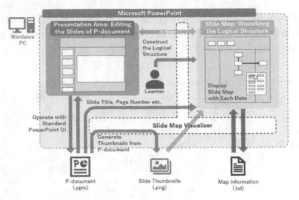

Fig. 3. Framework of Slide Map Visualizer

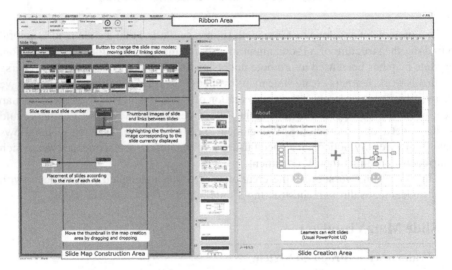

Fig. 4. Overview of Slide Map Visualizer

buttons for constructing a slide map on this tab. Learners click the start button if they want to start constructing a slide map, and then the slide thumbnails are exported and displayed on the slide map area. After clicking the button, it becomes inactive until finishing the map construction. Moreover, the learners can save the slide map constructed. The proposed system records the structure of the map with its own data format, and exports this data file according to the learners' operation. The system also loads the slide map constructed previously with this file, and the learners can continue to construct the slide map.

2) **Slide Map Construction Area.** Slide Map Construction Area is located at the left of the PowerPoint user interface (left part of Fig. 4). Thumbnails of all slides are displayed in this area as mentioned in Sect. 2.1. At first, no nodes are linked, and

all nodes are located at the top of this area. The number and title of each slide are displayed on each node.

There are two modes for construction a slide map, the slide moving mode and the link setting mode. In the slide moving mode, learners can move each slide and connected slides by means of drag and drop operation within the sequence area that corresponds to the connected links as mentioned in Fig. 1(b). In addition, the linked node cannot be moved to the above of the previous nodes because the logical flow must be from top to bottom.

In the link setting mode, learners can connect and disconnect slides. Dragging from the source node to the destination node brings about the link setting menu. Learners consider and select their logical relationships while looking at the example and explanation of the logical conjunction displayed in the menu.

3) **Slide Creation Area.** Slide Creation Area is located at the right of the PowerPoint user interface (right part of Fig. 4). The thumbnails of slides are vertically displayed at the left of this area. This area is the same as the regular PowerPoint user interface except for one thing. In choosing a slide, the corresponding slide thumbnail on the slide map construction area will be highlighted with red. At the right of this area, learners can edit any slide in the same way as the PPT user interface. During constructing the slide map, learners can also add new slides, and delete any slides. The nodes added/deleted are also put on/removed from the slide map construction area.

4   Case Study

The case study was conducted with 6 undergraduate and graduate students in science and technology. The purpose of the study was to ascertain whether the slide map helps learners to appropriately grasp the logical structure of P-document. The participants were required to logically and appropriately rearrange the order of slides included in a research P-document created by a student of our lab, which are randomly sorted in advance.

The participants were divided into two groups called SM group and PP group. SM group conducted the rearrangement task with the slide map, and PP group conducted it without the slide map and only with the PowerPoint user interface. We conducted this study as between-participants design, and each participant were assigned to one of the two groups mentioned above.

As for evaluation, we focused on the differences in the results of slides rearranged by SM group and PP group. All participants were given the same P-document, which was randomly sorted, and we compared the original order with the order after rearrangement by means of Damerau-Levenshtein distance for each segment of the P-document. Segment means the topic boundaries, and each segment contains several slides. The P-document used in this case study has four segments, and the segment was labeled by the author. Damerau-Levenshtein distance was calculated by how many times the slides rearranged has to be deleted, added, replaced, or replaced with the next slide in order to be consistent with the original slide order. The lower the value of this distance, the more correctly the slides are rearranged.

Table 1 shows the evaluation results based on average Damerau-Levenshtein distance for each segment and total segments in SM group and PP group. In the table, the numbers indicate the average distances, and the numbers in parentheses also indicate the standard deviations. Although there is no significant difference between the groups, the average distance for total segments in SM group (Average distance: 8.3, SD: 2.9) tend to be slightly shorter than the PP group (Average distance: 9.0, SD: 2.6). As a reason for this, the P-document used in this study was quite sophisticated and used in actual master's thesis presentation. It accordingly seems to be easy to understand the logical structure in the P-document even without constructing the slide map.

The results shown in Table 1 also suggest that it was difficult to rearrange Segment 3. According to the post-questionnaire with five-point Likert scale (1: "I don't know", 5: "I know well"), the PP group participants had knowledge required for understanding this segment more than the SM group as shown in Table 2. Although the average distances of the SM group in the segments except Segment 3 were shorter than the PP group, the average distance of the PP group in Segment 3 was shorter than the SM group. We think the arrangement task for this segment requires more knowledge for understanding it.

In this case study, we did not deal with slide map construction during P-document creation, which is our main goal. In future, we will conduct another case study in the contexts of constructing a slide map to refine a P-document.

Table 1. Average and Standard Deviation of Damerau-Levenshtein distance of each segment

SM group				
Total	Seg 1	Seg 2	Seg 3	Seg 4
8.3 (2.9)	0.7 (0.6)	0.7 (0.6)	6.0 (1.7)	1.0 (0.0)
PP group				
Total	Seg 1	Seg 2	Seg 3	Seg 4
9.0 (2.6)	1.0 (0.0)	2.0 (1.7)	4.7 (0.6)	1.3 (0.6)

Table 2. Five Point Likert Scale

	1(I don' know)	2	3	4	5(I know well)
SM group	2	1	0	0	0
PP group	1	0	0	2	0

5 Conclusion

This paper describes a support for P-document creation involving constructing and visualizing slide map. The proposed support system enables seamless connection between creating the contents of slides and visualizing the logical structure. The results of the case study with the system suggest that learners are allowed to think about the logical relationships between slides.

In future, we plan to conduct another case study to evaluate effectiveness of the system in more detail. In particular, we will investigate whether P-document with a solid logical structure can be created in building a slide map.

References

1. Mitsuhiro, G., Akihiro, K.: Understanding Presentation Document with Visualization of Connections between Presentation Slides, In: Proceedings of 20th International Conference on Knowledge-Based and Intelligent Information & Engineering Systems (KES2016), Procedia Computer Science Volume 96, 2016, pp. 1285–1293, York (2016)
2. Tomoko, K., Fumihiro, Y.: Automatic estimation of topic flow from slides for supporting presentation slide creation. J. Inf. Syst. Educ. 11(1), 24–31 (2013)
3. Shinobu, H., Akihiro, K.: A mining technique for extraction of presentation schema from presentation documents accumulated in laboratory, In: The Journal of Research and Practice in Technology Enhanced Learning (RPTEL), vol. 8, no.1, pp.153–169 (2013)
4. Tomoko, K., Naoya, I.: Presentation speech creation support based on visualization of slide relations. IEICE Trans. Inf. Syst. 97, 893–900 (2014)
5. Kei, I.: The Sentences are determined by connection words. 8th edn. Kobunsha, Japan (2013)
6. Mitsuhiro, G., Akihiro, K.: Evaluating visualization for slide-based investigative learning with connection between presentation slides, In: The 18th International Conference on Cognition and Exploratory Learning in Digital Age (CELDA 2021), pp. 235–242 (2021)

Generation of Instruction Range Map Based on Analysis of Demonstrative Words and Spatial Domain for Reduction of Miscommunication Among Chinese, Vietnamese and Japanese in Care Facilities

Binyu Wang[✉], Weiqing Xiang, Masanari Ichikawa, and Yugo Takeuchi

National University Corporation Shizuoka University, Hamamatsu, Japan
{wang.binyu.19,xiang.weiqing.20,ichikawa.masanari.18}@shizuoka.ac.jp,
takeuchi@inf.shizuoka.ac.jp

Abstract. In care facilities, demonstrative words such as "this" and "that" are frequently used to quickly share information and work instructions between staff members in the same space. According to the related research, Chinese and Vietnamese demonstrative words are not synonymous with Japanese ones, suggesting that there are differences in the spatial domain indicated by demonstrative words between the mother tongues. Therefore, it is considered that Chinese and Vietnamese are prone to miscommunication with Japanese in dialogues involving instructions irrespective of their proficiency in Japanese language skills. There are many cases of taking and getting of medical drugs in care facilities. Caregivers often use demonstrative words instead of specific medical drugs names or locations of medications because of busyness. If Chinese or Vietnamese caregivers do not understand the spatial domain of instruction well, they may get the wrong medication, which may lead to health risks for the elderly. So, it's necessary to eliminate such problems, and it is important for caregivers in the same space to be able to understand each other's instructions in care facilities. In our research, different perceptions of the spatial domains of the instructions between Japanese, Vietnamese and Chinese are Interpreted by something like "instruction range map" that organized the correlations between which demonstrative words are selected for which spatial domain by experimenters in different countries. The proposed map is expected to be useful for Japanese and foreigners to understand and share the differences in their perceptions when they interact or give instruction by pointing to each other. The proposed idea is expected to reduce miscommunication among cross-cultural staff in care facilities.

Keywords: Chinese · Vietnamese · Japanese · spatial domains · instruction · demonstrative words

1 Introduction

In recent years, Japan's aging population has been accelerating, and according to the Annual Report on the Aging Society Japanese (2019), the aging rate reached 28.1% in 2018 [5]. It is expected that the number of elderly people who require support in their daily lives will continue to increase. However, according to the supply-demand projections announced by the Ministry of Health, Labor and Welfare, in the fiscal year 2025, there will be a shortage of approximately 380,000 caregivers, as the projected supply of approximately 2.15 million falls short of the estimated demand for approximately 2.53 million [2]. In response to this gap between supply and demand, various measures are being taken to promote the entry of diverse workers, such as foreign caregivers, young people, and people with disabilities.

Since 2008, the acceptance of foreign caregivers has been started through economic partnership agreements. Furthermore, in 2016, a new residency status called "caregiver" was established, and in 2017, institutional reforms such as a review of the Technical Intern Training Program for foreign workers have been carried out. With the reform of the care system, the number of foreign caregivers is increasing, and it is thought that communication between staff of different cultures is more likely to occur in care facilities. In care facilities, sudden requests for staff may occur, such as responding to rapid changes in the physical condition of the elderly. To quickly give instructions among staff, communication with demonstrative words like "bring that quickly" frequently occurs. This phenomenon was observed by the author during visits to care facilities. For example, even though foreign caregivers did not understand the words they were instructed with, they could understand the instructions when Japanese caregivers pointed to the location. When a Japanese caregiver instructed a foreign caregiver, "take the rag," the foreign caregiver did not understand the word "rag," but when the Japanese caregiver pointed in the direction of the kitchen, the foreign caregiver could understand the instructions.

Demonstrative words do not have a concrete meaning in and of themselves, but instead derive their meaning by pointing to things around them. In the world's languages, there are languages like Japanese that have three series of demonstrative words, such as "ko," "so," and "a," and languages like Chinese that have two series, such as "zhe" (ko) and "na" (a). In Japanese, the demonstrative words "ko," "so," and "a" are usually translated into English as follows:

1. "ko" is translated as "this" and refers to objects close to the speaker.
2. "so" is translated as "that" and refers to objects relatively far from the speaker but close to the listener.
3. "a" is translated as "that over there or "that one" and refers to objects far from both the speaker and the listener.

On the other hand, the three series of demonstrative words are composed of proximal, medial, and distal forms, with the medial form serving as the addressee form in principle. The two series of demonstrative words are composed of proximal and non-proximal (distal forms), with the addressee form that should be served by the medial form not existing, and the non-proximal form serving in its place [1]. However, there is a tendency to think that the usage of "ko" in Japanese and "zhe" in Chinese is the same [6], but Chinese demonstrative words do not carry categorical concepts and only serve as demonstrative concepts, so the use of Chinese demonstrative words is heavily dependent on the subjectivity of the speaker [3]. The area they indicate may not be the same as in Japanese. Moreover, there are nuances between languages that have the same three series of demonstrative words, such as Japanese's "ko," "so," and "a," which are distinguished from the addressee's perspective [8], while Vietnamese's "ko," "so," and "a" are distinguished from the speaker's perspective. In addition, in the usage of pointing to an object, the usage of the medial and distal forms in Vietnamese can be interchangeable depending on the difference in orientation between the speaker and the addressee [9], and when using the medial form, it is necessary to consider not only the distance between the speaker and the addressee but also the presence or absence of shared knowledge between them [7].

Once learned, demonstrative words tend to be deeply ingrained in a person and their spatial division is based on the language they have learned [10]. Therefore, in the caregiving field where dialogues involving demonstratives are frequently exchanged, problems may arise when Japanese and foreign people communicate with each other. Therefore, it is desirable for Japanese people to be aware that spatial recognition of "ko," "so," and "a" may differ depending on the country when giving instructions to foreign people in the workplace. This research aims to clarify the spatial area surrounding the body by differentiating between the use of demonstratives by foreign people. We have captured the differences in spatial recognition between countries and examined the factors that can cause mistakes when giving instructions to foreign staff in the workplace.

Therefore, this research aims to experimentally verify the recognition of spatial domains for demonstrative words between Japanese and non-Japanese speakers, and consider new instructional methods for non-Japanese caregivers who are less affected by their Japanese language abilities, in communication situations.

2   Experiment

2.1   Conditions and Objective

The experiment involved 38 Japanese university students, 10 Chinese university students, 5 Vietnamese university students, and 3 students from a vocational school. The experiment was conducted in pairs of two, consisting of a Japanese student and either a Chinese student, a Japanese student and either a Japanese student, a Japanese student and either a Vietnamese student. Each pair was assigned the roles of "instructor" and "listener." It is worth noting that among the foreign participants, 17 individuals had passed the Japanese Language Proficiency Test N2 or higher, while one student had passed N3.

The specific placement of participants and tags of experiment is shown in Fig. 1, and involved placing cards with numbers ranging from 21 to 84 at equal intervals in a random pattern on an 8×8 grid on the ground. The spacing between the cards was 245 [cm] wide and high, and each card had a width and height of approximately 30 cm. The instructor would look at a random number between 21 and 84 displayed on a computer screen and point to the corresponding card while asking the listener, "Which one is number x?" based on the instructions provided by the instructor. The listener would then predict which card was being referred to based on the instructor's pointing gesture.

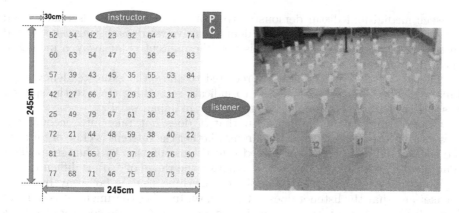

Fig. 1. Specific placement of participants and tags.

The instructor was instructed not to correct the listener's answer, even if it was incorrect. Each trial lasted for 30 s, and this process was repeated 64 times. If the instructor could not find the number within 30 s, they would move on to the next trial. The numbers displayed on the computer (ranging from 21 to 84) and the type of demonstrative words used by the speaker ("ko," "so," and "a") were recorded.

The procedure was repeated twice. For foreign participants, the first trial involved foreign participants as instructors and Japanese participants as listeners, while the second trial involved a role reversal.

The objectives of the experiment were to investigate the differences in spatial recognition domain of demonstrative words among Japanese, Chinese, and Vietnamese based on extracted instruction range map.

2.2 Hypothesis

Once learned, demonstrative words tend to be deeply ingrained in a person and it has been reported that the spatial division of demonstrative words is based on the language learned. As a result, the following predictions are expected.

The use of "ko" in Vietnamese is predicted to be the same as in Japanese. Vietnamese demonstrative words are generally distinguished based on the spatial distance between the speaker and the listener. When the speaker and listener are facing each other, the closer one to the speaker is expressed with a proximal demonstrative [9]. This method of use was the same as in Japanese.

The use of "so" and "a" in Vietnamese is predicted to be different from that in Japanese. When the speaker and listener are facing each other, the closer one to the listener is expressed with a medial demonstrative in Vietnamese. However, in Vietnamese, the distinction between medial and distal demonstrative words is often interchangeable in direct referential [11]. Also states that the distinction between medial and distal demonstrative words in Vietnamese is relative and not clear [8]. The use of Vietnamese demonstrative words is distinguished based on the speaker, so if the speaker feels that the referent is far away, a medial or distal demonstrative can be used.

The use of "ko" in Chinese is predicted to show the same tendency as in Japanese. The Chinese "ko" is used to indicate something close to the speaker in space, which is the same as the use of "ko" in Japanese [4].

Chinese differs from Japanese in that it does not take into account the presence of the listener when determining whether the referent is close or far from the speaker. Therefore, it is predicted that the use of "so" by Chinese speakers is at the discretion of the speaker. Predicting the range of "so" is difficult.

The Chinese "a" is used to indicate something that is far away from the speaker and that the listener does not yet know. In this experiment, it is difficult to predict the range of "a" because it is difficult for Chinese speakers to judge whether the Japanese listener knows the referred object when pointing to a number [4].

2.3 Result of Spatial Recognition Domain of Demonstrative Words Among Japanese, Chinese, and Vietnamese

Three groups of students from different countries conducted a study on the sensitivity of choice probabilities towards numbers. They picked out features of squares where the "ko," "so," and "a" option was chosen with a probability of over 70% out of 64 squares representing positions. Figure 2 shows the range of squares where "ko" was chosen when the participants from each country acted as the speaker. It was observed that the range of selection for "ko" tended to spread around the speaker for Japanese and Chinese participants. On the other hand, Vietnamese participants tended to move their selection range towards the listener's side.

Figure 3 shows the distribution of "so" in a similar manner. The selection range of Chinese participants was the same as that of Japanese participants, whereas Vietnamese participants tended to concentrate their selection on the

Japanese (n=10)

8	9	9	10	10	10	8	8
6	9	9	8	9	9	9	5
2	4	7	8	8	6	6	1
1	1	2	2	1	2	1	
		1		1			

Chinese (n=10)

9	8	10	10	10	9	10	7
9	8	10	10	9	8	10	5
4	6	9	9	8	9	5	5
1	4	3	5	4	4	1	
				1	1	2	
			1			1	

Vietnamese (n=8)

5	8	8	8	8	7	8	6
5	7	8	8	7	8	7	1
2	3	6	6	6	6	2	
1	1		3	1	2		
					1		1

Fig. 2. The comparison in spatial recognition domain of demonstrative words "ko (this)" among the three countries.

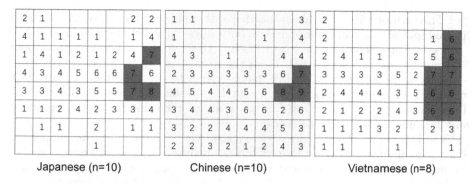

Fig. 3. The comparison in spatial recognition domain of demonstrative words "so (that)" among the three countries.

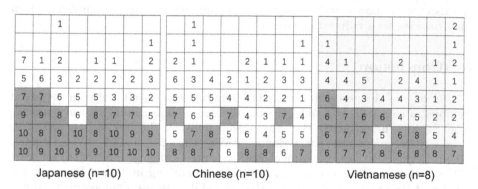

Fig. 4. The comparison in spatial recognition domain of demonstrative words "a (that over there/that one)" among the three countries.

listener's right side more than Japanese and Chinese participants. Figure 4 shows the distribution of "a". The selection ranges for both Japanese and Vietnamese participants were far from both the speaker and the listener, while this tendency was not observed in Chinese participants.

2.4 Discussion

The hypothesis presented in Sect. 2.2 regarding the demonstrative words "ko" was supported, indicating that Vietnamese, Japanese and Chinese students have the same spatial understanding of "ko." The hypothesis regarding the demonstrative words "so" in Vietnamese was not supported, as Vietnamese primarily use the distance between the speaker and the object to select a demonstrative words, yet in the experiment, it was found that Vietnamese speakers tend to use "so" as a listener-oriented expression when the speaker and listener are facing each other.

But the hypothesis regarding the demonstrative words "so" in Chinese was supported. Some Chinese people recognize "so" within the domain of "ko" and "a." Furthermore, 70% of Chinese participants could only recognize "so" within a limited spatial range in front of and on both sides of the listener within 30 [cm].

As for the demonstrative words "a," the hypothesis in Sect. 2.2 about Vietnamese was not supported. From the results, it can be inferred that when Vietnamese people use "a" while facing the listener, they tend to use it in a listener-oriented manner, which is similar to how Japanese people use "a." Therefore, the domain of usage for "a" is almost the same for both Vietnamese and Japanese people in this context.

The hypothesis about Chinese demonstrative "a" in Sect. 2.2 was supported. The experiment revealed that Chinese people have a narrower spatial understanding of "a" compared to Japanese people, but it was not possible to determine the domain of usage for "a." The experiment was conducted under the condition where the listener did not know which number was being referred to. The speaker pointed to the number with their finger, but it was difficult for the listener to know whether they knew the number for distant numbers, which may have led to a reduced use of "a."

3 Conclusion

The novelty of this research lies in clarifying the relationship between the use of demonstrative words by students from different countries and spatial domains. The research investigated the relationship between the use of demonstrative words by foreigners and spatial domains. With the exception of one participant, all participants in the experiment had Japanese language proficiency at level N2 or higher, which is considered sufficient for working in Japan. However, the results of the experiment revealed that the ability to use demonstrative words is not necessarily at the same level as that of Japanese speakers, regardless of their proficiency in Japanese.

Based on the results of the experiment, we believe that it is possible to extract a "Instruction Range Map" that organizes the correlation between which demonstrative words student from different countries choose for which spatial domains.

This map is expected to be useful for Japanese and foreign people to understand and share their differences in perception when they communicate and point to objects. It could also be an effective tool in communication education between Japanese and foreign people. It was also found that there were differences in the recognition of physical spaces in the medial and distal among students from three different countries. Because the recognition of the same physical space can differ depending on the country, it is possible to propose methods to reduce mistakes between multicultural staff in the field of care. Since the number of participants in this experiment was small, it is necessary to increase the number of participants for further verification in order to improve the accuracy of the results.

In the future, investigations on the usage of directional words among care staff in actual care settings will be conducted, and discussions on specific ways of using directional words in care settings will continue.

References

1. Fillmore, C.J.: Towards a descriptive framework for spatial deixis. In: Speech, Place and Action: Studies in Deixis and Related Topics, pp. 31–59 (1982)
2. Ministry of Health, Labour and Welfare: Estimation of supply and demand for care workers toward 2025 (2015). http://www.mhlw.go.jp/stf/houdou/0000088998. html
3. Hideki, K.: Chinese indicative "far and near". On the distance contrast of chinese demonstratives: a comparison with "Ko-so-a". In: Japanese and Chinese Contrastive Studies, pp. 181–211 (1992)
4. Hui, L.: "ko-so-a" and "na": a comparison of Japanese and Chinese. Bull. Soc. Dialectology **116**, 9–18 (1986)
5. Ministry of Internal Affairs and Communications: Annual report on the aging society (2018). https://www8.cao.go.jp/kourei/whitepaper/w-2019/zenbun/s111. html
6. Linsheng, Z.: Error analysis for Japanese language education: mother-tongue interference in 20 cases of Chinese speakers. 3A Network (2008)
7. Masanobu, G.: Gomi Learner's Vietnamese Dictionary. Musashino University Press (2015)
8. Mayumi, A.: Demonstratives, sentence-final particles, and interjections derived from demonstratives in Vietnamese. Ph.D. thesis, University of Tokyo (2016)
9. Phong, N.: Vietnamese Grammar Issues: Types of Subject and Object. National University of Hanoi Press (2002)
10. Shuji, Y.: Spatial division types observed in demonstratives and their universality. Bull. Natl. Mus. Ethnology **5–4**, 833–950 (1980)
11. Tomita, K.: The World of Vietnamese - Vietnamese Basic Dictionary. Daigaku-sho (2000)

Learning and Training Technologies

Tiktok as a Learning Tool for Elementary School Students

Paulina Magally Amaluisa Rendón$^{(\boxtimes)}$ ⓘ, Carlos Alberto Espinosa-Pinos ⓘ,
and María Giovanna Núñez-Torres ⓘ

Universidad Indoamérica, Ambato 180103, Ecuador
paulinaamaluisa@indoamerica.edu.ec

Abstract. The large number of users of the social network Tiktok worldwide and the studies that demonstrate the advantages of its use in relation to its educational capacity encourage us to seek new ways of teaching. The present study was conducted at the Indoamerica Educational University in the city of Ambato-Ecuador during the 2021–2022 school year, comparing the motivation of students of General Basic Education: specifically, Basic Middle (Sublevel 3): fifth, sixth and seventh grade corresponding to boys and girls of 9, 10 and 11 years old respectively, and the use of Tiktok as a learning tool demonstrated in their academic performance. Group A has used Tiktok as a tool for the development of academic activities, while group B has not used it. A quantitative methodology was used with a descriptive-inferential procedure and a qualitative analysis through interviews with educators. A pre-test and a post-test were carried out to demonstrate the children's motivation at the end of the school year. It is confirmed that the children who used Tiktok as a learning tool consider themselves more motivated and show a greater dedication to the proposed subject matter than children who do not use it, which is evidenced in their academic record. On the other hand, the teachers interviewed expressed heterogeneous opinions.

Keywords: Basic education · Tiktok · Motivation

1 Introduction

Currently Tiktok is one of the most important digital platforms worldwide, it was created in China by the company Byte Dance in 2016. This social network was launched in Ecuador at the end of 2018 [1]. The confinement due to COVID-19 originated an exponential growth of TikTok [2] increased the use of mobile devices in order to find new ways of employment, study, purchase goods and services, get information and communicate in moments of confinement [3]. As a result, by the year 2021 in Ecuador, 2,300,000 Tiktok users were already registered [4]. Through social networks, users become prosumers or active actors [5], in other words, they are innovative emitters, competent to produce and consume content simultaneously and cooperatively [6]. Tiktok is the largest, most influential and successful social network and contains a great diversity of topics with the most active users. In the area of education, several studies show its great potential

C. Stephanidis et al. (Eds.): HCII 2023, CCIS 1834, pp. 187–193, 2023.
https://doi.org/10.1007/978-3-031-35998-9_26

to improve educational pedagogies [7]. A study by Bossen and Kottasz on the use of the social network TikTok found that pre-adolescents are more active consumers than adolescents on TikTok [8]. Likewise, according to Toetenel [9], any user with a mobile device and from an early age has the means to create and publish content at any time and in any format they want. This paper analyzes the capacity of the use of Tiktok in the motivation of middle school students (pre-adolescents) and their dedication to the content transmitted, compared to students who have not used Tiktok whose results are reflected in academic performance.

2 Materials and Methods

2.1 Objectives

– To analyze the motivation for the use of the social network Tiktok as part of the teaching process in middle school students as demonstrated in their academic performance.
– To interpret the educators' criteria about their experience of using Tiktok as a teaching tool.

2.2 Participants

The study considered a sample of 148 students (69% female and 31% male) of the Indoamerica Educational Unit in the city of Ambato in the period between 2021–2022. They correspond to 6 parallels of 3 different levels organized as follows: Group A that did use Tiktok was made up of: fifth A (25 students), sixth A (25 students) and seventh A (25 students). Group B was made up of students in Fifth B (24 students), Sixth B (25 students) and Seventh B (24 students) who did not use the Tiktok social network with their teacher. Group A used Tiktok as a tool for the development of academic activities, while group B did not use Tiktok.

There are three teachers in group A, corresponding to fifth A, sixth A and seventh A; there are three teachers in group B: fifth B, sixth B and seventh B. After carrying out the SHAPIRO-WILK test, it can be seen that the sample responds to normal parameters ($p = 0.176$). The following table shows the data related to the number of students in the groups (Table 1).

Table 1. Study participants (grop, school grade, Tiktik use, number of students).

Groups	School grade	Use of Tiktok	Number of students
A	Fifth grade A	YES	25
	Sixth grade A	YES	25
	Seventh grade A	YES	25
B	Fifth grade B	NO	24
	Sixth grade B	NO	25
	Seventh grade B	NO	24

2.3 Analysis Used

The study is quantitative-qualitative, quantitative (descriptive and inferential) and qualitative (interviews). A pretest and a post-test were also applied to record in which dimension the students' motivation varies after the end of the school year.

Quantitative. A descriptive method (means and SD) and an inferential method (Anovas) were performed on group A and group B separately. The pretest and posttest data processing was carried out using the analysis factors, reflecting whether relevant disparities were found in the factors between the groups before and after the end of the school year.

Qualitative. Interviews were conducted with teachers through structured information gathering. The data found were examined by thematic content analysis [10] and periodic comparison of the data [11]. The content analysis was established in the investigation of patterns in the text, collecting the data matching the cross-patterns [12]. By means of a reflective conversation the themes found in the first study were independently critically investigated. Reliability was substantiated through participatory analysis and continuous feedback. The objective was to use the information collected to provide greater intelligibility in conveying the results. The categories emerging from the survey are shown in the results section [13].

The WEFT QDA tool was used to summarize, structure and saturate the information using the categories derived from the questions asked to the teachers.

2.4 Instrumentos Utilizados Para Recopilar Información

Quantitative. The information was collected using the accredited evaluation questionnaire in initial education [14]. The students responded to 15 questions according to the statement on the Likert scale whose values range from 1 = not at all to 5 = a lot corresponding to the Evaluation Systems Scale. The reliability of Cronbach's Alpha of the questionnaire is 0.87 with a confidence level of 95%.

For the final form, a Principal Component Factor Analysis was performed, where values for the KMO index of 0.85 were reached, in the same way as in Bartlett's test of sphericity ($p > .00$). The indicators obtained in the covariance matrix showed satisfactory agreement for the RMSEA index = 0.080, as well as for the GFI = 0.79. Thus, the questionnaire is made up of 2 factors:

1. *Motivation to study (10 components):* components related to the stimulation shown by the student towards the work proposed by the teacher, as well as autonomy and self-control during the teaching period.
2. *Dedication to the proposed subject matter (5 components):* the degree of perseverance and research that the student demonstrates during the school year, showing an effective predisposition towards the proposed actions.

Qualitative. A semi-structured interview was conducted with the teachers in the study in order to examine the opinions and appreciation of the teachers interviewed to reach an internal position of the experience [15]. In accordance with the study variables, 3 initial questions were asked to the teachers at the end of the school year:

- Do you know the benefits and difficulties of using Tiktok as a tool in the teaching process?
- Do you think that student motivation depends on the proposed topic or the methodology in which it is shared?
- Do you consider that the use of Tiktok can improve students' academic performance?

2.5 Study Design and Procedure

The fifth, sixth and seventh parallel A and B school grades that make up the sample are developed by school years. The research is retrospective, since the students have answered the questionnaire once the school year has ended and their grades have been socialized. The following paragraphs describe the process used by the teachers in each of the cases:

- *Group A uses Tiktok as a training tool*: Students perform their assignments in video format and these are uploaded in the virtual classroom as evidence of their execution. The student delves into the information acquired in the classroom, and elaborates group videos linking them to web pages and experts' criteria, creating constructive forums on specific topics. A hashtag was defined to share the information. On the other hand, the teacher constantly monitors the process through the virtual classroom and provides continuous feedback.
- *Group B does not use Tiktok as a training tool:* The methodology is traditionalist, the teacher sets the tasks, provides the material and resources to be used by the student. The development of the subject matter is done during class time and there is no previous research by the student. At the beginning of the school year, informed consent was given to the parents of both groups. At the end of the school year, the students individually answered the questionnaire in one hour of class. Anonymity was assured in order to obtain reliable answers, and confidentiality was guaranteed regarding the use of the information (Table 2).

3 Results

Table 2. Number of students by group, sex and pre-test and post-test average in academic performance.

Group	Men	Women	Pre-test average	Post-test average
Group A	15%	36%	7,15	8,70
Group B	16%	33%	7,32	7,02
Full	31%	69%		

Quantitative Analysis. No considerable disparities are observed in any element between the groups in the pre-test. On the other hand, at the end of the school year, the means of the elements increased in group A, while in group B they decreased. In relation to the dedication to the proposed subject matter, significant discrepancies were found in group A between the pre-test and the post-test and also between groups, which is reflected in the academic performance.

Inferential Analysis. Group A, which did use Tiktok, is of the opinion that the proposed methodology makes it possible to acquire a greater body of knowledge. By means of factor analysis and according to the components related to learning, important differences in academic performance are achieved. In group B, which did not use Tiktok, differences are found in the variable of the use of Tiktok outside the classroom, and those who use it frequently are the ones who most appreciate the teaching achieved.

Qualitative Analysis

- The teachers of group A who have used Tiktok distinguish the advantages of Tiktok in the educational process as opposed to the teachers who have not used it.
- The educators who did use Tiktok consider that in order to keep students motivated, both the content and the way it is taught are important. On the contrary, teachers who did not use it consider that students will not necessarily always be motivated by the proposed content, therefore, they are not concerned about the use of different methodologies.
- The educators of group B believe that students should strive for their grades and base the evaluation on the score. This is in contrast to the teachers in group A, who perceive teaching as a process that ensures learning.

4 Discussion

According to Cárdenas and Ruíz, the use of the Tiktok tool improves the students' academic achievement and this is reflected in their grade point average [16]. The children in group A who used the Tiktok tool showed a higher academic average and even a better attitude towards the knowledge imparted.

The study confirms that Tiktok used as a formative tool motivates students. However, the dedication to the proposed subject matter is the component in which notable irregularities are found among the groups at the end of the school year. Likewise, a previous study carried out with young university students affirms that the use of Tiktok as part of the learning resources makes them feel more motivated and show greater enthusiasm for the contents [17]. This factor is important because school performance is one of the lowest indicators in developing countries [18]. Children, adolescents and preadolescents in the educational system generate a large amount of information to be studied in order to bring about changes in contemporary educational standards [19].

In the pretest, both groups A and B did not present relevant differences. With respect to the qualitative part of this study, there is an important difference between the opinions of the teachers in each of the groups. The teachers who did use Tiktok think that both the content and the way of presenting the information are important and show a better attitude towards the use of technology as an educational tool. On the other hand, the educators in the group that did not use Tiktok maintained a traditionalist posture, considering the content as such and offering only one way of teaching.

5 Conclusions

It is evident that the use of technology in the educational field and in this case of Tiktok motivates the students of basic secondary education and improves their dedication to the proposed topics, which is demonstrated in their academic record.

On the other hand, the educators who have used Tiktok as a teaching tool accept its benefits in contrast to the teachers who have not used these technological resources.

References

1. Muñoz, V.O.: «El efecto Tiktok: Plataformas digitales y reconfiguración del escenario político electoral en Ecuador.» Sociología Y Política HOY 175–184 (2021)
2. Coman, C., Tiru, L.G., Meseşan-Schmitz, L., Stanciu, Bularca, M.C.: «Online teaching and learning in higher education during the coronavirus pandemic: students' perspective.» Sustainability 12(24), 10367 (2020). https://doi.org/10.3390/su122410367
3. Chang, C.J.R., et al.:«Análisisdel contenido de #CirugíaPlástica más visto de TikTok: una oportunidad para la divulgación educativa,» Cirugía Plástica y Reconstructiva 2022(149) (2022)
4. E. d. Ecuador, «Estadística de usuarios de redes sociales en Ecuador,» 2021. [En línea]
5. Condeza-Dall'Orso, A.R., Bachmann-Cáceres, I., Mujica-Holley «News consumption among Chilean adolescents: Interest, motivations and perceptions on the news agenda.» Comunicar 22(43), 55–64 (2014). https://doi.org/10.3916/C43-2014-05
6. Herrero-Diz, P., Ramos-Serrano, M., Los menores como usuarios creadores en la era digital: del prosumer al creador colaborativo. Revisión teórica 1972–2016.» Revista Latina de Comunicación Social 71, 1301–1322. https://doi.org/10.4185/RLCS-2016-1146
7. Tan, K.H., Rajendran, A., Muslim, N., Alias, J.: «The potential of TikTok's key features as a pedagogical strategy for ESL classrooms.» Sustainability (Switzerland) 14(24), (2022). https://doi.org/10.3390/su142416876
8. Bossen, C.B., Bossen, K.R.: «Uses and gratifications sought by pre-adolescent and adolescent TikTokconsumers.» Young Consum. 21(4), 1747–3616 (2020)
9. Toetenel, L.: «Social networking: a collaborative open educational resource.» Comput. Assist. Lang. Learn. 27(2), 149–162 (2014)
10. Libarkin, J.C., Kurdziel, J.P.: «Research methodologies in science education: qualitative data.» J. Geosci. Educ. 50, 195–200 (2002)
11. Denzin, N.K., Lincoln, Y.S.: Denzin, «Handbook of Qualitative Research.» Sage, Thousand Oaks (1994)
12. Saldaña, J.: «The Coding Manual for Qualitative Researchers,» Thousand Oaks. Sage (2009)
13. Cohn, P.J.: «An exploratory study on peak performance in golf.» Sport Psychol. 5, 1–14 (1991)
14. F. S. M. &. P. A. Castejón, «Cuestionarios obremetodología y evaluación en formación inicial en EducaciónFísica,» Revista Internacional de Medicina y Ciencias de la Actividad Física y el Deporte, vol. 12, n° 1, pp. 1–32, 2013.
15. Patton, M.Q.: «Qualitative Research and Evaluation Methods.» Sage, Thousand Oaks (2002)

16. Cárdena, M.I.G., Ruíz, M.G.M.: «Influencia de las redes sociales en el rendimiento académico de los estudiantes de Nivel Medio Superior de la UAEMéx,» Diversidad Académica 2(1), 216–240 (2022)
17. Rendón, P.A., Jordán, N., Arias, D., Núñez, G.: Tik tok as a teaching tool: the motivation of university students in Ecuador. In: 2022 IEEE 2nd International Conference on Advanced Learning Technologies on Education & Research (ICALTER) (2022)
18. Espinosa-Pinos, C.A., Núñez-Torres, M.G., Jordán-Buenaño, N., Jordán-Buenaño, C.:«Methodological strategy for asynchronous learning mathematical operations with real numbers.»In: de IEEE 2nd International Conference on Advanced Learning Technologies on Education & Research (ICALTER) (2022)
19. Espinosa-Pinos, C.A., Ayala-Chauvín, I., Buele, J.: Predicting academic performance in mathematics using machine learning algorithms. In: Valencia-García, R., Bucaram-Leverone, M., Del Cioppo-Morstadt, J., Vera-Lucio, N., Jácome-Murillo, E. (eds.) Technologies and Innovation. CITI 2022. Communications in Computer and Information Science, vol. 1658. Springer, Cham (2022). https://doi.org/10.1007/978-3-031-19961-5_2

Automated Content Generation
for Intelligent Tutoring Systems

Andrew Emanuel Attard[✉] and Alexiei Dingli

University of Malta, Msida, Malta
andrew.attard.18@um.edu.mt

Abstract. The demand for eLearning systems has grown as education becomes a priority and the need for better technological assistance in learning increases. One type of software aimed at providing a more engaging and educational experience is the Intelligent Tutoring System (ITS). The ITS system featured in this research is called FAIE, which focuses on using Artificial Intelligence (AI) in learning. The blueprint-based approach allows educators to design content for students, but this raises two challenges. First, designing the content requires technical skills that can be time-consuming for educators with many tasks. Second, it is difficult to immediately codify an educator's intrinsic knowledge. To tackle these challenges, a Blueprint-designer was created to generate content based on a text prompt from the educator containing key information. The content consists of problems to be answered with correct answers and distractors meant to challenge the student. The process of generating QA-Pairs involves determining a list of possible answers using a Named Entity Recognition (NER) model and passing the answers to a Question-Generation (QG) model. The QG model is based on the T5 Transformer model, which was trained to output questions based on the context and answer. Finally, distractors are generated by training a sequence-to-sequence model, BART, on the RACE dataset.

Keywords: eLearning systems · Intelligent Tutoring System · Artificial Intelligence (AI)

1 Introduction

As technology grows, it has brought about significant advancements in many fields of interest, including the field of education. As education becomes a priority, the demand for systems that effectively assist learning has grown. An example of such as system is the Intelligent Tutoring System (ITS) which makes use of technology to produce an engaging and personalized experience for students [1].

One such system is called FAIE, a system that focuses on using Artificial Intelligence (AI) to enhance the learning process. This system makes use of a blueprint-based approach, thus allowing educators to design content for their students, however, the design process presents its own set of challenges, such as the need for technical skills and difficulties in codifying an educator's intrinsic knowledge.

C. Stephanidis et al. (Eds.): HCII 2023, CCIS 1834, pp. 194–201, 2023.
https://doi.org/10.1007/978-3-031-35998-9_27

The goal of FAIE is to provide an effective learning experience through the usage of AI, by automating the content generation process, educators can focus on more important tasks. The system is designed to test the student's understanding and critical thinking. This research demonstrates the potential for AI to transform the learning experience and highlights the importance of continued innovation in the field of education technology.

2 Literature Review

2.1 Intelligent Tutoring Systems

ITS are computer systems that are designed to provide educational support to their students, aimed at delivering educational content, these systems make use of various evaluation methods. The goal of an ITS is to create a personalized and engaging learning experience for students by providing them with customized instruction and feedback [2].

ITS monitor their student's progress and adjust their content delivery accordingly by making use of AI techniques, an example of this would be the ITS analyzing the learning style of a student to identify their strengths and weaknesses within a topic and then adjust the difficulty of the material presented to them such that it matches their ability. Furthermore, ITSs provide immediate feedback to the student and help them identify where they need to focus more [1,2].

This personalization and adaptability are the key features of ITSs as these lead to increased engagement, motivation, and better learning outcomes. Furthermore, they provide data on student performance, which educators can use to better assist the student.

Overall, ITSs offer a promising solution to the challenges of traditional classroom instruction by providing students with a more personalized and engaging learning experience. By leveraging AI and other technologies, ITSs are becoming increasingly sophisticated and effective at delivering educational content and evaluating student performance.

2.2 Natural Language Processing

Natural Language Processing (NLP) is a branch of AI that deals with the interaction between computers and humans through natural language. The main concern of NLP is to develop algorithms and models that can understand, process, and generate human language. This field has been growing throughout recent years with applications in a variety of areas such as sentiment analysis, machine translation, chatbots, and text classification [3].

NLP can be divided into the following two categories:

- Syntactic NLP: This area focuses on the structure of languages, like grammar and syntax. Examples of this include part-of-speech tagging, parsing, and named entity recognition.

- Semantic NLP: This area focuses on the meaning of language. Examples of this include sentiment analysis, summarization, and question-answering.

The main challenge of NLP is the ambiguity and variability of natural language, as it is highly context-dependent. Thus making it difficult for machines to understand the meaning of a text without additional information. To overcome this challenge, NLP models are trained on large datasets of text to learn the patterns and rules of language. The quality and size of the training set play a critical role in the performance of NLP models and how they learn [4].

The main important technique of NLP is word representation which means converting words into a numerical representation that can be then further processed by machine learning algorithms. A popular approach to this is word embeddings which map words to dense vectors of real numbers that capture the word's semantic meaning [5].

Another important aspect of NLP is processing the text, which involves transforming the raw text into a representation that can be further processed by machine learning algorithms. This includes tasks like tokenization, stemming, and lemmatization. Tokenization means breaking down a sentence into its words and phrases while stemming and lemmatization mean reducing words to their root form [6].

NLP models can be considered as either:

- Rule-Based models: These models rely on a set of predefined rules and patterns to process language and while this leads to good performance for certain tasks, these models tend to be unable to generalize new language patterns.
- Statistical models: These models use machine learning to learn from a dataset of text and are more capable of adapting to new language patterns, an example of such a network is the Recurrent Neural Network (RNN)

Recently, there has been a huge increase in interest in deep learning in NLP, with the Transformer architecture being one of the most prominent models in this field. This is due to its state-of-the-art performance on a wide range of NLP tasks.

NLP has a wide range of applications in industry and academia. In industry, NLP is used for sentiment analysis, chatbots, and machine translation. Sentiment analysis is used to automatically determine the sentiment of a piece of text, such as whether it is positive, negative, or neutral. Chatbots are used for customer service, providing information and support to users. Machine translation is used to automatically translate text from one language to another, making it possible for people to communicate across language barriers.

In academia, NLP is used for information retrieval, text classification, and question-answering. Information retrieval involves finding relevant information in a large corpus of text, such as documents or web pages. Text classification involves automatically categorizing text into predefined categories, such as spam or not spam. Question answering involves automatically answering questions based on information.

2.3 Transformers

Transformers are a type of deep learning architecture that has become the dominant method in Natural Language Processing (NLP) tasks. They were introduced in 2017 by Vaswani et al. in the paper "Attention is All You Need", and since then have taken the NLP community by storm due to their effectiveness in a wide range of NLP tasks such as machine translation, text classification, and question answering [7].

Transformers make use of word embeddings to represent the data, which are fed into its architecture where multiple attention layers process the input to produce the output. The attention mechanism allows the model to learn the relationships between the words instead of learning the relationship between them linearly, this is a key difference from RNNs [8].

A primary advantage of transformers is their ability to handle large inputs in parallel, making them efficient when handling large datasets. Furthermore, the model is capable of handling long-term dependencies, making transformers well-suited for tasks that require an understanding of the context [7].

The transformer architecture has been widely adopted in NLP due to its effectiveness and versatility. Pretrained models such as BERT, GPT-2, and T5 have been released by research institutions and companies such as OpenAI and Google, allowing NLP practitioners to fine-tune these models for their specific use cases without the need for extensive training from scratch [9–11].

Despite their advantages, transformers have their limitations. One of these limitations is the memory required to store the model's parameters, apart from this transformers are computationally expensive, making them difficult to deploy in real-time applications. Furthermore, the attention mechanism in transformers can lead to the model learning superficial patterns in the input data, rather than truly understanding the underlying meaning of the text.

Despite these limitations, however, transformers have proven to be significant to the field of NLP and show promise in areas beyond NLP such as computer vision and speech recognition.

2.4 BART

BART, which is a Denoising Autoencoder-based Pre-training for Sequence Generation, is a transformer-based model that has shown great success in various NLP tasks such as text generation, summarization, and question answering. Developed by Lewis et al. in 2020, BART is designed to be a denoising autoencoder, which means that it is trained to reconstruct a sentence from a corrupt version of it. This pre-training step allows the model to learn rich representations of the text that can be fine-tuned for various NLP tasks [12].

One key advantage of BART is its ability to handle both text generation and text modification tasks, making it a versatile tool in NLP. For example, BART can be fine-tuned for summarization by training it to generate a condensed version of a text while preserving its meaning, or for text translation by training it to translate text from one language to another.

As a sequence-to-sequence model, BART takes a sequence of text as input and outputs another sequence of text as the model prediction. BART consists of a series of transformer encoder and decoder blocks with the attention mechanism, allowing the model to weigh the importance of each word in the input when generating the output.

A strength of BART is its resilience in handling noisy text, thus making it suitable for handling real-world input which is often noisy by nature. During the pre-training, the model is trained to reconstruct text from a masked version of the input, allowing it to learn how to handle missing data. This step, known as Masked Language Modelling, has been shown to lead to improved performance in NLP tasks [9,12].

Despite these successes, BART struggles to generate text which is of high quality as it is trained to focus on reconstructing text instead of generating text. Apart from this, like all transformer models, BART requires a large amount of memory and computation, making it difficult to work with.

Despite these limitations, BART has become a widely used tool in NLP and has shown great success in a wide range of NLP tasks. With ongoing research and development, BART will likely continue to play a central role in the advancement of AI in NLP.

3   Methodology

In this section, the approach taken to solve challenges discussed in Sect. 1 is discussed. The proposed solution to these challenges is to automate content generation by designing a process that makes use of multiple machine-learning models that are combined to achieve the aforementioned goal from a given piece of text.

One of the more common forms of assessment is the use of multiple choice quizzes, hence, the content generated by this process is modelled after this format and contains questions with a selection of multiple options that are comprised of the correct answer and a set of distractors meant to confuse the student into choosing the wrong answer.

The given text is analyzed to generate question and answer (QA) pairs, however, as most question generation models require an answer for the question to be generated to be supplied beforehand, a list of answers needs to be generated first, thus a Named Entity Recognition (NER) model is applied to scan the text for any named entities. The NER model is a finetuned XLM-Roberta model that was trained upon the conll2003 dataset to recognise entities from text [13,14].

Once the named entities have been generated, they are then supplied to the Question generation model along with the given text to generate the questions. The question generation model is a T5 model that has been finetuned to generate a question from a given context giving an answer to the question to be generated [15].

Once the question and answer pairs have been determined, the distractors are generated by making use of a distractor generation model, which is a BART model that was fine-tuned using the RACE dataset. The generated distractors are then injected into the QA pairs. Once the distractors have been generated, the student is then presented with a multiple-choice quiz [16] (Fig. 1).

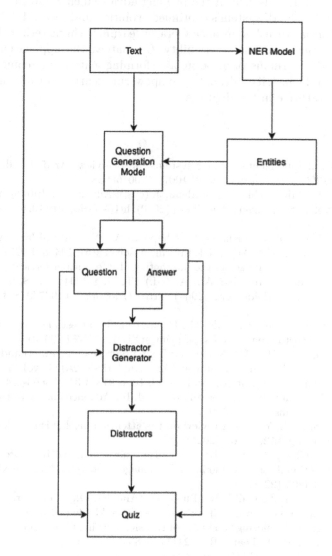

Fig. 1. Proposed Solution Diagram

4   Conclusion

In conclusion, the FAIE system represents a revolutionary approach to utilizing AI technology in education. The system's intricate blueprint designer and AI models are highly innovative solutions that are tailored to address the various challenges faced by educators in the contemporary educational landscape. Their versatility is evident in their potential to be integrated across a range of educational settings and fields. Given the ongoing advancements and investments in AI technology, the FAIE system's continued evolution and successful deployment have the potential to usher in a new era of learning, characterized by greater efficiency, interactivity, and accessibility. Ultimately, the application of AI in education holds enormous promise in transforming learning outcomes and promoting greater inclusivity, ultimately empowering learners of all backgrounds and abilities to thrive in the digital age.

References

1. Nwana, H.S.: Intelligent tutoring systems: an overview. Artif. Intell. Rev. **4**(4), 251–277 (1990). https://doi.org/10.1007/BF00168958
2. Nkambou, R., Mizoguchi, R., Bourdeau, J. (eds.): Advances in Intelligent Tutoring Systems, vol. 308. Springer, Heidelberg (2010). https://doi.org/10.1007/978-3-642-14363-2
3. Nadkarni, P.M., Ohno-Machado, L., Chapman, W.W.: Natural language processing: an introduction. J. Am. Med. Inform. Assoc. **18**(5), 544–551 (2011)
4. Baeza-Yates, R.: Challenges in the interaction of information retrieval and natural language processing. In: Gelbukh, A. (ed.) CICLing 2004. LNCS, vol. 2945, pp. 445–456. Springer, Heidelberg (2004). https://doi.org/10.1007/978-3-540-24630-5_55
5. Mikolov, T., Chen, K., Corrado, G., Dean, J.: Efficient estimation of word representations in vector space. arXiv preprint arXiv:1301.3781 (2013)
6. Anandarajan, M., Hill, C., Nolan, T.: Text preprocessing. In: Anandarajan, M., Hill, C., Nolan, T. (eds.) Practical Text Analytics. AADS, vol. 2, pp. 45–59. Springer, Cham (2019). https://doi.org/10.1007/978-3-319-95663-3_4
7. Vaswani, A., et al.: Attention is all you need. In: Advances in Neural Information Processing Systems, vol. 30 (2017)
8. Niu, Z., Zhong, G., Yu, H.: A review on the attention mechanism of deep learning. Neurocomputing **452**, 48–62 (2021)
9. Devlin, J., Chang, M.W., Lee, K., Toutanova, K.: BERT: pre-training of deep bidirectional transformers for language understanding. arXiv preprint arXiv:1810.04805 (2018)
10. Radford, A., Wu, J., Child, R., Luan, D., Amodei, D., Sutskever, I.: Language models are unsupervised multitask learners. OpenAI Blog **1**(8), 9 (2019)
11. Raffel, C., et al.: Exploring the limits of transfer learning with a unified text-to-text transformer. J. Mach. Learn. Res. **21**(1), 5485–5551 (2020)
12. Lewis, M., et al.: BART: denoising sequence-to-sequence pre-training for natural language generation, translation, and comprehension. arXiv preprint arXiv:1910.13461 (2019)
13. Conneau, A., et al.: Unsupervised cross-lingual representation learning at scale. arXiv preprint arXiv:1911.02116 (2019)
14. Tjong Kim Sang, E., De Meulder, F.: Introduction to the CoNLL-2003 shared task: language-independent named entity recognition. In: Proceedings of the Seventh Conference on Natural Language Learning at HLT-NAACL 2003, pp. 142–147 (2003)

15. Romero, M.: T5 (base) fine-tuned on SQUAD for QG via AP (2021). https://huggingface.co/mrm8488/t5-base-finetuned-question-generation-ap
16. Chung, H.L., Chan, Y.H., Fan, Y.C.: A BERT-based distractor generation scheme with multi-tasking and negative answer training strategies. In: Proceedings of the 2020 Conference on Empirical Methods in Natural Language Processing: Findings, pp. 4390–4400. Association for Computational Linguistics (2020)

E-Newspaper in International Chinese Language Education

Shasha Cai(✉)

School of Film Television and Communication, Xiamen University of Technology, Xiamen, China
550863947@qq.com

Abstract. Newspapers in Education prevails in many countries around the world and has great achievements. The research finds that the use of e-newspaper in international Chinese language education through the following ways has a significant effect. First, it can improve the timeliness of the Chinese Newspaper Reading course; second, it integrates with other courses to expand and enrich the knowledge of Chinese culture with the times; third, it improves the Chinese media literacy of foreign students; fourth, the students' newspaper reading proposals and teachers' comments promote class teacher-student interaction; and fifth, it promotes teachers' exploration of sustainable teaching reforms. Through the integration and use of high-quality e-news and multi-media optimization of learning contents, E-newspaper in Education innovates international Chinese language education, making it multi-dimensional and diversified, closely following China's social and cultural development, improving international students' Chinese language application ability and enhancing their Chinese cultural identity.

Keywords: E-newspaper · Multi-media · Chinese Language Education · International Student

1 Introduction

Newspapers in Education (NIE), which is prevalent in Europe, the United States and Japan, aims to foster a lifelong reading habit in students and their families by bringing newspapers into the classroom. As students improve their reading levels, their media literacy improves, and participating media outlets develop groups of faithfully audiences, resulting in a win-win situation for both education and media outreach. With the advent of the new media era, in which cell phones, tablets and other mobile devices are used as reception tools, the way people read newspapers has changed dramatically, and newspapers have built multi-media channels to suit the needs of their audiences. As the most popular mass communication content nowadays, if e-news can be properly selected and applied to international Chinese language education, it will be a useful supplement for international students to learn Chinese and understand China in an "acceptable way and in an easy-to-understand language" both in and out of class.

C. Stephanidis et al. (Eds.): HCII 2023, CCIS 1834, pp. 202–209, 2023.
https://doi.org/10.1007/978-3-031-35998-9_28

2 Origin and Development of NIE: Long History, Far-Reaching Impact

In the United States, NIE is a systematic, nationwide program that provides teachers with a variety of teaching aids, learning resources, and training opportunities. Information indicates that the history of NIE dates back to the 1890s. Before 1950, educators and newspaper publishers were already aware of the important role that newspapers could play in the school curriculum and had publicly expressed their views on the subject. In the 1950s, systematic research on NIE emerged, and a series of workshops for teachers began. In the 1960s and 1970s, the Newspaper Association of America promoted the further development of NIE by funding academic conferences, workshops, assessments, and survey projects. By 2000 there were 950 daily newspapers in the US that regularly conducted NIE projects [1]. As the Internet became popular and newspapers began to offer online newspapers to students and faculty (e.g., The Wall Street Journal, The Miami Herald), the growth of the online media business compensated for the loss of offline readers [2]. Sweden has been implementing NIE in primary and secondary schools since 1960, with an emphasis on methods of applying it to teaching and learning. Since then, Finland, Norway and Denmark have been influenced by Sweden to carry out NIE one after another, and the four countries hold "NIE Engineering Liaison Conference" every year to deepen exchanges and contacts [3]. The Japanese NIE Committee was established in 1988 by the Japan Press Association following the example of the US and the four Nordic countries, and as of 2015, more than 500 elementary and middle schools throughout Japan had introduced NIE for teaching purposes [4]. In 2004, the French Ministry of Culture and Communication offered a free one-month the daily newspaper subscription for students in their final year of secondary school and a free subscription for young people aged 18. In 2005, four more innovative programs for national support to promote newspaper reading among young people were approved, including the inclusion of national and local daily newspapers in information centers in 1,000 secondary schools and the creation of a supplement for writing by young people with the help of the Internet and mobile networks [5]. In addition, NIE is widely carried out in countries such as Germany and Singapore.

3 Application of NIE in China's Education: Language and Journalism

Although NIE has not yet developed into a system of long-term cooperation and inter-action between newspapers and schools in China, it has been used in the curriculum of universities, middle schools and primary schools since the 1980s. At the second International Chinese Language Teaching Seminar in 1987, Chen J.H. of Peking University put forward "Research on the setting and teaching of newspaper reading classes". In recent years, researches show that newspapers are also applied in English and Chinese teaching in primary and secondary schools and have achieved good results.

3.1 The Application of NIE in Language Teaching

Through three years of NIE practice, Jiang Q.L. (2010) found that most students developed a strong interest in reading English newspapers and periodicals, greatly improved their ability to analyze sentences, speed reading and appreciation, and achieved significant results in improving their interest and ability in reading [6]. Liu Y. (2010) tried to use English newspapers as an aid to English reading teaching, and found that the active newspaper reading promoted the teaching, as well as the change of students' reading strategies and reading habits [7]. Jin S.Y. (2015), as a foreigner learning Chinese, likes Chinese newspaper class, because she can understand the way of thinking of Chinese people and develop their language habits. She believes that since the readers of newspapers are mainly Chinese native speakers, which is somewhat difficult, the target of Chinese teaching through newspapers is mainly intermediate and above learners [8].

3.2 The Application of NIE in Journalism Major

The application of NIE in college courses, apart from language majors, is most common in journalism majors. Huang J.Y. (2009) emphasizes that "reading and reviewing newspapers" can help new students to form a strong perceptual accumulation of news and lay the foundation for theoretical learning. After developing the habit of following the news, students' ability to read and review newspapers professionally, their news sensitivity, analytical judgment and expression skills are enhanced. It should be integrated into all courses, especially practical courses, throughout the four years of journalism education [9]. Zhang X.Y. (2014) believes that newspaper covers a wide range of social issues, is a teaching material for life, a powerful bridge connecting school education and social reality, and is helpful to cultivate college students' ability to solve problems. Independent, timely and scientific news commentary is suitable for newspaper textbooks, which can effectively improve students' language application ability in speaking, reading and writing, as well as improve their critical understanding of news [10].

According to the literature review, although there have been many studies on the application of newspaper reading education in China, e-newspapers in education has not yet been mentioned, and there are few studies on its application in international Chinese education. Therefore, on the basis of previous studies, this study clarified the meaning of e-newspapers in education, made suggestions and analysis on the selection of multimedia, and designed practical measures to integrate into the teaching of international Chinese education.

4 E-NIE Definition and Media Selection: Mobile Viewing and Listening, Preferred Authoritative Media

In the multi-media era, the media are rich in content and diversified in forms. E-Newspapers in Education (E-NIE) on the basis of the NIE, the media viewed by the audience has changed from newspapers to graphic, audio and video electronic news presented on mobile phones, tablet computers and other devices. In addition, E-NIE can reduce the expenditure of schools to purchase printed newspapers, break the limitation of funds required by the paper media, lower the threshold and cost, and expand the content sources. Newspapers cultivate young audiences to boost sales, while at E-NIE it shows up as an increase in readership and followers. E-NIE, therefore, is an educational practice that uses mobile audiovisual content on various official or authoritative new media platforms, and through the selection of the content, uses it as a teaching material for education.

In China, the media chosen by E-NIE should be preferred to platforms founded by official media. The official media are authoritative and credible, with high quality content, a firm position in the international public opinion struggle, and the courage to speak out [11]. The new media platform of official media not only has the characteristics of timeliness, large amount of information and various forms of expression, but also becomes the perfect choice for E-NIE because of its rich experience in telling Chinese stories and spreading Chinese voices at home and abroad for nearly 100 years and its faithful and rational writing of news facts. The People's Daily, Guangming Daily, Xinhua News Agency and other provincial and municipal officials have social platform accounts such as Weibo, WeChat and Tik Tok, with informative content, diversified topics and high activity.

WeChat is the most frequently used communication tool by international students in China, so E-NIE with WeChat as the carrier has a good foundation for application and promotion. In our questionnaire on Chinese language learning for 150 international students at Xiamen University of Technology, 68.9% of the respondents said they were willing to use WeChat for Chinese language learning, 29.7% said they could, and 1.4% said they were not. It is clear that most international students welcome the Chinese language learning from WeChat. Through the study of several WeChat public platforms (with August 2022 as the observation time), we found that national media like People's Daily and Xinhua News Agency usually have more than 100,000 readers per news article, and the average daily posting is about 15 articles. Local official newspaper WeChat public platform such as Xiamen Daily, have thousands to tens of thousands of views for each news, with an average of about 15 articles per day. China Daily Bilingual News is basically read by tens of thousands of people for each news, with an average of about 7 articles per day. The English news in it helps learners understand the meaning of the Chinese news and is therefore more suitable for first- and second-year college students to read. Just the above four official newspaper WeChat public platforms have sufficient quantity and high quality news content available for study every day, covering international, domestic and local news, social, financial, cultural and educational, sports news, etc. As a result, students and teachers can easily and comfortably select content related to their respective courses.

The text part of the WeChat public platform news is suitable as reading material, while the video number news can be used for listening practice. Most of the short videos are captioned, so it is advisable to practice them as listening material without looking at the screen first and then watch them when checking the answers and explanations. You can also follow the WeChat public platform of some broadcasting channels, such as "Voice of China", and listen to the live broadcast directly, or click on the corresponding audio in each news article to listen to it. These audios correspond one-to-one with the text in the news and are current, high-quality Chinese listening materials that can also be applied in courses that use the listening and speaking method.

5 E-NIE Applied to International Chinese Teaching: Complementary Courses, Teacher-Student Interaction

Learning in class is the most direct and important way for Chinese learners to acquire knowledge of Chinese and understand Chinese culture. E-NIE enables the learning content to be more closely related to real life, allowing foreign students to fully immerse themselves in Chinese culture, and the cultural understanding in turn helps them learn the language. The integration of E-NIE and classes reflects the combination of science and art of teaching, and the article has the following thoughts on how to make the most of it.

5.1 Difficulties in Implementing an Independent Course

Similar courses have been established in most of the current curriculum systems for teaching Chinese as a foreign language, such as "Chinese News" and "Reading Chinese Newspapers", and many scholars have also conducted research on them. As a course, the latest version of the textbook that can be searched is the "New Edition of Learning Chinese by Reading Newspapers - Reading Chinese Newspapers" (published by Peking University Press in August 2017), which is also six years old now. For foreign students who get news from various sources every day, the content of the textbook lacks timeliness. However, if all or most of the teaching content is based on timely and recent news, it will make the course materials in a constant iteration, and teachers will need to prepare a new lesson every time, and it is difficult to form a system, which is not conducive to the accumulation and repeated polishing of the curriculum. Therefore, the article concludes that if E-NIE is established as an independent course, it will be difficult to implement for a long period of time because of the variable nature of its teaching materials, the excessive amount of preparation work, the difficulty of practicality, and the weakness of continuity.

5.2 Integrating Multiple Courses to Expand the Scope of Application

In other courses, if E-NIE is used, teachers can add several recent news items related to the original course content as supplementary extensions during lesson planning. E-NIE can be combined into many courses such as Chinese Reading, Chinese Listening, Chinese Writing, Overview of Chinese Society, and Intercultural Communication. Timely multimedia news can compensate for the relative obsolescence of the material, and also enhance the interest due to the inclusion of the audio-visual format. E-NIE does not need to take up too much class time, five to fifteen minutes is appropriate. Design a good introduction from the textbook to the e-newspaper, so that the course content is seamlessly integrated and students naturally accept it. This makes the knowledge in books "come alive". Teachers guide students to use what they have learned to understand the content of e-newspaper, so that foreign students can feel the connection between theory and practice, and learn to apply their knowledge. Integrating E-NIE into other courses in appropriate sections and allocating time reasonably can continue the systematic and structured curriculum, but also continuously enrich the curriculum and keep it fresh. In addition, students' media literacy can be improved, and E-NIE can better play its role in improving international students' Chinese language proficiency, expanding their knowledge and enhancing their Chinese cultural identity. Therefore, it is feasible to integrate E-NIE into other courses.

5.3 Teacher-Student Interaction for Thinking and Discernment

E-NIE operation can combine teacher choice with students choice, promote cooperative interaction between teachers and students, enliven the class atmosphere, and develop students' ability to explore-discover-grasp knowledge on their own. The diversity of subjects will make the e-newspaper content richer and more multi-layered, while making the class more democratic and harmonious. The content chosen by the teacher conveys the teacher's intention to teach and can be selected from a combination of student level, class needs and moral guidance. The teacher sends the e-news to the students three days before the class for pre-reading and asks them to give feedback on the words and sentences they need to focus on before the class. Being "prepared" makes the class more efficient. Teachers can also prepare some short and concise e-news as a time-limited reading exercise in class to test students' mastery of the application of knowledge.

Students read the e-news in general outside of class and then in class for proposals. As much as possible, every student is given the opportunity for public expression and full participation in the class. Within the scope of the theme, allowing students to choose their own learning content can mobilize and bring into play students' subjective initiative and enthusiasm, highlight students as the main subjects of learning activities, fully respect their individual choices and expressions, allow teachers to also understand students' interests, and facilitate two-way communication between teachers and students. By reading aloud the e-news of their choice, refining summaries, expanding vocabulary, setting questions, and summarizing by association, students are not only impressed with the content of the readings, but are also able to think deeply about how to choose and the meaning of their choices, exercising their critical thinking skills and comprehensive language skills. During the process, teachers should appropriately comment and guide students to correctly view various types of e-news and recognize their characteristics. E-NIE allows international students to learn the Chinese language while learning to recognize different multi-media, learn to screen and select the most appropriate content from the vast amount of information, and also improve their Chinese media literacy to be able to independently and rationally discern media information, thus transforming it for their own use and acquiring new knowledge.

Both student prep and feedback in instructor's choice and student choice should be assessed as part of the regular grade for the course. Each time there is a corresponding score and announced in time to improve the assessment management of the E-NIE and add appropriate pressure to get students' attention. Teachers summarize their work in a timely manner to identify shortcomings and correct them, and at the same time, they are humble enough to pick up students' unique ideas and learn each other.

5.4   Conduct Multiple Measures to Safeguard

To guarantee the smooth running of E-NIE, the first step is to strengthen the sense of identity and the department is able to provide strong institutional support. If group lesson preparation and resource sharing can be carried out, it can reduce teachers' pressure to prepare lessons and create a good sustainable environment for E-NIE to be carried out in the long term. Secondly, teachers can carry out teaching reforms and seminars on E-NIE, and through feedback collection and research studies, understand the changes in students' abilities after implementation, whether students' frequency of reading e-news has increased, and whether reading habits have been developed, which will make the development of E-NIE more scientific. Third, the combination of E-NIE and Chinese language teaching places higher demands on the quality of teachers as organizers and promoters. In addition to continuous professional growth, teachers' moral quality and media literacy also need to be improved in the long run. Finally, when conducting E-NIE, always be inclusive, accepting and affirming of students' choices of content, so that students can grow in confidence towards enhancing their interest in the class. The integration of E-NIE in international Chinese education allows the curriculum to be in dynamic improvement, and at the same time puts teachers, teaching materials, e-news, and students in an interconnected system, allowing teaching to be scientific, interesting, and communicative in one. At the same time, it broadens students' horizons, improves their quality, develops their habits of active inquiry, cultivates their self-learning and communication skills, makes them more concerned about society, and enhances their sense of social responsibility and civic consciousness.

6   Conclusion

Through the integration and use of quality e-newspaper and multi-media optimization of learning contents, E-NIE innovates international Chinese language education, making it multi-dimensional and diversified, closely following China's social and cultural development, improving international students' Chinese language application and enhancing their Chinese cultural identity. At the same time, insisting on the long-term selection of e-news from official media, cultivating international students' habit of contacting and reading e-news, enhancing their trust and dependence on official media, guiding them to actively pay attention to objective and neutral media and news, and forming correct judgment, which in turn has a positive and significant impact on their Chinese cultural identity.

Funding. This work was supported by 2021 Educational Research Projects for Young and Middle-aged Teachers in Fujian Province, China, "A Study on the Influence of E-NIE on Chinese Cultural Identity of International Students" (Funding Number: JAS21294).

References

1. Tian, F.: The "NIE Project" in the U.S. newspaper industry. Young Journalists **8**, 73–74 (2005)
2. Ye, C.: U.S. NIE in the network era. Media **2**, 70–71 (2007)

3. Xu, P.: Preliminary exploration of Japanese newspaper education project. Shanxi University, Shanxi (2012)
4. Southern Weekend Homepage. http://www.infzm.com/contents/117765?source=124&source_1=117580. Accessed 23 Sept 2022
5. Zhang, Z.R.: The only way to become a true citizen is to read the newspaper. Journalists **12**, 69–71 (2005)
6. Jiang, Q.L.: Analyzing the effective use of NIE in secondary school English teaching. Contemp. Educ. Forum **5**, 100–101 (2010)
7. Liu, Y.: An attempt to assist English reading teaching with English newspapers and magazines. Teach. Manag. **11**, 146–147 (2010)
8. Jin, S.Y.: A study on the teaching model of Chinese newspaper classes for foreigners based on NIE theory. Shandong Normal University, Shandong (2015)
9. Huang, J.Y.: More "reading and commenting on newspapers" in journalism education. News Knowl. **6**, 85–86 (2009)
10. Zhang, X.Y., Gao, G.D.: Development and implementation of NIE in university classes. News Knowl. **11**, 107–109 (2014)
11. Li, D.Q.: Exploration, reform and innovation in the external communication of Chinese official newspapers. Publishing Wide Angle **9**, 21–23 (2021)

The iMagic E-Learning System on University Students' Achievement During the COVID-19 Pandemic: Based on Learner-Centered Instruction

Wei-Ting Chen[1(✉)] and Mengping Tsuei[2]

[1] Office of Research and Development, National Chung Hsing University, Taichung, Taiwan
joycechen@email.nchu.edu.tw
[2] Graduate School of Curriculum and Instructional Communications Technology,
National Taipei University of Education, Taipei, Taiwan
mptsuei@mail.ntue.edu.tw

Abstract. E-learning tools have played an important role during the COVID-19 pandemic. This study introduced the iMagic E-Learning System which was developed based on the theory of learner-centered instruction. The system is equipped with e-learning platform and apps. It provides five modules for planning learner-centered instruction, including team building, teaching material distribution, assignment, online test, and assessment. In this study, we carried out a series of paired t-test of the changes in teachers' use of the system and students' achievement in 25 undergraduate courses over two Fall semesters (2020 and 2021). In Taiwan, Fall semester 2020 was the last semester before the outbreak of the COVID-19 pandemic in Spring 2021; and Fall semester 2021 was the HyFlex semester when the pandemic restrictions were eased. Our results showed that teachers' use of the system increased in Fall semester 2021 as compared to Fall semester 2020. Moreover, there was a significant increase in students' course grades between Fall semester 2020 and Fall semester 2021. Accordingly, we identified a positive trend of an increased use of features in the iMagic E-Learning System and learning outcomes. This may indicate that some teachers started to integrate more e-learning activities into their course designs, which benefit students.

Keywords: E-Learning System · Learner-Centered Instruction · University Students

1 Introduction

Due to the ongoing impact of the COVID-19 pandemic, higher education institutions have had to shift from the traditional face-to-face model of delivering quality education to a flexible, distance-based learning approach [1]. The advancements in technology have made it essential to distribute learning materials to a large number of students at the same time. With the use of online learning platforms, it is now easier to produce and manage content distribution, while also allowing for flexibility in catering to individual learners' needs, abilities, pace, and overall learning goals.

© The Author(s), under exclusive license to Springer Nature Switzerland AG 2023
C. Stephanidis et al. (Eds.): HCII 2023, CCIS 1834, pp. 210–215, 2023.
https://doi.org/10.1007/978-3-031-35998-9_29

The learning management system (LMS) is a platform that has been created to help administer online teaching and learning processes. This includes tasks such as creating and managing curricula, organizing and delivering training materials, implementing assessment tools, facilitating interactive activities among users, and generating reports on learners' progress and activities [2]. LMS can be a valuable tool for improving the quality of education and learning outcomes.

As a result of the shift to online learning, teachers are now required to adopt new pedagogical strategies [3]. Various suggestions have been proposed to help teachers in developing these new approaches [4]. [5] indicated that LMS is widely used to focus on the delivery of learning materials rather than the creation and development of interactive practices. Research on integrating pedagogical strategies into the e-learning platform is also limited. In the current study, a learner-centered LMS: the iMagic e-learning system, was presented. Moreover, the relationship between the use of the system and educational effectiveness was explored.

2 E-Learning Platform

E-learning platforms enable teachers to carry out online instructions through a managed learning management system (LMS). There are many learning management systems such as Blackboard, Moodle, Google Classroom, Canvas LMS, Edmodo. According to [6], an LMS usually comprises of four main components. The content management system assists teachers in organizing digital teaching materials, including text documents, multimedia files, and hyperlinks. The students' account management system comprises a database that keeps track of students' profiles, including their username, password, email, and learning logs. The communication system includes various tools for teachers and students, such as chat rooms, personal messaging, and discussion forums. Lastly, the evaluation system comprises various measurement tools like quizzes, assignments, and grade books. Previous study revealed that most of LMSs included similar features that allow the delivery and management of different courses [7]. However, [8] indicated a lack of communication support for LMS, which leads to using social networks outside the LMS.

LMS functions and tools help and enrich the learning environment. Previous study indicated that many educators recognize the advantages of LMS and finds the possibility of it in improving students' learning experiences [9]. Research by [10] suggested that LMS platforms should be more adaptive and customized to support instructors with limited technical skills.

Therefore, this study aims to propose the iMagic e-learning system as innovative platform for teachers to use various instructional strategies.

3   iMagic E-Learning System

The iMagic e-learning system includes five modules for teachers to plan learner-centered instruction, including team building, teaching material distribution, assignment, online test, and assessment (see Fig. 1). In the team building module, teachers can assign teaching materials to groups and individual students either intentionally or randomly. The teaching material can be linked with the Google Drive. In the assignment module, teachers can also deliver assignments to groups or individual students. In the assessment module, teachers can adopt self-assessment, within-group and between-group peer assessment or teacher assessment for classroom activities.

The five modules can be combined in various ways to form different learner-centered instructional strategies. To facilitate the implementation of commonly used learner-centered instructional strategies among teachers, the system provides teachers with six templates, including project-based learning, group investigation, jigsaw cooperative learning, flip instruction, problem-based learning, and student teams-achievement divisions. Teachers can choose between different instructional strategy templates that best fit the characteristics of their curriculum activities.

To facilitate student-teacher interactions, the system provides five interactive teaching tools: Interactive Response System (IRS), assignment gallery, whiteboard, discussion board, and student random drawing. Moreover, the system provides game-based learning to enhance students' motivation in formative assessment. Students use mobile tablets to participate in these interactive activities.

Teachers can conduct online tests using IRS (see Fig. 2). Students can respond to questions using mobile devices. The system records and analyzes the learning process in real time. Thus, teachers can immediately monitor students' learning and reinforce their concentration and learning outcomes.

In the assignment gallery, students can view, comment on, and provide feedback to each other's work and vote for their favorite ones.

The game-based learning tool provides the Tic Tac Toe game. Teachers pick questions from the item bank. Students then try to line up 3 Os (correct answers) in a 3x3 grid. Students who succeed in placing three of their marks in a horizontal, vertical, or diagonal row win the game.

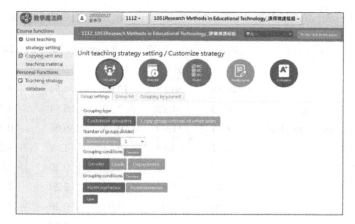

Fig. 1. The screenshot of the iMagic E-Learning System.

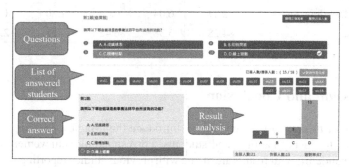

Fig. 2. The iMagic-IRS system.

4   Results

In this study, we focused on teachers' use of nine different features of the iMagic e-learning system that were available for them: course announcement, teaching material distribution, assignment, assessment, IRS, online test, assignment gallery, discussion board, and student random drawing. Paired t-tests were carried out using course-specific data collected from the system database. Only courses delivered over two consecutive Fall semesters (2020 and 2021) and with teachers' frequency of feature use above 2 times a semester were included in this study. In sum, 25 undergraduate courses were identified.

As shown in Table 1, teachers' overall use of the system increased during the COVID-19 pandemic ($M = 48.16$, $M = 75.66$). However, the difference was nonsignificant. Moreover, "teaching material distribution" ($M = 28.94$, $M = 29.77$), "discussion board" ($M = 9.47$, $M = 30.04$), and "course announcement" ($M = 2.90$, $M = 7.30$) were used most frequently, while "assessment" ($M = 0.00$, $M = 0.04$), "online test" ($M = 0.00$, $M = 0.04$), and "assignment gallery" ($M = 0.62$, $M = 1.08$) were used least frequently by teachers. Finally, we observed that during the COVID-19 pandemic, students' course grades increased significantly ($t = -2.18$, $p < .05$).

Table 1. Results of paired *t*-test on teachers' use of the system and students' achievement.

Feature	Fall semester 2020		Fall semester 2021		*t*(24)
	M	*SD*	*M*	*SD*	
Overall	48.16	50.12	75.66	94.54	−1.68
Course announcement	2.90	4.22	7.30	6.84	−4.11***
Teaching material distribution	28.94	31.90	29.77	36.68	−0.17
Assignment	2.57	3.43	6.41	8.09	−3.27**
Assessment	0.00	0.00	0.04	0.20	−1.00
IRS	1.40	3.04	0.53	2.20	2.05
Online test	0.00	0.00	0.04	0.20	−1.00
Assignment gallery	0.62	2.04	1.08	4.17	−0.95
Discussion board	9.47	24.99	30.04	81.74	−1.29
Student random drawing	2.27	6.04	0.45	1.80	1.45
Course grade	84.28	5.38	86.42	4.68	−2.18*

* $p < .05$. ** $p < .01$. *** $p < .001$.

5 Discussion and Conclusion

The purpose of this study was twofold: to introduce the iMagic e-learning system and to investigate teachers' use of it and students' corresponding achievement during the COVID-19 pandemic. Our results are in line with previous studies reporting increased use of e-learning platforms and improved achievement among students who have participated in e-learning platforms in higher educational institutions during the COVID-19 pandemic [1, 11]. Moreover, we found that the system was used more frequently for information (i.e., course announcement), content management (i.e., teaching material distribution), and communication (i.e., discussion board) purposes and less frequently for evaluation purposes (i.e., assessment, online test, and assignment gallery). Previous studies argued that teachers' and students' perceptions of e-learning platforms directly influence the actual use of e-learning platforms [11, 12]. Future studies are recommended to explore factors that influence teachers' and students' use of different features of the system in order to improve its application.

References

1. Sobaih, A.E.E., Hasanein, A.M., Abu Elnasr, A.E.: Responses to COVID-19 in higher education: social media usage for sustaining formal academic communication in developing countries. Sustainability **12**(16), 6520, 1–18 (2020)
2. Srichanyachon, N.: EFL learners' perceptions of using LMS. Turk. Online J. Educ. Technol. **13**(4), 30–35 (2014)
3. Vandeyar, T.: The academic turn: social media in higher education. Educ. Inf. Technol. **25**(6), 5617–5635 (2020). https://doi.org/10.1007/s10639-020-10240-1

4. Marek, M.W., Chew, C.S., Wu, W.-C.V.: Teacher experiences in converting classes to distance learning in the COVID-19 pandemic. Int. J. Distance Educ. Technol. **19**(1), 89–109 (2021)
5. Christie, M., Jurado, R.G.: Barriers to innovation in online pedagogy. Eur. J. Eng. Educ. **34**(3), 273–279 (2009)
6. Department of E-Learning and Educational Technology, RMUTI: LMS user guide. https://lms.rmuti.ac.th/LMS-UserGuide.pdf. Accessed 17 Mar 2023
7. Aldiab, A., Chowdhury, H., Kootsookos, A., Alam, F., Allhibi, H.: Utilization of learning management systems (LMSs) in higher education system: a case review for Saudi Arabia. Energy Procedia **160**, 731–737 (2019)
8. Kraleva, R., Sabani, M., Kralev, V.: An analysis of some learning management systems. Int. J. Adv. Sci. Eng. Inf. Technol. **9**(4), 1190–1198 (2019)
9. O'Leary, R.: Virtual learning environments. https://www.alt.ac.uk/sites/default/files/assets_editor_uploads/documents/eln002.pdf. Accessed 17 Mar 2023
10. Almarashdeh, A., Sahari, N., Zin, N., Alsmadi, M.: The success of learning management system among distance learners in Malaysian universities. J. Theor. Appl. Inf. Technol. **21**(2), 80–91 (2010)
11. Alameri, J., Masadeh, R., Hamadallah, E., Ismail, H.B., Fakhouri, H.N.: Students' perceptions of E-learning platforms (Moodle, Microsoft Teams and Zoom platforms) in the University of Jordan Education and its relation to self-study and academic achievement during COVID-19 pandemic. Adv. Res. Stud. J. **11**(5), 21–33 (2020)
12. Mahdizadeh, H., Biemans, H., Mulder, M.: Determining factors of the use of e-learning environments by university teachers. Comput. Educ. **51**(1), 142–154 (2008)

Effect of Online Synchronous Peer-Tutoring Writing on the Writing Performance and Attitude of Children

Wei-Ting Chen[1] and Mengping Tsuei[2]([✉])

[1] Office of Research and Development, National Chung Hsing University, Taichung, Taiwan
joycechen@email.nchu.edu.tw
[2] Graduate School of Curriculum and Instructional Communications Technology,
National Taipei University of Education, Taipei, Taiwan
mptsuei@mail.ntue.edu.tw

Abstract. Writing serves as the primary means by which students demonstrate their knowledge in all academic areas. The purpose of this study was to develop the mobile peer-tutoring writing system (iPTW) for elementary students. Twenty-six and 24 sixth-grade students participated in the experimental and control groups, respectively. The study results indicated that students in the experimental group outperformed the control group in sentence expression and basic techniques. Students in both groups had positive attitude toward the iPTW. Boys in the experimental group had significantly more positive attitude than girls toward writing preferences, peer tutoring, and system preferences and usability. This study supports the use of the online synchronous peer-tutoring writing model with elementary students.

Keywords: Peer Tutoring · Synchronous Peer-Tutoring System · Writing Instruction · Elementary Education

1 Introduction

Writing is not only a basic skill in all subjects, but also an important job skill [1]. [2] found evidence for the impact of students' writing performance on their academic achievement becoming more influential as they progress into higher grades. Students who do not develop strong writing skills may experience lower grades, particularly in courses where written assessments such as tests and reports are the primary ways of evaluating progress [3].

Traditional writing instruction is teacher-centered and focuses less on writing processes (planning and revising) [4]. Collaborative writing can encourage equal participation during writing and could better assist students with the writing process. In addition, the feedback provided during collaborative writing can promote mutual learning, self-revisions, and subsequently writing skills [5]. Some academic writing instructors have implemented collaborative writing to help students compose better essays [6]. However, there are some issues with collaborative writing. The research [7] found that disagreements among group members were common in collaborative writing. Moreover, students with low writing proficiency were less engaged in discussions. While collaborative writing might hold promise for a more thoughtful writing process, empirical findings suggest that it is important to provide scaffolding instruction to younger and less proficient students [8].

This study applied a reciprocal peer tutoring (RPT) writing model: the PT-ORDER model. The RPT is designed to program mutual assistance by combining peer management procedures and a supportive structure framework through all stages of the learning process [9]. In recent years, peer tutoring has been increasingly influenced by the integration of information technology in various forms. For example, [10] applied the ICQ software to second language writers. The study [11] developed the mobile peer-tutoring writing system (iPTW) for elementary students. However, studies examining the effect of online synchronous systems on children's writing remain limited. This study aimed to investigate the effect of the iPTW on elementary students' writing performance and attitude.

2 Related Works

The study [6] examined the effect of collaborative writing on 62 sophomore students using a quasi-experimental design and found that the number of words written collaboratively in the posttest was significantly higher than that in the pretest. This indicates that collaborative writing had great effects on students' writing fluency in both collaborative and individual writing essays. Furthermore, students expressed positive attitudes toward collaborative writing.

The study by [10] compared the interactional dynamics of face-to-face and online peer-tutoring writing in a university writing center. The results revealed significant differences in the patterns of tutor-client interaction between face-to-face and online tutoring sessions. In face-to-face tutoring, tutors did most of the talking as well as deciding what was to be talked about, whereas in online tutoring, clients were more proactive about setting the agenda and tutors responded more to client ideas. This suggests that face-to-face interactions were more hierarchal and less egalitarian than were online interactions. Moreover, textual issues such as grammar, vocabulary, and style were discussed more in face-to-face tutoring, whereas global issues such as content and process were discussed more in online tutoring.

Previous study [12] implemented a collaborative writing system named Paired Writing with 28 10–11-year-old students. The results of individual writing quality indicated that all groups reported significant improvements in writing. Furthermore, students who wrote in pairs showed greater pre-post gains in writing scores and had more positive self-esteem as writers than those who wrote alone.

In sum, most research on peer-tutoring writing showed positive results for university students. Very little research has been carried out on children's experiences of online synchronous peer-tutoring writing.

3 Method

3.1 The Mobile Peer-Tutoring Writing System (iPTW)

The iPTW featured a multiuser frontend interface designed using HTML5 and a server environment based on a Smartfox server. Teachers of each class could manually divide students into a heterogenous group of 2–4 students. In this study, students were grouped in pairs for experimental teaching through peer tutoring. Teachers could set the writing topics. When students logged into the system, the topic was displayed at the top of the page. The student logged into the system together with their partner on a 10-in tablet. After the student logged in, they could view the writing topic and collaboratively write with their partner.

Figure 1 shows the screenshot of the iPTW. After the student logged into the system, they could see their partner's name and login status. The collaborative writing area was on the left side of the interface and was synchronous. The student could engage in collaborative writing with their partner by discussing the order of sentences and writing structure. Sentences in white were written by the student and could be revised, deleted, and rearranged, whereas sentences in grey were written by the partner.

The iPTW consisted of three peer writing tools: (a) Word Bank: The student could select the vocabulary suggested by the teacher directly, and the selected vocabulary would then be filled in automatically. This encouraged the student to expand their vocabulary. (b) Peer Instruction Tool: When the student clicked the menu below the sentence in which their partner made corrections, the instructions provided by the partner appeared. When the student followed the instructions, their partner was notified. (3) Peer-Tutoring Messaging Tool: Buttons that read "Please help me fix the sentence" and "I want to fix the sentence" could be pressed by the student to facilitate collaborative writing. The system allowed the student's partner to make modifications once the student agreed to allow their sentence be revised.

Fig. 1. Screenshot of the iPTW: (1) writing topic; (2) collaborative writing area; (3) sentence correction; (4) pair grouping; (5) word bank; (6) peer instruction tool; (7) peer-tutoring messaging tool.

3.2 The PT-ORDER Model

The PT-ORDER model was designed by the researchers and teachers participated in the study. In the O (organizing) stage, students discussed the structure of their writing and created a draft. The students in the same group then wrote individually. In the R (writing) stage, students engaged in collaborative writing with their partner. If students encountered words that they did not know how to write or words that they could not think of, they could ask their partner online or face-to-face for assistance and a demonstration. Students in the experimental group could send messages to their partner by using the peer instruction tool in the iPTW. Students in the control group, however, discussed their writing face-to-face. In the D (drafting) stage, students discussed the sentences to be revised in their drafts. In the E (evaluation) and R (revising) stages, students revised the sentences. During revisions, students could add descriptors (e.g., adjectives describing people and things or descriptions of events, locations, and moods) or insert appropriate phrases and sentences from the word bank to complete their final draft.

3.3 Participants

Two classes of sixth-grade students from an elementary school in Taipei, Taiwan participated in the study. The experimental group consisted of 26 students (14 boys, 12 girls) and the control group consisted of 24 students (12 boys, 12 girls). Students in the experimental group all had experience using tablets. However, students in both groups had no experience in peer-tutoring writing or collaborative writing.

3.4 Procedure

Students in both groups were trained on the peer-tutoring writing activity before the experiment. Students in the experimental group were trained online to familiarize them with operating the system. Students in the control group were trained face-to-face.

3.5 Instruments

Writing Performance Scale. A writing performance scale was developed based on [13]. The scale encompassed four dimensions: sentence expression, content, structure, and basic techniques. Each dimension was divided into two subdimensions, and each subdimension was scored on a 0–5-point scale. The grading scale has a total score of 40 points. Before the experiment, two teachers with a tenure of over 15 years were invited to conduct a pretest writing activity individually, and the inter-rater reliability was .92.

Writing Attitude Questionnaire. This study adopted [14] writing attitude questionnaire. It was composed of 23 items. Twenty questionnaire items were categorized into four dimensions: writing motivation, self-efficacy, writing preferences, and attitude toward peer-tutoring writing. Students in both groups completed the questionnaire. Students in the experimental group were asked to answer three more questions about their thoughts on system preferences and usability. The overall Cronbach's α reliability was .89.

4 Results

4.1 Students' Writing Performance

This study implemented three peer-tutoring writing activities: "If I Were to Teach a Class," "Rainy Scenes in the Four Seasons," and "Fun Field Trip Stories." The mean of the scores graded by the two expert teachers is presented in Table 1. Repeated measures analysis of variance was conducted to analyze the differences in the total scores and the scores for each dimension between the two groups. The results are displayed in Table 2. The results revealed that after the peer-tutoring writing activities, students in both the experimental and control groups improved their writing scores regardless of whether they used the writing master system. However, the difference was nonsignificant. Regarding their writing performance, the experimental group had higher performance than the control group in sentence expression and basic techniques ($F = 4.19, p < .05$; $F = 59.37, p < .001$). The writing length (i.e., the total word count) of students in the experimental group was significantly shorter than that of students in the control group ($F = 21.16, p < .001$). However, the length of sentences of students in the experimental group was significantly longer than that of students in the control group ($F = 11.84, p < .01$).

Table 1. Descriptive statistics of students' writing performance.

Dimension	Experimental group ($N = 26$)			Control group ($N = 24$)		
	$M1(SD)$	$M2(SD)$	$M3(SD)$	$M1(SD)$	$M2(SD)$	$M3(SD)$
Overall	29.62 (5.24)	31.23 (4.60)	33.54 (5.14)	29.13 (2.95)	30.58 (3.05)	32.67 (4.05)
Sentence expression	7.38 (1.30)	7.31 (1.72)	7.92 (1.80)	6.17 (0.72)	6.67 (0.76)	7.83 (1.26)
Content	6.08 (1.81)	6.85 (1.83)	8.31 (1.75)	7.08 (0.88)	7.58 (1.28)	8.42 (1.38)
Structure	7.54 (1.86)	8.38 (1.42)	8.62 (1.76)	8.04 (1.43)	8.58 (1.59)	8.75 (1.55)
Basic techniques	8.62 (0.64)	8.69 (0.62)	8.69 (0.48)	7.67 (0.87)	7.75 (0.44)	7.67 (0.49)
Total word count	491.54 (160.57)	514.23 (187.19)	597.46 (312.11)	677.17 (85.03)	730.17 (109.79)	805.83 (147.74)
Sentence length	10.71 (1.21)	9.59 (1.16)	10.38 (0.77)	8.36 (1.45)	9.01 (14.79)	9.84 (1.70)

Table 2. Results of repeated measures analysis of variance on students' writing performance.

Dimension	Experimental group (N = 26)		Control group (N = 24)		F
	M	SD	M	SD	
Overall	33.54	5.14	32.67	4.05	0.35
Sentence expression	7.92	1.80	7.83	1.26	4.19*
Content	8.31	1.75	8.42	1.38	2.63
Structure	8.62	1.76	8.75	1.55	0.44
Basic techniques	8.69	0.48	7.67	0.49	59.37***
Total word count	597.46	312.11	805.83	147.74	21.16***
Sentence length	10.38	0.77	9.84	1.70	11.84**

$^{*}p < .05. ^{**}p < .01. ^{***}p < .001.$

4.2 Students' Attitude Toward Peer-Tutoring Writing

The students in the experimental and control groups were asked to fill out a questionnaire after the peer-tutoring writing activities. The results are shown in Table 3. Because the control group did not use tablets, the fifth dimension was exclusively used to evaluate students in the experimental group. The results of the remaining four dimensions were compared and analyzed using independent samples t-test. Generally, the two groups of students expressed positive attitude toward the peer-tutoring writing activity ($M = 4.03$, $M = 3.88$), particularly toward writing preferences ($M = 4.33, M = 4.11$). No significant differences were present in the overall attitude of the two groups. Nevertheless, the experimental group expressed significantly positive attitude toward peer tutoring than the control group ($t = 2.09, p < .05$).

The attitude of boys and girls was explored using a nonparametric Mann–Whitney U test, and the results are presented in Table 4. No significant differences were observed in the overall attitude toward peer-tutoring writing between boys and girls in the experimental group. However, boys had significantly more positive attitude toward writing preferences, peer tutoring, and system preferences and usability compared with girls ($z = -2.97, p < .01, z = -1.98, p < .05, z = -2.79, p < .01$). Regarding the control group, no significant differences were observed in the overall attitude toward peer-tutoring writing between boys and girls. Nonetheless, girls had a significantly more positive attitude toward writing preferences than boys ($z = -2.19, p < .05$).

Table 3. Results of independent samples t-test on the Writing Attitude Questionnaire ($N = 49$).

Dimension	Experimental group		Control group		t
	M	SD	M	SD	
Overall	4.03	0.59	3.88	0.67	0.41
Writing motivation	3.67	0.75	3.77	0.83	−0.43
Self-efficacy	3.81	0.85	3.75	0.73	0.27
Writing preferences	4.33	0.71	4.11	0.87	0.96
Peer tutoring	4.33	0.76	3.91	0.61	2.09*
System preferences and usability	4.04	0.67	–	–	–

$^*p < .05.$

Table 4. Results of Mann–Whitney U test on students' attitude toward peer-tutoring writing.

Dimension	Experimental group ($N = 25$)			Control group ($N = 24$)		
	Boy	Girl	Mann–Whitney U	Boy	Girl	Mann–Whitney U
	M (SD)	M (SD)	(z)	M (SD)	M (SD)	(z)
Overall	4.23 (0.35)	3.84 (0.69)	44.00 (−1.35)	3.76 (0.70)	4.01 (0.66)	57.00 (−0.87)
Writing motivation	3.64 (0.75)	3.69 (0.81)	74.00 (−0.22)	3.72 (0.81)	3.81 (0.87)	69.50 (−0.15)
Self-efficacy	3.73 (0.79)	3.90 (0.94)	61.50 (−0.61)	3.77 (0.73)	3.73 (0.77)	67.50 (−0.26)
Writing preferences	4.77 (0.32)	3.86 (0.73)	25.00 (−2.97)**	3.77 (0.78)	4.46 (0.84)	35.00 (−2.19)*
Peer tutoring	4.67 (0.40)	3.92 (0.90)	38.00 (−1.98)*	3.79 (0.74)	4.02 (0.43)	57.50 (−0.85)
System preferences and usability	4.38 (0.52)	3.67 (0.63)	27.50 (-2.79)**	–	–	–

$^*p < .05. ^{**}p < .01.$

5   Discussion and Conclusion

In the present study, peer-tutoring writing activities were implemented in elementary school classes. The results revealed that the iPTW improved students' writing performance. Although no significant differences in the total writing scores were observed between students in the experimental and control groups, the writing scores of both groups improved. Thus, peer tutoring facilitated the learning of writing. Moreover, online peer tutoring improved the sentence expression and basic techniques of students in the experimental group significantly more than the control group, which was consistent with the results of [6, 11, 12]. When writing on tablets, students organized their thoughts before writing. Therefore, their writing was simple but could accurately express concepts without the use of redundant words. Additionally, through peer instruction, students used more vocabulary in their sentences. Therefore, the sentences were longer and higher quality than those of the control group. Concerning writing attitude, students had positive attitude toward the iPTW. Students in both groups were positive about the performance of their peers. In the experimental group, boys had significantly more positive attitude toward writing preferences, peer tutoring, and system preferences and usability than girls, and found that peer tutoring improved their writing. Girls in the control group expressed significantly positive attitude toward writing preferences than boys. These results were consistent with those of literature on the effect of face-to-face peer tutoring on improving students' writing attitude [15, 16]. Boys were fonder and more familiar with tablets and consequently were more engaged when using the iPTW, whereas girls focused more on revising their sentences.

This study investigated students' writing performance and attitude toward the iPTW. The system featured a peer instruction tool and word bank to facilitate online peer writing activities. Future studies are recommended to build upon the system and design more interactive tools or functions that promote writing skills. Moreover, future studies should discuss the effects of different iPTW designs on students' writing performance.

Acknowledgments. This work was supported by funding from the Ministry of Science and Technology of Taiwan (MOST109-2511-H-152-006).

References

1. Graham, S., Dolores, P.: A meta-analysis of writing instruction for adolescent students. J. Educ. Psychol. **99**(3), 445–476 (2007)
2. Montague, M., Graves, A.: Improving students' story writing. Teach. Except. Child. **25**(4), 36–37 (1993)
3. Graham, S.: Writing. In: Alexander, P.A., Winne, P.H. (eds.) Handbook of Educational Psychology, pp. 457–477. Erlbaum, Mahwah (2006)
4. Cutler, L., Graham, S.: Primary grade writing instruction: a national survey. J. Educ. Psychol. **100**(4), 907–919 (2008)
5. Pham, V.P.H., Nguyen, N.H.V.: Blogging for collaborative learning in the writing classroom: a case study. Int. J. Cyber Behav. Psychol. Learn. **10**(3), 1–11 (2020)
6. Pham, V.P.H.: The effects of collaborative writing on students' writing fluency: an efficient framework for collaborative writing. SAGE Open **11**(1), 1–11 (2021)
7. Ansarimoghaddam, S., Tan, B.H., Yong, M.F.: Collaboratively composing an argumentative essay: wiki versus face-to-face interactions. GEMA Online J. Lang. Stud. **17**(2), 33–53 (2017)
8. Topping, K., Nixon, J., Sutherland, J., Yarrow, F.: Paired writing: a framework for effective collaboration. Reading **34**(2), 79–89 (2000)
9. Wolter, C.F., Pigott, H.E., Fantuzzo, J.W., Clement, P.W.: Student-administered group-oriented contingencies: the application of self-regulation techniques in the context of a group to increase academic productivity. Techniques **1**(1), 14–22 (1984)

10. Jones, R.H., Garralda, A., Li, D.C.S., Lock, G.: Interactional dynamics in on-line and face-to-face peer-tutoring sessions for second language writers. J. Second Lang. Writ. **15**(1), 1–23 (2006)
11. Tsuei, M., Huang, H.-W.: A mobile synchronous peer-tutoring system for elementary students' learning in Chinese language arts. In: Cheung, S.K.S., Kwok, L.-F., Kubota, K., Lee, L.-K., Tokito, J. (eds.) ICBL 2018. LNCS, vol. 10949, pp. 253–262. Springer, Cham (2018). https://doi.org/10.1007/978-3-319-94505-7_20
12. Yarrow, F., Topping, K.J.: Collaborative writing: the effects of metacognitive prompting and structured peer interaction. Br. J. Educ. Psychol. **71**(2), 261–282 (2001)
13. Zheng, B.-Z., Wang, W.-Q.: The effects of teaching strategy of revision on elementary school students revision performance, revision ability, writing quality, and writing attitude. Educ. Res. Inf. **5**(6), 82–100 (1997)
14. Tsuei, M.: Using synchronous peer tutoring system to promote elementary students' learning in mathematics. Comput. Educ. **58**(4), 1171–1182 (2012)
15. Medcalf, J., Glynn, T., Moore, D.W.: Peer tutoring in writing: a school systems approach. Educ. Psychol. Pract. **20**(2), 157–178 (2004)
16. Paquette, K.R.: Integrating the 6+1 writing traits model with cross-age tutoring: an investigation of elementary students' writing development. Literacy Res. Instr. **48**(1), 28–38 (2008)

Investigation of Chromatic Perception of School Children During HCI in Computer-Supported Collaborative Learning

Niki Choudhury(⊠) and Jyoti Kumar

Indian Institute of Technology Delhi, New Delhi, India
nikichoudhury124@gmail.com, jyoti@design.iitd.ac.in

Abstract. Color is a powerful communication tool that may be used from an early age to convey activity, modify emotion, and even influence psychological responses. Colors are efficient in evoking various emotions and capturing their attention. Color also has an important effect on the cognitive development of young students, and it influences intentions, performance, and emotional processes. Therefore, colors are used as an important medium to aid teaching. In HCI, digital content consists of colored texts, colored images, and other visual elements that serve as a platform for interaction. Previous studies have demonstrated indisputably the association between positive/negative perception and color, but a significant area that has not yet been investigated is how children associate color with emotions in Computer Supported Collaborative Learning (CSCL). In order to get an understanding of how children perceive color in the context of emotions in a collaborative setting, the researchers in this study invited students to use an online platform to a pool of 60 students from different schools that allowed them to create color and emotion-based digital content. The results showed that students used a monochromatic color scheme primarily to establish their emotions.

Keywords: Chromatic perception · computer supported collaborative learning · Human computer Interaction

1 Introduction

Color is a prominent aspect of the child's environment. Further, children are aware of color as a distinct visual element. Color contrast aids in visual recognition between foreground and background. As today HCI-based systems are available for both designing and educating, there is an opportunity y to understand how students can be taught color using CSCL. In this research students of grade 9 were taught color and its meaning in a CSCL environment and they were asked to express their emotions using colors. Observations dominantly revealed the choice of a monochromatic scheme to express emotions. Moreover, in art and design, warm and cool colors are often used strategically to create contrast, mood, and visual interest [1]. Color theories are often used in art and design to create harmonious color palettes and convey moods and emotions. Some of the most well-known color theories include the color wheel theory [2, 3]. This theory

© The Author(s), under exclusive license to Springer Nature Switzerland AG 2023
C. Stephanidis et al. (Eds.): HCII 2023, CCIS 1834, pp. 225–230, 2023.
https://doi.org/10.1007/978-3-031-35998-9_31

organizes colors into a wheel, with primary colors (red, blue, and yellow) forming the center and secondary colors (green, orange, and purple) forming the spokes. Colors that are located next to each other on the wheel (analogous colors) are believed to be harmonious and create a sense of unity, while colors that are opposite each other on the wheel (complementary colors) are thought to be contrasting and develop a sense of tension. Psychological theories of color suggest that different colors have different psychological effects on the viewer and that some of these effects are universal across cultures [4]. The Munsell color system uses a three-dimensional color space to describe colors based on their hue, value, and chroma [5, 6]. Several color schemes are used in art and design to create harmonious color combinations based on the relationship between individual colors. These color schemes are often derived from color theory and are used to create visual interest, convey a particular mood or emotion, or reinforce brand identity. Some of the most common color schemes [7] include the Monochromatic color scheme. The monochromatic scheme uses different shades, tints, and tones of a single color. This creates a harmonious look that is easy on the eyes. An analogous color scheme uses colors that are next to each other on the color wheel, such as blue, blue-green, and green. This creates a sense of unity and coherence in the design. A complementary color scheme uses colors opposite each other on the color wheel, such as red and green or blue and orange. This creates a strong contrast that can be visually striking and energetic. A triadic color scheme uses three colors equidistant from each other on the color wheel, such as red, yellow, and blue. This creates a vibrant and balanced look that is great for designs that need to be attention-grabbing. The tetradic color scheme uses four colors arranged into two complementary pairs. This can create a balanced and varied look, but it can also be challenging to execute effectively. The way colors are perceived in a scheme depends on how they interact with each other. (i) In a monochromatic scheme, the colors are similar and create a harmonious look. (ii) In an analogous scheme, the colors are related and create a sense of unity. (iii) In a complementary scheme, the colors are opposite and create a sense of contrast. (iv) In a triadic scheme, the colors are balanced and create a dynamic look. (v) In a tetradic scheme, the colors can create various effects depending on which pairs are used together [8]. In terms of color schemes, there are several different approaches to creating harmonious and visually appealing combinations of colors. Chromatic Perception [9] is influenced by various factors, including lighting conditions, color contrast, and individual differences in color vision. Color contrast aids in seeing content by combining the contrast ratio between foreground and background. Through the above schemes, colors communicate meanings. There is a dearth of research on how specific color schemes may be selected to communicate specific emotions.

2   Literature Review

2.1   Perception of Colors

Color is a personal experience [10]. It is essential to the visual sense and emotional experience [11]. On the other hand, perception is the subjective conscious experience of the impact of an outside stimulus on a sensory system [12]. Colors on the blue spectrum have been known as cool colors, which include green, blue, and purple. These colors are often described as calm and evoke emotions like grief and indifference [13]. Our experience of color falls into different categories, which have been under discussion in literature since the 19th century [14]. The psychological perception of color in humans is a fascinating and complex subject that has been studied for many years. Research has shown that color can have a significant impact on our mood, emotions, and behavior [15]. Studies have also found that color can influence our cognitive processes, such as memory and attention. Color can also play an important role in child development, as children are particularly sensitive to color and its effects. Children are drawn to bright colors and patterns from a young age, and these visual stimuli can help stimulate their senses and promote cognitive development. Color usage in child art and the interpretation of color have been discussed in many curricula [16]. It has been reported that chromatic sensitivity increases gradually between 3 months and 15 years of age [17]. Children aged 3–4 have a comprehensive collection of intuitive and learned color associations that they activate while drawing and looking at picture book illustrations. With children aged 11–12, color is not the dominant aspect of the visual language anymore [18]. While they work on enriching their collection of realistic, 'adult-like' representations, they concentrate on complex form and color variations.

2.2 Relation Between Color and Emotion:

Color can also have a significant impact on children's emotions and behavior. Colors and emotions are closely linked [19]. Warm colors can evoke different emotions than cool colors similarly bright colors can create different feelings than muted colors. Colors may create different emotions and feelings [20]. The way different colors can affect emotions depends largely on a color's brightness, shade, tint, or tone and whether it's cool or warm-toned.

(i) Happy colors: Yellow, orange, pink, and red are reported to be cheerful [21]. Literature suggests further that brighter and lighter hues are more cheerful [22].
(ii) Sad colors: Colors that are dark and muted. Grey is often used as the quintessential sad color, but dark and muted cool colors like blue, green, or neutrals like brown or beige can also evoke sadness [23].
(iii) Calming colors: Colors like blue and green can make you feel calm. Pastel colors and particularly cool-toned pastels like baby blue, lilac, and mint, have a calming and relaxing effect [24]. Cool colors like green, blue, and purple are calming and soothing but may also express sadness [25].

2.3 Impact of Color in HCI

Color can have a significant impact on children's learning and academic performance. For example, studies have found that presenting information in color can improve reading comprehension, memory retention, and attention span [26, 27]. Additionally, using color-coded systems for note-taking and organization can help children retain information and stay organized. However, it is important to note that individual differences in color perception and preferences can also affect how children respond to different colors. Some children may have a preference for certain colors, while others may find certain colors overwhelming or unappealing. Understanding the ways in which color can influence our perceptions and attitudes can help us create more effective communication materials, promote healthy development in children, and enhance our overall understanding of the role that color plays in our lives.

3   The Methodology

Context and Participants: A total of 60 school students (35 boys and 25 girls) with a mean age of 14.6 years and a standard deviation of 2.3 years were taught the color fundamentals. They were asked to create a book cover using the online software "Canva" tool as a group activity. The students were seated in a group setting arrangement with six students in a group. All students used Canva on HP Chromebook MediaTek Kompanio 500 - (4 GB/64 GB EMMC Storage/Chrome OS) Chromebook (11.6 inches, Black).

Procedure: Students were instructed on the relationship between emotion and color. They were instructed on the fundamental color theory schemes, which were monochromatic, analogous, complementary, triadic, and split-complementary. In the subsequent phase, the class was divided into ten groups of six students each. Each group of six students was tasked with designing a digital book cover. The book cover was expected to express one emotion of their group's choice using any one of the five schemes they had learned A total of 90 min was allotted for the assignment. This was followed by a semi-structured interview. The semi-structured interview with a group together was conducted for 20 min. Each group was asked to share the emotions they selected and the way they tried to depict the emotions. The thought process behind depicting the emotions in the selected composition was probed upon by the interviewees.

4   Analysis and Results

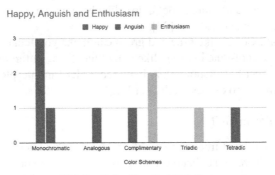

Fig. 1. Color-Emotion Relation

The book cover designs were collected from each group and assessed using color content analysis. Specific sets of color perception were extracted from the book covers, and the data was then A total of 10 book cover designs were collected one from each group of six students in the class of 60 students. Each design was first categorized under one of the five categories namely, monochromatic, analogous, complementary, triadic, and tetradic. As, the students had chosen to depict three emotions namely happiness, anguish, and enthusiasm, the frequency of occurrence of these emotions against the five categories was noted in (Fig. 1). Specific color usage was noticed from the book covers, and the data was then tabulated. The result of the color content was triangulated with the interview data.

It was observed that the monochromatic scheme though being a single color scheme yet was preferred by the majority of the students. The monochromatic scheme was used by students to express emotions through different shades, tones, and tints for depicting emotions. The colors predominantly used by students to depict their emotions using the Canva software in a monochromatic scheme were blue, yellow, and red.

5   Conclusion

In a computer-supported collaborative learning space, it was observed that the students are more comfortable using monochromatic color schemes when they were asked to portray their emotions. It appears that young students find it easy to relate a specific emotion to a specific color more easily than a mix of colors when asked to express their emotions through colors. Further, the three emotions namely happiness, anguish, and enthusiasm seem to be emotions easily available to young minds in the group studied when asked to represent emotions. Also, the use of shade, tint, and tone of single color helped the young students express their emotions.

References

1. Kadry, A.: The role of composition in advertising design. مجلة الفنون والعلوم التطبيقية **4**, 1–20 (2017)
2. Basic color theory. https://www.colormatters.com/color-and-design/basic-color-theory. Accessed 17 Mar 2023
3. Mollica, P.: Color Theory: An Essential Guide to Color-From Basic Principles to Practical Applications. Walter Foster Publishing (2013)
4. O'Connor, Z.: Colour psychology and colour therapy: caveat emptor. Color Res. Appl. **36**, 229–234 (2011)
5. Nickerson, D.: History of the Munsell color system and its scientific application. J. Opt. Soc. Am. **30**, 575 (1940)
6. A brief introduction to the Munsell color system. Smartermarx (2017). https://www.smarter marx.com/t/a-brief-introduction-to-the-munsell-color-system/481. Accessed 17 Mar 2023
7. Dutcher, K.: Understanding color schemes & choosing colors for your website. In: Web Ascender (2022). https://www.webascender.com/blog/understanding-color-schemes-choosing-col ors-for-your-website/. Accessed 17 Mar 2023
8. Benve, R.: Color harmony: color schemes explained. In: FeltMagnet (2012). https://feltma gnet.com/drawing/Harmonious-Painting-Color-Schemes. Accessed 18 Mar 2023
9. Caivano, J.L., López, M.A.: Chromatic identity in global and local markets: analysis of colours in branding. https://ncscolour.co.za/images/natural-colour-system/online-training/jose-luis-caivano/2007coldes.pdf. Accessed 17 Mar 2023

10. Zhang, L., Dempsey, N., Cameron, R.: Flowers – sunshine for the soul! How does floral colour influence preference, feelings of relaxation and positive up-lift? Urban For. Urban Greening **79**, 127795 (2023)

11. Alves, A.L., de Giuli, M.R., Zitkus, E., Paschoarelli, L.C.: Color influence on the use satisfaction of kitchen utensils: an ergonomic and perceptual study. Int. J. Ind. Ergon. **90**, 103314 (2022)

12. Lehar, S.: Gestalt isomorphism and the primacy of subjective conscious experience: a Gestalt Bubble model. Behav. Brain Sci. **26**, 375–408 (2003)

13. Reyna, J.: The importance of visual design and aesthetics in e-learning. Train. Dev. https://doi.org/10.3316/aeipt.202706

14. Wright, A.: The beginner's guide to colour psychology. Kyle Cathie Limited (1995)

15. Valdez, P., Mehrabian, A.: Effects of color on emotions. J. Exp. Psychol. Gen. **123**, 394–409 (1994)

16. Vigus, R.E.: The teaching of color in art education. J. Educ. Res. **48**, 241–253 (1954)

17. Knoblauch, K., Barbur, J.: Development and aging of chromatic sensitivity. Science

18. Zentner, M.R.: Preferences for colours and colour–emotion combinations in early childhood. Dev. Sci. **4**, 389–398 (2001)

19. Steinvall, A.: Colors and emotions in English. In: Anthropology of Color, pp. 347–362 (2007)

20. Zhao, S., Gao, Y., Jiang, X., Yao, H., Chua, T.-S., Sun, X.: Exploring principles-of-art features for image emotion recognition. In: Proceedings of the 22nd ACM International Conference on Multimedia, pp. 47–56. Association for Computing Machinery, New York (2014)

21. Hynes, N.: Colour and meaning in corporate logos: an empirical study. J. Brand Manag. **16**, 545–555 (2009). https://doi.org/10.1057/bm.2008.5

22. Hemphill, M.: A note on adults' color-emotion associations. J. Genet. Psychol. **157**, 275–280 (1996)

23. Jonauskaite, D., Althaus, B., Dael, N., Dan-Glauser, E., Mohr, C.: What color do you feel? Color choices are driven by mood. Color Res. Appl. **44**, 272–284 (2019)

24. Rubert, R., Long, L.D., Hutchinson, M.L.: Creating a healing environment in the ICU. In: Critical Care Nursing: Synergy for Optimal Outcomes, p. 27 (2007)

25. Hanada, M.: Correspondence analysis of color–emotion associations. Color Res. Appl. **43**, 224–237 (2018)

26. Dahlin, K.I.E.: Working memory training and the effect on mathematical achievement in children with attention deficits and special needs. J. Educ. Learn. **2**, 118–133 (2013)

27. Jacobson, L.A., et al.: Working memory influences processing speed and reading fluency in ADHD. Child Neuropsychol. **17**, 209–224 (2011)

Learning Experience of Students:

A Framework for Individual Differences Based on Emotions to Design e-Learning Systems

Jelle de Boer[1]([✉]) [iD] and Jos Tolboom[2] [iD]

[1] Institute of Communication and Media, Hanze University of Applied Sciences, Groningen, The Netherlands
`je.de.boer@pl.hanze.nl`
[2] Mathematics and Computing Curriculum Developer, SLO, Netherlands Institute for Curriculum Development, Groningen, The Netherlands

Abstract. This research aims to build a framework to classify individual differences between students in terms of learning outcomes, based on theories about emotional behavior. Some of these theories incorporate affective and emotional states from students.

We investigate the emotions of a student while learning, so an important aspect in this research is the determination of the emotional state of a student. We suggest using face reading technology (Emotion or VicarVision) to measure the emotion of a learner in only three states (normal flow, bored, and anxious). In this way we can increase classification accuracy for spontaneous affective behavior.

Keywords: Learning Experience · Emotional Behavior · Facial Expressions

1 Introduction

This research aims to build a framework to classify individual differences between students in terms of learning outcomes, based on theories about emotional behavior. There is already a framework for User Experience of Zarour [3], which incorporates Brand Experience (BX), User Needs Experience (NX), Technology Experience (TX), but not Learning Experience (LX).

Some of these theories incorporate affective and emotional states from students. Katuk [4] incorporated the flow model of Csikszentmihalyi [1] into the design of e-learning systems. We aim at incorporating more recent theories about affectional states of students like frustration [5] or confusion [10] into this design. This way, we could understand more about the learning experience and the individual differences between students while learning.

We investigate the emotions of a student while learning, so an important aspect in this research is the determination of the emotional state of a student. According to Cowen, there are 28 different emotions conveyed by naturalistic expression [7]. Ideally, this should be done continuously during the learning process itself, and preferably not

C. Stephanidis et al. (Eds.): HCII 2023, CCIS 1834, pp. 231–237, 2023.
https://doi.org/10.1007/978-3-031-35998-9_32

afterwards through interviews or observations [8]. One method to determine the emotional state during the learning process is the analysis of facial expressions of a student [2].

The research question that we want to answer with this research is: what are the individual differences between student's emotional state and the learning outcome (long-term and the short-term)? Designers can improve e-learning systems from a perspective with an individual and emotional component, using such a framework.

2   Relevant Work

Some of these theories that are described in this section address the affective and emotional states from students. Firstly, we will discuss theories about emotions such as Cowen (based on Ekman). Secondly, we will discuss theories such as Katuk, and D'mello who apply the Flow model.

2.1   Emotions

While there are differing views among experts, most emotion scientists agree that there are at least five core emotions. Research of Ekman [9] shows the strongest evidence to date of seven universal facial expressions of emotions. These seven universal emotions do not exist as a single affective or psychological state. Instead, emotions are comprised of a family of related emotional states which are variations on a shared theme.

2.2   Emotion Categories

According to Cowen, there are 28 different emotions conveyed by naturalistic expression [7]. Guided by new conceptual and quantitative approaches, they explored the taxonomy of emotion recognized in facial-bodily expression.

Participants judged the emotions captured in photographs of facial-bodily expression in terms of emotion categories, appraisals, free response, and ecological validity. They found that facial-bodily expressions can reliably signal at least 28 distinct categories of emotion that occur in everyday life.

Emotion categories, more so than appraisals such as valence and arousal, organize emotion recognition. However, categories of emotion recognized in naturalistic facial and bodily behavior are not discrete but bridged by smooth gradients that correspond to continuous variations in meaning.

Their results support a novel view that emotions occupy a high-dimensional space of categories. They offer an approximation of a taxonomy of facial-bodily expressions, visualized within an online interactive map.

2.3   Flow/Katuk

This paper reports [4] on differences in learning experience from the learner's perspectives when using an adaptive e-learning system, where the learner's knowledge or skill level is used to configure the learning path.

Central to this study is the evaluation of a dynamic content sequencing system (DCSS), with empirical outcomes being interpreted using Csikszentmihalyi's flow theory (i.e., Flow, Boredom, and Anxiety). A total of 80 participants carried out a one-way between-subject study controlled by the type of e-learning system (i.e., the DCSS vs. the non-DCSS).

The results indicated that the lower or medium achievers gained certain benefits from the DCSS, whilst the high achievers in learning performance might suffer from boredom when using the DCSS. These contrasting findings can be suggested as a pragmatic design guideline for developing more engaging computer-based learning systems for unsupervised learning situations (Fig. 1).

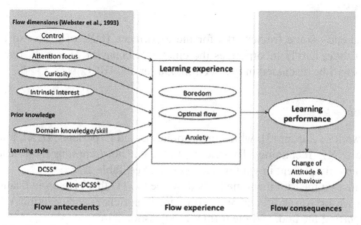

Fig. 1. Katuk: Boredom and anxiety versus (optimal) flow. High achievers might suffer from boredom in learning performance.

2.4 Frustration

Students' cognitive–affective states were studied by Baker [5] using different populations (Philippines, USA), different methods (quantitative field observation, self-report), and different types of learning environments (dialogue tutor, problem-solving game, and problem-solving-based Intelligent Tutoring System).

They found that boredom was very persistent across learning environments and was associated with poorer learning and problem behaviors, such as gaming the system. Frustration was less persistent, less associated with poorer learning. Confusion and engaged concentration were the most common states within all three learning environments. Experiences of delight and surprise were rare.

2.5 Confusion

D'Mello tested if [10] if the prediction of a theoretical model positing that confusion, which accompanies a state of cognitive disequilibrium that is triggered by contradictions, conflicts, anomalies, erroneous information, and other discrepant events, can be beneficial to learning if appropriately induced, regulated, and resolved.

Confusion was experimentally induced via a contradictory information manipulation involving animated agents expressing incorrect and/or contradictory opinions and asking the (human) learners to decide which opinion had more scientific merit.

The results indicated that self-reports of confusion were largely insensitive to the manipulations. However, confusion was manifested by more objective measures that inferred confusion based on learners' responses immediately following contradictions.

The conclusion of this section is that if we want to incorporate emotional behavior into a model that incorporates individual differences of learners with different abilities, we should only use three emotional states: normal flow, bored, and anxious.

3   Frameworks

There are already some frameworks for the experience (UX) of a user of a system, but none of them hardly incorporates the emotional behavior of a user. Two of these frameworks will be discussed in this section, Zarour and HILL.

3.1   Zarour

The framework of Zarour [3], which incorporates Brand Experience (BX), User Needs Experience (NX), Technology Experience (TX), but not Learning Experience (LX). Emotions are only present in via fun and hedonic. See Table 1.

There are two measurement methods described in [1] that give an indication of the emotions of a user. Attrakdiff and 3E (Expressing Experiences and Emotions). The latter is a self-reporting method, and the former is a questionnaire.

3.2   HILL

The HILL framework of Dochy [6] consists of seven elements, which all should be in coherence:

1. Create a sense of emergency
2. Involvement of the student
3. Collaboration and tutoring
4. Hybrid training
5. Action and knowledge sharing
6. Flexibility - Formal and informal training
7. Include evaluation as part of the training

This model is widely used in higher education, but also lacks the aspect of emotional behavior. Furthermore, it is more a model from the perspective of the teacher, and not the student.

Table 1. Suggested categories for UX aspects and their relationship to UX dimensions [1]

UX aspect	Aspect category	Dimension
Branding	Brand	Brand Experience (BX)
Everyday Operations	Brand	Brand Experience (BX)
Marketing	Brand	Brand Experience (BX)
Business Communications	Brand	Brand Experience (BX)
Context of use	Context	Brand Experience (BX)
Spatio-Temporal	Context	Brand Experience (BX)
User Journey	Context	Brand Experience (BX)
Cultural	Context	User Experience (UX)
Emotional	Hedonic	User Experience (UX)
Hedonic	Hedonic	User Experience (UX)
Trustworthiness	Hedonic	User Experience (UX)
Aesthetics	Hedonic	User Experience (UX)
Fun	Hedonic	User Experience (UX)
Privacy	Hedonic	User Experience (UX)
Sensual	Hedonic	User Experience (UX)
Usability	Pragmatic	User Experience (UX)
Functionality	Pragmatic	User Experience (UX)
Usefulness	Pragmatic	User Experience (UX)
Platform Technology	Development Technology	Technology Experience (TX)
Infrastructure	Hardware	Technology Experience (TX)
Service Response time	Operation	Technology Experience (TX)
Visual Attractiveness	UXD	Technology Experience (TX)

3.3 Proposed Model

The conclusion is that most models or frameworks hardly address the emotional aspect over the user in general and the learner.

We could add to the model of Zarour Learning Experience (LX) as the 4th dimension. The aspect category could remain hedonic. However, UX aspect emotional and fun should change. Furthermore, the Attrakdiff questionnaire and the Expressing Experiences and Emotions (3E) methods that are used are not very good.

There is a Learning Experience Questionnaire (LEQ), but this is more about course development.

4 Methodology

4.1 Research Question

The research question that we want to answer with this research is: what are the individual differences between student's emotional state and the learning outcome (long-term and the short-term)?

It has been driven by the above description of theories that use the emotional state of students in the context of learning, with some very interesting consequences for learners with different abilities. A student with a high ability is often confronted with boredom in classes. A student with low ability is often anxious in class which inhibits the learning outcomes. We propose to use face reading technology to overcome these consequences in the use of adaptive learning environments.

4.2 Measures

Dupre [2] has done a performance comparison of eight commercially available automatic classifiers for facial affect recognition. Commercial automatic classifiers for facial affect recognition have attracted considerable attention in recent years. Less is known about the relative performance of these classifiers, when facial expressions are spontaneous rather than posed.

Analyses per type of expression revealed that performance by the two best performing classifiers (Emotion and VicarVision) approximated those of human observers, suggesting high agreement for posed expressions. However, classification accuracy was consistently lower (although above chance level) for spontaneous affective behavior.

We want to detect only three states of a student (normal flow, bored, anxious) using one of those automatic classifiers (Emotion and VicarVision). In this way we can increase classification accuracy for spontaneous affective behavior.

The conclusion is that we propose to use face reading technology to overcome these limitations and replace existing methods to generate knowledge about the emotional state of a student while learning.

5 Conclusion and Discussion

One of the conclusions is that if we want to incorporate emotional behavior into a model that incorporates individual differences of learners with different abilities that success more guaranteed with these three states: normal flow, bored, and anxious. Katuk's [3] research shows some promising results using this approach.

Most models or frameworks hardly address the emotional aspect over the use in general and the learner. We propose to use face reading technology to overcome these limitations and replace the existing methods to generate knowledge about the emotional state of a student while learning.

We could add to the model of Zarour Learning Experience (LX) as the 4th dimension. The aspect category could remain hedonic. However, UX aspect emotional and fun should change. Furthermore, the Attrakdiff questionnaire and the Expressing Experiences and Emotions (3E) methods that are used are not very good.

There is a Learning Experience Questionnaire (LEQ), but this is more about course development.

Student's welfare is at a very low, after or due to Corona. A better understanding of the emotions of a student with this research can also contribute to on overall experience.

Designers can improve e-learning systems from a perspective with an individual and emotional component, using such a framework.

References

1. Nakamura, J., Csikszentmihalyi, M.: The concept of flow. In: Nakamura, J., Csikszentmihalyi, M. (eds.) Flow and the Foundations of Positive Psychology, pp. 239–263. Springer, Dordrecht (2014). https://doi.org/10.1007/978-94-017-9088-8_16

2. Dupre, D., Krumhuber, E.G., Kuster, D., McKeown, G.J.: A performance comparison of eight commercially available automatic classifiers for facial affect recognition. PLoS One **15**, e0231968 (2020). https://doi.org/10.1371/journal.pone.0231968

3. Zarour, M., Alharbi, M.: User experience framework that combines aspects, dimensions, and measurement methods. Cogent Eng. **4**, 1421006 (2017). https://doi.org/10.1080/23311916.2017.1421006

4. Katuk, N., Kim, J., Ryu, H.: Experience beyond knowledge: pragmatic e-learning systems design with learning experience. Comput. Hum. Behav. **29**, 747–758 (2013). https://doi.org/10.1016/j.chb.2012.12.014

5. Baker, R.S.J., D'Mello, S.K., Rodrigo, M.M.T., Graesser, A.C.: Better to be frustrated than bored: the incidence, persistence, and impact of learners' cognitive–affective states during interactions with three different computer-based learning environments. Int. J. Hum. Comput. Stud. **68**, 223–241 (2010). https://doi.org/10.1016/j.ijhcs.2009.12.003

6. Dochy, F., Segers, M.: An Executive Summary of the HILL Model. Routledge (2018)

7. Cowen, A.S., Keltner, D.: What the face displays: mapping 28 emotions conveyed by naturalistic expression. Am. Psychol. **75**, 349–364 (2020). https://doi.org/10.1037/amp0000488

8. da Silva Vieira Coelho, R., Selleri, F., dos Reis, J.C., Pereira, F.E.D., Bonacin, R.: An ontology-based approach to annotating enactive educational media: studies in math learning. In: Zaphiris, P., Ioannou, A. (eds.) HCII 2022. LNCS, vol. 13328, pp. 40–59. Springer, Cham (2022). https://doi.org/10.1007/978-3-031-05657-4_4

9. Ekman, P., Sorenson, E.R., Friesen, W.V.: Pan-cultural elements in facial displays of emotion. Science **164**, 86–88 (1969). https://doi.org/10.1126/science.164.3875.86

10. D'Mello, S., Lehman, B., Pekrun, R., Graesser, A.: Confusion can be beneficial for learning. Learn. Instruct. **29**, 153–170 (2014). https://doi.org/10.1016/j.learninstruc.2012.05.003

Augmented Reality as a Promoter of Visualization for the Learning of Mathematics in Ninth-Year of Basic Education

Carlos Alberto Espinosa-Pinos(✉), Paulina Magally Amaluisa Rendón⬤,
María Giovanna Núñez-Torres⬤, and Juan Quinatoa-Casicana⬤

Posgrado, Facultad de Ciencias de la Educación, Universidad Indoamerica, 180103 Ambato,
Ecuador
{carlosespinosa,paulinaamaluisa,
giovannanunez}@indoamerica.edu.ec

Abstract. This research focused on developing a mobile application in Metaverse augmented reality to improve the learning of notable products, factoring, and linear equations in ninth-grade students of the intercultural bilingual educational unit of the millennium "Pueblo Kisapincha" based on the notional method. The methodology applied was quasi-experimental and longitudinal, where related samples were compared using a diagnostic test versus a subsequent evaluation of knowledge. The sampling technique was by non-probabilistic convenience comprising 25 students and 15 teachers to whom a structured questionnaire was applied to determine the predisposition to work in the classroom with augmented reality, which was validated with Cronbach's alpha statistic ($\alpha = 0.844$). The students' scores improved significantly after participating in both evaluations, with the post-evaluation being the one that showed the highest score according to the Bayesian T-test applied to related samples. A proposal of activities was designed to motivate the study of algebraic expressions; this product was implemented considering the ADDIE instructional model, guiding each movement with its respective resolution process as a form of feedback. The proposal was evaluated by two experts in technology and two experts in education with more than ten years of experience. In conclusion, developing an augmented reality mobile application in Metaverse to improve the learning of introductory algebra proved to be a valuable and effective tool to contribute to student learning. The mobile application provided an interactive and engaging learning experience, so it is recommended to incorporate this mobile application in the curriculum of the Kisapincha educational unit and its possible implementation in other similar educational institutions.

Keywords: ADDIE · Metaverse · Educational Activities · Augmented Reality

1 Introduction

According to the Organization for Economic Cooperation and Development (OECD) [1], in terms of educational innovation, the Measuring Innovation in Education program provides a basis for countries to measure their creative growth in the field of education along with the development of research, a compendium of rules, organization of learning centers and the implementation of ICTs for the achievement of objectives. Mathematical learning in high school students is dull and unattractive; this can be attributed to traditional teaching methods, such as reading texts and solving exercises on paper [2]. ECLAC's statement [3] shows that children and young people are joining the world of technology on a massive scale since connectivity has increased among young people between 13 and 19 years of age; the highest level of connectivity is found in families formed by people over 20 years of age. With the democratization of access to digital devices, the context of teaching in education, in general, is moving towards a more participatory approach to teaching activities, demonstrating that emerging technology is beneficial [4].

Currently, technology in households has increased the use of cell phones, tablets, computers, and the internet; this is demonstrated in the last national survey in Ecuador on the use of ICT, where the results reveal that nine out of ten people have a cell phone. In contrast, regarding internet access, the percentage corresponds to 37.2%, where an increase of about 11.8% is observed in both urban and rural areas [5]. In Pujos' research [6], he states that technology is gaining ground in all areas of knowledge, education one of the most booming; in this research, he developed a didactic guide based on AR augmented reality to strengthen the understanding of high school students in terms of calculation, measurement of figures and geometric bodies. The mentioned application was developed using SketchUp together with Aumentaty; it was determined that AR is an essential digital educational material for learning [7].

2 Methodology

2.1 Type and Design of Research

Once the need to dynamize the learning of elementary algebra has been identified, a solution is presented for implementing a mobile application developed in AR Metaverse [8]. The learning method that supports the proposal is the notional one, which consists of manipulating the material, observing how the elements work, solving specific problems, and concrete modeling exercises [9]. The present study is quasi-experimental and longitudinal since it studies how the variables of interest change over time; also, because the assignment of participants cannot be randomly controlled [10]. The unit of analysis consisted of 15 mathematics teachers and 25 students in the ninth year of general primary education, for whose research the non-probabilistic convenience sampling technique was applied. The method used for data collection was the survey, and the structured questionnaire was used as an instrument for both students and teachers (objective: Predisposition to apply augmented reality in the teaching of algebra). For the validity and reliability of the device, Cronbach's alpha statistic was calculated since the questions are on a Likert scale, where each question has at least five response options, obtaining a favorable result of 0.844 after a pilot test. The data were processed with specialized free-use statistical software Jasp. The normality of scores before and after applying the proposal was determined by means of the Shapiro-Wilk.

3 Results

The student questionnaire reveals that in questions one through four, the majority of students, about 67%, mention that they are never motivated to use AR during mathematics classes; furthermore, most students show interest and curiosity in applying AR in classroom learning during mathematics classes. For questions five through seven, it is determined that a large percentage, about 62.27%, indicate that technological resources are never used for mathematics learning in the classroom. Reviewing questions eight, nine, and ten, the students show that approximately 69.33% have problems learning mathematics.

The information from the teachers shows that 63.33% have experience in the use of technological resources and would be interested in applying augmented reality in the learning of mathematics, considering that it is an innovative resource, as well as motivating the active participation of the student; it should be emphasized that this section refers to the summary of questions one to four. Regarding questions five to seven, 60% of the teachers are convinced that multimedia resources, pedagogical materials with real-time activities, are indispensable for academic training in the classroom; regarding questions eight through ten, about 56% of the teachers they were stated that the application of educational activities based on AR would significantly improve mathematics learning. Contrasting the information from students (66.33%) with that of teachers (59.63%), it is observed that most of them are predisposed on both sides to apply technological resources based on AR for the teaching-learning process of mathematics; they consider that the use of AR would improve the understanding of the primary algebraic operations such as multiplication, factoring and the solution of algebraic equations. Once the predisposition of both students and teachers is verified, we proceed to work with the augmented reality mobile application developed with Metaverse following the ADDIE instructional design; for each activity, the student must install the application on the phone, scan the code, visualize the proposed exercise, try to solve the movement by hand manually, interact with the application to verify the result or know the steps to solve it; the process is fed back with links to video tutorials of the application according to the subject (phases of the proposal see Fig. 1).

Before starting workshop, one related to linear equations, students are evaluated with a diagnostic test on the subject, then proceed to reinforce the topics according to the diagnosis made to subsequently reapply the same assessment by changing only the data of the algebraic problem posed (this period is four weeks).

The normality of data is fulfilled only with Group1 (diagnostic evaluation taken at the beginning of workshop one) according to the Shapiro-Wilk statistic (p_value $>=$ 0.05) see Table 1, which indicates applying a Bayesian T-test to compare the means of two related samples, obtaining a p_value of BF $= 3.058 \times 10^{-12}$ which ratifies rejecting the null hypothesis, i.e., the standards are not equal. Finally, it is established that group 2 (monthly evaluation after the start of workshop one) has a better score than group 1. A descriptive statistical report is presented below, together with the p_values, to determine the significance in terms of mean difference. significance in terms of difference in scores. See Fig. 2.

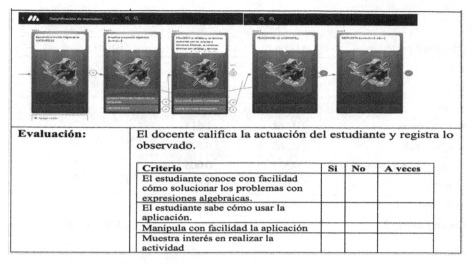

Evaluación:	El docente califica la actuación del estudiante y registra lo observado.			
	Criterio	**Si**	**No**	**A veces**
	El estudiante conoce con facilidad cómo solucionar los problemas con expresiones algebraicas.			
	El estudiante sabe cómo usar la aplicación.			
	Manipula con facilidad la aplicación			
	Muestra interés en realizar la actividad			

Fig. 1. Details on the structure of each activity.

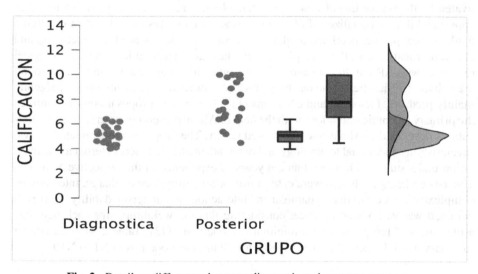

Fig. 2. Detail on differences between diagnostic and post-test averages.

Table 1. Descriptive and inferential statistics of group ratings.

Diagnostic posterior	Group 1	Group 2	BF BF
Valid	25	25	
Missing	25	25	
Mean	5.072	7.996	
Std. Deviation	0.664	1.814	
Shapiro-Wilk	0.965	0.878	
P_valor of Shapiro-Wilk	0.533	0.006	
Minimum	4.000	4.500	
Maximum	6.400	10.000	
Group 1-Group 2			3.058×10^{-12}

4   Discussion

After applying the data collection instruments, it was determined that students are unmotivated by the scarce use of innovative technological resources; they are interested in applying AR as a visualizer of algebraic concepts; they present difficulties in solving mathematical problems related to algebraic operations such as products, factoring, and algebraic equations. In the case of teachers, they are interested in using technological resources with AR but do not have a didactic guide for its application in the classroom; they observe difficulties in the teaching process in topics related to introductory algebra, mainly products, factoring, and equations [11]. The present proposal aims to reinforce the primary algebraic operations with the help of AR by presenting several mobile applications developed in Metaverse augmented reality. The proposal was evaluated by two specialists in educational technology and two mathematics teachers external to the institution under study, with more than ten years of experience in the respective area [12]. The aspects being evaluated were ease of use, accessibility, free of charge, interactivity, complexity in accessibility, dynamism and interaction, and understandability. The result obtained was 91.25% acceptance, considering that the weightings for each item had a maximum of ten points and a minimum of one point [13]. Table 2 shows a tabular summary of all the activities developed with Metaverse, coded from N1 to N10.

Table 2. Activities and code developed in Metaverse.

Actividad	Código		Actividad	Código	
N1		Simplificacion de expresiones algebraicas	N6		Producto notable 2
N2		Simplificacion de expresiones algebraicas	N7		ecuación
N3		ecuacion 1	N8		Expresión algebraica
N4		ecuaciones	N9		Trinomio de la forma ax2+bx+c
N5		Producto destacado 1	N10		Trinomio de la forma ax2+bx+c

5   Conclusions

The present mobile application based on AR developed with Metaverse was executed taking into consideration the ADDIE instructional model [14]; it responds to the solution of both students and teachers to improve the teaching-learning process of basic mathematical principles; It contributes to student learning because once the code is scanned with Metaverse, the proposed exercise is displayed on the cell phone, with possible answer options; as feedback, the possibility of reviewing detailed video tutorials on the subject is given, as well as the opportunity to review the solution step by step if required by the student. On the other hand, teachers ally with these mobile applications in teaching fundamental algebraic problems since, in a way, it replaces the face-to-face accompaniment, strengthening the autonomous work at home by the students [15].

For future research, it is worth mentioning that mobile technological applications are rapidly updated, so new academic content should be created at least every semester [16]. M-learning has proven effective in the changing educational world, contributing to learning by eliminating time and space constraints. It will be necessary to carry out more in-depth evaluations to determine the proposal's effectiveness in the essential algebra domain; it is also necessary to carry out an experimental study involving more participants, guaranteeing better measurements. Developing more activities will diversify algebraic learning, contributing to the improvement of basic mathematical skills and educational inclusion [17].

Acknowledgement. To Universidad Indoamérica for its support of this research.

References

1. Martínez-Usarralde, M.J.: Comparative educational inclusion in UNESCO and OECD from social cartography. Educación XX1 **24**(1), 93–115 (2021). https://doi.org/10.5944/educXX1. 26444
2. Espinosa-Pinos, C.A., Ayala-Chauvín, I., Buele, J.: Predicting academic performance in mathematics using machine learning algorithms. In: Valencia-García, R., Bucaram-Leverone, M., Del Cioppo-Morstadt, J., Vera-Lucio, N., Jácome-Murillo, E. (eds.) Technologies and Innovation. CITI 2022. Communications in Computer and Information Science, vol. 1658. Springer, Cham (2022). https://doi.org/10.1007/978-3-031-19961-5_2
3. Rendon, P.A., Jordan, N., Arias, D., Nunez, G.: Tik tok as a teaching tool: The motivation of university students in Ecuador. Paper presented at the Proceedings of the 2022 IEEE 2nd International Conference on Advanced Learning Technologies on Education and Research, ICALTER 2022 (2022),https://doi.org/10.1109/ICALTER57193.2022.9964670. www.scopus.com
4. Buele, J., Espinoza, J., Ruales, B., Camino-Morejón, V.M., Ayala-Chauvin, M.: Augmented reality application with multimedia content to support primary education. In: Botto-Tobar, M., Gómez, O.S., Rosero Miranda, R., Díaz Cadena, A., Luna-Encalada, W. (eds.) Trends in Artificial Intelligence and Computer Engineering. ICAETT 2022. LNNS, vol. 619. Springer, Cham (2023). https://doi.org/10.1007/978-3-031-25942-5_24
5. INEC: Programa Nacional de Estadística 2021–2025. Instituto Nacional de Estadística y Censos. Quito-Ecuador (2021). Recuperado en 28 de febrero de 2023, de http://www.ecu adorencifras.gob.ec/docuemntos/web-inec/Sistema_Estadistico_Nacional/Plnificacion_Est adistica/Programa_Nacional_de_Estadistica_2021-2025.pdf
6. Pujos, J.: Realidad Aumentada para mejorar el aprendizaje de la geometría en estudiantes de octavo grado de la unidad educative "12 de noviembre". Ambato, Universidad Tecnológica Indoamerica. https://repositorio.uti.edu.ec/handle/123456789/2305
7. Martínez, O.M., Mejía, E., Ramírez, W.R., Rodríguez, T.D.: Incidencia de la realidad aumentada en los procesos de aprendizaje de las funciones matemáticas. Información tecnológica **32**(3), 3–14 (2021). https://doi.org/10.4067/S0718-07642021000300003
8. Barreto, O., Andrea, S., Fonseca, V., Nathaly, J.: Realidad aumentada, una herramienta para la motivación en el aprendizaje de la Geometría. Conrado **16**(75), 56–60. (2020). Epub 02 de Agosto de 2020. Recuperado en 02 de marzo de 2023, de http://scileo.sld.cu/scielo.php?scr ipt=sci_arttext&pid=S1990-86442020000400056&Ing=es&tlng=es
9. González-Artunduaga, J., Cacca-Acosta, J., Díez-Fonseca, C.: Creación e implementación de una aplicación móvil con realidad aumentada para la enseñnza de la suma y la resta de polinomios.In: Serna, E. (ed.) Revolución en la formación y la capacitación para el siglo XXI (4th ed., pp. 540–553). Instituto Antioqueño de Investigación (2021). https://doi.org/10.5281/ zenodo.5708704
10. Hernández y Mendoza. Metodología de la investigación. Las rutas cuantitativa, cualitativa y mixta (2018). Obtenido de http://virtual.cuautitlan.unam.mx/rudics/?p=2612
11. Acosta, C.: Metodología para mejorar el aprendizaje de algebra en primer año de bachillerato de la Unidad Educativa Jorge Washington. Ambato, Universidad Tecnológica Indoamerica. http://repositorio.uti.edu.ec//handle/123456789/2373
12. Espinosa-Pinos, C.A., Núñez-Torres, M.G., Jordán-Buenaño, N., Jordán-Buenaño, C.: Methodological strategy for asynchronous learning mathematical operations with real numbers. In: 2022 IEEE 2nd International Conference on Advanced Learning Technologies on Education & Research (ICALTER), Lima, Perú. 2022, pp. 1–4 (2022). https://doi.org/10. 1109/ICALTER57193.2022.9964528

13. Rebollo, C., Remolar, l., Rossano, V., et al. Multimedia augmented reality game for learning math. Multimed. Tools Appl. **81**, 14851–14868 (2022). https://doi.org/10.1007/s11042-021-10821-3

14. Ligia, J.-A., Magaly, A.R.P., Patricio, S.S.R., Elizabeth, S.S.P.: Assistive technological tools to strengthen interaction, communication and learning in children with different abilities. In: Rocha, Á., Ferrás, C., Montenegro Marin, C.E., Medina García, V.H. (eds.) ICITS 2020. AISC, vol. 1137, pp. 340–350. Springer, Cham (2020). https://doi.org/10.1007/978-3-030-40690-5_34

15. Azman, M.N.A., Ruslan, S., Ab-Latif, Z., Pratama, H.: The development of mobile application software MyNutrient in home science subject. Asian J. Univ. Educ. **19**(1), 28–38 (2023). https://doi.org/10.24191/ajue.v19i1.21232

16. Junaid, S.M., et al.: Smartphone as an educational tool" the perception of dental faculty members of all the dental colleges of khiber Pakhtunkhwa – Pakistan. BMC Med. Educ. **23**(1). https://doi.org/10.1186/s12909-023-04093-8

17. Sumartini, T.S., Priatna, N.: Identify student mathematical understanding ability through direct learning model. J. Phys. Conf. Ser. **1132**(1). https://doi.org/10.1088/1742-6596/1132/1/012043 www.scopus.com

Wordhyve: A MALL Innovation to Support Incidental Vocabulary Learning

Mohammad Nehal Hasnine[1](✉) ⓘ, Junji Wu[1,2], and Hiroshi Ueda[2] ⓘ

[1] Hosei University, Tokyo 184-8584, Japan
nehal.hasnine.79@hosei.ac.jp
[2] Waseda University, Tokyo 169-8050, Japan

Abstract. In today's world, vocabulary learning is equipped with novel ways and techniques to engage language learners with the app and attract them to new learning. Research has shown that Mobile-assisted Language Learning (MALL) is a primary tool for enhancing the memorization of new words, sharing knowledge, and tracking performance. Although an increasing number of studies have focused on using mobile-assisted language learning for intentional vocabulary learning, there is a lack of studies regarding incidental learning. Therefore, this study introduces a new MALL innovation called Wordhyve to support incidental vocabulary learning. Wordhyve is a native android app that contains ubiquitous learning functionalities. Wordhyve uses deep learning methods to analyze learners' captured images, which we believe will open doors to new research along with the existing techniques such as learning through television programs, newspaper reading, movies, and listening to songs.

Keywords: AI in Education · Image Analytics for Vocabulary Acquisition · Incidental Learning · Intentional Learning · Mobile-assisted Language Learning (MALL) · Ubiquitous Learning · Vocabulary Learning

1 Introduction

Mobile learning is concerned with learner mobility in the sense that learners should be able to engage in learning activities without the constraints of having to do so in a tightly delimited physical location [1]. Devices that fall within the scope of mobile learning research include smartphones, palmtops and handheld computers, PDAs, Tablet PCs, laptop computers, and personal media players. With the convenience of mobile learning devices, learning, and teaching have become more accessible. Mobile learning certainly affected how second language acquisition was learned before. Now, we can find many mobile learning applications that are precisely developed for second language learners. Learners get many benefits while learning using mobile and computer-assisted learning environments, such as learning at any place and any time, track own's learning, sharing knowledge, and interacting with peers. More importantly, data collected through mobile and computer-assisted learning platforms opened doors to many complex learning problems that were not solved in earlier research. Today's mobile learning is open to advance research using sophisticated technologies such as AR, VR, Gaming, Robotics, and Chatbots.

© The Author(s), under exclusive license to Springer Nature Switzerland AG 2023
C. Stephanidis et al. (Eds.): HCII 2023, CCIS 1834, pp. 246–250, 2023.
https://doi.org/10.1007/978-3-031-35998-9_34

Incidental vocabulary learning refers to learning unknown vocabulary that is not intentionally meant to be learned but instead learned by accident or in the context. Incidental learning is a complex process, and much of it is unknown. It is widely agreed that learning occurs incidentally while the learner is engaged in extensive reading [2], watching television [3], listening to music, reading L2 materials, and reading newspaper. It is also found that [4], learning context (hereafter, context) play a crucial role in incidental vocabulary learning as contexts contain contextual clues that learners could use to learn incidental words. However, many critical aspects of incidental learning remained to be unsolved. As stated in the literature review by [2], several unresolved issues include- "the actual mechanism of incidental acquisition, the type and size of vocabulary needed for accurate guessing, the degree of exposure to a word needed for successful acquisition, the efficacy of different word-guessing strategies, the value of teaching explicit guessing strategies, the influence of different kinds of reading texts, the effects of input modification, and, more generally, the problems with incidental learning".

2 Apps in MALL Literature

As mobile learning technologies become increasingly popular, language learning apps are built to support language learning. Mobile and ubiquitous learning apps such as SCROLL, Duolingo, Lingvist, SuperMemo, Beelinguapp have shown promise in collecting data to produce feedback, location-based recommendations, and knowledge sharing. However, the above-mentioned tools do not address incidental learning.

To fill the research gaps and address the following research questions, we designed and developed Wordhyve [5]. First, how to recommend incidental vocabulary that is concrete nouns? Second, how to design a mobile learning app that could analyze the visual contents of a learning log to generate new words and context to represent those words? and Third, to what degree does a learner accept the recommended vocabulary and context? In Wordhyve, a learner can record learning experiences and track his/her learning activities. The app recommends incidental vocabularies and learning contexts to the learner to broaden the learning scope.

3 The Wordhyve

This section discusses the app's mechanism to generate incidental vocabularies, mainly concrete nouns, and their associated contexts. This section details the method to generating incidental vocabulary using a learning log (in 3.1). After that, the app's design is discussed (in 3.2). Under the 3.2 subsection, we present the user interfaces of the log-in, user registration, and log capture (refer to Fig. 1). Finally, the key functionalities of the Wordhyve app are provided (in 3.3). We discuss the recommendation panel, dashboard, and word card generation systems here.

3.1 Method

Wordhyve generates incidental words and their associated contexts by analyzing the scene of the image captured and uploaded by the learner. In the study design, we assume that the image uploaded by the learner is authentic (that is, personal). Authentic images could be captured during the learning activity and may contain objects, people, places, and text. A foreign language learner could capture an authentic image during traveling to a new place and experiencing cultural events. In the app, based on the complexity of the scene of the image, a number of vocabularies and contexts that we refer to as the smartly-generated learning contexts are generated. The associated contexts (i.e., the smartly-generated learning contexts) are small and long sentences generated based on the contents of the image. Wordhyve uses a couple of image-to-text and image-to-sentence generation APIs in the backend. Based on image captioning APIs (image-to-text and image-to-sentence generation models) of Wordhyve, the app generates and recommends vocabularies and contexts to the learner.

3.2 Design

The Wordhyve app has basic functions such as registering a new user and log-in in using a username and password. The mobile and ubiquitous learning system guidelines are followed in designing the app. We aimed to design simple interfaces without providing too much information on the interface, as the screen size of mobile devices is small. The app lets a user capture and uploads images in real-time with the camera function to create a log of new a learning experience. The app is designed in a way to track learning activities on the dashboard. The app has the option to customize user profile. Figure 1 shows the app's log-in, user registration, and log-capturing UIs.

Fig. 1. User log-in (left), user registration (middle) and log capture (right) in the Wordhyve app

3.3 Key Functions

Recommendation Panel. In this panel, multiple vocabularies and their associated contexts are recommended to the learner to elect the words to be learned. Research suggests that to guess the meanings of unknown words in context, the learner must be able to recognize on sight most of the surrounding words [2]. Therefore, in Wordhyve's recommendation panel, the learner can glimpse the recommended words (yellow, in Fig. 2) before choosing which words to learn. Consequently, the learner can read the recommended contexts (red, in Fig. 2), typically sentences, before electing the proper context. This helps the learner to read sentences in an unknown language.

Dashboard. It provides analytics on the number of logs the learner has logged so far and how many of them are memorized, the location of log capturing, customization based on the time of learning, frequent study time, and lets the learner access the word cards.

Word Card. Each word card contains information about the learning logs, either a self-captured log or an incidental log that was recommended to the learner. When a word card is accessed, a flashcard is popped up the learner gets details on the log. In the word card, a learner can also listen to the word's pronunciation.

Figure 2 shows the recommendation panel, dashboard and word card of the app.

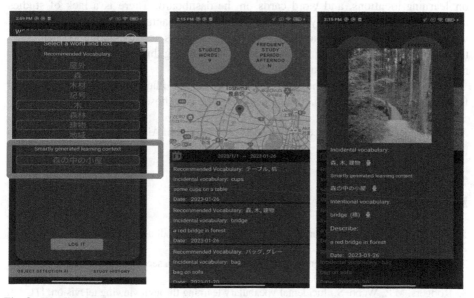

Fig. 2. Wordhyve's recommendation panel (left), dashboard (middle) and Word card (right) (Color figure online)

4 Discussion

In foreign language learning, incidental vocabulary acquisition depends on various exposures to a word in different contexts [2]. However, there has yet to be an argument on how many and what kinds of exposures are needed. It is argued that incidental learning and an associated context are easy to memorize. Several factors need to be considered in mobile learning to support incidental learning. For example, how to design an app that could support incidental learning and the right time and place to recommend incidental vocabulary. Furthermore, the limitations of incidental learning, the effectiveness of the mobile app, and the complexity of explicit strategies for recommendation and analyzing the knowledge source are critical for the researchers to understand. Therefore, designing a study using existing mobile learning apps takes time and effort.

To overcome this challenge, we designed and developed a new mobile learning app called Wordhyve. To support incidental learning, the app analyzes each of the logs, primarily the visual contents of the image uploaded by a learner and its EXIF information. Then, Wordhyve recommends a list of incidental vocabulary and smartly generated learning contexts on the recommendation panel, allowing a learner to save word(s) that s/he could learn in the future. By this, Wordhyve recommends incidental vocabulary and assists learners in memorizing that recommended vocabulary by analyzing various learning contexts. As for feedback to learners, the app provides statistics on the number of words a learner has logged and learned, the primary time of learning, information on learning locations, and word cards on the dashboard. There is a lack of studies that applied the image analytics method to learners' captured images for incidental vocabulary enhancement. Therefore, Wordhyve uses this new technique to open doors to new research and existing techniques such as learning through television programs, newspaper reading, movies, and listening to song.

A public test version of the app is released on Google Play and could be downloaded from https://play.google.com/store/apps/details?id=com.hosei.myapplication.

Acknowledgement. This project is funded by JSPS Grant-in-Aid for Early-Career Scientists project no. 21K13651.

References

1. Kukulska-Hulme, A., Traxler, J.: Mobile Learning: A Handbook for Educator and Trainers (2005)
2. Huckin, T., Coady, J.: Incidental vocabulary acquisition in a second language: a review. Stud. Second. Lang. Acquis. **21**(2), 181–193 (1999)
3. Rodgers, M.P., Webb, S.: Incidental vocabulary learning through viewing television. ITL-Int. J. Appl. Linguist. **171**(2), 191–220 (2020)
4. Webb, S.: The effects of context on incidental vocabulary learning. Reading Foreign Lang. **20**(2), 232–245 (2008)
5. Hasnine, M.N., Wu, J.: Wordhyve: a context-aware language learning app for vocabulary enhancement through images and learning contexts. Procedia Comput. Sci. **192**, 3432–3439 (2021)

Evaluating Young Children's Computational Thinking Skills Using a Mixed-Reality Environment

Jaejin Hwang[1]([✉]) [iD], Sungchul Lee[2] [iD], Yanghee Kim[3] [iD], and Mobasshira Zaman[1] [iD]

[1] Department of Industrial and Systems Engineering, College of Engineering and Engineering Technology, Northern Illinois University, DeKalb, IL, USA
jhwang3@niu.edu
[2] Division of Computer Science and Engineering, Sunmoon University, Asan, South Korea
[3] Department of Educational Technology, Northern Illinois University, DeKalb, IL, USA

Abstract. This study aimed to develop an innovative mixed-reality environment to promote early computational thinking skills in young children using augmented reality (AR) technology and a socially interactive robot. The learning objectives were focused on developing STEM problem-solving skills and adeptness in advanced technology use. The environment involved children walking on a chessboard-like grid to assist a robot in finding an optimal path towards a destination while holding a tablet. The robot provided instructions, cues, and motivational encouragement utterances, while the tablet displayed an equivalent map and AR obstacles. Motion capture and logging measures were used to assess children's learning progress and performance. Results from data collection of seventeen children aged six to eleven, of Caucasian, Asian, and African American ethnicities, revealed a range in abilities and computing experiences. The poster session presents the outcomes of the analysis and discusses the implications of this advanced technology in enabling young children's effective learning and ecologically valid assessment of computational thinking skills.

Keywords: Robot · Mixed-Reality · Computational Thinking

1 Introduction

The National Science Board [1] predicts that by 2026, jobs requiring STEM skills will increase, but K-12 mathematics and science performance in the United States has not improved and is still lower compared to other countries. The report highlights the ongoing problem of underrepresentation of gender and ethnic minorities in the STEM workforce. Additionally, the COVID-19 pandemic has exacerbated the challenge of equitable development of young STEM talents. With the shelter-in-place rule, online technology has become a widespread option for education and work. However, the Northwest Evaluation Association [2] predicts that academic growth for all age groups will be negatively impacted, especially in mathematics and more severely for younger children in elementary school and those from low-income families or of color [3].

© The Author(s), under exclusive license to Springer Nature Switzerland AG 2023
C. Stephanidis et al. (Eds.): HCII 2023, CCIS 1834, pp. 251–258, 2023.
https://doi.org/10.1007/978-3-031-35998-9_35

Current online learning methods may not be enough for young children. Educators and principals have identified a need for resources that engage children in hands-on activities and encourage social and emotional learning [4]. Children naturally interact with their surroundings through multiple senses, and STEM learning environments should reflect this by engaging children cognitively, socially, emotionally, and physically [5]. Early positive experiences in STEM tasks can foster a positive STEM identity and encourage further interest in STEM fields [6]. It is crucial to explore innovative ways to use advanced technologies to provide equitable STEM learning opportunities for all children, regardless of their real-life circumstances.

The project team aimed to help children view technology as a valuable tool for play, learning, and daily life, and become skilled in both creating and using advanced technology. We envisioned combining emerging technologies to create a personalized STEM learning environment for children. Studies showed that young children willingly engaged with digital virtual characters and robots, even forming social connections with them [7].

The objective of this study was to develop an innovative mixed-reality environment that would combine a socially interactive humanoid robot and augmented reality (AR) for children in K-2 to engage in computational tasks during play with the robot. This hands-on experience aimed to help children understand crosscutting and foundational concepts of STEM literacy and problem-solving, such as sequences and symbols. Grounded in embodied cognition and culturally responsive/sustainable pedagogy, this environment aimed to provide an equitable AR-enhanced play experience with a non-judgmental and socially unbiased robot playmate, promoting positive feelings towards working with and on advanced technologies.

2 Methods

2.1 Mixed-Reality Learning System

The aim of this study was to create a novel mixed-reality environment that fosters early development of computational thinking. Children in K-2 were instructed to walk on a floor mat resembling a 5 x 5 chessboard, with the goal of helping a robot (Linibot) navigate a path towards a destination while holding a tablet. The robot provided guidance to children through instructions, cues, and feedback, including corrections and motivational encouragement. The tablet displayed a corresponding map and AR obstacles for the child to avoid.

The primary learning objectives of this study were to develop children's foundational STEM problem-solving skills, specifically their understanding of symbols and sequences that are relevant across various STEM domains, and to increase their confidence in using advanced technology. To assess the children's progress unobtrusively while they played in the mixed-reality environment, we utilized multimodal behavioral data collection technology such as automated interaction logs that recorded their walking path and the time taken to reach the goal, as well as an optical motion capture system that precisely recorded their bodily gestures [8]. The mixed-reality environment was developed iteratively over a year and a half, with ongoing testing of our designs on 25 children in informal settings such as our lab, a community center, and a STEM showcase event. The focus of each test varied depending on the developmental progress of the environment.

2.2 Experimental Procedures

At a local STEM showcase event, we recruited seventeen children between the ages of six and eleven, with ethnicities including Caucasian, Asian, and African American. The children and their parents voluntarily visited our booth, and after obtaining parental consent, each child played two episodes of a path-finding game. Game 1 took five to ten minutes, and Game 2 took ten to twenty minutes. Before playing, children wore a motion capture suit and hat with the help of a research assistant. The suit had reflective markers to track their movements during the session. When approaching the game, a social robot greeted the children with programmed utterances, which were instantly controlled by a human operator behind the scenes. The social robot provided encouragement when a child struggled to find the next step during the game, and its various utterances were controlled by the human operator. The robot could also move, and this was controlled using a tablet controller by the human operator. The social robot acted as a peer, following the child's path without interfering with the task.

2.3 Data Analysis

The interaction logs were used to assess each child's walking path, total distance traveled, and time taken to reach the goal. For each subtask of finding a gem, the child's travel distance and time spent were recorded for each grid cell. The optimal path was calculated separately from the starting point to the gem, and then compared to the actual path taken by the child. Additionally, the data from optical motion capture technology was used to compare these two data sets and understand how they could be used to assess the child's learning progress authentically. Reflective markers attached to the child's head and neck, the tablet, and the social robot were used to compute several behavioral measures, including the distance between the head centroid and the tablet, the distance between the head centroid and the social robot, neck angle, neck angular velocity, and neck displacement. These measures had been previously used in a study to assess children's gestures.

3 Results

3.1 Performance of Path-Finding Tasks

The graph in Fig. 1 depicts the trend of the difference in total distance (in centimeters) between the child's actual path and the theoretically optimal path based on age groups. The performance of the 9 to 11-year-old group was consistently higher than the 6 to 8-year-old group throughout the session. In particular, the older group did not exhibit significant lower performance in the early stage of the learning session, which was contrary to the younger group.

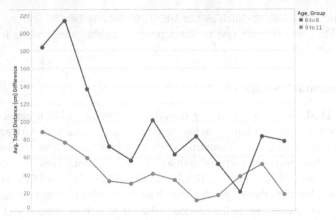

Fig. 1. The line chart displays the difference in total distance between the actual and optimal path for two distinct age groups, one ranging from six to eight years old and the other ranging from nine to eleven years old.

In order to conduct a detailed evaluation of the children's performance, a comparison was made between the actual path and the optimal path, and a heatmap was generated to display the time spent in each cell, as shown in Fig. 2. This approach provided insights into the individual children's path-finding strategies and the efficiency of their spatial thinking.

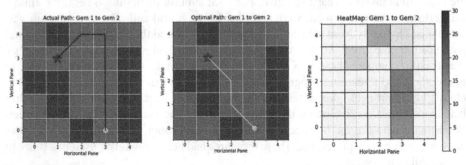

Fig. 2. This figure illustrates the visualization of both the actual path and the optimal path, along with a heatmap that displays the time spent in each cell. The example shown is from one child's trial of finding a gem.

3.2 Children's Bodily Movement

To gain a more in-depth understanding of the bodily movements and behavioral strategies employed by children, the researchers utilized motion capture-based measures as illustrated in Fig. 3. The first image in the figure (Fig. 3.a) shows a child maintaining a static posture with their head positioned far from the tablet. In contrast, the second image

(Fig. 3.b) displays a child exhibiting more dynamic bodily movement while searching for a path. This analysis of bodily movement and postures provides valuable insight into the children's behavioral patterns during the path-finding task, and can be used to inform the development of more effective and engaging learning tools for children.

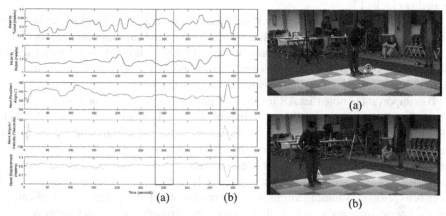

Fig. 3. It shows an instance of the multimodal assessment, which involves evaluating bodily movement and video capture during a child's task of finding a path. The first image (a) depicts a child with a considerable distance between their head and the tablet, while the proximity between the child and the robot was high. In the second image (b), the child's head was nearer to the tablet, and there was a dynamic movement of the head.

4   Discussion

We examined the potential of using a mixed-reality learning environment for young children with the help of multimodal data measurement. Our findings revealed that children found this new technology enjoyable and interacted well with a social robot while solving the path-finding task. The preliminary results indicated that children initially exhibited lower performance, but their performance improved significantly after participating in a few trials. This trend was more prominent for the younger age group (6 to 8 years old). These findings suggest that the system we developed was user-friendly and has the potential to enhance children's STEM thinking ability in the long run.

According to the theory of embodied cognition, our cognition is rooted in our bodily interactions with the social, cultural, and physical environment [9]. Sensory motor systems, which are the neural systems that process sensation and perception, are involved in cognition, and cognition is influenced by bodily movements and processes. In the past two decades, a substantial amount of evidence has accumulated to support the crucial role of the body in knowledge development and learning [10].

It is noteworthy that embodied cognition aligns with child development theory, which recognizes the fundamental interconnectedness of intellectual, social, emotional, and sensory-motor development. Typically, children between the ages of six and eight are in the process of developing both fine and gross motor skills, and as a result, they are unlikely to be able to sit still for extended periods of time. Furthermore, the development of their visual-motor skills is closely tied to their future success in academic subjects such as mathematics and science [11]. Similarly, research on embodied cognition has shown that children aged six to eight use their bodies to reason about time when reading an analog clock [12].

A mixed-reality environment such as the one we propose could provide an inclusive setting that enables every child to utilize their individual and cultural resources, or "funds of knowledge" [13], during the learning process. It also grants children a sense of agency and independence, allowing them to engage in a STEM learning community, voluntarily sharing their interests and assets to enhance the community's overall capabilities.

It is important to note that AR technology promotes embodied learning experiences. A mixed-reality environment that combines physical and virtual realities using AR technology allows learners to use their bodies to generate and manipulate relevant ideas presented in digital form and observe how the ideas work in a vivid and interactive manner. In a science learning application utilizing AR, for instance, a student playing the role of an augmented bee navigated physically to find nectar and communicate with other bees [14]. This finding aligns with the results of our study. Such AR applications aim to support students' conceptual understanding through experiential learning.

Social (or sociable) robots are robots that have a physical, lifelike appearance and interact with humans in a human-like manner [7]. With features like anthropomorphism, physical embodiment, socio-emotional presence, and mobility [15], a humanoid social robot has the potential to induce even stronger relational dynamics with children. In fact, several review studies on social robotics have confirmed that children develop highly emotional and social relationships with their physically embodied social robots [16].

It is important to highlight the use of a social robot as a means of promoting inclusive and equitable experiences. Previous research on human/computer interaction has shown that adolescent girls and individuals from ethnic minorities demonstrated higher self-efficacy and more positive attitudes towards learning mathematics, and performed better when assisted by virtual pedagogical agents, as compared to their white male counterparts [17]. These students felt encouraged to try and make mistakes, and felt supported by the agents' verbal encouragement, which was free from biases and judgments. A similar trend was observed in our data collection in this study.

Despite the study's rigorous design, there were some limitations. Firstly, the sample size was restricted as it was only in the preliminary testing phase, which resulted in low statistical power, and statistical analysis was not conducted. Secondly, there was no comparison of the proposed system's effectiveness to a control group, as the focus was solely on verifying the preparedness of the mixed-reality system for further steps. In future studies, the degree of spatial thinking between the control and intervention groups will be compared.

5 Conclusion

The study explored the practicality of using a mixed-reality learning environment that combined embodied cognition theory, social robotics, and AR learning to teach spatial thinking skills to young children. Through this advanced technology, children were able to learn while playing and receiving emotional and social support from a social robot. The motion capture system was able to accurately measure each child's behavior during the learning session. This innovative learning environment could be a valuable tool for developing young children's computational thinking skills and could be integrated into the curriculum by teachers.

References

1. Boroush, M.: Research and development: us trends and international comparisons. Science and engineering indicators 2020. NSB-2020–3. Natl. Sci. Found. (2020)
2. Kuhfeld, M., Soland, J., Tarasawa, B., Johnson, A., Ruzek, E., Liu, J.: Projecting the potential impact of COVID-19 school closures on academic achievement. Educ. Res. 49(8), 549–565 (2020)
3. Higgins, C.D., Páez, A., Kim, G., Wang, J.: Changes in accessibility to emergency and community food services during COVID-19 and implications for low income populations in Hamilton, Ontario. Soc. Sci. Med. 291, 114442 (2021)
4. De Felice, S., Hamilton, A.F.D.C., Ponari, M., Vigliocco, G.: Learning from others is good, with others is better: the role of social interaction in human acquisition of new knowledge. Philos. Trans. R. Soc. B 378(1870), 20210357 (2023)
5. Bremner, A.J., Lewkowicz, D.J., Spence, C.: The multisensory approach to development (2012)
6. Radovic, D., Black, L., Williams, J., Salas, C.E.: Towards conceptual coherence in the research on mathematics learner identity: a systematic review of the literature. Educ. Stud. Math. 99, 21–42 (2018)
7. Breazeal, C., Scassellati, B.: Robots that imitate humans. Trends Cogn. Sci. 6(11), 481–487 (2002)
8. Ailneni, R.C., Syamala, K.R., Kim, I.-S., Hwang, J.: Influence of the wearable posture correction sensor on head and neck posture: sitting and standing workstations. Work 62(1), 27–35 (Jan.2019). https://doi.org/10.3233/WOR-182839
9. Núñez, R.: On the science of embodied cognition in the 2010s: research questions, appropriate reductionism, and testable explanations. J. Learn. Sci. 21(2), 324–336 (2012)
10. Alibali, M.W., Nathan, M.J.: Embodied cognition in learning and teaching: action, observation, and imagination. In: International Handbook of the Learning Sciences, Routledge, pp. 75–85 (2018)
11. Radesky, J.S., Schumacher, J., Zuckerman, B.: Mobile and interactive media use by young children: the good, the bad, and the unknown. Pediatrics 135(1), 1–3 (2015)
12. Walkington, C., et al.: Grounding mathematical justifications in concrete embodied experience: the link between action and cognition. In: The Annual meeting of the American Educational Research Association, pp. 1–36 (2012)
13. González, N., Moll, L.C., Amanti, C.: Funds of Knowledge: Theorizing Practices in Households, Communities, and Classrooms. Routledge (2006)
14. Peppler, K., Thompson, N., Danish, J., Moczek, A., Corrigan, S.: Comparing first-and third-person perspectives in early elementary learning of honeybee systems. Instr. Sci. 48(3), 291–312 (2020)

15. Park, H.W., Gelsomini, M., Lee, J.J., Breazeal, C.: Telling stories to robots: the effect of backchanneling on a child's storytelling. In: Proceedings of the 2017 ACM/IEEE International Conference on Human-Robot Interaction, pp. 100–108 (2017)
16. Martínez-Miranda, J., Pérez-Espinosa, H., Espinosa-Curiel, I., Avila-George, H., Rodríguez-Jacobo, J.: Age-based differences in preferences and affective reactions towards a robot's personality during interaction. Comput. Hum. Behav. **84**, 245–257 (2018)
17. Kim, Y., Thayne, J., Wei, Q.: An embodied agent helps anxious students in mathematics learning. Education Tech. Research Dev. **65**(1), 219–235 (2016). https://doi.org/10.1007/s11 423-016-9476-z

Exergame to Promote Exercise Outside Physical Education Classes During a Pandemic

Akari Kanei[✉] and Hiroyuki Manabe

Shibaura Institute of Technology, Tokyo, Japan
ma22037@shibaura-it.ac.jp, manabehiroyuki@acm.org

Abstract. The novel coronavirus caused a pandemic at the end of 2019. Most university classes were also forced to move online. Physical education (P.E.) is one of the subjects that could not be easily transferred to online classes. The purposes of P.E. includes not only developing motor skills but also promoting the students' relationship-building skills and health maintenance. Since the content of P.E. had been developed assuming face-to-face situations, the educator faced difficulties in replicating the material online. The students lost opportunities to acquire such skills and negative effects were found both in and outside of P.E. classes. We propose an exergame that can be adapted to university P.E. classes and encourages the students to exercise outside the classes. It is assumed as a flipped classroom tool during pandemics or similar emergencies. The proposed exergame has two versions, one for single players and the other for pairs. Each student performs the former outside the class, while the latter is used in the class. The results of the one player game reflected in the in-class game. We evaluated the suitability of the proposed exergame for online P.E. Questionnaire results suggest that respondents might do the single-player version if their efforts at home had a positive impact on the in-class variant.

1 Introduction

A pandemic started at the end of 2019 due to a new type of coronavirus infection. The pandemic severely restricted all daily activities, including opportunities for physical activities associated with school classes and commuting to school. Schools went online, but while some subjects were easy to adapt to the online environment, others were not. One such subject was physical education (P.E.). The purpose of P.E. is not only to improve students' athletic ability, but also to build relationships and promote health maintenance. To achieve the objectives of P.E., sports such as soccer and basketball were utilized before the outbreak of the novel coronavirus. The instructors often encouraged students to cooperate with others because group learning was important. However, the online P.E. classes made it difficult to replicate these activities, and the classes consisted mainly of a combination of some limited skills training such as muscle training and fitness that students could do alone at home, and the teacher's talk. Student interaction was limited to online discussions, and the ability to encourage

Fig. 1. The game screen and the two-player exergame variant; the players are in different rooms.

communication with others was also limited. In addition, depending on the type of class, students may watch on-demand videos or use handouts for individual study, which leads even greater social isolation. Although the situation has been improving recently, we believe that we need to be prepared in case a pandemic occurs again.

Not only P.E. classes but in daily life, exercise facilities such as gyms have been closed, and opportunities for exercise have been drastically reduced. Supplementing opportunities for exercise in daily life and encouraging people need to be included as one of aims of P.E., especially in a pandemic disaster. We propose an exergame that can be adapted to university P.E. classes and encourages students to exercise outside the classes.

2   Related Work

This study is related to three main areas: P.E. in a novel coronavirus pandemic, flipped learning, and technology-enhanced sports. This section presents some of the existing research in these three areas.

2.1   P.E. in the COVID-19 Disaster

P.E. during the new coronavirus epidemic has been discussed in several countries. In Japan, distance learning was the main approach to practical skill courses in university P.E. in the first semester of 2020 [7]. That report indicated that more than 50% of the students were taking classes alone. In Indonesia, a study was conducted on students' perceptions of online learning and the preferred platform for online learning in P.E. classes during the novel coronavirus outbreak [4]. According to this study, Indonesian students consider online learning to be important in a pandemic disaster and prefer Zoom as the platform. In China, it was found that students were dissatisfied with online learning in general and with communication and question-and-answer sessions in particular during the pandemic disaster [13].

Participation in P.E. classes is said to provide a variety of benefits in the physical, social, emotional, and cognitive domains [1]. Moreover, it has been reported that cooperative learning may promote outcomes in these four learning domains [3]. However, interaction among students in online classes is more limited than in face-to-face classes. Therefore, it is difficult to conduct cooperative learning in online P.E. classes.

2.2 Flipped Classroom

Flipped learning is a learning method that involves video learning, assignment in advance, and group learning in class. Students' perceptions of flipped classes are generally positive overall, and students tend to prefer face-to-face lectures over video lectures and interactive activities in the classroom over lectures [2]. They also report that although flipped classes have been suggested to improve student learning compared to traditional classes, few studies have investigated this in depth. In flipped P.E. classes, it is reported the number of lessons tends to be between 3 and 5 and seems to be tied to a regular educational unit on a topic such as a specific sport or endurance [8]. They also report that such classes have a positive impact on student motivation and may increase opportunities for motor skill development and autonomy in the classroom.

Combining flipped learning with online classes in a pandemic disaster may have the potential to improve students' motivation to learn and provide opportunities to maintain their health conditions in daily lives.

2.3 Technology-Enhanced Sports

Exergame is a term coined for the combination of exercise and games [11]. Exergames not only provide fun, but are also known to have a variety of benefits. For example, Nintendo Ring Fit Adventure (RFA) has been shown to increase self-efficacy and reduce pain in patients with chronic low back pain [10]. It has also been reported that the use of RFA for four weeks improved the running performance of students [16]. An indoor exergame for the elderly using Kinect was studied in China because of the difficulty of exercising outdoors due to heavy air pollution [6]. Examples of the implementation of exergames in P.E. have been reported in the literature [14], and the use of exergames in schools has been shown to offer positive results in combating obesity. It was also shown that exergames have the potential to contribute to P.E. classes to motivate users by supporting the use of the games in large groups.

3   Proposed Method

We developed an exergame that is effective for university P.E., especially during a pandemic. It can be used as a tool for flipped learning to promote physical activity outside the class and it is also used in the P.E. class. It provides the opportunities for students to exercise in and outside the class and could contribute to achieve the purpose of P.E.

For an exergame to be considered effective for online P.E., it must meet the following requirements, (1) People in different locations can freely communicate with each other, (2) It can be used in small spaces in the home, (3) Students find enjoyment in playing the exergame, (4) The intensity of the exercise is at the same level as in a regular P.E. class, and (5) The equipment used is not easily broken. One of the key elements of an exergame is that it must be both engaging and effective as exercise [12] Since the proposed exergame is intended to promote exercise outside the class, the content of the game must be enjoyable for students and encourage continued exercising. It is also important to implement a mechanism to motivate the students to exercise at home as a tool for flipped learning.

4   Implementation

The implemented exergame is based on a shooting game and has two types: the single-player version and the pair version. The single-player version is used outside the class, while the pair version is used inside the class. The highest score and the number of times played in the single-player version are reflected in the score for the pair version. Both versions have the same controls to avoid confusion. Players wear leg straps with Joy-Cons attached to their feet and hold Ring-Cons in their hands, these devices are easy to get and unbreakable. There are three types of movements: (1) pushing the Ring-Con, (2) pulling the Ring-Con, and (3) squatting. These actions are assigned to the inputs of the shooter. The two objects at the bottom of the game screen represent player 1 and 2 (for two players, the pink and light blue objects in Fig. 1). The player can move this object to the right and left and can shoot upward from the position of this object. In the single-player version, each player's movement is assigned to (1) move the object to the right, (2) move the object to the left, or (3) shoot the gun. In the pair version, (3) is changed to "shoot the bullet from the object of the other who the player plays together with." This requires the player to communicate and cooperate with their partner. There are three types of targets to shoot at: diamond-shaped gems, pentagonal gems, and bombs. If a bullet hits a diamond-shaped gem, the player scores 20 points; a pentagonal gem, scores 15 points; and a bomb, -5 points. The player also gains 5 points for each movement. To achieve a high score, the player must hit the gems quickly and accurately. In the pair version, points which the highest score earned in a single-player version/100 are credited to the player who fired the bullet when it hits the gem. Also, 5 * (the number of times the player played the single-player version + 1) points are added for each movement. The highest score and the number of times in the single-player version are reflected in the pair version, thus students are encouraged to exercise outside the class. The exergame can be played at different locations, allowing communication and interaction between students through sports.

5 Experiment

An experiment was conducted to clarify whether the proposed exergame is suitable for online physical education, whether the game can contribute to the objectives of P.E., and to compare whether the motivation to play the game changes before and after reflecting the results gained when playing the single-player version of the game. The experiment was conducted with two participants simultaneously, each participating in a different room. The experiment was explained to the participants, and their heart rates were measured for one minute. This heart rate was defined as the resting heart rate. Zoom meeting was used for communication during the game, and the cameras and microphones were turned on. First, the participants played the pair version twice. Note that the scores attained in this trial were not altered. After a 10-minute break, the participants played the single-player version for 15 min. While playing the single-person version, the participants turned off the cameras and microphones in the Zoom meeting. Immediately before playing the single-player version, the participants were informed that their score and the number of times they played this game would alter their score in the next pair game. After a 10-minute break, the participants played the pair game twice with the camera and microphone turned on. At the end of the session, the participants answered a questionnaire. The total number of participants was six (six males) in three groups of two, all of whom were university seniors to second-year graduate students. After the experiment, participants received an Amazon gift card worth 1,500 JPY.

6 Results

Exercise intensity was measured using heart rate reserve and subjective exercise intensity. Heart rate reserve, known as the Karvonen method, is often used to calculate the target heart rate for exercising at a self-defined exercise intensity. The exercise intensity (%) is calculated: heart rate during exercise × 100/(maximum heart rate - resting heart rate) [5]. The estimated maximum heart rate was calculated as "220 - age" [9]. Subjective exercise intensity was measured using the Borg scale [15]. The Borg scale is rated on a 15-point scale from 6 to 20. Exercise intensities in the single-player and the pair version before and after score alteration were calculated from the maximum heart rate during the game. The calculated exercise intensity was 64.0% for the single-player version, 54.6% for the pair version before, and 72.0% after reflection. According to the ACSM Guidelines for exercise testing [9], exercise intensity between 40 and 60% is considered moderate, and between 60 and 90% is considered vigorous. Therefore, the exercise intensity determined from the maximum heart rate during

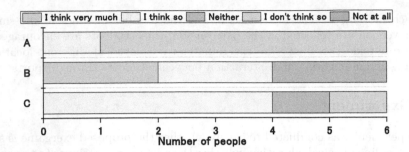

Fig. 2. Questionnaire on the exergame: (A) Would you like to continue playing the single-player version?, (B) Would you like to play the pair version in your P.E. class?, (C) If the pair version was played once a week in your P.E. class, would you play the single-player version before each class?

play was moderate to high. Subjective exercise intensity was 15.3 for the pair version before score alteration, and 16.3 for the single-person and 16.3 for the pair variant after score alteration. According to the ACSM Guidelines for exercise testing [9], a Borg scale of 15 is considered to be a hard (heavy) exercise intensity. Therefore, the exercise intensity is suitable for online classes in P.E.

In the questions on communication, many participants felt that it was easy to communicate with each other because "I had to give directions" and "we could talk to each other." However, they demonstrated little communication by voice during the play. The questions on whether the games played were interesting revealed that both the pair version before and after score alteration were interesting. One of the comments on the pair version score alteration was "it was challenging because the score increased with the amount of body movement," and comments after the reflection include "the score increased very quickly." A questionnaire asking the respondents whether they "would like to play the pair version in P.E. classes" shows a positive result (Fig. 2(B)). To a question asking if they would like to continue playing just the single-player version, one respondent said yes and five said no (Fig. 2 (A)). Some said that "I feel no change doing it and muscle training because I seek to exceed my past self (score)" and "I don't want to do it too many times because it is monotonous." However, to a question asking "if you play the pair version with score alteration once a week in P.E. class, would you play the single-player version?", four students agreed, one student did not agree, and one gave a neutral response (Fig. 2 (C)). One comment was "I can visualize my effort as a high score, which makes me want to work harder to achieve a higher score." The results indicate that the students didn't want to continue to play just the single-player version, but suggest that they might do so if their efforts at home had an impact on their classroom scores.

7   Disscusion

The results of this experiment show that the pair version was interesting both with and without score alteration; just the single-player game by itself was not interesting. Participants mentioned that the pair games were fun because they had a partner. Many participants said with regard to the single-player version that they "I felt more lonely than with a partner" and "it's not funny because the game was monotonous," and few wanted to continue to play the game. However, when their efforts were reflected in the classroom scores, they said they would play the single-player version. It is necessary that a long-term experiment should be conducted to verify whether students actually continue to play single-player version. However, in order for students to actively play the game outside the class, it is desirable for the content of the game to be such that they will want to continue playing it. One solution is to provide many kinds of games in addition to the current one. There are two reasons for this. First, there is a possibility that there are games that match one's own preferences. Since people have different preferences in games, the games they find enjoyable also vary from person to person. If there is at least one game that they find enjoyable, they may continue to exercise. Second, it could refresh the player.may reduce the number of people who feel bored with games. Some students said that even if they initially had fun playing the game, they may become bored with the game after playing it several times. If multiple game types and difficulty levels are prepared, players can change the game to suit their feeling and avoid boredom. In the future, it will be necessary to conduct long-term experiments by increasing the number of games, types of muscle training, and difficulty levels of the games played outside of class.

8   Conclusion

We proposed an exergame that can support university P.E. classes by encouraging students to exercise outside the class. The game is intended to be used as a flipped classroom tool during a pandemic. The single-player version is played outside the class, and the pair version is played in the class. The number of times the single-player version is played and the highest score are reflected in score of the pair version, thus encouraging students to exercise in their daily lives. The pair version is designed to allow remote players to communicate and cooperate with each other. The experiment suggests that students will exercise outside the class when the results of the single-player version are reflected in the pair version.

References

1. Bailey, R., et al.: The educational benefits claimed for physical education and school sport: an academic review. Res. Pap. Educ. 24(1), 1–27 (2009)
2. Bishop, J., Verleger, M.A.: The flipped classroom: a survey of the research. In: 2013 ASEE Annual Conference & Exposition, pp. 23–1200 (2013)
3. Casey, A., Goodyear, V.A.: Can cooperative learning achieve the four learning outcomes of physical education? A review of literature. Quest 67(1), 56–72 (2015)

4. Jumareng, H., et al.: Online learning and platforms favored in physical education class during COVID-19 era: exploring student'perceptions. Int. J. Hum. Mov. Sports Sci., 11–18 (2021)

5. Karvonen, M.J.: The effects of training on heart rate: a longitudinal study. Ann. Med. Exp. Biol. Fenn. **35**, 307–315 (1957)

6. Liu, Z., Liao, C., Choe, P.: An approach of indoor exercise: Kinect-based video game for elderly people. In: Rau, P.L.P. (ed.) Cross-Cultural Design, pp. 193–200. Springer International Publishing, Cham (2014). https://doi.org/10.1007/978-3-319-07308-8_19

7. Namba, H., et al.: Verification of the educational effect of online university physical education with COVID-19 from the perspective of teachers. Jap. J. Phys. Educ. Sport High. Educ. **18**, 21–34 (2021). (in Japanese)

8. O'Flaherty, J., Phillips, C.: The use of flipped classrooms in higher education: a scoping review. Internet High. Educ. **25**, 85–95 (2015)

9. Pescatello, L.S., et al.: ACSM's Guidelines for Exercise Testing and Prescription. Lippincott Williams & Wilkins, Philadelphia (2014)

10. Sato, T., et al.: Effects of Nintendo ring fit adventure exergame on pain and psychological factors in patients with chronic low back pain. Games Health J. **10**(3), 158–164 (2021). https://doi.org/10.1089/g4h.2020.0180

11. Sinclair, J., et al.: Considerations for the design of exergames. In: Proceedings of the 5th International Conference on Computer Graphics and Interactive Techniques in Australia and Southeast Asia, p. 289–295. GRAPHITE 2007, Association for Computing Machinery, New York (2007). https://doi.org/10.1145/1321261.1321313

12. Sinclair, J., et al.: Considerations for the design of exergames. In: Proceedings of the 5th International Conference on Computer Graphics and Interactive Techniques in Australia and Southeast Asia, pp. 289–295 (2007)

13. Tang, T., et al.: Efficiency of flipped classroom with online-based teaching under COVID-19. Interact. Learn. Environ., 1–12 (2020)

14. Vaghetti, C.A.O., et al.: Exergames experience in physical education: a review. Phys. Cult. Sport. Stud. Res. **78**, 23–32 (2018)

15. Williams, N.: The Borg rating of perceived exertion (RPE) scale. Occup. Med. **67**(5), 404–405 (2017). https://doi.org/10.1093/occmed/kqx063

16. Wu, Y.S., et al.: Effect of the Nintendo ring fit adventure exergame on running completion time and psychological factors among university students engaging in distance learning during the COVID-19 pandemic: randomized controlled trial. JMIR Ser. Games **10**(1), e35040 (2022). https://doi.org/10.2196/35040, https://games.jmir.org/2022/1/e35040

Development and Application Study of Coding Learning Game Using Augmented Reality-Based Tangible Block Chips for Children of Low Age Groups

Nayoung Kim[✉]

School of Games, Hongik University, 2639 Sejong-si, Sejong-ro, Sejong, South Korea
nayoung@hongik.ac.kr

Abstract. As the importance of coding education has recently increased, various methods are being attempted to increase learning efficiency rather than conventional education platforms. Among them, due to the educational effect and change in perception of games, research on coding education platforms that combine games and learning is being actively conducted. In particular, by solving various problem situations through games, not just games for fun, the positive effects of education using games such as logical thinking, problem-solving ability, and ability to deal with situations are currently attracted. In this study, a coding education game was developed in which the game itself becomes a coding education by integrating coding education with games. Furthermore, a computational thinking training game using an augmented reality-based tangible block chip was developed for children of low age groups who are inexperienced in mobile or PC environments. Then, after playing the coding game learning for children and parents, feedback on the user experience was investigated. A questionnaire and individual interviews were conducted on the usefulness, interest, recommendation, and overall satisfaction of a coding learning game for parents with children of the low-age group. Finally, by examining the pros and cons of a coding learning game using an augmented reality-based tangible block chip, we suggest effective coding learning for children of the low-age group.

Keywords: Educational game · Augmented reality coding game

1 Introduction

In recent years, game-based coding learning has emerged as a promising approach in coding education. Using games in coding education can effectively engage students and promote their interest in coding, while enhancing their problem-solving skills and creative thinking abilities [1]. Game-based coding learning has the advantage of allowing learners to develop programming skills naturally while playing the game. Learners can learn computational thinking through play, making it more interesting and sustainable for them [2]. This study aimed to create a game-based coding education program that

© The Author(s), under exclusive license to Springer Nature Switzerland AG 2023
C. Stephanidis et al. (Eds.): HCII 2023, CCIS 1834, pp. 267–272, 2023.
https://doi.org/10.1007/978-3-031-35998-9_37

leverages the characteristics of both coding education and gaming to make game play an educational experience. We developed an augmented reality coding education game for young children using smartphone-based tangible block chips, and conducted research to analyze the effects of game-based coding education and learner preferences. The game prototype was used to examine the usefulness, fun and usability of coding education for young children. Our findings suggest that game-based coding education can be an effective approach to enhance engagement and learning in coding education.

2   Theoretical Background

2.1   Educational Coding Game Learning

In Recently, coding education for young children has been designed in the form of games and play, which has been shown to improve their creativity and problem-solving skills. As an example, the coding learning tool "Bee-Bot" consists of 7 easy commands and allows children to learn coding through simple manipulations. Bee-Bot learning can also provide young children with simple mathematical experiences and increase their algorithmic and creative thinking skills through problem-solving activities [3]. The study in Fig. 1 is research on gamifying coding education for young children, similar to the coding toy "Bee-bot," with simple commands that help develop cognitive skills such as spatial awareness, observation, classification, and serves as a pre-education for coding. However, it was argued that a learning solution that reflects the learning environment is necessary [4]. This educational tool has limited programmed learning, making it difficult to expand for more systematic and diverse learning (see Fig. 1).

Fig. 1. A coding learning tools for young age groups

2.2   Engaging Students in Coding Education Through Coding Puzzle Games to Enhance Learning Immersion

In this study, a preliminary study was conducted on the educational effectiveness of web-based coding games. The developed games use models, puzzles, and tools that create a sense of familiarity and facilitate learning for young children, who would otherwise struggle with unfamiliar programming languages presented solely in textual form. Through learning sequences, loops, conditions, analysis, pattern recognition, abstraction, and other related skills, children are able to naturally develop computational thinking skills and problem-solving methods. This game was developed based on the "Light Bot" game, and through puzzle-solving gameplay, learners are trained to think algorithmically. The results of the study show that coding education using games was successful, particularly when the game was well-designed with satisfying gameplay. Higher learning achievements were observed when learners experienced highly polished games [5] (see Fig. 2).

Fig. 2. Preliminary research - Coding puzzle educational game

3   Body

3.1   Augmented Reality Game Design

Based on previous research, it has been found that using tangible blocks in a physical environment for learning is more helpful for younger children than learning through mouse manipulation, as it contributes to their confidence and satisfaction [6]. Therefore, we developed an augmented reality-based coding game learning program that allows teachers and friends to learn coding games systematically according to their levels by placing tangible Tensible blocks. Our ultimate goal was to develop mobile-based learning that is user-friendly and accessible. The content of the coding education is designed to share the same world view and game rules as the existing online coding game. The game's story is an adventure where players explore alien planets such as desert and ice planets with their own robots, defeat villains who pollute the planets, and purify the planets (see Fig. 3). The game mechanics involve solving coding puzzles in the game by using commands such as forward, turn left, turn right, and jump to move the robot. The game is designed based on an augmented reality textbook to provide systematic step-by-step learning of concepts such as sequences, loops, and functions (see Fig. 4).

3.2   Implementation of Augmented Reality Game System

In this study, an augmented reality command chip was implemented to recognize multiple marker-based commands simultaneously, consisting of five regular commands and three

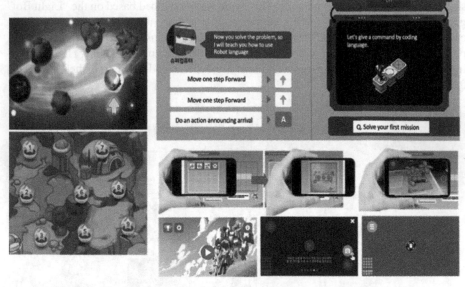

Fig. 3. Sequential logic learning problems puzzle map contents

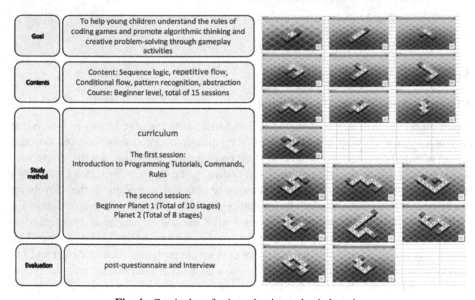

Fig. 4. Curriculum for introduction to basic learning

function call commands, with the ability to recognize up to 30 commands simultaneously. Marker-based commands were developed into image-based command chips to diversify the color and shape of the commands, as the marker-based commands had limitations in visually appealing to children. The AR recognition system used ArUco markers to ensure stable simultaneous recognition based on OpenCV for Unity [7]. Command chips were placed on a 4x4 command board, and recognized commands were displayed on the screen as command icon UI. The implemented commands included move forward, turn right, turn left, jump, and action, and for function learning, function main and G1, G2 commands were used (see Fig. 5).

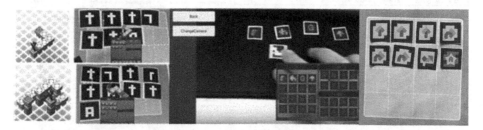

Fig. 5. Tangible blocks UI icons: executable commands and function commands

3.3 Augmented Reality Coding Game Questionnaire

The study on augmented reality coding game-based learning conducted in this research was targeted towards 20 parents with children aged 6 to 12. The survey was conducted with the purpose of using augmented reality coding puzzle games for children's education. First, participants confirmed the problems given in the learning material, then played the augmented reality coding game, and evaluated the satisfaction of learning coding puzzles using augmented reality. The questionnaire consisted of usability and gameplay questions, evaluating the usefulness of learning, fun, reusability, and overall satisfaction. The survey consisted of a total of 16 detailed questions, and responses to the survey were composed of a 5-point scale ranging from "very negative" to "very positive" (see Fig. 6).

The results of the survey collected through this study were analyzed as follows. The 16 detailed questions were integrated into four categories: "game usability," "willingness to reuse the game," "recommendation to others," "game fun," and "overall satisfaction," and the answer results for each category were graphed. As a result, the usability of the learning game received a positive response of 78%, game fun received 77%, willingness to reuse and recommendation to others received 85%, and overall satisfaction was evaluated at 90%.

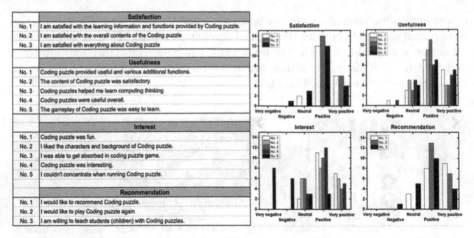

Satisfaction	
No. 1	I am satisfied with the learning information and functions provided by Coding puzzle.
No. 2	I am satisfied with the overall contents of the Coding puzzle
No. 3	I am satisfied with everything about Coding puzzle
Usefulness	
No. 1	Coding puzzle provided useful and various additional functions.
No. 2	The content of Coding puzzle was satisfactory.
No. 3	Coding puzzles helped me learn computing thinking.
No. 4	Coding puzzles were useful overall.
No. 5	The gameplay of Coding puzzle was easy to learn.
Interest	
No. 1	Coding puzzle was fun.
No. 2	I liked the characters and background of Coding puzzle.
No. 3	I was able to get absorbed in coding puzzle game.
No. 4	Coding puzzle was interesting.
No. 5	I couldn't concentrate when running Coding puzzle.
Recommendation	
No. 1	I would like to recommend Coding puzzle.
No. 2	I would like to play Coding puzzle again
No. 3	I am willing to teach students (children) with Coding puzzles.

Fig. 6. Survey results of satisfaction with augmented reality coding game learning

4 Conclusion

The post-interview results indicated that young children who are more accustomed to physical tools such as books or toys found it advantageous to solve problems through learning with block chips, rather than digital devices such as mobile or web-based platforms. They positively evaluated the learning environment where parents or teachers can participate together, which is difficult to achieve in online learning that requires group participation. However, they also mentioned difficulties in understanding the initial usage of the augmented reality blocks as the method of recognizing them was unfamiliar. Additionally, they suggested that more visually appealing features using augmented reality are needed to enhance the fun and interest of the game.

References

1. Hacker, M., Kiggens, J.: Gaming to learn: a promising approach using educational games to stimulate STEM learning. In: Fostering Human Development Through Engineering and Technology Education, pp. 257–279 (2011)
2. Jun, S.: The effect of convergence education based on reading and robot SW education for improving computational thinking. J. Industr. Convergence **18**(1), 53–58 (2020). https://doi.org/10.22678/JIC.2020.18.1.053
3. Yi, Y., Sung, H.: Influence of program using the coding robot. "Bee-Bot" Child. Math. Probl. Solv. Ability **16**(3), 261–281 (2017)
4. Hong, D.S., Yoo, M., Lee, H.K.: The development and application effect of coding game for the childhood cognitive development. J. Korean Soc. Game Stud. **18**(5), 103–112 (2018)
5. Kim, N.Y.: Game platform investigation for effective coding education. J. Korean Soc. Comput. Game **30**(3), 59–67 (2017)
6. Jeon, S.J.: Effects of SW training using robot based on card coding on learning motivation and attitude. J. Korean Assoc. Inf. Educ. **22**(4), 447–455 (2018). https://doi.org/10.14352/jkaie.2018.22.4.447
7. Seo, B.J., Jo, S.H.: Development of AR-based coding puzzle mobile application using command placement recognition. J. Korean Soc. Game Stud. **20**(3), 35–44 (2020)

Challenges in Cybersecurity Group Interoperability Training

Virgilijus Krinickij and Linas Bukauskas^(✉) (iD)

Cybersecurity Laboratory, Institute of Computer Science, Vilnius University,
Vilnius, Lithuania
{virgilijus.krinickij,linas.bukauskas}@mif.vu.lt

Abstract. The risk of becoming part of a cyber incident is increasing daily. The gap in skills in human-human, human-computer interaction is one of the biggest challenges facing the cyber security industry. It is essential to raise questions within the cyber security community about the importance of communication issues and challenges faced during cyber security events. Information exchange is the most important aspect of successfully mitigating a cyber event. Information is key, and communication while exchanging information in a particular situation enables the person in a cyber security event to perform rational decisions. While many security issues can be mitigated by artificial intelligence and machine learning, there are other tasks that people can only solve. Computer systems are manifestations of tasks and processes that sometimes require adaptation. Humans are working in groups separated by work position or tools. Therefore it is imperative to understand that software tools can not interact the way human-human communication works. One way to address the ongoing problem is to expand and reevaluate our own requirements when it comes to hiring and implementing apprenticeship programs and training for groups. Group training preparing for cyber security events is crucial. Gaps may appear in the group training chain. This work describes a multi-step methodology for assessing group performance in training of challenging cyber security events. The prototype created from the research assesses the groups working capabilities and decision making while using adaptive chaining communication dissemination. The prototype tries to identify the missing or broken links in interoperability of the group and groups. Also, the prototype tries to simulate stress levels in the group per different cyber events.

Keywords: Cybersecurity · training event · group interoperability

1 Introduction

Group interoperability training for cybersecurity personnel can present some unique challenges [2]. These challenges may range from confidentiality to personal stress level management. Confidentiality concerns are mostly related to cybersecurity personnel working with highly sensitive information and volatile systems, which can make it difficult to share information openly and transparently with others outside their organization. Technical expertise challenges are evident when cybersecurity personnel require a high level of technical expertise to perform their jobs effectively, making it challenging to find training programs that meet their specific needs. Communication barriers are a challenge when cybersecurity professionals work in highly technical fields and may need help communicating complex ideas to others who lack the same expertise. Challenges of stress level management put for cybersecurity personnel facing stress while making timely decisions, prolonged monitoring, and performing mitigation tasks in response to cybersecurity events are very important for individuals.

Addressing the mentioned challenges, group interoperability training for cybersecurity operators should be designed to address their unique needs and concerns. This can include providing specialized training tailored to their technical expertise, establishing clear guidelines for sharing sensitive information, and providing opportunities for communication, collaboration and mitigating stress. In addition, group interoperability training can include simulations and exercises that help cybersecurity personnel develop their skills in a safe and controlled environment, which can help them better prepare for real-world scenarios and stay in a comfort zone.

2   Related Work

To demonstrate or learn new skills achieved in prior experiences, a cybersecurity expert often participate in cybersecurity exercises provided by the organization. These types of educational activities are conducted globally. The most basic intention is to see how good the "blue team" will be while defending against the "red team" and vice versa. Due to the considerable preparation time and effort, the organizations neglect other challenges presented to the group.

One of the top games released for cybersecurity personnel training is Cyber-SIEGE [3]. It combines both human factors and the technical background of a single player. Although for one person to play the game is a boot camp level experience. Applying the same methods for the group training, it lacks teaming experience. In this game, a player is put in a simulated organization with the role of an IT specialist hired to protect the "inside" of the organization, but there is little to do with group interoperability. The game establishes a one-to-one relationship between the cyber event and stress. However, the result is only shown in a way that a player did not succeed in his job, without any additional explanation on how to maintain the stress levels.

Different approaches are suggested for cybersecurity range that was created to demonstrate a holistic approaches, ignoring the stress, confidentiality concerns [7] and other issues that may come across while playing. Cyber range is an important piece of the plan but concerns arise what will a group do if the training fails based on the given challenges.

Based on the research, Japan faces a shortage of human resources [11] and the production for a cyber range is very costly on a massive scale. Human resources was always a problem in different spheres of work and for a country this means that less effort then needed is being put through from any direction to produce cybersecurity training results.

Bayes networks are widely used in many different systems to evaluate causality. These networks help determine the probabilities of an action that may occur. For example, some event directly influences another event, or a result is made in conclusion based on the probabilities that those events had. While working, we can use Bayes networks to model the stress level of an employee who works within the system. Depending on the difficulty of the alert and the amount, we can determine an employee's comfort zone while working. In most cases, low, medium, and hard stress levels are presented as classes. If a person can not handle the level that was initially given to him, we can say that level of work is too hard, and the comfort zone is breached [12].

3   Model

In this section, we propose a model that would help cybersecurity groups to undergo more maintained and balanced training in cybersecurity exercises. In our model, we propose to use the key assumption check technique [9] with Bloom's Taxonomy [4] to evaluate groups' interoperability training. Bloom's Taxonomy is a framework for categorizing educational goals into six levels of cognitive complexity, ranging from lower-order thinking skills to higher-order thinking skills. While it is not specifically designed for key assumption checks, it can be used as a helpful tool to guide the process of assessing assumptions underlying an argument or idea [5].

Bloom's taxonomy uses six cognitive complexity steps for categorizing educational goals. With the key assumption check, we can validate all six steps:

- **Knowledge Level:** checking the factual knowledge based on the technical security assumption or skills.
- **Comprehension Level:** checking the technical knowledge about the meaning of terms and concepts that must be explicitly put to the test by the security environment.
- **Application Level:** checking assumptions if applicability of a security principle or concept to a particular situation or context.
- **Analysis Level:** checking assumptions about the risk, technical failures, and misconfiguration relationships among different threat factors or variables.
- **Evaluation Level:** checking assumptions about the value of significance of a particular conclusion or outcome securing the infrastructure.
- **Synthesis Level:** checking newly created assumptions about the validity or reliability of configured and integrated resources or evidence to defend assets.

In this work, we will not touch the Synthesis level with the revised Bloom's taxonomy called "Create" [8]. We focus on skills or learning features that improve from the basic level. Using Bloom's cognition taxonomy to guide the key assumption checks for the cybersecurity domain is not new but mostly observed in computing curricula. We assess the assumptions based on the scenario that the groups must perform on average. We present the model encapsulated in the cyber range. We treat cyber range as a physical or virtual environment, or a simulated TableTop simulation of a cyber range can be used.

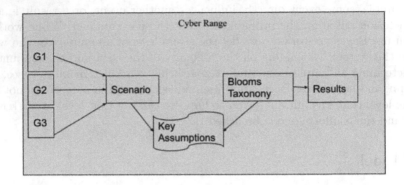

Fig. 1. Group Interoperability Training Model

In Fig. 1 you can see G1, G2, and G3 are the cybersecurity groups that participate in the cybersecurity exercises. A group goal is to secure network infrastructure assets given a scenario where the groups are having cybersecurity incidents. All groups face similar cyber incidents. We propose a scenario where a group of cybersecurity specialists train in cybersecurity exercises. Alternatively, team exercises could be established in a Tabletop environment [1,6] or in a virtualized cyber range environment proposed in [7]. If all the groups are expected to follow very similar solutions the possible detours in solutions can be observed and evaluated.

For example, in the scenario provided by [6] G1 must establish communication with a supervisor from IT department to an industrial observer to manage the systems that release pressure/open pipe. However non-negotiated release of pressure on the pipe could damage the other dependent groups' imaginary system. Based on the situation, evaluation of the choices made by one team could be validated as well as possible dependencies observed. One of the possible assumptions to test from the *knowledge level* is to check the management computer that controls the pipe really needs to be opened and is compatible with the other team infrastructures. As a result calculation of a score is based on the provided key assumptions mixing both infrastructure status and the facts teams understand about each other.

4   Results

By adding key assumptions to the Blooms Taxonomy and giving them to the scenario, we accumulate specific comprehensive reasoning which correlates between these two aspects and answers the taxonomy's level assumptions:

- Knowledge Level: as mentioned earlier in the given scenario, groups G1, G2, and G3 need to establish communication with a supervisor from a computer (level 2) to manage the hardware that releases the pressure of the network. After this, the teams think of a possible solution for the given scenario chapter or use the generated solutions provided by the scenario system. The solutions may be:
  1. Send a message to the supervisory computer level (level 2) to release pressure/open the pipe.
  2. Keep watching the monitor. Maybe the pressure will go down on its own.
  3. Send a message to level 2 to stop all of the flow.
  4. Block network traffic to the supervisory computer to protect the pipeline.
  The factual assumption here could be in a question form where we ask the group if the pipe is really in danger. Here we find the challenges in the communication barriers between groups or even one group's internal team members. If we also add a counter to the problem (majority voting), meaning that the time needed to solve the problem would be in a small time frame, the stress level of the group would increase dramatically after the first visible failure.
- Comprehension Level: The scenario chapter may present terms or concepts that are unclear or vague as instructions for computer specialists. Meaning that communication between teams or communication over the system that needs to be protected must be logical and at the corresponding experience level. The group needs to check the assumption about these terms and concepts. An internal or external triage within the groups is conducted for such activities. They can be conducted through a system called MISP [10] or in any other way. The challenge here is information sharing and common security-related dictionary usage. Organizations or teams that associate themselves with organizations tend not to use the given systems or disclose cybersecurity event information in general because of knowledge leakage. Despite this, information sharing, even in cybersecurity exercises, is vital for teams' successful defence against a threat actor.
- Application Level: when a group figures out the fact of a problem and the facts of terms, it is then when a group can check assumptions about the applicability of a principle or concept to a particular situation. Meaning that a group's provided solution should be implemented to stop a threat actor.
- Analysis Level: when a group adds a solution, we can check if that solution is working in that specific situation. One can conclude that the key works in the scenario event the implemented solution is successful.
- Evaluation Level: If the implemented solution is working, then we can check the assumptions about the value or significance of a particular conclusion or outcome. Meaning that we can say in a predicate form whether the solution was successful in execution or not. This gives the group much-needed relief, mostly in their stress levels.

5 Conclusions

In state-of-the-art cybersecurity defence exercises, groups and group members do not simulate or go through the evaluation process when knowledge levels are evaluated. By Using Blooms Taxonomy with key assumption checks and producing a systemic approach, we can use the presented methodology to address the cybersecurity challenges in a moderated, safe environment.

These challenges are unmet because of the time constraints allocated for training and preparing a feasible cybersecurity event scenario. Because the challenges in group interoperability training are multidimensional, the major problem arises in group confidentiality concerns. Even in exercise-level cybersecurity exercises, groups often are reluctant to share sensitive data. This leads to bad group communication and possibly failed exercises.

References

1. Brilingaitė, A., Bukauskas, L., Krinickij, V., Kutka, E.: Environment for cybersecurity tabletop exercises. In: ECGBL 2017 11th European Conference on Game-Based Learning, pp. 47–55. Academic Conferences and publishing limited, Manchester (2017)
2. Brilingaitė, A., Bukauskas, L., Juozapavičius, A., Kutka, E.: Overcoming information-sharing challenges in cyber defence exercises. J. Cybersecur. **8**(1), tyac001 (2022). https://doi.org/10.1093/cybsec/tyac001
3. Cone, B.D., Irvine, C.E., Thompson, M.F., Nguyen, T.D.: A video game for cyber security training and awareness. Comput. Secur. **26**(1), 63–72 (2007)
4. Kennedy, D.: Writing and Using Learning Outcomes: A Practical Guide. University College Cork, Cork (2006)
5. Krathwohl, D.R.: A revision of bloom's taxonomy: an overview. Theory Pract. **41**(4), 212–218 (2002)
6. Kvietinskaitė, G., Bukauskas, L., Krinickij, V.: Cyber security table-top exercise gamification with dynamic scenario for qualification assessment. In: HCI International 2022-Late Breaking Posters: 24th International Conference on Human-Computer Interaction, HCII 2022, Virtual Event, June 26-July 1, 2022, Proceedings, Part I, vol. 1654, pp. 54–62. Springer, Cham (2022). https://doi.org/10.1007/978-3-031-19679-9_8
7. Leitner, M., et al.: AIT cyber range: flexible cyber security environment for exercises, training and research. In: Proceedings of the European Interdisciplinary Cybersecurity Conference, pp. 1–6 (2020)
8. Mizbani, M., Chalak, A.: Analyzing reading and writing activities of Iranian EFL textbook prospect 3 based on bloom's revised taxonomy. J. Appl. Linguist. Lang. Res. **4**(2), 13–27 (2017)
9. Pherson, R.: Overcoming analytic mindsets: five simple techniques. In: Annual Meeting on Emerging Issues in National and International Security, Washington, DC (2005)
10. Van Haastrecht, M., et al.: A shared cyber threat intelligence solution for SMEs. Electronics **10**(23), 2913 (2021)
11. Wilhelmson, N., Svensson, T.: Handbook for planning, running and evaluating information technology and cyber security exercises. Försvarshögskolan (FHS) (2011)
12. Zeng, W., Germanos, V.: Modelling hybrid cyber kill chain. In: PNSE@ Petri Nets/ACSD, pp. 143–160 (2019)

Research on the Preference of University Students for the Form of Library Desktop Partition

Jinzhu Li and Zhanying Gao(✉)

School of Design, South China University of Technology, Guangzhou 510006, China
202221055594@mail.scut.edu.cn

Abstract. Performance and psychological perception of humans are impacted by the physical environment. The library study room is one of the most important learning spaces for college students. Desktop partition is a crucial component of a shared desk, and how it is configured can have a significant impact on users. This study uses Pearson correlation coefficients and perceptual images to discuss students' preferences for desktop partition. According to the findings, increasing the prevalence of desktop partitions is in line with student expectations. Students attach more importance to privacy and spatial independence when using shared desks, which is supposed to relieve stress. In addition, due to the various sensory experiences, different materials could be appropriate for different learning intensities.

Keywords: Desktop partition · Perceptual preference · University library · Learning performance

1 Introduction

Library study areas are the main places where university student study on a daily basis. For students who live on campus, such spaces are basically the second space, which is a dedicated study space outside the dormitory [1]. Libraries are short-time study spaces, users do not have fixed seats, so there is a problem of seat selection. Researchers from Korea have studied the relationship between student achievement and library use, and they discovered that there is a definite positive association between the two [2]. The learning environment and facilities are particularly important for encouraging students to spend more time in the library. In public learning environments, the movements of others can cause visual distractions that have a negative impact on concentration.

The study and reading area, the desktop computer area, the seminar room, the sofa lounge area, and the corridor seat make up the sittable area at college libraries [3]. Wook, Lee Jin classified library furniture into reading furniture, storage furniture, reading room furniture, and lounge furniture [4]. In this paper, we focus on the influence of desktop partition. Common library study desktops in Chinese and foreign universities can be classified according to the degree of obstruction to the view: open, semi-open, frontal

C. Stephanidis et al. (Eds.): HCII 2023, CCIS 1834, pp. 279–287, 2023.
https://doi.org/10.1007/978-3-031-35998-9_39

cover, and a wrap-around cover. Open type refers to the desktop without partition; semi-open type uses some objects or low partitions to divide the desktop area; frontal cover is to block the front view with different materials partitions; wrap-around blocking often consists of three baffles in the left, right, and front three directions. The desktop arrangements in the College libraries are mainly open, semi-open, and frontal shielding desktops (see Table 1).

The desktop partitioning method also has an impact on psychological aspects including the perception of privacy and security. The purpose of this paper is to investigate the preference of college students for desktop partition in library study areas and what specific effects desktop partition has on their study process. Based on the theory of Kansei engineering, we further investigate the influence of desktop partition material, structure, student personality, and study tasks on their preferences [5]. In a space under a learning atmosphere, it is discussed how the design of desk partition can reduce anxiety, distractions, and increase learning efficiency during the learning process. The results of the discussion can help to understand the psychological state of students when studying in college libraries, which can be used to improve the design of college library desktops and attract more students to use them.

Table 1. Common seating types in self-study areas in university libraries

Structure	Partition form	Material
Open	No partition	
Half open	1.Desktop lamps 2.Short partition 3.Arch	Wood
Front cover	1.Full screen baffle 2.Hollowed-out baffle	Glass, Wood, plywood, Acrylic board
Surrounding cover	Three sides baffle	Glass, Wood, plywood, Acrylic board

2   Theoretical Background

Ronald Beckers divided students' preferences for the study environment into social and physical dimensions, focusing respectively on personal privacy, interaction, autonomy and comfort, aesthetics, ICT facilities, and layout [6]. This study focused on desk partitioning facilities in the library study area and explore its impact on students both on the physical dimension and psychological dimensions.

Previous studies on concentration and reading performance have focused on auditory interference and background noise, and there are fewer studies related to visual aspects. Researchers found that different work surface illumination and light source color temperature can bring sensory differences to users and affect their learning efficiency [7]. Considering the overall environment, Korean scholars investigated the usage behavior of users in book cafes and found that users prefer to stay in a single café environment, which reflects the fact that factors such as furniture arrangement and openness of view can influence the psychological patterns of users [8].

Hwan-Hee Cho et al. proposed a revised model of cognitive load emphasizing the physical learning environment in 2014 [9]. In this revised model, the learning task is separated from the physical learning environment, and environmental factors are considered an integral part of performing the learning task. It is evident that a self-study environment in college libraries that does not meet the psychological expectations of most students can cause problems such as reduced motivation and less efficient assignments.

For the library, Kaeli Nieves-Whitmore has studied the relationship between college library design and students' library anxiety, which may originate from multiple factors such as space layout, usage skills, and noise level, and finally suggested that improving the academic library environment is one of the effective ways to reduce anxiety [10]. Lim, Lisa & Kim, and Minseok have studied seating choice in college libraries to clarify the relationship between seating preference and visual environment; this study showed that individuals tend to reduce their own visual exposure when choosing a seat [11].

Users who share a desk may also suffer from discomfort due to distance. Szpak et al. found that social discomfort can lead to physiological anxiety and increased attentional withdrawal [12]. For users of library common desktops, a two-dimensional division of the desktop is also necessary to reduce anxiety and discomfort by delineating the boundaries of personal space.

3 Conceptual Model

The object of this experimental study is a desktop partition device, which is a physical product and its physical properties are conceivable. Different structures can have a great impact on the students' view and interpersonal distance, so it is one of the most important factors. And it is to be further explored whether physical attributes affect the user's preference for the type of desktop.

According to the cognitive load model proposed by Hwan-Hee Cho, the effects of the physical environment include three categories: cognitive, physiological, and affective effects [13]. Combining this view, the following hypothesis was made for the conceptual model of this experiment (as shown in the figure) that the three elements may have an impact on desktop partition preference.

In order to understand the preference of college students for desktop partition forms, the following aspects need to be studied mainly: (1) What is the preference of students for the physical properties of baffles? For what reasons? (2) What are the differences in students' psychological performance in choosing different partitions? (3) What is the impact of the type of desktop partition on students' minds and bodies?

Due to a large number of elements and the possible interrelationship between them, the experimental results were tested using correlation coefficient analysis (Fig. 1).

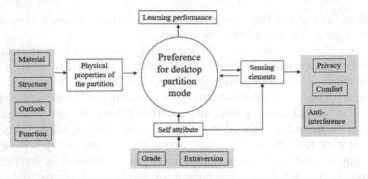

Fig. 1. Concept model

4 Research Methods

A questionnaire was developed with propositions to measure the preference for the desktop partition, based on findings from a collection of relevant literature and fieldwork. Students participating in the study were asked to mark their opinions after carefully reading the propositions. For the perceptual level, based on the Likert scale, from (1) = It is completely inconsistent with me to (5) = It is exactly for me. For the physical characteristics, from (1) = Very unimportant to (5) = Very important. Students' opinions about library desk partitions were also collected to determine the validity of the questionnaire respondents and to provide more references for subsequent improvements.

To make the experiment more generalizable, the type of devices respondents use most often in the library was collected. In terms of individual personality, subjects were asked to self-perceive the introversion-extroversion type of their personality in the questionnaire as a data reference for the experiment. According to perceptual engineering, a stimulus map is needed to trigger the subjective evaluation of the user. Firstly, actual pictures of the five most common forms of partitions in libraries were collected from the Internet for subjects to choose. Through the first round of perceptual selection of the available pictures, the respondents were divided into a group choosing no partitions and a group choosing partitions and answered different follow-up questionnaires to explore the psychological elements influencing their choices. Users who preferred partitions were asked to rate six forms of desktop partitions, which were designed using common forms and materials in colleges and universities, and users them perceptually in order to further understand preferences and needs (Table 2).

Table 2. Stimulus image

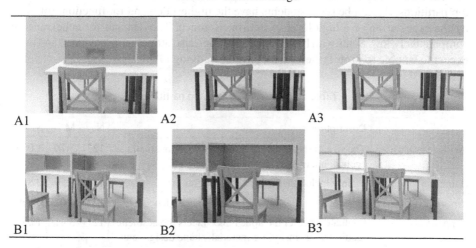

A1   A2   A3

B1   B2   B3

5 Data Analysis

The questionnaires were collected online, and 160 valid questionnaires were collected from full-time college students across China. 127 of them regularly go to the library for self-study, and these samples were extracted as the focus of analysis. 33 respondents never go to the library for self-study. Among them, 51.5% disliked the study atmosphere in the library, 48.5% said they were easily disturbed by others, 30.3% thought the current seating arrangement in the library was unreasonable, and some of the reasons for not going were out of social fear.

5.1 Basic Analysis

Further data analysis was presented for the 127 respondents who frequently visit the library for self-study.

Different study devices and study tasks were the decisive factors in users' perceptions. 43.3% of users use laptops most frequently in the library, ranking first; 39.4% often use paper books and the rest chose tablets. The results reflected that the learning tasks most frequently performed in the library were problem-solving (77.95%), followed by writing (61.42%), and the remaining were memorization tasks (25.98%) and creative work (14.96%). On the question of whether they would choose different types of seating when performing different learning tasks, 46.46% chose yes, 48.03% chose no.

The 123 subjects first selected the five pictures of partition structures. Respondents who selected P1 and P2 preferred open seating, set as group A, while those who selected P3, P4, and P5 preferred closed seating, set as group B. As the results shows, the reliability Alpha of Group A was 0.920 and Group B was 0.860, and the reliability coefficients of each section were in the range of 0.75–1, indicating that the scale had good internal consistency.

The following tables gives further descriptive statistics for each attribute of the desktop partitions. As can be seen, students have the highest demand for function, followed by the expectation of a high level of anti-interference. The demand for appearance is comparatively low. Seats with better space divisions also attract more students, and users expect to be able to protect their privacy while studying (Table 3).

Table 3. Properties of Desktop partitions.

	Description	N	M	SD
Wideness of view	The size of the range of desktop occlusion, small occlusion means bigger wildness of view	127	3.76	1.059
Function	Mainly including the socket and lightning	127	4.50	0.805
Space division	Desktop area division and space independence	127	4.02	0.930
Appearance	Evaluate whether the appearance meets the aesthetic requirements, including material, shape design, etc	127	3.41	1.049
Intimate feeling	Protection of user privacy	127	4.39	0.807
Anti-interference	The ability to reduce visual and acoustic interference in use	127	4.30	0.857

5.2 Correlation Analysis

P test results are as follows. The correlation results are significant at 0.01 (bilateral) and * at 0.05 (bilateral).

According to the results, Grade and extraverted degree did not show correlations with a preference for desk dividers, whereas perceptions of anxiety had more correlations with preferred outcomes. However, a linear correlation was shown between the physical properties of the partition and the perceived elements and learning performance.

For group A, the wide vision will make them feel more comfortable, but the independence of the desktop is also strongly related to comfort. At the same time, the division of the desktop is strongly related to anxiety and exposure, indicating that even for no partition, there is a need for a reasonable desktop division. The sense of privacy is strongly related to anti-interference and social distance, indicating that students need to maintain social distance to protect privacy, and a sense of privacy can reduce interference in the learning process.

Group B, pay more attention to desktop independence, which is strongly related to visual interference, social pressure, and learning pressure. Meanwhile, the privacy and security of the seat can improve the comfort of group B, when using the seat. Compared with group A, group B attaches more importance to the sense of privacy and security and has higher requirements for social distance. When the distance from strangers is reduced, group B will show a higher stress level (Table 4).

As for the correlation between physical elements and learning performance, a comfortable learning environment can improve learning enthusiasm and efficiency but has no effect on learning endurance (Table 5).

Table 4. Correlation analysis 1 of group A

Variable		1	2	3	4	5	6	7	8	9	10	11	12
1	Function	1											
2	Appearance	0.132	1										
3	Wideness of view	−0.001	0.115	1									
4	Comfort	0.089	0.133	.921**	1								
5	Space division	−0.078	0.074	.905**	.902**	1							
6	Intimate feeling	0.260	0.321	0.272	0.178	0.209	1						
7	Anti-interference	.377*	0.096	0.321	.386*	0.245	.499**	1					
8	Social distance	0.329	0.261	0.194	0.104	0.185	.665**	0.263	1				
9	Anxiety	−0.116	0.251	.879**	.884**	.893**	0.233	0.209	0.044	1			
10	Exposure	0.024	0.077	.863**	.899**	.903**	0.089	0.227	0.004	.872**	1		
11	Embarrassment	−0.142	0.012	0.090	0.020	0.101	−0.062	0.039	0.191	0.127	0.023	1	
12	Leisure	−0.105	0.154	.939**	.889**	.907**	0.183	0.177	0.087	.902**	.897**	0.078	1

Table 5. Correlation analysis 1 of group B

		1	2	3	4	5	6	7	8	9	10	11	12
1	Wideness of view	1											
2	Function	.208*	1										
3	Appearance	.355**	0.152	1									
4	Space division	0.049	0.155	0.069	1								
5	Anti-interference	.195*	.323**	0.136	.208*	1							
6	Social distance	.213*	.277**	0.119	.418**	.378**	1						
7	Intimate feeling	0.070	0.064	0.079	.715**	0.119	.396**	1					
8	Sence of safty	0.138	.216*	0.125	.713**	.267**	.398**	.752**	1				
9	Learning pressure	0.034	−0.155	0.038	.341**	0.122	0.107	.284**	.428**	1			
10	social pressure	0.128	−0.034	-0.039	.490**	0.196	.306**	.481**	.516**	.613**	1		
11	Visual interference	.232*	0.031	0.111	.699**	.221*	.409**	.685**	.629**	.211*	.449**	1	
12	comfort	0.038	0.092	−0.084	.647**	0.144	.335**	.539**	.665**	.400**	.488**	.608**	1

5.3 Perceptual Images Analysis

For Group B respondents, stimulus image selection was conducted to explore the impression gap given by different material baffles, including frosted glass, warm wood, and white acrylic panels, with the choice of the material referenced to libraries in national and international universities. The difference in the degree of user preference between the two structures of single-sided baffles and three-sided baffles is also discussed. Some common adjectives for library desktops, including calming, closed, positive, depressing, stable, and anxious, were summarized by randomly selected interviewees from the field and related literature, and the respondents in Group B were asked to choose by their own visual perception through a Likert scale, and their combined preference for the six images was rated.

B1 has got the highest score, which is structured as a three-sided baffle with warm wood material. For the perception of closure and positive feeling, the score of closure of B1, B2, and B3 is significantly higher than that of the frontal baffle; and the wood material is significantly better than the frosted glass and white acrylic panel in blocking the line of sight. The white acrylic material of the frontal blocking is more likely to give a positive feeling.

Stability and sedation are two similar feelings. As shown, B1 and A1, which are two made of wood, give the strongest sense of stability. Meanwhile, B1 has a higher sense of sedation, indicating that a relatively strong sense of closure can somehow bring calmness to people. Frosted glass scores lower on both characteristics, probably because of its translucent characteristics, which reduces the sense of stability brought to people.

All six types of baffles got a low level of depression and agitation. In contrast, acrylic panels and glass give a lower level of depression; wood gives a sense of stability and calmness while bringing a certain level of depression and a relatively high likelihood of causing impatience, which means that wooden partitions may be suitable for short periods of intense study, such as doing problems, but not for long periods of low-intensity tasks, such as reading and writing.

6   Discussion and Conclusions

Today's students are under increasing strain. According to the analysis, Students attach the most importance to desktop segmentation, which can improve the independence of personal space; Students are also concerned about their privacy and need an environment that is more anti-interference. However, dark materials and some of the wraparound baffles will give off a sense of closure, which may have the opposite effect. As learning tools advance, the function of library seating should be regarded seriously. More consideration should be given to the allocation of different types of seats in university libraries, and more partitioned seats should be installed. More students will visit the library to study as a result of these actions.

Introversion did not significantly correlate with a preference for desktop selection, in line with the findings of Fatema's experiments on the effect of noise on attention. Users are more focused on the anxiety associated with stress levels than the stress of socializing with strangers. The complex relationship between library design and library anxiety, which has been researched by Nieves-Whitmore, needs to be explained in light of information science and behavioral psychology.

The shortcoming of this experiment is that the influence of interior decorative elements on users is not discussed; however, the general library environment is uniform, mainly in wooden tones, although it is to be further examined whether the shades of wooden tones and the angle of shelf placement bring about changes in the psychological perception of users. Furthermore, the location of seats in the library should also be considered.

References

1. Oldenburg, R., Brissett, D.: The third place. Qual. Sociol. **5**(4), 265–284 (1982)
2. Park, J.-B.: The relationship analysis between academic library usage and academic achievement. J. Korean Libr. Inf. Sci. Soc. **45**(2), 5–27 (2014)
3. Applegate, R.: The library is for studying: student preferences for study space. J. Acad. Librariansh. **35**(4), 341–346 (2009)
4. Wook, L.J.: A study on the symbolism of library designed furniture. J. Korean Inst. Cult. Architect. **72**, 51–58 (2020)
5. Kanda, T.: Beginning of Kansei engineering and development of Kansei goods. ICIC Expr. Lett. **4**(3A), 601–605 (2010)
6. Beckers, R., van der Voordt, T., Dewulf, G.: Learning space preferences of higher education students. Build. Environ. **104**, 243–252 (2016)
7. Li, T.: The influence of illumination environment on visual comfort and learning efficiency under different reading modes. China Illum. Eng. J. **33**(02), 109–116
8. Lee, S.Y., Myung-A, L.: A study on the spatial characteristics and user behavior of public book cafes. Korean Inst. Inter. Des. J. **31**(4), 93–102 (2022)
9. Choi, H.-H., van Merriënboer, J.J.G., Paas, F.: Effects of the physical environment on cognitive load and learning: towards a new model of cognitive load. Educ. Psychol. Rev. **26**(2), 225–244 (2014). https://doi.org/10.1007/s10648-014-9262-6
10. Nieves-Whitmore, K.: The relationship between academic library design and library anxiety in students. Portal-Libr. Acad. **21**(3), 485–510 (2021)
11. Lim, L., et al.: Seat-choosing behaviors and visibility: a case study of library reading rooms as study environments. J. Archit. Plan. Res. **35**(4), 271–290 (2018)
12. Szpak, A., et al.: Too close for comfort: the effect of interpersonal proximity on spatial attention. In: Cognitive Processing, vol. 16: pp. S79-S80 (2015)
13. Gheewalla, F., McClelland, A., Furnham, A.: Effects of background noise and extraversion on reading comprehension performance. Ergonomics **64**(5), 593–599 (2021)

Exploring the Potential of Augmented Reality in English Language Learning: Designing an Interactive Pronunciation Training App

Farzin Matin(✉)🆔 and Eleni Mangina🆔

School of Computer Science, University College Dublin, Dublin, Ireland
farzin.matin@ucdconnect.ie

Abstract. Augmented reality (AR) has the potential to transform teaching and learning by providing real-time interactions, displaying information in various ways, and connecting the physical and digital worlds. While AR technology is becoming more accessible through mobile devices and head-mounted displays (HMDs), its widespread adoption in education depends on providing an engaging and interactive user experience. Designing appropriate AR user interfaces is crucial for ensuring the technology is easily adopted and enjoyed by users. One area where AR can be particularly beneficial is in the teaching of the English language and correct pronunciation, especially at an early stage of education. In the English language, vowels play a key role as they appear in every syllable of every word. Understanding vowel sounds is closely tied to reading skills. To address this, an AR-based pronunciation training app has been developed, based on linguistic theory and with a focus on usability for students learning English as a second language. The app is implemented using a Microsoft HoloLens head-mounted display and provides an AR-based learning experience. This study describes the factors that led to the development of the AR-based pronunciation app. This is an app that allows a user to be assessed on the pronunciation of selected 3D learning objects and receive meaningful feedback. As hardware advances and becomes more widely available, realistic holograms will be created. This will enable better technology integration with the physical world and more intuitive input methods. This will further enhance the user experience and increase technology acceptance.

Keywords: Augmented reality (AR) · AR-based pronunciation · User experience · English language pronunciation · Second language learning · Pronunciation training

This document is the result of the research supported by European Union's Horizon 2020 research and innovation program under grant agree-ment No 856533, project ARETE.

1   Introduction

The concept of augmented reality (AR) combines virtual objects with the real world, allowing users to experience both in real-time [1]. It is possible for users to interact with AR in multiple ways, including visually, auditorily, and physically [2]. With its ability to create innovative and immersive experiences, AR is increasingly used across various industries, and its potential applications are endless [3]. From enhancing educational experiences to revolutionizing how we market and sell products, AR is poised to have a significant impact on how we interact with the world around us. AR technology has become an increasingly popular tool in education, offering creative and engaging ways for learners to engage with educational content [4]. It can improve education by enhancing the interaction and perception of real-world objects, promoting active learning, and integrating 3D objects as teaching materials to improve learners' achievement [5].

Learning a foreign language can be challenging for young children, but the rewards can be enormous. According to studies conducted by Harvard University over a period of time, children who learn foreign languages at a young age experience a boost in their critical thinking abilities, as well as an increase in creativity and mental flexibility [6]. Establishing a motivating learning environment for young learners is essential [7]. Traditionally, English is introduced to children through songs, textbook exercises, and storybooks. The advancement of technology, however, has led to different learning preferences for today's children.

Many studies have demonstrated that AR can effectively enhance English language skills such as speaking, reading, and listening, despite the possibility of technical difficulties [8]. Mastery of English at an early age with proper pronunciation is crucial to effectively communicating in English. Pronunciation plays a crucial role in language acquisition because it directly impacts one's ability to communicate. The vowels play one of the most crucial roles in pronunciation as they can be found in every syllable of every English word. Learners' ability to understand vowel sounds is directly linked to their reading skills and can positively impact their English proficiency [9, 10].

The importance of correct vowel pronunciation in English language learning has been demonstrated by some studies. These studies have found that it can significantly improve learners' reading proficiency and contribute to their overall language development [11, 12]. However, despite its crucial role in language acquisition, vowel pronunciation has often been neglected in English language teaching, particularly in primary schools. To address this gap, this study investigates the potential of augmented reality (AR) technology to teach English vowel sounds to primary school students. The purpose of this paper is to explore the effectiveness of using AR technology for teaching basic English to non-native young learners, with a particular focus on pronunciation. Through the use of AR, we hope to increase learners' motivation and engagement in language learning. This is a new approach to teaching English that departs from traditional methods.

1.1 Related Work

While augmented reality is relatively novel to the educational field, many researchers suggest that it enhances the school curriculum [13]. Augmented reality boosts students' motivation to learn English [14]. Moreover, it offers the potential to enhance the educational system. It is considered an effective tool to facilitate learning English and increase student motivation [15].

According to Barreira et al. [16] children who played augmented reality games learned the language faster than those who received only traditional instruction. It appears that augmented reality can enhance educational experiences.

Augmented reality (AR) has been explored for superimposing digital objects on real-world environments. Thorne et al. developed an environmental education game that increased learner engagement [17]. Similarly, Sykes et al. developed an AR game called Mentira that uses spatial context to teach Spanish [18].

The use of augmented reality in the classroom could enhance reading comprehension and help students learn reading skills, according to Rau et al. [19].

In another study, Küçük and colleagues examined how augmented reality influences the attitudes, cognitive loads, and achievement of secondary school students studying English as a foreign language (EFL) [20]. Using augmented reality as a tool for studying English was found to be comfortable and effective by students [21]. To determine whether AR combined with speech recognition technology can enhance learning outcomes and improve user satisfaction, Che Dalim and colleagues conducted two experiments. A significant advantage was shown between the experiment and control groups in terms of learning outcomes and enjoyment of the practice [22].

After obtaining promising outcomes, it is hypothesized that augmented reality (AR) could improve pronunciation training by enhancing muscle control, which is commonly associated with mimicry in other exercises. Moreover, AR provides a captivating and interactive visual representation of articulation that learners can manipulate and explore from different perspectives. This makes the learning experience more stimulating and engaging. Providing children with such opportunities can enhance their learning experience and increase their motivation to succeed academically.

2 Material and Method

This section describes the materials and methods used in this project that produced a vowel trainer application for Microsoft Hololens2. With the vowel trainer, users can assess their pronunciation of selected 3D learning objects and receive meaningful feedback. By utilizing WordsWorthLearning's literacy program [23], Soapbox API [24], the project advanced current paper-based assessment methodologies and assisted users in learning vowel pronunciation. The project also utilized Soapbox API, a cloud-based speech recognition API, to analyze and provide feedback on the user's pronunciation. The animations used for the project were created using Character Creator 3 software [25], 3dsMax [26], and Unity. Orkestra was used for communication between the teacher and the student [27].

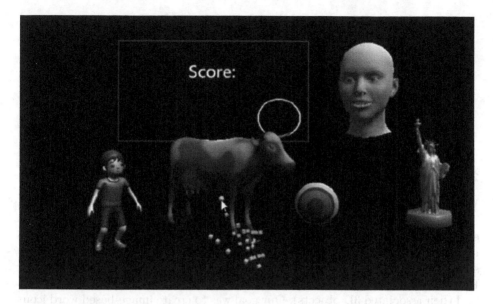

Fig. 1. Selecting an item triggers mouth animation when selecting a 3D object.

2.1   Application Development

This section describes the technical process of creating the vowel trainer application.

- Using the Character Creator 3 software, unique facial animations were created for vowel training. These animations blended some of the main characteristics of male and female models.
- A series of editing and polishing steps were performed using Photoshop to enhance the mouth texture.
- To create the reference poses, CC3 poses were exported and imported into 3DsMax. All mouth poses are linked to morph targets with the morpher modifier. To indicate the order, intensity, and duration of each morph target, keyframes have been placed into the timeline.
- Models were exported from 3dsMax (incorporating morpher modifier animations) as fbx files and animation keyframes were added. Following the import of the models into Unity, they were tested with some changes and tweaks to determine the right speed and pauses. There was also an alternative model developed with the mouth separated from the head to be further utilized for users who prefer not to view the full-face model.
- With the assistance of WordsWorth Learning vowel charts and 3D modeling software, a model with four different animations relating to the vowel shape to be made by the user was created.
- Students and teachers communicate through the orchestra. Orchestra allows users to subscribe to JSON events. Depending on whether the user is a student or teacher, a different JSON is sent, and a different method is called when received.

Table 1. Different vowel shapes and their associated 3D objects.

Vowel Shape	3D Objects
Spread	Bee, Ink, Apple, Mail
Round	Tooth, Bald, Sauce
Resting	Bird, Cup, Hammer
Moving	Boy, Cow, Eye, Statue

2.2 Vowel Trainer Description

When a teacher selects a menu option, objects related to vowel shapes are displayed for students. The student can select an object and hear an audio clip that explains how to pronounce it correctly. A 3D face model shows an animation to highlight the vowel shape. The menu options display different objects that correspond to the shape of the mouth when pronouncing a particular word, including Resting, Round, Spread, and Moving (Table 1. shows the different vowel shapes and their associated 3D objects). Our goal was to create image-based word icons that simulate this process in an AR scene to help students accurately reproduce the target phoneme/vowel. This was done to test whether users responded better to learning when word icons were supplied with a 3D model of face/mouth movement (As seen in Fig. 1, selecting an item activates an animation when a 3D object is selected). After selecting an object, the correct pronunciation of the object is played, and then a countdown begins, prompting the user to repeat the word. The audio is analyzed using the Soapbox API, and a score is received based on pronunciation accuracy. The higher the score, the better the pronunciation. Figure 2 illustrates a detailed analysis of a student's attempt displayed to the teacher.

3   Research Design and Methodology

This experiment examines whether augmented reality technology can enhance English language learning outcomes by using this technology. Usability tests are conducted on potential app users. As a result of usability testing feedback, the study will refine the prototype app. It will recruit 20 participants with no prior knowledge of applying AR to English language learning via social media and email distribution. During the experiment, participants will be divided into two groups, one using an app with AR and the other without. Participants in both groups will practice listening, repeating, recording sounds, evaluating peer recordings, and taking assessments and intrinsic motivation inventory tests. Participants will spend 10 min using the app during the study, which lasts two days. In exchange for their participation, participants will receive a gift card.

In addition to usability testing, we will conduct an experiment as part of our study. Participants will be asked to complete the Intrinsic Motivation Instrument (IMI) [28], and their answers will be entered into Qualitrics. Additionally, we will measure motivation and enjoyment every day through informal feedback. This will allow us to gather more usability data as a result.

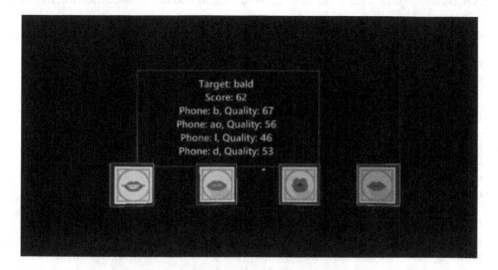

Fig. 2. Detailed analysis of the Student's attempt displayed to the Teacher.

4 Discussion

There is potential for using augmented reality (AR) technology to teach English pronunciation to non-native young learners. With AR, real-world objects can be interacted with and perceived better, active learning can be promoted, and 3D objects can be integrated as teaching materials to improve learners' learning outcomes. The rise of mobile devices and head-mounted displays makes AR technology more accessible to consumers, but its widespread adoption in education depends on how engaging and interactive it is for users. An AR-based pronunciation training app is described in the paper, which allows users to be assessed on their pronunciation of selected 3D learning objects.

This AR language learning system was designed with theoretical and pedagogical objectives in mind. Using a Microsoft HoloLens 2 head-mounted display, the app provides AR-enabled learning experiences. There are several studies that support the claim that AR can effectively improve English language skills such as speaking, reading, and listening. This is regardless of technical difficulties. Students' ability to understand vowel sounds is directly related to their reading skills, and it can boost their English proficiency.

5 Conclusions and Future Work

This paper examines the potential benefits of AR for young children's language learning, with a particular focus on language learning. Further research is needed on developing appropriate AR interfaces. It is also important to explore how AR can be used across different fields of education to create new learning experiences. AR technology is rapidly advancing, resulting in endless possibilities for AR in education. The effect of this is to improve learning outcomes for young children as well as promote their overall development.

In this project, we explored, developed, and experimented with vowel trainer augmentation. As well as assessing users' pronunciation of selected 3D learning objects and providing meaningful feedback, it advances current paper-based assessment methods. Help users learn the correct pronunciation of vowels by providing 3D models of faces/mouth movements along with word icons.

The vowel trainer will focus on creating an immersive experience by addressing the issue of not seeing each other's assets. Students and teachers will be able to interact with the same objects in real-time, and the teacher will be able to monitor the student's progress. As a result, students will benefit from increased immersion but also receive better feedback and assessments.

An additional improvement will be the use of a smaller mouth animation to highlight the mouth vowel shape. In this way, the student will understand the correct pronunciation of vowels through mouth animation. In addition, vowel trainers can be further enhanced by integrating machine learning algorithms that adjust learning experiences to individual student's learning styles and progress. As a result, the vowel trainer could provide customized feedback and learning materials to each student to help them improve their pronunciation skills.

References

1. Rauschnabel, P.A., Babin, B.J., tom Dieck, M.C., Krey, N. and Jung, T.: What is augmented reality marketing? its definition complexity, and future (2022)
2. Zachary, W., Ryder, J., Hicinbothom, J., Bracken, K.: The use of executable cognitive models in simulation-based intelligent embedded training. In: Proceedings of the Human Factors and Ergonomics Society Annual Meeting (1997)
3. Chen, Y., Wang, Q., Chen, H., Song, X., Tang, H., Tian, M.: An overview of augmented reality technology. J. Phys. Conf. Ser. **1237**, 022082 (2019)
4. Lee, K., et al.: Augmented reality in education and training. TechTrends **56**(2), 13 (2012)
5. Khan, T., Johnston, K., Ophoff, J.: The impact of an augmented reality application on learning motivation of students. Adv. Hum.-Comput. Interact. **2019** (2019)
6. Kuhl, P.K.: Early language learning and literacy: neuroscience implications for education. Mind, Brain Educ. **5**(3), 128–142 (2011)
7. Weiland, C., Yoshikawa, H.: Impacts of a prekindergarten program on children's mathematics, language, literacy, executive function, and emotional skills. Child Dev. **84**(6), 2112–2130 (2013)
8. Ustun, A.B., Simsek, E., Karaoglan-Yilmaz, F.G., Yilmaz, R.: The effects of AR-enhanced English language learning experience on students' attitudes, self-efficacy and motivation. TechTrends **66**(5), 798–809 (2022)
9. Parmaxi, A., Demetriou, A.A.: Augmented reality in language learning: a state-of-the-art review of 2014–2019. J. Comput. Assis. Learn. **36**(6), 861–875 (2020)
10. Tosto, C., et al.: The potential of AR solutions for behavioral learning: a scoping review. Computers **11**(6), 87 (2022)

11. Godwin-Jones, R.: Augmented reality and language learning: from annotated vocabulary to place-based mobile games (2016)
12. Sinyagovskaya, D., Murray, J.T.: Augmented reality in Chinese language pronunciation practice. In: 2021 IEEE International Symposium on Mixed and Augmented Reality Adjunct (ISMAR-Adjunct), pp. 403–408. IEEE (2021)
13. Jumani, A.K., Siddique, W.A., Laghari, A.A., Abro, A., Khan, A.A.: Virtual reality and augmented reality for education. Multimedia Comput. Syst. Virtual Real. 189–210 (2022)
14. Kamińska, D., et al.: Virtual reality and its applications in education: survey. Information 10(10), 318 (2019)
15. Tiede, J., Matin, F., Treacy, R., Grafe, S., Mangina, E.: Evaluation design methodology for an AR app for English literacy skills. In: 2021 7th International Conference of the Immersive Learning Research Network (iLRN), IEEE (2021)
16. Barreira, J., et al.: Mow: Augmented reality game to learn words in different languages: case study: learning English names of animals in elementary school. In: CISTI 2012, IEEE (2012)
17. Sydorenko, T., Hellermann, J., Thorne, S.L., Howe, V.: Mobile augmented reality and language-related episodes. Tesol Q. 53 (2019)
18. Holden, C., Sykes, J.M.: Complex l2 pragmatic feedback via place-based mobile games. Technol. Interlang. Pragmatics Res. Teach. (2013)
19. Rau, P.-L.P., Zheng, J., Guo, Z., Li, J.: Speed reading on virtual reality and augmented reality. Comput. Educ. 125, 240–245 (2018)
20. Weninger, C., Kiss, T.: Culture in English as a foreign language (EFL) textbooks: a semiotic approach. TESOL Q. 47(4), 694–716 (2013)
21. Küçük, S., Kapakin, S., Göktaş, Y.: Learning anatomy via mobile augmented reality: effects on achievement and cognitive load. Anat. Sci. Educ. 9(5), 411–421 (2016)
22. Dalim, C.S.C., Sunar, M.S., Dey, A., Billinghurst, M.: Using augmented reality with speech input for non-native children's language learning. Int. J. Hum.-Comput. Stud. 134, 44–64 (2020)
23. Learning to Read and Spell kernel description. https://wordsworthlearning.com. Accessed 30 Jun 2022
24. Children's speech recognition and voice technology solutions kernel description. https://www.soapboxlabs.com. Accessed 30 Sep 2022
25. Character creator 3, Computer software (2021)
26. Autodesk Inc., 3ds max, Computer software (2023)
27. Collaborative AR learning experiences using Orkestra library. https://www.areteproject.eu. Accessed 23 May 2022
28. Buchner, J., Zumbach, J.: Promoting intrinsic motivation with a mobile augmented reality learning environment. Int. Assoc. Dev. Inf. Soc. (2018)

Integrating 360 Degree, Virtual Reality (VR) Content via Head Mounted Displays (HMD) into Social Sciences Classes

Brian J. Mihalik[1]([⊠]), Hyunsu Kim[2], and Linda Mihalik[1]

[1] University of South Carolina, Columbia, SC, USA
bmihalik@hrsm.sc.edu, mihalikl@mailbox.sc.edu
[2] California State University at Fullerton, Fullerton, CA, USA
hyunsukim@fullerton.edu

Abstract. This paper discusses using activity theory as a foundation for the successful integration of 360-degree Virtual Reality content into classes at a major, US research university. The authors produced multiple, 360-degree Virtual Reality, Olympic themed video projects, subsequently integrated them in sport management and global tourism classes and then assessed student opinions on the use of inexpensive HMD coupled with smart phones for viewing. The results of this research revealed overall, strong student support towards the integration of 360-degree VR content with several statistically significant results. With regards to activity theory, this research supported the work of Dai et al. (2022), Loup et al. (2016) and Reiners et al. (2014) as this research demonstrated that ITC can raise student's class interaction, increase satisfaction, and found that learners using HMD displays were more engaged and took immersive VR experiences more seriously.

Keywords: 360-degree videos · Virtual Reality · Olympic Games · Tourism

1 Introduction

Activity theory (AT) helps explain the relationship between technology and students in educational settings and is being integrated into human-computer interaction. Scanlon and Issroff (2005) examined AT and learning technologies in higher education. Scavarelli et al. (2021) looked at integrating technology and more specifically, virtual reality (VR) and augmented reality (AR) into the classroom while examining social interaction models from a variety of learning theories including activity theory. Multiple studies have projected that these technological platforms would grow significantly from as far back as Cheong (1995). However, then came COVID-19. Kim et al (2021) investigated millennials VR experience pre- and post- COVID-19. Yet while select retail products worldwide saw declines due to COVID-19, the International Data Corporation (IDC 2020) again projected that the use of VR and AR will be positive in the long term. Scavarelli et al. (2021) even stated that the use of VR and AR was generating even

C. Stephanidis et al. (Eds.): HCII 2023, CCIS 1834, pp. 296–302, 2023.
https://doi.org/10.1007/978-3-031-35998-9_41

more attention because of the relatively inexpensive Oculus Quest head mounted display (HMD). They wrote that there is "an explosion of experimentation and development of novel applications within VR/AR forms such as…educational endeavors."

In 2018, two of the authors of this paper decided it was important to begin to integrate 360-degree VR content into classes in two academic disciplines within a major research university. However, when the authors visited YouTube and other video hosting platforms, they discovered a dearth of free and public, 360-degree VR educational content related to the academic disciplines in question. Thus, two of the authors began, at their own expense, to produce, edit and host specific 360-degree VR educational specific content to You Tube related to the hospitality and tourism management and sport and entertainment management fields of study. More specifically, these 360-degree VR projects were concentrated on global tourism destination management and the use and management of Olympic Games physical legacies which also can serve as global tourism attractions. This team has subsequently produced, edited, and hosted to YouTube approximately N = 50, 360-degree VR educational projects viewed over 10,000 times on YouTube. It was discovered that this was one of the first attempts by faculty at this institution to successfully produce and integrate 360-degree, immersive VR educational content into the classroom experience.

This preliminary research then examined student outcomes of the integration of faculty produced, 360-degree virtual reality (VR) content (*AT Object*) incorporating HMD (*AT Tools*).

2 Methodology

The authors integrated predominately 360-degree faculty produced VR content accompanied by select publicly produced VR videos (N = 10) hosted on YouTube into a 15-week, academic term. Students used inexpensive HMDs ranging from USD$10-$40 coupled with predominately iOS (Apple) smart phones for an "immersive" experience. Student opposition was verbally expressed when asked if they would prefer to purchase the "relatively inexpensive" Oculus Quest HMD priced at USD$300 for a better-quality, immersive experience as suggested by Scavarelli et al. (2021).

Below is a partial list of the 360-degree VR links produced by Mihalik and Mihalik, published in YouTube and were used most frequently in classes. The links are accompanied by a brief description:

- Participants "experience" a virtual bobsled ride on the 1932 Olympic bobsled track: *Lake Placid Van Hoevenberg 1932 Olympic Bobsled Run in 360*: https://youtu.be/cVsywi4VRvg
- Participants "experience" a virtual visit to two Lake Placid, NY Olympic Games legacy ice rinks: *Lake Placid 1980 and 1932 Olympic Rinks*: https://youtu.be/rTlA_R B_tAE
- Participants "experience" a virtual visit to the Berlin, Germany 1936 Olympic stadium, and other historic Olympic structures: *Berlin Olympic Stadium Tour in 360*: https://youtu.be/63oOto1C3ek
- Participants "experience" a virtual visit to the interior entertainment facilities at the Berlin, Germany 1936 Olympic stadium: *Historic Tour of Berlin Olympic Stadium in 360:* https://youtu.be/0__c-z-ond0

- Participants "experience" a virtual visit to the 2008 Beijing Olympic "Birds Nest" Stadium and "Water Cube" Olympic Pool: *Beijing Olympic Venues Night Walk:* https://youtu.be/rSn-RCFF8nk
- Participants "experience" a virtual visit at dusk to *The Eiffel Tower*, Paris, France whose park at the foot of the Tower will become a Paris 2024 Olympic temporary venue: https://youtu.be/UNZc_kzbSwo

After watching each 360-degree VR project, the authors asked multiple questions via a 7-point Likert scale with (1) labelled "Strongly disagree" to (7) identified as "Strongly agree." The survey instrument was partially based on the work of Tussyadiah et al. (2018) and expanded to assess student opinions of the integration of human-computer interaction, i.e., multiple, 360-degree VR immersive learning experiences. Student cooperation was further incentivized by the presence of a class grade for the completion of each survey instrument administered after viewing each of the N = 10, 360-degree VR videos. The presence of a grade for the completion of each survey iteration allowed this research effort to be classified as "exempt" by our Institutional Review Board. Each student's name was removed from the subsequent aggregate research analysis to ensure student participant anonymity.

After completing each Likert-scale assessment, students then utilized a second technological tool to enhance knowledge retention. Students participated in an on-line learning game titled Kahoot. Students were asked questions based on the 360-degree immersive images, embedded factual text and embedded voice narration. Game participation was incentivized by awarding class participation points to all students who played the entire Kahoot game regardless of the final game score. Further, students were informed that these Kahoot questions would be replicated in a graded examination.

3   Results

Seven survey questions were analyzed in this research project as seen in the "Note" in Figs. 1, 2 and 3. They included a student's subject content understanding, sense of engagement, support of 360-degree VR, sense of enjoyment, willingness to see more VR content in class, production quality of the VR projects viewed, and illness experienced while wearing a HMD. The statistically significant results of this preliminary research are discussed after Fig. 2 and Fig. 3. A response pool of N = 800 viable and completed student surveys were used for this study.

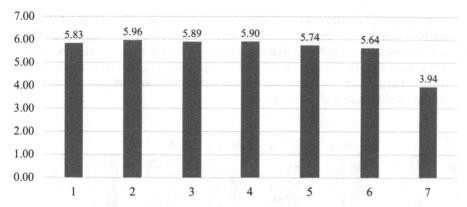

Fig. 1. Mean Scores across 7 Variables with N = 800

Note: 1 = The integration of 360 VR improved my understanding of HRTM/SPTE Management. 2 = I felt more engaged in this class because of the use of 360 VR. 3 = I looked forward to our 360 VR classes. 4 = I enjoyed being "immersed" when "visiting" sport/global tourism destinations. 5 = I would like to see more 360 VR in my classes. 6 = I was pleased with the quality of this 360 VR production. 7 = Viewing content with a 360 VR headset made me feel ill.

In six of the seven questions, student responses were positive and well above a neutral rating of four as seen in Fig. 1. Question 2, "engagement" (5.96), Question 4 "being immersed" (5.90) and Question 3, "I looked forward to our 360 VR classes" (5.89) received the highest ratings. The question related to headset viewing illness (Q. 7) revealed that far more students had no adverse physical effects from viewing 360-degree VR content inside inexpensive 360-degree VR HMDs.

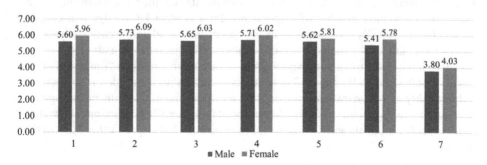

Fig. 2. Gender differences

Note: 1 = The integration of 360 VR improved my understanding of HRTM/SPTE Management. 2 = I felt more engaged in this class because of the use of 360 VR. 3 = I looked forward to our 360 VR classes. 4 = I enjoyed being "immersed" when "visiting" sport/global tourism destinations. 5 = I would like to see more 360 VR in my classes. 6 = I was pleased with the quality of this 360 VR production. 7 = Viewing content with a 360 VR headset made me feel ill.

Regarding gender differences, all differences were statistically significant at p = .05 except Items #5 & #7. Females were statistically more likely to have improved their content understanding then their male counterparts. Females significantly were more engaged, more welcoming, and more likely to enjoy being immersed in the use of 360-degree VR. Further, female students were more acceptable towards the 360-degree VR production quality then male students.

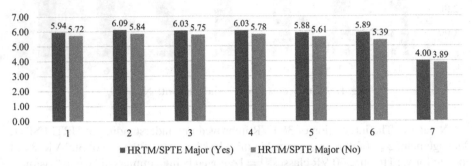

Fig. 3. Academic major differences

Note 1: 1 = The integration of 360 VR improved my understanding of HRTM/SPTE" Management. 2 = I felt more engaged in this class because of the use of 360 VR. 3 = I looked forward to our 360 VR classes. 4 = I enjoyed being "immersed" when "visiting" sport/global tourism destinations. 5 = I would like to see more 360 VR in my classes. 6 = I was pleased with the quality of this 360 VR production. 7 = Viewing content with a 360 VR headset made me feel ill.

With regards to academic "majors", all differences were statistically significant at p = .05 except Item #7 regarding feeling ill when viewing 360-degree VR content which again represented a smaller number of respondents. Prior content knowledge that could be present by successfully completing more courses in one's academic area of study (major) proved to be statistically more beneficial to improved subject understanding, being more engaged, more welcoming and experiencing more enjoyment when "immersed" in the world of 360-degree VR content. Those students enrolled in the academic subject areas of hospitality and tourism management and the sport and entertainment management also were more supportive of the quality of the 360-degree VR productions shown to all course enrolled students and desired to see more similar 360-degree VR content in their classes.

4   Implications of the Current Work

The results of this research revealed overall, strong student support towards the integration of 360-degree VR content (Fig. 1) with several statistically significant results as seen in Figs. 2 and 3.

Female students were significantly more responsive to 360-degree VR experiences in HMD then their male counterparts in five of the seven questions. Students who were more familiar with the content contained in the 360-degree VR videos as noted by their academic "major" were significantly more in support of the integration of 360-degree VR content via HMD in all six questions except for the "viewing illness" question #7.

Further, supporting this data analysis of the survey questions were anonymous, written class evaluation comments conducted during the last week of class. When students had an opportunity to respond in writing to the following question: "Assignments and tasks which were especially useful to your learning process", approximately 50% of the students wrote about the 360-degree VR content in their class.

With regards to activity theory, this research supported the work of Dai et al. (2022) as this research also demonstrated that ITC can raise student's class interaction and satisfaction via teaching strategies incorporating diverse technology such as 360-degree VR. It also supported the work of Loup et al. (2016) who found that learners using HMD displays were more engaged and the work of Reiners et al. (2014) who observed that their research audience took immersive VR experiences more seriously.

5 Limitations

While the students strongly supported the use of inexpensive 360-degree head mounted displays using an Apple iOS phone, recent developments have revealed that what is commonly referred to as the Google cardboard icon in YouTube is no longer available to those using an iOS phone inside an inexpensive HMD. It does appear that those that use an Android operating system on their phone can still see this cardboard 360-degree icon and experience 360-degree VR immersive video inside inexpensive HMDs. However, most of our research subjects use iOS Apple iPhones. Thus, the ability to truly be immersed inside an inexpensive HMD has been suspended by either Google which owns YouTube or by Apple, all to direct 360-degree immersive experiences to their respective and more expensive platforms and HMDs. Initially, estimates are that the soon to be released Apple headset will cost USD$1,500 thus making the USD$300 Oculus Quest the only viable alternative for in class, 360-degree immersive experiences. And again, this runs contrary to the expressed wishes of students who said the purchase of a 360-degree HMD priced at USD$300 was still too expensive.

A second limitation of this study is the fact that it was confined to college age students at a major research-intensive university. While gender and academic major differences were investigated, other demographic variables such as family income, adult ages, family life cycles, and workplace occupation could impact the successful integration of 360-degree, VR content through HMDs.

A third limitation of this research was the use of self-produced, educational, 360-degree VR content. Production quality was assessed in survey question six. While the production quality of faculty, self-produced 360-degree VR educational projects received strong viewer ratings (5.69/7.00), it is possible that results of this research would have been enhanced with the integration of commercially produced, 360-degree educational VR content aligned with specific subject matter. However, the development of affordable, commercial VR, subject specific, educational content is still lacking in the marketplace in the areas of hospitality and tourism management and the Olympic Games legacy management.

Finally, a fourth limitation of this study relates to survey Question #7, which states that "Viewing content with a 360 VR headset made me feel ill." Those that experienced motion sickness while viewing 360-degree VR content may have evaluated their other educational experiences lower than those that did not experience motion sickness. It is possible that further analysis by eliminating participants that experienced motion sickness from this project would result in even stronger support for the integration of 360-degree VR content for those remaining study participants. This suggestion is also supported by the 2019 study by Rupp et al. who investigated the 360-degree video experiences in educational settings. These authors also suggested that motion sickness "may have led to suboptimal educational experiences."

References

Cheong, R.: The virtual threat to travel and tourism. Tour. Manage. **16**(6), 417–422 (1995)

Dai, Z., Xiong, J., Zhao, L., He.: The effectiveness of ICT-enhanced teaching mode using activity theory on raising class interaction and satisfaction in an engineering course. Interact. Learn. Environ. (2022). https://doi.org/10.1080/10494820.2022.2086574

International Data Corporation. AR and VR Headsets Will See Shipments Decline in the Near Term Due to COVID-19, But Long-term Outlook Is Positive (March 18, 2020). According to IDC. https://www.idc.com/getdoc.jsp?containerId=prUS46143720

Kim, H., So, K., Mihalik, B., Pedo-Lopes, A.: Millennials' virtual reality experiences Pre- and post-COVID-19. J. Hosp. Tour. Manag. **48**, 200–209 (2021)

Loup, G., Serna, A., Iksal, S., George, S.: Immersion and persistence: Improving learners' engagement in authentic learning situations. vol. 9891 LNCS. 11th European Conference on Technology Enhanced Learning, EC-TEL 2016, pp. 410–415 (2016)

Reiners, T., Wood, L.C., Gregory, S.: Experimental study on consumer-technology supported authentic immersion in virtual environments for education and vocational training. Paper presented at the 31st Annual Conference of the Australian Society for Computers in Tertiary Education, ASCILITE 2014 (2015)

Rupp., M., Odette, K., Kozachuk, J., Michaelis, J., Smither, J., McConnell, D.: Investigating learning outcomes and subjective experiences in 360-degree videos. Comput. Educ. **128**, 256–268 (2019)

Scanlon, E., Issroff, K.: Activity theory and higher education: evaluating learning technologies. J. Comput. Assist. Learn. **21**(6), 387–451 (2005)

Scavarelli, A., Arya, A., Teather, R.J.: Virtual reality and augmented reality in social learning spaces: a literature review. Virtual Reality **25**, 257–277 (2021)

Tussyadiah, I., Wang, D., Jung, T., tom Dieck, M.: Virtual reality, presence, and attitude change: empirical evidence from tourism. Tour. Manage. **66**, 140–154 (2018)

Design of BPM Processes in Higher Education in Ecuador

Rosa Molina-Izurieta[1,3] (iD), Jorge Alvarez-Tello[3,5] (iD), Mireya Zapata[2(✉)] (iD), and Pedro Robledo[2,4] (iD)

[1] Facultad de Ciencias Matemáticas y Físicas, Universidad de Guayaquil, Guayaquil, Ecuador
rosa.molinai@ug.edu.ec

[2] Centro de Investigación en Mecatrónica y Sistemas Interactivos – MIST, Universidad Indoamérica, Av. Machala y Sabanilla, Quito 170103, Ecuador
mireyazapata@uti.edu.ec

[3] Escuela Superior de Ingeniería, Tecnología y Diseño, Universidad Internacional de la Rioja (UNIR), Logroño, Spain

[4] Facultad de Empresa y Comunicaciones, Universidad Internacional de la Rioja (UNIR), Logroño, Spain
pedro.robledo@unir.net

[5] Centro de Innovación Social y Desarrollo (CISDE), Quito, Ecuador
jorge.alvarez@cisde-ec.com

Abstract. Introduction: This manuscript addresses the strategy for digital transformation in university management as an improvement for the development of the link with society, where the digital transformation strategy for the Academy in Ecuador is taken as a reference. **Objective:** To design the planning sub-process through a Business Process Management Suite as a proposal for improvement in the Information Technology degree programme at the University of Guayaquil. **Method:** To carry out the design proposal for automation, the problem definition, the AS-IS model, the Hammer PEMM diagnosis for the company and processes are presented. The model is optimised based on the process mining analysis to obtain the TO-BE process. For the implementation, the database, formats, and the end-user interface are designed. Together with the ROI estimation for the justification of the feasibility of the proposal. **Results:** With the TO-BE process optimised by a business process analysis (BPA) software package, a time reduction of 51% and a total cost reduction of 41% is achieved. The estimated return on investment (ROI) is 1.61. **Conclusion:** Optimisation through process mining increases the assertiveness in the design of the proposal, exceeding even the initial projection of optimising the process by 30% in contrast to the 51% obtained. The estimated return on investment facilitates the justification for technical implementation, according to the institutional investment programme.

Keywords: Process mining · digital transformation · Social Knowledge Management · process automation · High Education

C. Stephanidis et al. (Eds.): HCII 2023, CCIS 1834, pp. 303–310, 2023.
https://doi.org/10.1007/978-3-031-35998-9_42

1 Introduction

Data production in organisations is currently developing exponentially and real-time decision making is relevant to organisational development. Society demands innovative products and processes that are vital for organisational development, potentially enhancing exploration, autonomy, and the development of change challenges, as well as fostering improved access to expertise, funding, and minimising bureaucracy [1]. Higher Education Institutions (HEIs) compete in terms of student recruitment and funding. This is a basis for establishing performance indicators for HEI management [2]. In this sense, HEIs are no exception and are starting the organisational transformation to functional and operational structures, in which the university management has the space for the interaction of services for students, teachers and the public. These challenges for HEIs make it possible to use current curricula, update them and thus improve the educational process and student satisfaction [3], it is about organising high performance through digital transformation, based on five pillars: policy, work management, learning management, human resources management and infrastructure [4]. On the other and, the outreach practices managed by universities are related to social action and lifelong learning activities, as well as technology transfer and business creation. This properly managed relationship with the construction of ecosystems between academia and society is a cornerstone for the economic development of a country [5]. Processes that are managed manually or semi-automated based on physical or virtual files and regulations as management support, consume a lot of resources and generate problems in the traceability of information. To make each of these improvements, it is necessary not only to have a clear purpose, but also to use methodological and innovative tools that allow an organised, standard, and controlled work with respect to the improvements made, thus promoting the generation of new opportunities for the improvement of the organisations' strategy in the knowledge value chain [6, 7]. HEIs should organise, distribute, and design strategies in the implementation of a platform, where resources for the support of teaching and learning are integrated [8]. The universities must fulfil their mission based on three components: education, research, and links with society; these components relate to each other, creating and maintaining two-way communication between them [9]. In the Universidad de Guayaquil, the linkage has the institutional nomination as Social Management of Knowledge, where activities are carried out through which the student fulfils requirements that will allow him/her to complete his/her academic training with the obtaining of his/her respective degree. The techno-logical and social trends towards digitalisation contribute to the development of a framework for digital transformation in 8 axes, which are listed below: University city, ICT infrastructure, administration, research, transfer, marketing, communication, and governance of digital transformation [10]. The alignment of this automation exercise of the planning sub-process of the linkage projects gives way to the pre-professional internships, is aligned with the digital agenda of Ecuador, which is based on 5 lines of action [11]: infrastructure, digital culture and inclusion, digital economy, emerging technologies for sustainable development, digital governance. The BPM lifecycle sets the roadmap for digital transformation in an organisation and the importance of processes lies in the efficiency they can bring to the organisation through the identification of processes, which enables the development of process architecture and the ease of efficient information management [12].

With this background, the applied research question is established: How to design the automation of the planning sub-process through a Business Process Management Suite for digital transformation as a proposal for improvement in the Information Technology career at the Universidad de Guayaquil?

2 Method

To establish the route for digital transformation in the Social Management of Knowledge of the Information Technology department of the University of Guayaquil, a framework is generated based on the BPM life cycle, to take the relevant strategies and activities for the BPM design (see Fig. 1).

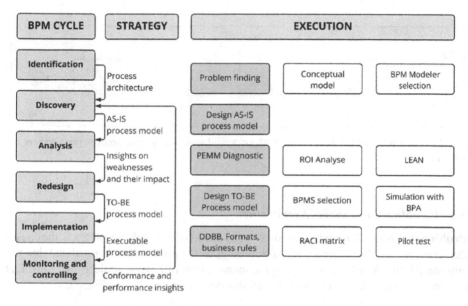

Fig. 1. Method: The BPM cycle [12] as a strategy. Source: prepared by the authors

We proceed to investigate the current project management and the drawbacks or shortcomings of the process. Within the Social Knowledge Management department, the problem to be solved is determined. Then we proceed to formalise the concept of the current situation with the people who manage the process to identify the activities that make up the project management process that give way to the pre-professional practices, obtaining the conceptual model for the design). A process maturity diagnosis is also performed according to Michael Hammer's Process Enter-prise Maturity Model (PEMM), together with the personnel who work directly with the process. With this information, the benefits are determined through the analysis of the return on investment (ROI) and the quantitative and qualitative benefits that will be obtained at the time of implementation and integration in the automation of this process design. The process must have the selection of an improvement methodology for the production phase, for which the LEAN methodology is defined, which continuously systematises the efficiency of the processes. Then, the design of the AS-IS model is carried out, assisted by a Low Code process modeller, BPM.

3   Results

3.1   Linkage Process

In the Universidad de Guayaquil, there is a process of Social Linkage with Society called Social Management of Knowledge, which is based on the project cycle, with the formalisation of activities by means of an agreement with the institution with which the community service practices are developed. The sub-process to be designed is planning (see Fig. 2).

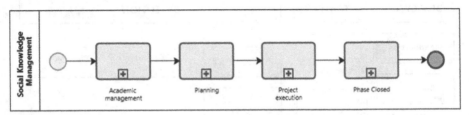

Fig. 2. Social Knowledge Management of Universidad de Guayaquil Source: prepared by the authors.

3.2   Identification: Process Architecture

Problem Finding. Through the evaluation by means of the Ishikawa diagram, the causes that comprise the limitations and shortcomings of the process that is regulated, but not automated, are identified, addressing the management of linkage projects and the effect that in this case is the problem for which this design was made (see Fig. 3).

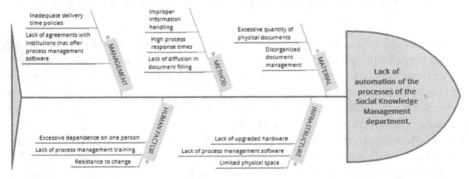

Fig. 3. Ishikawa diagram for problem definition (cause-effect). Source: prepared by the authors

3.3 Discovery: AS-IS Model

Based on the description of the start, resolution and completion of project management, the elements involved in the AS-IS process can be the form visualised with respect to the initial starting situation (see Fig. 4).

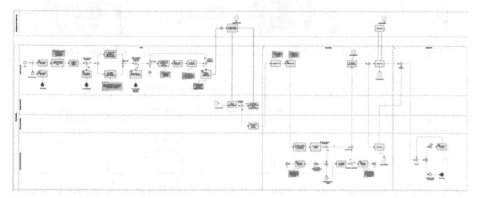

Fig. 4. A figure caption of the AS-IS process model done by BPMS Bizagi modeler. Source: prepared by the authors (see Annex 1)

3.4 Analysis: Insights on Weaknesses and Their Impact

Process Maturity Assessment: Hammer Diagnostic. Through Hammer's PEMM diagnosis, the maturity level of the process is determined, which identifies the areas of urgent intervention marked in blue in Fig. 5 (see Annex 2a & 2b).

ROI Analysis. To estimate the ROI, an analysis is carried out based on the quantitative benefits, which will help me to configure the simulation scenario and qualitative and quantitative analysis of the implementation. Among the benefits (25120.00 USD) is the maintenance of the system, staff training, delay time and expenses (9600.00 USD) are the annual licenses, the cloud environment and BPM consulting hours, which gives an ROI of 1.61, return on investment, indicating the desirability of developing the automation of the planning sub-process, since the time is within one year of implementation.

3.5 Redesign: TO-BE Process Model

Business Process Analysis & Simulation. For the improvement of the processes [13], there are several options, testing, trial, and error, having the simulation option as the most appropriate, which needs to have an initial model, which in the case of processes is the AS-IS model, also the initial data for the configuration of the programme (see Fig. 6).

Likewise, the data for the definition of the business, such as its rules, policies, data traffic, documentation that the system uses and on which the activities in the process are

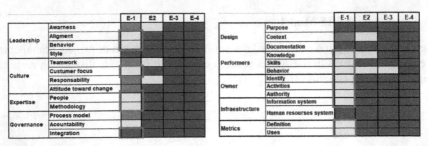

Fig. 5. A figure caption of PEMM diagnostic of enterprise (left) and process (right).

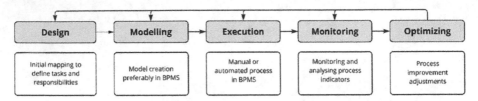

Fig. 6. A figure caption of the BPM simulation process by SYDLE. Source: adapted by the authors

Table 1. Results of simulation in time & costs

Model	t Execution (min)	t wait (min)	t inactive (min)	t Trans (min)	t Run (min)	Cost (Non personal)	Cost personal	Total Cost
AS-IS	2278	2439	360	20	4731	4,70	465	470
TO-BE	1270	992	320	0	2307	1,60	278	279
Reduction	44%	59%	11%	1%	51%	66%	40%	41%

based, with the assignment of the roles that intervene in each phase of the process (see Table 1).

TO-BE Process Model. Based on the description of the TO-BE model, because of the optimisation of the AS-IS model, which is available for project planning, which is visualised in the sub-process according to the following diagram (see Fig. 7).

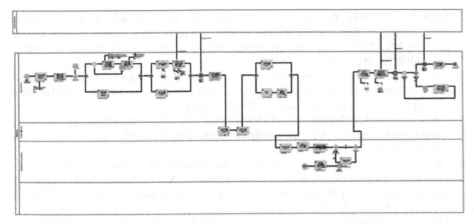

Fig. 7. A figure caption of the TO-BE process model done by BPA Adonis. Source: prepared by the authors (see Annex 3).

4 Conclusion

BPM is a methodology used to analyse, model, optimise and monitor business processes, administrative processes, among others, such as improving the agility of services, student registration, organisation of class schedules, etc. It will depend on the needs of each institution. In the case of the management of linking projects for the Information Technology degree programme at the University of Guayaquil, the proposal was designed with the following limitations in mind: The feasibility on the part of the public institution, technical and infrastructure limitations based on the analysis of the institution's history. Among the initial objectives of 30% efficiency in automating the sub-process, this objective has been exceeded, reaching 41% in costs and 51% in process management time. The ROI of 1.61 indicates the feasibility of implementing this proposal.

Finally, it is concluded that the automation of the planning sub-process promotes agility in the services of the department and that this method of development can be replicated in the other workspaces at the University of Guayaquil, which will help greatly for national and international accreditations or certifications.

It is also recommended that from this optimisation can continue with the implementation with an innovation Business Process Suite (iBPMS) the design of databases, formats and adapt the business rules, according to the policies and organisational structure to improve the results of operations with intelligent analysis.

Annexes

https://github.com/JAlvarezT/HCII2023-BPM-TD-UG

References

1. Espinoza-Guano, M., Álvarez-Tello, J., Ramos-Guevara, J., Maturity of innovation culture in Ecuadorian companies, RISTI - Revista Iberica de Sistemas e Tecnologias de Informacao. **2022**(Special Issue E50), 237–249 (2022)

2. Multisilta, J., Mattila, T., Digital transformation in finnish higher education: a perspective from a university of applied sciences. In: Proceedings of the International Conference on E-Learning 2022, Part of the Multi Conference on Computer Science and Information Systems 2022, MCCSIS 2022, pp. 93–100 (2022)

3. Shalina, D., Larionova, V., Stepanova, N., Network interaction as a way of innovative development of the university: Case of Ural Federal university. In: Proceedings of the European Conference on e-Learning, ECEL, pp. 416–426 (2021)

4. Rujira, T., Nilsook, P., Wannapiroon, P., Synthesis of vocational education college transformation process toward high-performance digital organization. Int. J. Inf. Educ. Technol. **10**(11), 832–837 (2020)

5. Véliz, V.: Calidad en la Educación Superior. Caso Ecuador. Atenas **1**(41), 165–180 (2018)

6. Álvarez-Tello J., Martínez-Crespo J., Zapata-Rodríguez M.: Evaluation methods review of the innovation capacity of companies based on knowledge management. Commun. Comput. Inf. Sci. **1655** CCIS, 248–257 (2022)

7. Chamorro L., Cuesta L., Proyecto de automatización para la coordinación de investigación y gestión del conocimiento –UG– módulo de convocatorias (PPI). http://repositorio.ug.edu.ec/handle/redug/49606 (2020)

8. Villarreal, V.D., Mora, D.F.: Merchan, F., et al.: University digital transformation plan through the implementation of digital resources: the case of the technological University of Panama. In: Proceedings - 11th International Conference on Virtual Campus, JICV 2021 (2021)

9. Rueda, I., Acosta, B., Cueva, F.: Universities and their practices of outrearch with society.Educação Sociedade **41** (2020)

10. Almaraz-Menéndez, F., Maz-Machado, A., López-Esteban, C., et al., Analysis of the digital transformation of Higher Education Institutions. In: A Theoretical Framework, pp. 181–202 (2017)

11. Michelena, A., Muñoz, J., Puente, G., Ribadeneira C.: Agenda de Transformación Digital Ecuador – Ministerio de Telecomunicaciones y de la Sociedad de la Información. https://www.telecomunicaciones.gob.ec/agenda-de-transformacion-digital-ecuador/. Accessed 14 Mar 20223

12. Dumas, M., La Rosa, M., Mendling, J., et al.: Fundamentals of Business Process Management. 2nd edn, p. 23. Springer, Cham (2017)

13. Kopp, A., Orlovskyi, D.: A method for business process model analysis and improvement. In: CEUR Workshop Proceedings, vol. 2403 (2019)

Model Educational ReVIso Based on Virtual Reality

Jose Ricardo Mondragon Regalado[1][(✉)] ⓘ, Alexander Huaman Monteza[1] ⓘ,
Julio César Montenegro Juárez[1] ⓘ, Jannier Alberto Montenegro Juárez[1] ⓘ,
Abelardo Hurtado Villanueva[1] ⓘ, Nazario Aguirre Baique[2] ⓘ,
Julio Arévalo Reátegui[3] ⓘ, and Norma Judit Padilla Suárez[4] ⓘ

[1] National University of Jaen, Jaen, Peru
jose.mondragon@unj.edu.pe
[2] National Intercultural University of the Amazon, Ucayali, Perú
[3] National University of Ucayali, Ucayali, Perú
[4] Local Educational Management Unit of Jaén, Jaén, Perú

Abstract. The accelerated technological advance has brought opportunities in all sectors of society, one of them and the one that will be addressed in this study is the use of virtual reality in the educational aspect, for this reason, the main objective of the research is to propose the theoretical intervention model based on virtual reality to improve learning in basic and higher education students. The purpose of the ReVIso educational model is to use virtual reality as a learning medium that moves the student from a reality of abstract knowledge to a scenic, graphic and objective reality. It is concluded that the ReVIso model proposal improves student learning using virtual reality, which consists of changing the traditional practice of the teacher who generates abstract knowledge towards a context of digital transformation or metaverse where the contents are presented in a scenic way, dynamic and graphic, situation in which the student is able to generate synergy in the achievement of real and significant learning. The model moves the student and teacher to a new dimension where the dynamics of teaching and learning allows the student to develop critical, creative, reflective thinking and promote the capacity for autonomy, as well as generate empowerment spaces to propose alternative solutions in scenarios real.

Keywords: Model Educational · ReVIso · Virtual Reality · technology

1 Introduction

The information presented below corresponds to the synthesized version of the study. Virtual reality is and will be one of the most powerful tools that man will have to conquer the world. From the point of view of education, most of our students will exchange their traditional notes for innovative systems based on virtual reality.

According to Odame and Tümler (2022) teaching through virtual reality presented a significant difference between groups, it is also more attractive, pleasant and useful.

© The Author(s), under exclusive license to Springer Nature Switzerland AG 2023
C. Stephanidis et al. (Eds.): HCII 2023, CCIS 1834, pp. 311–317, 2023.
https://doi.org/10.1007/978-3-031-35998-9_43

However, in order to incorporate virtual reality into education, it will be necessary against access to both software and hardware technologies. According to Colorado and Edel (2022), the usability of ICTs in training leads to improving skills and abilities in students.

For this reason, the reform of the curriculum in universities is a challenge that corresponds to the authorities of the education sector at a global level, mainly those that want to keep pace with technological progress and that generate opportunities to incorporate the digitization of their contents. In this sense, Li and Li (2022) argue that universities in alliance with companies seek to achieve social and ethical value through cooperation, which is a fundamental aspect to promote teamwork, solidarity and innovation through technology and entrepreneurship among students. Therefore, it is very important to highlight that the implementation of a virtual reality educational laboratory allows the combination of artificial intelligence and practical research of university students to develop talent that provides contributions to society.

In this context, the research carried out by Cheng et al. (2021) reveal that cognitive structures are supported by virtual reality, thus facilitating a good understanding in young students. The quality of education is associated with student learning outcomes. However, to achieve good learning results, concentration and the teaching methodology used by teachers are fundamental elements. Therefore, in order to measure it, virtual interaction can be applied and have as indicators the rate of visual focus and the mastery of educational activities of the various courses or subjects from the competences and capacities (Lin et al. 2022).

In a post-pandemic scenario, the educational context has been favored by the use of technology, since it promotes motivation, autonomy, collaborative work and improves student learning performance. Another contribution that technology based on virtual reality presents to us is the intervention in the field of health developing procedures, among others. If it is possible to carry out these processes, why would it not be feasible to transfer these experiences to the educational context? Kim and Im (2022) affirm that education based on virtual reality allows teaching and learning to be generated by educational actors.

Various studies proposed by Li and Madina (2022) regarding virtual reality in teaching and learning the English language; In addition, the study by Gong (2021) regarding the experience of teaching the artistic area and (Liu 2011) the teaching of the physical education area concluded that the method based on virtual reality favored autonomy and the comprehensive improvement of learning in the students.

From the above, it is considered that didactics in the teaching-learning process is crucial in education, because it maintains three fundamental elements related to content, student and teacher. In this sense, the study presented by Vallance (2021) proposes a didactic design for education in virtual reality with the incorporation of various interactive elements to develop effective teaching-learning processes.

The era of digitization commits educators to permanently strengthen digital competence, because information and other messages are disseminated in societies through technology and digital media such as the Internet, virtual reality, and augmented reality. Thus, a very important achievement for learning is online education integrating people located in various parts. However, this educational form still does not extend to the basic levels of education in the different countries of the world, as an example, it is specified that teaching is still carried out using books and manual drawings (Sun and Peng 2020).

In education, achieving good motivation and increasing students' interest in learning are elementary pedagogical processes for the development of a good class and achieving favorable learning results. Thus, technology contributes so that students can achieve excellent motivation and interest in learning through mobile devices incorporated into technological equipment such as virtual reality glasses (Abdelaziz et al. 2020).

The link between education and technology is getting closer, this is due to the fact that as part of technological progress, artificial intelligence guides education to new horizons. Emerging technologies contribute so that universities, secondary and primary schools develop the teaching and learning process incorporating virtual reality as a medium (Abdullah et al. 2018).

In addition, the study by Noah and Das (2021), among its findings, specifies that through augmented reality and virtual reality, inventions that contribute to digital evolution for the education sector globally can be intensified and thus develop teaching learning according to the interests of the students.

Currently, few innovative strategies are evidenced as a means or teaching-learning tools in regular basic education and higher education, being important factors to improve student learning. Therefore, the results of the evaluations that have been taken by national institutions and international organizations are not those expected in regular basic education. While in higher education it is also necessary to incorporate new teaching models in which technological advances are integrated in order to achieve better results in the future. Although it is true that a better education depends on many factors, it is nevertheless believed that a new model with a technological focus will contribute to strengthening learning levels. For this reason, the following research question is posed. Will the theoretical intervention model "ReVIso" based on virtual reality improve learning in basic and higher education students?

The ReVIso model is important from a theoretical point of view because it will allow researchers to take it as a scientific basis for other studies. From the social aspect, the level of learning performance will improve and from the practical aspect, teachers and students will have better means and dynamic instruments in the classroom to strengthen the teaching-learning process.

In accordance with the above, the following objective is proposed: to propose the theoretical intervention model "ReVIso" based on virtual reality to improve learning in basic and higher education students.

2 Methodology

The present study is of a descriptive propositive level, of a non-experimental design, its purpose was to propose an educational theoretical model based on virtual reality to improve learning through an innovative teaching practice that leads to better levels of academic performance in education students. Basic and higher (Fig. 1).

3 Representation of the Theoretical Model ReVIso

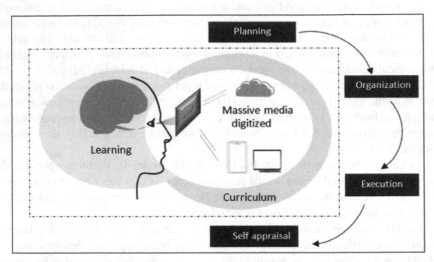

Fig. 1. The figure represents the ReVIso theoretical educational model based on virtual reality.

4 Approach

The ReVIso model estimates that it is possible to improve student learning using virtual reality, which consists of changing the traditional practice of the teacher who generates abstract knowledge towards a context of digital transformation or metaverse where the contents are presented in a scenic, dynamic way and graphic, a situation in which the student is capable of generating real and meaningful learning. In addition, that it invigorates self-learning, contributing to the retention of knowledge with greater fluidity and allows the development of critical, creative, reflective thinking and promotes the capacity for autonomy and empowerment to propose alternative solutions in real scenarios.

5 Methodology

Teaching based on the ReVIso model requires a team of teachers who are agents of change, as well as the implementation of laboratories with technological tools that allow access to virtual reality.

In this proposal it is notmention brands or models of technological equipment, but it is expected that when there is the will to implement it, it will be carried out with prior evaluation at the discretion of experts to demand the highest quality and thus obtain the greatest benefits from its use.functionality or performance.

To make the application of the ReVIso model effective, it is necessary to follow a process that is described below from the procedural point of view:

1. The curriculum is the fundamental basis on which the activities that will be taught in each area will be developed, taking into account the level of education.

2. The implementation of technological means such as lenses or visors, computers, cameras, cell phones, cloud storage, internet access, among others, is needed.
3. Training in strengthening digital skills for the teaching team is important.
4 Classification of the subject to be addressed by each specialty, grades or cycles and level. It must be clear what skills and abilities are expected to develop in students.
5. Digital transformation, consists of taking the theme chosen and classified by the teacher towards an environment of graphic and animated scenes or video recording that will be made up of real-looking objects. For this, suitable software and hardware will be used to develop the activity.
6. Digital content is previously stored on compatible devices such as cell phones, computers, or the cloud, the latter as long as certain transmission bandwidth standards are met.
7. The teacher plans the class plan according to the norms and standards required by the Ministry of Education or the highest authority in the case of higher education.
8. The academic activity is executed taking into account the processes of the learning session or class plan as appropriate.
9. It is necessary to carry out metacognition about the learning experience guided by the teacher, who can be found in person or online and expects the active and orderly participation of the students.
10. Self-assessment is a process that the ReVIso model requires and must be considered a priority during the intervention.

The ReVIso model involves in a wayholistic the institutional commitment in which the following processes are identified:

Planning. The authorities responsible for basic and higher education institutions assume the commitment to manage human and technological resources for the application of the ReVIso model.

Organization. Designate a person in charge of managing and coordinating to make effective the various activities that have been planned to achieve the proposed objectives regarding the application of the ReVIso model.

Execution. The ReVIso coordinator provides technical support to the teacher so that the execution of the activity is effective. Here the teacher develops and executes the plan or learning session according to current standards.

Self Appraisal. The self-assessment is not only in charge of prejudging oneself what has been learned, but also for students to critically assess why the expected was not achieved or if it was achieved, which was the main impact from the metaverse point of view.

6 Conclusions

It is concluded that the ReVIso model proposal improves student learning using virtual reality, which consists of changing the traditional practice of the teacher who generates abstract knowledge towards a context of digital transformation or metaverse where the contents are presented in a scenic way, dynamic and graphic, a situation in which the student is capable of generating real and meaningful learning.

In addition, the ReVIso model strengthens self-learning, contributing to the retention of knowledge more fluently and allows the development of critical, creative, reflective thinking and promotes the capacity for autonomy and empowerment to propose alternative solutions in real scenarios.

References

Abdelaziz, M., El-Bakry, H., Riad, A., Senousy, M.: The impact of using virtual reality on student's motivation for operating systems course learning. J. E-Learn. Knowl. Soc. 16(2), 25–33 (2020). https://doi.org/10.20368/1971-8829/1135076

Abdullah, R., Azman, M., Kamal, M., Riu, T., Yaacob, R.: Experiential learning: the effective application of virtual reality in teaching and learning. J. Soc. Sci. Res. 2018(Special Issue 6), 1208–1212 (2018). https://doi.org/10.32861/jssr.spi6.1208.1212

Cheng, K.-H., Tang, K.-Y., Tsai, C.-C.: The mainstream and extension of contemporary virtual reality education research: Insights from a co-citation network analysis (2015–2020). Educ. Tech. Res. Dev. 70(1), 169–184 (2021). https://doi.org/10.1007/s11423-021-10070-z

Colorado, A., Edel.: La usabilidad de TIC en la práctica educativa. Revista de Educación a Distancia (RED), (30). Recuperado a partir de (2015)https://revistas.um.es/red/article/view/232611

Gong, Y.: Application of virtual reality teaching method and artificial intelligence technology in digital media art creation. Ecol. Inform. 63 (2021). https://doi.org/10.1016/j.ecoinf.2021.101304

Kim, D., Im, T.: A systematic review of virtual reality-based education research using latent dirichlet allocation: focus on topic modeling technique. Mob. Inf. Syst. 2022 (2022). https://doi.org/10.1155/2022/1201852

Li, M., Li, Q.: Universitas Potensi Utama's curriculum reform for virtual reality education laboratory system. In: Proceedings of the 5th International Conference on Big Data and Education (ICBDE '22). Association for Computing Machinery, New York, NY, USA, pp. 7–14 (2022). https://doi.org/10.1145/3524383.3524411

Li, M., Madina, Z.: Analysis of english education classroom student interaction and performance based on virtual reality. Secur. Commun. Netw. 2022 (2022). https://doi.org/10.1155/2022/904255

Lin, Y., Lan, Y., Wang, S.: A method for evaluating the learning concentration in head-mounted virtual reality interaction. Virtual Real. 27, 863–885 (2022). https://doi.org/10.1007/s10055-022-00689-5

Liu, J.: The Study on Physical Education Method Based on Virtual Reality (Vols. 271–273), pp. 1164–1167. https://doi.org/10.4028/www.scientific.net/AMR.271-273.1164

Noah, N., Das, S.: Exploring evolution of augmented and virtual reality education space in 2020 through systematic literature review. Comput. Animat. Virtual Worlds 32(3–4) (2021). https://doi.org/10.1002/cav.2020

Odame, A., Tümler, J.: Está listo el software de realidad virtual estándar para la enseñanza médica? In: Chen, J.Y.C., Fragomeni, G. (eds.) Realidad virtual, aumentada y mixta: diseño y desarrollo. HCII 2022. LNCS, vol. 13317. Springer, Cham (2022). https://doi.org/10.1007/978-3-031-05939-1_15

Ryu, J., Han, S., Hwang, S., Lee, J., Do, S., Kim, J., Park, J.: Effects of virtual reality education on procedural pain and anxiety during venipuncture in children: a randomized clinical trial. Front. Med. 9 (2022). https://doi.org/10.3389/fmed.2022.849541

Sun, S., Peng, L.: Study of the virtual reality education and digitalization in China. J. Phys. Conf. Ser. 1456 (2020). https://doi.org/10.1088/1742-6596/1456/1/012042

Vallance, M.: Work-in-progress: Didactical design for virtual realityeducation. In: 2021 IEEE International Conference on Engineering, Technology & Education (TALE), pp. 1167–1170 (2021). https://doi.org/10.1109/TALE52509.2021.9678772

From Physical to Digital Storytelling.
A Comparative Case in School Education

María Giovanna Núñez-Torres$^{(\boxtimes)}$ ⑩, Paulina Magally Amaluisa Rendón⑩,
and Carlos Alberto Espinosa-Pinos⑩

Universidad Indoamérica, Ambato 180103, Ecuador
{giovannanunez,paulinaamaluisa,
carlosespinosa}@indoamerica.edu.ec

Abstract. The advantages of narratives and stories in school teaching are known, however, nowadays the use of information and communication technologies are consolidated with common practices, opening the way to the use of strategies such as storytelling. The research was carried out at the Indoamerica Educational Unit in the 2022–2023 academic period in Ambato-Ecuador. Its main objective was to analyse the practice of reading comprehension based on storytelling in physical and digital format as a strategy in the teaching process in the subject Language and Communication. The study collects information from two groups of 6-year-old students with the same level of schooling (second year of primary school), group one with 60 students and group two with 61 students. The teacher of group 1 used illustrated pictures based on infographics to tell the stories (physical format). The teacher of group 2, on the other hand, used Tiktok as a digital narrative resource (digital for-mato). The central theme of the stories is respect and protection of animals. On the other hand, and beforehand, the teachers have completed some training stages on both physical and digital storytelling techniques. A mixed quantitative-qualitative methodology and a reading comprehension test were used, in addition to assessing the most striking graphic resources in both formats. The results show that students who have used digital storytelling as a learning tool have shown better reading comprehension and in less time, which is due to the use of movement, sound and light in the digital format. The teacher of group 1, on the other hand, finds that the use of storytelling in digital format captures the children's attention and facilitates concentration.

Keywords: School education · Tiktok · storytelling

1 Introduction

From the moment a person begins to coordinate ideas, he or she tries to tell, to narrate this, one could say, is an inherent quality of the human being, hence, it is appropriate to refer to Bruner whose thought marks two stages, the first, the stage of the cognitive revolution in which he develops a theory of learning from models of representation that allows understanding based on sensory stimuli from the context, expectations and experiences, the succession of concepts and objects. The second stage determines a cultural revolution in which great interest is shown in narrative thinking [1].

C. Stephanidis et al. (Eds.): HCII 2023, CCIS 1834, pp. 318–324, 2023.
https://doi.org/10.1007/978-3-031-35998-9_44

Likewise, and from the perspective of narrative, storytelling has been applied as the art of storytelling in order to encourage students to understand and create an orderly continuity of events with an approach, characters, knot and denouement from both the physical and digital storytelling as methodological strategies to measure levels of understanding, assimilation and also to ensure communicative effectiveness.

According to Bruner, storytelling is the form of expression that is best understood by children, perhaps because it is the most familiar and most characteristic form of popular culture. Bruner states that narration, in this case storytelling, is a form of expression that simplifies the understanding of the contents it transmits, which allows the exceptional to become comprehensible; therefore, by using oral, written and graphic narrative representations in the teaching of the mother tongue, we are adapting this learning to the forms proper to the culture that is simpler and closer to the person. In the conviction that the stories that are told in one way or another, are susceptible to being reinterpreted or reinvented [2].

2 Materials and Methods

2.1 Objectives

- To analyse the practice of reading comprehension based on the use of storytelling in both physical and digital formats in the subject Language and Literature.
- Determine the most attractive graphic resources for children in each of the formats and which encourage reading comprehension.
- To describe the effectiveness of the physical and digital formats based on the didactic praxis experienced.

2.2 Participants

The study collects data from two groups of 6-year-old students with the same level of schooling (second year of primary school), group one with 60 students and group two with 61 students. The teacher of group 1 used illustrated pictures based on infographics to tell the stories (physical format). The teacher of group 2, on the other hand, used Tiktok as a digital narrative resource (digital format).

The two participating teachers are female. The Kolmogorov-Smirnov test confirms that the sample is within normal parameters ($p = 0.169$). The following is the information related to the number of students in the sample, organised according to their group (Table 1).

Table 1. Members of the study by groups, types of formats used and narrative resources

Groups	Number of estudents	Format	Narrative resource
1	60	Physical-Print	Infographics
2	61	Digital- Video	Tiktok

2.3 Analysis Used

A quantitative-qualitative methodology was used, the quantitative part being inferential, while the qualitative component was based on interviews. Also, a reading comprehension test was applied in order to recognise the effectiveness of both physical and digital resources and to assess the variations in the students' level of comprehension after applying each of the techniques separately, in addition to assessing the most striking graphic resources of both forms.

Cuantitative. A descriptive procedure (means and SD) and an inferential Anova procedure were developed for group A and group B individually. The treatment of the information in the reading comprehension test was carried out through the analysis factors, recapitulating if main differences in the factors were discovered between group one and group two.

Cualitative. Information was collected through structured interviews with teachers, whose findings were probed through thematic content study [3] and the constant comparison of information [4]. The themes found were critically analysed independently. The aim was to organise the data collected in order to provide greater transparency in the delivery of the information.

The use of the WEFT QDA tool made it possible to summarise, structure and control the saturation of the information on the basis of the qualities of the pre-questions asked to the teachers.

2.4 Instruments Used to Collect Information

Cuantitative. A descriptive procedure (means and SD) and an inferential Anova procedure were developed for group A and group B individually. The treatment of the information in the reading comprehension test was carried out through the analysis factors, recapitulating if main differences in the factors were discovered between group one and group two.

Cualitative. Information was collected through structured interviews with teachers, whose findings were probed through thematic content study [3] and the constant comparison of information [4]. The themes found were critically analysed independently. The aim was to organise the data collected in order to provide greater transparency in the delivery of the information.

For the final form a Principal Component Factor Analysis was performed, where values for the KMO index of 0.85 were reached, in the same way as in Bartlett's test of sphericity ($p > .00$). The indicators obtained in the covariance matrix showed satisfactory agreement for the RMSEA index $= 0.080$, as well as for the GFI $= 0.79$. Thus, the questionnaire is made up of 2 factors:

1 .*Reading comprehension:* The comprehension of the message is estimated using the storytelling technique in both physical and digital formats.

2. *Most eye-catching graphic resources*: visual elements of design, form, colour and texture in the physical format and the same plus added resources in the digital format such as light, movement and sound are valued.

Cualitative. At the end of the first term of the 2022 academic year, a semi-structured interview was conducted with the two teachers who were part of the study in order to find out their criteria and reach an internal position on the experience [6]. According to the variables of the study, 3 questions were asked to the teachers

- What has been your experience with the use of storytelling in training?
- Do you think that reading comprehension practice can be improved through the use of creative techniques such as storytelling?
- Do you think that the use of different formats contributes to children's reading comprehension?

2.5 Study Design and Procedure

In order for teachers to optimise the use of storytelling as a teaching resource as didactic material, the teachers were subjected to a prior training process consisting of the following stages:

1. Approval of a 40-h course on storytelling as a training tool.
2. Selection of the topic "Respect and protection of animals" after analysing the basic education curriculum of the Ministry of Education.
3. Creation and narration of stories with different animals of the Ecuadorian Sierra.
4. Elaboration of didactic material: Group 1. Printed infographics (physical format) that tell stories of different types of animals whose message has to do with respect for them. Group 2. Use of Tiktok (digital format) to tell the same stories.

The process used by the teachers in each of the groups is explained below:

- *Group 1. Use of infographic plates (physical format)*: The teacher presents the pictures to the children and tells the story according to the infographic sequence of the story. The children ask questions and the teacher answers their initial questions, then hands the material to the children. This has been the constant training for the subject matter during 3 weeks of work. At the end of this academic period, the teacher has applied a reading comprehension test to each of the children individually on the subject.
- *Group 2. Use of Tiktok (digital format):* The teacher exposes the material to the children as a group using a digital screen. After doing so, the children start to ask questions and the teacher gives feedback. Prior to this research process, informed consent was obtained from the parents of both groups. At the end of the first training period, the teacher gave a reading comprehension test to each of the children individually on the topic. The information collected was kept confidential and anonymity was guaranteed.

3 Results

Quantitative Analysis. There are no inequalities with respect to the considerations of the message and the recognition of main ideas with coherence between the groups. On the other hand, in the evaluation of the meaning of words and time, the mean values of the items increase in group 2 and decrease in group 1 (Table 2).

Table 2. Reading comprehension by groups

Group	Message	Meaning of words	Main ideas	Time
Group 1	Describes, explains, narrates and argues	5–10	Coherent ideas	15 min
Group 2	Describes, explains, narrates and argues	10–15	Coherent ideas	6 min

The assessment of the physical format shows that colour is the most striking basic design element for children. In contrast, in the digital format, movement, sound and light are the ones that capture attention and allow for greater concentration (Tables 3 and 4).

Table 3. Eye-catching storytelling resources physical format

Group	Form	Colour	Texture
Group 1	30%	70%	0%

Table 4. Eye-catching storytelling resources in digital format

Group	Form	Colour	Texture	Light	Sound	Moviment
Grupo 1	6%	15%		25%	26%	28%

Inferential Analysis. Group 2, which used storytelling in digital format (Tiktok), values the achievement of a greater set of knowledge attained. Through factor analysis and according to the elements concerning the practice of reading comprehension, significant divergences are obtained. In group 1, which used storytelling in physical format, differences are found in the variable of word meaning and message assimilation times, which are lower than in group 2.

Qualitative Analysis

- Both teachers consider the use of storytelling in education a positive experience, the teacher of group 1 says that storytelling makes it easier for the children to understand the messages, while the teacher of group 2 says it is a more natural and attractive way of transmitting them.
- Both the teacher of group 1 and group 2 reflect that the use of techniques such as storytelling allows the message to be grasped more quickly and easily, generating meaningful learning.

- the physical format, mentioned that it is an alternative around which the children can improve even their social aspect, the interaction with the format allows them to be closer to the materials used. The teacher in group 2 experimented with the digital format and said that she observed greater attention, concentration and motivation on the part of the children.

4 Discusión

The use of storytelling has been shown to improve children's reading comprehension practice. This is also demonstrated by a study conducted by Abbott and McCarthey in which it was found that practices such as storytelling favour the circumstances of responsibility in the reading comprehension process, significantly influencing students' creation of narratives [7].

On the other hand, children belonging to group 1 who used storytelling in physical format through infographics are able to describe, expose, narrate and argue the message as well as coherently express the main ideas of the story. In the same way, infographics improve the communicative potential as they consist of visual images, texts and colours, being a type of media that facilitates information, using only the most important elements to make effective communication possible and optimising the latter by interrelating the image with the text [8].

However, group 2 that used the storytelling in digital format Tiktok, as well as the physical format based on infographics, was able to describe, explain, narrate and argue the message as well as coherently express the main ideas of the story, and the teacher in her interview states that there is greater attention, concentration and motivation on the part of the children. On the other hand, it is the meaning of the words and the time in which inequalities are registered between the two groups. In addition, a study has shown that the use of Tiktok as a learning tool makes the students more motivated and more enthusiastic about learning [9].

With respect to the visual resources of design used in both physical and digital storytelling: form, colour and texture, it has been found that in the digital format colour is the most striking. In the same way, Javier Nó mentions it, who deeply exploits the communicative probabilities of colour and its capacity to execute functions such as provoking attention, conserving it, informing, insinuating and developing associations [10] On the other hand, in the digital format, light, movement and sound are the elements that capture children's attention. The screen brings sensory resources highly attractive to the human brain, light and movement are accompanied by sound capturing the full attention of the senses [11].

5 Conclusions

It is evident that the use of storytelling as an educational tool facilitates the practice of reading comprehension in primary school children. There are differences according to the use of different formats. Storytelling in digital format is the one that captures children's attention and makes it easier for them to concentrate.

On the other hand, the most striking resource in the printed format is colour, while in the digital format it is light, movement and sound.

In the qualitative component, the teachers positively evaluate the use of this narrative technique.

References

1. Mex, D., Hernández, L., Cab y M. Castillo, J.: «El desarrollo cognoscitivo de la parábola según Bruner, en el empleo del software educativo» Scielo 5 (2021)
2. Bruner, J.: Realidad mental y mundos posibles. Los actos de la imaginación que dan sentido a la experiencia., Estados Unidos: gedisa (2004)
3. Libarkin, J.C., Kurdziel, J.P.: «Research methodologies in science education: qualitative data,» J. Geosci. Educ. **50**, 195–200 (2002)
4. Denzin, N.K., Lincoln, Y.S.:«Handbook of Qualitative Research» Sage, Thousand Oaks (1994)
5. MD educación. «Instructivo para la aplicación de la evaluación estudiantil,» Quito-Ecuador (2018)
6. Patton, M.Q.: «Qualitative Research and Evaluation Methods.» Sage, Thousand Oaks (2002)
7. Abbott, J.A., McCarthey, S.J.: «Classroom Influences on first-grade students' oral narratives.» J. Lit Res. **33**(3), 389–421 (2001). https://doi.org/10.1080/10862960109548118
8. Amaluisa Rendón, Amaluisa Rendón, A.K.:«La imagen visual comoelemento clave para informar a la población sobre el Covid-19 en Sudamérica.» Zincografía **6**(12), 181–200 (2022)
9. Rendon, P.A., Jordán, N., Arias, D., Núñez, G.: Tiktok as a Teaching Tool: The Motivation of University Students in Ecuador (2022)
10. Nó, J.:«Color y comunicación. La estrategia del color en el diseño editorial.» Departamento de Ediciones y Publicaciones de la Universidad, Salamanca (2006)
11. Alba, G.:«¿Pegados a la pantalla? Videojuegos en la vida cotidiana de niños, niñas y jóvenes de Bogotá.» Revista Latinoamericana de Ciencias Sociales, Niñez y Juventud **8**(1), 65–77 (2010)

Interactive Course Materials in Higher Institute Learning

Jabez Ng Yong Xin[✉], Chia Wen Cheng, Trinh Tuan Dung,
and Owen Noel Newton Fernando

Nanyang Technological University (NTU), Singapore, Singapore
{jabe0001,wchia017,c170017}@e.ntu.edu.sg, ofernando@ntu.edu.sg

Abstract. The COVID-19 pandemic has accelerated the shift to online learning and softcopy materials, highlighting the value of interactive learning experiences. For higher education institutes, converting course materials, lecturers use into an interactive application can provide a more engaging way for students to learn. This paper explores online teaching materials and conceptualizes features that could be implemented in an interactive course materials application, enhancing current learning experiences and providing additional functionalities to support learning in ways that traditional material cannot.

Keywords: E-Learning · Interactive E-Learning · Interactive Course Materials

1 Introduction

The onset of a technological revolution beginning in the 1950s has brought about significant transformations in the education sector globally. Since the unprecedented COVID-19 crisis, there has been a surge in the implementation of e-learning technologies in schools to enable remote learning. These innovative tools have allowed students to acquire knowledge from anywhere, anytime [1]. Although the flexibility of learning and greater interconnectedness between students and educators are benefits of e-learning towards efficacious learning [2–4], the lack of interactivity still needs to be improved [5, 6]. The absence of interaction may cause students to lose interest and disengage from the lesson [7].

Given this, we feel that there is space for technology to fill the gap and improve a student's learning journey, mainly by enhancing online course materials to promote greater interactivity. An excellent way to achieve this would be to incorporate key functionalities in interactive electronic books (eBooks) useful in interactive course materials [8]. Online course materials should not be viewed as merely the digitalization of printed media content that hardcopies offer. It can offer many meaningful features that far surpass traditional course materials. Examples could include animated illustrations, embedded videos, and even cutting-edge technologies such as mixed reality techniques that can cater to different types of learners. By developing an application to achieve meaningful interactions with learning materials, students will break the monotony and stereotypes of route learning, boosting their learning experience while improving information retention [9], concentration, and learning abilities [10].

C. Stephanidis et al. (Eds.): HCII 2023, CCIS 1834, pp. 325–333, 2023.
https://doi.org/10.1007/978-3-031-35998-9_45

2   Literature Review

In its simplest form, digital course material could be any digitalized teaching material, such as a PDF file containing lecture information or a video file for a lecture recording. However, with the increasing prevalence of digital course materials and the growing number of technology native students, enhancing the software used for learning is becoming increasingly important. In addition, studies have emphasized that interactive digital course materials need to be developed as current course materials need to be compiled in an integrated way [11].

Learning management systems (LMS) have become increasingly prevalent in universities as a communication, content delivery, and assessment platform. However, despite their popularity, LMS has limitations in terms of multimedia integration [12]. For instance, text and video materials are delivered separately, and some videos require page navigation that can be inconvenient and negatively impact students' learning experience. These shortcomings suggest a need for more effective software solutions to offer students an integrated and seamless experience.

Interactive eBooks contain advanced features enabled by integrating multimedia components, which can improve the learning experience [13]. However, the selection and development of these multimedia tools suitable for students learning remain a crucial but challenging problem [14] for many educators. The underlying reason was the mismatch in expectations and a need for more convenient and intuitive features, denying a student an authentic learning experience.

Previous studies investigating the obstacles to students' learning with eBooks concluded that students met with more barriers than affordances when faced with difficulties navigating and printing/downloading content [15]. Moreover, certain course materials may not be readily available in such an interactive eBook format. Therefore, we will now analyze some distinctions in features between eBooks and present-day digital course materials.

Table 1. Comparing electronic books and digital course materials

Feature	Electronic books	Digital course materials
Organization	eBooks combine various multi-media components into a unified package that is simple to navigate and search [16]	Course materials are often presented in separate PDF/lecture video files, with troublesome navigation between them
Interactivity	Interactive elements such as quizzes, animation, and simulations are included in eBooks to enhance the learning experience [17, 18]	Course materials are typically static and do not allow for much interactivity beyond clicking hyperlinks
Customizability	Bookmarking, note-taking, and highlighting are built into eBooks [19]	Students must manually organize and customize their course materials by creating their own bookmarks, notes, and highlighting in separate applications
Compatibility	eBooks can be designed to work with a variety of devices and platforms, including mobile phones, tablets, laptops, and desktop computers [20]	Course materials may not be compatible with all devices or platforms, necessitating the download of separate software or applications to view them

Table 1 underscores the existing problem concerning the inadequate integration of various course materials. Our solution aims to compile these isolated course materials into a single interactive application for an enhanced learning experience.

3   Design and Implementations

Understanding some of limitations of current digital course materials outlined in the previous section, we laid out and implemented some features and components for our interactive course materials application. Our implementation was executed using React-Native which is an open-source mobile application framework (Table 2).

Table 2. Features implemented and their description

Features Implemented	Description
Fast and Smooth Navigation (Organization)	Simple and intuitive navigation using common hand gestures. Users can select modules and preview their pages and read pages in full screen. A progress bar is also incorporated to track a user's progress
Bookmark (Customizability)	Users can bookmark or remove bookmarks on pages. A bookmark list allows users to toggle between displayed bookmarks
Quick-flip (Interactivity)	Users can save a page by performing a long press on it. A widget allows the user to navigate back to the saved page
Image and Video Viewing (Organization)	Provides users with customized image viewing with interactions such as rotating, enlarging, or shrinking. Moreover, video viewing from streaming services like YouTube

3.1   Fast and Smooth Navigation

Our application employs easy and swift navigation by making use of simple and familiar hand gestures, such as swiping and double tapping (Fig. 1).

In our application, the Module Scroll Screen allows users to select a module or chapter and preview the pages within it. They can navigate to different modules by swiping left or right, and they can select a specific page by scrolling through the Page Preview List. By spreading their fingers or double tap the preview page, they can view the page in full screen mode. In the Page Preview List, the Page Slider displays the user's progress (Fig. 2).

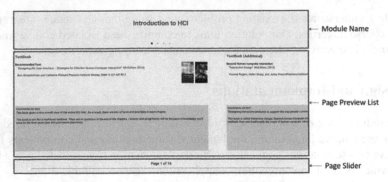

Fig. 1. Module scroll screen

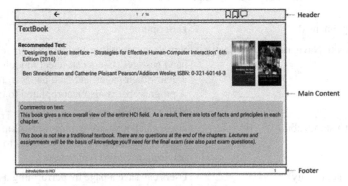

Fig. 2. Page Reader Screen

The Page Reader Screen allows users to read pages in full screen. Page contents are displayed in the Main Content section, and users can navigate to previous or next pages in the module by swiping left or right. Users can also jump to a specific page by entering the page number in the Header part of the screen (Fig. 3).

3.2 Bookmark

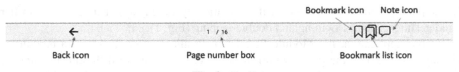

Fig. 3. Toolbar

The Page Reader Screen has a Header component with icons, including a Back, Bookmark, and Bookmark List icon. The Bookmark icons allows users to bookmark or remove the bookmark of the current page, while the Bookmark List icon displays a vertical list of bookmarks indicating page and module numbers, limited to 3 bookmarks. Double tapping on a bookmarked item navigates to the bookmarked page (Fig. 4).

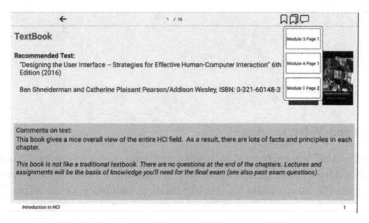

Fig. 4. Page Reader Screen with Bookmarked pages

3.3 Quick-Flip

Users can long-press on a page in the Page Preview List to save it for quick flipping, which will be indicated by a black border. This allows users to easily navigate back to the saved page (Fig. 5).

Fig. 5. Table 2. Black Border Indication

As the user scrolls past the saved quick-flip page, a small widget will be shown at the bottom of the Page Preview List. The user is allowed to scroll back to the saved page by clicking on this widget (Fig. 6).

Fig. 6. Quick-flip widget indicating page 1 has been saved

3.4 Image and Video Viewing

The application allows users to view images and videos in a customizable full-screen mode, accessed by spreading two fingers on an image. In the Image Viewer Screen, users can manipulate the image using actions like rotating, enlarging, or shrinking (Fig. 7).

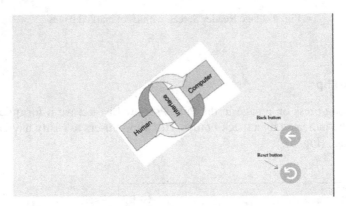

Fig. 7. Customized image viewing

The Image Viewer Screen has 2 buttons: Back and Reset. The Reset button allows users to return the image to its original state after rotating, enlarging, or shrinking it, while the Back button brings the user to the previous screen. The application also supports video viewing from YouTube or mp4 files stored on the server (Fig. 8).

Fig. 8. Video viewing

4 Discussion and Future Works

Although the current application has potential, its storage capacity and scalability could be improved. For example, all static assets, such as images, videos, and icons, are currently stored locally, which can cause memory issues as the number of assets grows. To address this limitation, the development team intends to deploy a content delivery network (CDN), a distributed network of servers optimized to deliver static content to end users. This enables the application to store static assets on cloud servers, increasing scalability and storage capacity.

Moreover, the application can only support the Human-Computer Interaction course materials. However, the team plans to broaden its scope by developing a development framework to be built upon and scaled for use in multiple NTU courses. This framework will allow the team to easily create interactive course materials for various courses, enhancing students' overall learning experience.

To ensure the effectiveness of the interactive course materials application, we plan to conduct user research on 400 students currently enrolled in the Human-Computer Interaction course to ensure the effectiveness of the application. This research will allow us to gather feedback on the efficacy of learning experiences and identify areas of improvement. By incorporating user feedback, we can improve the application and provide students with a more personalized and enhanced learning experience.

Plans include a text summarizer feature powered by OpenAI's GPT-3 model, natural language processing techniques, and gamification using mixed-reality enhanced course materials for interactive and engaging learning experiences.

5 Conclusion

This paper has successfully demonstrated that it is possible to implement educational aiding features and solutions using a very widely shared programming language library. The application paves the way for a promising long-term vision of creating learning materials that are simple to create and that educators can use to increase student engagement.

As a result, we can revolutionize today's traditional learning environment by making education more dynamic, interactive, and effective for learners of all levels. With the help of innovative technology and a strong commitment to education, we can empower educators and students to unlock their full potential and achieve tremendous success in the classroom and beyond.

References

1. Yuhanna, I., Alexander, A., Kachik, A.: Advantages and disadvantages of online learning. J. Educ. Verkenning **1**(2), 13–19 (2020). https://doi.org/10.48173/jev.vli2.54
2. Castro, M.D.B., Tumibay, G.M.: A literature review: efficacy of online learning courses for higher education institution using meta-analysis. Educ. Inf. Technol. **26**, 1367–1385 (2021). https://doi.org/10.1007/s10639-019-10027-zM
3. Blackburn, G.: Effectiveness of e-learning in statistics: pictures and stories. E-learn. Digit. Media **12**(5–6), 459–480 (2015). https://doi.org/10.1177/2042753016653704
4. Gamage, D., Perera, I., Fernando, S.: A framework to analyze effectiveness of eLearning in MOOC: Learners perspective. In: 2015 8th International Conference on Ubi-Media Computing (UMEDIA), Colombo, Sri Lanka, 2015, pp. 236–241 (2015). https://doi.org/10.1109/UMEDIA.2015.7297461
5. Farrah, M., Jabari, S.: Interaction in online learning environment during Covid-19: factors behind lack of interaction and ideas for promoting it. Bull. Adv. English Stud. **5**. 47–56 (2020). https://doi.org/10.31559/BAES2020.5.2.3
6. Alzahrani, J.G., Ghinea, G.: Evaluating the impact of interactivity issues on e-learning effectiveness. In: International Conference on Information Technology Based Higher Education and Training (ITHET), Istanbul, Turkey, pp. 1–5 (2012). https://doi.org/10.1109/ITHET.2012.6246017
7. Dhawan, S.: Online learning: a panacea in the time of COVID-19 crisis. J. Educ. Technol. Syst. **49**(1), 5–22 (2020). https://doi.org/10.1177/0047239520934181
8. Rahmatina, F., et al.: Exploring the effectiveness of e-book for students on learning material: a literature review. J. Phys. Conf. **1481**(2020). https://doi.org/10.1088/1742-6596/1481/1/012105
9. Ha, Y., Im, H.: The role of an interactive visual learning tool and its personalizability in online learning: flow experience. Online Learn. **24** (2020). https://doi.org/10.24059/olj.v24i1.1620
10. Phadung, M.: Interactive E-book design and development to support literacy learning for language minority students. In: 2015 World Congress on Sustainable Technologies (WCST), 14–16 December 2015, pp. 95–97 (2015). https://doi.org/10.1109/WCST.2015.7415126
11. Yuliana, F.H.: A Need Analysis in Developing Interactive Digital Teaching Materials Using Contextual Approach in Microeconomic Theory Course (2020). https://doi.org/10.2991/assehr.k.201230.113
12. Onah, D.O., Nzewi, U.M.: Examining barriers to multimedia integration in teaching and learning of science. IOSR J. Res. Method Educ. **11**(5), 07–13, e-ISSN:2320-7388, p-ISSN: 2320-737x(2021)
13. Guedes, G.P.: Multisensorial books: improving readers' quality of experience. In: 2018 XIII Latin American Conference on Learning Technologies (LACLO), 1–5 Oct. 2018, pp. 33–36 (2018). https://doi.org/10.1109/LACLO.2018.00017
14. Bidarra, J., Martins, O.: Exploratory learning with Geodromo: an interactive cross-media experience. J. Res. Technol. Educ. **43**(2), 171–183 (2010). https://doi.org/10.1080/15391523.2010.10782568

15. Pierard, C., Svihla, V., Clement, S., Fazio, B.: Undesirable difficulties: investigating barriers to students' learning with ebooks in a semester-length course. College Res. Lib. **81**(2) (2020). https://doi.org/10.5860/crl.81.2.170
16. Neil, P.M., James, L.: Multimedia Interactive eBooks in laboratory bioscience education. Higher Educ. Pedag. **2**(1), 28–42 (2017). https://doi.org/10.1080/23752696.2017.1338531
17. Smeets, D.J.H.: The interactive animated e-book as a word learning device for kindergartners. Appl. Psycholinguist. **36**(04), 1–22 (2014). https://doi.org/10.1017/S0142716413000566
18. Zhang, X., Tlili, A., Shubeck, K., Hu, X., Huang, R., Zhu, L.: Teachers' adoption of an open and interactive e-book for teaching K-12 students Artificial Intelligence: a mixed methods inquiry. Smart Learn. Environ. **8**(1), 1–20 (2021). https://doi.org/10.1186/s40561-021-001 76-5
19. Huang, R., Chen, N-S., Kang, M., Mckenney, S., Churchill, D.: The roles of electronic books in the transformation of learning and instruction. In: Proceedings - 2013 IEEE 13th International Conference on Advanced Learning Technologies (2013). https://doi.org/10.1109/ICALT.201 3.180
20. Jardina, R., Chaparro, B.S.: Investigating the usability of E-Textbooks using the technique for human error assessment. J. Usability Stud. **10**(4), 140–159 (2015)

Data-Driven Approach for Student Engagement Modelling Based on Learning Behaviour

Fidelia A. Orji[✉], Somayeh Fatahi, and Julita Vassileva

Department of Computer Science, University of Saskatchewan, Saskatoon, Saskatchewan, Canada

{fidelia.orji,Somayeh.fatahi}@usask.ca, jiv@cs.usask.ca

Abstract. A great number of people around the world learn through MOOCs platforms offered by higher institutions of learning. Effective utilization of the platforms for self-directed learning will help to foster the United Nations' agenda of inclusive and equitable education. However, low engagement and high attrition rates are common issues in the platforms. We believe that automatic modelling of student engagement levels based on their learning behaviour (access and interaction with various learning activities) will enable the construction of effective personalization methods that will improve student engagement in the platforms. In this study, statistical techniques were utilized to investigate the relationship between students' self-reported perception of their learning and their actual learning behaviour. Moreover, machine learning algorithms were applied to develop models for effective modelling of engagement levels in real-time. Our experiments with a de-identified dataset from Canvas Network open courses show promise in building predictive models that can automatically detect student engagement levels based on learning behaviour. The results revealed that significant differences in academic performance exist among different learner types and that machine learning models can be applied to automatically detect learners with low engagement. The models developed in this research can be applied to provide tools for instructors to observe student involvement in their learning activities so that they can devise pedagogical mechanisms/interventions to improve engagement through instructional design.

Keywords: Student Engagement Modelling · Learner Engagement · MOOC · Machine Learning · Learning Behaviour · Engagement Detection · Prediction

1 Introduction

In recent years, technology is playing a crucial role in our daily lives and using technology for education has been one of the most active research topics in applied computer science, attracting much attention from academics and practitioners [1]. Massive Open Online Courses (MOOCs) systems emerged as one of the new forms of learning utilizing technology. MOOCs provide a great variety of programs and courses offered by different universities and made accessible to anyone worldwide for free or very low cost, as there is no limit on class sizes. However, online courses have known disadvantages,

C. Stephanidis et al. (Eds.): HCII 2023, CCIS 1834, pp. 334–342, 2023.
https://doi.org/10.1007/978-3-031-35998-9_46

mostly related to the high dropout rate, lack of learner engagement and persistence to accomplish all course learning goals. A study presented a high dropout rate of between 66.09% and 92.93% for 79,186 students who enrolled in 39 courses [2]. Estimated dropout rates in online courses were 10% to 20% higher than in their face-to-face counterparts [3]. These issues have led to investigations on the link between various factors such as behavioural engagement, motivation, and academic performance in online environments. Several methods exist for measuring student engagement, such as validated survey tools, physiological sensors, and interaction-based approaches. The interaction-based approach allows measuring student engagement levels in real-time without the need for expensive equipment for capturing data. The approach uses learning behaviour such as access and interaction of students with various learning activities. The learning behaviours are logged by online learning systems. There is increasing interest in automatic modelling of student engagement levels in real-time and some studies [4, 5] that model student engagement levels using the interaction-based approach combined learning behaviour and assessment data. However, students that enroll in MOOCs have various goals that they intend to achieve. Some students intend to get a certificate (therefore they will participate and submit assignments and assessments as required by the course design), while others might want to gain skills that will help their work or career and thus might not submit assessments. Yet, to fulfill any of their objectives, students need to take part in the learning process. Therefore, there is a need to investigate how to develop effective predictive models that can detect students' engagement levels automatically based on their learning behaviour so that personalized interventions can be provided to students to support learning pathways adapted to their needs. The models also can be applied to provide tools for instructors to observe student involvement in their learning activities so that they can devise pedagogical mechanisms to improve engagement through instructional design.

Several studies on student engagement modelling in online contexts can be found in literature. Sharma et al. [6] proposed an approach that analyzed eye tracking, head movement, and facial expression to predict student engagement in an online learning context. Engagement was categorized into 3 levels: "very engaged", "nominally engaged," and "not engaged at all". Hussain et al. [5] used machine learning algorithms to recognize low-engaged students in a social science course. The researchers considered the data about the highest education level of the learners, their final results, their score on assessment, and the number of clicks during activities in a virtual learning environment, as input variables. The engagement levels of students in various activities served as the output variable. The findings show that the J48, decision tree, JRIP, and gradient-boosted models exhibited better performance in terms of accuracy, kappa value, and recall compared to the other tested models. A dashboard was implemented based on the models that instructors can use to monitor students' engagement during learning.

This study explored learning behaviours that are indicative of student engagement such as the number of events, number of days, number of discussion posts, and number of contents viewed as the feature vectors. We hypothesize that combining these features in engagement modelling will produce models that can predict the exact engagement level of a student in MOOCs. The following research questions guide this study:

RQ1: Are there differences in learning behaviour and academic performance among various learner types reported by students? RQ2: Can models for predicting student engagement levels in MOOC be developed using only learning behaviour data and machine learning? RQ3: Which models are more effective at predicting the engagement levels of students? RQ4: What are the most important learning behavioural features for predicting student engagement in MOOCs?

2   Methodology

2.1   Data Description

The de-identified dataset from Canvas Network open courses published online [7] is used in this study. The dataset contains data about courses, grades, demographic, course surveys, and student learning activities in 238 Canvas Network courses and over 325,000 students' records. Table 1 provides descriptions of some features contained in the dataset that we considered relevant for this study.

Table 1. Dataset description

Features	Description
User_id	Randomly generated user identifier
completed_%	Indicate the percentage of total required content modules a student completed
grade	Indicate actual final grade in a course as a percentage
learne_type	Standardized type of learner obtained from course survey
nevents	Page view counts
ndays_act	Count of distinct days with one or more events
ncontent	Number of unique modules viewed in a course
nforum_posts	Total number of posts made in discussion forums throughout the course

2.2   Data Preprocessing

Previous studies indicated that student engagement in learning activities on MOOCs can be determined based on their level of participation in activities such as watching lecture videos, posting forum posts, post content reviewing and number of clicks to activities [5, 8]. Since this study focuses on modelling student engagement levels, records of students who did not participate in any course activities were deleted. The retained dataset consists of 125,917 records of students that participated in at least one activity in a course.

We expressed student engagement as $E = \{E_1, E_2,...\}$, where E is the composite engagement score of a student, representing the percentage of total required content modules completed. $E_1, E_2,..$ Are input feature vectors of E, and they represent various learning activities students performed in the MOOCs system. The total number of times

Table 2. Pearson correlation analysis of engagement variables

	nevents	ndays_act	ncontent	nforums_posts	Grade
nevents	1	0.32	0.2	0.06	0.14
ndays_act	0.32	1	0.35	0.15	0.38
ncontent	0.2	0.35	1	0.11	0.24
nforum_posts	0.06	0.15	0.11	1	0.32
grade	0.14	0.38	0.24	0.32	1

a student accessed specific learning activity is an indicator of engagement in that activity. To examine the association among the engagement features E_i and also with grade we performed Pearson correlation analysis using Python. The r-values of these variables are shown in Table 2. The significance level for r is taken to be 0.05. The engagement features have significant positive correlations with themselves and with grade.

We categorized students using a data-driven approach. Highly engaged students will complete a greater percentage of course modules. Thus, we define composite engagement score of a student as S_i, where $i \in \{1,0\}$. S_i represents the student engagement level (high or low): S_1 represents highly engaged students with *completed_%* equal to or greater than 50% and S_0 represents low-engaged students. As shown in the equation below, engagement level is modelled based on the four input feature vectors (*nevents, ndays_act, ncontent, and nforums_posts*) represented as E_1 to E_4.

$$S_i = (E_1, E_2, E_3, E_4) \to (1, 0)$$

2.3 Investigating Learning Behaviour Based on Learner Types

For this analysis 21,695 records of students that provided their learner types were used. Four categories of learner types provided include *active, passive, drop-in, and observer*. *Active* participants describe students that plan to participate fully in all the course activities. *Passive* participants plan to complete the course on their own schedule and without engaging with assignments or other students. *Drop-in* participants intend to learn specific topics within the course. *Observer* participants aim to browse the course content, discussion and videos but will not take part in assessments. The distribution of the various learner types is shown in Fig. 1. Most of the students reported that they are *active* learners. We investigated students' actual involvement in learning and their reported learner types to find out if learning patterns and grades differ across the various types. Based on the mean rank of various learning activities and grades in Table 3, we can say that the students in the *drop-in* learning group were more engaged in learning activities except forum posting than other groups. The *active* group was best in forum posing and academic performance. To determine if there are significant differences in learning behaviour among the various learner types, we performed a non-parametric test called the Kruskal-Wallis H test because the features in the dataset were not normally distributed and the test can perform multiple comparisons among many groups.

Fig. 1. Distribution of the learner types

Table 3. Mean of learning features based on learner groups

| Learning features | Learner types | | | |
	Active (Mean Rank)	Passive (Mean Rank)	Drop-in (Mean Rank)	Observer (Mean Rank)
nevents	10796.53	10791.90	11443.49	10834.02
ndays_act	10830.13	10790.87	11268.30	10790.78
ncontent	10929.56	10715.86	11208.92	10499.10
nforum_posts	12136.13	9727.13	9348.93	8838.98
grade	9576.08	8585.61	7390.64	7237.05

2.4 Modelling of Student Engagement

The purpose of the modelling process is to detect students' engagement levels automatically based on their learning behaviour in MOOC so that personalized interventions can be used to improve their engagement. The features for the modelling process were described in Sect. 2.2. In the modelling experiment, a number of machine learning algorithms were applied to develop predictive models of student engagement levels. Diverse algorithms were chosen for building the predictive models and the sklearn libraries in python were utilized to develop the models. The classification algorithms that were used include Random Forest (RF), Extra Trees (ET), Gradient Boosting (GB), AdaBoost (AB), Extreme Gradient Boosting (XGB), Logistic Regression (LR), K-nearest Neighbors (KNN), Multilayer Perception (MLP), and Support Vector Machine (SVM). These classifiers are commonly used and they have been applied to educational data mining to study the learning behaviour patterns of students. We applied the downsampling method using resample library in sklearn to balance our dataset. The downsampling process resulted in a total of 9,352 records (i.e. 4,676 records for each class). In building our models, we applied a percentage split to our dataset (80% for the training set and 20% for the test set) and the best hyperparameters for tuning our models were selected using Grid Search Cross-Validation (GridSearchCV) in sklearn.

3   Results

Relationship Between Learner Types and Learning Behaviour. The results of the Kruskal-Wallis H test show that significant differences in learning behaviour in terms of *nevents (H(3)* = *17.93, p < .001), ndays_act (H(3)* = *9.12, p < .03), ncontent (H(3)* = *27.92, p < .001), nforums_posts (H(3)* = *1003.49, p < .0001), and grade (H(3)* = *412.80, p < .0001)* exist among the four learner types. The results show that the groups differ with respect to learning behaviour and grade. The results of the post-hoc test using Bonferroni correction for multiple comparisons revealed that significant differences in learning behaviour in terms of nevent exist between *drop-in* and *active* (p <.0001), *drop-in* and *passive* (p <.0001), and drop-in and observe (p <.038). For *ndays_act*, significant differences exist between drop-in and active (p <.034), and drop-in and passive (p < .020). For *ncontent*, significant differences exist between *active* and *passive* (p <.011), *active* and *observer* (p < .007), *drop-in* and *passive* (p <.0001), and *drop-in* and *observer* (p <.0001). For *nforums_posts*, significant differences exist be-tween *active* and *passive* (p <.0001), *active* and *observer* (p < .0001), *active* and *drop-in* (p <.0001), and *passive* and *observer* (p <.0001). For *grade*, significant differences exist between *active* and *passive* (p <.0001), *active* and *observer* (p < .0001), *active* and *drop-in* (p < .0001), *passive* and *drop-in* (p < .0001), and *passive* and *observer* (p < .0001).

Student Engagement Modelling. The performance of our predictive models for student engagement was evaluated based on standard evaluation metrics (accuracy, f1, precision, and recall) for machine learning algorithms. The best result was generated by GB, XGB, AB, and LR while the least accuracy result of 0.898 was achieved by the SVM. Figure 2 summarizes the accuracy, f1, precision and recall of the four best models. The results demonstrated that behavioural features of students can be applied to detect low-engaged students so that interventions that can motivate them to improve their engagement can be personalized to them.

To determine the impact of each activity feature in predicting the levels of student engagement, we applied the Shapley Additive exPlanations (SHAP) framework [9]. The framework is used to improve interpretability and understanding of machine learning models. It estimates the impact of each feature on a model prediction and outputs the values (called SHAP values) obtained. Figure 3 explains model prediction using SHAP. The SHAP values show that the *ncontent* and *nevents* were the most predictive features.

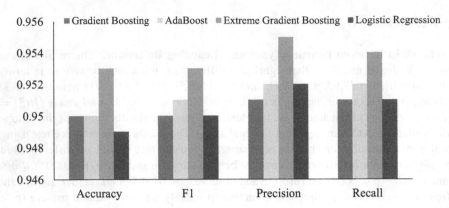

Fig. 2. Engagement recognition models with the best performance

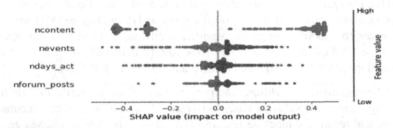

Fig. 3. The impact of learning features on engagement recognition model

4   Discussion

The results of our correlation analysis showed that there exist positive associations among the engagement features (*nevents, ndays_act, ncontent, and nforums_posts*). The features represent various learning behaviour demonstrated by students during their learning process. Overall, the features are important in automatically determining composite engagement levels of students using MOOCs. Investigations on the relationship of the features with self-reported learner types using the Kruskal-Wallis test showed that significant differences exist in learning behaviour and academic performance. However, the post-hoc results indicate that learner types could not be differentiated based on learning behaviour across various learning activities. This means that the four standard categories reported by MOOCs users did not represent various learning activity patterns of students. The *drop-in* group engaged in the course longer than the other groups, although *active* and *passive* groups performed better in forum posting and academic performance. The *passive* group participated well in forum posting and assessments even when they indicated that they are not interested in assessments and interaction with other students. This means that self-reported learner types do not represent the actual learning behaviour of students in MOOCs. Determining students' actual learning behaviour in MOOCs should be based on their performance of learning activities, not on self-reported surveys.

While the statistical analysis investigated significant differences in learning behaviour and performance among student groups, it did not provide information that could be used to assess the level of engagement of individual students. To understand the level of engagement of each student based on their learning behaviour, learning analytics method involving machine learning techniques was employed to detect low- and high-engaged students. In general, the performance of the machine learning models developed in this study demonstrated that learning behavioural features alone can be applied to detect low- and high-engaged students in MOOCs. This answers our second research question on whether student engagement levels in MOOCs can be predicted using only learning behaviour data and machine learning. The models that are more effective at predicting the engagement levels of students based on their learning behaviour are Gradient Boosting, Extreme Gradient Boosting, AdaBoost, and Logistic Regression. The models we developed in this study can be applied in detecting the engagement of certificate- and noncertificate-earning students because assessment features were not included. Also, our models can be applied in developing learning analytics dashboards that instructors can use in tracking student engagement in a course to aid them in designing improved scaffolding systems and adapting interventions that can improve students' engagement and sustain them to achieve their learning goals. The dashboard could also help students to monitor their learning activity patterns and apply their self-regulatory skills to improve their learning. For our fourth research question, the most important learning features for predicting student engagement in MOOCs are *ncontent* and *nevents, i.e.* the number of unique modules viewed in a course and the page view count.

5 Conclusion

In this study, we compared students' self-reported learner types (four groups) with their actual learning behaviour in MOOC using a Canvas dataset. Our results revealed that the learner types did not represent various learning behaviour of students. This means that students' perception of their own learning may perhaps not affect their learning behaviour. Although the perception might impact students' academic performance as indicated by significant differences in academic performance among the self-reported learner types. Moreover, we proposed an automatic approach for assessing students' engagement based on their learning behaviour. The results of our models indicated that they can be applied to predict low-and high-engaged students. The models may be employed in learning analytics dashboards to help instructors in understanding student engagement in a course to assist them in enhancing scaffolding design and adaptation of intervention that will promote engagement in learning.

References

1. Kumar Basak, S., Wotto, M., Bélanger, P.: E-learning, M-learning and D-learning: conceptual definition and comparative analysis. E-Learn. Digit. Media. **15**, 191–216 (2018). https://doi.org/10.1177/2042753018785180
2. Zhang, T., Yuan, B.: Visualizing MOOC user behaviors: a case study on XuetangX. In: Yin, H., et al. (eds.) IDEAL 2016. LNCS, vol. 9937, pp. 89–98. Springer, Cham (2016). https://doi.org/10.1007/978-3-319-46257-8_10
3. Scheuermann, M.: Online Student Engagement Tools and Strategies (2012)

4. Raj, N.S., Renumol, V.G.: Early prediction of student engagement in virtual learning environments using machine learning techniques. E-Learn. Digit. Media. **19** (2022). https://doi.org/10.1177/20427530221108027

5. Hussain, M., Zhu, W., Zhang, W., Abidi, S.M.R.: Student engagement predictions in an e-learning system and their impact on student course assessment scores. Comput. Intell. Neurosci. **2018** (2018). https://doi.org/10.1155/2018/6347186

6. Sharma, P. et al.: Student engagement detection using emotion analysis, eye tracking and head movement with machine learning. In: Reis, A., Barroso, J., Martins, P., Jimoyiannis, A., Huang, R.Y.M., Henriques, R. (eds.) Technology and Innovation in Learning, Teaching and Education. TECH-EDU 2022. Communications in Computer and Information Science, vol. 1720, pp. 52–68. Springer, Cham (2022). https://doi.org/10.1007/978-3-031-22918-3_5

7. Canvas Network Person-Course (1/2014–9/2015) De-Identified Open Dataset - Canvas Network Dataverse. https://dataverse.harvard.edu/dataset.xhtml?persistentId=doi:10.7910/DVN/1XORAL. Accessed 31 Jan 2023

8. Bonafini, F.C., Chae, C., Park, E., Jablokow, K.W.: How much does student engagement with videos and forums in a MOOC affect their achievement? Online Learn. J. **21**, 223–240 (2017). https://doi.org/10.24059/olj.v21i4.1270

9. Lundberg, S.M., Allen, P.G., Lee, S.-I.: A unified approach to interpreting model predictions. Adv. Neural Inf. Process. Syst. **30** (2017)

Enhancing First-Generation College Students' Prosocial Motivation in Human-Computer Interaction Design: A Review of Literature

Hye Jeong Park[1(✉)], Yongyeon Cho[2], and Huiwon Lim[3]

[1] University of Northern Colorado, Greeley, CO, USA
hyejeong.park@unco.edu
[2] Iowa State University, Ames, IA, USA
yongyeon@iastate.edu
[3] Pennsylvania State University, University Park, PA, USA
hjl5360@psu.edu

Abstract. The enrollment number of first-generation college students (FGCS) has been raised. It makes HCI educators put efforts into understanding FGCS and supporting them for their academic success. In particular, prosocial motivation is a significant consideration for a better understanding of user-centered perspective and allows FGCS to involve in the classes. The aim of this study is to identify how prosocial motivation can be integrated into HCI design and how it can be taught to promote FGCS' prosocial motivation for generating user-centered solutions for others. Through a review of the literature, the current study applied the Hierarchy of Needs Theory proposed by Maslow (1943) to understand human motivation and find the link in how prosocial motivation can be synthesized into HCI design education. Meeting the love and belonging need, which is the third tier of the theory, and diverse in- and outside-class activities are suggested to develop FGCS' prosocial motivation in the context of HCI design education.

Keywords: Diversity · First-generation College Students · Prosocial Motivation · The Hierarchy of Needs Theory · Human-Computer Interaction Design · Higher Education

1 Introduction

The body of college students' demographic has been diverse, and one of the reasons is the growth of the number of first-generation students whose parent has not obtained a college degree or one of the parents graduated from a college [23, 26]. According to previous studies, 34% of first-generation students registered for four-year colleges and 53% of first-generation students entered two-year colleges in 1995 and 1996 [3], and recently one-third of first-generation students are comprised of the student body of U.S. colleges [2]. Therefore, institutions should understand the traits of first-generation college students (FGCS) and consider developing course curricula and class environments to engage them successfully.

© The Author(s), under exclusive license to Springer Nature Switzerland AG 2023
C. Stephanidis et al. (Eds.): HCII 2023, CCIS 1834, pp. 343–350, 2023.
https://doi.org/10.1007/978-3-031-35998-9_47

The Human-Computer Interaction (HCI) design field should consider FGCS. Since team diversity drives HCI designers' holistic design approaches, including a high degree of understanding of their users [13, 31], FGCS' cultural backgrounds and perspectives can support generating useful design solutions. Therefore, FGCS' engagement in the class can help build broad and diverse perspectives of their peers and make synergy for generating user-centered design solutions in the design process.

Several studies examined the traits of FGCS in higher education. FGCS seems to have fewer interactions with faculty, less participation in class activities, less contribution to generating ideas, less motivation, and left institutions easily; and these are negatively related to their learning outcomes, such as critical thinking and writing skills [19, 23, 26]. In spite of these negative traits, FGCS tends to show similar abilities, such as learning achievement, critical thinking, and openness to non-first-generation students (NFGCS) [23]. In addition, when FGCS is connected to their communities, they tend to have higher prosocial values and be more willing to engage in prosocial learning compared to NFGCS [2]. Previous studies demonstrated that motivation, academic achievement, and prosocial values positively affect FGCS' perspectives. When FGCS are intrinsically and extrinsically motivated, they have shown positive learning performance [23] and are motivated by the help of others [21]. Table 1 presents the summary of previous studies' findings about the relationships between teaching tools and values to enhance FGCS' learning achievements in higher education. Articles included in the review are denoted with * in the reference list.

Table 1. A Summary of Previous Findings: Understanding the Impact of Teaching Strategies and Values on Learning Performance of FGCS and NFGCS in Higher Education

Sources	FGCS' learning achievement	NFGCS' learning achievement
Castillo-Montoya and Ives (2021) [2]	FGCS showed higher prosocial motivation and goals when they can: • Build connections between FGCS' academic content and community. This method enhanced FGCS' classroom engagement and leadership. • Collaborate with other disciplines to help their communities. This strategy fostered FGCS' comprehensive and collaborative learning experience.	N/A

(continued)

Table 1. (*continued*)

Sources	FGCS' learning achievement	NFGCS' learning achievement
Goldman et al. (2021) [7]	• Intrinsic, utility, and achievement values are significantly associated with FGCS' Transformative Experience (TE), and it drove positive learning outcomes. • Positive emotion (e.g., hope, curious, happy) was no significant difference to FGCS' learning achievement.	NFGCS tended to show a higher level of positive emotions than negative emotions (e.g., hopelessness, disappointment) compared to FGCS. It helped NFGCS easily engage in their learning and academic success.
Hecht et al. (2021) [11]	FGCS showed lower institutional matches than NFGCS. However, when interactions between friends and family are associated with their academic life, motivation for attending universities, academic confidence, and math scores are increased.	N/A
Kim and Sax (2009) [15]	Student-faculty interaction strongly impacted FGCS' academic achievement and educational goals: • Research-related faculty interaction positively promoted FGCS' GPAs, degree aspirations, critical thinking, and communication. • Course-related faculty interaction facilitated FGCS' degree aspirations, critical thinking, communication, and satisfaction with college. However, course-related faculty interaction did not arouse FGCS' GPAs.	Student-faculty interaction strongly influenced NFGCS' academic achievement and educational goals: • Research and course-related faculty interaction were importantly correlated to NFGCS' GPAs, degree aspirations, critical thinking, communication, and satisfaction with college.

(*continued*)

The previous studies (Table 1) demonstrated that motivation plays an important role in impacting FGCS' learning experience and achievement. Motivation also affects HCI students' creativity, persistence, and ability to solve design problems; accordingly, motivation can contribute to creating user-friendly interfaces [17]. The aim of this study is to understand FGCS' motivation from the perspective of HCI design through the

Table 1. (*continued*)

Sources	FGCS' learning achievement	NFGCS' learning achievement
Pascarella et al. (2004) [20]	• Classroom activities, such as reading assigned books and completing written assignments positively impacted FGCS' writing skills, openness to diversity, critical thinking, higher academic involvement, and academic success rather than NFGCS. • Volunteering in events or activities had either a slightly positive or negative impact on FGCS' academic involvement.	Volunteering in school or non-school activities growth NFGCS's learning achievements rather than FGCS.
Próspero and Vohra-Gupta (2007) [23]	• Intrinsic motivation and academic integration increased FGCS's GPAs; however, extrinsic motivation and amotivation decreased GPAs. • Intrinsic motivation promoted FGCS's academic achievement to engage in the college.	Academic integration and motivation did not contribute to NFGCS's GPAs.
Soria and Stebleton (2012) [26]	In- and outside classroom interaction with faculty, class discussions, generating ideas during the class supported FGCS' academic engagement.	N/A

review of the literature. Particularly, FGCS' prosocial motivation will be highlighted to arouse their user-centered idea generation ability.

2 Motivation in HCI Design

2.1 The Hierarchy of Needs Theory in HCI Design

HCI designers' motivation is an essential element in developing a positive user experience [10]. Human motivation can be described by the Hierarchy of Needs Theory proposed by Abraham Maslow (1943) [16], and it can be applied to HCI design to contribute to users' personal growth, well-being, and social development [25, 29]. The Hierarchy of Needs consists of five-tier human needs, physiological needs, safety needs, love and belonging, esteem, and self-actualization, and the lower tiers must be satisfied before moving on to meet higher tiers [16]. Table 2 exhibits how the five tiers can be integrated into HCI design.

Table 2. Integration of the Hierarchy of Needs Theory into the HCI design.

Tiers	Traits of each tier	Applying to the HCI design	Expected outcomes to the HCI design
Tier 1	Human survival: Food, water, and rest	The tier 1 and 2 can impact ergonomic interface design that can meet users' basic physical and security needs (e.g., encryption, authentication, and privacy settings) [14, 24].	Designers can prioritize user security in device design to create a sense of trust and safety in users [6, 32].
Tier 2	Protection: Shelter, stability, and protection from harm		
Tier 3	Interpersonal relationship and related behaviors: Social connection and relationships with others	The tier 3 can be associated with users' needs of interaction with others using devices (e.g., online-based communications: text, online forum, social media).	Designers can create a sense of community and belonging for users [18, 22] through developing a website and application functions that can facilitate social interaction.
Tier 4	Esteem for oneself & reputation from others: Achievement, mastery, and prestige	The tier 4 and 5 can be correlated to users' feedback to enhance personalization and customization design. Accordingly, the two tiers can positively develop user satisfaction [10].	Designers can arouse users' satisfaction, confidence, personal growth, and self-actualization [18] when they designed a product that can meet users' personal styles or identities.
Tier 5	Self-fulfillment: Pursuing personal growth and fulfillment		

HCI designers can create more responsive interfaces and user-friendly interactions when Maslow's the Hierarchy of Needs is synthesized into the design process. It will ultimately lead to a higher degree of designers' prosocial motivation which is related to developing a user experience that can meet users' satisfaction and fulfillment.

2.2   Prosocial Motivation in the HCI Design Education

From the perspective of HCI design education, understanding prosocial motivation is crucial for designing a product since it allows designers to take others' perspectives [9]. Prosocial motivation, which is benefiting and helping others [8], is closely associated with the HCI design process. In other words, since designers are required to solve social challenges with diverse creative methods, designers' prosocial motivation cannot be described separately in HCI design [30]. Prosocial motivation can be particularly correlated to the third tier of the Hierarchy of Needs Theory, love and belonging, in the HCI design education context. Since the traits of love and belonging desire social connection, when designers feel connected to others for their projects, they are more likely to behave prosocially and contribute to others' well-being [28].

In line with this, HCI students with a high level of prosocial motivation tend to show robust social relationships that can drive their project involvement and completion which is related to their higher academic performance [1]. Developing students' prosocial motivation can create compassion and empathy that can allow students to generate creative outcomes for their users and actively engage in the design process [4, 5].

2.3 Educational Strategies to Promote FGCS' Prosocial Motivation in the HCI Design Education

Through the review of previous studies, the current article suggests teaching methods to develop FGCS' prosocial motivation that can positively arouse their user-oriented design solutions. Firstly, HCI design educators should focus on enhancing FGCS' motivation for their learning achievement based on Maslow's (1943) [16] the Hierarchy of Needs Theory. For example, educators should build an inclusive learning environment and a positive connection with FGCS related to the third tier, love and belonging. Thibodeaux and Samson (2021) [27] examined that belongingness drove FGCS' academic achievement, and it can be influenced by an interaction between students and faculty [15, 26]. When FGCS meets the third tier, they will naturally move to the fourth, esteem needs, and fifth, self-actualization, tiers. Through the process, FGCS can arouse their degree of academic engagement, achievement, and satisfaction, and it can positively impact FGCS' design process. Eventually, FGCS' prosocial motivation can be amplified and contribute to generating user-oriented design solutions to meet users' needs.

Secondly, HCI design educators should apply effective in- and outside-classroom teaching strategies to arouse FGCS prosocial motivation. For example, according to Pascarella et al. (2004) [20], involving volunteering events and activities did not impact FGCS's academic involvement even though it is an effective method for developing individuals' prosocial motivation [9]. However, when volunteer work is related to their assignments or projects, it may positively affect FGCS learning achievement; and will affect fostering FGCS's prosocial motivation. Castillo-Montoya and Ives (2021) [2] posit that FGCS tends to show a higher degree of helping their communities. Therefore, engaging their potential users, family, and friends in the design process will effectively support developing FGCS' perspective taking and understanding of others [11]. It will help FGCS set a higher prosocial goal to generate more meaningful solutions for their users. The transformative experience (TE) can be an effective method to elevate FGCS' academic success [7]. In other words, the TE allows students to integrate their learning in class into daily life [12]. Therefore, TE can support FGCS to not only make connections between the knowledge gained from universities and their life but also get intrinsically, extrinsically, and prosocially motivated to develop their ideas with a user-centered perspective.

3 Conclusion

Engaging FGCS in the class is crucial to develop students' diverse perspectives and learning experiences in HCI design education. This study reviewed how FGCS was taught and how motivation impacted their learning achievement in higher education. Based on the findings, the current study focused on prosocial motivation since it can directly impact students' design outcomes with a user-oriented perspective in HCI design education. From the review of previous studies, the current study demonstrated that the Hierarchy of Needs Theory [16] could be applied to HCI design explaining the relationship between human motivation, HCI design, and prosocial motivation. Students' prosocial motivation is associated with the love and belonging of the theory, and it can be developed through an inclusive learning environment and positive relations with faculty. Several teaching tools such as volunteer work related to FGCS' assignments, involving their family and friends in the design process, and applying what they learned from class to daily life are suggested. These teaching strategies will enhance FGCS' class and project engagement; thus, it will lead to having other-oriented viewpoints for generating their design solutions.

References

1. Caprara, Barbaranelli, C., Pastorelli, C., Bandura, A., Zimbardo, P.G.: Prosocial foundations of children's academic achievement. Psychol. Sci. **11**(4), 302–306 (2000)
2. Castillo-Montoya, M., Ives, J.: Transformative practices to support first-generation college students as academic learners: findings from a systematic literature review. J. First-Gener. Student Success **1**(1), 20–31 (2021)
3. Choy, S.: Students whose parents did not go to college: postsecondary access, persistence, and attainment. Findings from the Condition of Education, 2001. ED Pubs, P (2001). https://eric.ed.gov/?id=ED460660
4. Dovidio, J.F., Piliavin, J.A., Schroeder, D.A., Penner, L.A.: The Social Psychology of Prosocial Behavior. Psychology Press (2017)
5. Eisenberg, N., Fabes, R.A., Spinrad, T.L.: Prosocial development (2006)
6. Gao, L., Waechter, K.A., Bai, X.: Understanding consumers' continuance intention towards mobile purchase: a theoretical framework and empirical study–a case of China. Comput. Hum. Behav. **53**, 249–262 (2015)
7. Goldman, J., Cavazos, J., Heddy, B.C., Pugh, K.J.: Emotions, values, and engagement: understanding motivation of first-generation college students. Scholarship of Teaching and Learning in Psychology, No Pagination Specified-No Pagination Specified (2021)
8. Grant, A.M.: Does intrinsic motivation fuel the prosocial fire? Motivational synergy in predicting persistence, performance, and productivity. J. Appl. Psychol. **93**, 48–58 (2008)
9. Grant, A.M., Berry, J.W.: The necessity of others is the mother of invention: intrinsic and prosocial motivations, perspective taking, and creativity. Acad. Manag. J. **54**(1), 73–96 (2011)
10. Hassenzahl, M., Tractinsky, N.: User experience-a research agenda. Behav. Inf. Technol. **25**(2), 91–97 (2006)
11. Hecht, C.A., Priniski, S.J., Tibbetts, Y., Harackiewicz, J.M.: Affirming both independent and interdependent values improves achievement for all students and mitigates cultural mismatch for first-generation college students. J. Soc. Issues **77**(3), 851–887 (2021)
12. Heddy, B.C., Sinatra, G.M., Seli, H., Taasoobshirazi, G., Mukhopadhyay, A.: Making learning meaningful: Facilitating interest development and transfer in at-risk college students. Educ. Psychol. **37**(5), 565–581 (2017)

13. Issa, T., Isaias, P.: Usability and human–computer interaction (HCI). In: Issa, T., Isaias, P. (eds.) Sustainable Design: HCI, Usability and Environmental Concerns, pp. 23–40. Springer, London (2022). https://doi.org/10.1007/978-1-4471-7513-1_2

14. Johnston, J., Eloff, J.H., Labuschagne, L.: Security and human computer interfaces. Comput. Secur. **22**(8), 675–684 (2003)

15. Kim, Y.K., Sax, L.J.: Student–faculty interaction in research universities: differences by student gender, race, social class, and first-generation status. Res. High. Educ. **50**(5), 437–459 (2009)

16. Maslow, A.H.: A theory of human motivation. Psychol. Rev. **50**(4), 370–396 (1943)

17. Norman, D.: Emotion & design: attractive things work better. Interactions **9**(4), 36–42 (2002)

18. O'Brien, H.L., Toms, E.G.: What is user engagement? A conceptual framework for defining user engagement with technology. J. Am. Soc. Inform. Sci. Technol. **59**(6), 938–955 (2008)

19. Ostrove, J.M., Long, S.M.: Social class and belonging: Implications for college adjustment. Rev. High. Educ. **30**(4), 363–389 (2007)

20. Pascarella, E.T., Pierson, C.T., Wolniak, G.C., Terenzini, P.T.: First-generation college students: additional evidence on college experiences and outcomes. J. High. Educ. **75**(3), 249–284 (2004)

21. Petty, T.: Motivating first-generation students to academic success and college completion. Coll. Stud. J. **48**(1), 133–140 (2014)

22. Preece, J., Sharp, H., Rogers, Y.: Interaction Design: Beyond Human-Computer Interaction. Wiley, Hoboken (2015)

23. Próspero, M., Vohra-Gupta, S.: First generation college students: motivation, integration, and academic achievement. Community Coll. J. Res. Pract. **31**(12), 963–975 (2007)

24. Rogers, Y., Preece, J.: Interaction Design: Beyond Human-Computer Interaction. Wiley, Hoboken (2007)

25. Ryan, R.M., Deci, E.L.: Self-determination theory and the facilitation of intrinsic motivation, social development, and well-being. Am. Psychol. **55**(1), 68 (2000)

26. Soria, K.M., Stebleton, M.J.: First-generation students' academic engagement and retention. Teach. High. Educ. **17**(6), 673–685 (2012)

27. Thibodeaux, J., Samson, J.E.: Perceptions of school belongingness and goal motivation in first-generation students. J. First-Year Experience Students Trans. **33**(1), 121–137 (2021)

28. Twenge, J.M., Campbell, W.K.: The Narcissism Epidemic: Living in the Age of Entitlement. Simon and Schuster (2009)

29. Vallerand, R.J.: Toward a hierarchical model of intrinsic and extrinsic motivation. In: Advances in Experimental Social Psychology, vol. 29, pp. 271–360. Academic Press (1997)

30. Wang, H., Jiang, X., Wu, W., Tang, Y.: The effect of social innovation education on sustainability learning outcomes: the roles of intrinsic learning motivation and prosocial motivation. Int. J. Sustain. High. Educ. (2022)

31. Wright, P., McCarthy, J.: Empathy and experience in HCI. In: Proceedings of the SIGCHI Conference on Human Factors in Computing Systems, pp. 637–646 (2008)

32. Zhang, J., Luximon, Y., Song, Y.: The role of consumers' perceived security, perceived control, interface design features, and conscientiousness in continuous use of mobile payment services. Sustainability **11**(23), 6843 (2019)

Investigating Factors that Influence Learning Outcomes in K-12 Online Education: The Role of Teachers' Presence Skill and Students' Grade

Lingli Pi[1,2], Jiayi Hou[1,2,3], Fei Wang[1,2,4] (iD), and Jingyu Zhang[1,2(✉)] (iD)

[1] CAS Key Laboratory of Behavioral Science, Institute of Psychology, Beijing 100101, China
zhangjingyu@psych.ac.cn
[2] Department of Psychology, University of Chinese Academy of Sciences, Beijing 100049, China
[3] Department of Psychology, Renmin University of China, Beijing 100872, China
[4] State Key Laboratory of Cognitive Neuroscience and Learning, Beijing Normal University, Beijing 100875, China

Abstract. The present study examined the influence of teachers' presence skill and students' grade on learning performance across 15 weeks in a whole semester. Data were collected from 148 online extra-curricular English courses for more than 200,000 Chinese primary students. Teachers' presence skill was evaluated by experts familiar with K-12 online education. Using Hierarchical Linear Modelling (HLM) analyses, the results suggested that students taught by teachers of high presence skills achieved higher scores than those taught by teachers lacking such skills. Besides, high-grade students remained stable performance across the semester. However, the performance of middle-grade students tended to drop quickly after some critical milestone (e.g., the first class and the mid-term examination) but improved quickly before examinations. The different patterns may be attributed to the differences in students' self-control abilities and time allocation strategies between online and offline courses. The findings were beneficial to human-computer interaction (HCI) researchers and practitioners who develop new methods to improve teachers' presence skill and also important to design more age-adaptive courses.

Keywords: Teaching presence skill · Learning performance · Grade · K-12 online education

1 Introduction

K12 online education has gained popularity in recent years [1]. This trend has been strengthened by the outbreak of COVID-19 as it can reduce the risk of infection compared to traditional face-to-face education [2]. However, maintaining pupils' attention and motivation in online classes is challenging as it is hard for teachers to manage students who are less capable of self-regulation. Previous studies on adult online education suggest that teachers' presence skills might be essential to mitigate such a problem.

C. Stephanidis et al. (Eds.): HCII 2023, CCIS 1834, pp. 351–357, 2023.
https://doi.org/10.1007/978-3-031-35998-9_48

Presence skills refer to the ability to make online audiences feel like they are in a real classroom [3, 4]. In adult education, many studies have revealed that teaching presence can facilitate learning [4–6]. These studies have found that teaching presence relates to relevant aspects of the online learning experience [4] and is one of the key factors influencing students' assessment of course quality [5]. In addition, the online course instructors' perceptions of their teaching presence can greatly affect students' learning experience and outcomes [7].

However, little research has examined this issue in K12 online education. Compared to adults, children are more susceptible to teachers' influences [8–10]. A recent study on K12 online education found that teachers' presence skills can positively influence the learning motivation of course participants [11]. Although it did not directly investigate the effects of teachers' presence skills on more objectively measured learning behaviors and performance, it implied that teachers' teaching presence might also influence the learning outcomes in K12 education as motivation was the key determinant of learners' engagement and performance [12].

In K12 online education, the student's age is another crucial aspect that should be considered [13]. Students in different age groups may differ in their metacognitive abilities and self-regulation skills. Younger children might find it more challenging to balance their time between on-campus courses and extra-curricular cram courses [1]. Therefore, it is likely that there will be differences in learning outcomes between elementary school students in higher grades and those in lower grades.

Based on the analyses above, this study explored the effects of teachers' presence skills on the online learning outcomes of primary school students in different grades. Rather than using self-reported data from unrepresentative samples, this study utilized real class-level records from 148 classes from a large online education company. As the data records students' attendance and performance across the whole semester (15 sessions for each class), this study was able to take the time dimension into consideration. The time course has been considered necessary in online education [14], and initial studies on adult online education have already found that the learning outcomes are subject to change over time [15]. However, such a topic has been rarely examined in previous studies on adult education, let along K12 education. Therefore, this study will examine how the joint influence of teachers' presence and students' grades would affect the whole semester.

2   Method

2.1   Data Description

The course records from a large online extra-curriculum education institution in China was used. In this paper, we analyzed the homework full-mark rates of all 15 courses in a semester from 148 classes. Among these classes, 55 were for middle grades (3rd–4th grade), and 93 were for upper grades (5th–6th grade). Additionally, a monthly exam was administered in the 4th, 8th, and 15th weeks.

2.2 Research Instrument

Teaching Presence Skill. Four experts familiar with K-12 online education were invited to score the instructional videos. Teaching presence skill was rated based on two factors: visible materials and suitable language. Each factor was identified by eight to nine questions. Each question was measured on a 5-point Likert scale ranging from 1 (strongly disagree) to 5 (strongly agree).

Homework Full-Mark Rate (HFR). To measure learning outcomes, we used the homework full-mark rate, which was calculated as the percentage of students who receive full marks on their homework. This indicator was particularly valuable since students completed the homework independently without any explanation from the teacher. As such, the full mark rate directly reflected students' mastery of the course material.

2.3 Data Analysis

We first used SPSS 26.0 to conduct descriptive statistics on the longitudinal data, followed by repeated measures of variance (RMANOVA) to examine the mean-level differences on learning outcome over the semesters. Specifically, the independent variables were divided into within-group and between-group factors, where time was within-group, and grade and teaching presence were between-group factors. Teaching presence and grade were categorical variables. Middle-grade courses were coded as 0 and higher-grade courses were coded as 1. The expectation maximization method in SPSS was used to impute missing data. Results of the analysis using the dataset with missing values imputed did not diverge from the analysis of the complete dataset. Therefore, in this study, only the analyses using the complete data were reported.

3 Result

3.1 Descriptive Analysis

The descriptive data analysis was shown in Table 1. The dependent variable was learning outcomes, while the independent variables included student grade, teaching presence skill and time.

Table 1. Descriptive data analysis

Variables	N	Minimum	Maximum	Mean ± SD (%)
Grade 3–4	65			43.9%
Grade 5–6	93			62.8%
TPS	148	0	1	0.49
HFR	148	0	1	0.30

3.2 Repeated Measures of Variance (RMANOVA)

Longitudinal data on academic performance underwent a repeated measures ANOVA. Levene's test revealed no violation of the assumption of homogeneity of variance. Results demonstrated significant interactions between time and grade level ($F = 7.50, p < 0.001$, $n_p^2 = 0.05$), but no significant interactions between time and instructional presence ($F = 0.96, p = 0.49, n_p^2 = 0.05$). As shown in Fig. 1, simple effects analysis revealed that high-grade students maintained stable performance throughout the semester.

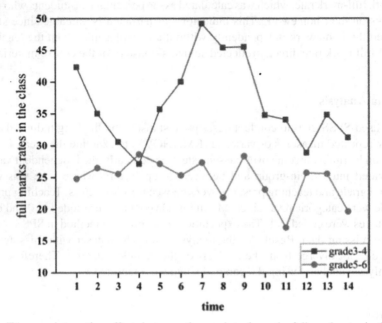

Fig. 1. Two-way interaction effects between time and grade on the full-mark rates in the rates.

However, middle-grade students (grades 3–4) showed more pronounced fluctuations in performance, with rapid declines after key events (such as the first class and mid-term examination) and quick improvements before examinations (including the mid-term exam in week 8 and the final exam in week 15). Furthermore, the main effect of teaching presence was found to be significant ($F = 3.98$, $p = 0.05$, $n_p^2 = 0.03$), indicating a positive impact on academic performance (see Fig. 2).

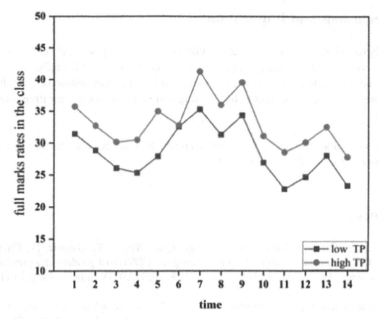

Fig. 2. The effect of teachers' presence skills on the full-mark rates in the class.

4 Discussion

This study explored how teachers' presence skills influence primary school students' learning outcomes throughout a semester across different grade levels. The study yielded several noteworthy findings that warrant discussion.

First, we found that teaching presence positively impacts students' academic performance. This finding is consistent with previous research in adult education [16, 17]. Teaching presence can encourage students to participate actively in various aspects, including behavior, cognition, and emotion, thereby improving their learning outcomes [18, 19]. Training is needed to improve the skills of teachers.

Our research also revealed that students' grades played a significant role in shaping their academic performance trajectory. Specifically, students in higher grade levels tended to have more consistent academic performance, whereas students in middle-grade levels experienced more fluctuations. These distinction patterns may be attributed to differences in self-control and time management strategies employed by students of different ages in online and offline courses. Teachers must provide guidance and support to help students develop time management and effort regulation skills.

Several limitations of the present studies must be addressed. Firstly, our study only used the evaluation from experts from schools rather than behavioral scientists so that the evaluation accuracy might be improved in future studies. Secondly, our research mainly focused on course-level outcomes. Future studies may benefit from considering the attitudes and behaviors measured at the individual level.

5   Conclusions and Implications

This study found that teachers' presence skills and students' grades influenced the online learning performance of primary school students. On the one hand, teachers and institutions are recommended to cultivate the presence skills of online instructors. On the other hand, more efforts must be paid to help younger students manage their time effectively during the semester.

Acknowledgements. This study was supported by the National Natural Science Foundation of China (Grant No. U2133209 and 52072406).

References

1. Yan, L.X., Whitelock-Wainwright, A., Guan, Q.L., Wen, G.X., Gasevic, D., Chen, G.L.: Students' experience of online learning during the COVID-19 pandemic: a province-wide survey study. Br. J. Edu. Technol. **52**(5), 2038–2057 (2021). https://doi.org/10.1111/bjet. 13102
2. Fernandez-Batanero, J.M., Montenegro-Rueda, M., Fernandez-Cerero, J., Tadeu, P.: Online education in higher education: emerging solutions in crisis times. Heliyon **8**(8), e10139 (2022). https://doi.org/10.1016/j.heliyon.2022.e10139
3. Joksimovic, S., Gasevic, D., Kovanovic, V., Riecke, B.E., Hatala, M.: Social presence in online discussions as a process predictor of academic performance. J. Comput. Assist. Learn. **31**(6), 638–654 (2015). https://doi.org/10.1111/jcal.12107
4. Morales, R., Frenzel, M., Bravo, P.R.: Teaching presence vs. student perceived preparedness for testing in higher education online english courses during a global pandemic? Challenges, tensions, and opportunities. Front. Psychol. **13**, 891566 (2022). https://doi.org/10.3389/fpsyg. 2022.891566
5. Ni, A.Y., Van Wart, M., Medina, P., Collins, K., Silvers, E., Pei, H.: A profile of MPA students' perceptions of online learning: what MPA students value in online education and what they think would improve online learning experiences. J. Public Aff. Educ. **27**(1), 50–71 (2021). https://doi.org/10.1080/15236803.2020.1820288
6. Poluekhtova, I.A., Vikhrova, O.Y., Vartanova, E.L.: Effectiveness of online education for the professional training of journalists: students' distance learning during the COVID-19 pandemic. Psychol. Russia-State Art **13**(4), 26–37 (2020). https://doi.org/10.11621/pir.2020. 0402
7. Turk, M., Muftuoglu, A.C., Toraman, S.: Teaching presence in online courses: similar perceptions but different experiences from multiple instructor perspectives. Online Learn. **25**(4), 7–28 (2021). https://doi.org/10.24059/olj.v25i4.2885
8. Freeman, S., et al.: Active learning increases student performance in science, engineering, and mathematics. Proc. Natl. Acad. Sci. U.S.A. **111**(23), 8410–8415 (2014). https://doi.org/ 10.1073/pnas.1319030111
9. Tanveer, M.A., Shabbir, M.F., Ammar, M., Dolla, S.I., Aslam, H.D.: Influence of teacher on student' learning motivation in management sciences studies. American Journal of Scientific Research **67**(1), 76–87 (2012)
10. Alfarimba, R., Ardianti, S.D., Khamdun, K.: The impact of online learning on the learning motivation of primary school students. Prog. Pendidikan **2**(2), 94–99 (2021). https://doi.org/ 10.29303/prospek.v2i2.146

11. Zuo, M.Z., Hu, Y., Luo, H., Ouyang, H.J., Zhang, Y.: K-12 students' online learning motivation in China: an integrated model based on community of inquiry and technology acceptance theory. Educ. Inf. Technol. **27**(4), 4599–4620 (2022). https://doi.org/10.1007/s10639-021-10791-x

12. Wang, C.-H., Shannon, D.M., Ross, M.E.: Students' characteristics, self-regulated learning, technology self-efficacy, and course outcomes in online learning. Distance Educ. **34**(3), 302–323 (2013). https://doi.org/10.1080/01587919.2013.835779

13. Ke, F.F.: Examining online teaching, cognitive, and social presence for adult students. Comput. Educ. **55**(2), 808–820 (2010). https://doi.org/10.1016/j.compedu.2010.03.013

14. Barbera, E., Gros, B., Kirschner, P.A.: Temporal issues in e-learning research: a literature review. Br. J. Edu. Technol. **43**(2), E53–E55 (2012). https://doi.org/10.1111/j.1467-8535.2011.01255.x

15. Tang, H., Xing, W., Pei, B.: Time really matters: understanding the temporal dimension of online learning using educational data mining. J. Educ. Comput. Res. **57**(5), 1326–1347 (2019). https://doi.org/10.1177/07356331187847

16. Lim, J., Richardson, J.C.: Predictive effects of undergraduate students' perceptions of social, cognitive, and teaching presence on affective learning outcomes according to disciplines. Comput. Educ. **161**, 104063 (2021). https://doi.org/10.1016/j.compedu.2020.104063

17. Wang, Y., Stein, D., Shen, S.: Students' and teachers' perceived teaching presence in online courses. Distance Educ. **42**(3), 373–390 (2021). https://doi.org/10.1080/01587919.2021.1956304

18. Wang, Y., Stein, D.: Effects of online teaching presence on students' cognitive conflict and engagement. Distance Educ. **42**(4), 547–566 (2021). https://doi.org/10.1080/01587919.2021.1987837

19. Wang, Y.: Effects of teaching presence on learning engagement in online courses. Distance Educ. **43**(1), 139–156 (2022). https://doi.org/10.1080/01587919.2022.2029350

Research on the Personalized Design of Gamification Element in E-learning

Qiuyue Zhao[1], Dong Min Cho[2(✉)], and Maoning Li[3]

[1] Department of Design and Manufacturing Engineering, Jeonbuk National University, Jeonju, Jeollabukdo 54896, South Korea
[2] Department of Industrial Design, Jeonbuk National University, Jeonju, Jeollabukdo 54896, South Korea
202055162@jbnu.ac.kr
[3] Department of Digital Media Art, GuangZhou University, 230 Wai Huan Xi Road, Guangzhou, People's Republic of China

Abstract. Gamification refers to the application of game design elements in non-game environments for the purpose of engaging users, motivating action, facilitating learning, and solving problems. Self-directed electronic learning (SDEL) is one of the favorite learning environments for many adult learners and is an environment where gamification is often applied. However, there is still a "one-size-fits-all" approach to gamification in many e-learning environments, and most gamification is still dominated by PBL (points, badges, leaderboards).

Personalization is defined as "the process of changing the functionality, interface, information content, or uniqueness of a system to increase its relevance to the individual". Personalization gives the user a greater sense of control, and this increased perceived control is related to the level of enjoyment of the user experience. Therefore, there is a need to create a personalized design with "learner-centered" gamification elements.

Through user interviews and empirical research, this paper proposes evaluation dimensions for personalized design of SDEL gamification elements from the perspective of "system-user" interaction: Rewards, Entertainment, Social interaction, and Visual appeal, and provides guidance solutions for designers of e-learning platforms to personalize the design of gamification elements.

Keywords: Self-directed Electronic Learning · Gamification Element · Personalized Design

1 Introduction

1.1 Research Background

With the rapid development of society, adults need to constantly learn new knowledge and skills for personal development or career advancement. Advances in the Internet and electronic technology have changed the way learners learn, and more and more adult learners are using the Internet and electronic devices to learn. According to 2020 U.S. Online Learning Statistics, the online learning rate for adult learners in the U.S. has increased by nearly 400% since 2012.

© The Author(s), under exclusive license to Springer Nature Switzerland AG 2023
C. Stephanidis et al. (Eds.): HCII 2023, CCIS 1834, pp. 358–363, 2023.
https://doi.org/10.1007/978-3-031-35998-9_49

According to the 48th Statistical Report on the Development Status of China's Internet by the China Internet Information Center (CNNIC), the online learning rate of adult learners in China is also growing. As of December 2022, the scale of online education users in China has reached 415 million, of which adult learners' learning purposes are mainly vocational training, skill improvement and hobby courses. In order to meet the demand of learners to learn anytime and anywhere, more and more educational institutions have developed self-directed electronic learning platforms.

Self-directed electronic learning (SDEL) refers to the way learners use electronic technology and the Internet to learn at their own pace in their own space [1], and has the advantages of flexibility, convenience, autonomy, personalization, and diversity of learning content [2, 3]. Examples include MOOCs, blogs, video lectures, educational apps, etc.

However, surveys have shown that most adult learners do not persist to the end of their studies in SDEL. Reports indicate that dropout rates (abandoning the learning program midway and not meeting learning goals) for e-learning can be as high as 70–80% [4].

Dichev et al. state that e-learning requires more self-regulation and intrinsic motivation from the learner [5]. Virginio Cantoni states that e-learners need to have some self-control and self-management when engaging in self-directed e-learning in order to keep up with a freer and unconstrained learning process and schedule [6]. Learners with a higher sense of self-efficacy are more likely to adopt proactive learning strategies and are more likely to complete their learning tasks. Therefore, learners need to be constantly self-motivated when learning in SDEL in order to maintain their ability to learn autonomously over time.

What kind of learning environment is one that fosters learner autonomy? In "Toward a theory of intrinsically motivating instruction" published in 1981, game educator T.W. Malone proposed that interesting games satisfy three elements, namely challenge, curiosity and fantasy. These three elements can be effective in motivating people intrinsically. Deterding defines this approach of applying game design elements to non-game situations as gamification [7].

In recent years, gamification has been widely used by domestic and international e-learning platforms. on February 8, 2020, the report Digital Learning Innovation Trends, jointly released by several educational organizations, identified gamification and game-based learning as one of the major trends in the development of digital learning.

For example, Duolingo's leveling system allows learners to freely choose the course material they need and complete the previous level of the challenge to unlock the next level of learning (see Fig. 1).In Bai Ci Zhan's contests, learners choose their opponents to compete and earn points by comparing the time and quantity of learning to enter the ranking (see Fig. 2).Mootools (MOOC), Coursera awards badges to learners who complete the learning tasks (see Fig. 3).

Fig. 1. Duolingo   **Fig. 2.** Baicizhan   **Fig. 3.** Mooc

1.2 Research Purpose

However, there is currently a "one size fits all" approach to gamification in e-learning environments, with the majority of gamification designs still dominated by PBL (points, badges, leaderboards) [7]. While gamification has created some encouraging results, inappropriate design approaches can also pose serious risks [8]. Therefore, learner-centered, personalized design solutions for gamification need to be proposed from the learner's perspective.

Personalization is defined as "the process of changing the functionality, interface, information content, or uniqueness of a system to increase its relevance to the individual. Personalization allows users to feel more control, and the increase in perceived control is related to the pleasantness of the user experience", thus increasing active user stickiness. Then, how to evaluate the personalization of gamification design, there are few related studies. This study understands the personalization needs of e-learners for gamification design through user interviews and questionnaires, and constructs the evaluation dimensions of personalization through empirical analysis.

2 Experiment

2.1 Experiment 1

Step1. Firstly, we combed through the literature of relevant studies on gamification elements.

Step2. Conduct in-depth user interviews with the cases to extract and summarize the components of gamification.

Step3. Combine with expert interviews, merge similar elements, and summarize the representative components of personalized design for SDEL gamification elements (See Table 1).

Table 1. Representative components of SDEL gamification elements.

Project	Components
Representative components of SDEL gamification elements	Constraints, Emotions, Progression, Relationships, Challenges, Competition, Rules, Goals, Growth, Constraints, Exploration, Status, Cooperation, Points, Leaderboards, Feedback, Rewards, Roles, Badges, Missions, Social, Collections, Levels

2.2 Experiment 2

Based on the literature and expert opinions, a questionnaire was developed, SPSS 22.0 was applied to process the data to verify the reliability of the questionnaire, and the evaluation dimensions of SDEL gamification elements and personalized design were analyzed empirically through Exploratory Factor Analysis (EFA).

To validate the research questions, an open online questionnaire was administered to adult learners with experience in self-directed e-learning. The questionnaire questions consisted of two parts, containing six basic questions (gender, age, educational background, monthly income, occupation, and user proficiency) and 21 questions on gamification elements. The questions in the second part were based on a 5-point Likert scale. The time period of questionnaire distribution was from May 12 to May 17, 2022, and 211 valid questionnaires were collected, containing 81 males and 130 females, including 129 college students and 82 masters and above.

3 Data Analysis

In this study, factor analysis and reliability analysis were conducted using SPSS 22.0. The results of data analysis showed that $P < 0.05$, $KOM = 0.943 > 0.6$, and $Sig = 0.000 < 0.01$, indicating high reliability and suitability for factor analysis. Four evaluation dimensions of personalized design of gamification elements were extracted by Exploratory Factor Analysis (See Table 2).

(1) Rewards in gamification systems are positive feedback given to e-learners in recognition of their services and efforts to encourage users and keep them motivated
(2) Entertainment: Entertainment in the learning process aims to stimulate e-learner to achieve a psychological state of pleasure and immersion.
(3) Social interaction: social interactions embody personal and social interactions to enhance users' gaming experience in a gamified environment
(4) Visual appeal: Visual appeal refers to the aesthetic experience that e-learner can perceive.

Table 2. Exploratory Factor Analysis of Elements.

Variables	Measurement items	Composition				Cronbach alpha
		Factor 1	Factor 2	Factor 3	Factor 4	
Rewards		.777				.900
		.740				
		.728				
		.728				
		.641				
		.534				
		.513				
Entertainment			.785			.876
			.763			
			.759			
			.589			
			.547			
Social interaction				.848		.862
				.802		
				.594		
				.540		
				.504		
Visual appeal					.745	.884
					.729	
					.624	
					.552	
Intrinsic value		11.005	1.511	1.133	.957	
KMO		.943				
Bartlett's Test of Sphericity		Approximate cardinality		3181.644		
		df		210		
		Sig		.000		

4 Conclusion

This study extracts and investigates the dimensions of gamification elements and personalized design of SDEL through literature review, actual case analysis, user interviews and questionnaire surveys.

The personalized design of gamification elements of SDEL mainly contains four dimensions: Rewards, Entertainment, Social interaction, Visual appeal.

Rewards, Entertainment, Social interaction and Visual appeal can give intrinsic motivation to e-learners through external factors. These four elements constitute the evaluation dimensions of personalized design of SDEL gamification elements and provide design guidance solutions for e-learning designers.

References

1. Jones, A.C., Scanlon, E., Clough, G.: Mobile learning: two case studies of supporting inquiry learning in informal and semiformal settings. Comput. Educ. **61**, 21–32 (2013)
2. Reinders, H.: Supporting self-directed learning through an electronic learning environment. In: Supporting Independent Learning: Issues and Interventions, pp. 219–238 (2006)
3. Park, J.-H., Choi, H.J.: Factors influencing adult learners' decision to drop out or persist in online learning. J. Educ. Technol. Soc. **12**(4), 207–217 (2009)
4. Long, L., Dubois, C., Faley, R.: A case study analysis of factors that influence attrition rates in voluntary online training programs. In: EdMedia+ Innovate Learning Online 2022, vol. 8, no. 3. Association for the Advancement of Computing in Education (AACE) (2009)
5. Dicheva, D., et al.: Gamification in education: a systematic mapping study. J. Educ. Technol. Soc. **18**(3), 75–88 (2015)
6. Cantoni, V., Porta, M., Semenza, M.: The e-learning myth and the new university. In: Image: e-Learning, Understanding, Information Retrieval, Medical, pp. 60–68 (2003)
7. Deterding, S., et al.: From game design elements to gamefulness: defining "gamification". In: Proceedings of the 15th International Academic MindTrek Conference: Envisioning Future Media Environments (2011)
8. Pedreira, O., et al.: Gamification in software engineering–a systematic mapping. Inf. Softw. Technol. **57**, 157–168 (2015)

Interacting with Cultural Heritage and Art

Research on the Design of Building a Personalized Intelligent Art Interaction System from the Perspective of Scenes

Yihui Cai[1]([✉]), Yi Ji[1], Xudong Cai[1], Yinghe Xiao[2], Zhenni Li[1], and Shaolong Zheng[1]

[1] Guangdong University of Technology, No. 729 Dongfeng East Road, Yuexiu District, Guangzhou, China
yihuicai2001edu@foxmail.com
[2] South China Normal University, No. 55, West Zhongshan Avenue, Tianhe District, Guangzhou, China

Abstract. The National College Entrance Examination in art is essential for selecting outstanding artistic talent in China. However, the current art education scene in China is unable to meet the individual needs of art candidates. In addition, the existing art education software does not yet enable personalized art education based on students' abilities. Therefore, this paper analyzes the traditional art education scene regarding teachers, students, learning spaces, and learning tools and summarizes the problems of China's current art education scene. And a personalized art interaction system is proposed. The technologies involved in the system's generating drawing steps function and drawing scoring function are demonstrated. The system is designed to help meet the needs of students' learning development and personalized learning paths and build a learner-centered personalized art education scene.

Keywords: Scene theory · Art education · Intelligent system · Personalized education

1 Introduction

The elements of a scene include "hard" aspects, such as objects and places, and "soft" parts, such as space and atmosphere associated with them [1]. The scene's core is the relationship between people and the surrounding elements in a specific space and time. Thus art teachers, students, learning spaces, and learning tools constitute the art education scene.

In terms of teachers, in the current Chinese art teaching, teacher-centered teaching and student-centered learning are in an unbalanced state, with teaching, in general, being more important than learning. Teachers mainly focus on the aspect of education, imparting the basic skills of painting and art knowledge through the use of technical means and modern teaching methods. Although this teaching method maximizes the teacher's leading role, it could be more conducive to developing students' creative thinking and imagination and limits their potential for individual growth [2].

C. Stephanidis et al. (Eds.): HCII 2023, CCIS 1834, pp. 367–375, 2023.
https://doi.org/10.1007/978-3-031-35998-9_50

On the students' side, on the one hand, the examination result-oriented learning process leads to a process in which students only passively learn painting skills and lack a deep understanding of painting. This single learning mode needs to meet the diverse learning needs of students. On the other hand, due to the imbalance of regional educational resources, many students, and learning tasks, the large classroom model of art teaching is still the main form of teaching in current art education. This teaching model of one teacher tutoring multiple students makes the interaction between students and teachers lacking, making it easier for students to get immediate teaching guidance [3].

In terms of learning space, the current art education model is mainly based on the collective teaching mode of large classes, mainly in the form of one teacher tutoring multiple students offline and one teacher tutoring one student online. Therefore, the learning space can be divided into offline space and online space.

At this stage, online training in Chinese art education is mainly based on online courses and forum exchanges, which only support teaching. Learning in the online space was supposed to have the feature of breaking through time and space limitations. However, the current Chinese market with a single teaching video-based approach has lost this advantage. At the same time, because teachers need to demonstrate frequently in art education, learning in the offline space depends on teachers' guidance, resulting in students' offline area being confined to the studio, making it challenging to build a space for independent learning. With the empowerment of today's technology, contemporary art education spaces should be deeply integrated with modern information technology to continuously broaden the depth and breadth of knowledge in the art education scene [4].

In terms of learning tools, in China's current art education model, the offline teaching space is used as the educational venue, and the large class system is used as the education form, making the rapidly developing technology and mobile terminal devices only as auxiliary tools and does not play their proper role. At the same time, among the current online art teaching software, only a few art software can realize personalized function design, and the degree of intelligence is weak, which is challenging to meet the personalized learning needs of learners [5].

The rapid development of artificial intelligence technology brings an opportunity to construct intelligent painting assistance systems [6–8]. In response to the current problems in the art education scene, this paper creatively proposes a personalized art interaction system. This system can be set up according to the individual needs of students to build a personalized educational intelligent scenario for actual teaching.

2   System Design

Based on the above problems, this paper combines artificial intelligence technology and scene theory to reprogram and reconfigure factors such as teachers, students, learning spaces, and learning tools in the art education scene. And an interactive system capable of personalized art tutoring for students is developed to build up a personalized art education intelligent scene.

2.1 Teacher's Perspective

Build a learning guidance mechanism in the system, providing immediate guidance function, step-by-step diagram generation function, and drawing evaluation. At the same time, the system can generate a series of step-by-step process diagrams based on the work entered by the students. The module of the drawing guide can score and evaluate the analysis of the individual student's work. In addition, the system can also generate the remaining steps based on the students' unfinished drawings and guide them to complete their work, see Fig. 1.

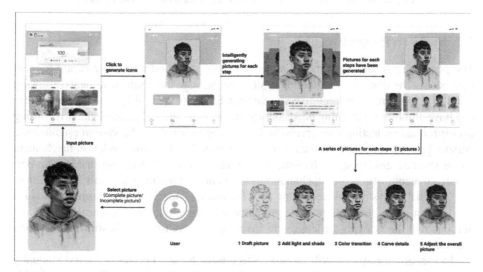

Fig. 1. Generate step function sketch avatar step diagram generation case

During the process, the system acts as an "AI teacher" to advise students on step changes and correct errors. After the painting is completed, it will be evaluated and scored. Based on the grading scale of Chinese art exams, the grading will be divided into four grades and scores: A, B, C, and D, to evaluate the work. In this process, the system will construct a data model of the learner to provide a basis for real art teachers to teach for personalized instruction. Therefore, this system can effectively alleviate the problem of insufficient teachers and too much repetitive work. It allows real art teachers to pay more attention to their students and guide them in teaching scenarios. This system redefines the role of teachers in teaching scenarios and helps art teaching become more accurate and personalized, see Fig. 2.

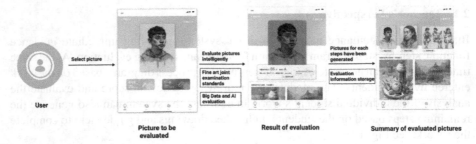

Fig. 2. Scoring function function drawing evaluation feedback process

2.2 Student's Perspective

The personalized education model's primary motivation and ultimate goal are to meet the needs of the students. The model requires attention to the needs of students, allowing them to participate as protagonists in learning. Students are at different learning stages and have different art learning needs depending on their age and education. By recording user information, testing user levels, and collecting user habits, the system establishes a personal profile for students, thus forming a personalized recommendation mechanism and a learning guidance mechanism according to the user's learning needs. The personalized recommendation mechanism can recommend learning tutorials, information, and materials for students according to their learning level. In the learning guidance mechanism, the system can provide guidance according to the user's learning situation, demonstrate the drawing process, and give suggestions for modification, scores, and evaluation.

In user use, the system will further collect users' habitual preferences and gradually generate an educational learning model that better meets users' needs. The system builds learner-centered art education scenarios through precise matching of students' personalized needs to meet different students' learning development needs and personalized learning paths. The personalized recommendation mechanism is shown in Fig. 3.

Fig. 3. Personalized real-time assistance, intelligent studio recommendation, tutorial information push, painting material push and other function diagrams

2.3 Personalized Learning Space

In response to the current situation that Chinese students' art learning space is limited to the offline area of the studio and the single form of teaching in the online learning space, it is impossible to build an independent learning space. The system's learning guidance mechanism can provide students with instant guidance, enabling them to study in an informal area outside the studio with the assistance of AI teachers. At the same time, the personalized recommendation mechanism generates an educational model that better fits the user's learning needs. In addition, this system has an online self-study space that allows learners to communicate online, creating a learning atmosphere in a formal area from visual and auditory aspects. Through online and offline human-machine collaboration, the learning space for students expands and breaks through the limitations of time and space, building a learner-centered, personalized intelligent art education scene.

2.4 Personalized Learning Tool

Based on artificial intelligence technology and big data, this system integrates art subjects' knowledge, learning resources, and learning strategies and proposes an interactive system for personalized art education. This system can be used on tablets or cell phones and will become an important learning tool in offline art education scenarios. The system also develops a user portal for the teacher role, where art teachers manage student accounts in their classes. Through the system, the teacher can better grasp the students' learning situation. The system realizes the linkage between online and offline education scenes, reconstructs the relationship between people and people, people and things, and people and the environment in the education scene, and forms a student-centered personalized education model.

3 Technology Realization

In this study, drawing, color, and sketching image data with scores for different categories of mock exams were collected from art institutions and publishers with long experience in art education for database and model building. The data were mainly divided into scoring data, drawing step data, and picture evaluation data. The data samples were sourced from various studios and publishers in Guangdong Province (China).

3.1 The Function of Generating Drawing Steps

Our module divides the painting process into 5 steps, namely forming, removing dark surfaces, rubbing, in-depth characterization, and bright gray surface characterization. The paintings in this process are photographed and recorded during the painting process. Taking sketch portraits as an example, a total of 6,700 sets of data were entered at this stage, with a total of 33,500 pieces. In practice, this research utilizes a generation confrontation network CycleGAN (Cycle Generative Adversarial Networks) [9, 10], as shown in Fig. 4, to develop the intelligent generation step function of sketching paintings.

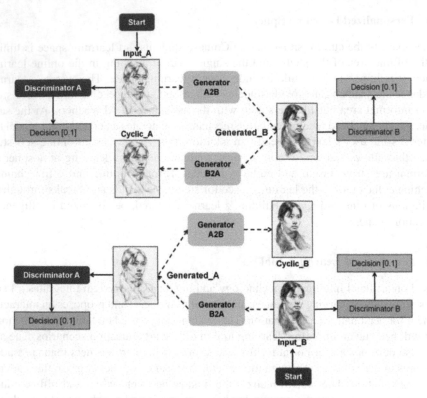

Fig. 4. Schematic diagram of CycleGAN structure

In reality, it is difficult and expensive to find paired data. However, in the absence of paired images, the CycleGAN model uses a method that learns to transform images from the source domain X to the target domain Y. The goal is to learn the mapping G: X → Y, using an adversarial loss such that the image distribution of G(X) is indistinguishable from that of Y. The model has two generators and two discriminators. In addition to the original GAN (Generative Adversarial Networks [11]) loss, the loss also introduces a new cycle consistency loss. We take the loss of the two and train to reduce the overall loss value, and finally obtain the best Model.

We classify the collected training samples according to the drawing steps, taking the first step (shape forming) to the second step (dark side row) of the sketch portraits as an example, the data set of the first step is used as the source domain X, and the first step is the source domain X. The second-step dataset is used as the target domain Y. By inputting pictures of their respective styles to the discriminator and generator for confrontation training, the probability distribution of images in the dataset is learned, and the mapping between the input image and the output image is obtained. After the model training is completed, input the test sample of the first step (shape forming) to get the second step (dark surface removal), and the other steps (rubbing, deep characterization, and bright gray surface characterization) are the same.

3.2 The Function of the Painting Score

At this stage, a total of 36,000 sketch avatar data with scores were entered. Its scoring standard refers to the scoring standard of the Art College Entrance Examination in Guangdong Province, China. Comprehensive scoring will be made from four perspectives: composition, structure and proportion, in-depth details and local depiction, and expressive means and techniques. In practice, we proposes a new type of lightweight attention convolutional network (depthwise separable convolutional network with multi-head self-attention module, DCMnet), which is used to develop an intelligent scoring and evaluation mechanism for sketch head portraits. Realize the accurate evaluation of portraits by artificial intelligence. Among them, the depth-separable convolution module requires fewer parameters than the conventional convolutional network, which is conducive to building a lightweight network, speeding up model inference time, and achieving fast scoring [12]. At the same time, convolutional neural networks have great advantages in extracting local features [13–15]. As a supplement to the convolutional network, the attention mechanism is used to mine the global features of the sketch portraits. In order to imitate the actual grading methods of teachers, our grading framework is divided into the following three stages [16]. In Stage 1, we first train a DCMnet to pay attention to the difference between grades of sketch head portraits, and divide the works into four grades: below 60 points, 60–69 points, 70–79 points, and above 80 points. On the basis of stage 1, train several subdivided classifiers (DCMnet) to further subdivide the works into eight grades. Finally we give the corresponding scores of the works. Through this method of classification from coarse to fine and then scoring, the precise scoring of works is realized, as shown in Fig. 5.

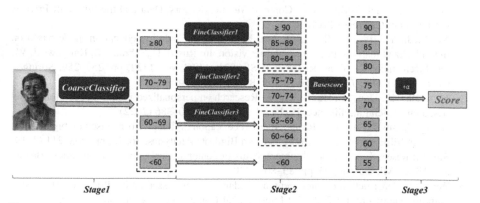

Fig. 5. A coarse-to-fine scoring framework. Among them, both the coarse classifier and the fine classifier are composed of DCMnet

During the training process, we used an effective pre-training strategy. The main idea is to warm up the model on the simple high-low classification task first, and then train the classifier in the framework, which is conducive to speeding up the model convergence speed and classification accuracy. In the classification layer, we added a softmax layer to optimize the model with multivariate cross-entropy, and reduce the value of the loss function through training to obtain the best classification model.

4 Conclusion and Future Work

Against the background of the rapid development of intelligent technology, personalized and diverse educational needs have put forward new requirements for the art education scene. This paper analyzes the traditional art education scene at the levels of teachers, students, learning spaces, and learning tools. It points out that the current Chinese art education model needs more personalization at all levels. We combine the concept of artificial intelligence technology and personalized education with building a personalized intelligent art interaction system based on personalization. It is also designed and functionally developed at the levels of teachers, students, learning spaces, and learning tools. This system helps to realize the personalized art learning style and build a personalized art education scenario. All in all, this system attempts to develop personalized art education interactive systems in the context of the intelligent era. It provides a case reference for the development of personalized art education.

Foundation Item. Guangzhou Philosophy and Social Science Planning Project, No. 2022GZGJ258;

Guangzhou University Innovation and Entrepreneurship Education Project, No. 2020kc007;

Guangzhou Philosophy and Social Science Development "13th Five-Year Plan" Young Scholar Project, No. 2020GZQN24.

Guangdong Science and Technology Innovation Strategy Special project, No. pdjh2023b0170.

References

1. Scoble, R., Israel, S.M.: Age of Context: Mobile, Sensors, Data and the Future of Privacy. Patrick Brewster Press (2014)
2. Xu, Y., Ji, Yi., Tan, P., Zhong, Q., Ma, M.: Intelligent painting education mode based on individualized learning under the internet vision. In: Russo, D., Ahram, T., Karwowski, W., Di Bucchianico, G., Taiar, R. (eds.) IHSI 2021. AISC, vol. 1322, pp. 253–259. Springer, Cham (2021). https://doi.org/10.1007/978-3-030-68017-6_38
3. Ji, Y., Zhu, Z., Han, M., Hu, B., Hu, J.: Research on personalized painting education model based on artificial intelligence. Packag. Eng. **43**(S1), 380–386 (2022)
4. Xiang, Z., Zhi, L., Jiang, J.: Research on art education digital platform based on big data. In: 2019 4th IEEE International Conference on Big Data Analytics, no. 10, pp. 208–211 (2019)
5. Shi, L.: Research on the development status of contemporary online art education. Beauty and Times (Middle), no. 05, pp. 85–86 (2020)
6. Zeng, Q.: Construction of intelligent art guidance system based on intelligent robot-assisted painting equipment. In: 2022 3rd International Conference on Electronics and Sustainable Communication Systems (ICESC), pp. 1345–1348 (2022)
7. Kim, M., Kang, D., Lee, N.: Feature extraction from oriental painting for wellness contents recommendation services. IEEE Access **7**, 59263–59270 (2019)
8. Luo, R.C., Hong, M.-J., Chung, P.-C.: Robot artist for colorful picture painting with visual control system. In: 2016 IEEE/RSJ International Conference on Intelligent Robots and Systems (IROS), pp. 2998–3003 (2016)
9. Zhu, J.-Y., Park, T., Isola, P., Efros, A.A.: Unpaired image-to-image translation using cycle-consistent adversarial networks. In: 2017 IEEE International Conference on Computer Vision (ICCV), Venice, Italy, pp. 2242–2251 (2017)

10. Lee, S., Ko, B., Lee, K., Yoo, I.-C., Yook, D.: Many-to-many voice conversion using conditional cycle-consistent adversarial networks. In: ICASSP 2020 - 2020 IEEE International Conference on Acoustics, Speech and Signal Processing (ICASSP), Barcelona, Spain, pp. 6279–6283 (2020)

11. Goodfellow, I., et al.: Generative Adversarial Nets. Neural Information Processing Systems. MIT Press (2014)

12. Sandler, M., Howard, A., Zhu, M., Zhmoginov, A., Chen, L.-C.: MobileNetV2: inverted residuals and linear bottlenecks. In: 2018 IEEE/CVF Conference on Computer Vision and Pattern Recognition, Salt Lake City, UT, USA, pp. 4510–4520 (2018)

13. He, K., et al.: Deep residual learning for image recognition. In: Proceedings of the IEEE Conference on Computer Vision and Pattern Recognition (2016)

14. Simonyan, K., Zisserman, A.: Very deep convolutional networks for large-scale image recognition. arXiv preprint arXiv:1409.1556 (2014)

15. Tan, M., Le, Q.: Efficientnet: rethinking model scaling for convolutional neural networks. In: International Conference on Machine Learning. PMLR (2019)

16. Vaswani, A., et al.: Attention is all you need. In: Advances in Neural Information Processing Systems, vol. 30 (2017)

Insights on Metrics' Correlation of Creativity Assessment for Museum Cultural and Creative Product Design

Hui Cheng[1,2,3](✉) ⓘ, Shijian Luo[3], Bingjian Liu[2], Liang Xia[2], Jing Xie[2], and Xiao Qiu[1]

[1] Zhejiang University of Finance and Economics Dongfang College, Haining 314408, China
chenghui2050@163.com, hui.cheng@zufedfc.edu.cn
[2] University of Nottingham Ningbo China, Ningbo 315100, China
[3] Zhejiang University International School of Design, Ningbo 315100, China
sjluo@zju.edu.cn

Abstract. The museum's cultural and creative industries face some problems in the product aspect. The dominant issues are the phenomenon of product homogenisation and the shortage of creativity in the product. Herein, several questions underlie this phenomenon and problem: (1) What does cultural creativity mean when referring to museum cultural and creative products? (2) What measurements can we take to evaluate creativity? and (3) Can we calculate an overall creativity score for museum cultural and creative products to guide design decisions? Unfortunately, after reading the literature, few answers have been discovered. We explored as many potential metrics and models as possible in this realm of creativity research, highlighted some potentials and invited 224 participants to verify through a survey using 5-point Likert Scales. From the survey results (Cronbach $\alpha = 0.95$), we found: (1) There are gender and experience differences in the measurement of creativity; (2) The products with high creativity share the same order of six metrics; thus, there may be a "recipe" for improving product creativity; (3) In cases of high creativity product, *Emotion* is the leading dimension; thus, this dimension may be dominant in creativity assessment; (4) *Novelty* is not predominant in the sample assessment, and this phenomenon may happen in other museum's cultural and creative products; (5) *Usefulness* is easily influenced by other factors, which may include the preferences and interests of customers; (6) *Importance* ranks the last in all dimensions among all products and this may be caused by the fact that we used products with the same function.

Keywords: Product Design · Creativity Assessment · Museum Culture and Creativity

1   Literature Review

1.1   Creativity Research

With Guilford's significant presidential address to the American Psychological Association in the 1950s, the research on creativity started (Mumford, 2003; Rhodes, 1961; Weisberg, 2015), but the definition of creativity is still vague through years of development, one literature contended there are at least 164 definitions of creativity (Sarkar & Chakrabarti, 2008). In the inquires of creativity definition, the researchers have developed four categories of creativity research to understand better what creativity is, which are known as the *"4P Model"*: *Process, Person, Press (i.e., Environment)*, and *Product* (Besemer & Treffinger, 1981; Kaufman & Glăveanu, 2021; Oman, Tumer, Wood, & Seepersad, 2012; Rhodes, 1961).

The Aspect of the Person. Rhodes used *"Person"* to cover information about personality, intellect, habit, behaviour, and value system. (Rhodes, 1961). Put differently, this aspect is on the human capacity to develop ideas or products that are novel and useful (Martinsen, 2011).

The Aspect of the Process. This aspect applies to perception, motivation, learning, thinking and communicating (Rhodes, 1961). It is a field where researchers from the design discipline often attend, and the process of design thinking and the methods for innovative or creative design are intensively studied.

The Aspect of the Press. In this facet, the *"Press"* means the relationship between human and their contexts, including society and culture (Rhodes, 1961). Csikszentmihalyi is one of the most significant figures in this aspect, and he put forward a model including the *field* (social system), the *domain* (cultural system), and the *person* to demonstrate how creativity is accepted by the culture (Csikszentmihalyi, 1998). This notion provides a theoretical foundation for assessing creativity in outcomes (Hennessey, Amabile, & Mueller, 2011).

The Aspect of the Product. Influenced by the previous three aspects, the *"Product"* in this aspect covers all the outcomes of creative behaviours, including artworks, poems, ideas, and industrial products. Compared with the former three facets, product creativity is an area where the research is somewhat deficient and has been long ignored (O'Quin & Besemer, 2006). Researchers have put forward several models for product creativity assessment and verified them through experiments. Mainly, there are three approaches to assessing product creativity: the CAT (*Consensual Assessment Technique*), the CPSS (*Creative Product Semantic Scale*) and the PCMI (*Product Creativity Measurement Instrument*). Among them, the PCMI model is of high compatibility theoretically because it is based on CPSS and designed for assessing the creativity of industrial products. The PCMI model has been developed in recent years. The metrics of the initial version include novelty, resolution, emotion, attraction, importance and desire (D. Horn & Salvendy, 2006), and the current simplified version only covers affect, novelty and importance(Diana Horn & Salvendy, 2009). The initial version of the model has been used in our study because this model does not have a long history and is immature. Moreover, it is still rare to see the model be applied to assess the product in the context of museum culture and creativity; thus, as a model development, we need to start validation from the beginning version.

2   Description of the Survey

In Horn's model validation stage of the initial model, they identified 41 potential pairs of adjectives and finally reduced to six pairs in total by evaluation; we chose the one with the highest factor loading for each dimension because these adjective pairs can better represent each assessment metric (see Table 1). We selected the positive polars of the six pairs only (*Rare, Functional, Appealed, Favourable, Important, Desire*) from the adjective-pair list, proposed a survey questionnaire on "Wenjuan Wang", and invited design experts who owned cultural and creative product design expertise over three years to rate five museum cultural and creative products with 5-point Likert Scales (1 represents the lowest score and 5 means the highest score).

Table 1. Creativity Dimensions and the Corresponding Adjective Pairs with Factor Loadings

Dimension	Corresponding Adjective Pair	Factor Loading
Novelty	Rare - Standard	0.71
Usefulness (Resolution)	Functional - Impractical	0.69
Emotion (Pleasure)	Appealed - Revolted	0.64
Attraction (Arousal)	Favourable - Unfavourable	0.73
Importance (Applicability)	Important - Unimportant	0.85
Desire (Centrality)	Desirable - Undesirable	0.64

The category of museum cultural and creative product we chose in the survey is "Strom Glass" because this is a novel and bestseller category for museum culture and creativity. Moreover, few customers are familiar with this category. Thus, it may evoke a sense of pleasure and curiosity in the participants and the assessment process, making the survey more pleasant. The storm glass is a mixed solution invented by *Robert FitzRoy* in the 1800s, which can be used to "forecast" the weather for the hybrid solution will crystallise or dissolve as per the temperature. Although the nearest experiments show the inaccuracy of such weather forecast instruments, many people still prefer to own one for home decoration because of the pleasant phenomenon of crystallisation and dissolution. We selected five different storm glasses, each with a unique cultural heritage element from three world-leading museums (*the British Museum in London, the Metropolitan Museum of Art in New York*, and *the Palace Museum in Beijing*) (see Fig. 1).

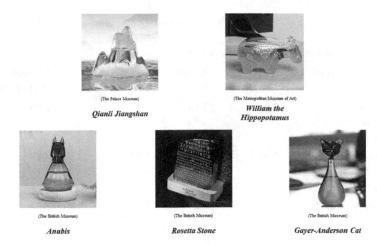

Fig. 1. Samples for the Survey

3 Results

We received 224 responses at the end of the survey. After reviewing them individually, we deleted two duplicates and reserved the rest 222 answers (*Cronbach $\alpha = 0.95$*). On the age scale, 32.58% of the 221 participants are males, and 67.42% are females. On the scale of design experience, 43.44% of the participants have 3–5 years of experience, 19% have 5–7 years, 14.03% have 7–10 years, and the rest, 22.53%, have more than ten years of experience. We calculated the average score for the five products in different scales (see Table 2).

Table 2. Average Score of the Five Samples in Different Scales

Scale	Sample Name (Average Score)				
	Anubis	Qianli Jiangshan	Rosetta Stone	Gayer-Anderson Cat	William the Hippopotamus
Males	3.30	3.21	3.29	3.38	3.10
Females	3.31	3.04	3.21	3.30	3.00
Experts with 3-to-5-year Experience	3.36	3.25	3.32	3.39	3.06
Experts with 5-to-7-year Experience	3.10	3.04	3.17	3.35	3.06

(continued)

Table 2. (*continued*)

Scale	Sample Name (Average Score)				
	Anubis	Qianli Jiangshan	Rosetta Stone	Gayer-Anderson Cat	William the Hippopotamus
Experts with 7-to-10-year Experience	3.36	3.06	3.13	3.23	2.99
Experts with Over-10-year Experience	3.35	2.88	3.20	3.23	2.99
On All Scales	3.31	3.10	3.24	3.32	3.03

From Table 2, the sample with the highest average score, *i.e.*, the highest creativity score, can be identified, and the ranking of each product in each scale shows as follows (see Table 3).

Table 3. The Ranking of the Five Samples in Different Scales

Scale	Sample Name (Ranking, 1 represents the top, and 5 represents the bottom)				
	Anubis	Qianli Jiangshan	Rosetta Stone	Gayer-Anderson Cat	William the Hippopotamus
Males	2	4	3	1	5
Females	1	4	3	2	5
Experts with 3-to-5-year Experience	2	4	3	1	5
Experts with 5-to-7-year Experience	3	5	2	1	4
Experts with 7-to-10-year Experience	1	4	3	2	5
Experts with Over-10-year Experience	1	5	3	2	4
On All Scales	2	4	3	1	5

The average scores and their Standard Deviations of each dimension for each sample also have been figured out and presented in Table 4.

Table 4. The Average Scores and Ranking of Each Dimension

Sample Ranking	Sample Name	The Ranking of Each Dimension	The Average Score of Each Dimension	The Standard Deviations of Each Dimension
1	Gayer-Anderson Cat	Emotion	3.58	1.02
		Attraction	3.49	1.10
		Novelty	3.48	1.05
		Desire	3.33	1.08
		Resolution	3.14	1.02
		Importance	2.92	1.06
2	Anubis	Emotion	3.73	1.07
		Attraction	3.57	0.97
		Novelty	3.51	1.09
		Desire	3.27	1.06
		Resolution	3.10	1.10
		Importance	2.67	1.07
3	Rosetta Stone	Novelty	3.62	1.00
		Emotion	3.46	1.06
		Attraction	3.31	1.02
		Desire	3.24	1.01
		Resolution	2.98	1.01
		Importance	2.82	1.06
4	Qianli Jiangshan	Novelty	3.26	1.11
		Attraction	3.25	1.08
		Emotion	3.24	1.15
		Desire	3.06	1.09
		Resolution	3.05	1.05
		Importance	2.73	1.10
5	William the Hippopotamus	Novelty	3.34	1.09
		Emotion	3.12	1.16
		Attraction	3.11	1.15
		Resolution	2.98	1.06
		Desire	2.92	1.14
		Importance	2.72	1.04

4 Discussion

From the above tables (Table 2, Table 3 and Table 4), we discovered the following insights:

(1) There are gender differences in rating the most creative products: males voted *Gayer-Anderson Cat*, while females chose *Anubis*. Differences can also be found in the scale of design experience: participants with design experience of fewer than seven years voted *Gayer-Anderson Cat,* and the ones with more than seven years of experience chose *Anubis*. If years of experience can be interpreted as the duration they expose to museum culture and creativity, surely they will be more critical of the novelty than the ones who have less experience because research revealed novelty is associated with surprise, which is a kind of first-sight emotion (Chang & Wu, 2007; Desmet, 2002), the more a person exposed to a novel product, the less emotion will be evoked. It may lead to a lower creativity score. However, this mechanism of how emotion impacts the perception of a product's novelty and indirectly influences overall creativity needs to be investigated.

(2) The products with the predominant creativity score (*Gayer-Anderson Cat* and *Anubis*) share the same order of six dimensions. In contrast, the same phenomenon cannot be discovered in the inferiors (*Rosetta Stone, Qianli Jiangshan,* and *William the Hippopotamus*). This exciting phenomenon may imply that there is a "recipe" for designing products with high creativity. More specifically, we could develop a system to predict the overall creativity score, perfect the creativity performance and assist the design practice after constructing an assessment model and understanding the correlations of metrics in the context of museum culture and creativity.

(3) In traditional creativity research, *Novelty* is the predominant metric; however, it may not apply to museum cultural and creative products because *Novelty* only ranks third in *Gayer-Anderson Cat* and *Anubis* (the two cases of high creativity score). However, it ranks first in the inferiors (*Rosetta Stone, Qianli Jiangshan, and William the Hippopotamus*). This finding corresponds with the discovery of O'Quin and Besemer (2006). Based on the result and the literature, we may conclude that *Novelty* is not a determining factor for creativity assessment, especially in the museum cultural and creative products category.

(4) In *Gayer-Anderson Cat* and *Anubis*, the two cases of high creativity score, *Emotion* is the leading dimension, which may indicate that emotion is an essential metric in the creativity assessment of museum cultural and creative products, and it may be a metric that impacts the overall score of creativity to a great extent. Suppose data can validate this finding. In that case, the *Affect* dimension will replace the traditional positions of *Novelty* and *Usefulness* in assessing creativity, especially for museum culture and creativity products.

(5) The traditional creativity study also emphasises the importance of *Usefulness*. However, this dimension ranks fifth in *Gayer-Anderson Cat* and *Anubis, and* design experts still rate these two products with high scores. Moreover, we offered the participants products with the same function but have not received similar scores. This phenomenon tells us that raters may easily be affected by their preference and interests, which is what Diana Horn and Salvendy (2009) contended. In their research

(Diana Horn & Salvendy, 2009), *Attraction* refers to customers' interest, which is subjective. In this survey, we discovered that *Attraction* ranks second or third place in all samples, which may indicate that this personal dimension is also an influential aspect of creativity assessment. In other words, the score of creativity for a product may be deeply impacted by assessor's preference. Although we tried our best to obtain objective creativity scores of products, it is unavoidable that the score will be impacted by raters' subjectivity. And this may create a gap between the theoretical score and the practical score and make the task of creativity measurement more difficult to accomplish.

(6) An exciting phenomenon is that *Importance* ranks sixth among all dimensions in the result of five products, which means design experts contended that these museum's cultural and creative products are not vital to them because they all give low scores. Since we used products of the same function, the scores may be influenced, and we need to use products of different functions to conduct another survey.

5   Conclusion

From the survey result, we summarised seven significant insights for further validation, and they are: (1) There are gender and experience differences in the measurement of creativity; (2) The products with high creativity scores share the same order of six metrics; thus, there may be a "recipe" for improving product creativity; (3) In cases of high creativity score, *Emotion* is the leading dimension; thus, this dimension may be dominant in creativity assessment; (4) *Novelty* is not predominant in the sample assessment, and this phenomenon may happen in other museum's cultural and creative products; (5) *Usefulness* is easily influenced by other factors, which may include the preferences and interests of customers; (6) *Importance* ranks the last in all dimensions among all products and this may be caused by the fact that we used products with the same function.

The drawbacks of this research are: (1) We only based on the average score to summarise the insights; (2) We have not validated the results through statistical analysis tools such as *Stata* and *SmartPLS*.

In the future, we will prove our insights and validate them to improve their validity and reliability. Furthermore, we will validate the metrics of the assessment model through biosensors, including *Electrodermal Screening (EDS)*, *Electroencephalograph (EEG)* and *Eye Tracker*.

Acknowledgement. This research is supported by the Major Project of Zhejiang Social Science Foundation (21XXJC01ZD) and the Provincial Fundamental and Commonweal Research Projects of Zhejiang (LGF22G030015).

References

Besemer, S.P., Treffinger, D.J.: Analysis of creative products: review and synthesis. J. Creative Behav. **15**(3), 158–178 (1981). https://doi.org/10.1002/j.2162-6057.1981.tb00287.x

Chang, W.-C., Wu, T.Y.: Exploring types and characteristics of product forms. Int. J. Des. **1**(1), 3–14 (2007). http://www.ijdesign.org/index.php/IJDesign/article/view/7/9

Csikszentmihalyi, M.: Implications of a systems perspective for the study of creativity. In: Sternberg, R.J. (ed.) Handbook of Creativity, pp. 313–336. Cambridge University Press, Cambridge (1998)

Desmet, P.: Designing Emotions. Doctoral Degree. Delft University of Technology (2002)

Hennessey, B.A., Amabile, T.M., Mueller, J.S.: Consensual assessment. In: Runco, M.A., Pritzker, S.R. (eds.) Encyclopedia of Creativity, 2nd edn., pp. 253–260. Academic Press, San Diego (2011)

Horn, D., Salvendy, G.: Product creativity: conceptual model, measurement and characteristics. Theor. Issues Ergon. Sci. **7**(4), 395–412 (2006). https://doi.org/10.1080/14639220500078195

Horn, D., Salvendy, G.: Measuring consumer perception of product creativity: impact on satisfaction and purchasability. Hum. Factors Ergon. Manuf. Serv. Ind. **19**(3), 223–240 (2009). https://doi.org/10.1002/hfm.20150

Kaufman, J., Glăveanu, V.P.: An overview of creativity theories. In: Kaufman, J.C., Sternberg, R.J. (eds.) Creativity: An Introduction, pp. 17–30. Cambridge University Press, Cambridge (2021)

Martinsen, Ø.L.: The creative personality: a synthesis and development of the creative person profile. Creat. Res. J. **23**(3), 185–202 (2011). https://doi.org/10.1080/10400419.2011.595656

Mumford, M.D.: Where have we been, where are we going? Taking stock in creativity research. Creat. Res. J. **15**(2–3), 107–120 (2003). https://doi.org/10.1080/10400419.2003.9651403

O'Quin, K., Besemer, S.P.: Using the creative product semantic scale as a metric for results-oriented business. Creativity Innov. Manag. **15**(1), 34–44 (2006). https://doi.org/10.1111/j.1467-8691.2006.00367.x

Oman, S.K., Tumer, I.Y., Wood, K., Seepersad, C.: A comparison of creativity and innovation metrics and sample validation through in-class design projects. Res. Eng. Design **24**(1), 65–92 (2012). https://doi.org/10.1007/s00163-012-0138-9

Rhodes, M.: An analysis of creativity. Phi Delta Kappan **42**(7), 305–310 (1961). http://www.jstor.org/stable/20342603

Sarkar, P.K., Chakrabarti, A.: Studying engineering design creativity-developing a common definition and associated measures. Paper presented at the NSF Workshop on Studying Design Creativity (2008)

Weisberg, R.W.: On the usefulness of "value" in the definition of creativity. Creat. Res. J. **27**(2), 111–124 (2015). https://doi.org/10.1080/10400419.2015.1030320

Research on Folk Belief Space in Fengzhou Ancient Town Based on GIS

Yue Cui[✉], Jie Zhang, Ying Zhang, Chenglin He, and Dashuai Liu

School of Art Design and Media, East China University of Science and Technology,
Shanghai 200237, China
cuiyue619@163.com

Abstract. Folk belief space is the concrete embodiment of folk belief in the settlement space, and it is also an important activity space of folk belief. For a long time, the study of folk belief is mainly based on qualitative analysis, and more objective and rational quantitative research has gradually become a research trend. This paper takes the folk belief space in Fengzhou Town, Nan'an City, Fujian Province as the research object. Firstly, through field investigation, the beliefs categories and geospatial information of folk belief spaces in the research area are collected. Second, organize survey data through 91wemap and produce vector data for further analysis. Finally, the kernel density analysis method based on GIS is used to conduct data simulation and data visualization on the distribution form and influence range of various folk belief spaces in the research area. Thus, the radiation range of folk belief spaces in the research area can be summarized. In the end, this paper proposes some suggestions on the spatial planning of ancient towns and provides theoretical reference for the protection and reconstruction of ancient towns.

Keywords: Folk belief space · GIS · Ancient village protection

1 Research Background

1.1 Folk Belief Space in Fengzhou Ancient Town

Fengzhou town is an ancient land with a history of more than 1,700 years [1]. Due to its location in the southeast coast far away from the political center, its unique production and life style in coastal areas, as well as many factors such as immigrants from the Central Plains in history, rampant knife fighting and profound tradition of "believing in ghosts and witches" [2], the folk beliefs in Fengzhou town not only have distinct local characteristics of southern Fujian, but also inherit the tradition of folk beliefs in the Central Plains [3]. Nowadays, Fengzhou still has a large number of traditional buildings, where we can clearly see the important spiritual role of various folk beliefs in people's lives [4]. These folk belief spaces not only represent the formalization of folk beliefs, but also integrate people material and spiritual activities under different cultures [5], connecting people's spiritual world and real life.

C. Stephanidis et al. (Eds.): HCII 2023, CCIS 1834, pp. 385–392, 2023.
https://doi.org/10.1007/978-3-031-35998-9_52

The folk beliefs in Fengzhou Town have a broad mass base, and the influence of this scattered and unsystematic folk belief almost extent the whole city. However, under the impact of modernization, the original folk belief space in Fengzhou ancient town has been broken, and the old and new buildings are distributed in disorder. However, folk belief still plays an important role in people's spiritual world, and the renovation of family belief space has always been an important appeal for Fengzhou people. Therefore, by studying the folk belief space in Fengzhou, this paper proposes the regional characteristics and protection strategies of the folk belief space in Fengzhou Town, so as to provide theoretical reference for the protection and development of the folk belief space in Fengzhou Town.

1.2 GIS and Ancient Village Protection

Since the 1990s, UNESCO has applied high-tech technologies such as geographic information system (GIS) and remote sensing (RS) into the protection planning and management of cultural heritage, and conducted pilot projects in Vietnam, Laos, Thailand, Cambodia and other Southeast Asian countries, achieving fruitful results [6]. In 2000, UNESCO and the School of Architecture of Southeast University jointly established the GIS Center to improve the planning and research level of China's cultural heritage, promote the application of GIS in the protection and management of historical cultural heritage, and apply GIS technology to the whole process of current situation investigation, conservation planning, management and control of historic blocks [7].

Based on its powerful spatial data management ability [8] and analysis ability, GIS can comprehensively consider social development, economic growth, natural conditions and other factors in the urban planning area in the face of complex spatial data, and objectively evaluate the program content under the condition of reasonable screening, so as to propose better planning decision content. Thus, the design cycle can be shortened and better planning and design effects can be obtained, and the protection planning and design scheme can be changed to a more reasonable direction [9]. Juan A [10] investigated and studied the characteristics of historical buildings in rural areas of Valencia, Spain, and drew the characteristics of historical buildings in the region through the establishment of PPGIS (Geographic Information System for Public Participation) database, so as to assist the evaluation and management of historical buildings. Andre Soares Lopes [11] developed a GIS computing tool to identify and represent the information elements of cultural heritage sites, protected buildings and the surrounding environment, and to achieve the common visibility of this information element. Jing Fu [12] conducted a systematic survey of traditional houses and built a spatial database of villages based on GIS, so as to provide convenience for the evaluation and evaluation of architectural value. Ren Yue [13] built a document-type protection model of traditional village culture through GIS system, which was composed of four modules: data front-end collection module, database construction and data platform display module, protection planning system module and background monitoring and maintenance module. Song Guanfu [14] elaborated five systems of GIS from the perspective of IT industry: The big data GIS, Artificial intelligence GIS, 3D GIS, Distributed GIS technology and Cross-platform GIS technology, and the difficulties and innovations of each technology system are discussed and summarized.

2   Research Design and Methods

2.1   Research Object Overview

The research object is part of Fengzhou town, and the area involves Fengzhou Village and Taoyuan Village, which covers 1.4 square kilometers. In terms of geographical space, it reaches Fengzhou Road in the south, Taoyuan Tianqian in the north, Qiaozhong Road in the west, East Ring Road in Fengzhou Village and Nanmen Street in Taoyuan Village in the east. In terms of belief types, Buddhism and Taoism are the main basis of all beliefs, and they are combined with ancestor worship and polytheism, reflecting the characteristics of mutual penetration of superstition, customs and religious beliefs. In terms of folk belief space, as of December 2022, 320 buildings with traditional features have been preserved in the research area, which is the most important space for local belief activities.

2.2   Research Design and Methods

The research content of this paper can be divided into three parts: data collection, data collation and data analysis of folk beliefs in Fengzhou. The research methods include field investigation method and kernel density analysis method based on GIS tools.

Field Investigation. In the data collection stage, this study adopts the field survey method to collect data. First of all, it is necessary to consult a large amount of literature to make a complete research plan and research objectives. Secondly, the buildings in the research area should be numbered and the building survey information table should be made before the research work. The building survey information sheet should include: building number, building age, religion category, etc. These two preliminary works can prevent omissions during the investigation, facilitate the search of building location during the visit and investigation, and facilitate the information sorting after the investigation is completed. Finally, conduct research. With the help of the building number, record the information of each building according to the building survey information sheet; For key buildings, in-depth interviews can be conducted with the buildings or residents around the buildings to dig out the folk stories behind the beliefs and make records.

Kernel Density Analysis Based on GIS Tool. The data sorting stage is based on the relevant data of the folk belief space in Fengzhou that collected in the previous research. Firstly, the data screening was carried out to select the architectural space and its information with folk belief, while the architectural space and its information without folk belief were screened out. Secondly, according to the corresponding building number, divide the layer for different belief types in 91 wemap and drop points as the specific belief space location.

In the data analysis stage, import the data layer from 91wemap into the ArcGIS, take the survey area as the raster boundary, and use the kernel density analysis tool in ArcGIS to present the relationship between the belief space inside the boundary and the radiation range of the belief space. The analysis results of kernel density and the visual presentation of data can better assist the research and discussion in the following paper.

2.3 Research Tool

In different research stages different research tools are needed. In the data collection stage, this study adopts the field survey method, which requires architectural map drawings, cameras and other research tools, and prepares architectural information sheets as the recording tools. In the stage of data collation, this study selected 91 wemap software as the data collation tool and ArcGIS as the kernel density analysis tool.

3 Research Results and Analysis

3.1 The Number and Distribution of Various Belief Spaces

Taking the belief space in Fengzhou as the research object, 320 traditional buildings with folk belief function were investigated. After sorting out GIS data, it was found that: In the research area, there are 16 folk beliefs, such as Landowner, Avalokitesvara, God of Wealth, Guan Gong, Matsu, Emperor Bao Sheng, City God, Buddha and Emperor Taizong of Tang and Chieftain star, and so on (see Table 1). Among all the belief Spaces, there are 16 temples and the rest are ancestral houses or dwellings. In addition, according to the number of worship Spaces, it can be clearly seen that among the various folk beliefs in this area, the most common beliefs are Landowner and Avalokitesvara.

Table 1. The number of belief Spaces for various beliefs.

Name of belief	Number of belief Spaces	Number of temples
Landowner	138	4
Avalokitesvara	102	1
God of Wealth	5	1
Guan Gong	4	0
Matsu	4	1
Emperor Bao Sheng	3	1
City God	1	1
Buddha	1	0
Emperor Taizong of Tang	1	1
Chieftain star	1	0
Five Directions Heavenly God	1	1
Yellow River water god	1	1
Emperor of Heavenly Master	1	1
Emperor Zhen Wu	1	1
King Hirozawa's	1	1
Mrs. Su mother	1	1

After sorting and visualization of specific survey data, the distribution of various belief Spaces is shown in Fig. 1.

Fig. 1. The spatial distribution of all folk beliefs.

Then complete the vector point positioning in 91wemap, import the vector graphic file into ArcGIS, and use the kernel density analysis tool to get the following analysis diagram (as shown in Fig. 2).

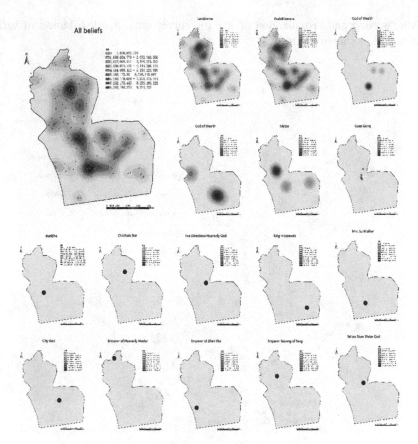

Fig. 2. Kernel density analysis diagram of belief space in the research area.

4   Research Conclusion and Enlightenment

4.1   Research Conclusion

Based on the above research, analysis and exploration of the folk belief space in the research area of Fengzhou, the following conclusions can be concluded (see Fig. 2).

There are Many Kinds of Folk Beliefs in the Fengzhou Research Area. This is the most obvious conclusion of the study. The study area is only 1.4 square kilometers, but there are 16 faith types surveyed. This is due to the strong inclusiveness of local folk beliefs. No matter it is the ancient official belief, such as God of Wealth, the local protector god, such as Mrs. Su mother, or the exotic belief, such as Yellow River water god, all have special temples. Moreover, more than ten folk belief palaces and temples in the research area play an important role in maintaining and inheriting folk beliefs.

In the Research Area, the Influence of Folk Belief Space Mainly Covers Taoyuan Street, Nanmen Street and the Inner Area of the Ancient City East of Nanmen Street, and These Three Areas as the Center to Fade Away. Based on the research and life experience in Fengzhou, Taoyuan Street, Nanmen Street and the area to the east of Nanmen Street are the most intensive regional space for people's daily life, social interaction and trade, which reflects that folk belief is an indispensable part of people's life.

In the Research Area, the Space of Folk Belief Overlapped with Each Other Without Clear Boundaries. There is no obvious division between different belief categories in Fengzhou, showing a close fusion and overlapping state. From the micro point of view, even in the ancestral hall or palace temple, two or more folk beliefs are enshrined.

The Kernel Density Analysis of GIS is of Great Significance to the Study of Folk Belief Space. Kernel density analysis can establish connections for the distribution points of folk belief space in vector files, so as to simulate the influence relationship between folk belief Spaces, the range of activities of folk beliefs and other information that cannot be directly recorded and expressed.

4.2 Discussion

In addition, based on the above investigation, research and discussion, this paper puts forward the following suggestions for the protection and development of folk belief space in Fengzhou Town.

Taoyuan Street, Nanmen Street and the area inside the ancient city to the east of Nanmen Street should be regarded as a priority for protection. The specific architectural space is: Taoyuan Street folk belief activity area from Taoyuan Palace to Fu Ancestral Hall and then to Longevity Palace, folk belief activity area from Yanshan Huang Ancestral Hall to the southern section of Cizhu Tang Taoyuan Street, folk belief activity area from Nanyi Town God Temple to Wurong Tzu Chi Palace, and ancient house group east of Nanmen Street.

4.3 Deficiency and Prospect

Although there are some interesting findings, the study has limitations. In the research, some individual buildings did not open doors due to force majeure, so the belief information could not be collected. However, based on the existing sufficient research data, this part of the deviation has little impact on the research conclusion. In addition, the research data of this study can only reflect the spatial distribution of folk beliefs in the research area as of December 2022, which is indicated here.

References

1. Compilation group of Fengzhou Annals: Fengzhou Annals (1996)
2. Feng, L., Zhengyi, F.: Minnan Culture Theory. Chinese Academy of Social Sciences Press, Beijing (2008)
3. Xinhao, L., Zhiming, Z.: Folk Beliefs of Southern Fujian. Fujian People's Publishing House, Fuzhou (2008)

4. Qiong, C.: The fusion of the sacred and the profane and the expansion of the space of belief. Qinghai J. Ethnol. **30**(3), 215–221 (2019)
5. Livingstone, D.E.: Space for religion: a Belfast case study. Polit. Geogr. **17**(2), 145–170 (1998)
6. Paul, B.: GIS and cultural resource management: a manual for heritage managers. UNESCO Principal Regional Office for Asia and the Pacif, Bangkok (1999)
7. Mingxing, H., Wei, D.: Managerial information system for conservation of historic areas with GIS. Planners (3), 71–73 (2002)
8. Mingxing, H., Wei, D.: Studies on the application of the GlS technology to the preservation planning for historic blocks. Archit. J. (12), 63–65 (2004)
9. Weiwei, C.: Design and application of spatial experience system for urban village reconstruction based on GIS. Sci. Program. (2022). https://doi.org/10.1155/2022/5423927
10. Juan, A., Garcia, E., Pablo, A, T.: A GIS-based methodology for the appraisal of historical, architectural, and social values in historic urban cores. Front. Archit. Res. (9), 900–913 (2020)
11. Andre, S.L., Daniel, V.M., Anderson, Y.B., et al.: Assessment of urban cultural-heritage protection zones using a co-visibility-analysis tool. Comput. Environ. Urban Syst. (76), 139–149 (2019)
12. Jing, F., Jialu, Z., Yunyuan, D.: Heritage values of ancient vernacular residences in traditional villages in Western Hunan, China: spatial patterns and influencing factors. Build. Environ. (188), 107473 (2021)
13. Yue, R., Sijia, L.: Construction of the archiving protection model of traditional village culture based on GlS. Arch. Sci. Study (4), 69–74 (2020)
14. Guanfu, S., Yong, C., Qiang, Q., et al.: Development and prospect of GIS platform software technology system. J. Geo-Inf. Sci. (23), 2–15 (2021)

Digital Construction Strategy of Yangtze National Cultural Park Based on Digital Twinning Technology

Lingjing Duan and Yangshuo Zheng[✉]

Wuhan University of Technology College of Art and Design, Wuhan, China
k3623640@gmail.com

Abstract. As a super-large public cultural space in the Yangtze River valley, the construction and design of the Yangtze River National Cultural Park should be distinguished from the indoor cultural space such as museums and exhibition halls and the outdoor small cultural places such as cultural parks and squares. Based on the comprehensive heritage theory like linear cultural heritage, it is necessary to integrate the huge and diverse cultural heritage resources of the Yangtze River by means of coherent media and diverse forms. With the development and application of new information technology such as cloud computing, intelligent sensing and Internet of Things, digital technology represented by digital twin provides a new way of thinking to understand complex systems. The research and development of access to the existing website of the digital twin platform, multi-types of the Yangtze River Cultural Heritage Digital Model for unified management, multi-terminal display, it is of great practical significance to the construction of the online website and offline exhibition hall of the Yangtze National Cultural Park.

Keywords: Yangtze National Cultural Park · cultural heritage · digital construction · digital twinning

1 Research Status of Digital Twinning Technology at Home and Abroad

1.1 Current Situation of Research and Construction Abroad

The study on the theory of digital twinning and its application is relatively early in foreign countries. In the field of digital twinning theory and concept definition, 2003 GRIEVESM. W. Professor in the product life cycle management course of its conceptual model, "Digital Twins" is also known as "Mirror Space Model. NASA used the concept of "Digital twinning" in its technology roadmap released in 2012 [1]. Gartner, an IT research and consulting firm, has ranked digital twinning as one of the top 10 strategic technology trends of the year for two consecutive years (2017 and 2018), making the concept a major concern [2].

In terms of digitizing the cultural heritage, the British State Bureau of Surveying and Mapping produced a professional map of the Hadrian's Wall in 1964 based on an aerial

C. Stephanidis et al. (Eds.): HCII 2023, CCIS 1834, pp. 393–398, 2023.
https://doi.org/10.1007/978-3-031-35998-9_53

photo archive established in 1920 [3]. Small expounds the method and process of digital mapping and archive recording by analyzing more than 27,000 aerial photographs taken by NMP in the UK in 2002 [4]. Tony Wilmott describes the Newcastle University team's use of airborne laser scanning technology to conduct an archaeological demonstration of fort El Oued in "Double wall dialogue.", the technique of motion recovery structure for accurately generating 3D data is described [5].

1.2 Current Situation of Research and Construction in China

In recent years, the research on digital twinning has attracted much attention in China. In theoretical research, Tao Fei proposed four key problems in 2017, which are physical fusion, model fusion, data fusion and service fusion, and related technical paths [6]. In 2018, Liu Datong made a literature review and prospect of digital twinning technology, and summarized the research results of digital twinning at home and abroad in recent years [2]. Beihang digital twinning technology research team first proposed the concept of digital twinning five-dimensional model in 2018, which has been widely concerned by the academic community [7]. In 2019, some contents of the standard system and ten application fields were collected by 2020 Digital Twin Application White Paper, digital twin and other industry white papers and works [8]. On this basis, Qin Xiaozhu et al. [9] in the course of studying the digital construction of the Han Buddhism cultural heritage in Guangxi-yunnan-guizhou region, in 2018, the application of digital twinning technology in the digital construction of material and cultural heritage was first described, which makes digital twinning research go out of military, manufacturing and urban construction fields. In terms of practical application, 51WORLD, a state-owned high-tech enterprise, launched the "Earth Cloning Project 4" in 2020, the core technology of DST1.0, such as SuperAPI3.3.0, visual editing component (WDT2.0), real-time cloud rendering platform (Cloud5.0) and dynamic simulation converter (DST1.0) has been improved in September 2020, the SA + MEC Smart Cloud XR digital twinning platform of Erlitou archaeological site park in Henan province officially launched, and in February, the 2021 digital twinning visualization platform of Haidian District in Beijing officially launched, let the digital twinning have the new landing application in the domain and so on literature travel, city management.

1.3 Review of Research at Home and Abroad

First of all, in the field of research, the existing domestic and foreign digital twin research in aerospace, machinery manufacturing and other fields more in the cultural heritage, less research in the humanities and social sciences. Secondly, at the research level, the current digital level of the Yangtze River cultural heritage is low, digital research is mainly focused on the display level, for the core metadata and digital standards system less research; Most of the cultural heritage records are still displayed as "Picture + image + text", but there are some deficiencies in 3D model, platform R & D, AR/VR/XR multi-level display And lack of "Physical entity, virtual model, service system, twin data and connection" of the closed-loop comprehensive study.

From the concept of digital twinning and its development process, the application fields gradually transfer from aerospace, military and other fields to modeling and processing, design and manufacturing fields [10]. Combined with the concept of digital twins and technical features, it can be seen that there are many common features between digital twins and digitization of material and cultural heritage, the theory and technology of digital twinning can provide a brand-new idea, method and application scene for the research of digital construction of Yangtze National Cultural Park.

2 The Value of Digital Twinning Technology in the Construction of Yangtze River National Cultural Park

2.1 To Complement the Theoretical System of Digital Construction of Cultural Heritage in China

As a public carrier of large-scale cultural heritage resources in the Yangtze River Basin, the Yangtze River National Cultural Park is a major cultural project to construct the protection and utilization system of cultural heritage resources in the Yangtze River, systematically elaborate the spiritual connotation of the Yangtze River culture, and promote the prosperity and development of Chinese culture in the new era. As of August 2022, the construction design of the Yangtze River National Cultural Park is still in the initial exploration stage, and a relatively mature general design paradigm has not yet been formed. The Yangtze River has a wide distribution area. At present, it has not yet formed an effective activation of the ancient and splendid Yangtze River cultural treasure resources. The practical applicability of the Yangtze River cultural heritage based on the large differences in preservation conditions still needs to be further studied and refined. At the same time, how to shape a more effective design cognition of the Yangtze River culture for the public still requires a lot of theoretical and practical research.

The digital twins of the Yangtze River can digitally restore its historical formation process, important historical space-time and real-time status quo, and provide reliable digital resources and strong data support for the protection, restoration and display of the Yangtze River. At the same time, the AI calculation of the Yangtze River and its surrounding environment through massive data provides visual intelligent simulation for the future construction of the Yangtze River. Therefore, the construction of digital twin of Yangtze River cultural heritage is not only a new exploration of digital twin technology in the field of cultural heritage, but also an innovative supplement to the existing theoretical system of digital construction of Yangtze River cultural heritage.

2.2 To Comprehensively Help the Digital Construction of the Yangtze National Cultural Park

On May 22, 2022, the General Office of the Communist Party of China and State Council General Office issued the opinions on promoting the implementation of the National Strategy for digitizing culture, which clearly stated that by the end of the 14th five-year plan period, cultural digital infrastructure and service platform have been basically completed, and an online and offline integration and interaction, three-dimensional coverage of cultural services supply system has been formed. As the public carrier of the large-scale cultural heritage resources in the Yangtze River Valley, the research on the digitalization construction of the Yangtze River National Cultural Park is to promote the implementation of the national cultural digitalization strategy, it is a major cultural project serving the construction of a national cultural power. At present, the exhibition mode of the cultural heritage resources in the Yangtze River area mainly depends on the offline museums and exhibition halls. In the construction of cultural heritage databases (such as material and non-material heritage data resources, the Red Gene Bank and the Yangtze River culture special database that has been built or is under construction), taking the Hubei Intangible Cultural Heritage Network (Hubei.gov.cn) as an example, most of the displays have not yet broken through the traditional "Picture + text" format. In the application of digital twinning technology, the current landing plan only 2021 September launch of the Shanghai Digital Twinning Museum. Therefore, the research and development of access to the existing website of the digital twin platform, multi-types of the Yangtze River Cultural Heritage Digital Model for unified management, multi-terminal display, it is of great practical significance to the construction of the online website and offline exhibition hall of the Yangtze National Cultural Park.

3   Research Path and Content of Construction

"Digital twin" is a technical form with the characteristics of virtual and real fusion, full life cycle, dynamic/intelligent/total factor mapping, etc. By means of virtual-real interaction feedback, data fusion analysis, decision iterative optimization and so on, it simulates the behavior of physical entities in the real environment, and adds or extends new capabilities for them. Based on the concept of digital twin technology, the Yangtze River National Cultural Park can more intuitively and stereoscopically show the comprehensive information of cultural heritage. Visitors can also use AR, VR and other multiple means to communicate with cultural heritage beyond time and space. This study will focus on the theoretical and practical value of digital transformation and digital twin technology for the construction of the Yangtze River National Cultural Park, to explore the digital construction strategy of large-scale and cross-regional public cultural space represented by Yangtze River National Cultural Park.

3.1   Yangtze River Cultural Heritage Database

The core metadata element set, heritage classification and coding system and digital standard system of the Yangtze River cultural heritage resources, namely the "Yangtze River Cultural Heritage Database", should be established on the basis of ensuring cultural security, resource integrity and data sharing and circulation. In the process of digital elements generation and dissemination, it is necessary to draw on the traceability and independence of blockchain technology to strengthen the protection of cultural security and intellectual property rights. This will become the theoretical research foundation of the digital twin system of the Yangtze River cultural heritage and the Yangtze River National Cultural Park.

3.2 The Digital Twins of the Yangtze River Cultural Heritage

By retrieving the database of the Yangtze River cultural heritage, we can restore the information elements of the heritage entity, its protection status, development history and production process, so as to construct the "Digital twin of the Yangtze River Cultural Heritage", so that the real-time data, historical data and other related data of the physical entity can fed back to the virtual model to realize its dynamic and intelligent visualization mapping. In practice, the digital mapping of cultural heritage needs to avoid the problem of being homogeneous, which means differentiating the reconstruction methods of cultural relics resources of different categories.

3.3 Digital Twin System of Yangtze National Cultural Park

The "digital twin of the Yangtze River National Cultural Park" should be constructed by simulating the environment quality, economic development and industrial planning of the Yangtze River basin, it also needs to integrate the real-time and multi-dimensional dynamic data such as government business data and environmental weather data, so that the trial-and-error cost can be effectively reduced, and the efficiency of the actual construction can be improved in the design stage. Due to the continuous development of the digital twin system, its service scene will be expanded along with the practical application, which puts forward the extremely high request to the dynamic computing capabilities and intelligent sensing systems. In the future construction of core data platform, it is necessary to emphasize the study of the coupling relationship between digital twin technology and practical application. We should pay attention to the deep cultivation of cultural content, and constantly enrich the interactive experience of the five senses to meet the needs of the new era of mass cultural experience.

4 Conclusion

In today's generation Z population in China, the way of cultural experience presents digital, fragmented and personalized characteristics, which not only provides an opportunity for the digital transformation of traditional public cultural space, but also implies the public's need to pursue the diversity of cultural experience. The digital field that is not limited by time and space provides a good space carrier for efficient cultural display and communication, it can also effectively eliminate the shortcomings of traditional offline travel experience in a fixed form and one-way output. The digital transformation of public cultural space led by the Yangtze River National Cultural Park will stimulate stronger cultural self-confidence and cultural influence, and provide a more forward-looking and comprehensive theoretical and practical paradigm for promoting the formation of a pluralistic and integrated human civilization pattern.

References

1. Yu, Y., Fan, S., Peng, G., et al.: Application of digital twin model in product configuration management. Aviat. Manuf. Technol. (7), 41–45 (2017)
2. Liu, D., Guo, K., Wang, B., et al.: Review and prospect of digital twin technology. J. Instrum. **39**(11), 1–10 (2018)
3. Ordnance. Survey Map of Hadrian's Wall. London (1964)
4. Small, F.: Hadrian's Wall NMP Project, Brampton to Birdoswald: National Mapping Project Report. English Heritage Research Dept. Report Series69, Swindon (2008)
5. Wlmott, T.: Hadrian's Wall Survey and Excavation (2020)
6. Tao, F., Cheng, Y., Cheng, J., et al.: Cyber-physical fusion theory and technology of digital twin workshop. Comput. Integr. Manuf. Syst. **23**(8), 1603–1611 (2017)
7. Tao, F., Liu, W., Liu, J., et al.: Digital twin and its application exploration. Comput. Integr. Manuf. Syst. **24**(1), 1–18 (2018)
8. Tao, F., Liu, W., Zhang, M., et al.: Digital twin five-dimensional model and its application in ten fields. Comput. Integr. Manuf. Syst. **25**(1), 1–18 (2019)
9. Qin, X., Zhang, X.: The application of digital twin technology in the digital construction of material cultural heritage. Inf. Work (2), 103–111 (2018)
10. Cui, M., Bai, Y., Luo, Y., et al.: Basic characteristics, diagenetic process and mineralization of Alaska-type intrusions. Ore Deposit Geol. **39**(3), 397–418 (2020)

Research on the Digital Protection and Inheritance of Yao Nationality Costumes—Take the Yao Nationality in Liannan, Guangdong as an Example

Yixin Fan and Xiaoping Hu[✉]

School of Design, South China University of Technology, No. 382, Daxuecheng Outer Ring East Road, Panyu Guangzhou, Guangdong, People's Republic of China
huxp@scut.edu.cn

Abstract. Digitization of Intangible Cultural Heritage is an important initiative for the sustainable development of Intangible Cultural Heritage protection and inheritance, and it is also particularly important for the intangible heritage of Yao costume. Yao costume is an important carrier of Yao culture and is known as the wordless history book of the nation and is an important part of China's intangible cultural heritage. The digital protection and inheritance of Yao costumes benefit the conservation of resource integrity of Yao costumes, promote the economic redevelopment of Yao costumes, and expand new ways of inheritance of Yao costume culture. This article takes the Yao of Liannan, Guangdong as an example, investigates the local dilemmas faced in the protection and inheritance of the costumes through fieldwork, constructs strategies for the digital protection and inheritance of Yao costumes on the basis of existing digital technologies, and puts forward targeted suggestions in five aspects: data collection, storage and retrieval, exhibition and communication, dissemination and promotion, and innovative development.

Keywords: Intangible Heritage Preservation · Digitization · Protection and Inheritance of Culture · Yao Costumes

1 Introduction

The Yao is one of the oldest ethnic groups in China. They have been suppressed by the central government for a long time and were forced to migrate south into the Lingnan region, where they lived in the mountains to escape from the outside world. Due to the scarcity of resources in the mountains, the Yao people had to disperse into many small groups and move into different mountains, eventually forming a major dispersion with minor gatherings, which is commonly referred to as "there are no mountains in Lingnan without Yao". In the process of migration, the Yao people developed the habit of recording their lives with patterns and expressing what they saw in their lives in an artistic form on the costumes they wore, contributing to Yao's colorful costume culture.

However, culture is dynamic, and nothing stays the same, as time goes by, many Yao people gradually assimilate with the Han people. With the establishment of New China,

C. Stephanidis et al. (Eds.): HCII 2023, CCIS 1834, pp. 399–407, 2023.
https://doi.org/10.1007/978-3-031-35998-9_54

the social status of ethnic minorities was raised and communication with Han people became more and more frequent. After the Reform and Opening up, more and more young Yao people came out of the mountains and entered the cities, replacing their traditional ethnic costumes with modern clothes. Since the 21st century, modernization has accelerated, and information dissemination has grown at a rapid pace. Young people are more interested in trends than in tradition, and various emerging cultures are impacting the original ethnic culture, so Yao traditional costumes are gradually abandoned. Visual patterns constituted by costume appearances have become the representation of a nation, the explanation and confirmation of identity. [1] At the same time, costumes have undergone social development and change over a long history, precipitating national spirit and emotion. Once a nation's unique costumes are lost, the people of that nation will lose their identity and cultural traits, then that nation will also cease to exist in name. The protection and inheritance of Yao costume culture are now facing a serious situation, and the rescue of Yao costumes and the inheritance of related costume crafts need to be given high priority.

Since the 1990s, technologies have developed rapidly, and the world has entered the digital era. Digitization of Intangible Cultural Heritage means adopting technologies such as digital acquisition, digital storage, digital processing, digital exhibition, and digital dissemination to convert, reproduce and restore Intangible Cultural Heritage into shareable and renewable digital forms, and interpret them with new perspectives, preserve them in new ways and utilize them with new demands. [2] Digital technologies have injected new vitality into the career of world Intangible Cultural Heritage protection and inheritance.

The article takes the Yao costumes in Liannan, Guangdong as the object of study. Liannan, Guangdong, is one of the most important Yao settlements, surrounded by mountains and only one road to the outside, with a relatively closed environment and a strong ethnic atmosphere, where traditional costumes are well preserved. In addition, the local government pays great attention to the development and dissemination of ethnic culture, constructing the Chinese Yao Museum and the Yao Culture Center, and supporting traditional handicraft industries. All these provide good conditions for investigating and studying Yao costume culture. We hope to promote the protection and inheritance of local costume culture through digitalization, and we also hope to apply this example to nationwide Yao costume protection and inheritance and promote the development of various costume intangible heritage in digital protection and inheritance.

2   The Dilemma Faced by Liannan Yao Costumes

2.1   Disintegration of the Social Inheritance Mode

Social inheritance refers to skills learned by people who are naturally influenced by their environment in a community setting. [3] Taking embroidery as an example, in the past costume embroidery was a necessary skill for Yao girls in Liannan, the general social environment encouraged girls to learn embroidery, and the ability to embroider became a criterion for evaluation, girls who were good at embroidery were able to make a name for themselves at events, and there was even a saying that if you were good at embroidery you could be married well. Yao girls learn the skill from an early age under the influence of their mothers, grandmothers, and other female relatives. In this atmosphere, even some girls who had not yet been exposed to embroidery learned the skill naturally through the influence of each other. During this period, the Yao of Liannan were in a relatively closed environment, with backward production methods, low production levels, and high interdependence between individuals. From a macro perspective, cultural inheritance is a necessity for the continued development of any ethnic group. From a microscopic perspective, adapting to traditional culture and inheriting it is the only option for any member of society to obtain the right to social survival. [4] Therefore, the Yao costume culture has flourished, and the costume craft has been inherited widely and steadily.

After the Reform and Opening up, with the development of the economy, the country interconnected and broke the original closed state of the Yao community. The change in the socio-economic system brought a huge transformation to the Yao society in Liannan, as young people who were supposed to inherit traditional culture came out of the mountains to seek new employment opportunities. These young people are not only leaving their hometowns in a physical sense, but also in a spiritual sense. They have become distant from the traditional Liannan Yao society, and their minds are constantly changing in the external environment. Young people have become more individual and are no longer simply part of a group. The social environment that originally bound them has gradually lost its influence.

2.2 Impacts Caused by Industrialized Production Methods

The process of making traditional Yao costumes is delicate and slow, requiring a lot of time for both embroidery and weaving. In the early days, women carried sewing kits with them when they went to the mountains to pick and work, and when they had time, they would take out the kits and embroider with great care, expressing their thoughts and feelings about life in the embroidery patterns. [5] The embroidered costumes they made were mainly for themselves and their families, or for sale in the local area of Liannan. However, in this era, the market for costumes was much larger than the original one, and the speed of manual production was not able to keep up with the market demand.

By mechanizing the assembly line to quickly manufacture large quantities of homogeneous products, this industrialized production method is the adaptation to the modern market demand. In this rapidly developing society, time costs are compressed to improve economic efficiency. Although machine embroidery is slightly bulkier and less sophisticated than hand embroidery, there is no overwhelming difference between the two effects (see Fig. 1). The fact that a costume pattern that would have taken a year to make with human labor now took just one day with industrial machines was certainly a boon to business. As a result, the market and capital have gladly abandoned human labor, intangible heritages have been edged out, and the culture of Liannan Yao costumes has been increasingly eroded in this industrialized era. In the process of producing clothes on the assembly line, the patterns of the costumes, which were originally rich in cultural connotations, gradually became simple and repetitive graphics.

Fig. 1. Liannan Yao costume embroidery.

2.3 Decrease in Daily Demand for Traditional Costumes

According to fieldwork, the needs of the Yao people in Liannan to wear traditional costumes can be divided into two types, one for specific occasions and one for daily life. During festivals or events, the local Yao people, both men, and women, both young and old, will attend in the full dress of the nation, which is a tradition of the Yao people, The colorful full dress is the formal wear of the nation. With the development of tourism in Liannan, the Yao people also perform their folk customs in gorgeous costumes to impress tourists. These specific occasions maintain the demand for traditional full dress among the Yao of Liannan, however, the demand for traditional costumes faced in daily life is not optimistic. In the context of modern society, traditional costumes no longer fit into contemporary life situations and daily aesthetics. As a result, the young people of the Liannan Yao no longer live wearing traditional costumes. Middle-aged and elderly women, who are the main wearers, are also replacing some of their traditional costumes with modern clothes, and there is a relatively common phenomenon of mixed costumes (see Fig. 2). Compared with traditional costumes, modern clothes are more suitable for people's body shapes and more functional. Moreover, under the influence of the offspring in the family, the aging elders are also gradually assimilated into modern aesthetics, which makes the demand for traditional costumes in daily life decrease repeatedly. With the decreasing demand in daily life, Liannan Yao's traditional costumes will soon disappear into the landscape.

Fig. 2. The phenomenon of mixing traditional costumes with modern clothes.

2.4 Aging of Intangible Cultural Heritage Inheritors

The vast number of inheritors of the Liannan Yao costume craft are middle-aged and elderly, with most inheritors from the 1940s to the 1960s. [3] These inheritors have experienced a period of prosperity in costume culture and have stuck to their ethnic culture as the costume craft has been declining. Most of them have only primary and secondary education, and they do not know how to give lectures or tell the story of the reasoning behind these costumes, they just do it quietly. But for modern young people, the spread of electronic devices lets them get in touch with the outside world too early, fragmented high-speed information makes it difficult for them to do things slowly and calmly, they receive higher and higher degrees of education, they are eager to go to a bigger platform to engage in higher-paying jobs. It is difficult to retain these young people in small rural counties, and fewer young people are willing to carry on the traditional intangible cultural heritage, leaving an aging population of inheritors.

The essence of Intangible Cultural Heritage lies in the "inheritance" of culture, the core of which is the person who inherits the culture, without which the existence and inheritance of Intangible Cultural Heritage cannot be separated from the inheritors. [4] When this group of inheritors ages without the emergence of young inheritors, the inheritance of Liannan Yao costume culture will be broken. Consequently, it is especially important to protect and inherit Liannan Yao's traditional costume culture through new methods.

3 The Significance of Digital Protection and Inheritance

3.1 Digital Acquisition and Storage Benefit the Conservation of Resource Integrity of Yao Costumes

Documentation through photography and video recording is one of the important ways to preserve Yao costumes, and modern digital acquisition technology has developed various new ones on top of this. Converting ancient materials into digital files through graphic scanning technology, collecting 3D data of Yao costumes through stereo scanning technology, recording the 3D effect of Yao costumes in the wearing state through holographic photography, restoring the real color representation of Yao costumes in the natural environment through digital photography, storing the traditional wearing steps and production process of Yao costumes through motion capture technology, and so on. These technologies can not only collect accurate data related to Yao costumes more effectively but also help to record the cultural environment in which the NRM is located. Then, with the help of digital storage technology, effective protection of ICH resources can be achieved through databases, disk arrays, CD-ROM towers, optical fiber and network connections, and a series of related regulations and protocols. [2] With the help of digital acquisition and storage technology, Yao costume cultural resources can break through the original conservation methods and remain completer and more authentic. In this way, even if Liannan Yao costumes do disappear someday, they can survive in the virtual world in the form of data.

3.2 Digital Restoration and Reproduction Benefit the Economic Redevelopment of Yao Costumes

The challenge of inheriting the Liannan Yao costume can be summarized as the opposite of this goal and the goal of modernization. On the one hand, the traditional costume culture needs to be continuously inherited by people, while on the other hand, the value and demand for the use of traditional costumes are decreasing. Digital restoration and reproduction technologies are constantly developing, now it is possible to virtually restore the original appearance of the intangible heritage. Through restoration technologies such as graphic processing and 3D modeling to produce Liannan Yao digital costumes, through animation technologies such as 3D scene modeling, special effects rendering, and virtual scene coordination display to revert to real scenes of how Liannan Yao costumes were made and used, through knowledge visualization, digital animation, and other technologies to analyze and interpret the cultural stories of the Liannan Yao costumes, helping people to inherit the costume culture. The digital heritage reverted by digitization technology can also be made into virtual products, which are convenient for redevelopment and utilization. Meanwhile, the strengthening of virtual reality technology and the popularization of the metaverse concept promise to explode new values and demands for Liannan Yao costumes in the virtual world. It is possible to transform the Liannan Yao costumes into digital collections, to develop Yao virtual fashion costumes based on them, and to transform the process of making Liannan Yao costumes into virtual reality experiences. In addition, creative design based on the original data of the Liannan Yao costumes to create new cultural design products that meet modern aesthetics is also a way to renew their values and demands.

3.3 Digital Presentation and Communication Benefit the Expansion of New Ways to Inherit Yao Costumes

The digital exhibition is to use the Internet, multimedia, human-computer interaction, virtual reality, and other technologies to present the acquired and stored data to the public based on digital restoration and reproduction, such as online digital museums that can be visited anytime anywhere, and immersive experience museums that integrate text, sound, image, video, and culture. Digital dissemination is to use of the Internet and multimedia as a medium to present various data information of a certain regional culture to more people in a more convenient way, such as using graphics and short videos to let the intangible heritage culture spread and circulate on social media, while live streaming and linked mike forms also provide more opportunities for people who are separated from each other to communicate. Digital exhibition and dissemination have broken the original spatial boundaries, expanded the ways for people to get in touch with intangible heritage, innovated the way to experience intangible heritage, and provided a new method to inherit the culture of Liannan Yao costume. The dissemination of Liannan Yao culture through social media can attract potential inheritors who are interested in the craftsmanship of Liannan Yao costumes, and the data on Liannan Yao costumes in the digital museum allows these people to learn the relevant culture, and the virtual interactive experience in the immersion museum allows those who are interested to further experience the fun of Liannan Yao costume culture and even get to know some of the production skills, and the online live broadcast allows those who are willing to pass on Liannan Yao costume to have the opportunity to learn from a teacher even if they are not in the local area.

4 Strategies for Digital Protection and Inheritance

4.1 A Develop Digital Collection Standards of Yao Costumes

The acquisition of original costume data is an important part of the protection of the Liannan Yao costume, and a unified standard is needed to ensure the accuracy and universality of the acquired data, so it is necessary to develop digital acquisition standards.

The data to be collected for Liannan Yao costumes include basic information such as costume pictures, names, classifications, etc., as well as specific information such as wearing styles and plane effects, etc. The data will be summarized into an information data card for Liannan Yao costumes (see Fig. 3), and the data will be unified according to the standardized units and presentation in the card.

Fig. 3. An information data card for Liannan Yao costumes.

4.2 Establish a Database of Yao Costumes

Based on the information acquired on Liannan Yao costumes, we will establish a database of Liannan Yao costumes to store the data and set up search tags according to the content of the basic information (see Fig. 4), the search tags can make the search efficient greatly improved. In addition, the database will be linked to electronic resources for resource sharing, so that the public can have more accessibility to the Liannan Yao costumes.

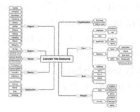

Fig. 4. Liannan Yao Costume Retrieval Tags.

4.3 Build the Digital Museum of Yao Costumes

Based on the Liannan Yao costume database, we will use digital technology to recreate virtual costumes, establish the Liannan Yao Costume Museum, and organize thematic exhibitions to exhibit related collections online so that more people can have access to the Liannan Yao costume culture. At the same time, the online museum will set up a communication platform to encourage visitors to discuss and exchange ideas. Interactive links will be designed during the online viewing process to increase enjoyment, making the Liannan Yao Costume Digital Museum a new form of general education and a cradle for training potential inheritors of Intangible Cultural Heritage.

4.4 Digital Dissemination of Yao Costumes Through New Media

Use new media to promote the Liannan Yao Costume Digital Museum, plan related promotional activities, spread information on various media platforms through those who participate in the activities, attract people who love Intangible Cultural Heritage to watch the online costume thematic exhibition, and even attract them to come to Liannan for field trips and delve into the local culture to drive the development of the local tourism economy.

4.5 Design Creative Products for Yao Costumes

The popularity of Liannan Yao costume culture on new media platforms is bound to give rise to more related cultural products. Designing and developing related creative cultural products is an important way to revitalize protection and inheritance. By developing new products that adapt to modern aesthetics and needs through creative design, the economic value of traditional intangible heritage skills can be rekindled, to ensure the continued development and inheritance of Liannan Yao costume intangible heritage in contemporary China.

5 Conclusion

The development of digital technology has given the dying Liannan Yao traditional costume a new way of existence in today's world and established a new connection between people and traditional costumes. The five digital preservation and inheritance strategies proposed in the article are not only to preserve the original costume culture but also to bring more young people in touch with the Yao costume culture through digitalization, creating awareness and enthusiasm for it. Heritage culture is dependent on people, and only by constantly establishing connections with them can Yao costumes continue to be inherited and developed today.

References

1. Feng, M., Zhang, L.: Discussion on ethnic costumes and intangible cultural heritage protection. J. Sichuan Minzu Coll. **20**(05), 16–21 (2011)
2. Huang, Y.L., Tan, G.X.: Research on digital protection and development of intangible cultural heritage in China. J. Central China Normal Univ. (Humanit. Soc. Sci.) **51**(02), 49–55 (2010)
3. Chen, H.: The protection and inheritance of the clothing embroidery of the Lian Nan Yao Ethnic Group. Guangdong Polytechnic Normal University (2012)

4. Xu, J.H.: Research on the Inheritance and Development of Miao Costume Handicraft in Guizhou under the Perspective of Intangible Heritage. Guizhou University of Finance and Economics (2014)
5. Hu, X.P., Luo, L.L.: Study on the traditional dress of Guoshan Yao Women in Ruyuan the Northern Guangdong Province. J. Silk **57**(01), 76–80 (2020)

Connecting Historic Photographs
with the Modern Landscape

Michalis Foukarakis[1], Orestis Faltakas[1], Giannis Frantzeskakis[1],
Emmanouil Ntafotis[1], Emmanouil Zidianakis[1], Eirini Kontaki[1], Constantina Manoli[1],
Stavroula Ntoa[1], Nikolaos Partarakis[1(✉)], and Constantine Stephanidis[1,2]

[1] Institute of Computer Science, Foundation for Research and Technology—Hellas (FORTH),
70013 Heraklion, Crete, Greece
{foukas,faltakas,giannisf,ntafotis,zidian,ekontaki,cmanoli,
stant,partarak,cs}@ics.forth.gr

[2] Computer Science Department, School of Sciences and Engineering, University of Crete,
70013 Heraklion, Crete, Greece

Abstract. We present a mobile application that is bringing to life historic photographs of Heraklion by mapping them in historical routes within the city and offering the visitor a dialogue with its social and historical context. At the same time while visiting the public library where these historic photographs are exhibited, the mobile app enhances the provided information by virtually replacing the photographs with alternative views from different historic periods.

Keywords: Augmented Reality · Mobile technology · Mobile Guides · Cultural Heritage

1 Introduction

The invention of photography, more than one and a half-century in the past, revolutionised the way we capture and communicate reality. This new form of communication arrived in Crete, Greece in a troubled period of the Cretan State (1898–1913). Several photographs taken during this period were used to create postcards used mainly by soldiers sending their news back home. These postcards today are an important part of the Cretan cultural heritage and are considered a window into the past as they allow us to virtually visit locations and sites altered in the modern appearance of the island.

For a long time this treasure, possessed by the Municipal Library of Heraklion, has been on display and its digital version can be found on the web. In this work, we move a step further by geolocalising these historical sources in the city of Heraklion, allowing modern visitors to explore these sources at their place of photographic origin. This is done through a mobile app available for download through the device app store.

C. Stephanidis et al. (Eds.): HCII 2023, CCIS 1834, pp. 408–414, 2023.
https://doi.org/10.1007/978-3-031-35998-9_55

2 Background and Related Work

Designing mobile applications for the presentation of multimedia collections requires appropriate browsing and visualization approaches, because several new forms of querying are available, such as localization and RGB-based image features detection by utilizing the photographic sensor of the devices. As a consequence, a mobile app can create more interesting user experiences, by supporting queries such as "Retrieve all the images relevant to the location I'm currently in" [1]. Another consideration that should be taken into account is the screen size of the device and the interaction style, which means that all interactions should be meaningful and information should be attractive and intuitive [2, 3].

At the same time, Augmented Reality (AR) [4–6], a research domain for three decades that found a new ground of application through the evolution of mobile devices, can be used to create compelling encounters with photographs of the past. More specifically, using Mobile Augmented Reality the results of these queries can be visualized in place and even blended with the reality as seen by the user's camera [7, 8]. With this novel approach, a tourism information provision system can enhance information provision before, during and after the visit. Furthermore, while visitors are in a destination such systems can augment the physical landscape with information by integrating visual information to the video stream retrieved by the mobile device camera [9].

Today approaches that blend reality with digital content are exploited both in the cultural and tourism sectors [10–15]. Some of these approaches combine mobile AR with a web information system. Thus when at home, visitors may use the web to access information which is in turn augmented when using the mobile while visiting the actual site [16, 17]. Finally, in the AR domain using 3D content and virtual humans has made possible the revival of the past through the physical remains of the present (e.g. daily life at Pompei) [18–24].

In this work, motivated by the potential offered through the augmentation of physical paper with digital information [25, 26], we build on the state of the art in mobile technology applied in the domain of tourism and culture [27–29] and its application in real-world scenarios [30, 31]. As such we propose a system that digitally augments and brings to life historic postcards. The developed mobile application provides a twofold augmentation by presenting postcards from the past when visiting the city centre of Heraklion, and by augmenting the exhibition room of the Vikelaia municipality public library by virtually replacing the post-cards with other historic photographs or photographs of the modern landscape from the location of the postcard.

3 Overview of the Tour Guide

Vikelaia Postcards is a mobile app that provides an AR-powered presentation of postcards from the audiovisual archive of the city of Heraklion's public Vikelaia library. The app also offers city route suggestions for visiting historical landmarks, buildings and important locations.

The Vikelaia library owns a significant amount of new and old postcards which are displayed in an exhibition room. The majority of them are old photographs from places around the city, including famous streets, squares, the Venetian port, gardens, etc. The app offers an interactive map of the exhibition room that shows where each postcard is located. Visitors can use the app to view detailed information for each postcard exhibit and open the city map to see where each postcard's location resides in the city.

Every postcard displayed in the library can be brought to life by interacting with it through the device's camera and viewing its contents through a different lens. Some of them are transformed into different versions of the same landmark or location, while others are replaced by images of their modern-day status, highlighting the difference between then and now.

For users that want to see the modern-day locations that are depicted in the postcards, the app suggests three different routes through the city, each with several stops that highlight the most important sights depicted in the postcards. Walking directions are also available to facilitate the tour.

The application is multiplatform and runs on iOS and Android phones and tablets. On iOS, it is written in the Swift language [32], using the latest SwiftUI framework [33]. Augmented Reality features are powered by the RealityKit framework. On Android, it is written in Kotlin [34], using standard Android mobile development practices. Augmented reality features are powered by the AR Core framework [35]. Both versions of the app share a common JSON data source containing information on postcards, routes and localized strings in both Greek and English. The Google Maps API [36] is used to integrate the city map and its markers into the application.

4 UI Overview

The main page of the application provides the available options for interacting with the collection of the municipal library (see Fig. 1, a). From these options, the „Bring the postcard to life" and „Then and now" provide different forms of augmentation. A typical usage scenario is illustrated in Fig. 1 (b and c) where the user is selecting a postcard from the list to access its details while having the option to activate AR for further augmentation. Another provided option is the localisation of the postcard on the map of the city centre of Heraklion as shown in Fig. 1 (d).

The city tour options are structured in a collection of alternative tours that the user can take to explore different aspects of the city both today and in the past. The tour is visualised on the mobile device providing also a suggested path within the city. When on the move the user's location is also visualised by using the GPS data from the mobile device.

Fig. 1. (a) Mobile App home page, (b) Selecting a postcard, (c) Postcard visualisation, (d) Localising postcards in the city, (e) Available routes, (f) Route visualisation on the city map.

5 Evaluation Results

The application has been developed following an iterative design approach, alternating prototype development with expert-based evaluation, with the involvement of User experience (UX) experts and curators from the Vikelaia Municipal Library. The expert-based evaluation was conducted based on the 10 heuristic guidelines [37], but also on heuristic guidelines for mobile design [38] and mobile AR [39]. The problems identified throughout the various iterations fall into four major categories: user guidance, navigation, interaction, and AR UX.

In terms of user guidance, it was pointed out that succinct instructions should be provided for each AR functionality supported, allowing users to clearly understand how they can initiate the AR experience and manipulate the virtual objects, thus supporting them to fully engage with the AR content. Clear instructions were also important for the city tour component, allowing users to understand how to personalize the experience.

Regarding navigation, issues mostly pertained to the usability of the city navigation part, ensuring that information is consistently provided regarding the user's current location and orientation, nearby points of interest (POIs), and route from one POI to another. Navigation in the short tours provided in the Library was also scrutinized to safeguard that users could successfully start a tour, pause, and resume it according to their needs.

Interaction issues concerned primarily AR interactions, ensuring the accurate recognition of AR-augmented postcards, system responsiveness to user actions for initiating the AR functionality, short loading time, and adaptation to the user's position and camera movements.

Finally, AR UX considerations focused mainly on the discoverability and findability of AR features, the visibility of UI elements across different backgrounds, the minimization of UI to make sure that it does not interfere with the AR experience, and the alignment of the physical and virtual worlds.

6 Conclusion

In this paper, we have presented a simple, yet efficient approach to using historic photography to provide an alternative form of visiting experience to the visitors of the city centre of Heraklion. The approach uses modern AR features to present historic photographs in the place where they were taken, thus opening a dialogue between the present and the past. This dialogue also connects with the location within the city where these historic photographs are on display providing even further features by replacing the past with the present or providing views from other historic periods in a photographic timeline of captured moments of history.

Acknowledgement. This project was funded by the European Regional Development Fund, Regional Programme Crete 2014–2022, under a public tender by the Vikelaia Municipal Library of Heraklion.

References

1. Sauter, L., Rossetto, L., Schuldt, H.: Exploring cultural heritage in augmented reality with gofind! In: 2018 IEEE International Conference on Artificial Intelligence and Virtual Reality (AIVR), pp. 187–188. IEEE (2018)
2. Garcia-Lopez, E., Garcia-Cabot, A., de-Marcos, L., Moreira-Teixeira, A.: An experiment to discover usability guidelines for designing mobile tourist apps. Wirel. Commun. Mob. Comput. 1–12 (2021)
3. Shukri, S.A.I.A., Arshad, H., Abidin, R.Z.: The design guidelines of mobile augmented reality for tourism in Malaysia. In: AIP Conference Proceedings, vol. 1891, no. 1, p. 020026. AIP Publishing LLC (2017)
4. Azuma, R.T.: A survey of augmented reality. Presence Teleoperators Virtual Environ. **6**(4), 355–385 (1997)
5. Carmigniani, J., Furht, B.: Augmented reality: an overview. In: Handbook of Augmented Reality, pp. 3–46 (2011)
6. Papagiannakis, G., Singh, G., Magnenat-Thalmann, N.: A survey of mobile and wireless technologies for augmented reality systems. Comput. Animat. Virtual Worlds **19**(1), 3–22 (2008)
7. Cavallo, M., Rhodes, G.A., Forbes, A.G.: Riverwalk: Incorporating historical photographs in public outdoor augmented reality experiences. In: 2016 IEEE International Symposium on Mixed and Augmented Reality (ISMAR-Adjunct), pp. 160–165. IEEE (2016)
8. Rainio, K., Honkamaa, P., Spilling, K.: Presenting historical photos using augmented reality. Area **15**, 11–12 (2015)
9. Jingen Liang, L., Elliot, S.: A systematic review of augmented reality tourism research: what is now and what is next? Tour. Hosp. Res. **21**(1), 15–30 (2021)
10. Tscheu, F., Buhalis, D.: Augmented reality at cultural heritage sites. In: Inversini, A., Schegg, R. (eds.) Information and Communication Technologies in Tourism 2016, pp. 607–619. Springer, Cham (2016). https://doi.org/10.1007/978-3-319-28231-2_44
11. tom Dieck, M.C., Jung, T.H.: Value of augmented reality at cultural heritage sites: a stakeholder approach. J. Dest. Mark. Manag. **6**(2), 110–117 (2017)
12. Casella, G., Coelho, M.: Augmented heritage: situating augmented reality mobile apps in cultural heritage communication. In: Proceedings of the 2013 International Conference on Information Systems and Design of Communication, pp. 138–140 (2013)
13. Choudary, O., Charvillat, V., Grigoras, R., Gurdjos, P.: MARCH: mobile augmented reality for cultural heritage (2009)
14. Angelopoulou, A., Economou, D., Bouki, V., Psarrou, A., Jin, Li., Pritchard, C., Kolyda, F.: Mobile augmented reality for cultural heritage. In: Venkatasubramanian, N., Getov, V., Steglich, S. (eds.) MOBILWARE 2011. LNICSSITE, vol. 93, pp. 15–22. Springer, Heidelberg (2012). https://doi.org/10.1007/978-3-642-30607-5_2
15. Stricker, D., et al.: Design and development issues for archeoguide: an augmented reality based cultural heritage on-site guide (2001)
16. Mathioudakis, G., et al.: InCulture: a collaborative platform for intangible cultural heritage narratives. Heritage **5**(4), 2881–2903 (2022)
17. Mathioudakis, G., et al.: Supporting online and on-site digital diverse travels. Heritage **4**(4), 4558–4577 (2021)
18. Machidon, O.M., Duguleana, M., Carrozzino, M.: Virtual humans in cultural heritage ICT applications: a review. J. Cult. Herit. **33**, 249–260 (2018)
19. Papagiannakis, G., Schertenleib, S., Ponder, M., Arévalo, M., Magnenat-Thalmann, N., Thalmann, D.: Real-time virtual humans in ar sites. In: 1st European Conference on Visual Media Production (CVMP), no. CONF, pp. 273–276 (2004)

20. Magnenat-Thalmann, N., Papagiannakis, G., Chaudhuri, P.: Applications of interactive virtual humans in mobile augmented reality. In: Encyclopaedia of Multimedia, 2nd edn. Springer, Heidelberg (2008)
21. Karuzaki, E., et al.: Realistic virtual humans for cultural heritage applications. Heritage **4**(4), 4148–4171 (2021)
22. Carre, A.L., et al.: Mixed-reality demonstration and training of glassblowing. Heritage **5**(1), 103–128 (2022)
23. Stefanidi, E., Partarakis, N., Zabulis, X., Papagiannakis, G.: An approach for the visualization of crafts and machine usage in virtual environments. In: Proceedings of the 13th International Conference on Advances in Computer-Human Interactions, Valencia, Spain, pp. 21–25 (2020)
24. Papagiannakis, G., et al.: Mixing virtual and real scenes in the site of ancient Pompeii. Comput. Animat. Virtual Worlds **16**(1), 11–24 (2005)
25. Margetis, G., Ntoa, S., Antona, M., Stephanidis, C.: Augmenting natural interaction with physical paper in ambient intelligence environments. Multimedia Tools Appl. **78**, 13387–13433 (2019)
26. Woods, E., et al.: Augmenting the science centre and museum experience. In: Proceedings of the 2nd International Conference on Computer Graphics and Interactive Techniques in Australasia and South East Asia, pp. 230–236 (2004)
27. Kim, D., Kim, S.: The role of mobile technology in tourism: patents, articles, news, and mobile tour app reviews. Sustainability **9**(11), 2082 (2017)
28. Law, R., Chan, I.C.C., Wang, L.: A comprehensive review of mobile technology use in hospitality and tourism. J. Hosp. Market. Manag. **27**(6), 626–648 (2018)
29. Dorcic, J., Komsic, J., Markovic, S.: Mobile technologies and applications towards smart tourism–state of the art. Tourism Rev. **74**(1), 82–103 (2019)
30. Partarakis, N., et al.: Digital heritage technology at the archaeological museum of heraklion. In: Stephanidis, C. (ed.) HCI 2018. CCIS, vol. 852, pp. 196–203. Springer, Cham (2018). https://doi.org/10.1007/978-3-319-92285-0_28
31. Partarakis, N., et al.: Interactive city information point: your guide to heraklion city. In: Stephanidis, C. (ed.) HCI 2018. CCIS, vol. 852, pp. 204–212. Springer, Cham (2018). https://doi.org/10.1007/978-3-319-92285-0_29
32. Swift. https://developer.apple.com/swift/. Accessed 15 Feb 2023
33. SwiftUI. https://developer.apple.com/xcode/swiftui/. Accessed 15 Feb 2023
34. Kotlin. https://kotlinlang.org/. Accessed 15 Feb 2023
35. ARCORE. https://arvr.google.com/arcore/. Accessed 15 Feb 2023
36. Google maps platform. https://developers.google.com/maps. Accessed 15 Feb 2023
37. Nielsen, J.: Enhancing the explanatory power of usability heuristics. In: Proceedings of the SIGCHI Conference on Human Factors in Computing Systems, pp. 152–158 (1994)
38. Yáñez Gómez, R., Cascado Caballero, D., Sevillano, J.L.: Heuristic evaluation on mobile interfaces: a new checklist. Sci. World J. (2014)
39. Endsley, T.C., Sprehn, K.A., Brill, R.M., Ryan, K.J., Vincent, E.C., Martin, J.M.: Augmented reality design heuristics: designing for dynamic interactions. In: Proceedings of the Human Factors and Ergonomics Society Annual Meeting, vol. 61, no. 1, pp. 2100–2104. Sage Publications, Los Angeles (2017)

Artificial Intelligence Painting Interactive Experience Discovers Possibilities for Emotional Healing in the Post-pandemic Era

Tanhao Gao⍟, Dingwei Zhang⍟, Guanqing Hua⍟, Yue Qiao⍟,
and Hongtao Zhou(✉)⍟

College of Design and Innovation, Tongji University, Shanghai, China
tanhaogao@gmail.com

Abstract. The COVID-19 pandemic has significantly impacted mental health worldwide. However, many individuals are reluctant to seek professional treatment due to a lack of awareness and passive social judgment. In order to help those "silent majority" groups, we discover an adaptive and inclusive strategy to help individuals overcome mental sub-health states. We chose an Artificial Intelligence (AI) painting platform called "Mid journey" and invited six participants with different professional backgrounds to create interactive healing experiences. "Mid journey" generates paintings based on their input keywords. The AI algorithm generates four images within 30 s, which can be further modified through continuous iteration, resulting in a final picture that meets the participant's psychological expectations. They created six paintings with the common theme of childhood memories, recreation, and entertainment linked to healing. The paintings incorporated elements of nature, the sky, and the ocean, which might reflect the connection between "healing" and unrestrained freedom. The results show that the interactive experience of AI painting can help residents experience the emotional healing journey and reduce their psychological stress. In addition, AI painting can surpass human creativity and imagination, providing a unique and potential way for future research on design research and practice related to emotional healing.

Keywords: Artificial Intelligence Painting · Emotional Healing journey · Post-Pandemic Design

1 Introduction

COVID-19 is a highly transmissible pandemic caused by the SARS-CoV-2 virus. The virus primarily spreads through respiratory droplets, and its high transmission rate has resulted in numerous outbreaks globally [1]. The emergence of the Omicron variant, with multiple mutations in the spike protein, has led to increased transmissibility and immune escape. The number of COVID-19 cases worldwide has been growing exponentially [2]. As of February 18, 2023, the global COVID-19 case count has surpassed 750 million, with approximately 6.8 million deaths (see Fig. 1).

© The Author(s), under exclusive license to Springer Nature Switzerland AG 2023
C. Stephanidis et al. (Eds.): HCII 2023, CCIS 1834, pp. 415–425, 2023.
https://doi.org/10.1007/978-3-031-35998-9_56

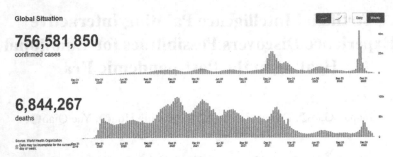

Fig. 1. COVID-19 Global Infection and Death Case Statistics. Source: https://covid19.who.int/

The pandemic has driven the world into a physical and psychological public health catastrophe. In this "protracted battle" against the entire human immune system and the operating structures of society, many citizens have been forced to carry a substantial psychological burden, while healthcare providers are under intense pressure to work and are confused about their professional identity [3]. Worse still, the majority of mental disorder residents are unwilling to seek psychological therapy at healing centers or hospitals due to the lack of mental health awareness and the pressure of negative social judgment [4]. Due to the fear of the pandemic and the confusion about the uncertain future, many community residents suffer heavier mental stress burdens. The impact of COVID-19 on the global economy, healthcare systems, and public systems has been significant and continues to be a severe challenge [5].

1.1 The Painful "Long Covid" Sequelae

The COVID-19 pandemic has been ongoing for four years, and despite global efforts to control its transmission, individuals have had to learn to live with the painful consequences of COVID-19. The sustained and prolonged effects of the pandemic have garnered increasing attention, especially for those suffering from "Long Covid" sequelae and associated psychological subhealth [6]. "Long Covid" refers to the long-term symptoms and sequelae that occur after a COVID-19 infection, resulting in not only physical discomforts such as fatigue, difficulty breathing, headache, insomnia, and cardiovascular problems but also psychological challenges such as anxiety, depression, and social isolation [7]. These symptoms may persist for several months or even longer, significantly affecting the quality of life and workability of those infected and posing challenges to overall community health and social development. Worse still, even mild or asymptomatic infections can also suffer from "Long Covid", leading to widespread concern among public health agencies and medical institutions [8]. Currently, many unknown factors remain regarding the treatment and prevention of "Long Covid" sequelae. Therefore, it is crucial to provide psychological health support and assistance to alleviate residents' psychological stress.

1.2 Trategies from Various Design Fields to Ease the Impact of "Long Covid"

To alleviate the negative impact of COVID-19, various design fields have taken active measures to create warmer, more humane, and closely connected social environments through different approaches.

In Architecture design, many architects are actively considering how to design environments better adapted to the pandemic, such as spaces with good ventilation and abundant natural light [9], as well as broader public areas to maintain social distancing [10]. Additionally, many architects are also exploring how to integrate natural elements into the design [11], such as creating more greenery and natural landscapes to provide more relaxing and stress-relieving places [12].

In product design, many designers focus on more humane products, such as healthy furniture [13] and kitchenware with high-quality antibacterial materials or more practical and easy-to-clean medical equipment [14]. These designs not only protect people's health, but also improve their efficient and comfortable experience.

In graphic and digital design, many designers create more visually appealing and interactive online platforms and applications, such as virtual exhibitions and online educational tools [15], to alleviate people's feelings of loneliness caused by the COVID-19 pandemic and social isolation [16].

In fashion design, many designers are considering how to design more comfortable, practical, and protective clothing [17], such as sports and work clothes with breathability and high antibacterial properties or masks and gloves that can resist viruses [18].

Furthermore, some designers are attempting to combine emerging technologies such as artificial intelligence with emotional healing journeys to create warmer, healthier, and more closely connected social environments.

2 The Evolution of Artificial Intelligence (AI) Painting Platform

As the world has to adapt to the "new normal" of coexisting with the pandemic, society needs to adopt various measures to alleviate the psychological and physical impact of COVID-19 on community residents. People have gradually discovered the emotional healing potential of some emerging technologies. Among them, constructing an adaptive and inclusive mental health system with the help of AI technology can assist community residents experiencing mental sub-health status [19]. This platform could promote public attention to mental health issues and provide new possibilities for research and practice related to emotional therapy [20].

2.1 Definition and Characteristics of AI Painting Platform

AI painting refers to using AI algorithms and technologies to create artwork. Unlike traditional painting processes, AI painting relies on inputting specific data and rules to create artwork [21]. AI painting has several distinctive characteristics:

1. **Autonomous creation based on databases:** AI painting technology is based on machine learning generative models, which can learn art styles, colors, patterns, and other elements from vast amounts of training data and use them to generate new artworks [22]. During the training process, AI can automatically adjust and optimize its algorithm to improve the quality and accuracy of the generated paintings [23].
2. **Efficiency and precision:** Compared to traditional hand painting, AI painting can adjust different parameters such as color, texture, shape, and theme in several seconds. Moreover, there are almost no errors during the painting process, which makes it highly efficient and precise [24].
3. **Real-time interactivity:** By inputting keywords and adjusting the painting elements, AI painting allows users without professional art backgrounds to participate in the painting creation process. This experience can increase participant engagement and interest while providing satisfaction and positive emotions [25].
4. **Customization:** AI painting algorithms can generate various paintings based on different inputs, and users can customize their painting experience by inputting different keywords or adjusting painting elements.
5. **Diverse artistic forms:** AI painting technology can create diverse possibilities, such as abstract art, realism, impressionism, and cubism. Furthermore, AI-generated paintings can demonstrate the fusion of various styles and expressions to generate unique artworks [26]. This collaboration can promote interdisciplinary cooperation to stimulate broader cultural exchange and innovation.
6. **Sustainability:** AI painting can continuously learn and optimize its algorithms, improving quality and accuracy. This sustainability ensures the long-term stability and development potential of AI painting.

In conclusion, AI painting technology is an innovative art form with many unique characteristics and advantages. The continuous development of these technologies will provide more opportunities and experiences for future artists and audiences, as well as broad application prospects and value in fine arts, cultural and creative industries.

2.2 The Healing Potential of AI Painting Platform

"Long Covid" have had a significant impact on individual's mental health, and many are reluctant to seek professional training because of their lack of awareness or social pressure. However, AI painting interactive experiences provide an innovative, effective, and inclusive solution for these individuals [27]. Community residents can access AI painting platforms from home, participate in interactive painting processes, and generate and modify artwork that meets their psychological expectations, helping them release anxiety and improve their mental health.

More specifically, in addition to providing an innovative, effective, and inclusive experience, AI painting technology has the following advantages for emotional healing:

1. **Color therapy:** Colors can impact people's emotions and mental health. AI painting can generate different color combinations based on input keywords, helping users relieve stress and anxiety through colors.
2. **Emotional resonance**: During the painting process, participants can focus on creating without worrying about the results or being judged. Meanwhile, they can show the painting to their friends to share their happiness, which can help them express themselves and release emotions through painting while also promoting communication and emotional resonance among people [28].
3. **Promoting focus and attention:** AI painting can arouse participants' attention and interest by providing visual and emotional stimulation. During the painting process, they can forget about the environment and problems around them and focus on creation.
4. **Enhancing self-esteem and self-affirmation:** AI painting can provide an opportunity for those without professional art backgrounds to experience the pleasure of creation, helping them feel a sense of accomplishment and self-worth, thus enhancing self-esteem and self-affirmation and obtaining positive emotional value [29].

In conclusion, AI painting can help alleviate the psychological pressure brought about by COVID-19 and improve people's mental health. This technology has great potential to discover innovative inspirations and possibilities for emotional treatment and artistic creation research.

3   Aim

In order to help those "silent majority" who are in a mental sub-health state but are reluctant to seek professional treatment. From the perspective of socially sustainable development, it is necessary and critical to design a more adaptive and inclusive system to help more community members alleviate their alienation more smoothly and comfortably. The Artificial Intelligence painting interactive experience allows residents to experience it at home without going to a specific healing place and has the potential to carry emotional healing touchpoints in the community. At the same time, we could further explore the potential direction of emotional healing by analyzing the images generated by Artificial Intelligence.

4 Methodology

We chose an AI painting platform called "Mid journey" and invited six participants with different professional backgrounds. The only limitation is they need to add "healing installation" as one of the keywords, and the rest are free to spare their inspirations. The algorithmic painting generation logic of the "Mid journey" platform is as follows:

5. First, the participants need to enter the "/imagine: prompt" in the "Mid journey" platform and then enter a series of keywords to define the proportions, colors, materials, elements, and other characteristics of the picture. They can also add artists, games, movies, or rendering software to describe the picture style further.
6. Mid journey's AI algorithm generates four images at a time within 30 s.
7. The participants can select one of them individually and execute the "U" command (U is to upscale the chosen picture and further generate richer details) or the "V" command (V is to use the selected picture based on Similar composition and elements and create the variation of four images).
8. The picture after "U" or "V" can be further upscale or variation. Through continuous iteration, they can keep modifying the keywords in the process, and finally, they can find a picture that obtained their psychological expectations.

5 Outcome

As shown in Fig. 2, the participants created six works of "Swing", "Balloon", "Ferris Wheel", "Roller Coaster", "Ocean Bubble", and "Butterfly". The creation is usually very conceptual at the beginning. It is necessary to continuously brainstorm according to the generated intention and add more qualifiers to make it concrete. Interestingly, "healing" in the Artificial Intelligence database is often linked to childhood memories, recreation, and entertainment and incorporates the intentions of the sky, nature, and ocean, which may reflect the link between "healing" and unrestrained freedom. The color tendency derived from it is also a potential exploration direction.

More specifically, we take the "Ocean Bubbles" painting as an example. Here are the final keywords: mirror reflection, colorful crystal clear bubbles above the crystal palace on the sea, fishes, Symmetrical composition above and below sea level, Jesus light, volume light, hyper-realistic, light blue, unreal engine, clean, transparent color, dreamy, 8k, lots of details, by Miyazaki Hayao, by Ivan Aivazovsky, by Greg Rutkowski (Figs. 3 and 4).

Fig. 2. The participants created six paintings based on the "Mid Journey" AI platform

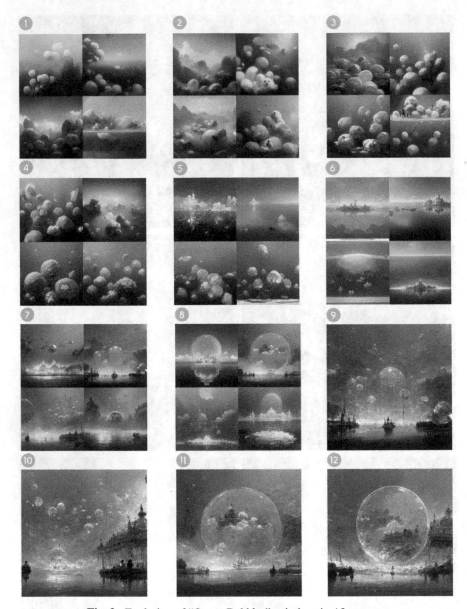

Fig. 3. Evolution of "Ocean Bubbles" paintings in AI systems.

Fig. 4. Final outcome of "Ocean Bubbles" paintings in AI systems.

6 Conclusion

Artificial intelligence technology has been widely used in various fields, including painting. Corresponding image processing technology has also developed rapidly, bringing innovation and diversified art forms development. Compared with traditional art, artificial intelligence art has a broader connection with people's lives. It lowers the threshold for community residents to participate in art creation, which is entirely different from the interactive experience obtained by watching other artists' paintings. Everyone can instantly get the images they expect and even discover a bunch of surprises, which is precisely in line with the value direction of contemporary art, breaking the boundaries between artists and residents. During this process, residents subtly completed the process of art healing and relieved their psychological pressure.

From another perspective, the characteristics of Artificial Intelligence algorithms can transcend human creativity and imagination, as well as cultural and environmental constraints, and be free from these influences. Imaginary images bring some new possibilities to artistic creation. It also provides a unique and potential way for future research on design research and practice related to emotional healing.

References

1. Bohlken, J., Schömig, F., Lemke, M.R., Pumberger, M., Riedel-Heller, S.G.: COVID-19 pandemic: stress experience of healthcare workers-a short current review. Psychiatr. Prax. **47**(4), 190–197 (2020)
2. Tian, D., Sun, Y., Xu, H., Ye, Q.: The emergence and epidemic characteristics of the highly mutated SARS-CoV-2 Omicron variant. J. Med. Virol. **94**(6), 2376–2383 (2022)
3. Wu, Z., McGoogan, J.M.: Characteristics of and important lessons from the coronavirus disease 2019 (COVID-19) outbreak in China: summary of a report of 72 314 cases from the Chinese Center for Disease Control and Prevention. JAMA **323**(13), 1239–1242 (2020)
4. Benfer, E.A., Wiley, L.F.: Health justice strategies to combat COVID-19: protecting vulnerable communities during a pandemic. Health Aff. Blog **10** (2020)
5. Mazza, M.G., et al.: Anxiety and depression in COVID-19 survivors: role of inflammatory and clinical predictors. Brain. Behav. Immun. **89**, 594–600 (2020)
6. Tansey, C.M., et al.: One-year outcomes and health care utilization in survivors of severe acute respiratory syndrome. Arch. Intern. Med. **167**(12), 1312–1320 (2007). https://doi.org/10.1001/archinte.167.12.1312
7. Rudroff, T., Fietsam, A.C., Deters, J.R., Bryant, A.D., Kamholz, J.: Post-COVID-19 fatigue: potential contributing factors. Brain Sci. **10**(12), art. no. 12 (2020). https://doi.org/10.3390/brainsci10121012
8. Raveendran, A.V., Jayadevan, R., Sashidharan, S.: Long COVID: an overview. Diabetes Metab. Syndr. Clin. Res. Rev. **15**(3), 869–875 (2021). https://doi.org/10.1016/j.dsx.2021.04.007
9. Gregory, D.D., Stichler, J.F., Zborowsky, T.: Adapting and creating healing environments: lessons nurses have learned from the COVID-19 pandemic. Nurse Lead. **20**(2), 201–207 (2022)
10. Salama, A.M.: Coronavirus questions that will not go away: interrogating urban and socio-spatial implications of COVID-19 measures. Emerald Open Res. **2** (2020)
11. Bhalla, R., Chowdhary, N., Ranjan, A.: Spiritual tourism for psychotherapeutic healing post COVID-19. J. Travel Tour. Mark. **38**(8), 769–781 (2021)
12. Zhang, X., Zhang, Y., Zhai, J.: Home garden with eco-healing functions benefiting mental health and biodiversity during and after the COVID-19 pandemic: a scoping review. Front. Public Health **9**, 740187 (2021)
13. Martín López, L., Fernández Díaz, A.B.: Interior environment design method for positive mental health in lockdown times: color, textures, objects, furniture and equipment. Designs **6**(2), 35 (2022)
14. Irfan Ul Haq, M., et al.: 3D printing for development of medical equipment amidst coronavirus (COVID-19) pandemic—review and advancements. Res. Biomed. Eng. 1–11 (2020)
15. Juliantino, C., Nathania, M.P., Hendarti, R., Darmadi, H., Suryawinata, B.A.: The development of virtual healing environment in VR platform. Procedia Comput. Sci. **216**, 310–318 (2023)
16. Gong, Y.: Application of virtual reality teaching method and artificial intelligence technology in digital media art creation. Ecol. Inform. **63**, 101304 (2021)

17. Karim, N., et al.: Sustainable personal protective clothing for healthcare applications: a review. ACS Nano **14**(10), 12313–12340 (2020)
18. Li, J., Liu, X.: The study of sustainable strategy in design of protective clothing and accessories after coronavirus (COVID-19) outbreak. J. Phys. Conf. Ser. **1790**(1), 012027 (2021)
19. Vaishya, R., Javaid, M., Khan, I.H., Haleem, A.: Artificial Intelligence (AI) applications for COVID-19 pandemic. Diabetes Metab. Syndr. Clin. Res. Rev. **14**(4), 337–339 (2020)
20. Bullock, J., Luccioni, A., Pham, K.H., Lam, C.S.N., Luengo-Oroz, M.: Mapping the landscape of artificial intelligence applications against COVID-19. J. Artif. Intell. Res. **69**, 807–845 (2020)
21. Liu, X.: Artistic reflection on artificial intelligence digital painting. J. Phys: Conf. Ser. **1648**(3), 032125 (2020)
22. DiPaola, S., McCaig, G.: Using artificial intelligence techniques to emulate the creativity of a portrait painter. Electron. Vis. Arts 158–165 (2016)
23. Ragot, M., Martin, N., Cojean, S.: Ai-generated vs. human artworks. A perception bias towards artificial intelligence?. In: Extended Abstracts of the 2020 CHI Conference on Human Factors in Computing Systems, pp. 1–10 (2020)
24. Floridi, L.: Artificial intelligence, deepfakes and a future of ectypes. Ethics Gov. Policies Artif. Intell. 307–312 (2021)
25. Mazzone, M., Elgammal, A.: Art, creativity, and the potential of artificial intelligence. Arts **8**(1), 26 (2019)
26. Foster, D.: Generative Deep Learning: Teaching Machines to Paint, Write, Compose, and Play. O'Reilly Media (2019)
27. Sandoval, C., Pirogova, E., Lech, M.: Two-stage deep learning approach to the classification of fine-art paintings. IEEE Access **7**, 41770–41781 (2019)
28. Ivzhenko, I., Demchenko, I., Dzhyhun, L., Lytvynenko, V., Kacherova, O.: Art therapeutic techniques to provide psychological assistance. BRAIN Broad Res. Artif. Intell. Neurosci. **13**(4), 68–80 (2022)
29. Bi, C., Wang, H., Cao, W., Liu, L., Liu, Y.: Application and design of capacitive hand-painted screen in psychotherapy of painting art. In: Artificial Intelligence in China: Proceedings of the 3rd International Conference on Artificial Intelligence in China, pp. 646–653 (2022)

Research on Protection of Village Cultural Heritage Based on Residents' Perception and Experience—A Case Study of Fengzhou Ancient Town, Nan'an City, Fujian Province

Chenglin He[✉], Jie Zhang, Dashuai Liu, Yue Cui, and Ying Zhang

School of Art Design and Media, East China University of Science and Technology, Shanghai 200237, China
hechenglinecust@163.com

Abstract. In recent years, the protection of traditional village cultural heritage and sustainable tourism development have gradually received high attention from the state, society, and enterprises, while the residents' experience perceptions have not received sufficient attention, thus the study selects the residents of Fengzhou ancient town in Nan'an City, Fujian Province, which is located in the southeast coastal region of China, surrounded by mountains on three sides and the sea on one side, creating unique advantages of natural resources and humanistic endowments. It fully demonstrates the architectural characteristics of the traditional settlements in southern Fujian and the diversified trade exchanges. However, the once glorious ancient town as the starting point of the Maritime Silk Road is gradually declining in the tide of development, facing the loss of historical architecture, the residents' living conditions, the decline of regional folk customs, people and emotions, and other issues. Based on residents' perceptions, this study uses in-depth interviews to investigate the overall perceptions of different groups of residents on the current state of conservation in Fengzhou ancient town, summarize the residents' perception tendencies, and identify the factors related to residents' perceptions of conservation. We also identify the factors related to residents' perceptions of conservation, and determine the influence of each factor on the current state of conservation, with a view to providing development strategies for the conservation of Fengzhou ancient town in the new era, and providing some reference and inspiration for the conservation and development of similar historical and cultural towns.

Keywords: Fengzhou ancient town · residents' perceptions · influencing factors · cultural heritage preservation

1 Introduction

In China, traditional villages, as "living fossils", are rich in tangible and intangible cultural heritage, carrying the cultural essence of the Chinese nation, presenting high historical, cultural, scientific, artistic, social and economic values, and in recent years, ancient towns have set off a tourism boom, and their moderate tourism development is conducive to both the renewal and development of traditional villages of renewal and development, but also to promote the residents out of poverty and wealth. However, in the process of its development, negative phenomena such as demolition of old and construction of new, improper use or repair of ancient buildings often occur, causing constructive damage. Previous studies on cultural heritage conservation show that the majority of attention is focused on core departments, heritage conservation experts, tourists, etc. while ignoring the opinions and views of local residents. In fact, local residents are better able to judge the changes before and after conservation and compare the level of conservation. Their perceptual evaluation of cultural heritage conservation work plays an important reference significance for the in-depth improvement of specific measures and details of conservation work. We use a systematic concept to sort out the specific perceptions and evaluations of traditional village residents on cultural heritage conservation, explain the current status of implementation of specific conservation work, extract the influencing factors and problems, and then propose reasonable and effective suggestions and measures for improvement.

2 Literature Review

Research related to the preservation of cultural heritage in ancient villages covers the following three main areas:

2.1 Protection Subject

Frank Masele found that private enterprise poses a challenge to the conservation and management of cultural heritage in Tanzania, and therefore cultural heritage conservation efforts must be carried out in partnership with local government and communities [1]. Yoshio Onuki, while conducting archaeological excavations at Kuntue Wasi in northern Peru, found that maintaining good relations with the local population helps to preserve cultural heritage [2]. Wuxin et al. systematically summarized the means to increase the cultural consciousness of residents and enhance the cultural consciousness of traditional village residents for the conservation of intangible cultural heritage in their villages [3]. Chen Zhenhua et al. summarized the effective methods of traditional village conservation in Taiwan, China, which include avoiding the model of government hegemony, advocating bottom-up community self-development, and proposing a leading model combining village community spontaneity and civil society [4]. Thus, it can be seen that the main body of cultural heritage conservation in ancient towns should be both local government departments and residents, and it needs to be carried out in close cooperation.

2.2 Protection Measures

Hongmei Song et al. used Hongcun, China as a research sample to analyze residents' attitudes and perceptions towards sustainable development from four main aspects: economic, environmental, social and cultural, so as to propose measures for sustainable tourism in traditional villages [5]. Shahrul Yani Said et al. argued that in the process of heritage conservation, public awareness of conservation should be raised, stakeholders should be given full play to their role, coordinate heritage and tourism management with the government, and introduce effective financing mechanisms [6]. Zhang Ruoshi et al. explored the framework of a multi-dimensional data-supported method for assessing the conservation and development of traditional villages in order to provide builders, managers, and residents with sustainable traditional village interventions and research logic references [7]. Du Xiang et al. implemented the classification of traditional villages according to the overall dimension to determine their development evolution patterns and indicate the various conservation and development strategies required. A consensus was reached on three aspects: the holistic awareness of conservation and utilization, the establishment of a coordination mechanism for village management, and the main role of villagers [8]. Zhang Zhi et al. used geographic information technology such as RS and GIS to construct a technical solution for cultural heritage conservation and utilization research to fundamentally achieve effective conservation and sustainable utilization of the cultural heritage system [9]. Liu Zhihong proposed the application of digitalization and intelligence in the study of traditional village cultural heritage conservation and proposed to construct a path to realize the digital conservation strategy of traditional village cultural heritage [10].

2.3 Protection Effects

In their study of Italian cultural heritage, Galogero Guccio et al. found that the professionalization of contract commissioners and the openness of the bidding process had a negative impact on the effectiveness of contract implementation for the conservation of cultural heritage sites, while potential competition had a positive and significant impact on the implementation of cultural heritage conservation contracts [11]. In in-depth interviews with 50 local residents, Lepp Andrew et al. found that a village in Uganda used both government and community-led approaches, where the community-led approach had a positive impact on heritage conservation [12]. Bryan Liu et al. constructed an evaluation system of conservation implementation effects in four aspects: conservation effectiveness, social effects, economic benefits, and environmental effects, examined and tested them, analyzed the advantages and disadvantages they brought, and promoted the importance of heritage conservation monitoring and management [13]. Zhu Yue aims to preserve and pass on the regional culture of traditional villages through the living renewal of traditional villages [14]. Li Bohua et al. proposed to create a theory and path for organic renewal of the habitat of traditional settlements, which to a certain extent promoted the organic renewal of rural settlements [15].

3   Research Methods

3.1   Survey Subjects

The research object of this paper is the residents of Fengzhou ancient town, which has the representative characteristics of traditional villages. Fengzhou ancient town in Nan'an City, Fujian Province, has been listed as a famous historical and cultural town in China, and has a good cultural heritage protection status (see Fig. 1), with 2 national cultural relics protection units, 3 provincial cultural relics protection units, 9 municipal cultural relics protection units, and 26 cultural relics protection points. And immovable cultural relics are scattered all over the town, among which the cliff carvings on the JiuRi Mountain and the Taoyuan Palace Dharani Sutra Building in Nan'an are the most famous. Intangible cultural heritage is divided into traditional music, traditional skills, folklore, folk beliefs and other items totaling 22. In particular, the wind prayer ceremony on JiuRi Mountain has witnessed the prosperity of marine trade in the port of Citong in Quanzhou, one of the important starting points of the Maritime Silk Road.

Fig. 1. Current status of cultural heritage in the ancient town of Fengzhou.

3.2   Survey Methods

As a conventional method of field research, in-depth interview mainly obtains real ideas from respondents' personal experiences and inner activities, and digs deeper ideas, and is able to continue to ask questions and explore, with greater flexibility, openness, and room for interpretation. The materials, cases, and distilled ideas obtained from in-depth interviews are an important basis for qualitative research. This study uses semi-structured interviews to obtain corresponding textual data to explore the overall perception of the residents of Fengzhou ancient town on the current status of ancient town conservation and its changing trends, and to identify the influencing factors. Drawing on previous studies, the study tends to explore the perceived status of the residents of Fengzhou ancient town from three aspects: demographic factors, physical environment variables, and social environment factors, while focusing on distinguishing whether the relatively independent geographical environment of Fujian and the influences of overseas Chinese culture have their uniqueness (see Fig. 2).

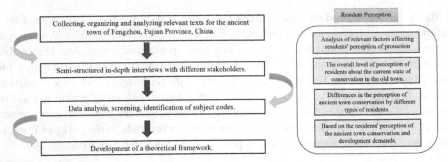

Fig. 2. Basic framework of the study, analysis of the dimensions of residents' perception inquiry.

3.3 Survey Method and Data Processing

In-depth interviews were conducted from February 7, 2023, from 9:00 a.m. to 20:00 p.m. for a total of 10 days. It was conducted by heterogeneous and snowball sampling. There were 56 in-depth interview texts and 48 valid texts (numbered A1-A48) (see Table 2). The majority of respondents were interviewed for 30–60 min. Respondents were aware that the interviews were only used as basic data for the study, and the following interview outline was used (see Table 1).

Table 1. Semi-structured interview outline.

Interview Outline	Specific issues (part)
Personal Information	Age, education level, length of residence, nature of household registration
Social Environment	Do you and your family and friends know the past history of the ancient town of Fengzhou? Are government departments actively engaged in environmental protection? Do you think the folklore now is the same as in the past? Have they changed?
Physical Environment	Are you satisfied with the current status of heritage conservation/public service facilities/transportation facilities? Do you think the old houses are well preserved and utilized?

Table 2. Basic information about the in-depth interview sample (part).

Number	Gender	Age	Residential nature	Interview Location	Basic Information
A1	Female	80↑	Local residents	Interior	Resident, not involve in commercial operations
A2	Male	50↑	Local residents	Field	Resident, engage in vegetable farming
A3	Male	50↑	Out-of-town migration	Restaurant	Specialty restaurant owner
A4	Female	70↑	Local residents	Interior	Resident and merchant, sell daily chemical products
A5	Female	40↑	Out-of-town migration	Government	Resident cadre
A6	Male	30↑	Local residents	Nearby	Young people returning to their hometown Run a special bed and breakfast
A7	Male	40↑	Local residents	Interior	Resident and worker, engage in the restoration of ancient buildings
A8	Male	60↑	Local residents	Interior	Resident and merchant, Seafood products for sale
A9	Male	40↑	Local residents	Interior	Resident Elementary School Math Teacher
A10	Female	50↑	Out-of-town migration	Store	Cell phone repair store owner

Nvivo12 software is widely used for decoding and analyzing content from interviews, questionnaires, social media, etc. It can analyze the received text data to extract the topics needed for research. Based on the rooting theory, open-ended coding, spindle coding and selective coding of all in-depth interviews were predicted using the software, following the principle of theoretical saturation, and after several rounds of validation and revision, a total of 745 main reference words and 16 core indicators were formed into 6 core categories after abstract naming (see Tables 3 and 4).

Table 3. Demonstration of the interview text coding process (Personal factors).

Selective coding	Spindle type coding	Number	Open coding (partial)	Example of interview text
Personal factors	Personal Experience	17	Childhood Memories, Missing Home	"I went to elementary school at Fengzhou College."
	External Experience	11	Change of style, Bookish Family	"The ancient town is rich in architectural types and many ancient officials were born here."
	Personal Background	20	Length of residence, Educational Background	"After a long time, I don't know what's interesting except for the architecture and scenery."

Table 4. Demonstration of the interview text coding process (External factors).

Selective coding	Spindle type coding	Number	Open coding (partial)	Example of interview text
Regional Spirit	Customary Rituals	70	JiuRi Mountain praying for the wind ceremony, Taoyuan snake shedding ancient formation	"The street stomping ceremony held by the Fu family is divided into 'big points' and 'small points'."
	Local legends	33	Emperor Fuyou,, Second Lady Jinsu, King Xianying	"Baosheng Da Di is the predominant folk belief in the god of medicine in Fujian and Taiwan"
	Overseas Chinese Culture	24	Famous overseas Chinese,, giving back to home	"Many foreign buildings and schools were built by them back home."
Local elements	Traditional Cuisine	52	Shiting green tea, Putou water balls, Taoyuan fish sticks	"The fish sticks have a tender taste and are loved by the locals."

(continued)

Table 4. (*continued*)

Selective coding	Spindle type coding	Number	Open coding (partial)	Example of interview text
	Architectural monuments	66	Taoyuan Palace, Fengzhou Academy, Wurong Ciji Palace	Our ancient town has a variety of buildings such as ancient houses, Fanzai buildings and foreign buildings
	Natural Environment	43	Jiuri Mountain, Lotus Peak,, Jinji Barrage, Qingyuan Mountain	"Our air here is very fresh and pleasant, and the elderly live a very long and hard life."
Development Opportunities	Time Environment	47	Prosperous Past, Maritime Silk Road, Tourism Development	"The ancient town of Fengzhou was once the starting point of the Maritime Silk Road and was very prosperous, but has since declined."
	Regional Linkage	77	Taoyuan Ancient Street, Nanmen Street	"The government plans to integrate the scenic area with the township's businesses to enhance the ecological and economic benefits."
Protection measures		85	measures that are not understood, Application complexity	"I don't know why this building repair was terminated halfway through."
Survival Development	Business Performance	81	Income gap, business status, hours of operation	"These years of epidemic, business is not good."
	Security	55	Road potholes, building quality, worrying emotions	"Many old houses are dangerous and unsafe to live in, but there are not enough funds to repair them.'

(*continued*)

Table 4. (*continued*)

Selective coding	Spindle type coding	Number	Open coding (partial)	Example of interview text
	Traffic Disputes	33	Parking planning, mixing of motorized and non-motorized vehicles	'Many sections of the road mixed with vehicles, there is a greater safety hazard, should be planned more reasonable.'
	Infrastructure	31	Public toilets, signage, open space, parking	'The lack of management in public toilets makes hygiene a concern.''

4   Analysis of Influencing Factors

Combined with the results of Nvivo12 analysis, the 16 key factors extracted were divided into six categories according to their different nature and emotional tendencies. Among them, the categories that positively influence residents' perceptions of conservation are regional spirit, local elements and development opportunities; while the conservation measures to be improved and the urgent needs for survival and development negatively influence the perceptions of residential conservation, and the personal factors of residents have both positive and negative influences.

4.1   Personal Factors

Personal factors include personal background, outside experiences, and personal experiences. The length of residence, as an important influencing factor, largely reflects the depth of residents' emotion for the place, which in turn affects their perception of conservation. In the actual research of Fengzhou ancient town, compared with middle-aged people, older people have a stronger sense of emotion and responsibility for the ancient town. They showed a more profound view of ancient town conservation and a stronger sense of local conservation due to the length of residence. The "education level" directly affects the residents' perceptions of the physical and cultural environment of their homes. In this interview process, residents with higher education level maintain positive perceptions of the original value of the ancient town, but also realize that there are many problems and obstacles in the conservation of ancient buildings, which is accompanied by a sense of powerlessness and frustration, thus weakening the perception of local conservation. It can be seen that education level has both positive and negative effects on residents' perceptions of local conservation. The interaction between "personal experience" and the place itself promotes and generates residents' local emotions, which in turn strengthens their perceptions of local conservation. For example, "Our old town has many kinds of buildings, such as ancient houses, fanzai buildings, and foreign buildings, and there is a great variety of building forms and sizes." (A7). It can be seen that the residents are able to look at themselves and the outside world through their own observations, and through their interaction with the outside world, they have developed a sense of pride in their place, which contributes positively to the formation of their "pride". This positive sense of self-esteem supports the residents' positive perceptions of place protection.

4.2 Regional Spirit

The "spirit of the region" is represented by overseas Chinese culture, customs and rituals, and local legends, indicating that residents have a high level of local conservation perception in this area. "Overseas Chinese culture" is the core topic in the interview, mainly referring to the construction of the ancient town of Fengzhou after the overseas Chinese went to Hong Kong and other places to return home, with 54 reference nodes. The residents of Fengzhou ancient town pay more attention to the local spiritual culture, with the following statement: "We have a strong culture of education here, and many talents came out in ancient times, and they love to work hard and come back to build their hometown when they earn money" (A21). This shows that memories and beliefs related to the environment are extremely important to individual residents. The sense of belonging brought about by their values is reflected, effectively promoting local identity and local attachment, and thus enhancing residents' perception of local conservation. "Customary rituals" are local cultural activities with distinctive characteristics that reflect regional spiritual worship and survival wisdom. Located in southern Fujian, the ancient town of Fengzhou has developed a unique clan belief and maritime culture. The most famous wind prayer ceremony is held at Zhaohui Temple to pray for a smooth and safe voyage. The continuation of the "ritual" is an important manifestation of cultural heritage preservation and is also the intrinsic evidence of local residents' perception of preservation. "Local legends" refers to the interpretation of stories about mountains, rivers and relics, which is a kind of nostalgia, and is more a reflection of the spirit of the region. For example, the residents mention "Tiandu Marshal, who has been worshiped by the locals for a long time to bless peace." It can be seen that this power inspires the cultural imagination of the residents, and its power to motivate people to stay constitutes an important part of the regional cultural heritage.

4.3 Local Elements

The ancient town of Fengzhou gives residents a unique experience in five dimensions: sight, sound, smell, taste and touch. As the audience of the ancient town, the residents are left with a deep impression. "Traditional food" refers to the unique food formed by the specific climate and geographical location, carrying the local culture of Fengzhou ancient town. Shiting green tea and Taoyuan fish sticks spread among visitors, providing a new channel of communication and a positive effect on the continuation of the sense of local attachment. The "architectural monuments" refer to the ancient houses, houses, houses, study halls, temples and other buildings, as well as ancient wells, inscriptions and other environmental elements of the ancient town. The conservation status of the monuments directly affects the overall conservation perception of the residents. In interviews, with a total of 101 reference points, ancient houses have 3 levels of significance to local residents: first, as a physical environment and a shelter for living, but also as an important social place; second, to assume certain economic functions. The residents use the buildings as the basis for commercial operations and gain potential benefits, and the third is spiritual nourishment, as the Minnan culture is deeply embedded in the hearts of the residents of the ancient town of Fengzhou. In different spatial and temporal dimensions, nostalgia produces significant positive effects through local attachments. Therefore, the effective protection of architectural monuments should be the top priority of the town's conservation. The "natural environment" includes the overall landscape pattern of Fengzhou township, such as Jinjiang River, Qingyuan Mountain, Ninth Day Mountain and Lotus Peak. The protection status of the natural environment directly affects the protection perception of the residents. For example, "when you climb the Ninth Day Mountain, you can see the whole ancient town with beautiful scenery and a sense of relaxation" (A29). To a certain extent, the natural landscape nourishes the residents of the ancient town both spiritually and materially, giving them not only rest and comfort, but also "imagery" in the thinking and emotion of the residents. A unique spiritual outlook and a strong sense of vernacular has emerged, thus establishing a strong sense of local preservation.

4.4 Development Opportunities

The "regional linkage" refers to the creation of the Fengzhou ancient town cultural and tourism economic development planning circle, the state of tourism development and residents' income, local self-confidence tightly linked. Local residents say "after the completion of the Qingyuan Mountain Scenic Area, the business of the ancient town has become much better, and we are also very happy". The perception of local identity and town preservation. For ancient towns and residents, the "environment of the times" mainly refers to urban changes, the impact of the Internet and the planning and layout of the large economic circle in southern Fujian, whose role should not be underestimated. To a certain extent, the ancient town will inevitably face population loss, and the ancient town, the new shopping method to break the stable business model. But also greatly improve the visibility of the ancient town, and promote the development of regional tourism. How to preserve the old and welcome the new is Fengzhou ancient town protection and development of the urgent need to solve the problem.

4.5 Protection Measures to Be Improved

"Conservation measures" refers to the publicity, repair and planning work carried out by the relevant departments to protect the ancient buildings. In-depth interviews were mentioned 95 times, but the negative attitude of the residents is obvious. 4 residents directly said in the interview that the government policy did not really protect the ancient buildings, and blind renovation and reconstruction led to the loss of authenticity in some areas of the town; the protection of cultural heritage should be a common topic between the government and local residents, and close cooperation between the two sides can greatly enhance the residents' sense of belonging. However, in Fengzhou ancient town, the cooperation mechanism has not yet been formed, and the residents have gradually formed passive inertia dependence and spectator mentality, and the residents' perception of conservation is constantly being weakened.

4.6 Survival and Development Needs

According to Maslow's hierarchy of needs theory, human needs from low to high are physiological needs, security needs, social needs, respect needs, and self-development needs. The results of the interviews show that the residents of the ancient town of Fengzhou still have low-level needs, including business performance, safety issues, traffic disputes, and infrastructure (see Fig. 3).

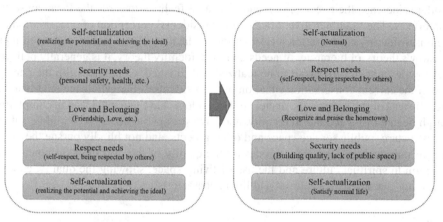

Fig. 3. Comparison of Maslow's Hierarchy of Needs and the Current Perception of Residents in Fengzhou Ancient Town.

"Business performance" is a factor that affects residents' well-being, and was mentioned 80 times in the in-depth interviews, "affected by the epidemic, many times there is no business. When business performance is difficult to meet the daily needs of residents, residents are stuck with the basic quality of life, and it is more difficult to focus on the conservation of the ancient town." The "safety issue" mainly refers to the safety hazards of the ancient town's buildings and roads. As a basic element of survival, it largely affects the degree of local attachment of the residents. Otherwise, the residents' sense of belonging and identity will be difficult to maintain, and the awareness of the ancient town's protection will continue to decrease. Traffic controversy" refers to the contradiction of whether traffic control should be implemented in some streets of the ancient town. At present, there are many problems in the ancient town such as indiscriminate parking of motor vehicles, mixed traffic and road width restrictions. A traffic controversy and security problems, it is easy to make the residents upset negative emotions, which leads to the overall protection of the ancient town of negative emotions. "Infrastructure" refers to the infrastructure within the ancient town, such as public toilets, open spaces, and guided tours. During the interview process, residents focused more on the actual use and quality of the space. However, the current facilities inside the ancient town are relatively old and lacking. The uneven use of various public spaces and the lack of leisure and entertainment functions are urgently needed to be improved and implemented in the later stage of optimization in order to improve residents' awareness of the current state of conservation in the ancient town.

5   Conclusions and Policy Recommendations

Based on the above analysis, it can be found that most of the positive effects on residents' perceptions of conservation are the existence of famous ancient buildings, the characteristic landscape patterns, especially the continuation of the good spiritual qualities carried by them, and the benefits of the development process, which can make the residents increase their recognition and favorable feelings towards the local conservation effects. The main negative aspects of the residents' perception of conservation are the unsatisfactory conservation measures and the lack of related facilities. According to Maslow's theory of hierarchy of needs and local identity theory, it is generally believed that low-level needs are easier to be realized and satisfied. Combined with the perception of the current conservation situation of the residents of Fengzhou ancient town, the overall signs of the inverse, the ancient town residents have taken the lead in completing a high degree of local cultural identity, and have stronger demands for building safety, infrastructure, public service space and other aspects, and not blindly pursue the quantitative improvement, but should focus on the quality of the overall environment, pay attention to spiritual culture and the use of living space, showing the quality, cultural and living characteristics cultural and living characteristics.

References

1. Masele, F.: Private business investments in Heritage sites in Tanzania: recent developments and Challenges for heritage management. Afr. Archaeol. Rev. **29**, 51–65 (2012)
2. Onuki, Y.: The archaeological excavations and the protection of cultural heritage in relation with the local society. Archaeologies **3**(2), 99–115 (2007)
3. Xin, W., Heping, Y., Wenpu, W., Yubin, C.: Strategies for the protection of intangible cultural heritage of traditional villages based on cultural consciousness: a case study of Shawan town, Panyu district, Guangzhou. Small Town Constr. (04), 82–87 (2020)
4. Zhenhua, C., Lin, Y.: The construction and sustainable development of village communities in Taiwan and its enlightenment. Famous Cities China (03), 17–23 (2014)
5. Song, H., Zhu, C., Fong, L.H.N.: Exploring residents' perceptions and attitudes towards sustainable tourism development in traditional villages: the lens of stakeholder theory. Sustainability **13**, 13032–13048 (2021)
6. Yani, S.: Heritage conservation and regeneration of historic areas in Malaysia. Procedia Soc. Behav. Sci. **105**, 418–428 (2013)
7. Ruoshi, Z., Yuting, D., Zhaoxin, S.: Research on multi-dimensional affective association evaluation method for the protection and development of traditional villages: a case study of Yangchan Tulou in Xiao County, Huangshan City, Anhui Province. Archit. J. **S1**, 231–238 (2022)
8. Xiang, D., Qiuxiang, L.: A new method for the classification of traditional village types and the formulation of conservation and development strategies: a case study of four traditional villages in Linhai City, Zhejiang Province. Archit. Heritage **02**, 42–52 (2020)

9. Zhi, Z., Anrong, D., Miaole, H., Dongfan, W.: Construction of information technology method framework for the protection and utilization of cultural heritage of the great wall. J. Remote Sens. **12**, 2339–2350 (2021)
10. Zhihong, L.: Research on digital protection strategies of cultural heritage of traditional villages. Famous Cities China **12**, 55–61 (2022)
11. Guccio, C.: Evaluating the efficiency of public procurement contracts for cultural heritage conservation works in Italy. J. Cult. Econ. **38**, 43–70 (2014)
12. Andrew, L.: A comparison of attitudes toward state-led conservation and community-based conservation in the village of Bigodi, Uganda. Soc. Nat. Resour. **19**(7), 609–620 (2006)
13. Shulu, L., Dawei, X., Juan, F.: Exploration of evaluation methods for the implementation effect of traditional village protection. Small Town Constr. **6**, 85–90 (2014)
14. Yue, Z.: Research on the living renewal of traditional villages from the perspective of regional cultural landscape: a case study of Qiqiao village, Gaochun district, Nanjing. Decoration **7**, 142–144 (2022)
15. Bohua, L., Fuduan, Y., Yindi, D.: Organic renewal of human settlements in traditional villages: theoretical cognition and practical paths. Geogr. Res. **5**, 1407–1421 (2022)

The Future of the Performing Arts with Extended Reality

Tanja Kojić[1]([✉]), Iva Srnec Hamer[2], Maurizio Vergari[1], and Sebastian Möller[1,3]

[1] Quality and Usability Lab, Technische Universität Berlin, Berlin, Germany
tanja.kojic@tu-berlin.de
[2] Empiria Teatar, Zagreb, Croatia
[3] German Research Center for Artificial Intelligence (DFKI), Berlin, Germany

Abstract. Extended Reality (XR), an umbrella term for AR and VR, is growing in academic and business applications. Each technology simulates reality differently regarding immersion, content, and environment interaction. This gives content providers various chances to deliver material in innovative ways and from faraway locations. XR's freedom allows for a lot of creativity in different aspects, including such as design and art. XR technology has already been included and used in several events and venues recently, but this work will discuss possibilities with XR and the performing arts. During the last several years, XR and performing arts have gotten closer. The power and necessity to integrate developing technologies into arts are becoming more apparent, especially with COVID-19. XR technology's expansion and the performing arts digital transition provide a dilemma: how to construct the future of performing arts with XR? This study theoretically addresses the challenge by building the prototype experience and testing this prototype XR performance with a live audience.

Keywords: Extended Reality · Performing Arts · UX

1 Introduction and Motivation

Extended Reality (XR) as an umbrella term for Augmented Reality (AR) and Virtual Reality (VR) is rapidly getting popular in academic and industry applications. Each of those technologies allows different degrees of simulation of reality in terms of immersion, content, and interactivity levels with the environment. This generates many opportunities for content creators so that the audience can enjoy content in new ways and from different remote locations.

This high degree of flexibility of XR results in a additional room for expression, especially from the design and artistic value of an experience. In recent years, this technology has been embedded and utilized in many different events and spaces, but within this work, the focus will be given to the performing arts. The intersection between performing arts and XR has grown significantly over the past few years. Especially with the outbreak of COVID-19, the strength and

C. Stephanidis et al. (Eds.): HCII 2023, CCIS 1834, pp. 440–445, 2023.
https://doi.org/10.1007/978-3-031-35998-9_58

needs to apply emerging technology to arts are increasingly evident. On the one hand, the extensive and immersive experience taken by XR is gradually seen by the public. A research project [1] showed that the acceptance rate by various groups of the population who had chances to experiment with the XR technologies is significantly high, which can be interpreted as a significant market opportunity. On the other hand, it has been discussed that sometimes people are initially skeptical about incorporating XR into performance [2]. The conflict between the explosion of XR technology and the difficulty of the performing arts' digital transformation leaves a problem: how to develop the future of performing arts with XR technology?

This work approaches the problem from the theoretical side and by prototyping the experience itself and trying out the XR performance with a live audience.

2   Related Work

Although art and technology may appear to be two distinct fields, they have a long and interconnected history. The word "technology" derives from the Greek words "techne" and "logia" which mean "art, craft, and skill" respectively. Together, they comprise "technologia," which originally referred to the study of practical arts but, over time, expanded to include the practical application of scientific knowledge [3]. Throughout history, artists have frequently been at the forefront of technological advancement, using new materials, methods, and equipment to push the boundaries of their work. Similarly, technological developments have frequently inspired and shaped creative trends and styles, influencing how artists create and engage with their work [4].

As human cultures developed and became more complex, so did the instruments used to create art. Technological advancement has greatly influenced the evolution of art history, from traditional painting over to the invention of the printing press and photography. As new technologies emerged, artists began experimenting with new forms of expression and media. This resulted in the emergence of artistic movements such as video art and digital art, which included technology as an integral part of their creative processes [5].

With new digital tools and technologies like VR, AR, and artificial intelligence, artists have greater access to resources than ever before [6]. However, artists struggle with the ethical and aesthetic repercussions of using modern technology to create and participate in their work [7].

In any case, artists and technologists continue pushing the limits of what is possible [8], creating new opportunities for innovation and creativity.

2.1   Objective

The objective of this research was to investigate the creative potential of humans in combination with the immersive technological capabilities that can connect the real and virtual worlds. This not only allows artists to explore new possibilities for their work, but also permits them to experiment with novel ways of combining their work with that of other creatives.

The main goal was to construct a bridge between traditional creative arts and the expanding technological possibilities of expression in such a way that it does not pose a threat of replacement and does not interfere with the artist's statement but rather functions as yet another tool for expression. This performance wanted to attract an audience, as well as artists from a variety of diverse backgrounds, due to the fact that it combines a variety of art forms and, consequently, individuals who are interested in other art forms. Additionally, it attempted to introduce those who have only been interested in technology to the art world. With this prototype, we aimed to establish an improvisational style of performance art, as this opens up new avenues for connecting different forms of art with technology and enables artists to collaborate.

3   Exploration Prototype

Our primary goal was to create a new artistic means of communication between performance artists. Considering the wide range of use cases and possible extensions of the project (such as an online format), on a macro level, we targeted artists of any kind who wanted to explore immersive technologies and expand their vision of artistry. As it can be seen in Fig. 1, the performance included a dance that was augmented with visual artifacts based on the dancer's heartbeat, and it was possible to only remotely observe a fully virtual world created based on the same artifacts.

Fig. 1. Example of rehearsal for performance that could have been followed in AR and VR.

However, we believed that our digital stage could serve as a means of communication between artists and people with a background in technology. We aimed to bring together:

- artists wanting to explore new possibilities with XR technologies;
- people with a technical background wanting to expand their skill sets artistically.

3.1 Set-Up

To use the application, a Polar Chest Strap has been needed (tested with version H10, and should also work with H7). The heart rate sensor must have been activated by mildly moistening the electrode area. The strap should have been fastened around the chest and adjusted to fit snugly.

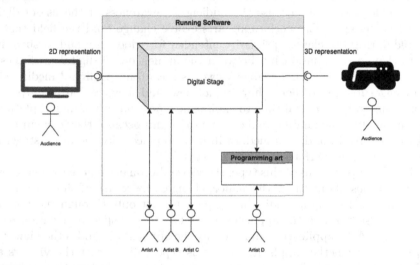

Fig. 2. High-level architecture for implementing the Digital Stage that is designed with 3D and a 2D representation, enabling artists to contribute synchronously.

To use the application, the user was required to activate Bluetooth and GPS on their device and launch the app. For the initial usage, it was necessary to configure the Device ID of the Polar device, whereby the Bluetooth scan identified the device with the corresponding Device ID. The Device ID was typically located on the sensor's top surface (e.g., ID: 35815C28). Subsequently, the "Change Device ID" button was pressed to input the Device ID, which was a one-time process. Once the Device ID was entered, the user clicked on the "Connect to Polar Belt" button to establish the device's connection and commence the simulation. This app was created with the specific purpose of generating a "choreography" that was synchronized with the dancer's heart rate. As heart rate is an individualized biosignal, the app's functionalities were customized to align with the dancer's heart rate range. In the event of a different performer or different effects, it might have been necessary to make adjustments to the app. Accordingly, testing the app required performing activities such as jumps and running. The full architecture of the prototype is shown in Fig. 2.

4   Discussion and Conclusion

The process is one of the most important aspects of working in the performing arts. The process of creation, learning, working on yourself, and the possibility of making mistakes. The space of the unknown, unexplored, and controversial has been a field of interest for many theatre practicians. Unfortunately, the opportunity to explore digital possibilities in the theatre is rare. When the pandemic started, a whole new world opened up in the field of performing arts, not because digitization is a new field in the arts; theater companies have been using digital media for decades, but because the audience's awareness of the use of digital media has changed. The performing arts evolve change, and the field that we explored during the class is primarily intended for wider use; and as such, it is able to change the relationship between the audience and digital media, especially in the XR field. The average viewer is not afraid of digital media. They are no longer foreign to them, they are not new, and they can hardly surprise or shock them. So it's an ideal time to explore new possibilities of digital platforms because they become familiar and organic to us and because they can enrich our performance. And no, digital media will never replace a live actor on stage, but they can enrich his performance and concept.

Through applications of this type, the viewer becomes an active observer who brings attitudes about the performance, changes the course of the performance and tailors it, creating an individual experience not only through their organic senses but also through the application. We had to pay special attention to the dramaturgy of the application and the way the application guides the viewer the question arises whether applications of this type will distract the viewers and distract them from the live performer on stage. Through testing the application on a selected audience, we concluded that the process of watching the performance deepened; that is, using the application while watching the performance, either live or as pre-recorded video material, did not disturb the audience too rough the process must be meaningful for the viewer and meaningful for the story. Therefore, it can be concluded that the potential future for XR and performing arts is to be explored further, and it can include experiences such as immersive theater, virtual concerts, mixed reality performances, collaborative performances, and training and rehearsals in a virtual environment.

Acknowledgment. We would like to thank all the students who participated in the Advanced Projects at the Quality and Usability Lab during the Winter Semester of 2021/22 under the project Performing Arts with XR, for their dedication, hard work, and valuable contributions toward exploring new ways of integrating XR technology in the performing arts.

References

1. Novakova, H., ŠTarchoň, P.: Creative industries: challenges and opportunities in XR technologies. In: SHS Web of Conferences, vol. 115, p. 03011. EDP Sciences (2021)
2. Kamala Sankaram Composer: Why XR and the performing arts are made for each other, September 2020. https://www.zappar.com/blog/why-xr-and-performing-arts-are-made-each-other/
3. Drengson, A.: Definitions and examples of technology practice (2020)
4. National Research Council, et al.: Beyond Productivity: Information Technology, Innovation, and Creativity. National Academies Press (2003)
5. Kirk, C., Pitches, J.: Digital reflection: using digital technologies to enhance and embed creative processes. Technol. Pedagog. Educ. 22(2), 213–230 (2013)
6. Fung, S., Jacobson, K., Pike, J.: PXR2020: re-seeing the possibilities of theatre in virtual, augmented, and mixed reality (2022)
7. Hunter, E.: Theatre majors and immersive technology: an interview with HP's Joanna popper. In: Experiential Theatres, pp. 206–211. Routledge (2022)
8. Goldberg, A., Tetreault, S.: Live from the metaverse: virtual XR performances for audiences on-stage, online, in-game, and in-VR. In: ACM SIGGRAPH. Production Sessions 2021, p. 1 (2021)

Information and Communication Technology in Yogyakarta Heritage Tourism Marketing

Aromah Udaningrum Kusumadewi[⊠] and Filosa Gita Sukmono

Department of Communication, Universitas Muhammdiyah Yogyakarta, Bantul Regency,
Indonesia
`aromah.u.isip19@mail.umy.ac.id, filosa@umy.ac.id`

Abstract. Yogyakarta utilizes ICT for cultural heritage tourism promotion. This study aims to determine how ICT promotes the cultural heritage of Yogyakarta. In the promotion of cultural heritage tourism, ICT plays a crucial role. This study employs descriptive quantitative methods to describe the responses of tourists gathered through systematic sampling. This study reveals three aspects: proper sourcing, both sides, and step-by-step verification. According to this study, tourists evaluate the role of ICT in marketing differently in three categories: first, the role of social media on tourists with ratings (38.20%), second, tourist satisfaction with Yogyakarta Culture promotion content with ratings (43.50%), and third, the content of promotional content on social media with an evaluation (38.20%). This acceptability is demonstrated by the disparity between respondents and the information-seeking ICT they employ. This study clarifies the role of ICT in promoting Yogyakarta's cultural heritage tourism, which positively impacts tourists' decisions to visit the city.

Keywords: Cultural Heritage · Tourism Promotion · Information and Communication Technology · Yogyakarta

1 Introduction

Cultural heritage tourism is included in special interest tourism, which means tourists who like ancient buildings' history, culture, and architecture. These tourists also have interests such as adding educational value, especially in the field of culture or history when the tour takes place. In Roozana's view [1], cultural legacy is both tangible and intangible, representing the uniqueness of a civilization that is conserved over time. Cultural legacy documents the evolution and development of human society [2]. Additionally, communities must uphold safety and sustainability. For heritage tourism to promote sustainability, it must keep up with the digital revolution [3].

Yogyakarta is a well-known tourist destination for both Indonesians and international visitors from all over the world. According to Gratiano [4], Yogyakarta offers many timeless tourist experiences, including exquisite natural, historical, and cultural tourism. Yogyakarta is one of Indonesia's most popular tourist attractions due to its people's reputation for friendliness towards travelers.

© The Author(s), under exclusive license to Springer Nature Switzerland AG 2023
C. Stephanidis et al. (Eds.): HCII 2023, CCIS 1834, pp. 446–452, 2023.
https://doi.org/10.1007/978-3-031-35998-9_59

Adhiningasih Prabhawati's study [5] on the importance of ICT in heritage tourism marketing communications indicates that cooperation and collaboration between the Yogyakarta Palace and travel brokers through ICT have a significant impact. The research of Pei Tsai [6] demonstrates how ICT applications might enhance the happiness of heritage tourism destinations. According to a study by the Council [7], marketing communication methods efficiently build tourism destinations' image and brand recognition. It contrasts with research by Jinbo Xu [8] that discusses the role of ICT, which continues to encourage and support all content and interaction aspects for the growth of cultural heritage tourism, and eventually promotes a healthy industrial cycle.

Tourism benefits from marketing through digital media since it can disseminate information fast. However, many Yogyakarta cultural tours still require ICT in their deployment [9]. This study indicates that many need help to balance Yogyakarta's heritage tourism with modern societal advancements, like ICT. The frequency of cultural tourism visitors in Yogyakarta is decreasing due to competition from more popular tourist locations, such as shopping malls and other hurdles.

2 Theoretical Framework

The development of information and communication technology is constantly experiencing rapid increases in its increasingly diverse uses by modern human activities [10]. The technology is much used because of its portability and strong interaction [11]. Marketing communications through digital media are being intensively used by Yogyakarta heritage tourism in disseminating information and as tourism promotion to increase tourist attraction [12]. For example, tourists use ICTs to widely share their experiences and impressions of the sites they visit, competing with commercial and promotional materials and greatly influencing the decision-making processes of others [13]. ICT functions as a medium to promote cultural heritage widely [14]. Cultural heritage can develop if it is widely grown and advanced, one of which is using ICT [15]. ICT covers a variety of functions such as digital communication tools, devices, and technology, as well as various services and applications related to it, and information dissemination and promotion activities with the support of appropriate and comprehensive strategies can increase the competitiveness of tourism products and services so that they have high quality that can attract tourists. Tourists are interested in visiting heritage tourism in Yogyakarta through various information and communication technology applications, including social media [16]. In addition to the role of ICT, the commitment and proper management of cultural heritage can catalyze a destination's iconic development [17]. A city's brand and culture must conform to the marketing concept and have characteristics [18]. Factors such as cultural heritage attract tourists [19], and cultural forms such as typical dances, wayang, and traditional ceremonies make the city have characteristics and characteristics that are considered attractive [20, 21].

3 Method

This study used a quantitative method by analyzing the data obtained by distributing questionnaires to tourist visitors in the Yogyakarta Tourism Area. In addition, quantitative methods can produce more accurate research and more convincing results. Data is collected using survey results. This understanding is a form of simplification of the survey method as a complex and comprehensive research instrument. According to Susila Adiyanta [22], a survey provides questions for research about self-reported beliefs/behaviors. These questions become sharper when respondents answer a question with the desired variables.

4 Result and Discussion

In this study, 110 respondents were Yogyakarta tourists. In this study, men and women were local or came from Indonesia, namely 31 respondents from Yogyakarta, 16 from East Java, 13 from West Java, 13 from Central Java, ten from Jakarta, and the remaining 27 from other cities in Indonesia. Respondents are aged 15–25 years and actively use ICT in the form of social media. The characteristics of the 110 respondents who were sampled in this study were 39 men and 71 women. The age distribution of the respondents in this study was 28.2% aged 15–20 years, 60.9% old 20–25 years, and the remaining 10.9% aged over 25 years.

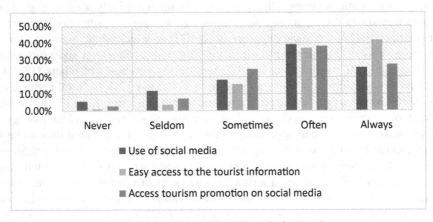

Graph 1. The Role of Social Media for Tourists

Graph 1, shows respondents assess the function of social media on tourists, with a percentage of 39.1% of respondents often using social media in seeking information on cultural tourism in Yogyakarta. Then on the ease of access to tourist information, a rate of 41.70% and 38.20% of respondents often seek information from Yogyakarta's promotional social media. This data shows that the ICT used by Yogyakarta tourists has used the right source selection. This finding confirms Yuni Fitriani's theory [23] that the internet is a communication tool for finding tourist information for the community. Furthermore, according to Ahmad Andhika [24], social media is more efficient,

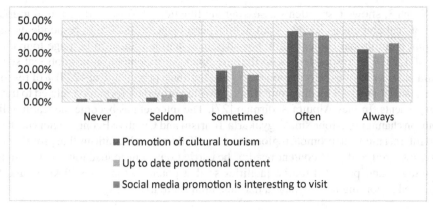

Graph 2. Tourist Satisfaction with Yogyakarta Cultural Promotion Content

and can easily find extensive information about cultural heritage tourist destinations in Yogyakarta.

Graph 2, shows respondents assess the function of tourism promotion carried out by social media, with a percentage of 43.50% of respondents stating that they often feel satisfied regarding the content of cultural tourism promotion in conveying information. Then the rate of 42.60% of respondents felt that promotional content on Yogyakarta tourism social media was often up to date in its delivery. Moreover, a percentage of 40.70% of respondents stated that the function of promotional content on Yogyakarta cultural tourism social media often attracts and makes tourists go to tourist destinations. Intense content creates an excellent response to Yogyakarta tourism. According to Ayu Salndri [25], promotion through content as an innovation in choosing the right digital tools can increase profits, expand markets, increase assets, and customer satisfaction. Tourism actors can also use social media to retain customers, fulfilling customer satisfaction and creating customer loyalty for the products or services offered by Yogyakarta tourism actors [26]. Therefore, tourists are satisfied with the function of Yogyakarta cultural heritage tourism promotion content in its delivery.

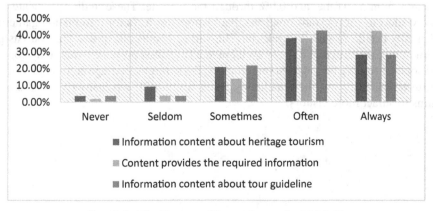

Graph 3. The Content of Promotion on Social Media

Graph 3, shows respondents assessing the function of Yogyakarta cultural tourism promotional content on social media, with a percentage of 38.20% of respondents stating that promotional content often provides information related to heritage tourism, a rate of 42.60% of respondents said that the function of content on promotional social media always provides information that is needed and a percentage of 42.70% of respondents stated that social media promotions also often provide information related to travel arrangements. In viewAlputra Sudirman [27], The internet has become the leading distribution channel in e-tourism. Yogyakarta Tourism and Creative Economy Service have used internet media to promote regional tourism. This research confirms that promotional activities through digital content need to be carried out to introduce tourist attractions, advantages, and provided tourist facilities so that potential tourists will know and be interested in coming to Yogyakarta heritage cultural tourism [28].

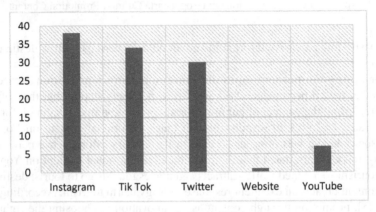

Graph 4. Use of ICT

Graph 4, explains that most respondents visited Yogyakarta's cultural heritage attractions because of information from Information and Communication Technology in the form of social media, with 34.5% from Social Media Instagram followed by the second highest percentage of 30.9% from Social Media Tik Tok. The rest are 27.3% from Twitter, 6.4% from YouTube, and 0.9% through the website. These findings indicate that these visitors use ICTs study confirms that visitors use ICTs for information gathering and finally decide to visit Yogyakarta. The survey results also prove that tourists get information from different ICTs or social media [29]. Respondents in this study considered social media by far the most important ICT. Therefore, heritage cultural or tourism institutions should focus their marketing resources on ICT, especially on social media. It aims to attract more visitors.

5   Conclusion

From the study results, promoting Yogyakarta's cultural heritage tourist attraction through ICT positively affects the intention to visit it. The promotion is running effectively. As evidenced by the survey results involving respondents from tourists visiting Yogyakarta, tourists are interested because they see advertisements from social media accounts. Yogyakarta tourism should prioritize ICT in the form of Instagram and Tik Tok social media because, based on the survey results, many visitors get information related to information on Yogyakarta heritage cultural tourism from these social media. Tourism uses information networks and media by tourism to be more involved with users and increase the interest of domestic and foreign tourists to visit Yogyakarta.

References

1. Roozana, O., Ritonga, M.: Pengembangan Wisata Warisan Budaya Sebagai Daya Tarik Kota Tangerang Cultural Heritage Tourism Development as Tourist Attraction in Tangerang. http://ejurnal.binawakya.or.id/index.php/MBI
2. Filipe, J., Ghosh, A., Prates, R.O., Zhou, L.: Communications in Computer and Information Science 1654 Editorial Board Members (2022). https://link.springer.com/bookseries/7899
3. Sulistyanto, B.: Warisan Budaya Sebagai Barang Publik Cultural Heritage as Public Property (2018)
4. Gratiano Mali, M.: Peran Pemerintah Dalam Pengembangan Pariwisata Era New Normal di Daerah Istimiewa Yogyakarta Melalui Aplikasi VIisiting Jogja (2021). http://ojs.stiami.ac.id
5. Adhiningasih Prabhawati, S.W.: Pertunjukan Tari Klasik Tradisional Gaya Yogyakarta Sebagai Daya Tarik Wisata Budaya di Keraton Yogyakarta (2018)
6. pei Tsai, S.: Augmented reality enhancing place satisfaction for heritage tourism marketing. Curr. Issues Tour. 23(9), 1078–1083 (2020). https://doi.org/10.1080/13683500.2019.1598950
7. Dewan, K., Prof, R., Astuti, W.: Susunan Dewan Redaksi
8. Xu, J., Wei, Y.: Analysis of the attainable design paths of non-heritage cultural tourism immersion experience - an example of the Tujia City living room project in Enshi Prefecture. In: Stephanidis, C., Antona, M., Ntoa, S., Salvendy, G. (eds.) HCII 2022. CCIS, vol. 1654, pp. 370–377. Springer, Cham (2022). https://doi.org/10.1007/978-3-031-19679-9_47
9. Cornellia, A.H.: Model Pemasaran Museum di Yogyakarta; Tantangan dan Kesempatan Berkembang di Era Digital (2018)
10. Penelitian, J.I., Deria, O., Wijaya, A., Saeroji, A., Prasetyo, J.S., Agfianto, T.: Strategi Pemasaran Berbasis Website di Kampung Wisata Baluwarti Surakarta
11. Zhou, J., Kong, Z.: Research on visual design of Tibetan medicine mud mask based on HTML5 technology - taking Tibetan medicine mud mask as an example. In: Stephanidis, C., Antona, M., Ntoa, S., Salvendy, G. (eds.) HCII 2022. CCIS, vol. 1654, pp. 284–291. Springer, Cham. https://doi.org/10.1007/978-3-031-19679-9_35
12. Yulianto, A.: Evaluasi Usability Pengembangan Website Desa Wisata Bejiharjo Gunung Kidul Yogyakarta (2019)
13. Hausmann, A., Weuster, L.: Possible marketing tools for heritage tourism: the potential of implementing information and communication technology. J. Heritage Tour. 13(3), 273–284 (2018). https://doi.org/10.1080/1743873X.2017.1334786
14. Halum, Y.S., Selamat, E.H., Rondas, T.F., Mbohong, Y.C., Nagi, Y.D.: Promosi Budaya dan Pariwisata Berbasis Media Digital: Meningkatkan Kesadaran Kaum Muda Terhadap Warisan Budaya Lokal. Randang Tana - Jurnal Pengabdian Masyarakat 4(3), 91–100 (2021). https://doi.org/10.36928/jrt.v4i3.874

15. Perdana, A., et al.: Nilai Budaya Naskah La Galigo dan Perahu Pinisi di Museum Untuk Generasi Millennial Cultural Values of La Galigo ManuScript and Pinis Boat in Museum for Millenials (2020)
16. Subejo, S., et al.: Strategi Komunikasi Dan Pemanfaatan Teknologi Informasi Dan Komunikasi Dalam Pengembangan Ketahanan Desa Wisata Pada Masa Pandemi Covid-19 Di Cirebon. Jurnal Ketahanan Nasional 27(1), 90 (2021). https://doi.org/10.22146/jkn.61859
17. Rakhmawati, Y., Kurniasari, N.D., Subastian, R.M.: Keris as branding destination tourism: Indonesian heritage daggers from Madura. Komunikator 14(1), 42–52 (2022). https://doi.org/10.18196/jkm.12818
18. Hidayat, D., Hafiar, H., Anisti, A., Suhartini, T.: Tofu product branding for culinary tourism of Sumedang, Indonesia. Komunikator 11(2), 82–92 (2019). https://doi.org/10.18196/jkm.112022
19. Hadi, W.: Menggali Potensi Kampung Wisata di Kota Yogyakarta Sebagai Daya Tarik Wisatawan (2019)
20. Putri, A.D.: Srategi Komunikasi Tepas Tandha Yekti Dalam Mengelola Citra Posisit Kraton Yogyakarta Melalui Media Ssosial Instagram, vol. 2 (2019). https://journal.student.uny.ac.id/
21. Sules, A.: Tino Sidin Art Project #1 'Art Transmission, Artcurrency' (2022)
22. Susila, F.C., Hukum, A.B., Negara, A.: Hukum dan Studi Penelitian Empiris: Penggunaan Metode Survey sebagai Instrumen Penelitian Hukum Empiris (2019)
23. Fitriani, Y.: Ciptaan disebarluaskan di bawah Lisensi Creative Commons Atribusi 4.0 Internasional. Pemanfaatan Media Sosial Sebagai Media Penyajian Konten Edukasi atau Pembelajaran Digital. J. Inf. Syst. Appl. Manag. Account. Res. 5(4), 1006–1013 (2021). https://doi.org/10.52362/jisamar.v5i4.609
24. Andhika, A., Islam, U., Muhammad, K., Al-Banjari Banjarmasin, A.: Penggunaan Video Promosi Wisata Melalui Youtube Untuk Meningkatkan Daya Tarik Wisatawan Ke Provinsi Kalimantan Selatan (2019)
25. Salindri, Y.A., et al.: Pemberdayaan UKM YAD Blangkon Yogyakarta Melalui Pemasaran Berbasis Digital Sebagai Upaya Menembus Pasar Global. Jurnal Inovasi dan Pengabdian Masyarakat Indonesia 1(4), 41–46 (2022). https://jurnalnew.unimus.ac.id/index.php/jipmi
26. Umami, Z.: Social Strategy Pada Media Sosial Untuk Promosi Pariwisata Daerah Istimewa Yogyakarta
27. Alputra Sudirman, F., Ode Dina Sarma, W., Tri Susilawaty, F.: Promosi Pariwisata Melalui Digital Diplomacy: Upaya Internasionalisasi Pariwisata Daerah (2020)
28. Kadarisman, A.: Peran Generasi Muda dalam Pemanfaatan Media Sosial untuk Mempromosikan Geopark Ciletuh. Jurnal Ilmu Komunikasi ULTIMACOMM 11(2), 92–108 (2019). http://ejournals.umn.ac.id/index.php/FIKOM/about
29. Hausmann, A., Schuhbauer, S.: The role of information and communication technologies in cultural tourists' journeys: the case of a World Heritage Site. J. Heritage Tour. 16(6), 669–683 (2021). https://doi.org/10.1080/1743873X.2020.1819300

Use of Semiotics on the Character Development of Choreography

Jui-Hsiang Lee[1](✉) and Shu-Ling Chiu[2]

[1] Department of Digital Multimedia Design, China University of Technology, Taipei, Taiwan
leockmail@gmail.com
[2] Department of Choreography, Sonia Dance Studio, New Taipei, Taiwan
soniadance@gmail.com

Abstract. Movement performance is a part of character development, and dance is one of the results of movement performance. Anthropologists believe that "dance" can be analogized to language, which can express what is in one's mind and is neither falsified nor abstract. Moreover, they regard "dance" as "culture," which is a kind of "human" thought, custom, belief, norm, and behavior. "Culture" also provides a rich source of inspiration for character developers and choreographers. French linguist Roland Barthes once pointed out that all human cultural phenomena are regarded as a sign system, or all cultural activities are regarded as message transmission. In this study, Roland Barthes's two orders of signification thinking mode were integrated into character development and choreography of the dance of the "Women's Mind". Based on a literature review, the study categorized the cultural signs in the framework of character development and choreography into four stages: (1) discovery of signs; (2) exploring the semantic meaning of signs; (3) context analysis of signs; (4) transformation and application of signs. Using qualitative methods, including descriptive documents, discussion records, diagram generation, work practice, and evaluation scale, the semantic data of the general public were collected to increase internal and external validity. In addition, focus groups were employed as participants to observe the role of the above-mentioned creation structure in the dance creation process. During the observation process, relevant research data were collected. The results showed that (1) cultural signs are hidden in daily life; (2) this coding link still needs the creativity, beautification, and sublimation of character developer and choreographers; (3) this study helps to find the source and awareness of sign coding; (4) Roland Barthes's two orders of signification process not only has the function of spreading creativity but also has the auxiliary function of providing creation methods.

Keywords: Character · Choreography · Cultural Code · Folk Culture

1 Introduction

In the field of academic research, anthropologists believe that "dance" can be analogized to language, which has unique functions and purposes. It can express what you think, neither falsified nor abstract; moreover, like "culture," "dance" is a kind of "human" thought, custom, belief, norm, and behavior [1]. Culture is also a rich source of inspiration for choreographers. Common people's life is common material for folk dance, and the narrative plot in classical ballet is expressed through dance movements instead of language. Modern dance draws material from the local cultural landscape and political issues using dance theater to show the phenomena occurring at present. Therefore, this study also focused on how to draw material from the life of common people to be used as the theme of contemporary choreography.

And what are women's concerns in their mind? Some people think that girls are inherently scared, or are more likely to worry? Some studies believe that women actually have more "reflection and introspection thinking" than men [2]. Being a woman, for example, mothers or wives always worry: "Is this enough? Is there something that I haven't noticed for my family? Is my performance good? How can I help my children or family avoid danger? Worrying about being not careful... etc." Women are more vulnerable than men, the stereotype of women's fear has always appeared, and it will be regarded as excessive reflection. Motherhood in common people's culture is most prone to these phenomena.

Roland Barthes used semiotics to discuss popular culture such as diet and clothing, and some product design scholars, such as Wei Wanli, applied Roland Barthes's two orders of signification thinking mode as the theoretical basis to design cultural goods [3]. Therefore, using Roland Barthes's semiotics methodology, this study shows the deductive process of cultural codes. In addition, appropriate signs are used in "character development" and "choreography".

2 Literature Review

2.1 Theoretical Basis of Cultural Signs

We live in a world of signs: the ubiquitous signs in our lives. In the cognitive system, a sign refers to an image with a certain meaning, which can be a picture image, a combination of words, a sound signal, an architectural modeling, or even an ideological culture and a current affairs figure. The function of signs is to carry and convey meaning [4]. Applying linguistic similarity to dance theory, Guest thought that dance, like literary language, must act if it wants to change. "Act" is a verb, each part of the body is a noun, and the way of performance is an adverb. Dance action is a kind of a language code [5].

According to Ferdinand de Saussure, language is the basic system of semiotics, and signs are composed of the signifier and the signified. Roland Barthes inherited Saussure's linguistic system from the origin of this thought, and besides extending the deeper concept using the relationship between the signifier and the signified, he also proposed a sign analysis system model of two orders of signification [6].

Roland Barthes believed that the word "sign" has two orders of meaning. The first order is denotation, also known as explicit meaning, which includes o the signifier and the signified of the first order, and refers to common knowledge, that is, the obvious meaning of the sign itself. Explicit meaning means the direct and clear superficial meaning of things. Cognition of "objectivity" means, for example, the mechanical reproduction of something in a photograph taken using a camera. Another example is that the audience directly sees the expressive significance of dance actions. The second order is the connotation, also known as implicit meaning, which includes a signifier of the so-called denotative sign formed by the signifier and the signified of the first order, and another signified with symbolic meaning, which refers to the interaction between this sign and the user's emotion or culture. Implicit meaning explains how signs interact with the feelings, emotions, and cultural values of sign users.

In addition, Barthes also pointed out that making the second-order signification includes hidden meaning (itself), myth, and sign, that is, when the first-order signification involves inherited historical heritage or established cultural discourse, it will produce connotation and myth (myth refers to a mythical concept).

2.2 Character Development and Choreography

Character development is the process of creating believable and realistic virtual characters by giving fictional characters emotional depth. In the storytelling of stories, the character plays the role of process development, plot interpretation, emotional sustenance, and symbolic symbols that bear specific meanings [7]. "Character" in English, which has the meanings of "letter or character", "personality, characteristic or style" and "character". To put it bluntly, it means to Character have a unique personality [8]. Usually, character development can easily be understood as modeling, which is a work of character outline design, but this is actually a big misunderstanding.

What makes the stories and the characters attractive is that the characters in the story are like "Human", that is, the characters in the story have the meaning of "humanity." Therefore, the role of the story must express the universal needs of human nature, such as love and being loved, helping others and happiness, even the character is a car or an animal. Another question is how to develop personality of a character? Propp emphasized that which kind of person a character belongs to is not determined by his identity, willingness or feelings, but depends on the significance of his actions to the protagonist and the entire course of action [9]. The third problem is the performance of the character's inner emotions must be presented by their body movements. For example, the action of the impatient character is quite hasty, while the action of the slow-tempered character is slow and smooth. The body movements of the character have an additive effect on character shaping.

As we summarize the concept by Rudolf von Laban, Dance begins with an emotional concept, an understanding of joy or sorrow. In a flash of lightning, understanding turns into modeling. Conceptual achievement is everything. Everything is unfolded from the power of dance posture [10]. The final stage of choreography mostly emphasizes the discussion of dance form and content. The content is the "message", "meaning", or "ideas" that a dance work is aimed to convey. These three are the spirit and soul of dance work, reflecting the inner intention of the choreographer. Chi pointed out that an experienced choreographer should have at least four basic abilities: first, the ability to organize dance signs; second, the ability to structure dance signs; third, the ability to choreograph dance actions in series; and finally, the ability to combine and rehearse [11].

3 Methods

In this study, a four-stage process of character development and choreography was developed. To understand the problems that choreography may encounter in this four-stage process, different methods or materials were used to verify the above points at different stages. 1. At the discovery of signs stage, choreography ideation (drawing materials from the observation of common people's culture and association of sign vocabulary) was mainly carried out, and magnolia flowers and flower-selling women were obtained from descriptive secondary data collection and non-participatory observation. 2. At the stage of exploring the semantic meaning of signs, we focused on the creation and discussion of sign vocabulary association. Through a random survey at street corners and an expert survey, we obtained the general public's semantic exploration samples of adjectives of magnolia flowers/flower-selling women, and data were collected using the semantic attitude scale. Then, the focus group, that is, the choreographers of the dance troupe, further interpreted the semantic samples of magnolia flowers/flower-selling women. 3. At the stage of context analysis of signs, the author focused on the creation and discussion of sign vocabulary association and understood the respondents' description of the situation based on the first layer of sign extension and signification analysis table of Roland Barthes's two orders of signification. 4. At the stage of transformation and application of signs, from the second-order sign connotation analysis table of Roland Barthes's two orders of signification, the respondents' transferability of sign operation was understood.

3.1 Discovery of Signs

From the late 1990s to the early 2000s, with the development of Taiwanese Minnan ballads, the creation of lyrics and songs, which are different from those of the martial law period, and the songs with the theme of Taiwan's political and economic transformation and impact appeared one after another. And it cannot be found which day to start, flower women selling magnolias can often be seen on busy streets. In this study, popular ballads about magnolia were collected in advance. From the lyrics, the meanings of magnolias and their meanings from the perspective of women were compared.

The most popular type of magnolia ballads describes the hard work of flower-selling women and the bleak world and also describes the real state of the streets in Taiwan and the mockery of the uselessness of life. In the song titled Magnolia, sung and composed by Lin Qiang, Hung Wen Fang, and lyricist was Wu Xiong, the lyrics state "Wearing a hat on the head and wearing cloth shoes on the feet, regardless of sunshine or wind, smiling and soliciting customers. The traffic in the city is no problem for her. The more the red lights, the better the business. If taxi drivers buy it, thank you. If they don't buy it, thank you, too. When there is a traffic jam, they are filled with anger" [12]. In the song titled Magnolia, sung by Jiang Hui and lyrics written by Wu Xiong, the heroine performs her duty and works hard, hoping to get food and clothing, and even becomes outstanding, singing out the aspiration of a woman to support her family [13].

3.2 Exploring the Semantic Meaning of Signs

To understand the general public's impression of magnolia, at this stage, the "adjectives" of personal feelings about magnolia signs were widely collected, and to show our discretion, non-repetitive opinions were collected as far as possible to carefully select the data. Opinion interviews through random sampling without specific subjects, random sampling at street corners, and interviews with people of different ages and occupations and different views and thoughts were included in order to gather diverse viewpoints and ensure the correct interpretation of data. Forty-two people were interviewed and, after excluding invalid questionnaires, 40 questionnaires were completed. Adjective collection method: Using the morphological pictures of the four stages of magnolia growth as prompts, an "adjective" describing "what semantic association the sign of magnolia gives you" was collected from 50 samples.

At the second stage, the focus group, that is, the choreographers of a dance troupe, referred to the above and selected adjectives for cross-selection to identify the adjectives at the four stages of magnolia growth that best conforms to the spirit of "Taiwan" and can be transformed into visual signs of abstract dance performance. The experts in the focus group were five members of the choreography team, all of whom had more than 10 years of creation and teaching experience in dance or related copywriting, with professional experience of at least 10 years and at most 20 years. One had a bachelor's degree and four had master's degrees.

Through group discussion, the five creation members added four adjectives (incomplete blooming, gaudy, dehydrated, and outwardly strong but inwardly weak), with a total of 54 samples. It was proposed to select the semantic meaning of magnolia that is of a Taiwanese nature, localized, and easy to interpret for transformation to the symbolic meaning of dance To allow the five members to judge independently and not influence each other, the selection was conducted using a questionnaire survey. The questionnaire was designed based on a five-point Likert scale, and the perception degree of the imagery vocabulary of each item was judged using scores from very weak (1) to very strong (5).

Considering the demands of choreography, it was agreed that the questionnaire should include four aspects: 1. original meaning of flower language; 2. message to be conveyed; 3. creative mood; and 4. expression of adjective lexicalization into action. For each aspect, five groups of imagery vocabularies were put forward, which could appropriately express the connotation of magnolia flower language. Therefore, a total of 20 items in each flower language were investigated using a questionnaire. The final analysis and statistical results were as follows.

The first characteristic of magnolia flowers is: single bud without calyx, bud, and single calyx without support. The first imagery vocabulary was extracted as follows: (1) original meaning of flower language—independence, diligence, and self-improvement; (2) message to be conveyed—self-improvement; (3) creative mood—fearless and striving; (4) expression of adjective lexicalization into action—independence and fearlessness.

The second characteristic of magnolia flowers is that they need to be picked before blooming. The second imagery vocabulary was extracted as follows: (1) original meaning of flower language—incomplete blooming and child bride; (2) message to be conveyed—striving for survival and child bride; (3) creative mood—waiting and striving for survival; (4) expression of adjective lexicalization into action—waiting and child bride.

The third characteristic of magnolia flowers is their unique fragrance. The third imagery vocabulary was extracted as follows: (1) original meaning of flower language—persistence and altruism; (2) message to be conveyed—purity and altruism; (3) the creative mood—persistence and vulgarity; (4) expression of adjective lexicalization into action—vulgarity and altruism.

The fourth characteristic of magnolia flowers is that when the flowers wither, such as drying, dehydration, and burning, the fourth imagery vocabulary is extracted as follows: (1) original meaning of flower language—sacrifice, dehydration; (2) message to be conveyed—sacrifice, outwardly strong but inwardly weak; (3) creative mood—sacrifice, outwardly strong but inwardly weak; (4) expression of adjective lexicalization into action—enduring pain and sacrifice.

3.3 Context Analysis of Signs

At the stage of context analysis, the members of the focus group concretized magnolia flowers into the signifier of selling flowers on the street, and the signified of independence and fearlessness. Flower-selling women (the denotation of the sign for the first time) represent women who sell magnolia on the street. Then, the members of the focus group continued to explore the second order of connotation through the above discussion (see Table 1).

Table 1. Interpretation of cultural signs of "selling magnolia flowers on the street"

	Selling magnolia flowers/ Women's Mind Creation or Brand style	Selling flowers on the street/ Signifier 1/ Existential image	Independence and fearlessness/ Signified 1/ Psychological concept	Selling magnolia flowers on the street
Selling on the street/ Cultural presupposition position		Flower-selling women/ Sign: first order of denotation/ 2 (Signifier) explicit meaning/ Meaning of the sign itself		Selling in the traffic/ symbolic meaning/ 2 (Signified)/Street selling culture produced by interaction
		Selling flowers on the street to earn money to feed themselves/ Sign: second order of connotation and hidden meaning/ Folk group and identity (the human part)		

3.4 Transformation and Application of Signs

At the fourth stage, the members of the focus group transformed and applied the first order of denotation and symbolic meaning to produce the second order: connotation, produce the development framework of choreography, and explain the four connotations.

4 Results

In this theoretical and empirical research on the dance narrative theme through continuous discussion and sharing with the expert group, a consensus on choreography and movement design of character development was reached, and through repeated reconstruction by coding and decoding, the following research focuses were found:

(1) Cultural signs are signs or cultural operations on which signs are based, and their main spirit lies in transforming social and cultural phenomena into sign representations. Based on street observation and data description, this study showed that the sellers of magnolia flowers have reasons for selling them on the street. However, including the analysis of popular ballads and the description of the semantic meaning of magnolia by the public, we can also observe people's association about magnolia, a sign that is representative of women, which makes us feel that cultural signs are hidden in the soil of daily life.

(2) The choreography method of using existing signs to shape cultural signs requires beautification and sublimation of artistic creation. The cited "reference object" and the "interpreted object" have the same or similar attributes, which are conducive to the close operation of codes. This refers to women who sacrifice themselves for their families and children and are unwilling to be defeated by reality and work hard, as if they were representative of the older generation of Taiwanese women.

(3) Although observing an appropriate substitute based on common cognition to serve as the source of sign coding is highly beneficial, how does this discovery come about? Is it from the inner psychological intuition of the choreographer or a keen sense of the environment? This study helps to find the source and awareness of sign coding. This can be proven by the process of sign language extraction.

(4) The respondents introduced the general public's adjective collection of magnolia semantics at the semantic analysis stage, and all the choreography team members expressed that this could prevent creative thinking from being influenced only by the participants' past experiences or knowledge and help to expand the horizontal thinking aspect of creativity. At the same time, using the denotation and connotation transformation of Roland Barthes's two orders of signification is beneficial to master the central idea in the choreography, as well as to explore the relationships among different dance codes and the deep meanings.

5 Discussion

The working style of modern choreographers and dancers has changed gradually, from creating one-way "teaching and learning" in the past to the relationship of creation sharing and cooperation. Whether the choreographer's creative communication and the dancer's physical performance can coordinate with each other affects the quality of dance communication. Creative communication must have substantive dialogue and produce meaningful content, even to communicate with curators, to co-produce programs with interdisciplinary talents, and to communicate ideas with audiences. The researchers observed that the creative workers in Taiwan worked hard in basic training and were keen on learning and observation. Therefore, identifying a way of creative works to work with cross interdisciplinary workers that can quickly and properly optimize is a topic worth considering.

References

1. Zhang, P.Y.: On the importance of preserving and inheriting the wedding ceremony dance in Paiwan ethnic group from the viewpoint of dance education. In: 2006 Dialogue between Art and Science of Speaking and Dancing-Presentation of Cross-school Dance research Papers (2006)
2. McLean, C.P., Anderson, E.R.: Brave men and timid women? A review of the gender differences in fear and anxiety. Clin. Psychol. Rev. (6), 496–505 (2009)
3. Wei, W.L.: The application of intangible cultural signs in commodity design procedures-taking the proverbs of ghosts and gods in southern Taiwan as an example. J. Des. **16**, 69–93 (2011). (in Chinese)
4. Wikipedia: Code (n.d.). https://zh.wikipedia.org/wiki/%E7%AC%A6%E7%A2%BC. Accessed 10 Feb 2016. (in Chinese)
5. Guest, A.H.: Choreographics-A Comparison of Dance Notation Systems from the Fifteenth Century to the Present, 194 p. Routledge Publish, Oxfordshire (1989)
6. Zhang, J.H., et al.: Communication Semiotics Theory (original author: Fiske, John.) Yuan-Liou Publishing Co., Ltd., Taipei (1995). (in Chinese)
7. Pope, B.R.: Character Development: 12 Steps, Arcs, & Guides [Worksheet]. https://self-publishingschool.com/character-development/. Accessed 10 Feb 2023
8. Character (noun). https://dictionary.cambridge.org/zht/%E8%A9%9E%E5%85%B8/%E8%8B%B1%E8%AA%9E-%E6%BC%A2%E8%AA%9E-%E7%B9%81%E9%AB%94/character?q=Character. Accessed 10 Feb 2023
9. Propp, V.: Morphology of the Folktale. University of Texas Press, Austin (1968)
10. Laban, R.V., Ullmann, L.: The Mastery of Movement, 4th edn. Northcote House, Plymouth (1980)
11. Chi, J.: Discussion on how choreographers strive for novelty and uniqueness in their creations (n.d.). http://big.hi138.com/wenxueyishu/yishulilun/201110/355632.asp#.VvAFQ7lJnVI. Accessed 5 Mar 2016. (in Chinese)
12. Wu, X., Lyrics, Lin, Q., Hung, W.F.: Composing (1992). Magnolia [Recorded by ROCK RECORDS & TAPES]. On title of Q. Lin, Chhun-hong siàu-liân hia album [Medium of recording CD.] Taipei, Rock Records Co., Ltd. Publishing (1992). (in Chinese)
13. Wu, X., Lyrics, Tseng, S.Y.: Composing (2010). Magnolia [Recorded by Sony Music]. On title of J. Chiang, When I Was Getting Married album [Medium of recording CD.] Taipei UMPG Publishing (2010). (in Chinese)

Interaction Design Practice of Luohua Bird Embroidery Jacket Information in Mixed Reality Context

Chenlu Li and Songhua Gao(✉)

Inner Mongolia Normal University, No. 81, Zhaowuda Road, Hohhot, China
1163221829@qq.com

Abstract. Current cultural relics are mostly exhibited in museums, exhibition halls and other display cases and shelves. Mostly in the form of physical presentation, the audience can not fully access the information of cultural relics, and the information of cultural relics can not be fully interpreted, resulting in the public's recognition of the cultural value of cultural relics information is reduced. The design practice to Luohua bird embroidery Jacket as an example, in terms of product target positioning, refining user needs; clear content type. In terms of content and function design, screen key content; refine key content; explore transformed content. In terms of interaction design and implementation, we enhance interaction efficiency based on natural interaction principles; strengthen multimodal sensory cooperation to enhance interaction experience; mobilize subconscious behavior to enhance interaction participation. In terms of visual performance design, scenario-based design creates a sense of reality; narrative design builds a sense of presence; artistic design enhances expressiveness. We explore the issue of how to design cultural heritage information interaction in the context of mixed reality. From the perspective of heritage information interaction design as an entry point, combined with mixed reality context and features, to provide a basis and reference for heritage information interaction design, which is conducive to help improve user experience.

Keywords: Mixed Reality · Information Interaction Design · Luohua Bird Embroidery Jacket

1 Design Practice Overview

1.1 Project Background

Mixed reality is the sum of technologies between augmented reality and virtual reality. When users use the product, they interact with the environment they are in around them, which also creates a mixed reality environment that consists of a combination of human, technological, and environmental factors. Context refers to the environment in which an event takes place, so mixed reality contexts are born. The creation of new contexts brings unlimited opportunities for design. Mixed reality devices are becoming increasingly

C. Stephanidis et al. (Eds.): HCII 2023, CCIS 1834, pp. 461–469, 2023.
https://doi.org/10.1007/978-3-031-35998-9_61

mature, providing a stable hardware foundation for commercial applications. However, there is a lack of quality experience applications in the industry, and a lack of such displays for the display of heritage information. The design link also lacks mature design strategies, which limits the development process of mixed reality commercialization. To address these phenomena and problems, a mixed reality interaction design project is planned to explore solutions, taking the Luohua bird embroidery jacket as an example.

1.2 Project Objectives

The goal of this design practice project is to try to provide users with the opportunity to explore and interact with the Luohua bird embroidery jacket and participate in the communication. Under the premise of satisfying the user's needs and the need to present the artifacts, a more natural way of interaction is used to create a realistic experience and a sense of presence, allowing the user to fully understand the information of the Luohua bird embroidery jacket.

1.3 Project Content

The Luohua bird embroidery jacket is an ancient textile excavated from the cellar of the former city, site of Yuan Jininglu, in the former banner of Chahar Right Wing, Ulanqab City, Inner Mongolia Autonomous Region, China. The body is 58 cm long and the sleeves are 107 cm wide. It is a jacket with various patterns of embroidered flowers, birds and figures, and the patterns are distributed on both shoulders and the front chest. In the case of the Luohua bird embroidery jacket, Luo refers to a traditional Chinese manufacturing process, the flower and bird embroidery refers to the content of the embroidery, and the jacket refers to the style of the lapel coat of the garment. On the jacket, there are ninety-nine groups of large and small patterns, and two groups of large patterns appear on both shoulders, which are recorded as "Manchijiao". The embroidery on the surface of the jacket is the most wonderful part of this costume. The patterns are very rich and have rich artistic connotations (Fig. 1).

Fig. 1. Luohua Bird Embroidery Jacket diagram

2 Design Elaboration of Mixed Reality Visualization Part of Luohua Bird Embroidery Jacket

2.1 User Requirements and Content Categories

Targeting User Demographics and Analyzing User Needs. The three main categories of users are "browsing visitors", "clothing culture researchers" and "clothing culture enthusiasts". The users are mainly located in the three categories of "browsing visitors", "clothing culture researchers" and "clothing culture enthusiasts". Browsing visitors need to bring users a better cultural perception, experience and real clothing restoration experience, and help them understand the background knowledge related to the Luohua bird embroidery jacket. Costume culture researchers, who need to provide digital research tools, as well as the search and editing functions of costume information, with some collaborative discussion functions. Fashion culture enthusiasts, who need to understand the connotation of fashion culture in depth. Provide more visualized and interesting content.

Presentation of Content by Category. Introducing and describing the body of the embroidered bird and rosette. Includes basic information on the body of the shirt, including size, fabric, shape, pattern, production techniques, embroidery techniques, colors and styles. The introduction of this information extends the information content. This includes both historical and social information, as well as cultural and artistic information. Historical and social information includes: the characteristics of the Luo Hua bird embroidery jacket, the social impact it had, and the cultural values it embodied. The aesthetic concepts and stories, the design ideas and cultural psychology embodied, and the cultural spirit manifested.

2.2 Content and Functional Design

First, select key content. The content is collected and collated from production techniques, clothing classification, clothing pattern composition forms, pattern themes and shapes, pattern characteristics, cultural values and other aspects, to uncover information about the Luohua bird embroidery jacket. Screening can reflect the material, information, behavioural information, institutional information, spiritual information, cultural information and other important contents of traditional clothing information. Second, refining the key elements. Analyze the information, the content is coded in terms of basic information, subject categories, motif themes, motif shapes, motif image features, composition forms, symbolic meanings, cultural values and production techniques. Combining the suggestions from the interviews with research experts and related personnel, as well as the analysis of the positioning and needs of the user population, coding the content in three aspects: classification, knowledge content and graphic elements. Prepare the content for the Mixed Reality Interactive Design of the rosette. Third, mining for transformative content. The four aspects of the interaction design experience: cultural content, behavioural habits, technical features and artistic presentation are transformed, and information transformation tables are created to transform the information required by the ontology and the ontology extensions into the information required by the interaction design.

2.3 Interaction Design and Implementation

Based on the Principles of Natural Interaction to Improve Interaction Efficiency. Combined with the content refinement and information transformation tables constructed. The following process is required for the user to experience the project: after wearing the mixed reality device, the device will automatically scan the surrounding environment, at which point the user can enter the corresponding start screen of the Luohua bird embroidery jacket mixed reality information visualization display project through natural interaction such as gaze, gesture or voice. When a command is given, the home screen of the project is launched, and all experience units will also return to the home screen when they are finished. The project experience consists of seven units, which are accessed through seven entrances on the home screen. These are: Production Process, Embroidery Process, Style Explanation, Pattern Matching, Typical Patterns, Color Matching Experience, and More Patterns. At the end of the experience you will return to the home screen (Fig. 2).

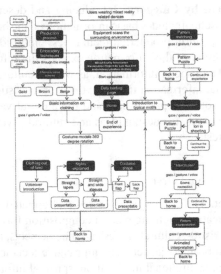

Fig. 2. Mixed Reality Interaction Design Flowchart for Luohua Bird Embroidery Jacket

Based on the content of the interaction information architecture diagram, corresponding to the information, a low-fidelity flowchart of the interaction of the Luohua bird embroidered jacket is drawn. The aim is to make the key interaction flow interaction logic clearly visible. In the typical pattern display unit, the design strategy was based on the comfort range of movement, incorporating Saara Kampari Miller's storyboard template and drawing typical pattern scenarios, placing the subject in the comfort zone at 30° left and right and 20° up and down. The most representative elements of the typical pattern are placed in the main content area at 85° on each side, 75° up and 67° down. In the peripheral areas, which extend 110° to the sides and more than 90° up and down, the corresponding supporting elements are designed. Improving the efficiency of the visualisation. The feasibility of a design strategy for visualising traditional garment information in a mixed reality context is demonstrated. In the design of the pattern matching unit, the concept of information anchoring is followed, placing the information position in front of the user's line of sight, fixed in a special position. It does not move with the device worn by the user, so that the user can only see the information when looking in the direction of the text during the experience. This helps the user to place multiple patterns in space for comparison when matching patterns, enhancing the efficiency of the user's interaction (Fig. 3).

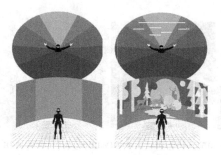

Fig. 3. Low fidelity diagram of the mixed reality interaction design of Luohua Bird Embroidery Jacket

Enhancing Multimodal Sensory Coordination to Improve the Interaction Experience. An interaction paradigm diagram was designed for the Luohua bird embroidery jacket. The design process takes into account the cognitive and behavioural patterns of human beings. Which analyses the stages of interaction experience and user emotions, aims to capture the different emotional states of the user at each stage, helping to mobilise subconscious behaviour and thus increase user engagement. The analysis of the interaction through the hardware, aims to match the hardware with the capabilities and corresponding logical judgements. Simplify data and information feedback with multimodal sensory interactions such as gesture, voice and eye movement. The rules of sound expression are analysed using background sound effects, feedback sound effects, atmospheric rendering and sound descriptions. The interaction jumping logic is analysed by means of behavioural script flowcharts. The behavioural scripting operation descriptions are explained according to the different behaviours of each stage. The exploration of the interaction design under each stage and each modality can be clarified (Fig. 4).

Mobilising Subconscious Behaviour to Enhance Interaction. On the one hand, the user is guided to make shooting actions through the dynamic design of geese flying by. After the shooting is completed, the interaction flows naturally and smoothly into the spring water and autumn mountain experience. Add guidance design. On the other hand, through the timely and accurate feedback on the action after shooting, a highlighting icon prompt appears. It fully mobilises the subconscious behaviour of the user and creates a natural and smooth interaction experience. Add natural feedback to the design (Fig. 5).

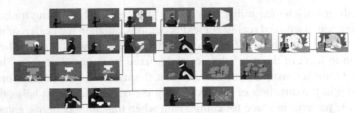

Fig. 4. Low fidelity diagram of the mixed reality interaction design of Luohua Bird Embroidery Jacket

Fig. 5. Low fidelity diagram of the mixed reality interaction design of Luohua Bird Embroidery Jacket

2.4 Visual Presentation Design

Scene Design to Create a Sense of Reality. The design of the interactive experience through aural visualisation allows for the materialisation of the language of thought. Through anthropomorphic design and realistic scene design, the immersion of the environment is experienced along with the flow of images, and the introduction of text. In conjunction with special sound effects, the user is made to feel as if they are walking through the scene, attracting them to stop and conveying the emotions and connotations of the product. Reasonable arrangement of the position of people and objects. The relationship between the size and position on the environment and the user is assumed and simulated. A strategy for rationalising the position of the user in relation to the virtual object is proposed using the interaction dimension. Makes it easier for the user to understand and receive information. Reduces the cognitive load on the user and improves the perceptibility and experience of the space (Fig. 6).

Fig. 6. Low fidelity diagram of the mixed reality interaction design of Luohua Bird Embroidery Jacket

Narrative Design Builds a Sense of Presence.   During the experience, the visualisation immersion is enhanced by setting up realistic interactions with virtual anthropomorphic objects, combined with natural interaction methods such as gesture manipulation, eye tracking and voice commands to string together the scene experience. The scene consists of a butterfly pattern extracted from the costume as a storytelling clue to build a three-dimensional spatial pattern of transforming lines. A fusion of art, science, technology, design and the natural world, it is intended to break down traditional boundaries and call for the future. The act of zooming in and out using natural gestures, with eye gaze, enables a natural interactive experience. Giving the user an artistic experience (Fig. 7).

Fig. 7. Low fidelity diagram of the mixed reality interaction design of Luohua Bird Embroidery Jacket

Artistic Design to Enhance the Power of Expression. Borrowing from the principles of artistry, the visual impact is created by magnifying the scale of objects or enlarging local elements to show clear details. This is reflected in the impact brought by style, visuals and kinetic effects. Combined with contrasting styles and realistic kinetic design, this brings about a real interactive experience and leaves a lasting memory for the user. Through movement, sound effects, visual patterns, voice explanation, etc., fully interpret the implicit information in the heritage information that cannot be vividly interpreted. To achieve the purpose of implicit information explicit expression (Fig. 8).

Fig. 8. Low fidelity diagram of the mixed reality interaction design of Luohua Bird Embroidery Jacket

Fig. 9. High-fidelity rendering of the mixed reality interactive design of Luohua Bird Embroidery Jacket

3   Conclusion

Through the analysis of the concept and characteristics of mixed reality contexts, new opportunities for digital product design from three dimensions: computer, human and environment are discovered. The design theory of natural interaction techniques, natural human interaction behaviors, and the theoretical support that can enhance user experience in rich application scenarios provide for heritage information interaction design. Further extends the application of mixed reality contexts in the field of heritage information dissemination. Extends the interpretive power of heritage information. From the level of public awareness: It helps to help the public to better understand heritage information, gradually love traditional culture, enhance the awareness of heritage information, and then create a sense of cultural identity. From the level of cultural promotion: to enhance the breadth and depth of heritage information popularization, help promote the dissemination and transmission of heritage information, while expanding the effective way of heritage information transmission (Fig. 9).

References

1. Azuma, R., Baillot, Y., Behringer, R., et al.: Recent advances in augmented reality. IEEE Comput. Graphics Appl. **21**(6), 34–47 (2001)
2. Ware, C.: Information Visualization: Perception for Design. Elsevier, Amsterdam (2012)
3. Arnheim, R.: Visual Thinking. University of California Press, California (2004)
4. Garrett, J.: The Elements of User Experience: User-Centered Design for the Web and Beyond. New Riders Press, California (2010)
5. Verhulst, I., Woods, A., Whittaker, L., et al.: Do VR and AR versions of an immersive cultural experience engender different user experiences? Comput. Hum. Behav. (7), 10 (2021)
6. Yan, Y., Yi, X., Yu, C., et al.: Gesture-based target acquisition in virtual and augmented reality. Virtual Reality Intell. Hardw. (3), 276–289 (2019)
7. Smith, K., Roughley, M., Harris, S., et al.: From Ta-Kesh to Ta-Kush: the affordances of digital, haptic visualisation for heritage accessibility. Digit. Appl. Archaeol. Cult. Heritage (8), 10 (2020)
8. Li, Y., Huang, J., Tlan, F., et al.: Gesture interaction in virtual reality. Virtual Reality Intell. Hardw. (1), 84–112 (2019)
9. Hajirasouli, A., Banihashemi, S., Kumarasuriyar, A., et al.: Virtual reality-based digitisation for endangered heritage sites: theoretical framework and application. J. Cult. Heritage (3), 10 (2021)

10. Laing, R.: Built heritage modelling and visualisation: the potential to engage with issues of heritage value and wider participation. Dev. Built Environ. (6), 10 (2020)

Research on Systematic Design Framework of Subway Public Art Based on Urban Spirit

Lian Liu[✉] and Boyuan Zhang

School of Art and Design, Wuhan University of Technology, No. 123 Luoshi Road, Hongshan
District, Wuhan 430070, China
526375339@qq.com

Abstract. In the current development of cultural cities, the role played by spiritual connotations in urban construction is crucial. The dissemination of urban spirit requires the help of a certain material medium. Systematic design is conducive to the full expression of urban spirit. The inherent spatial and temporal characteristics of the subway complement each other with public art. This article studies the relationship between urban spirit and subway public art, combines Chinese and foreign typical cases to illustrate the interaction between urban spirit and subway public art, proposes a design framework for subway public art system based on urban spirit, and explores the in-depth development direction of future urban subway design.

Keywords: Urban Spirit · Systematic Design · Subway Public Art

1 Introduction

The early 20th century had seen the commencement of public art research. After a century of growth, its study subfields have been honed, and several studies on public art in subways have surfaced. In 2018, the Los Angeles Metropolitan Transportation Administration conducted an in-depth study on many completed subway public art projects. The findings indicate that public art has a favorable impact on urban public transportation since it can increase citizens' use of the subway on a more frequent basis. Furthermore, scholars place a high value on the connection between urban growth and public art. They view public art as a vital medium for citizens to experience cities and think that public art can influence the economic development of communities. European and American countries are pioneers in urban subway engineering construction. The emergence of the public art subway can be traced back to the end of the 19th century and the beginning of the 20th century, and the Paris subway in France is the most famous. Paris in the 20th century was the center of the world's art and design field. Its subway construction has long been affected by the art and design movement, which is manifested in the artistic design of subway buildings and the implantation of a large number of public artworks. Public art is an important medium to create a subway space atmosphere, which is the most intuitive embodiment of a city subway different from other cities. At present, although there have been many studies on the relationship between subway public art and urban spirit, most of the creative themes of subway public art are the translation and presentation of cultural elements, and most of them are based on the individuality of a station, lacking the integrity and continuity of the expression of urban spirit from the perspective of the lack of layout of the whole line of the subway network. There are scattered creations, and the integrity of the public's understanding of the urban spirit has not yet been formed. A system that promotes memory reinforcement.

2   Systematic Design of Metro Public Art and Urban Spirit

2.1   The Subway Public Art Design

The term public art emerged in the United States in the 1960s, out of activities promoted by the National Endowment for the Arts and the Human Service Administration, such as "Art in the Public Domain", "Art in Architecture", etc. The subway public art limits the display space of public art within the entire subway field, and the form of expression will vary according to the carrying medium and space factors in the subway. As an important part of the city's public space, the subway carries the output and dissemination of urban culture and city image. Therefore, the subway space has become a display window for the integration of urban culture. Public art is an important part of urban cultural form, a concrete manifestation of urban culture, and an entity that spreads urban culture. Subway public art shows a city's natural geography, historical and cultural heritage, and the city's spiritual connotation and humanistic atmosphere through art forms. It can connect the history and future of a city, strengthen the image of the city in people's minds, and tell the story of a city. The story satisfies the behavioral and psychological needs of the people living in the city and the people from outside the city. Its forms of expression include paintings, art exhibits, installation art, sculptures, environmental facilities, images, landscape structures and artistic decorative design styles.

2.2   The City Spirit

The concept of city spirit can be traced back to the term spirit of place in ancient Rome. The ancient Romans believed that the world was a sacred space ruled by gods and gods. Every area in the world, such as a river, a forest, and a mountain, had its own patron saint, who gave life to people and places, and at the same time It also determines their essence and characteristics, from which the concept of local spirit arises. There is a similar concept in ancient China. Ancient Chinese Feng Shui believed that the earth contained natural aura, and there were also spirit beasts in the left, right, front, back and four directions, namely Qinglong, Baihu, Suzaku, and Xuanwu. Although people have long since given up superstitious belief in local gods, the concept of local spirits continues to this day. From the perspective of the form and expression of the urban spirit, it has the following three characteristics: the unity of the dynamics of the development of the times and the relatively stable connotation of the times; the unity of diverse and diverse content and the conciseness of expression; cultural inheritance, extension and distinctive regional characteristics sexual unity.

2.3 Systematic Design

"Systematic design" refers to the whole design process under the guidance of system science theory: in the process of design conception and preliminary planning, the system view of system science is used as the macro perspective of design, and technical science such as system theory, cybernetics, and information theory is used Based on the theory at the level of design, collect, analyze and organize information on the design subject and its environment; then use the "system engineering" theory at the engineering technology level in systems science to guide the implementation process of the design work; finally obtain the design results. The content of systematic design not only refers to the design results of self-contained systems, but also includes the whole design process from design conception, implementation planning, and step-by-step execution.

3 The Interaction Between Urban Spirit and Metro Public Art

Both urban spirit and public art are cultural. For urban spirit, urban culture is an important constituent element. For public art, culture can be the source of its creation. As an important part of the city's public space, the subway carries the output and dissemination of urban culture and city image. Therefore, the subway space has become a display window for the integration of urban culture.

3.1 Urban Spirit Promotes and Guides the Creation of the Public Art

The spirit of the city can play a guiding role in the creation of public art. First, the spirit of the city can guide the theme of public art works. An excellent work of art itself has a certain spirituality, which is closely related to its theme. Compared with non-public art, the characteristics of public art require its theme to be grasped to a certain degree and to pay attention to the real demands of the public. That is to say, the creation theme of public art can neither be a pure expression of personal emotion, nor can it be a simple accumulation of cultural symbols without doubt. The spirit of the city can provide clues to the theme of public art and help creators clarify their creative goals. Second, the spirit of the city can guide the form of public art works. At present, there are still many urban public art that are defined as "cosmetics" to beautify the urban space at the beginning of their creation, which leads to the lack of locality of the public art itself. There are many public sculptures in life, which are in the form of figurative imitation of trivial objective objects in life, and such forms are not only devoid of spirituality, but also far from satisfying the increasing aesthetic taste of urban residents. The urban spirit can provide creators with a perceptual perspective, and its rich connotations and constituent elements can provide more choices and possibilities for the implementation of public art.

The cities where "urban spirit" is relatively fully reflected in the development of subway public art mainly include New York and Paris. As a multiracial immigrant city, New York has an open, inclusive and diverse culture. The presentation of New York subway public art is mainly based on "tile murals". For example, the 12 works of Subway Portraits on 82nd Street and Second Avenue are all made by Chuck Close, made of millions of mosaic tiles. For the portraits, the artist chose artists from different countries and ages as the subjects of the paintings to reflect the diversity of passengers on the subway: old people, young people, Asians, Africans, etc. (Fig. 1). Starting from the level of "people", the diversity of races is used to reflect the richness of New York's cultural collection and to show New York's international, open, and diverse characteristics. The artwork "Life Underground" at the Eighth Avenue Subway Station on 14th Street consists of a group of bronze villains or animals hiding in corners, on wooden chairs, under stairs and other unexpected places for passengers. Multiple event scenes, such as a villain bitten by a crocodile, a villain standing on a money bag, etc. (Fig. 2). The way of expression and presentation of them breaks the limitation of scale and placement space of traditional public art, creates a relaxed and witty atmosphere for the subway space, and shortens the psychological distance between art and passengers.

Fig. 1. New York 82nd Street Second Avenue Subway "Subway Portraits"

Fig. 2. New York 14th Street-8th Avenue subway station "Life Underground"

The main feature of the public art of the Paris Metro is that the public art in its subway station is often related to the culture, history and scenic spots of the station, so that passengers can intuitively understand the information corresponding to the urban space on the ground when they are in the station. For example, the Louvre Station displays a series of sculptures and works of art that are exactly the same as the Louvre, which enhances the connection between the ground and the underground, avoids the problem of isolated underground space, and provides passengers with continuity and integrity of experience.

3.2 The Public Art Enhances and Leads the Expression of Urban Spirit

The urban spirit needs material media to be presented, and public art is a high-quality material carrier to present the urban spirit, and can vividly and concretely express and strengthen the connotation of the urban spirit, and promote the public's perception, memory and recognition of the urban spirit. People's perception of a city does not start with the city's official city spirit. Even if a city does not publish a clear expression of city spirit, the unique atmosphere of the city has already subtly affected the local residents' impression of it. In today's information age, even if people have never set foot in a city, they can learn about a city through various information sources and form a preliminary impression of the city, which may be one-sided. In short, people's perception of urban spirit starts from the interaction with the city, which is full of subjectivity. Public art can be used as an information source for people to perceive the urban spirit, making the urban spirit more obvious and intuitive.

Italian sculptor Eduardo Tresoldi created a permanent public art named "Opera" in Calabria, Italy (Fig. 3). This work takes the local cultural heritage as the basic prototype and extracts Italian classical architecture The shape of the pillars in the building is used as the material, and modern materials and technology are added with transparent attributes, so that these monuments can achieve a connected and balanced relationship with the surrounding environment, forming a majestic and transparent sense of place. The classical column structure is a reflection of the local architectural history. Under its emphasis, it aims to make people walking in it regain the admiration and pursuit of elegance and beauty passed down by Italian ancestors.

Fig. 3. "Opera" by Eduardo Tresoldi

4 Systematic Design Framework of Metro Public Art Based on Urban Spirit

4.1 Systematic Thinking Involved in Design

Design in the future will show a trend of systemization. The transformation of design from "things" to "people" represents the transformation of design from tradition to modernization, and the core value of going to the future is the transformation from "people" to "systems". The core of the design is no longer simply to meet the needs of "people", but needs to be based on the virtuous circle of the entire system, consider the three elements of "man-machine-environment", balance various relationships in the system, and integrate resources, is also the design trend of the development of subway public art in the future.

Subway public art is one of the elements in the urban public art system, and its design should first meet the overall requirements of urban public art, that is, to pursue the optimal solution within the scope of upper-level planning. From a conceptual point of view, subway public art refers to the collection of all public art works placed in the subway space. Even if it is a single piece of work, the theme, scale, form, shape, color, material, technology, etc. are all elements that make it up. For its design, it cannot only rely on the artist's personal inspiration and skills, because outside the work, The subway space environment, passenger behavior psychology and other public art works are all related elements, so it is necessary to regard the subway public art as a system.

4.2 Decomposition of Urban Spirit Elements

The generation of urban spirit comes from various characteristics of the city's natural and humanistic aspects. We can also look at the urban spirit from a systematic perspective, and regard the urban characteristics that constitute the urban spirit as elements in the system. These elements interact with each other. For example, the natural climate of a city has a great influence on the living habits of local residents, and living habits have a profound impact on the formation of residents' personalities. There is a hierarchical relationship between the elements of urban spirit. For example, a city with distinctive architectural cultural characteristics can be divided into multiple sub-elements such as landmark buildings, folk buildings, relic buildings, and religious buildings. The demand continues to be divided, which can be directly divided into various representative buildings, or divided into architectural modeling features, architectural structure features, and building material features. Therefore, the generation of urban spirit can be regarded as a layer-by-layer induction from specific elements to general elements, and its final presentation.

It is a simplified expression of urban spirit, and the reverse process is to peel off the urban spirit layer by layer, trace its source, analyze its connotation and decompose it into specific elements, so as to better embed urban spirit elements in public art in works.

4.3 Extraction of Systematic Design Elements

A public art work is composed of multiple design elements. The design elements include the theme concept, scale, expression form, technical means, shape, color and material of the work.. The urban spirit, as the condensed and sublimated characteristics of various aspects of the city, in the process of its promotion and publicity, its surface meaning is mostly abstract, so the main purpose is to highlight the urban spirit, whether it is for the planning of the public art system or for individual works The creation of each requires a process of translating the spirit of the city into design elements (Fig. 4).

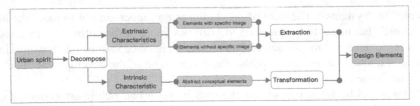

Fig. 4. The process of translation from urban spirit to design elements

4.4 Extraction of Systematic Design Elements

When extracting design elements from the more abstract urban spirit elements, it is necessary to transform the urban spirit elements first, that is, from abstraction to concrete transformation, using relatively clear objects to explain and express abstract concepts. Metaphors in rhetoric are relatively similar, so this study uses metaphors to complete the transformation of abstract urban spirit elements. The essence of metaphor is to understand and experience another thing through one thing. It is not only a language phenomenon, but also a thinking mode [1]. Linguist George Lakoff divides metaphors into entity metaphors, structural metaphors and orientation metaphors. These three methods can provide three transformation methods for abstract urban spirit elements.

First, the transformation method based on entity metaphor. Entity metaphor refers to the way of mapping abstract concepts to physical substances that people are more familiar with, and uses tangible things to represent abstract spirits, emotions, thoughts, etc. [2, 3]. For example, people often use roses to describe love, where rose is the source domain and love is the target domain. The mutual admiration between sentient individuals is invisible, but roses have remarkable characteristics such as bright colors, rich sweetness, and prickly stems. It is grief, and this similarity in feeling constitutes the relationship between roses and love. For the abstract concepts in the urban spiritual elements, we can look for the related ones, especially the physical things that can give people common or similar feelings as the transformation objects.

Second, the transformation method based on structural metaphor. Structural metaphor refers to explaining a concept with an internal structural relationship with another concept with an internal structural relationship [1]. The relationship between the two concepts is reflected in the structural correspondence, that is, each unit or component in the source domain can Corresponds to a unit or component in the target domain. For example, people often compare life to a journey. Life and travel are two independent big concepts. There are corresponding relationships between several small concepts in the two: the "birth" of life and the "starting point" of travel, and the "death" of life, and the "destination" of travel, "gain and loss" of life and "scenery along the way" of travel, "attitude" of life and "mood" of travel, etc. Using travel as a metaphor for life can be established.

Third, the transformation method based on the orientation metaphor. Orientation metaphor refers to the use of spatial orientation concepts such as up-down, front-back, inside-outside, etc. to explain and describe another concept [4]. Compared with the understanding of language and text, people's perception of spatial attributes is more intuitive and clear, so people often use the concept of space to describe abstract concepts, especially to express the degree of abstract concepts. There are many examples of orientation metaphors in everyday language, such as "high" and "low" to describe the degree of emotion, "deep" and "shallow" to describe the degree of thought. Based on the perspective of directional metaphors, openness and openness are more suitable to be expressed on a large scale, the character of perseverance and resistance is suitable to be compared to "thickness", and the sentimental and romantic literati elegance is suitable to be compared to "frivolity".

5 Research Result

As an important part of urban public transportation, the subway not only solves the travel problems of citizens, but also becomes an important carrier to promote the spiritual culture of the city due to the huge flow of people, the closed space structure and the criss-cross network of the subway. This research uses methods such as literature analysis, induction and deduction, and case study to study the systematic design framework of subway public art based on urban spirit: the decomposition of urban spirit elements, the extraction of systematic design elements, and the integration of entity metaphors, structural metaphors, and orientation metaphors. Transformation of design elements. The systematic public art design based on the urban spirit can connect the regional culture and the modern spirit, and use the subway public art design as a modern communication medium for the expansion of urban culture and the regeneration of knowledge, so as to raise public art to a higher level Cultural knowledge expansion.

References

1. Lakoff, G., Johnson, M.: Metaphors We Live By, pp. 2–9. University Of Chicago Press, America (2003)
2. Indurkhya, B.: Metaphor and Cognition. Springer, Germany, pp.101–109 (1899)
3. Wyatt, J.M.: Mrs. Dalloway: literary allusion as structural metaphor. PMLA **88**(3), 440–451 (1973)
4. Kovecses, Z.: Metaphor: A Practical Introduction, pp. 186–193. Oxford University Press, America (2002)

Newbie Guides for Omnidirectional Guidance in Head-Mounted-Device-Based Museum Applications

Yu Liu[1]([✉]), Yan Huang[2], and Ulrike Spierling[1]

[1] Hochschule RheinMain, Unter den Eichen 5, 65195 Wiesbaden, Germany
{yu.liu,ulrike.spierling}@hs-rm.de
[2] SAIC, Antuo Road 56, Jiading District, Shanghai 201800, China
huangyan06@saicmotor.com

Abstract. Novel digital museum guides using omnidirectional cues through head-mounted devices (HMDs) have been presented in previous research. However, due to the novel interaction technologies of HMDs, today's visitors are not yet familiar with these types of guides. We developed and tested instructions ("newbie guides") to help first-time users learn novel interaction patterns of HMDs, inspired by those used in website design or game tutorial design. First, we created three basic example patterns to direct attention using visual, auditory, and a combination of visual and auditory cues. Second, we created a newbie guide as an example showcase for each guidance pattern based on seven design criteria. The newbie guides were tested and evaluated in an exhibition situation, and the results indicate that the seven design criteria can assist HMD-based AR developers in creating effective newbie guides to support first-time users learn omnidirectional guidance patterns in the museum and exhibition context.

Keywords: Human-Computer Interaction (HCI) · augmented reality (AR) · head-mounted device (HMD) · spatial interface · interaction pattern · Newbie guide · omnidirectional guidance · Museum applications

1 Introduction

With the increasing prevalence of head-mounted-device (HMD)-based augmented reality (AR) applications in daily life, many developers are exploring the potential of HMDs to enhance user experiences and improve services across various areas [1,6,12]. One specific area has emerged as a significant challenge: directing user attention appropriately in the spatial interface [5,13,14]. While many individuals are accustomed to navigating 2D screen-based devices such as personal computers (PCs) and handheld devices (HHDs) [11,17,18], they may encounter difficulties with adapting to the 3D vision unit offered by HMDs, such as HoloLens 2 or Magic Leap, which require users to access interfaces in a spatial

C. Stephanidis et al. (Eds.): HCII 2023, CCIS 1834, pp. 478–485, 2023.
https://doi.org/10.1007/978-3-031-35998-9_63

environment and may present unfamiliar omnidirectional guidance patterns [3,8]. Thus, to provide positive user experiences for museum and exhibition visitors, so-called newbie guides that provide instructions on omnidirectional guidance patterns are necessary.

Newbie guides are often utilized in game design and website design to support users in learning interaction patterns and are typically integrated into applications at the outset [4,19]. These guides are intended to be used by users after the application has launched to familiarize them with the system's functionality. Employing a clicking-through interaction strategy, first-time users can learn interaction patterns step-by-step by following visual and audio cues on desktop and handheld platforms [7]. However, there is currently no project exploring how to create newbie guides for HMDs that support first-time users in learning omnidirectional guidance patterns in the exhibition sector.

In our study, we initially derived seven design criteria from the website and game design, which we adapted to create newbie guides that assist first-time HMD users in learning three omnidirectional guidance patterns (Table 1) during the exhibition visit phase [10]. Subsequently, based on the seven design criteria, we created a prototype that includes three newbie guides as example showcases for each guidance pattern. The prototypes were implemented in Unity3D and deployed to Microsoft HoloLens 2. Consequently, we evaluated the newly created newbie guide prototypes to determine whether the proposed seven design criteria can effectively serve as principles to support developers in creating newbie guides for museum visitors to learn omnidirectional guidance patterns on HMDs.

Table 1. Three Attention Guiding Patterns

	Guidance Patterns	Cues
1	Visual pattern	By displaying objects with visual flicker effect
2	Auditory pattern	By playing a series of spoken dialogues cues
3	Avatar pattern	By providing interactive visual and auditory cues

2   Related Work

Prior research has already explored how to guide users' attention on HMDs, such as with visual and audio cues [2,15,16]. Rothe et al. [16] conducted a study to investigate the effectiveness of diegetic and non-diegetic cues, including lighted objects, sound from a specific direction, movements of stationary objects (e.g., swinging), and locomotive objects, in directing viewers' attention in virtual reality environments. The study aimed to determine whether sound-connected objects attracted more attention than those without sound and whether moving objects or lights could influence the viewer's attention. Rothe and Hussmann [15] found that sound was effective in drawing the viewer's attention, but objects without sound could also guide the viewer in other directions. Chao et al. [2] investigated user behavior for guiding users' attention with both visual and audio cues. They suggested that visual attention diminishes dramatically when viewing the omnidirectional video (ODV) without sound (i.e. muted), and users' attention concentrates on salient regions when viewing ODVs with sound (i.e., mono and ambisonics). In particular, prominent auditory cues, such as human voices and sirens, and salient visual cues, such as human faces, moving objects, and fast-moving cameras, have more impact on the visual attention of participants. However, previous projects focused on the cinematic-virtual-reality sector instead of see-through augmented reality and no projects yet explored the influence of the novel gesture-based interaction patterns while learning the omnidirectional guidance pattern.

Training first-time users to learn newly developed interaction patterns is a common topic in the field of human-computer interaction (HCI). Hashimoto et al. [7] developed a flexible framework for a step-based recipe-guiding system that included grabbing and releasing interaction styles to guide users through the recipe. They concluded that their system was effective in guiding users through the cooking recipe and confirmed that step-based interaction patterns contributed to smoother human-computer interaction.

Wijaya et al. [19] analyzed the interface design for DOTA 2 to help first-time players using the ease-of-use principle. They suggested that displaying too many aspects or elements at once could overwhelm first-time users who are not yet adapted to the interface. The researchers recommended that first-time players complete the tutorial, watch matches of other players, and seek guidance from expert players.

Despite the existing research in human-computer interaction, no studies have yet proposed design guidance or principles to develop newbie guides to support first-time users in learning omnidirectional guidance patterns in museums and exhibitions.

3   Methodology

The objective of this research is to provide practical design criteria that developers can utilize to create effective newbie guides to teach first-time HMD users to use omnidirectional guidance patterns in museums and exhibitions. Initially, we developed three omnidirectional guidance patterns with visual, audio, and a combination of visual and audio cues (Table 1) based on the general visiting phase [10]. We then adapted first-time user instructions and tutorials from various fields such as game design and website design [4,19], and created newbie guide prototypes for these three patterns. Iterative pre-testing of the newbie guide prototypes was performed at an exhibition test field, resulting in the identification of seven design criteria, which are as follows:

1. Use simple and clear descriptions
2. Provide an arrow pointer as a visual cue
3. Provide a voice dialogue as an auditory cue

4. Explain the interaction workflow step by step
5. Provide a practice session for users to remember the interactive logic
6. Show the newbie guide before the use case starts
7. Repeat the newbie guide when use case changes

3.1 Prototype and Implementation

The prototype simulated a visiting pattern in which the user was first guided to the next point of interest (PoI) and then to explore the artifact at the PoI [10]. It comprised three guidance patterns, each offering both visual and audio cues.

In the visual guidance pattern, we incorporated objects with blinking effects (see Fig. 1, Left). Users had to follow blinking objects sequentially until the exploration task was completed. While testing, the user was required to locate and approach the blinking object in the scene, and we provided an arrow as an orientation pointer (see Fig. 1, Right) to guide the user in navigating the spatial interface in case of difficulty locating the mentioned object. The auditory pattern provided a series of audio dialogues that guided the user to find and follow a specified object, such as a picture of an apple on the wall. Users needed to hear the guiding dialogue instead of finding the blinking object in the physical world. Although the auditory pattern was designed to provide auditory cues only, we also used the orientation arrow to indicate the direction in which the user needed to look. In the avatar pattern, we provided an animated blue sphere (see Fig. 1, Middle) as the visual cue and a series of audio dialogues as the auditory cue to direct the user's attention. The blue sphere moved along the visit path, and the user had to locate and approach it to trigger movement to the next node. While moving from node to node, the user was prompted by an audio dialogue, such as "Please follow me" or "This way, please". We also introduced an orientation pointer to help the user follow the moving sphere around the scene.

Fig. 1. Left, object with blinking effect; Middle, the blue sphere; Right, orientation pointer arrow (Color figure online)

To provide clear and simple instructions for teaching users to learn the three guidance patterns, newbie guides were implemented in a straightforward language style [20], such as providing an auditory guiding dialogue and a written sentence "Please find the blinking object in the scene". Furthermore, we presented all the newbie guides before the first use case started and repeated them when the use case changed, for instance, when the user arrived at the PoI and before the exploration use case started. Additionally, all newbie guides were structured in a step-by-step manner, explaining the reasoning behind each interaction and how to proceed to the next step. For example, the user learns the visual guidance pattern as follows: The user had to find the blinking object in the scene first, then the user heard the guiding dialogue "please approach the blinking object" to understand the next interactions. Lastly, we included a practice session for each newbie guide in the prototype to ensure effective learning of the guidance patterns. Once the user completed the practice session, it was assumed that they had successfully learned the omnidirectional guidance patterns.

3.2   Test and Evaluation

To assess the effectiveness of the newbie guides based on seven design criteria, we conducted an initial evaluation on a testbed in an exhibition with eight participants who had no prior experience with HMD-based AR applications. Before the test session began, participants received instructions on the test and were asked to focus on learning three omnidirectional guidance patterns through separate newbie guides. During the test session, we tracked users' interactions and behaviors using the usability test method from Liu et al. [9] and provided only necessary support, such as how to wear the HMD and how to start/end the prototype. After the test session, the participants were asked to fill out a questionnaire to share their experiences and suggestions.

We assumed that our newbie guides can support first-time users in successfully learning the omnidirectional patterns. Thus, we designed the evaluation criteria based on our seven design principles. The topics we evaluated using a Likert scale in the questionnaire include the following:

1. To what extent did users understand the written descriptions and auditory guiding dialogues from the newbie guide interfaces
2. To what extent were users able to find and follow the mentioned object (e.g., blinking object/a picture of an apple/the blue sphere) in the scene
3. To what extent did the orientation pointer arrow help users find the mentioned object in the scene
4. To what extent did the step-based newbie guide explain the interaction clearly
5. To what extent did the practice session in each newbie guide support first-time users in remembering the interactive logic

3.3   Preliminary Results

Based on the results of the first test, it was found that 7 out of 8 participants agreed that they comprehended the written descriptions and auditory guiding dialogues provided by the newbie guides. However, only 6 participants agreed that they could immediately locate the mentioned object in the scene based on visual or auditory cues. Nonetheless, all participants agreed that the orientation pointer arrow proved to be useful in assisting them in locating the mentioned objects in the scene. Furthermore, 6 participants agreed that the step-based newbie guide approach facilitated their understanding of the interaction and aided in effectively following the guidance. Only 4 participants indicated that they needed to repeat the newbie guides when the use case changed. Finally, all participants agreed that the practice session played a significant role in aiding them in becoming familiar with the guidance patterns.

4   Discussion

The preliminary test results demonstrate that the step-based approach of the newbie guide, with clear and concise descriptions, is effective in facilitating users' understanding of the guiding logic and subsequent interactions. The orientation pointer arrow was found to be significant in guiding users' attention, as it can be displayed promptly on the interface when required. Additionally, participants reported that the auditory guiding dialogue was also crucial in instructing them on what to do, particularly when numerous objects were displayed on the interface, and they were able to follow the auditory cues effectively. Furthermore, the results indicate that it is essential to present the newbie guide before the use case starts, although repeating it when the use case changes may not be necessary. This may be attributed to the consistent cues provided in all use cases and the availability of a practice session that enables users to adapt to the interaction pattern effectively. Ultimately, the findings suggest that the proposed seven design criteria incorporated into our newbie guides were effective in teaching first-time users the omnidirectional guidance patterns and that they could be further developed and implemented in future HMD-based AR applications.

5   Conclusion

This research presents a set of seven design criteria that support the creation of effective newbie guides that can assist first-time users in learning omnidirectional guidance patterns on HMDs in museum and exhibition environments. A prototype was developed to demonstrate the implementation of the design criteria, which comprises three omnidirectional guidance patterns: visual guidance, auditory guidance, and a combination of both. The evaluation results indicate that providing both visual and auditory cues is essential for effective learning of the guidance patterns. The findings also suggest that the repetition of newbie guides may be necessary, depending on the complexity of the application, such as when using multiple guidance patterns to direct users' attention. Additionally, the practice session is considered a crucial opportunity for users to better understand and remember the guiding logic. Overall, the research offered insights into creating effective newbie guides for omnidirectional guidance patterns on HMDs and offers useful suggestions on how to organize effective guidance patterns to ensure positive user experiences.

References

1. Beccaluva, E.A., et al.: Using HoloLens mixed reality to research correlations between language and movement: a case study. In: Proceedings of the 2022 International Conference on Advanced Visual Interfaces, pp. 1–5 (2022)

2. Chao, F.Y., et al.: Audio-visual perception of omnidirectional video for virtual reality applications. In: 2020 IEEE International Conference on Multimedia & Expo Workshops (ICMEW), pp. 1–6. IEEE (2020)

3. Derby, J.L., Chaparro, B.S.: The challenges of evaluating the usability of augmented reality (AR). In: Proceedings of the Human Factors and Ergonomics Society Annual Meeting, vol. 65, pp. 994–998. SAGE Publications Sage CA, Los Angeles (2021)

4. Golbeck, J.: 'Back off, man. i'm a scientist'. using fiction to teach beginners HCI. Interactions 24(2), 70–73 (2017)

5. Hakulinen, J., Keskinen, T., Mäkelä, V., Saarinen, S., Turunen, M.: Omnidirectional video in museums – authentic, immersive and entertaining. In: Cheok, A.D., Inami, M., Romão, T. (eds.) ACE 2017. LNCS, vol. 10714, pp. 567–587. Springer, Cham (2018). https://doi.org/10.1007/978-3-319-76270-8_39

6. Hammady, R., Ma, M.: Designing spatial UI as a solution of the narrow FOV of Microsoft HoloLens: prototype of virtual museum guide. In: tom Dieck, M.C., Jung, T. (eds.) Augmented Reality and Virtual Reality. PI, pp. 217–231. Springer, Cham (2019). https://doi.org/10.1007/978-3-030-06246-0_16

7. Hashimoto, A., Inoue, J., Funatomi, T., Minoh, M.: How does user's access to object make HCI smooth in recipe guidance? In: Rau, P.L.P. (ed.) CCD 2014. LNCS, vol. 8528, pp. 150–161. Springer, Cham (2014). https://doi.org/10.1007/978-3-319-07308-8_15

8. Liu, Y.: Human-computer interaction patterns for head-mounted-device-based augmented reality in the exhibition domain. In: Doctoral Consortium ACM International Conference, pp. 21–26 (2022)

9. Liu, Y., Bitter, J.L., Spierling, U.: Evaluating interaction challenges of head-mounted device-based augmented reality applications for first-time users at museums and exhibitions (2023). (Prepared for publishing)

10. Liu, Yu., Spierling, U., Rau, L., Dörner, R.: Handheld vs. head-mounted AR interaction patterns for museums or guided tours. In: Shaghaghi, N., Lamberti, F., Beams, B., Shariatmadari, R., Amer, A. (eds.) INTETAIN 2020. LNICST, vol. 377, pp. 229–242. Springer, Cham (2021). https://doi.org/10.1007/978-3-030-76426-5_15

11. Myers, B.: Challenges of HCI design and implementation. Interactions 1(1), 73–83 (1994)

12. Neb, A., Brandt, D., Awad, R., Heckelsmüller, S., Bauernhansl, T.: Usability study of a user-friendly AR assembly assistance. Procedia CIRP 104, 74–79 (2021)

13. Pillai, J.S., Ismail, A., Charles, H.P.: Grammar of VR storytelling: visual cues. In: Proceedings of the Virtual Reality International Conference-Laval Virtual 2017, pp. 1–4 (2017)

14. Pillai, J.S., Verma, M.: Grammar of VR storytelling: narrative immersion and experiential fidelity in VR cinema. In: The 17th International Conference on Virtual-Reality Continuum and Its Applications in Industry, pp. 1–6 (2019)

15. Rothe, S., Hußmann, H.: Guiding the viewer in cinematic virtual reality by diegetic cues. In: De Paolis, L.T., Bourdot, P. (eds.) AVR 2018. LNCS, vol. 10850, pp. 101–117. Springer, Cham (2018). https://doi.org/10.1007/978-3-319-95270-3_7

16. Rothe, S., Hußmann, H., Allary, M.: Diegetic cues for guiding the viewer in cinematic virtual reality. In: Proceedings of the 23rd ACM Symposium on Virtual Reality Software and Technology, pp. 1–2 (2017)
17. Shneiderman, B., Plaisant, C., Cohen, M.S., Jacobs, S., Elmqvist, N., Diakopoulos, N.: Designing the user interface: strategies for effective human-computer interaction. Pearson (2016)
18. Westerman, W., Elias, J.G., Hedge, A.: Multi-touch: a new tactile 2-D gesture interface for human-computer interaction. In: Proceedings of the Human Factors and Ergonomics Society Annual Meeting, vol. 45, pp. 632–636. SAGE Publications Sage CA, Los Angeles (2001)
19. Wijaya, A.D., Baskara, F., Kusuma, M.R., Bernhard, R.S., Senjaya, R.: Ease of use analysis of in-game interface design in DotA 2 for beginners using SAW method. In: 2015 International Conference on Information & Communication Technology and Systems (ICTS), pp. 123–126. IEEE (2015)
20. Yampolskiy, R.V.: Human computer interaction based intrusion detection. In: Fourth International Conference on Information Technology (ITNG2007), pp. 837–842. IEEE (2007)

A Study on Exhibitions of Art Interventions for Environmental Sustainability in Rural Communities

Li-Shu Lu[✉] and Jia-Yi Liu

Department and Graduate School of Digital Media Design, National Yunlin University of
Science and Technology, Douliu, Taiwan
luls@yuntech.edu.tw

Abstract. In view of the increasing importance of artistic activities as a bridge
of interpersonal communication that also influences the vitality and attractiveness
of rural communities, this study aims to explore the models of exhibitions that
enable the integration of art into environmental sustainability in rural communities on the basis of the theory of strategy pyramids. Firstly, case studies on rural art
in Taiwan and Japan were presented. Then, in-depth interviews with experts were
conducted to reflect on the strategies of art intervention in exhibitions and explore
the methods of curation to propose the models of rural exhibitions. The results
show: (1) Rural curation might undergo comprehensive consideration and rolling
corrections based on the four strata of preliminary consideration, tactics, strategies,
and operational plans. (2) The dimensions concerning the curating strategies from
the four strata are the five ideas of curation from the perspective of preliminary
consideration (communication with regional leadership for recognition, the integration of resources and funds, the operation of regional characteristics, friendly
regional environments, and the joint engagement of regional residents). (3) The
objective of curation from the perspective of strategies is the joint creation of a
good rural living environment and the development of rural attractiveness, and the
means and methods of exhibitions from the perspective of tactics are the ways of
participatory design with an orientation to rural attractiveness in accordance with
the seasonal environmental features. (4) The action plans of various dynamic or
static exhibitions can be planned from the perspective of operational plans (such
as art installations, life experience, ecological tours, production applications, fair
events, trip passports, theme lectures, and propitious prayers in festivals and celebrations). Meanwhile, the integration of resources and the concerted efforts and
benefit sharing between related parties in communities are important aspects of
thinking for developing rural attractiveness. These two aspects are conducive to
the sustainable development of rural communities.

Keywords: Rural Communities · Exhibition Strategy · Art Intervention · Rural
Sustainability

C. Stephanidis et al. (Eds.): HCII 2023, CCIS 1834, pp. 486–498, 2023.
https://doi.org/10.1007/978-3-031-35998-9_64

1 Introduction

As the development of rural regions is limited by population aging, the outflow of young people, and the industrial decline, the central government departments of Taiwan have successively introduced targeting policies in the hope of restoring rural value and fashioning the new rural landscape. The Ministry of Culture has promoted the movement of life aestheticization in Taiwan since 2008 to enrich the culture and improve the quality of living environments. Since then, urban and rural regions in Taiwan started to conduct regional revitalization and to connect rural regions with the world through the means of art intervention spaces, such as art celebrations and art festivals. Many urban and rural areas convene these activities in cities, such as the Royal Edinburgh Military Tattoo and the Inside Out Project London. Meanwhile, quite a few of them in Japan are held on small islands or villages which lack access to transportation and are sparsely populated, including the famous cases of the Echigo-Tsumari Art Triennial and the Setouchi Triennale, to promote the tourism and economy in these rural regions. Therefore, an attractive design can be created by capturing the essence of the attractiveness of the product by understanding the consumption choices of consumers (Asano, 2001). Besides attracting visitors with an orientation to attractiveness, the protection of the ecological environment is also an important issue. Huang (2013) shared the ecological tour in Satoyama, Japan, and discusses the possibilities of building ecological communities based on the concept of Satoyama. The United Nations Educational, Scientific and Cultural Organization (UNESCO) (2010) defines Satoyama as a socio-ecological production landscape, or an interactive landscape of humans and land use under the long-term interaction between human and natural factors that simultaneously maintains biodiversity and provides humans with what they need for living (Lee, 2011). The Satoyama spirit emphasizes the close interaction and connection between the natural environmental ecology and humans' well-being. Moreover, with the aim of building a harmonious coexistence between human beings and nature, the Satoyama vision is in line with production, life, and ecology in rural construction, and in conformity with the idea of development for coexistence and common prosperity.

Manning (1983) construed festival events as exhibitions that are the theatrical representations of cultural symbols. As art festivals have the characteristics of popularity, collectivity, and the potential to integrate into the people the crowd, they are closer to the people than other artistic forms. It is a noteworthy trend in recent years that artistic exhibitions are leaving museums and entering regional society (Huang, 2014). Under the influence of street corner museums and the integration of artistic exhibitions into everyday life, the planning of the methods of exhibitions has become one of the instruments of strategic formulation for community construction. A case of street corner museums is the Daxi Wood Art Ecomuseum in Taoyuan, Taiwan. The museum adopts the idea of museums without walls, which also means that the community landscape of streets and street corners in everyday life that can be seen everywhere has become the cultural exhibits of the museum without walls, and the small stories and life experiences of everybody are the precious items on display in the museum without walls (Cheng, 2016). The integration of art creation into communities and the choice of social public spaces as the stages of exhibitions are all local cultural practices that cannot be ignored in recent years, as well as the ways and trends of regional revitalization. Meanwhile, the concept of post-museums emphasizes the process of local practices, which creates locally-specific patterns of exhibitions based on local features and characteristics. In this concept, it has also been mentioned that time is the process, and experiences and activities grant different cultural exhibitions on communities as time goes on. In general, the concept of regarding artistic activities as the bridge of interpersonal communication has received increasingly more attention, which is sufficient to manifest the influence of using the form of artistic exhibitions to unite people and revitalize regions. Due to this influence and the development of rural tourism, rural regions not only serve as bases of supply products but also have more possibilities for development. Therefore, this study aims to regard rural regions as spaces for exhibitions; in other words, it considered the possibilities of the whole rural communities being the art galleries and the museums of cultural representation. This study also explored the ideas and methods of integrating art topics into rural curation from the perspective of the theory of strategy pyramids.

2 Literature Review

2.1 The Theory of Strategy Pyramids and the Thinking of Curation

Hosoya (2011) proposed that formulating correct and successful strategies was like a pyramid of thinking, in which the top stratum was the thinking of strategies that focused on the consideration of visions, missions, objectives, and directions, the second stratum was the thinking of tactics, by which coping strategies and plans were considered and the optimal plan was selected with the basic assumptions on the stratum of strategies as the guideline, and the third stratum was the thinking of operational plans, which mainly involved action plans and project management, as well as the implementation of the action plans based on the needs of the tactical plans. Chen (2015) thought about exhibitions through a sequential route of strategies, tactics, and the operational plan. In this sequential route, the corresponding curators form a linear hierarchy of guidance, which means that the curators in the stratum of strategies would guide the curators in the stratum of tactics, while the latter would guide those in the stratum of operational plans. Meanwhile, the curating teams form an inverted linear hierarchy of support, which means that the achievement of the strategic objectives relies on the implementation of the tactical plan, while the effect of the tactical plan relies on the realization of operational plan. Shown in Fig. 1 (Isao Hosoya, 2011; Chen J. L., 2015).

The concept of curation signifies the endowment of value for exhibits or information and the subsequent creation of ideas that are sufficient to provoke resonance. And people who curate are called curators (He, 2012; Chen, Chen, and Lin, 2014). Both recognized collections and developing creations are a part of the history and the wealth of all humans. Therefore, the position of a curator has three key responsibilities, i.e., preservation and protection, research and discussion, as well as education and promotion (Lin, 2013). Blythe (1999) mentioned that in order to build a good channel of communication with visitors at exhibitions, it must be noticed: (1) We must make visitors engaged in the exhibitions; (2) the information delivered to visitors must be understandable; (3) the information must provoke their interest; and (4) the curators must communicate with visitors using the same language (Chen, Chen, and Lin, 2014). Today, as exhibitions have

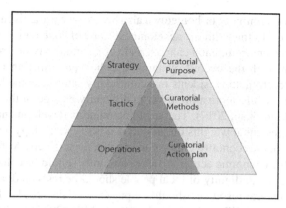

Fig. 1. The strategy pyramid is combined with the thinking of curation strategies.

become a common medium for marketing, curators are motivated to accept a proactive role in enhancing the significance and values of artists and their creations (Chen, 2016).

2.2 Art Intervention Spaces and the Concept of Post-museums

In recent years, the development of art intervention spaces has changed the definitions and perceptions of art so that art can intervene in public lives softly and in a low profile (Lu, 2014). In the perceptions of traditional society, the actions in art intervention spaces concentrate on the interactions between artists and society, and the importance of the process of intervention is larger than that of the final yield (Chang, 2011; Tung, 2013). Suzanne Lazy proposed the concept of the New Genre Public Art, which interacts with an extensive and diversified range of the public on the basis of participation. Its essence is a social intervention that has developed artistic creations with public value (Tung, 2013). In the process of art intervention, many artists reflect local histories, cultures, feature industries, and social topics in their works to promote the development of the cultural industry. Moreover, an ecological museum does not take a fixed form. It can be a community museum, a street museum, a regional cultural center, a museum of the living environment, and a regional cultural park. As the concept discussed above gradually emerges, the paradigm of post-museums is formed (Liao, 2014). Hooper-Greenhill (2000) emphasized that the process of practices and the empirical nature of post-museums in regions are jointly produced in the regional life of people from different community groups, and the concept of post-museums is dynamic (Liao, 2014; 2016). As the development of museums attaches increasingly more importance to rationality, Chen (2004) argued that museums are in the process of becoming community-based, and as the theory of community museums is inferred from practices, it shows a new direction for community construction.

2.3 Community Construction and Rural Attractiveness

Asano (2001) points out that by understanding the way consumers select products and the successful experience of product design, we can capture the attractiveness of products, and similarly, our community or hometown also has its own attractiveness and contains surprising treasures. In line with the development trend of "one region with one characteristic", the unique environmental characteristic of a community or a region is regional attractiveness. Through the overall planning and their participation in the process of community construction, the residents in a community can awake the love of all for the land and the home while motivating them to diligently engage in the actions of community revitalization (Kao, 2017). The key to community development is a sustainable approach that places equal weights on production, life, and ecology, which correspond to the dimensions of the economy, culture, and nature, respectively. As for the dimension of the economy, the economic activities in a community should be enhanced; as for that of culture, the ideas and dignity of local people should be respected; and as for that of nature, the local natural resources should be preserved (Hus, 2011). The three factors of rural attractiveness of villages proposed by Lu and Lin (2017) are human touch, natural landscapes, and the agricultural industries, which exactly correspond to the "life, ecology, and production" in rural regions. For "life - human touch", the interpersonal emotional communication between local residents are friendly and cordial, which fosters a lifestyle with the attractiveness of human touch. For **"ecology** - natural landscapes", due to the influence of the geological environments, villages have rich ecological resources, and the natural ecological landscapes become one of the factors of the attractiveness of villages. For "production - agricultural productivity", the production of a diverse range of crops that enables tourists to purchase local agricultural products also proves to be the attractiveness of villages. If the life, production, and ecology in rural regions can be comprehensively taken into consideration, not only the rural attractiveness can be fostered but also a sustainable approach to rural exhibitions can be created.

3   Research Methods and Process

The research procedure of this study includes two steps, discussions and in-depth interviews. The discussions about the strategies of artistic exhibitions in Taiwan and Japan mainly focused on case studies related to art seasons using the theory of strategy pyramids and exhibition strategies. In-depth interviews with regional curators were carried out and comprehensively summarized to form a model of strategies for exhibitions based on environmental sustainability in rural communities. The research process is shown in Fig. 2.

3.1   Case Study: The Art Seasons in Taiwan and Japan

The sources of cases were mainly from literature, websites, and relevant books. Furthermore, the inclusion criteria were cases in the face of the impact of population aging and population outflow, and those with the intervention of art festivals in rural regions. Our findings are detailed in Table 1.

As the method of analysis is based on the definition of the strategic curation proposed by Chen (2015), the strata of strategies, tactics, and operational plans are defined as the objectives of exhibitions, the methods and plans of exhibitions, and the operations and action plans of exhibitions, respectively. Moreover, the analysis was conducted in accordance with the definition of each stratum, which was also the basis of the subsequent interviews with regional curators.

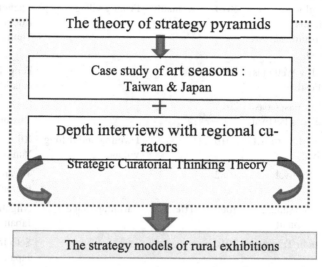

Fig. 2. The research process

3.2   In-Depth Interviews: Ideas of Curators

In-depth interviews were conducted with regional curation experts with more than five years of experience, and the relevant data are shown in Table 2.

The research process: Firstly, an interview with an expert was conducted, before the outline of the official interview was finalized through revisions. Then, the semi-structured interviews with two experts were conducted based on the outline of the official interview. Finally, the content of the interviews with the three experts was analyzed qualitatively, and the data of the interviews were encoded uniformly.

4   Result and Discussion

4.1   Case Studies Related to Art Seasons in Rural Regions

This study was based on the rural background types of the cases, and the cases concerned were either under the influence of population aging and population outflow or related to the intervention of art festivals in rural regions. Through case studies on the exhibitions of art seasons in rural regions and the application of the theory of exhibition strategies, the comparison of the individual cases of exhibitions of art seasons in rural regions and the relationship matching in the form of the pyramid of exhibition strategies were separately presented. The cases include four cases of farming villages (the Taiwan East Coast Land Arts Festival, the Xiluo Modern Art Festival, the Toga Festival, and the

Table 1. Cases of art seasons in rural regions (Compiled by this study)

Country	Name of Case	Period	Cycle	Type	Location
Taiwan	Chenglong Wetlands Environmental Art Season	2010	Annually	Fishing village	Chenglong Village, Kouhu Township, Yunlin County
	Mipaliw Wetlands Art Festival	2011			Fengbin Township, Hualien County
	Taiwan East Coast Land Arts Festival	2015			East coast of Taiwan
	Xiluo Modern Art Festival	2016		Farming and fishing village	Xiluo Township, Yunlin County
Japan	Toga Festival	1982			Togamura, Toyama Prefecture, Japan
	Echigo-Tsumari Art Triennial	2000	Triennial	Farmingvillage	Niigata Prefecture, Japan
	Setouchi Triennale	2010			Seto Inland Sea, Japan
	Oku-Noto Triennale	2017			Suzu-shi, Ishikawa Prefecture, Japan

Table 2. The relevant data (Compiled by this study)

N	Seniority	Gender	Educational and experiences	Experiences of curation
E01	11年	Male	Architectural art, regional curation	Elegant Farmers, Liberating Villages with Youth, and Togo Rural Village Art Museum
E02	11年	Female	Law, visual arts, urban design	City Yeast, Parent Child Market, Re-create Taipei Parks Project, and Design for Street Corners
E03	5年	Male	Regional cultural centers and community construction, urban revitalization	Coal · Memory - Taiwan-Japan Coal Mine Culture Special Exhibition, and Taoyuan City Daxi Wood Art Ecomuseum

Echigo-Tsumari Art Triennial), two cases of fishing villages (the Chenglong Wetlands Environmental Art Season and the Setouchi Triennale), and two cases of farming and fishing villages (the Mipaliw Wetlands Art Festival and the Oku-Noto Triennale). The forms and characteristics of all cases of rural art exhibitions are presented below, as Table 3.

Table 3. The forms and characteristics of all cases of rural art exhibitions

Case name	Description	Excemple of picture
Taiwan		
Chenglong Wetlands Environmental Art Season	International environmental artists were invited to join teachers and students in the Chenglong Elementary School and the local residents to complete a large-scale outdoor piece of artwork, and evoke the attention of the community and the social public to the topics of the environment of wetlands through the participatory process.	
The Mipaliw Wetlands Art Festival	Mipaliw means mutual assistance in Amis. Artists from various places were invited to live in the village, interact with the tribe, and collaborate with the tribe in artistic creation, so as to experience the relationship of mutual assistance in the artistic narration of social ecology and production in the Satoyama Initiative.	
Taiwan East Coast Land Arts Festival	An art festival with the theme of the natural environment, tribal life, and habitat of the East Coast. Through artist-in-residence, art installations, and events, tourists can generate dreams in the domain.	
Xiluo Modern Art Festival	With artistic creation, the proposal for the transformation of Xiluo Bridge was evoked, which echoed the process and spirit of the revitalization of Xiluo Old Street, and exhibited the abundant artistic and cultural features of Xiluo.	
Janpan		
The Toga Festival	The Toga Festival which first commenced in 1982 is Japan's first largest international theater festival. It has promoted the local economy through the development of sightseeing tours.	
The Echigo-Tsumari Art Triennial	With farmland as the stage and art as the bridge, artists entered the community and integrated into the local environment to create multiple pieces of artwork that are full of local natural and cultural features.	
The Setouchi Triennale	Through activities, such as art installations, the convention of catering parties, knitting workshops, the participation in community beautification, and local festivals, the island's economy has been effectively promoted. Furthermore, the migrated residents of the island have come back, and the vitality has gradually been restored.	
The Oku-Noto Triennale	Through the conversations between art and land, the international and the local, as well as artists and villagers, joint efforts were made to explore the potential local attractiveness, and new ideas were inspired through the collision of the festival culture and modern art.	

In this study, it was found that the main objective of the cases of art seasons is to activate the local region, convey spirits, ideas, and proposals by the means and medium of art, and attract tourists through art to bring a sense of identity to local residents. In general, the common operational methods for art seasons include inviting artists to live and create locally, hiring volunteers, the participation of school teachers and students, the participation of and cooperation with residents, the scattering of artworks throughout a village, using local materials for art creation, the planning of local tours, and re-purposing unused spaces. The action plans include the convention of art lectures, concerts, fairs, and workshops, selling cultural and creative products, promoting local specialties, and the implementation of touring passports for art seasons.

4.2   The Views of the Regional Curators

As for the dimensions of thinking and processes of practices of the three curators in terms of regional curation, including the objectives, methods, means of implementation, and dimensions of thinking of exhibitions, the analysis focused on items that were mentioned at least by two experts. Therefore, the exhibition objective is a good life, the means of implementation of exhibitions is the consideration of the concept of community construction, and the dimensions of thinking of exhibitions should at least include communication for regional recognition, the integration of resources and funds, long-term regional operations, friendly regional environments, and the engagement of regional residents. Meanwhile, the three experts used different exhibition methods, and they were the application of the features of the seasonal environmental scenarios, the utilization of unused spaces in old buildings, and the participatory design and interactions as Table 4.

The views of the experts towards exhibitions in the domain of rural regions are the shaping of exhibitions (the accumulation of experience, the policies in Taiwan, and the regional pulses) and the real situations (the rotation and short-term operations of ruling parties, and the environmental advantages of rural regions in Taiwan).

4.3   Case Studies and the Comprehensive Analysis of the Views of the Curators

In light of the case studies related to art seasons and the analysis of the interviews with curators, this study comprehensively presented the following summary. In the cases related to art seasons, the operational methods of scattering artworks throughout a village and using local materials for art creation corresponded to the curators' method of the application of the features of the seasonal environmental scenarios. Meanwhile, re-purposing unused spaces corresponded to the curators' method of utilizing unused spaces in old buildings. The operational methods of inviting artists to live and create locally, hiring volunteers, the participation of school teachers and students, and the participation of and cooperation with residents corresponded to the curators' method of the application of the participatory design and interactions. Furthermore, the planning of local tours corresponded to all three curators' methods. In conclusion, the hierarchy of strategic strata of regional exhibitions in rural regions proposed in this study is: (1) The stratum of preliminary thinking is the overall objectives; (2) the stratum of strategies is the exhibition objectives; (3) the stratum of tactics is the means and methods of implementation in sequence; and (4) the stratum of operational plans is the action plans, as Fig. 3.

Table 4. The dimensions of thinking and processes of practices of the three curators

		E01	E02	E03	Total
Purpose	Changing people's perception about rural regions, speaking for residents, and jointly creating a better life	●	●	●	3
Methods	Features of the seasonal environmental scenarios	●			1
	Utilization of unused spaces in old buildings		●		1
	Participatory design and interactions			●	1
Implementation	Ways of community construction	●		●	2
	Grounded studies on proposals		●		1
	Course education and training			●	1
Dimensions of thinking of exhibitions	Communication for regional recognition	●	●	●	3
	Integration of resources and funds	●	●	●	3
	Long-term regional operations	●	●	●	3
	Friendly regional environments	●		●	2
	Convenient transportation, catering, and accommodation			●	1
	Participation of regional residents	●	●	●	2
	Demand of tourists			●	1

The five dimensions of the overall objective are communication for regional recognition, the integration of resources and funds, long-term regional operations, friendly regional environments, and the participation of regional residents. Only by clarifying them can we further clarify the real needs of a region and formulate the implementation objectives for each stage as Table 5.

The exhibition objective focuses on changing people's perception of rural regions, speaking for regional residents, solving regional problems and jointly creating a better regional life. The means of implementation of exhibitions: Experts believe that local cultures can be preserved and revitalized by the means of seeking memories, preserving scenarios, recurring scenarios, and avant-garde reproduction. The exhibition methods: (1) the application of the features of seasonal environmental scenarios (scattering artworks throughout every corner of a village, and making them a part of the village's landscape and exhibits in a seasonal exhibition, thereby making them a feature of the village); (2) the utilization of unused spaces in old buildings (clearing unused spaces in a village, renovating them into exhibition spaces, restaurants, and bed and breakfast, granting them new values, and forming the pattern of "the environmental village is the

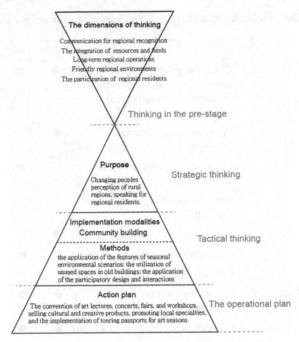

The dimensions of thinking

Communication for regional recognition
The integration of resources and funds
Long-term regional operations
Friendly regional environments
The participation of regional residents

Thinking in the pre-stage

Purpose

Changing peoples
perception of rural
regions, speaking for
regional residents.

Strategic thinking

Implementation modalities
Community building

Methods

the application of the features of seasonal
environmental scenarios; the utilization of
unused spaces in old buildings; the application
of the participatory design and interactions

Tactical thinking

Action plan

The convention of art lectures, concerts, fairs, and workshops,
selling cultural and creative products, promoting local specialties,
and the implementation of touring passports for art seasons.

The operational plan

Fig. 3. The strategic ideas for the exhibitions of art seasons in rural regions

exhibition space of life" through the connection between each other); and (3) the application of the participatory design and interactions (giving more possibilities to the events of artistic exhibitions in rural regions through inviting artists to live and create locally, hiring volunteers, the participation of school teachers and students, and the participation of and cooperation with residents). The operational plan includes the convention of art lectures, concerts, fairs, and workshops, selling cultural and creative products, promoting local specialties, and the implementation of touring passports for art seasons. Based on the results of the strategy pyramid for regional exhibitions in rural regions, the procedure of each stratum, including preliminary consideration, strategies, tactics, and operational plans.

Table 5. The five dimensions of regional curation.

Five dimensions of curation	Explanation
Communication for regional recognition	The strategies and techniques of communication with regions include taking advantage of the introduction and assistance of agencies, which can help you gain local information and trust more efficiently
The integration of resources and funds	You must learn about local human resources and find key persons to master local information and resources; the assistance of funds is also a necessary part of curation for bargaining
long-term regional operations	You must think about whether you can actually activate a rural domain, and formulate operational strategies from the perspective of long-term operations
Friendly regional environments	You must consider the environmental equilibrium and tourist load capacity of a region, think about the safety of an exhibit, or whether an exhibit can withstand the environmental factor and the climate, and you should not take into account a strategy that can devastate the landscape features of a region
The participation of regional residents	You must give a sense of engagement, belonging, achievement, glory, and recognition to regional residents

5 Conclusion

The diversity of terrain and environments in Taiwan, including cities, forestland, farmland, and mountainous areas, gives birth to different regional cultural features. When these features are integrated, a domain-based land arts season is generated, which also echoes the core concept of the Satoyama Initiative, the landscape of "social ecology and production". This concept refers to the landscape features generated through the long-term interactions between humans and nature, i.e., cultural heritage. This study proposes that above the entire strategy pyramid for exhibitions, there should be another stratum of preliminary consideration which includes five dimensions to serve as the overall objective. Through the comprehensive consideration of the four strata of exhibition strategies, the sustainable development of environmental artistic exhibitions in rural regions can be made possible. Based on the "life, ecology, and production" in rural regions, rural attractiveness can be inferred through discussions. As a result, the sustainable development of rural attractiveness, as well as environmental conservation, can be further achieved in line with the ideas of the Satoyama Initiative, and in virtue of the cooperation and resource sharing between different rural settlements.

References

Asano, H.: Practice of Attractiveness Engineering. Kaibundo, Kuala Lumpur (2001)

Blythe, J.: Visitor and exhibitor expectations and outcomes at trade exhibitions Marketing. Intell Plan. 17(2), 100–110 (1999)

Chen, C.-L.: The movement of community museums: a global perspective. Museol. Quart. 18(4), 43–57 (2004)

Hung,C.-P.: Beyond the Spectacle: The Study of Local Arts Festivals in Taiwan, Master's thesis, Taipei National University of the Arts (2009)

Chang, C.-W.: Art in public spaces as a new genre of art -a research on it's position of the art world. Art Papper Publ. 16(17), 55–70 (2011)

Cheng, W.T.: The Daxi street corner museum - experiencing the beauty of culture (2016)

He, F.P.: What do curators curate? Business Next (2012)

Hooper-Greenhill, E.: Museums and the Interpretation of Visual Culture. Routledge, London (2000)

Hosoya, I.: The problem-solving pyramid: Figuring out Why, What, and How makes you work without worries (The original author: Isao Hosoya). Commonwealth Publishing, Taipei City (2011)

Huang, S.H.: An article of a special interview: think nicely ~ the ecological life in japan (2013). Author: Jui-Kun Kuo from PTS News Network

Huang, C.Y.: Regional reproduction, artistic exhibitions, and citizen participation - an overview of society-based artistic exhibitions in Japan since the 1990s. Nat. Center Tradit. Arts Bimonth. 112, 62–73 (2014)

Chao, J.-T.: Satoyama, a type of socio-ecological production landscape 88, 04–13 (2014)

Chen,J.-L.: Strategic curation, doctoral dissertation. National Taiwan University of Arts Creative Industry Design Institute, Taipei (2015)

Kao, S.K.: Constructing the regional attractiveness and community aesthetics of Shui Fan Jiao (2017)

Lee, K.C.: A new thinking for rural landscape conservation - the Satoyama Initiative. Taiwan Forest. J. (2011)

Lu, J.-T.: Art intervention in communities conducted by Taipei fine arts museum-a case study. J. Art Calligrap. 16, 145–174 (2014)

Lu,L.-S., Yi-Wun, L.:. A Study on Exhibition Model of Traditional Display and Art Intervention in Rural Areas. Design Value and Sensibility Practice Papers. Fo Guang University, Yilan (2017)

Manning, F.E.: The Celebration of Society: Perspective on Contemporary Cultural Performance. Bowling Green State University Popular Press, Ohio (1983)

Qiu, M.-Y.: Bajen experience and the Satoyama vision in Taiwan. 88, 60–71 (2014)

Lin, T.S.: The cultivation of curators: examining the US principles and standards. J. Des. 18(4), 23–40 (2013)

Chen, M.-T.: An investigation of the requirements of curators in science museum. J. Sci. Technol. Mus. 20(2), 5–24 (2016)

Chen, S.-J., Chen, J.-L., Lin, C.-L.: A study on curatorial communicability: the case of "the origins of Taiwan" exhibition. J. Des. 19(3), 01–22 (2014)

Liao, S.-C.: Local practices of post-museums: treasure hill. Museol. Quart. 28(2), 35–71 (2014)

Liao, S.-C.: Post-museum art exhibitions: a case study of the rubber duck in Keelung City. Museol. Quart. 30(4), 73–97 (2016)

Tung, W.-H.: Art intervention into the community: a socially engaged aesthetics and art practice. J. Art Res. 2, 27–37 (2013)

Digital Information Provision on Gastronomic Tourism

Vassiliki Neroutsou[1], Michalis Methimakis[1], Eirini Kontaki[1,2],
Emmanouil Zidianakis[1], Argiro Petraki[1], Eirini Sykianaki[1], Stavroula Ntoa[1],
Nikolaos Partarakis[1(✉)], George Kapnas[1], and Constantine Stephanidis[1,2]

[1] Institute of Computer Science, Foundation for Research and Technology—Hellas (FORTH),
70013 Heraklion, Crete, Greece
{vaner,methimakis,ekontaki,zidian,argpet,eirinisi,stant,
partarak,gkapnas,cs}@ics.forth.gr
[2] Computer Science Department, School of Sciences and Engineering, University of Crete,
70013 Heraklion, Crete, Greece

Abstract. In this paper we present the design and implementation of a multi-modal solution for the promotion of gastronomic tourism in the municipal area of Heraklion city. The provided solution is comprised of standalone information systems accompanied by a mobile app for the presentation of thematic routes. By facilitating a rich knowledge base and a collection of audiovisual material, the applications allow the visitor to explore dimensions of tangible and intangible cultural heritage connected to gastronomy and plan a personalised experience orchestrated by their mobile device while on the move in the municipal area.

Keywords: digital information · mobile guides · info-kiosks · gastronomic tourism

1 Introduction

The concept of sustainable development can be perceived as a convergence between economic development and environmentalism [1]. It was officially illustrated at the Stockholm Conference on Humans and the Environment in 1972 promoting the concept of eco-development [2]. Recently, growing emphasis has been placed on tourism experiences, the culinary tradition of a destination and the existence of indigenous products that could support a gastronomic destination [3].

In this paper, we focus on the region of Crete which has remarkable natural, cultural, and historical resources [4, 5]. The main motivation behind this work is that although Crete as a destination is rich in resources, the island attracts, almost entirely, package tourism [6, 7]. For instance, in 2002 the three main activities of visitors to Greece were swimming/sunbathing, dining outside the accommodation establishment, shopping and visitating cultural sites [8].

C. Stephanidis et al. (Eds.): HCII 2023, CCIS 1834, pp. 499–509, 2023.
https://doi.org/10.1007/978-3-031-35998-9_65

In the domain of gastronomy and tourism, several works have underlined that a large number of destinations use gastronomy as a tourism marketing tool, and may also use tourism to promote gastronomy [9]. At the same time, this has been identified as a meaningful marketing tool that could contribute to a market segment on a destination [10].

In this paper, we are addressing the need for gastronomic experiences on the island of Crete and in particular the municipal area of Heraklion city and the villages nearby. To support the vision of seamless information provision, we start from standalone information points in key locations at the municipality complemented with a mobile app available on the go while exploring thematic routes and gastronomic destinations.

2 Background and Related Work

During the past two decades, there has been an increasing demand for presentation and interaction technologies that could reshape the way we understand and interact with various forms of cultural heritage [11–15]. In this context, interactive installations have been presented as a means of extending the services provided by city information points and museums through the exploitation of various pure digital and Mixed reality experiences. At the same time, digital technology for CH is extending its applicability to include interactive systems that model gastronomy [19] as a recognised form of intangible CH strongly connected with the land and place of its origin [16–18].

Today, Augmented Reality (AR) can be considered as a new medium for storytelling, as it can gracefully blend digital content with reality [20–23]. Additionally, recently several technologies for VR-based access to digital information have emerged, including hybrid AR-VR virtual experiences [24–28]. An advanced example supporting multi-platform and multimodal presentation modalities including web, AR, and VR is the Invisible Museum that comes with an authoring platform that supports web-based collaborative virtual-museum authoring [29].

Accessibility of digital information for culture and tourism is today considered by researchers [30–35] in order to expand the target base of such information systems and provide compliance with standards on digital accessibility that tend to become a prerequisite with the effect of new legislation [36].

3 System Overview

The system is comprised of an AR application and a standalone kiosk-based application implemented on top of the Unity Game Engine, thus making the solution available for windows based kiosks, android based devices and iOS-based devices.

3.1 AR Application

The goal of the AR application is the promotion and presentation of the gastronomic tradition of a tourism destination the digital augmentation of thematic routes by connecting tourist information with the products and the geographic locations of their production. The visitor, using the application, has the opportunity to discover themed routes, as well as POIs present in them and explore their surroundings with a mobile device. The application integrates the map of each thematic route and displays points of interest (POIs) that are included in that route. It automatically associates the user's location with POIs and displays them dynamically, grouped or individually, depending on the user's choices and location. Through AR the camera of the mobile phone can be used to discover these POIs in the surrounding space. This means that the landscape seen by the user through the camera of their mobile device is digitally augmented with the appropriate marker elements that correspond to their location and orientation. By selecting any of these items, corresponding information is displayed. Such information contains text descriptions and rich multimedia material such as photos, videos, 360 degrees assets, etc.

Routes and POIs are "filtered" through the user's profile, which includes, among other things, interests, the radius within which to look for points of interest, and whether they are immediately accessible (e.g. open wineries, restaurants, museums, workshops, etc.).

To combine sightseeing activities with gastronomy, the user can create routes and preview POIs that are precisely tailored to their food and drink preferences. City routes can be combined with a stop at a restaurant or a tavern, at a mezes tavern, for fast food, or for coffee and dessert to round out the user experience. For each point of interest, the system offers recommendations for places to visit nearby. In addition, the presence of wineries and vineyards, traditional tastes (e.g., local products and recipes), and gathering places (e.g., traditional coffee shops) can shape the suggested inland routes.

3.2 Interactive Kiosk-Style Information Systems

To accompany the AR app kiosk style information systems are designed to be operated within the city. A key feature of these systems is the presentation of interactive thematic routes consisting of historical and recreational points of interest, which the user can follow to discover and gain unique experiences during their visit. A route is an interactive map of several locations; for each of which, a brief description is provided together with relevant POIs that are accompanied by a short description and additional multimedia material.

In addition, the kiosks focus on the communication and promotion of local gastronomic specialities to the wider public, combined with their intangible dimension as manifested in works of folk art, customs and traditions. In this respect, users can create a personalized route that incorporates POIs aligned with their gastronomy, culture, or/and nature sightseeing preferences. To further promote gastronomy, the system also embeds recipes in textual and video formats, directly associated with specific routes, thus bringing to visitors the culinary customs and habits of different areas of the island.

3.3 Use Case

The use case of the system was implemented and deployed for the heraklion municipal area and the sourounding villages. To this end the AR app has been parameterised with cultural context of the specific destination. Furthermore, for the on-site presentation of key points of the municipal area of Heraklion, four interactive systems have been developed and permanently installed in three villages of the municipal area and at the city centre of Heraklion outside the central Information Point of the Municipality.

3.4 Design and Implementation

To ensure the usability and user-friendliness of the application, the human-centred design approach was followed and all international standards related to software usability were considered (ISO/IEC 9241-xx, 250xx [36, 37]). The iterative design was conducted in the form of interactive prototypes to achieve high-quality user interfaces. The essence of iterative design lies in continuous improvements. Therefore, iterative design can be represented as a cycle with three main components: i) Design, (which also includes phases of defining problems, ideation, empathizing and requirements specifications), ii) prototyping (mock-ups) based on these specifications and iii) the expert-based evaluation [38–40]. From an aesthetic point of view, the appearance of the applications, as well as the arrangement of their elements, followed a common theme and arrangement to create a uniform UX.

The mobile design was based on the design standards, principles and rules of Mobile Friendly Design to work with complete compatibility and ease of use on any device (tablet pc, smartphone, etc.). The implementation was done with cross-platform compliance in mind (for Android and iOS operating systems). For this reason, parameters were considered to ensure the responsiveness of the application, in each resolution, dimension and orientation of the device, always presenting a uniform image. The basic techniques of Mobile Friendly Design include, among other things, the automatic change of the layout of the application depending on the device used by the user as well as the adaptation of the content to different screen sizes (mobile phones, tablets, etc.). Also, the navigation logic was designed to be as intuitive as possible. This implies that the individual elements that make up the page as a whole (e.g. navigation menu, texts, video images, etc.) have been visually optimized according to the device so that they can be fully used with a limited number of keys and with the use of only one hand. Audits with usability experts were conducted to ensure the quality and functionality of the application.

For the design of the info-kiosk application, the efficient and easy interaction of users on a touch screen was targeted. The viewing and switching of digital content were framed by an attractive graphical environment without burdening the system's response and without imposing a limitation regarding the computing power of the system. At the same time, the user's interaction with the application has been enriched with the use of audio assistance and the support of multilingual content. Furthermore, info-kiosks were installed in special showcases designed for each specific point of installation to support both indoor and outdoor usage. The showcases were designed using approved materials and were installed elegantly, and fully in harmony with the environment. The construction materials were specially selected to protect the equipment from natural disasters and vandalism. For the outdoor case, a vitrine was used, embedding all equipment to be protected and vandal-proofed. The interaction was supported through the installation of a touch foil on the outer side of the vitrine. The final results are presented in Fig. 1.

The mobile application has been developed using the Unity 3D platform. It is a powerful cross-platform 3D game engine which gives developers the capability to create applications for mobile phones, desktop computers, the web, and consoles. For AR purposes, the AR + GPS Location package has been used. This package brings the ability to position 3D objects in real-world geographical locations via their GPS coordinates using Unity and AR. It works by mixing both GPS data and the AR tracking done by AR Foundation, a cross-platform framework that allows the developer to write augmented reality experiences. In addition, the application uses the Mapbox Maps SDK, a collection of tools for building Unity applications from real map data. This package was essential to spawning the required data on the map of Heraklion.

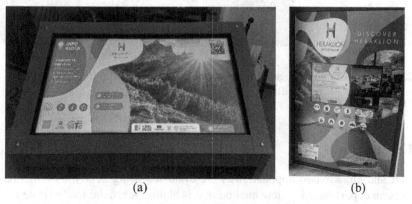

(a)   (b)

Fig. 1. (a) Design of the info-kiosk, (b) Design of the vitrine display.

4   UI Overview

Both the mobile and the standalone UI use the same look and feel to create a corporate look on the applications and support the same basic goals of accessing thematic routes and through them all the dimensions of gastronomy-related tangible and intangible CH. At the same time, they support the creation of personalised routes based on several criteria to allow visitors to create their travel plans through the supported destinations. The mobile app has the added functionality of map and AR-based visualisation of POIs and can be used while on the thematic route to visualise information within the landscape. Selected key features of these apps are presented in Fig. 2 and Fig. 3 respectively.

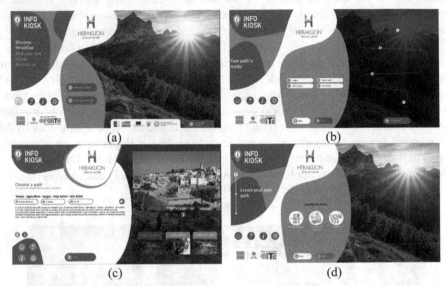

Fig. 2. (a) Info-kiosk home page, (b) Accessing a thematic route, (c) Information on a point of interest in the thematic route, (d) Creating a personalised route.

5   Evaluation

The AR and kiosk-based applications were evaluated using heuristic evaluation [43], which is an expert-based review method that is highly beneficial to eliminate usability problems before testing with representative end users [44, 45]. A small group of four evaluators examined the user interfaces to spot violations of established usability principles, commonly known as heuristics [46]. To find heuristic violations or other usability issues pertinent to the system, the evaluators performed multiple iterations. Each evaluator recorded the identified problems and specified the violated principles for each one. Then, all evaluation reports were combined into a single one, addressing each problem exactly once. To prioritize the problems, the evaluators reviewed the combined list and gave each problem a severity rating. The problems' final severity score was determined by averaging the results of each evaluator.

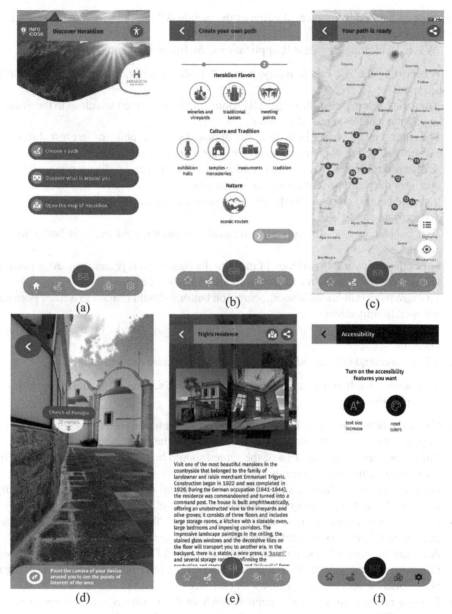

Fig. 3. (a) Mobile App home page, (b) Create personalised route, (c) Preview the route on your mobile phone, (d) On-site AR information, (e) Information point details, (f) Accessibility options.

Results in each iteration highlighted usability problems that should be rectified, ordering them by severity. Given the multiple iterations, numerous problems were identified and corrected until a prototype was identified as usable. This section summarizes key lessons learned from the evaluation of the mobile AR application and the interactive info-kiosks.

When developing mobile AR applications, the following should be considered:

- When using the AR functionality, it is preferable to minimize the number of clicks required.
- Augmented elements indicating POIs should not be displayed too close to the ground to provide a better sense of distance.
- The timing of messages indicating the approaching of a point of interest should be carefully selected when multiple nearby points are present.
- A distance indicator is not useful, and in fact, it can even be disorienting when the user is at the point of interest or very close to it.
- It should be easy to return to the previous page and the back button should behave as expected when clicked.
- Text bubbles can be difficult to distinguish on mobile devices. It is better to use pop-ups.
- For optimal viewing experience of multimedia content, it is recommended to present videos and 360° assets in full-screen mode on mobile devices.
- To make page transitions smooth, common buttons should remain in a fixed position across different screens.
- When placing elements over images, a dark overlay should be used for optimal visibility.
- It is recommended to avoid large white spaces in frames and containers.

Likewise, the following factors should be taken into account when developing kiosk-based applications:

- Given the large screens, it is crucial to pay attention to the icons' resolution.
- Pop-up windows should close automatically when the user clicks outside of them.
- Putting buttons on the top area of the screen should be avoided because they may be difficult for some users to reach.
- For crucial actions, the user should receive confirmation. For example, when sending an email through a public system, they should always know if it has been sent.
- Personal user information should not be retained from screen to screen, unless necessary, taking into account the public nature of the system.
- A reasonable time of inactivity should be accounted for, after which the system will return to its home screen. This time depends on how information-heavy is the system and should be decided after trials with end users.
- Buttons relevant to a specific context, such as the next/previous buttons to move between POIs in a route, should be easily associated with the specific elements to which they are relevant, by placing them at an appropriate screen location.
- It is helpful to have a controller for 360° assets, considering that all interaction is touch-based.
- 360° assets should have a representative starting point, providing a meaningful first view to users.
- To prevent inadvertent activation of buttons, they should not be placed too close together.

6 Conclusion

In this paper, we have presented a multimodal approach to the provision of gastronomic information. We have developed two systems one mobile and and interactive kiosk-style information point. As a use case of these systems, we present the ones created for the municipal area of Heraklion city. In this case four standalone information systems we installed to organize and plan a thematic route while the mobile app targeted the provision of gastronomic information while on the go in the municipal area. Both applications are deployed in production and can be accessed within the city and from mobile app stores [41, 42].

Acknowledgement. This research has been financed by the European Union and Greek national funds through the programme "Rural Development of Greece 2014 – 2020, CLLD/LEADER, Prefecture of Heraklion".

References

1. Hardy, A., Beeton, R.J., Pearson, L.: Sustainable tourism: an overview of the concept and its position in relation to conceptualisations of tourism. J. Sustain. Tour. **10**(6), 475–496 (2002)
2. Sagasti, F., Colby, M.: Eco-development and perspective's on global change from developing countries. In: Chourci, N. (ed.) Global Accord. MIT, London (1993)
3. Hjalager, A.M., Richards, G.: Still Undigested: Research Issues in Tourism and Gastronomy, pp. 238–248. Routledge, Oxfordshire (2003)
4. Anagnostopoulou, K., Arapis, T., Bouchy, I., Micha, I.: Tourism and the Structural Funds-the Case for Environmental Integration. RSPB, Athens (1996)
5. Andriotis, K.: Local community perceptions of tourism as a development tool: the island of Crete (Doctoral dissertation, Bournemouth University) (2000)
6. Andriotis, K.: Coastal resorts morphology: the cretan experience. Tour. Recreat. Res. **28**(1), 67–76 (2003)
7. Andriotis, K., Vaughan, D.R.: Urban residents' attitudes towards tourism development: the case of crete. J. Travel Res. **42**(2), 172–185 (2003)
8. Papanikos, G.: Greek Tourist Earnings [in Greek]. ITEP, Athens (2005)
9. Fields, K.: Demand for the gastronomy tourism product: motivational factors. Tourism Gastronomy, 50–64 (2003)
10. Kivela, J., Crotts, J.C.: Gastronomy tourism: a meaningful travel market segment. J. Culinary Sci. Technol. 4(2–3), 39–55 (2005)
11. Koutsabasis, P.: Empirical evaluations of interactive systems in cultural heritage: a review. Int. J. Computat. Methods Heritage Sci. (IJCMHS) 1(1), 100–122 (2017)
12. Mortara, M., Catalano, C.E., Bellotti, F., Fiucci, G., Houry-Panchetti, M., Petridis, P.: Learning cultural heritage by serious games. J. Cult. Herit. 15(3), 318–325 (2014)
13. Fidas, C., Sintoris, C., Yiannoutsou, N., Avouris, N.: A survey on tools for end user authoring of mobile applications for cultural heritage. In: 2015 6th International Conference on Information, Intelligence, Systems and Applications (IISA), pp. 1–5. IEEE, July 2015
14. Bekele, M.K., Pierdicca, R., Frontoni, E., Malinverni, E.S., Gain, J.: A survey of augmented, virtual, and mixed reality for cultural heritage. J. Comput. Cult. Heritage (JOCCH) 11(2), 1–36 (2018)

15. Partarakis, N., Zabulis, X., Antona, M., Stephanidis, C.: Transforming heritage crafts to engaging digital experiences. In: Liarokapis, F., Voulodimos, A., Doulamis, N., Doulamis, A. (eds.) Visual Computing for Cultural Heritage. SSCC, pp. 245–262. Springer, Cham (2020). https://doi.org/10.1007/978-3-030-37191-3_13

16. de Miguel Molina, M., de Miguel Molina, B., Santamarina Campos, V., del Val Segarra Oña, M.: Intangible heritage and gastronomy: the impact of UNESCO gastronomy elements. J. Culinary Sci. Technol. 14(4), 293–310 (2016)

17. Romagnoli, M.: Gastronomic heritage elements at UNESCO: problems, reflections on and interpretations of a new heritage category. Int. J. Intang. Heritage 14, 158–171 (2019)

18. Lin, M.P., Marine-Roig, E., Llonch-Molina, N.: Gastronomy as a sign of the identity and cultural heritage of tourist destinations: a bibliometric analysis 2001–2020. Sustainability 13(22), 12531 (2021)

19. Partarakis, N., et al.: Representation and presentation of culinary tradition as cultural heritage. Heritage 4(2), 612–640 (2021)

20. MacIntyre, B., Bolter, J.D., Moreno, E., Hannigan, B.: Augmented reality as a new media experience. In: Proceedings of the IEEE and ACM International Symposium on Augmented Reality, Austin, TX, USA, pp. 197–206, 1–5 December 2001

21. Azuma, R.: 11 Location-based mixed and augmented reality storytelling (2015)

22. Liestøl, G.: Augmented reality storytelling–Narrative design and reconstruction of a historical event in situ (2019)

23. Yilmaz, R.M., Goktas, Y.: Using augmented reality technology in storytelling activities: examining elementary students' narrative skill and creativity. Virtual Reality 21(2), 75–89 (2016). https://doi.org/10.1007/s10055-016-0300-1

24. Bonis, B., Stamos, J., Vosinakis, S., Andreou, I., Panayiotopoulos, T.: A platform for virtual museums with personalized content. Multimedia Tools Appl. 42, 139–159 (2009)

25. Flotyński, J., Dalkowski, J., Walczak, K.: Building multi-platform 3D virtual museum exhibitions with flex-VR. In 2012 18th International Conference on Virtual Systems and Multimedia, pp. 391–398. IEEE, September 2012

26. Schofield, G., et al.: Viking VR: designing a virtual reality experience for a museum. In: Proceedings of the 2018 Designing Interactive Systems Conference, pp. 805–815, June 2018

27. Camps-Ortueta, I., Deltell-Escolar, L., Blasco-López, M.F.: New technology in museums: AR and VR video games are coming. Commun. Soc., 193–210 (2021)

28. Oyelude, A.A.: Virtual reality (VR) and augmented reality (AR) in libraries and museums. Libr. Hi Tech News (2018)

29. Zidianakis, E., et al.: The invisible museum: a user-centric platform for creating virtual 3D exhibitions with VR support. Electronics 10, 363 (2021)

30. Partarakis, N., et al.: Supporting sign language narrations in the museum. Heritage 5(1), 1–20 (2022)

31. Kosmopoulos, D., et al.: Museum guidance in Sign Language: the SignGuide project. In: Proceedings of the 15th International Conference on PErvasive Technologies Related to Assistive Environments, pp. 646–652, June 2022

32. Li Liew, C.: Online cultural heritage exhibitions: a survey of information retrieval features. Program 39(1), 4–24 (2005)

33. Pisoni, G., Díaz-Rodríguez, N., Gijlers, H., Tonolli, L.: Human-centered artificial intelligence for designing accessible cultural heritage. Appl. Sci. 11(2), 870 (2021)

34. Neves, J.: Cultures of accessibility: translation making cultural heritage in museums accessible to people of all abilities. In: The Routledge Handbook of Translation and Culture, pp. 415–430. Routledge (2018)

35. Partarakis, N., Klironomos, I., Antona, M., Margetis, G., Grammenos, D., Stephanidis, C.: Accessibility of cultural heritage exhibits. In: Universal Access in Human-Computer Interaction. Interaction Techniques and Environments: 10th International Conference, UAHCI 2016, Held as Part of HCI International 2016, Toronto, ON, Canada, July 17–22, 2016, Proceedings, Part II 10, pp. 444–455. Springer, Cham (2016). https://doi.org/10.1007/978-3-319-40244-4_43

36. ISO 9241–11:2018(en) Ergonomics of human-system interaction. https://www.iso.org/obp/ui/#iso:std:iso:9241:-11:ed-2:v1:en. Accessed 08 Feb 2023

37. ISO/IEC 25010:2011 Systems and software engineering — Systems and software Quality Requirements and Evaluation (SQuaRE) — System and software quality models. https://www.iso.org/standard/35733.html. Accessed 08 Feb 2023

38. Nielsen, J.: Iterative user-interface design. Computer **26**(11), 32–41 (1993)

39. Nielsen, J.: The usability engineering life cycle. Computer **25**(3), 12–22 (1992)

40. Brown, T.: Design thinking. Harv. Bus. Rev. **86**(6), 84 (2008)

41. Mobile App on the App store. https://play.google.com/store/apps/details?id=com.ICS FORTH.com.forth.ics.herakliongastronomy. Accessed 02 Aug 2023

42. Mobile App on Google Play. https://apps.apple.com/app/heraklion-gastronomy/id1664 900666. Accessed 02 Aug 2023

43. Nielsen, J.: Usability Engineering. Morgan Kaufmann, Burlington (1994)

44. Ntoa, S., Margetis, G., Antona, M., Stephanidis, C.: User experience evaluation in intelligent environments: a comprehensive framework. Technologies **9**(2), 41 (2021)

45. Martins, A.I., Queirós, A., Silva, A.G., Rocha, N.P.: Usability evaluation methods: a systematic review. Human Factors Softw. Dev. Des., 250–273 (2015)

46. Nielsen, J.: Enhancing the explanatory power of usability heuristics. In: Proceedings of the SIGCHI Conference on Human Factors in Computing Systems, pp. 152–158 (1994)

What are the Drivers in Cultural Development

Matthias Rauterberg[1]([⊠]) [iD] and Pertti Saariluoma[2] [iD]

[1] Eindhoven University of Technology, Eindhoven, The Netherlands
g.w.m.rauterberg@tue.nl
[2] University of Jyväskylä, Jyväskylä, Finland
pertti.o.saariluoma@jyu.fi

Abstract. To understand the nature of driving forces for cultural development, we must distinguish between a physical and an ideal realm. However, the ontological status of the ideal realm in relation to the physical realm is heavily debated. We argue for the necessity and relevance of both realms; both are connected through the actions of agents based on their mental concepts. The dynamic forces for the actions of the ideal realm are drivers for cultural development.

Keywords: action · agency · culture · development · energy · information · matter

1 Introduction

Cultural development needs actors and agency [1]. But before discussing the cultural agency's metaphysical foundation, we must address the mind-body problem (MBP). We follow Wiener [2] and try to resolve this MBP by claiming a third quality next to 'matter' and 'energy' called 'information.' Wiener clearly distinguished: "information is information, not matter or energy" [2, p. 132]. It is now the time to acknowledge that the concept of 'information' is a new quality that can not be reduced to energy or matter [3].

Historically 'matter' was the first concept developed and investigated long before we could understand the concept of 'energy' [4]. We are now in a similar situation as we have been with 'energy' centuries ago, to define and understand 'information.' The concept of information is relevant for actors and agencies based on learning and adapting [5, 6]. All living systems are adapting, humans in particular [7]. Following Kahneman [8], we can separate the human mind into three major building blocks: perception, system-1 (intuition), and system-2 (reasoning). While perception and intuition operate in the natural world's presence, reasoning operates in a representational and symbolic space [9].

One of the tragedies in metaphysics is the common category mistake of confusing the natural world with symbols from this representational space [10]. So often, we confuse the map with the territory [11]. For example, in art, a significant part of the work of Rene Magritte is dedicated to this confusion. "The most important thing to look for in these paintings is the way Magritte questions our understanding of the relationship between objects and images and between words and things. Using the interplay between language and images, he seeks to shake up our bourgeois acceptance of the status quo, and of the unquestioning importance or meaning we give to everyday objects and events" [10, p. 62, 64]. Or, as Maxwell puts it, "the only real entities are the good old familiar ones which we sense directly every day" [12, p. 27].

However, many modern disciplines are entirely dependent on abstract concepts. Consequently, these disciplines treat all those abstract concepts as ontological essentials. For example, in information and data science, the concepts of information, knowledge, and data are unavoidable [13]. In law and jurisdiction, the abstract concept of a juridical person is used [14]. And physics is full of not observables [4]. Lastly, philosophy and mathematics are entirely based on representational language and symbols, while most other disciplines also include some practices in dealing with perceivable physical entities (i.e., objects and subjects). Hence, we must distinguish between a physical and an ideal realm (see Fig. 1). Although most people have no problem capturing the physical realm as *real* (based on matter and energy), we must accept that the ideal realm is as *real* as the physical one. The physical realm we can experience directly through our *perception*, but the ideal realm we can get in touch with through *apperception* [15]. People do not get information only through their senses; human mental representations entail non-perceivable concepts. People can think about *tomorrow*, but they cannot perceive it. They cannot directly perceive entities like infinity, eternity, possibility, redness, or thoughts of Allah either. Yet, they can experience them and construct non-perceivable content in their mental representations. Such information contents cannot be represented in human sensory-neural surfaces such as the retina. Thus, it makes sense to assume that mental concepts of abstract entities are *apperceived* rather than *perceived*.

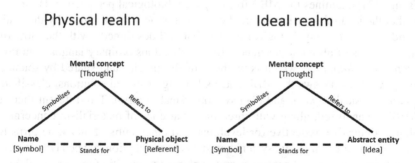

Fig. 1. The semiotic triangles for the physical (l) and the ideal realm (r) [16].

The ideal realm is the space for all abstract entities, like *information*. Nowadays, we cannot deny that information is as real and important as anything from the physical realm [17]. It is generally acknowledged that we live in the "information age." However, the ideal realm is only linked to the physical realm through the agency and action of a learning system.

Theleffsen, Theleffsen, and Sorensen [18] argue that understanding information as objective or subjective discursive leads to objective reductionism and signal processing, which has severe difficulties explaining how information could become meaningful.

Conversely, information is understood only relative to personal discursive intentions, agendas, etc. To overcome the limitations of defining information as either objective or subjective discursive, a semiotic analysis shows that information, understood as signs, is consistently sensitive to objective and subjective discursive characteristics of information (see Fig. 1). They argued that information should be defined with ontological conditions and inevitable epistemological consequences.

Meaning is the most critical problem in cognitive psychology because it controls memory and perception [19]. Moreover, meaning is the goal of communication and underlies social activities and culture. Harnad [20] described the *symbol grounding problem*: How can a formal symbol system's semantics be intrinsic to such a system rather than just parasitic on our mental concepts? To understand the new quality of the idea of meaningful information, we introduce the first-, second-, and third-person view [21]. Although the third-person view is the standard view in science, we also need the first-person view to understand ourselves as actors in the natural world. Our representational space of ideas and symbolic thoughts is the central mechanism for voluntary actions to reach into the world of the physical realm [22]. This teleological dimension [23] allows us – and any other symbolically controlled actors, too - to become drivers for cultural development.

2   The Mind-Body Problem (MBP)

For a long time, the MBP was and still is the subject of an intensive metaphysical debate. One of the main reasons why the MBP is still unresolved lies probably in the insufficient understanding of adequate metaphysical concepts to capture our world.

Bunge [24] examines the MBP from a psychobiological perspective. He intends to show that the idea of a separate mental entity is not only unwarranted by the available data and the existing psychological models but collides directly with the most fundamental concepts of all modern science. Bunge abandons ordinary language in favor of the *state space language*, which is mathematically precise and shared by science and philosophy. He overviews the MBP and its leading proposed solutions, classified into (1) psychophysical *monism* and (2) psychophysical *dualism*. Ten different theories of the MBP are analyzed, along with three main varieties of materialism concerning the problem: eliminative, reductive (or leveling), and emergentist. Finally, he turns to the notion of a concrete or material system based on the assumption that behavior is an external manifestation of neural processes and explores the specific functions of the central nervous system. In this respect, Bunge can be seen as a reductionistic materialist. Stoerig [25] added the *trialism* theories, like the three-world concept of Popper and Eccles [26]. Popper and Eccles tried to avoid a pure reductionistic outcome with this three-world approach. They call the collection of all physical objects *world-1*, all possible mental concepts *world-2*, and all likely abstract entities as outcomes from thought processes *world-3* (see Fig. 1).

3 Ontological Foundations

We follow a foundational approach [27]. Intelligent technologies are based on *information* and its processing [28]. Pure mechanical systems are determined, and they can hardly say to have any intelligence though they make sense as technical systems. One can expect a new technology revolution related to intelligent information systems because information and its processing open new possibilities for creating new kinds of technologies [e.g., ChatGPT is a variant of the Generative Pre-trained Transformer 3 'GPT-3' [29, 30]. These technologies can be multipurpose, and they can control their own actions in task-relevant situations. This capacity is unique in the history of technology design and innovation [31].

Before our times' technical artifacts had been renovated and innovated by means of finding a new solution based either on matter or energy [32]; stone and copper axes are examples of matter-grounded innovations wind, electricity, or nuclear power exemplify energy-based innovations [33]. Both means of advancing technologies are still relevant, but information makes creating new kinds of technologies possible. Because information is neither matter nor energy [32], innovations are based on renewing information processing in technical artifacts by making new utilizations possible for these technologies. Artificial Intelligence and other intelligent technologies are built on information. Davies and Gregersen [34, p. 3] find the "conceptual hierarchy: information → laws of physics → matter."

Information has referred initially to a picture or representation [35]. Much of the recent discourse has been devoted to measuring the amount of information and complexity [5, 36]. Paradoxically, this influential theory which underlies, for example, capacity-oriented cognitive psychology, does not discuss information contents and meaning at all; thus, it sets the contents of information outside the discussion [37–39]. Nevertheless, information refers to something, and thus it also means something [40]. The meaning can be called *information contents* and *mind mental contents* [41–45]. "Mental information includes the key quality of semantics; that is, human beings derive an understanding of their world from sense data and can communicate meaning to each other. The question here is what can and what cannot be explained merely by digital information, which is formulated in terms of bits without regard to meaning" [34, p. 4].

Pawlowski et al. [46] go a step further and discuss the idea of 'information causality' as a fundamental law in nature. "We suggest that information causality—a generalization of the no-signalling condition— might be one of the foundational properties of nature." [46, p. 1101].

4 Determination Through Action

According to Rauterberg [22], there is a fundamental and still largely unsolved problem in recognizing and naming unknown patterns in the totality of our perception. The perception of meaningful units in the visual world depends on complex operations that are not consciously accessible and can only be proven indirectly [47, 48]. This may be based on the still unsolved problem of universals: Do universals (in the sense of objective concepts) even have an independent existence outside of the mind of a cognitive and perceiving subject? If there is such a thing as universals – they do not exist as static entities (e.g., concepts) but as dynamic processes (e.g., actions).

From the abundance of differentiation possibilities that are made available by reality, those differences that are considered to be necessary for the constitution are defined by the determination process. The determination process is to be understood as a broad category of any cognitive system's actions. According to Neisser [49], the relationship between percipience and taking action is an irreversible, cyclical process: the exploration of perception as an action selects the relevant aspects from the quantity of all potentially available differentiation criteria, which in turn changes the individual knowledge structure of existing interpretation schemata and invariants.

As we have already argued before, symbols should be grounded. But we insist that they should be grounded in subsymbolic activities and the interaction between the agent and the world [48, 50]. The point is that concepts are not formed in isolation (from the world), in abstraction, or "objectively." Instead, they are created concerning the experience of agents, through their perceptual and motor apparatuses, in their world and linked to their goals and actions. A famous example is the French revolution [51], but any [scientific] discovery would cout as well [52], where actions based on ideals turned into fundamental changes in reality. Sun [53] takes a detailed look at this relatively old issue with a new perspective, supported by his work on computational cognitive model development.

In the work of Olier, Barakova [54], the problems of knowledge acquisition and information processing are explored concerning the definitions of concepts and conceptual processing and their implications for artificial agents. The discussion focuses on views of cognition as a dynamic property in which the world is actively represented in grounded mental states which only have meaning in the action context. Reasoning is an emerging property consequence of actions-environment couplings achieved through experience and concepts as situated and dynamic phenomena enabling behaviors. Re-framing concepts' characteristics is crucial to overcoming settled beliefs and reinterpreting new understandings of artificial systems.

Olier, Barakova [54] found support for grounded and embodied cognition views, describing concepts as dynamic, flexible, context-dependent, and distributedly coded. They argue to contrast with many technical implementations assuming concepts as categories while explaining limitations when grounding amodal symbols or unifying learning, perception, and reasoning. The characteristics of mental concepts are linked to methods of active inference, self-organization, and deep learning to address challenges posed and to reinterpret emerging techniques. In addition, an architecture based on deep generative models is presented to illustrate the arguments elaborated. This new architecture is evaluated in a navigation task, showing that good representations are created regarding situated behaviors with no semantics imposed on data beforehand. Moreover, adequate behaviors are achieved through a dynamic integration of perception and action in a single symbolic domain and process.

5 Conclusions

Living in an information age means taking abstract entities (e.g., information, knowledge, etc.) as *real* as any other physical object that can be experienced directly through our perception. However, these abstract entities need a physical carrier to unfold their relevance in the physical realm. These carriers are passive (e.g., written text, etc.) or active (e.g., mental concepts of agents). Any learning and adapting system can become those agents to link the ideal realm with the physical realm through their actions. Primarily the ideal realm contains the driving forces for cultural development!

References

1. Latour, B.: Science in Action: How to Follow Scientists and Engineers through Society. Harvard University Press, Cambridge (1987)
2. Wiener, N.: Cybernetics or Control and Communication in the Animal and the Machine, 2nd edn. MIT Press, Cambridge (1961)
3. Adriaans, P.: Information. The Stanford Encyclopedia of Philosophy 2012, 18 August 2020. https://plato.stanford.edu/entries/information/. Accessed 12 Mar 2023
4. Harman, P.M.: Energy, Force, and Matter: The Conceptual Development of Nineteenth-Century Physics. Cambridge University Press, Cambridge (1982)
5. Rauterberg, M.: About a framework for information and information processing of learning systems. In: Falkenberg, E.D., Hesse, W., Olivé, A. (eds.) Information System Concepts. IAICT, pp. 54–69. Springer, Boston, MA (1995). https://doi.org/10.1007/978-0-387-34870-4_7
6. Ahn, R., et al.: Interfacing with adaptive systems. Autom. Control Intell. Syst. 2(4), 53–61 (2014)
7. Rauterberg, M.: About non-living things and living systems as cultural determinants. In: Rauterberg, M. (ed.) Culture and Computing - 10th international conference as part of 24th HCI international conference, pp. 445–463. Springer, Cham (2022). https://doi.org/10.1007/978-3-031-05434-1_30
8. Kahneman, D.: Maps of bounded rationality: a perspective on intuitive judgment and choice. In: Frangsmyr, T. (ed.) Les Prix Nobel: The Nobel Prizes 2002, pp. 449–489. Nobel Foundation, Stockholm (2003)
9. Wang, X., Rauterberg, M.: Time travel in our mind based on system 2. In: Atmanspacher, H., Hameroff, S. (eds.) Book of Abstracts of the 13th Conference of the Science of Consciousness, pp. 130–131. Collegium Helveticum Zurich, Zurich (2019)
10. Alden, T.: The essential René Magritte. The Wonderland Press, New York (1999)
11. Wuppuluri, S., Doria, F.A. (eds.): The Map and the Territory. TFC, Springer, Cham (2018). https://doi.org/10.1007/978-3-319-72478-2
12. Maxwell, G.: The ontological status of theoretical entities. In: Feigl, H., Maxwell, G. (eds.) Minnesota Studies in the Philosophy of Science-Scientific Explanations, Space, and Time, pp. 3–27. University of Minnesota Press, Minneapolis (1962)
13. Zins, C.: Conceptual approaches for defining data, information, and knowledge. J. Am. Soc. Inform. Sci. Technol. 58(4), 479–493 (2007)
14. Adriano, E.A.Q.: The natural person, legal entity or juridical person and juridical personality. Penn State J. Law Int. Affairs 4(1), 363–391 (2015)
15. Saariluoma, P.: Apperception, content-based psychology and design. In: Lindemann, U. (ed.) Human Behaviour in Design: Individuals, Teams, Tools, pp. 72–78. Springer, Berlin, Heidelberg, New York (2003)

16. Ogden, C.K., Richards, I.A.: The Meaning of Meaning: A Study of the Influence of Language upon Thought and of the Science of Symbolism, 8th edn. Harcourt Brace & World, New York (1946)
17. Burgin, M.: Theory of Information: Fundamentality, Diversity, and Unification. World Scientific Series in Information Studies. Burgin, M. (ed). World Scientific Publishing, Singapore (2010)
18. Thellefsen, M.M., Thellefsen, T., Sørensen, B.: Information as signs: a semiotic analysis of the information concept, determining its ontological and epistemological foundations. J. Documentation **74**(2), 372–382 (2018)
19. Saariluoma, P., et al.: Cognitive mimetics: main ideas. In: Arabnia, H.R. et al., (eds.) Proceedings of the 20th International Conference on Artificial Intelligence, pp. 202–206. CSREA Press, Las Vegas (2018)
20. Harnad, S.: The symbol grounding problem. Physica D **42**(1–3), 335–346 (1990)
21. Neuwirth, K., Frederick, E.: Extending the framework of third-, first-, and second-person effects. Mass Commun. Soc. **5**(2), 113–140 (2002)
22. Rauterberg, M.: Reality determination through action. In: Ishida, T., Tosa, N., Hachimura, K. (eds.) Proceedings of IEEE International Conference on Culture and Computing - C&C, pp. 24–28. IEEE, Piscataway (2017)
23. Hennig, B., Rauterberg, M.: The significance of Aristotle's four causes for design. Des. Issues **38**(4), 35–43 (2022)
24. Bunge, M.: The Mind-Body Problem: A Psychobiological Approach. Pergamon Press, Oxford (1980)
25. Stoerig, P.: Leib und Psyche: Eine interdisziplinäre Erörterung des psychophysischen Problems. Wilhelm Fink, München (1985)
26. Popper, K.R., Eccles, J.C.: The Self and Its Brain-An Argument of Interactionism. Springer, Berlin (1985)
27. Saariluoma, P.: Foundational Analysis: Presuppositions in Experimental Psychology, 2nd edn. Routledge, New York (2016)
28. Salomon, G., Perkins, D.N., Globerson, T.: Partners in cognition: extending human intelligence with intelligent technologies. Educ. Res. **20**(3), 2–9 (1991)
29. Cotton, D.R., Cotton, P.A., Shipway, J. R.: Chatting and cheating. ensuring academic integrity in the era of ChatGPT, pp. 1–11. EdArXiv 2023(Preprints)
30. Brown, T., et al.: Language models are few-shot learners. In: Larochelle, H., et al. (eds.) Advances in Neural Information Processing Systems - NeurIPS 2020, pp. 1877–1901. NeurIPS, San Diego (2020)
31. Verbeek, P.-P.: What Things Do: Philosophical Reflections on Technology, Agency, and Design. Pennsylvania State University Press, University Park (2005)
32. Wiener, N.: Cybernetics. Sci. Am. **179**(5), 14–18 (1948)
33. Derry, T.K., Williams, T.I.: A Short History of Technology from the Earliest Times to AD 1900, 1993rd edn. Dover, New York (1960)
34. Davies, P., Gregersen, N.H.: Introduction: does information matter? In: Davies, P., Gregersen, N.H. (eds.) Information and the Nature of Reality: From Physics to Metaphysics, pp. 1–9. Cambridge University Press, Cambridge, New York (2010)
35. Adriaans, P., Van Benthem, J.: Philosophy of information. In: Gabbay, D., Thagard, P., Woods. J. (eds.) Handbook of the Philosophy of Science, North Holland, Amsterdam, Boston, London, New York (2008)
36. Shannon, C.E.: A mathematical theory of communication. Bell Syst. Tech. J. **27**(3), 379–423 (1948)
37. Broadbent, D.: Perception and Communication. Pergamon Press, London (1958)
38. Miller, G.A.: The magical number seven, plus or minus two: some limits on our capacity for processing information. Psychol. Rev. **63**(2), 81–97 (1956)

39. Saariluoma, P.: Chess and content-oriented psychology of thinking. Psicológica **22**(1), 143–164 (2001)
40. Floridi, L.: Semantic information. In: Floridi, L. (ed.) The Routledge Handbook of Philosophy of Information, Routledge, London, New York, pp. 44–49 (2016)
41. Fodor, J.A.: A Theory of Content and Other Essays. MIT Press, Cambridge (1990)
42. Myllylä, M.T. and P. Saariluoma, Expertise and becoming conscious of something. New Ideas Psychol. **64,** 1–9 (2022). (article 100916)
43. Newell, A.: Unified Theories of Cognition. Harvard University Press, Cambridge (1994)
44. Newell, A., Simon, H.A.: Human Problem Solving. Prentice Hall, Englewood Cliffs (1972)
45. Floridi, L.: The Philosophy of Information. Oxford Oxford University Press, New York (2011)
46. Pawłowski, M., et al.: Information causality as a physical principle. Nature **461**(7267), 1101–1104 (2009)
47. Treisman, A.: The perception of features and objects. In: Wright, R.D. (ed.) Visual Attention, pp. 26–54. Oxford University Press, New York, Oxford (1998)
48. Everett, D.L.: Dark Matter of the Mind: The Culturally Articulated Unconscious. University of Chicago Press, Chicago (2016)
49. Neisser, U.: Cognition and Reality. W.H. Freeman, San Francisco (1976)
50. Vogt, P.: The physical symbol grounding problem. Cogn. Syst. Res. **3**(3), 429–457 (2002)
51. McPhee, P.: The French Revolution 1789–1799. Oxford University Press, Oxford (2002)
52. Winston, R. (ed.): Science Year by Year: The Ultimate Visual Guide to the Discoveries that Changed the World. Dorling Kindersley, London (2013)
53. Sun, R.: Symbol grounding: a new look at an old idea. Philos. Psychol. **13**(2), 149–172 (2000)
54. Olier, J.S., et al.: Re-framing the characteristics of concepts and their relation to learning and cognition in artificial agents. Cogn. Syst. Res. **44**(1), 50–68 (2017)

Study on the Living Inheritance Strategies of Funan Wickerwork in the Context of Rural Revitalization

Tianxiong Wang[1(✉)], Jiaxin Fu[1], Liu Yang[2], and Xian Gao[2]

[1] School of Art, Anhui University, No. 111, Jiulong Road, Economic and Technological Development District, Hefei 230601, China
wangtx_2018@163.com
[2] School of Machinery and Electrical Engineering, Anhui Jianzhu University, No. 292, Ziyun Road, Shushan District, Hefei 230601, China

Abstract. In the perspective of rural revitalization, based on the industrial development of Funan willow weaving craft, the current situation of the inheritance mode and the characteristics of the weaving craft, the problems faced by its inheritance are analyzed and the strategy of its living inheritance is explored. Through promoting the value of wickerwork, building a collaborative design model between schools and enterprises, creating a brand IP and expanding wickerwork design derivatives, we explore strategies for the living heritage of Funan wickerwork and establish a concrete implementation path for the heritage of Funan wickerwork from a brand perspective. Based on the brand visual image, the project will promote the heritage and sustainable development of Funan's wickerwork craft from various aspects, stimulate the vitality of Funan's wickerwork industry, and thus contribute to rural revitalisation.

Keywords: Funan wickerwork · rural revitalization · living heritage · innovative design

1 Introduction

The 20th National Congress of the Communist Party of China once again emphasised the need to comprehensively promote the revitalisation of the countryside, solidly promote the revitalisation of rural industries and cultural revitalisation, and accelerate the building of a strong agricultural country. The revitalisation of the countryside means vigorously developing rural industries, taking multiple measures to enhance the vitality of agriculture and rural areas, promoting industrial revitalisation, promoting rural civilisation, strengthening rural governance, improving the lives of farmers and ultimately achieving the goal of comprehensive revitalisation of the countryside. Huanggang wickerwork in Funan County of Anhui Province has a long history and rich cultural heritage, and is distributed in Huanggang Town of Anhui Province. Funan wickerwork products are characterised by hand-woven, fine workmanship, tight structure, strong and durable and have high research value.

C. Stephanidis et al. (Eds.): HCII 2023, CCIS 1834, pp. 518–526, 2023.
https://doi.org/10.1007/978-3-031-35998-9_67

At present, with the rapid development of economic and cultural development in Funan County, Funan wickerwork techniques and cultural industries have ushered in new development opportunities, and research related to the inheritance of Funan wickerwork techniques has increased year by year, for example, Li [1] explains the historical origins, production process characteristics and cultural features of Funan wickerwork; Wang [2] explores the innovative design of Funan wickerwork techniques based on emotional design and creative design combined with consumers' aesthetic interests; Zhang and Zhang [3] explore the integration of wickerwork and ceramics in terms of material, colour and technology to achieve a breakthrough in the design of wickerwork and broaden its application in materials. The study also explores the application of wickerwork to the material. Due to the outdated image of product design in the development of the Funan wickerwork industry, the limited application of cultural genes and the weak brand awareness of the products have become the key problem in its living heritage. Therefore, based on the culture of Funan wickerwork, this study explore the problem of its inheritance from both the current situation of the industry and the characteristics of the craft, and proposed the innovative strategies for the living inheritance of Funan wickerwork techniques in the context of rural revitalisation, so as to promote the integration of Funan wickerwork techniques with the new economy and new consumption, so that to make it inherit and innovate, thus empowering rural revitalisation.

2   Review

2.1   The Current Situation of the Development of the Wickerwork Industry in Funan

Huanggang has a long history of wickerwork and a deep cultural heritage, and a history of more than 500 years of wickerwork. The rise of wickerwork products began at the end of the 17th century. In the late Ming and early Qing dynasties, the wickerwork industry flourished. According to Ming Zhengde's "Yingzhou Zhi", "Huai Meng produces water wattle in abundance, harvesting and processing, tough as rattan" [4]. Since the 1950s, the local community has held the "Huanggang Wickerwork Material Exchange Meeting" every year. In May 2011, the Huanggang wickerwork process in Funan County was included in the third batch of national intangible cultural heritage protection list, and has become an important regional cultural card in Funan with its unique craft characteristics and rich historical and cultural values. It has been named as "China Wickerwork Capital" and "Anhui Wickerwork Cultural Cluster (Base)". After years of development, the Funan wickerwork cultural heritage has been transformed from the traditional wickerwork to the willow wood cultural industry covering traditional wickerwork, household, decoration and art, mainly including two categories of household items and craft products: household items are divided into traditional ware, decorative ware and folklore items; craft products are mainly divided into willow weaving material combination products, willow weaving product sets and home decoration, as shown in Table 1 [1].

Table 1. The Funan Wickerwork Household and Craft Products

Product categories	Industrial Properties	Product definition	Related product images
Household goods	Traditional shapes	It mainly serves the traditional productive life.	
	Decorative objects	The shape varies, and each has its own aesthetic characteristics, both for appreciation and for practical use.	
	Folkloric objects	Wickerwork baskets, buckets and other wickerwork objects with symbolic connotations.	
		A ritual instrument used in rituals. The local people weave the dragon with wicker to pray for good weather and good health.	
Craft products	Wickerwork material combinations	By combining mixed weaving materials with other materials, the willow weavers' ingenious and creative designs form innovative solutions, presenting a personalised and artistic aesthetic.	
	Wickerwork product sets	This refers to willow weaving products that are similar in form, with slight differences in size and proportion, presented in sets, reflecting the ingenuity of the willow weavers.	
	Home decoration	Used in interiors as a decorative accent to give a distinctive artistic character[6].	

2.2 The Current Status of the Inheritance Model of Funan Willow Weaving

With the current progressive trend of globalisation and rapid economic and social changes, the mode of inheritance of the willow weaving craft mainly includes the traditional family inheritance, master-apprentice inheritance and organised production inheritance. Specifically, the family inheritance regards the willow weaving technique as a family tradition, and this mode of inheritance is usually passed on by the family elders or other skilled family members, and the young descendants learn the willow weaving technique under the teaching of the family elders. The master-apprentice inheritance is mainly through the master leading the apprentice, and the senior willow weaving inheritor selects the apprentice who is interested in learning the willow weaving technique, and carries on the inheritance through the way of oral and manual teaching, and the apprentice learns the willow weaving. Many organisations and associations are dedicated to promoting and protecting the traditional craft of willow weaving in Funan, usually organising training, exhibitions and exchange activities for willow weaving masters, and some enterprises have set up willow weaving research and development departments, responsible for developing innovative willow weaving techniques [6] in production. Some enterprises have set up R&D departments to develop innovative willow weaving techniques [6], and to teach them to practitioners of willow weaving through training prior to production. In short, the different modes of inheritance in Funan constitute a differentiated inheritance situation that allows for the inheritance and sustainable development of willow weaving techniques.

3 Types of Wickerwork Funan

The Funan wickerwork craft as a product of rural culture, is the crystallization of national wisdom, its Funan wickerwork weaving techniques can be divided into the following eight categories (Table 2):

Firstly, flat weaving is the more common weaving method in wickerwork, the weaving method is to cross the wicker warp and weft to design various cross patterns, it can also be mixed with bark, bushes and other materials for weaving. Secondly, diameter weaving is one of the traditional willow weaving handicraft techniques, and is also one of the most complex. Diameter weaving is characterised by its long endurance and long service life of the craft, but weaving is time-consuming and labour-intensive. Thirdly, the wicker weaving technique is also a traditional wicker weaving technique, mainly using hemp rope as the warp and wicker as the weft, and the weaving technique is a press together, with the woven pattern appearing to be diamond-shaped. The main advantage of the weave is that it is tight and sturdy, beautiful and durable. Fourthly, masonry is also a common method of traditional willow weaving, where the knotted material is polymerised into a handle and then pierced with a stronger gabion. Fifthly, the twist weave, also known as 'twist weave', is woven by first arranging the warp stakes and then using the weft strips to cross and wrap around the warp stakes in a circular motion. It is characterised by its unobtrusive warp strip, its strength, its richness of pattern and its beauty of shape. Sixthly, the wrap is mostly made of a hard material as the core, outside of which soft wicker is wound in a certain direction, which not only effectively holds it in place, but also has a certain aesthetic decorative effect. The wrap is arranged in

Table 2. Types of craft techniques in Funan willow weaving

Weaving	Specific features	Picture examples
Flat knitting	The pattern is continuous in four directions, with a strong sense of order and a flat, natural surface, and is woven in a warp and weft pattern, resulting in different patterns.	
Diameter knitting	Long endurance and long service life of the woven artefacts, but time, effort and energy consuming to weave.	
Strass knitting	Hemp rope for the path, with wicker for the weft.	
Masonry knitting	The knotted material is polymerised into a handle and threaded together with a stronger gabion.	
Twisted knitting	No warp stripes are shown. No warp stripes showing, stronger, richly patterned and beautifully shaped.	
Winding knitting	A hard material core with a thin soft wicker or peeled wicker bark wrapped around the outside to both secure the edge of the product and provide a decorative surface effect.	
Standing knitting	The weft is small and the warp is large, and the ratio of weft and diameter is well-defined, with a strong sense of three-dimensionality.	
Jumble knitting	The flowers are innovative, uniquely shaped, interesting and artistically beautiful.	

single or multiple strips, with the single strips arranged neatly and the multiple strips arranged in a variety of colours to create a beautiful pattern. Seventh, the vertical knitting is an innovative knitting method, mainly highlighting the weft less warp more, knitting out the product three-dimensional sense. Eighth, the chaotic weave is a new type of wicker weaving process resulting from the advancement of modern technology and the changing functional needs of the apparatus [7]. Its weaving technique mainly uses metal materials to make a good frame, and there is no fixed interweaving technique between the wicker strips, combining the principles of formal aesthetics and the aesthetic sense and artistic inspiration of the weaving artist to complete the improvised weave, creating novel, uniquely shaped and interesting wicker products.

4 Strategies for the Living Heritage of the Funan Wickerwork

4.1 Promoting the Value of Wickerwork

To increase recognition of the value of the willow weaving industry, it is important to treat willow weaving as a sunrise industry that keeps pace with the times, to bring together and inspire young rural talents with sentiment, ability and responsibility to choose the industry as a career choice, to increase their recognition of the value of willow weaving, to trigger a wave of innovation and entrepreneurship in rural industries, and to give new life to traditional willow weaving. Against the backdrop of strong demand for willow weaving crafts in domestic and international markets, the Internet, artificial intelligence and big data technology are used as promotional media to reconstruct the development pattern of diversified dissemination of handicrafts, showcasing the designs of craftsmen through digital methods such as video, live streaming and APP, establishing a bridge of communication between consumers, designers and craftsmen, and effectively linking production with production in an "Internet+" manner. The "Internet+" approach effectively connects the production and consumption value chains, changes the traditional offline marketing model of willow weaving products, and extends the new channels in the process of inheritance and development of traditional willow weaving through the intervention of new media platforms and online methods such as APP. With the advantage of the Internet, the multi-dimensional promotion and communication of the cultural value of willow weaving as a traditional national culture, thus promoting the inheritance and reshaping of its industrial culture.

4.2 Building the School-Enterprise Collaborative Innovation Design Model

Training traditional craftspeople in the theoretical aspects of the art. Although the craftspeople have a wealth of technical experience, most of them lack a wealth of theoretical knowledge. Through cooperation between design and art majors and traditional craftspeople, willow weaving handicrafts are introduced to universities by means of university-enterprise cooperation, lectures by inheritors, joint development of courses and subject setting. Firstly, based on the university platform, teachers and students provide modern design methods and novel technical support to promote the fashionable and modern transformation of willow weaving forms or craft products, and use the commercial power of enterprises to provide resource support and create more room for the growth of the inherited objects. Secondly, we are looking for suitable inheritance candidates among the young generation of university students to cultivate, expand the range of inheritors and attract more young people with a good design education to work in the willow weaving industry. The relevant government agencies and universities will provide financial support for the inheritors to enter the design practice of enterprises. On the one hand, this collaborative innovation model helps craftspeople to learn modern design concepts and improve the overall fashionability of their work, while on the other hand it promotes young students to learn about handicrafts, encourages them to engage in the craft industry and ensures that the ideas of university students are implemented with the support of enterprises and craftspeople, thus promoting the revival and sustainable development of the willow weaving industry.

At the same time, the establishment of professional competitions and award mechanisms in universities will raise the profile of the willow weaving industry, enable students to experience the artistic charm of traditional willow weaving techniques, and promote the fashionable transmission and improvement of willow weaving techniques from a creative design perspective. The competition will focus on willow as the main design material and will require participants to use a variety of modern creative expressions and means to create design themes such as space, landscape, stationery, furniture and APP interfaces, so as to explore the creative design and material expressions of Funan willow weaving and to promote the iterative upgrading of willow weaving skills through the design of new application scenarios and new functions of the material.

4.3 Create Brand and Enhance the Added Value of Products

Cultivating well-known brands is a key response to the revitalisation of rural industries. Factors such as brand positioning, image and experience will directly affect consumers' cognitive satisfaction [8]. IP (Intellectual Property), or intellectual property, is an intangible cultural asset [9], mainly referring to the connection and fusion between culture and products, and is a cultural symbol that can be realised in the long term [10]. IP, as an important carrier for spreading cultural genes, is also One of the key elements essential to brand image communication, its ability to enhance the brand's memorability and association, achieve high value output of brand culture and enhance the emotional resonance between the brand and the audience. With artistic design thinking and brand innovation strategies, we can deeply explore the natural ecology, history and culture of Funan County and other resources, refine a distinctive visual language and symbols, and shape a brand visual system with strong regional characteristics. To create a brand IP, it is necessary to use the power of culture to carry out an in-depth analysis of the cultural connotations of the enterprise and willow weaving, discover the cultural genes of the enterprise and the brand, and then build the values and world view of the IP. Secondly, it is necessary to shape the brand image and further design the basic brand image logo, as shown in Fig. 1. Specifically, the brand can be realised by means of explicit semantic features such as the external form, colour and material of the logo to convey the cultural connotation. This design enables consumers to better identify and remember the brand, while presenting a guarantee of product quality. The logo is designed in a simple and clear manner, eliminating as much detail as possible. The Chinese character '柳' is chosen as the prototype for the logo, and the striped texture of willow weave is used to fill in the content to convey the values and ideas of the brand.

Fig. 1. Wickerwork brand logo

The application of the brand logo is shown in Fig. 2. Building a complete brand visual identity by establishing a unified and effective visual message element is an important part of brand equity building.

Fig. 2. Funan willow weaving brand logo effect display

5 Conclusion

China's rural revitalisation strategy has opened up a new journey of revitalising poverty reduction with Chinese characteristics. Focusing on the sustainable development and inheritance of handicrafts helps to enrich and enhance rural culture and reshape rural characteristics. Funan willow weaving is a folk art that combines handicraft skills, artistic aesthetics and regional culture, and is closely related to the ecological environment. This study explores the current status of the inheritance mode and weaving process characteristics of Funan willow weaving craft, and explores its living inheritance strategy in terms of promoting the value of willow weaving craft, building a collaborative innovation design model between schools and enterprises, creating brand IP and expanding willow weaving design derivatives to enhance the value of willow weaving craft and provide relevant references for the high-quality development of the industry.

Acknowledgments. Our work is supported by the Project of Philosophy and Social Science Planning of Anhui Province in 2022, and its number is ANSKQ2022D148.

References

1. Li, X.: Study on the cultural characteristics of Funan willow art under the background of the protection of intangible cultural heritage. J. Huaihua Univ. **36**(04), 13–15 (2017)
2. Jin, J., Chu, Q., Wang, Z.: Exploration of innovative design of traditional handicrafts based on emotional design: taking Funan willow weaving as an example. Design **33**(15), 147–149 (2020)
3. Zhang, L., Zhang, X.: Research on the fusion application of Funan willow weaving and ceramic materials. J. Guangxi Normal Univ. Nationalities **37**(03), 84–87 (2020)
4. Gui, M.: Study on the inheritance and development of Funan willow weaving from the perspective of dynamic protection. Anhui University (2019)
5. Zhang, H., Liu, T.: Study on the dynamic inheritance of traditional folk handicraft willow weaving. Packag. Eng. **38**(18), 1–4 (2017)
6. Shi, J.: Study on the production technology and inheritance protection of Funan willow weaving. Anhui University (2019)
7. Wei, Y., Wang, L.: Artisan spirit in Chinese intangible cultural heritage: research on the history and living inheritance of willow weaving crafts in the Huaihe river basin. Ind. Eng. Des. **2**(01), 1–10 (2020)
8. Gong, M.: New forms of agriculture and rural economy and design value. Decoration (01), 26–31 (2022)
9. Liu, Y., Jia, S., Zhao, W.: Research on the design and development of museum role-based intellectual property from a multidimensional derivative perspective. Packag. Eng. **41**(16), 254–259 (2020)
10. Jia, S.: Research on creative design and development based on museum cultural intellectual property. Donghua University (2020)

Study of Development of Library Cultural and Creative Products from the Perspective of the Metaverse

Mengli Xu[(✉)] and Junnan Ye[(✉)]

East China University of Science and Technology, Shanghai, China
1921036356@qq.com, yejunnan971108@qq.com

Abstract. As the underlying technology that supports the development of the metaverse is gradually improving and maturing, new technologies and new thinking under the concept of metaverse are constantly pushing the development and change of the existing industry. The library industry needs innovative ideas of design and marketing. Firstly, the current research status of library cultural and creative product development are analysed through literature and the problems faced by the library cultural. Secondly, the solutions to problems and product opportunities brought about by new technologies and new thinking for library cultural and creative product development in the context of the metaverse industry are examined. Afterwards, a model of library cultural and creative product development are outputted from a metaverse perspective on the basis of the existing development models. Finally, this model is used for product practice.

Keywords: library · cultural and creative product · metaverse · product development

1 Introduction

Cultural consumption has become an important way to enhance the well-being of the nation. As a carrier of cultural storage and dissemination, libraries have driven the development of library cultural and creative products, and the development of library cultural and creative products has become a current research hotspot.

2 Library Creative Product Development

2.1 Library Creative Product Development Content

Cultural and creative product development is the process of providing consumers with tangible products and intangible services based on cultural resources through intellectual activity and design, with the ultimate goal of achieving cultural dissemination and satisfaction of users' spiritual needs [1]. It aims to achieve the ultimate goal of cultural dissemination and satisfaction of users' spiritual needs. Library cultural and creative product development focuses the design sources on library resources and library-related elements, aiming to make library resources "come alive" [2] (Fig. 1). Each stage is independent and interconnected.

C. Stephanidis et al. (Eds.): HCII 2023, CCIS 1834, pp. 527–534, 2023.
https://doi.org/10.1007/978-3-031-35998-9_68

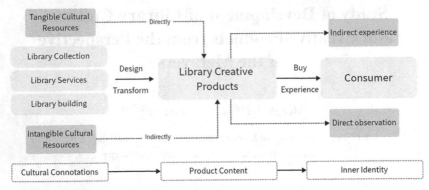

Fig. 1. Cultural connotations of library creative products delivered

2.2 Current State of Creative Product Development in Libraries

Many libraries have started to gradually lay out their cultural and creative industries and develop cultural and creative products, using cultural and creative product development as an important way to enhance library services [3]. However, there are still many problems in the development process of cultural and creative library products. There is still a lack of breakthrough development in terms of product carriers, immersion experiences, marketing and communication.

Firstly, libraries are not sufficiently innovative. Most libraries' creative product development is led by internal library staff, who lack the ability to fully integrate creativity with cultural product development and design.

Secondly, the content carrier of the library's cultural and creative products is thin. A large number of cultural and creative products with household items as the carrier are not able to bring about a good interactive experience.

3 Metaverse and Library Creative Product Development

3.1 Metaverse Concepts and Characteristics

Meta-universe is a new virtual society based on six core technologies: blockchain technology, interactive technology, video game technology, artificial intelligence technology, network and computing technology, and Internet of Things technology [4] The metaverse is parallel to the real world. The metaverse is parallel to the real world and allows each user to produce and edit content [5].

3.2 Meta-universe Empowers Creative Product Development in Libraries

Libraries are now turning to explore digital creativity, including 3D perception of culture through digital software, virtual interactive experiences through interactive installations, virtual product sales, etc. [6].

Meta-universe's application of higher-order audiovisual technology allows people's creative labour to be materialised and visualised in front of the user [7]. The metaverse represents the latest stage in visual immersion technology, featuring audio-visual, interactive, persistent and immersive features [8] The metaverse represents the latest stage of visual immersion technology, with characteristics such as audiovisuality, interactivity, permanence and immersion. In the advanced stage of Internet technology development, this integration of information technology, audiovisual technology and other technologies can present invisible and intangible products in virtual space, deepening users' intuitive experience of content and images. At the same time, the metaverse can broaden the application scenarios of cultural and creative industries in libraries and give rise to new cultural and creative industries. VR, AR, artificial intelligence and other technologies are developing rapidly and are widely used, providing a good opportunity for the development of cultural and creative industries and the development of cultural and creative products [6].

4 Exploring the Library's Cultural and Creative Product Development Model from a Metaverse Perspective

4.1 The Underlying Technical Layer

This layer includes the infrastructure and equipment that make up the metaverse and various development tools (Fig. 2). It mainly introduces various IoT technologies to manage the vast data resources of the library; interactive technologies such as AR, VR and MR to broaden the application scenarios and immersive experiences of the library's cultural creation; and various blockchain technologies to provide a safe and stable underlying technological ecological environment for the authentication and circulation of digital collections.

Fig. 2. Introduction of metaverse to library creative product development

4.2   Content Creation Layer

The unified metadata standard is used to structure the description of multimodal archival information resources such as text, image, video and space, and to further extract concepts, entities and relationships at different levels in digital resources based on ontology technology [9]. The knowledge graph between resource data is established through text analysis, content analysis, temporal analysis and spatial analysis [10]. The project aims to provide a traceable resource base for the development of cultural and creative products and to bridge the data silos [11]. Through metaverse technology empowerment, a library culture product creation platform featuring interaction and sharing is created.

4.3   Product Presentation Layer

Relying on the metaverse to develop library cultural and creative products broadens the idea of product design and provides a variety of media options for releasing and disseminating the value of library collection resources. The metaverse world is not bound by three-dimensional space, and the products can complete multimodal interaction with the five senses. In the marketing phase, the main tasks of libraries are to plan the sales channels and develop marketing strategies for their cultural and creative products [12]. The main tasks in the marketing phase are to plan the sales channels and develop marketing strategies. Accurate user marketing positioning can help the commercial success of the product. Extend the reach of library culture and creativity through the interconnection of the platform with social media platforms. Use big data to profile user demand preferences and accurately match corresponding products [13].

5   Design Practice

The Suzhou Library, with its rich collections, is committed to the integration of culture and industry to achieve the preservation and dissemination of culture and to create a more distinctive and quality library service. This design practice focuses on the Suzhou Library's valuable antique book collection and explores the development of the library's cultural and creative products.

5.1   The Underlying Technical Layer

Suzhou Library has the first design-themed library in China, located on the fifth floor of the North Library, focusing on 'design development' and 'design exhibition'. Based on this platform, the library can introduce various IoT technologies to manage the library's vast data resources, enabling designers, companies and design organizations to access information more quickly and easily, clarify cultural aspects and improve creative efficiency.

5.2   Content Creation Layer

Reconstructing the Ancient Books Resource System of Suzhou Library.   The Suzhou Library has a vast and complex collection of ancient resources. These precious resources include more than just the content itself. The colours, typography and text forms of ancient books can all be used as design objects. The typographic binding of these books contains many design possibilities (Figs. 3, 4 and 5).

Fig. 3. Color elements in antique books

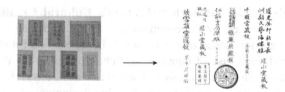

Fig. 4. Information elements of antique book bindings

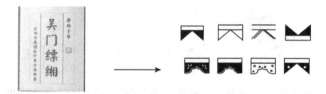

Fig. 5. Elements of motifs for the mouth of an antique book binding

Building a Platform for Co-creation of Cultural Products in Suzhou Libraries.   Using the Suzhou Library's Design Library as a basic platform. Build an online and offline cultural product co-creation platform, around cultural creativity and design research and development, providing literature resources and professional tools for professional designers and design institutions, design enthusiasts and consumers (Fig. 6).

Fig. 6. Cultural and Creative Online Co-creation Platform

5.3 Product Presentation Layer

Enriching the Expression of Suzhou Library's Cultural Creativity. The meta-universe is not constrained by three-dimensional space, and there are more options for representation carriers based on the resources in the Suzhou Library collection. In addition to the traditional use of common household items as the design carrier, the presentation form can also use patterns and text elements as basic elements to build an online platform where users can experience the cultural connotations in the auditory and visual senses to achieve a more multi-faceted product experience (Figs. 7 and 8).

Fig. 7. Silk scarf from the series of book mouth illustrations of ancient book

Fig. 8. Online display of the Antique Book Binding Information Text Series fashion

Product Marketing Layer. Through big data analysis of the characteristics of users who are interested in "ancient book binding", a portrait is drawn, and the promotion focus and marketing methods are planned in conjunction with the product demand and product design elements. The theme of the campaign is "Ancient Book Binding", with the text representing the printing information in the ancient book as the element and the auxiliary pattern redesigned with the book opening pattern of the ancient book binding, aiming to express the cultural atmosphere of the ancient book and promote the cultural heritage of Jiangnan. The marketing campaign holds online activities to showcase the ancient books, allowing people to experience and become interested in the culture of ancient books; users are encouraged to participate in the secondary creation of ancient book elements, forming a good ecology for product creation and consumption.

6 Conclusion

By combining the background of the metaverse industry, this paper aims to make the most of the library's resource advantages, enrich the library's service content, better meet the needs of users, and help the library's cultural creation out of the industrial dilemma. It also provides a new path for the development of library cultural and creative products from a metaverse perspective and further enriches theoretical research on the development of library cultural and creative products. Due to the limitations of the equipment and the author's knowledge reserve, the research on metaverse in this paper still lacks certain depth, and there is still much room for exploring the mode of combining with library cultural and creative development. Further research will be conducted on the application mode, path and theory of metaverse in library cultural and creative development to promote the flourishing development of cultural and creative industries.

References

1. Sun, X., Jin, W., Li, C.: Research on the design of nanjing museum cultural and creative product from the perspective of experience. In: Marcus, A., Wang, W. (eds.) DUXU 2017. LNCS, vol. 10290, pp. 529–539. Springer, Cham (2017). https://doi.org/10.1007/978-3-319-58640-3_38
2. Guo, Y.Y.: Copyright protection in the development and use of cultural and creative products in libraries. Libr. Work Res. (11), 20–26 (2022)
3. Su, Y., Lu, H.: Analysis and inspiration of product development categories and models of cultural and creative products in public libraries. J. Shan-Dong Libr. (1), 44–50 (2022)
4. Wang, Y., Su, Z., Zhang, N., et al.: A survey on metaverse: fundamentals, security, and privacy. IEEE Commun. Surv. Tutor. 1 (2022)
5. Dionisio, J.D.N., Iii, W.G.B., Gilbert, R.: 3D virtual worlds and the metaverse: current status and future possibilities. ACM Comput. Surv. 45(3), 1–38 (2013)
6. Lee, K.C.: Digital Creativity: Individuals, Groups, and Organizations. Springer, New York (2013). https://doi.org/10.1007/978-1-4614-5749-7
7. Fang, L., Zhao, X.: Metaverse and cultural digitization: an analysis based on property rights theory. Digit. Libr. Forum (9), 70–72 (2022)
8. He, S., Qin, J.: From VR/AR to metaverse: a study of immersive children's picture book interaction design for the alpha generation. Libr. Constr. (5), 66–72 (2022)

9. Xiang, A.-L., Gao, S., Peng, Y.-T., et al.: Knowledge reorganization and scene reconstruction: a meta-universe for digital resource management. Libr. Intell. Knowl. **39**(1), 30–38 (2022)
10. Wei, J., Liu, R.: A versatile approach for constructing a domain knowledge graph for culture. Proc. Assoc. Inf. Sci. Technol. **56**(1), 808–809 (2019)
11. Chen, W., Wang, D., Xu, Y., et al.: Construction of metadata model for digital construction of cultural and creative works. J. Agric. Libr. Inf. Technol. 1–10
12. Wang, G.: Research on the workflow and model of cultural and creative product development in libraries. Libr. Work Res. (10), 25–32+74 (2019)
13. Yang, H.: A comparative study on the development models of library cultural and creative products. Henan J. Libr. Sci. **39**(6), 59–61 (2019)

A Study on the Decoding of Regional Cultural Genes and the Design of Cultural and Creative Products

Junnan Ye and Yue Wu[✉]

East China University of Science and Technology, Shanghai, China
1060036118@qq.com

Abstract. Regional culture is an important aspect in the field of cultural studies and has become an important force for social development. In recent years, problems such as homogenization and lack of regional cultural characteristics have emerged in cultural and creative products. Taking Shanghai as an example, this paper uses design semiotics and other methods to study the decoding of regional cultural genes and cultural and creative product design. Firstly, the overall framework of regional cultural gene decoding is constructed. Secondly, the theoretical innovation of regional cultural gene decoding and the innovative design strategy of cultural and creative products are proposed. Finally, the feasibility of the system framework of cultural gene decoding is verified through the design practice of Fengjing town's product packaging. This topic summarizes the methodological theories of semiotics and design factors used in gene decoding, which provides theoretical support and methodological basis for the development of regional cultural and creative products.

Keywords: Regional Culture · Genetic decoding · Cultural and Creative Product Development · Design and Communication

1 Introduction

Regional culture is a unique cultural tradition of a specific region, and as a cultural wealth, it brings new opportunities and vitality to cultural and creative products. Integrating regional cultural elements into the design of cultural and creative products not only makes the products more representative and recognizable and enhances their artistic sense, but also helps to spread the regional culture.

Research on regional culture mainly involves the fields of landscape, furniture, and cultural and creative products. Scholars' research on regional cultural and creative products starts from cultural resources and symbol extraction; Efendy et al. [1] explored the process of library interior design under Javanese culture, and Li et al. [2] studied the highway landscape design method for regional culture. Some scholars have also proposed innovative research methods using interdisciplinary theories and new technologies. Song et al. [3] proposed an innovative design model for experiential cultural and creative products using the theory of cognitive psychology, and Xue Li et al. [4] compared the traditional and artificial intelligence-assisted models in product design, and the study summarized regional cultural characteristics and traditional graphic language. At present, many innovative products have emerged in the cultural and creative product market, but homogenization is also frequent, mostly manifested by direct copying of elements and abuse without connotation [5], so a systematic method is needed to decode and extract the cultural genes of the region and apply them reasonably in cultural and creative products, so that they have both cultural and artistic values.

Cultural and creative products are products with physical forms based on culture and derived from cultural symbols, and are an important part of cultural consumption [6]. Excellent cultural and creative design relies on decoding cultural genes, reflecting the mainstream values of society and showing the soft power of cities. Creating cultural and creative products with regional characteristics has become a universal demand for the development of cultural tourism industry. Shanghai, a representative international city, has maintained steady growth in the industry as a whole and has great potential in the cultural consumption market. This paper takes Shanghai as an example to study the decoding of regional cultural genes and cultural and creative product design.

2   Method

The cultural gene is a concept derived from the gene theory in biology, which is a design mindset used to study the spread and evolution of culture [7]. This is a word that corresponds to Gene. According to the research of many scholars, this paper summarizes the "four-step" process of decoding Shanghai's cultural genes, as shown in Fig. 1.

1. Source culture data collection and analysis

The methods of researching source culture include documentary method, fieldwork method, questionnaire survey method, and interview method. In the process of researching source culture, we can understand the basic information of culture by consulting historical documents and internet materials; collect relevant physical pictures from major museums, historical sites, and cultural gathering areas; and obtain perceptual knowledge through interviews or questionnaires with user groups who understand culture.

After the collection is completed the cultural genes are initially mined to analyze the elements that have potential in the source culture. The methods include perceptual mining, genealogical mining, geographical mining, meaning mining and tracking mining [8]. The perception mining method mainly analyzes the cultural elements with high recognition of the source culture; the genealogy mining method mainly analyzes the elements of cultural characteristics with strong inheritance; the regional mining method mainly analyzes the cultural ecological correlation factors that are compatible with the regional cultural characteristics; the meaning mining method mainly analyzes the cultural elements in the cultural heritage that do not have a specific inheritance mode; the tracking mining method mainly analyzes the historical development process of culture from the time lineage combing, the origin The method of tracing is mainly to analyze the historical development process, the source, the evolution and the development trend of culture from the time line.

2. Cultural Gene Classification and Extraction

Cultural genes are extracted in a variety of ways, and a common approach is to classify the source culture, which broadly includes three methods: dominant and recessive factors, semiotic four dimensions, and biogenetic methods.

Cultural genes are divided into dominant and recessive factors. Explicit factors refer to tangible factors that people can directly feel with their five senses, including patterns, forms, colors, etc.; implicit factors refer to intangible factors such as emotions, meanings, ideas, etc. From the cultural connotation, we analyze the cognitive style, value system, and cultural context. Implicit factors can use questionnaires to collect perceptual evaluation vocabulary, express it in the form of diagrams, and distill it in the same simplified and diffuse way as explicit factors features, and complete the extraction of cultural genes.

A symbol is a human means of conveying information. Semiotics proposes four analytical dimensions, semantic, semantic construction, semantic use and context, which help to decipher the symbolic connotation of artifacts [9]. The semantic dimension includes explicit and implicit semantics, reflecting the function of artifacts from the modeling ontology and interpreting the social value behind artifacts from the metaphorical perspective, respectively; the semantic construction dimension studies the structure of artifact elements and the performance of artifact elements, determining their spatial location, layout, and expression, and designing applications by means of deconstruction, combination, and dispersion; the contextual dimension refers to the artifacts and the user use environment, including visual style, natural environment, and Social environment; Contextual dimension refers to the user's mode of thinking and cultural background, to explore the cultural connotation and enhance the value of the recreated product (Fig. 1).

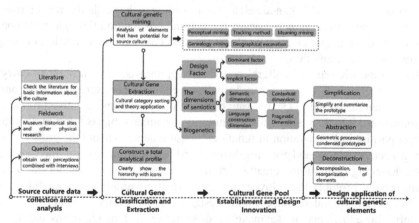

Fig. 1. Decoding process of regional cultural genes

Cultural genes can be regarded as the smallest information unit of linear cultural heritage. Therefore, the extraction method of biological genes can be used analogously to the extraction of cultural genes, and the representative cultural products of the region can be collected, and the core cultural elements can be obtained through function, principle and structure analysis to complete the inverse translation process, and then the cultural genes can be concentrated and refined to complete the reverse transcription process.

Finally, the total analysis mapping is constructed to clearly show the hierarchical relationship of cultural contents with diagrams. In order to visualize each hierarchical structure, the corresponding analysis mapping can be constructed and each design gene can be coded to facilitate further screening, transformation and application, showing the hierarchical relationship and categories of each design element.

3. Cultural Gene Pool Establishment and Design Innovation

The establishment of a gene bank allows the storage of rich cultural genes and is an important tool for the conservation of cultural elements [10]. Researchers can flexibly select, match, modify and store genes in the library and continuously enrich the gene pool with design activities. For innovative design methods of design factors, the main methods are simplification, abstraction and deconstruction and reorganization. Simplification method is based on retaining the main form of the original pattern, simplifying it, summarizing the content of the prototype and inheriting the original modeling characteristics. The abstract method is to condense the characteristics of the original pattern, use the geometric method, use the point line surface outline, transform the individual pattern into continuity, and do exaggerated and diffusion treatment appropriately. The deconstruction and reorganization method is to decompose the prototype partially or as a whole, and the specific techniques include superposition, addition, subtraction, scaling, transformation, etc., to reassemble freely.

4. Design application of cultural genetic elements

On the basis of the above research and sorting, elements from the regional cultural gene pool can be applied to the development of cultural and creative product design. The key is to select suitable genetic elements according to the aesthetic characteristics of different people, and accurately convey the cultural connotation through the shape and color of the cultural and creative products, so as to complete the extension of imagery and transmission of emotion.

Due to the diversity of cultural and creative products, it is difficult to carry out mass production, and it is necessary to balance cultural characteristics and economic benefits when designing [11]. Innovative design of cultural and creative products can be summarized into three strategies: changes in consumer subjects to promote younger product positioning, innovation in functional requirements to avoid the proliferation of homogeneous products, and grasping design trends to transition to diversified aesthetics. When designing cultural and creative products, creators should consider the needs of young people, promote the rejuvenation of product positioning, use modularization, gamification and digitalization, combine design with practicality, add interactive forms, and enrich the experience of use; make use of social networking platforms and regularly learn about the popular "Netflix" style in order to get closer to the aesthetic interests of the public and grasp the popular trends. We also make use of social media platforms to understand the current "netflix" style, so as to get closer to the aesthetic interest of the public, grasp the trend and make the design products more fashionable.

In terms of design theory innovation, unconscious design theory corresponds to the symbolic code and regional cultural symbolic environment formed after objective sketching of product appearance, structure and usage behavior, grafting the characteristics of the target product with the cultural symbolic environment and using the two spans for deep cultural excavation [12]. The combination of unconscious design theory and semiotics is applied to extract cultural genes, discover objective needs, and precisely transform cultural connotations into cultural and creative products with both practicality and cultural attributes [13]. In terms of user perception, the kano model can assess consumer preferences and requirements [14], which reflects the nonlinear relationship between each product attribute and user satisfaction. The kano model combining semi-structured interviews and fuzzy linguistic concepts can yield more accurate results during actual research [15], and the combination of quantitative and qualitative methods makes the design practice of cultural and creative products more reliable.

3 Case Study

In order to verify the practicality of the decoding process of regional cultural genes proposed in this study, the design practice is carried out with the derivative products of Fengjing Town in Jinshan District, Shanghai as an example. As a typical ancient water town in Jiangnan, Fengjing Town is one of the existing large scale and well-preserved water towns in Shanghai, with a deep historical heritage.

First of all, the cultural research of Fengjing town, using the regional excavation method to analyze the cultural and ecological factors associated with the regional cultural characteristics, which are summarized into four aspects: water township architecture, famous people in the past, the four treasures of Fengjing and three paintings a chess. The water township architecture is the most distinctive feature of Fengjing town, which is known as "two bridges in three steps and ten harbors in one look"; there are more than 600 famous people recorded in history since the Tang Dynasty, and there are many humanistic landscapes such as Zhu Xuefan's former residence and Ding Cong's cartoon museum; Fengjing Ding's feet, Jinfeng Yellow Wine, Tianxiang Dried Bean Curd and Fengjing Scholar's Cake are known as "Fengjing four treasures"; three paintings a chess refers to Jinshan peasant painting, Ding Cong cartoon, Cheng Shifa Chinese painting and Gu Shuiru's Go.

Second, the cultural genes are classified and extracted. Agriculture is the most prominent economic source of Fengjing town, so the cultural genes can be extracted around the agricultural products in the derivative product design. Five aspects of cultural symbols of Fengjing are mined. The agriculture of Fengjing Town can be divided into four industries: fruit industry, rice industry, aquatic industry and green vegetable industry. The explicit genes are the characteristic products of each industry, and the recessive genes start from the cultivation process of Fengjing farmers to explore the unique storytelling.

After completing the construction of cultural gene mapping, the obtained cultural gene elements are organized. In the design innovation, the simplification method is mainly used to draw illustrations based on the original products, remove the complicated details and adopt simple low-saturation colors; the abstraction method and deconstruction method are used to design the logo, and the elements are geometrically processed, as shown in Fig. 2, wheat, fish, radish and waves are extracted and recombined, and the main color distinction is made according to the four industries.

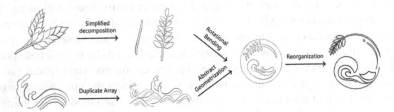

Fig. 2. Elemental extraction process

Finally, the design elements are applied to the package, using highly condensed phrases to describe the product, and finishing the whole package design with finishing elements such as seals and borders, so that the whole series of styles reach unity. The effect is shown in Fig. 3.

Fig. 3. Fengjing town products packaging design

4   Results and Discussion

The cultural elements in this case use the distinction between explicit and implicit factors in the extraction, and methods such as unconscious design can be introduced when the range of extracted objects is too large and the most important elements cannot be clearly identified. In terms of the communication of regional cultural and creative products, in order to help the development of Fengjing's agricultural culture, an agricultural products sales APP is designed in the case practice, which includes Fengjing's science popularization, soft promotion, personalized shopping recommendation, etc. Strategies such as offline exhibition and live broadcast with goods are proposed. In terms of integrated communication of cultural and creative products, firstly, it is necessary to open up communication channels and build a platform for integrated promotion: infiltrate into people's lives and improve the influence and visibility of cultural and creative products. Secondly, integrate high-quality resources and develop IP to increase traffic: take representative characters, architecture, historical facts and events as prototypes, refine attractive IP, tell regional stories, and accumulate fan groups through cooperation with popular anchors and other means, so that high-quality IP products can extend their market vitality. Optimize the sales model and plan online and offline activities. In terms of promotion and operation, we adopt cloud exhibition, "crowdfunding" marketing and live-streaming with goods online, and brand salon offline to create awareness in a short period of time. In terms of promotion and operation, we adopt cloud exhibition, "crowdfunding" marketing and live broadcast with goods on line, and brand salon offline to create awareness within a short period of time, and combine with consumers' behavior, so that more excellent cultural and creative products can enter thousands of households.

5 Conclusion and Forward

This study starts from regional cultural and creative products, focuses on regional cultural genes and design applications, takes Shanghai as an example to analyze the current situation of its cultural industry development, and proposes a process system for decoding regional cultural genes, uses the packaging of the products of Fengjing Town in Jinshan for design practice, verifies the feasibility and effectiveness of the system framework for decoding cultural genes, and proposes development strategies in terms of theoretical innovation of decoding regional cultural genes, innovative design and dissemination of cultural and creative products. The development strategy is proposed from three aspects: theoretical innovation of regional cultural gene decoding, innovative design of cultural and creative products and dissemination paths. The process method and design development strategy proposed in this study provide theoretical support and methodological basis for the development of regional cultural creativity, and have important practical significance for the inheritance and promotion of regional culture. However, due to time and energy constraints, there is a lack of in-depth user research in the research of regional cultural elements, and it is necessary to improve the design process in further research to continuously iterate and conduct follow-up surveys on regional culture to strengthen the universality of the method.

References

1. Hartini, B.W., Situmorang, R.: Interior design of postgraduate library based on cyber technology by applying Javanese cultural ornaments and eco-friendly materials. IOP Conf. Ser. Mater. Sci. Eng. **852**(1), 012145 (2020)

2. Li, Y., Chen, F., Jiang, D.: Research on highway landscape design based on regional culture. IOP Conf. Ser. Earth Environ. Sci. **330**(2), 022046 (2019)
3. Song, Y., Zhu, M., Kang, H.: Research on creative product design of experiential cultural tourism based on cognitive psychology. Psychiatr. Danub. **33**(8), 648–657 (2021)
4. Li, X., Lin, B.: The development and design of artificial intelligence in cultural and creative products. Math. Probl. Eng. **2021**, 1–10 (2021)
5. Fu, Z.: Innovative design of cultural and creative products based on regional culture. Pack. Eng. **40**(20), 215–218+222 (2019)
6. Yang, L., Mengfei, M., Mi, T.: Research on innovative design methods for cultural and creative products. Pack. Eng. **41**(14), 288–294 (2020)
7. Iloh, C.: Do It for the culture: the case for memes in qualitative research. Int. J. Qual. Methods **20**, 1–10 (2021)
8. Liu, Z., Jiang, Y.Y.: Construction and design application of cultural genealogy map of traditional bamboo weaving craft in Xiangxi. J. Bamboo **37**(4), 56–63 (2018)
9. Schielke, T.: The language of lighting: applying semiotics in the evaluation of lighting design. LEUKOS **15**(2–3), 227–248 (2019)
10. Cannizzaro, S.: Internet memes as internet signs: a semiotic view of digital culture. Sign Syst. Stud. **44**(4), 562–586 (2016)
11. Hsueh, S., Zhou, B., Chen, Y.: Supporting technology-enabled design education and practices by DFuzzy decision model: applications of cultural and creative product design. Int. J. Technol. Design Educ. **32**(4), 2239–2256 (2022)
12. Ding, F., Wei, W.: Naoto Fukasawa and his without thought design theory. J. Hunan Univ. Technol. (Soc. Sci. Ed.) **16**(2), 138–141 (2011)
13. Yang, L., Liu, W.: The application of without thought design in the civilian security product. In: 2019 IEEE 6th International Conference on Industrial Engineering and Applications (ICIEA). Tokyo, Japan: IEEE, 2019, pp. 150–153 (2019)
14. Južnik Rotar, L., Kozar, M.: The use of the Kano model to enhance customer satisfaction. Organizacija **50**(4), 339–351 (2017)
15. Yeh, H.-R., Lin, L.-Z., Lu, C.-F.: Classification of traditional cultural elements in temple street festivals using the fuzzy Kano model. Curr. Issue Tour. **22**(10), 1190–1215 (2019)

Analysis on the Characteristics of Advocating Business in the Decorative Art of ShanShaanGan Guild Hall from the Perspective of Image Semiotics

Zhao Yiming[✉]

College of Architecture and Urban Planning, Huazhong University of Science and Technology, No. 1037 Luoyu Road, Hongshan District, Wuhan, China
987685665@qq.com

Abstract. With the spirit of craftsmanship spirit and exquisite skills of craftsman, the beauty of Chinese traditional architecture has spread by adopting the elements of the Chinese culture for architectural decoration, forming many architectural art treasures. ShanShaanGan Guild Hall, located in Bianjing City (Bian Jing in Jin Dynasty), is a typical guild hall building in Central China. It collects a large number of architectural and carving decorative arts and contains rich historical, cultural and architectural art values. Based on the image triple interpretation method proposed by Bart Rowland, this paper analyzes the appearance,universal significance, deep significance and existing background of its decorative elements through the symbol extension layer and connotation layer.From the analysis on the characteristics of advocating business of guild building decoration symbols, this paper deduces the simple wealth view of businessmen and the great inclusiveness of business culture in the traditional sense.

Keywords: ShanShaanGan Guild Hall · Image semiotics · Architectural decoration · Characteristics of advocating business

1 Introduction

The origin of traditional culture often can be traced from tangible objects with profound historical culture. As a medium of cultural transmission, architecture has the dual role of being symbols itself and carrying symbols. As symbol carrier, architecture has the universal function of semiotic signifier and signified, demonstrating artful shapes and images and extending the profound implication of society, humanities and history. Guild hall, a commercial and cultural place built by businessmen from other regions in China, is the product of commercial development in the middle and late period of Chinese feudal society. What makes guild halls different from functional architecture such as ancestral halls is that they are usually magnificent and grandiose due to their commercial features and the comparison mentality of merchants. Other than that, the decoration is also particularly gorgeous. As a result, guild hall represents traditional architecture

C. Stephanidis et al. (Eds.): HCII 2023, CCIS 1834, pp. 543–553, 2023.
https://doi.org/10.1007/978-3-031-35998-9_70

with artistic expressive force. The beauty in the decoration of guild hall shows less in nationality and regionalism than ancestral hall, it is showed in merging the aesthetic of the public and humanism ideological trend of the period. Therefore, guild hall is an iconic product of social integration. ShanShaanGan Guild Hall represents all guild halls in Central China because it possesses superb social and cultural significance and high value of architecture form, in addition, it's artistic value is elevated even higher due to wood, stone and tile carving.

2   An Overview of Decorative Art and Image Semiotics of ShanShaanGan Guild Hall

Located in Bianjing, the capital of Song Dynasty, ShanShaanGan Guild Hall was built in the 41st year of the Qianlong Dynasty (1776). In the Qing Dynasty, Bianjing was renamed Kaifeng which was the capital of Henan, the commercial trade was developed with many commercial intercourse. ShanShaanGan Guild Hall was built by the wealthy merchants of Shanxi, Shaanxi and Gansu in the old residence of Xu Da of Zhongshan in order to provide a place for rest and business contacts for the villagers in this place.The hall building has the layout of traditional courtyard, and the architectural system is based on wooden frames.The organizational style is concise.In line with the layout of traditional Chinese buildings, the guild hall sits north and faces south with symmetrical structure on both sides of the axis.Along the central axis is the Wall, the opera building, the archway, the main hall, and the ancillary buildings which are distributed on both sides. The ShanShaanGan Guild Hall is different from the traditional guild hall. As the last hall enshrines and worships the Guansheng Emperor, it can use auspicious motifs such as the dragon and phoenix without the restriction of hierarchical regulations to fully decorate the guild building. As a result, the ShanShaanGan Guild Hall has rich historical and cultural values as well as architectural aesthetics.

The architectural aesthetics of the guild hall can be seen from its architectural design. From the Wall into the inside, the central axis of the main halls adopt the hip roof (the highest level of roofs) decorated with high relief flowers, both ends are featured by dragon-shaped animals and glazed green tiles. East and west sides of the compartment are connected by eaves corridor, under the eaves are lifelike wood carvings which are hollowed out. The carving art of "three wonders" in the guild hall makes it the greatest guild hall in the Central Plains, that is, wood carving, stone carving and brick carving. In the courtyard, everywhere has been carefully designed and polished by craftsmen from the construction of stone pier to the brick carving of the Wall, which reflects the developed handicraft industry and exquisite skills of craftsmen in the Ming and Qing dynasties.Decorative themes include birds and animals, characters, myths and stories, landscapes, etc.., and the totem culture lives in the utilitarian beliefs of merchants, all of which reflect the characteristics of advocating business in the decorative arts. The carving form is influenced by the minimalist aesthetics of the Northern Song Dynasty, showing the beauty of elegance and freshness. ShanShaanGan Guild Hall embodies the beautiful beliefs of the merchants beyond utilitarianism, and the intricate decorative patterns in the building are symbols of the integration of folklore, faith and social values, expressing traditional meanings by convention, as well as the deep meaning of the characteristics of advocating business.

Symbols are abstract expressions of images and real things, with a broad range of concepts across disciplines, including the four main disciplines of semantics, logic, rhetoric, and hermeneutics.In today's increasingly developed cold media, pictorial symbols act as language in some areas, enveloping all aspects of our lives.Modern semiotics can be traced back to the 19th century, when people began to realize the interrelationship between images and symbols, and Saussure, the philosopher and structuralist, proposed the dualism which is the most famous concept of 'signifier' and 'signifier'. At the same time, Pierce added the dynamism of semiotics to its foundation, scientifically and systematically constituting the triadism of semiotics, i.e., pictorial symbols, indicator symbols and symbolic symbols. Architecture, as an image symbol, is the turn and trend of contemporary visual culture communication, and architectural decoration is an important part of its imagery and it is very meaningful.In his book Image Rhetoric, Bart-Roland studies photographs, pictures, and paintings, based on the photographs, proposing the linguistics of images in an attempt to reveal the mechanisms by which sociocultural and ideological coding works in images. He decomposed the image into three layers: "linguistic information layer", "extended image layer" and "connotative image layer". The triple interpretation method is known for providing a systematic interpretation of traditional cultural symbols.As it is adopted for the interpretation of architectural decorative symbols, the elaboration of the extended meaning and connotation of the decoration can be achieved by combining the social and historical nature of architecture with the artistry of decorative symbols.

There are many architectural decorative elements of ShanShaanGan Guild Hall, but the architectural decoration graphics are different from the advertising image in linguistic information layer. Therefore, the language information layer can be regarded as the structural factor of the image ontology to discuss the extension layer and the connotation layer. The three-fold interpretation concept is abstract to some extent, but its three-layer concept can be interpreted in meanings as elements, superficial connotations and deep connotations. The deep significance of the architectural decorative graphics of signification can be depicted by the the modeling and colour of signifier and metalanguage and image category of the universal meaning of signified. The connotation is derived from the form expressed by the signifier and the relevant concepts and existing historical backgrounds referred to by signified, that is, the characteristics of advocating business of the decorative arts.

3 The Epitaxial Layer of the Decoration Image Symbol in the ShanShaanGan Guild Hall

3.1 The Epitaxial Layer of the Decoration Image Symbol in the ShanShaanGan Guild Hall

The guild hall building preserves the excellent part of traditional Chinese culture, accumulates the essence of the aesthetic practice of Chinese architecture, and forms the architectural beauty with national features.The decorative images and artistic expressions of the guild hall mainly find expression in the wood, stone and brick carving decorative components in the building, focusing on the eaves, door posts, window ledges, arches and walls, etc., visually exquisite and complex, but without losing the integrity of the architectural style. Wood material is the most commonly used material in traditional Chinese architecture, wood carving decorative pattern has also become an important part of the decorative components and it has formed a certain scale in the ShanShaan-Gan Guild Hall, distributed under the eaves of multiple layers, layers of carving through the exquisite pattern, fang, bucket arch, sparrow brace, baffle, hanging columns and other parts are decorated with exquisite auspicious patterns.According to the different functions of the building, different wood attributes are selected, basswood, poplar, pear wood and other materials are used, and the decorative carving often uses a whole log for carving, giving full play to its texture and color characteristics.Brick carving and stone carving decoration is the other two important decorative components of the ShanShaan-Gan Guild Hall, using granite, masonry, bluestone, etc. as the carving raw materials, mainly used in the green brick back carving pattern under the wall and the eaves, as well as the pillar foundation, the drum pattern decoration, the hard material sense of the masonry with the soft decorative pattern forming a harmonious coexistence between the force and the soft. The construction methods of elements mostly use symmetrical, continuous and single-piece types, and the construction methods are selected according to different themes. Symmetrical patterns include upper and lower symmetry, left and right symmetry and circular symmetry, they are mostly used in the the ridge of the roof, rafters, foreheads, the Wall and so on in order to pursue the balance and diversity of patterns. Continuous pattern is mostly used in the carving of mythological stories on the forehead, Wall and under the eaves, with wood or brick as the carving carrier, and depicted in the form of flat relief in order to form a colourful composition and bear folk cultural connotations.Single-piece type includes single-piece continuous pattern and single-piece independent pattern. The wood carving of rafters represents single-piece continuous type. Single-piece independent pattern often appears in brick carving and stone carving art and often appear in a specific position such as on drum-shaped bearing stone and has a special meaning.

3.2   The Signifier and Signified of the Epitaxial Layer

The epitaxial image layer emphasized by Bart Roland is the visual and perception image layer of the image, which refers to the real objects analogous to the image, and the signifier is the image of these real objects being copied in the image.The epitaxial layer contains the consistent signifier and the signifier under the paradigm, with relative fixation and procedural features.There are many architectural decoration patterns and themes in the ShanShaanGan Guild Hall, and the image symbols are synonymous repetitions according to the coding of objective things, and the signifier can be regarded as the element content of the image body as a symbol, and is discussed from its appearance and color, as shown in Table1. Divide by thematic elements and spiritual satisfaction so as to explore the conventional meaning.The decorative elements in the courtyard are most concentrated in the Guandi Temple of the main hall, spreading over the eaves of the façade of the building and beams and window flowers in the interior. The eight purlins under the eaves and seven layers of openwork carvings are clearly layered, and the intricate patterns are reflected in different themes on each layer. The decorative pattern under the eaves mainly consists of grass, wood and flowers, auspicious birds and animals and auspicious symbols, from the bat on the lower floor of the eaves, the cloud pattern on the second floor, the two dragons playing beads on the third floor, the lion and horse and walking beast on the fourth floor, the pine and bamboo plum blossoms on the fifth floor, the mandarin duck playing in the water on the sixth floor, and the phoenix and peony on the seventh floor, which has the extensiveness of decorative themes and the auspicious feature of decorative aesthetics.

In the animal decoration patterns in the guild hall, the shape of the dragon, phoenix and bat is not restricted by the ruling class and is widely used, which is a major feature of the ShanShaanGan Guild hall, from the Wall to the east and west wings to the main hall, from the drum-shaped bearing stone to the eaves, from the building façade to the indoor gallery, the merchant hopes to beautify life through the image of the dragon and phoenix symbolized by the totem of the Chinese culture.As for plants, grapes, pomegranates, golden melons and other plants are carved on the masonry to imply fruitful achievements and flourishing population.For example, the melon pattern of the drum-shaped bearing stone is very common in the guild hall.At the same time, the lotus flower pattern is usually applied to the circular pillar base by the four sides under the influence of Buddhist culture. Peony, which represents wealth and auspiciousness, is often used as a wood carving decoration under the eaves, and the petals can also be carved out of nine layers.Character patterns are often found in the masonry carvings in the guildhall, mostly based on historical and mythological stories. The story of the Three Kingdoms and the promotion of filial piety are the main content, for example,on the second floor of the archway, there are 8 story paintings of Guan Yu, including Guan Yu scraping bones to cure poison, hanging seals and sealing gold, chopping Huaxiong between the twinkling of an eye, peach garden sworn brothers etc., showing Guan Yu's loyalty and valor and skill on the battlefield.ShanShaanGan Guild Hall has the uniqueness of carving folk culture, in the past, few guild hall buildings wound adopt people's life as the theme for decorative construction, but city life and street scenery were used as the source of theme in this courtyard building, reflecting the aesthetic of the public.The pattern of utensils is often used in the ShanShaanGan Guild Hall, and a large number of patterns are "bottles", the number of which is more than 50, and the meanings of different shapes vary. They are mainly distributed on both sides of the hall and the Wall.The four treasures of the study room, including the string of money and the abacus also appear in the pattern, conveying the aesthetic value of suiting both refined and popular tastes. The auspicious symbols of the building are mostly based on words or the elements of their abstract meanings. Abstract elements can be seen in the brick carving of the back word pattern of the girder of the Wall and using the swastika-style pattern in the courtyard as a floor brick decoration is also a common sight influenced by Buddhism.In the specific location of the building, specific characters are used, such as the four characters of "loyalty, righteousness, benevolence and courage" on the Wall, as well as the presence of multiple plaques, which have a certain indicative effect.

The color of the hall is mainly cyan and gold. The roof is mostly covered with cyan glazed tiles and yellow glazed tiles for embellishment. In addition, wood carving patterns are also colored cyan and gold. For example, the wood carvings of seven layers of the hall, which are typical of the decorative style of the building, are cyan and gold with red and white embellishments, which can be described as vivid and gorgeous. Yellow, red, cyan, white and black are the most widely used colors in ancient Chinese palace architecture, corresponding to the five directions of heaven and earth, giving people a sense of divine and majestic.

Table 1. Signifier and signified of decorative images

1 signifier			2 signified
	Elements category	Elements	General significance of the epitaxial layer
Modeling	Animal elements	Dragon, phoenix, spider, bats, lion, monkey, horse, etc	With animal themes as decorative images, symbolic techniques and homophonic words are usually used to express the pursuit of auspiciousness and beautiful life. As auspicious symbols of traditional Chinese culture, animal elements has the general recognition of auspicious meanings
	Plant elements	Lotus, peony, pomegranate, grape, golden melon, etc	The elements of plants are often used in architectural decoration in an abstract way. They are attached to the beautiful meanings under the influence of the cultural connotations of different plant and the belief and culture of Buddhism and Taoism,, such as bringing the new couple children and happiness and remain blessed throughout the year
	utensils elements	Bottle, abacus, string of money, etc	The extensive use of bottles in the guild hall is based on customs, meaning peace and prosperity

(*continued*)

Table 1. (*continued*)

1 signifier			2 signified
	Elements category	Elements	General significance of the epitaxial layer
	Character elements	The story of eight immortals crossing the sea 、 The opera of Jingtai Hui 、 Carving patterns praying for generations of marquises and expressing 24 kinds of filial behaviors and so on	The use of myths and legends materials shows the aesthetic value of the public, which reflects the confidence attitude the citizens adopted towards life. In the mean time, it also spreads traditional religious philosophy and has indoctrination function to some extent. Guild merchants also hope to pray for their business through the beautiful myths and legends
	Special character element	Specific character symbols, as well as back word, swastikas, etc	Specific character symbols inside the guild hall usually have the function of anchoring architectural objects, and the back word lines and swastikas are symbols of auspiciousness and beauty in the perceptions all the time
Colour	Color elements	Cyan, yellow, red, etc	According to the use of color and consistent recognition of traditional Chinese architecture, the colors dominated by cyan and yellow symbolize majesty and sacredness

4   The Connotation Layer of the Decorative Image Symbol in the ShanShaanGan Guild Hall

The signifier of the connotation layer of the symbol resides under the signifier and the referred category of the epitaxial layer, and the connotative image information has a close relationship with its culture, which is a kind of transliteration coding of culture.In the field of semiotics, the ShanShaanGan Guild Hall is layered on top of each other, and the characteristic meaning of the connotation layer is proposed according to the previous period for the signage layer of the symbol and the connotation layer symbol derived from

Table 2. Triple interpretation of image symbols

Symbol epitaxial layer	Meta image meta language	1signifier	2signified	II signified
		Animals, plants, objects, characters, characters, color elements	It refers to the faith symbol of the Chinese folk tradition, has the symbolic role of blessing and wishes, and is the decorative pattern transformed by the traditional auspicious symbol.	ShanShaanGan Guild Hall has both history and formation background: the times background, formation motivation and cultural background
Symbol connotation layer	surface	3 signification I signifier The auspicious view under the concept of folk tradition Businessmen'view of wealth under the secular belief The historical reflection and artistic aesthetic of the hall		
	deep (layer)	III signification (1) The guild hall embodies the simple wealth and auspicious views of the merchants, and represents the utilitarian spiritual beliefs of the merchants (2) The business culture is highly inclusive and compatible (3) Businessmen are not only the operators of business, but also the designers of architecture, the creators of art and the disseminators of culture.		

the signifier, combined with the historical context and social context of the building.As shown in Bartholand's three-fold interpretation of image symbols, the proposal of the connotation of image symbols is not a simple superposition or relationship progression logically, but on the basis of the first two interpretations, the meaning of the previous double image symbol is the new symbol signifier, and then combined with the reference to produce the image symbol meaning that is, the connotation of the image [2].

According to the analysis of the image elements of the 1 signifier and the 2 signified, the 3 signification(I signifier) has the subjectivity of the connotation, which can be mainly attributed to the auspicious view under the influence of the traditional concept of folklore, the wealth value under the influence of the secular beliefs of the merchants and the historical reflection and artistic aesthetics of the guild hall architecture. The objective anchorage with connotation of II signified can be transformed into the existing history and formation background of the ShanShaanGan Guild Hall: 1) The development of the commodity economy in the Ming and Qing dynasties reached the highest peak in history, and the circulation and trade of goods increased.The atmosphere of advocating business in the two provinces of Shanxi and Shaanxi waextremely strong. At that time, businessmen run around to make a living and trade activities were mostly carried out through the guild hall. Therefore, Shan Shaan guild halls were opened all over the country. The architectural style is characterized by their grand scale and majestic structure, and the guild halls sooth the foreign merchants who are on the move with their strong regional features. The Shan Shaan merchants combined the Guandi Temple with the form of the guild hall in hope of being blessed by the Guan Emperor.The guild hall building was the embodiment of the spirit of Shan Shaan merchants.2) Kaifeng is located in the Central Plains and in the middle and lower reaches of the Yellow River, equipped with convenient transportation and dense population. During the Ming and Qing dynasties, Kaifeng was the capital of Henan and the political, cultural and commercial center. As Henan and Shan-shaan border, a large number of merchants were attracted to do business.Gansu merchants joined the market around 1890.The guild hall built by the merchants from Shanxi, Shaanxi and Gansu was of the top rank and its strong strength and the long history of traditional Chinese culture created a magnificent and beautiful guild hall building.3) Citizens of the Ming and Qing dynasties advocated auspicious art, and the literary works and patterns related to auspicious art were spread and applied. At that time, brick carving, stone carving and wood carving were popular, coupled with the circulation of brick and stone carving skills in Shaanxi and Henan provinces in the pre-Tang and Song dynasties, the exquisite carving technology of the Ming and Qing dynasties and a variety of expressions related to auspicious themes were formed, therefore,the traditional auspicious view of the people was expressed in the decoration of the building.

The ShanShaanGan Guild Hall, deduced by the I and II references, is a unique product of the business classes, reflecting their secular beliefs and pursuits."Garden Rule" begins with a truth:When people build houses and gardens, they like to find ordinary craftsmen to do it. Have you not heard that the skills of craftsmen account for only thirty percent of the success while their ideas and designs account for seventy? What we want is a skilled craftsman with ingenious ideas. Ancient Lu Ban and Lu Yun were exquisite in their skills and they also have brilliant ideas.If the craftsmen think the exquisite skill is all they need, he will never become successful. The merchant at this time had the triple identity of builder and artist,merging mercantilism into the building and decorative patterns. The bead in the pattern of the "Two Dragons Playing Pearl" carved on the Wall of the guild hall is different from the traditional kind of fire bead, and the spider is used, also known as the "Xi Zhu", which means that the commercial network is spread in all directions. Vase-shaped patterns are widely used in the guildhall, and the shape of the vase is generally small at the neck, implying that money only pours in. The word "Holy Land" is written in front of the Wall inside the hall, and the "loyalty, benevolence, and courage" of the merchants' creed is written on the back, which is the spiritual connotation given by the faith. Every decoration and character in the guild hall represents the simple view of wealth and auspiciousness of the merchants.

Compared with ordinary guild halls,The ShanShaanGan Guild Hall is different in its mercantilism, especially in the commercial themes that have not appeared in the architectural decoration, which has a strong sense of utilitarian.For example, the abacus, copper coins and account books that appear in the guild hall are the patterns that are difficult to be defined as refined art with the policy of physiocracy and restriction of business. As they became the decorative theme of the guildhall, merchants' psychology of summoning good luck and fortune is revealed, so is the integration of elegance and customs, making them the decorative pattern with the characteristics of advocating business.At the same time, although the social behavior of merchants is not recognized by Confucian culture, a large number of carvings on Confucian ethics and other themes are still presented in the guild hall, which reflects the strong inclusiveness and compatibility of business culture.

5 Conclusion

ShanShaanGan Guild Hall is not only a product of traditional Chinese architecture, but also a product of the ingenuity of craftsmen, which preserves the essence of historical aesthetics and forms a unique architectural art.Based on the analysis of the decorative image of the guild hall under the field of image semiotics, the analysis of the modeling color and referent of the epitaxial layer for the meta-image and language is derived from the signifier of the connotative layer, and the characteristics of the deep meaning are derived from its existing background.The characteristics of the ShanShaanGan Guild Hall are using decorative image with the features of advocating business. And the auspicious symbols of the hall are consistent with the auspicious concept of traditional Chinese culture. The exploration of its internal laws is conducive to the protection and inheritance of the architectural beauty of this cultural treasure house, and also provides inspiration for the diversified study of traditional Chinese architectural decorative symbols.

References

1. Liu, Y.: Research on Architectural Decoration of Kaifeng Shanshangan Guild Hall. Henan University (2011)
2. Zhiqiang, W.: Analysis of the female characteristics of the decorative art of lady wang's ancestral hall in Bailu village from the perspective of image semiotics. J. Jiangxi Univ. Technol.**41**(02), 96–99 (2020)

3. Rui, M., Peng, P.: Image coding and layering – Roland Barthes' image layering theory. Tianfu New Theory **06**, 150–152 (2009)
4. Wang, M.: Research on Auspicious Patterns in the Architectural Decoration Art of Kaifeng Shanshangan Guild Hall. Henan University (2008)
5. Guohua, C., Shuang, L., Haiwei, D.: Research on poster culture of china professional football club based on image layering theory. J. East China Univ. Technol. (Soc. Sci. Edn.) **38**(03), 263–268 (2019)
6. Zhang, Y.: On the design art thought of Yuanye. J. Southeast Univ. (Philos. Soc. Sci. Edn.) (01), 76–81 (2001)

Visualizing Ocean Fragility: Glitch Art and Social Media in Marine Conservation

Mickey Mengting Zhang[1]([⊠]), Yu Shen[1], and Ihab Salah Ali Mohamed[2]

[1] Faculty of Humanities and Arts, Macau University of Science and Technology,
Avenida Wai Long, Taipa, Macau, China
mtzhang@must.edu.mo
[2] Faculty of Hospitality and Tourism Management, Macau University of Science and
Technology, Avenida Wai Long, Taipa, Macau, China
isalahalimohamed@must.edu.mo

Abstract. Marine pollution is a significant environmental issue resulting from increasing urbanization and human activities. The contamination of the ocean by oil, red tide, marine debris, radiation substances, domestic wastewater, and heavy metals poses a threat to marine ecosystems. To tackle these challenges, it is crucial to raise awareness and increase efforts towards marine protection. In this paper, we explore the potential of glitch art, a digital art form that intentionally creates digital errors or distortions, to create an aesthetic connection with marine ecosystems' vulnerability. By subverting the audience's expectations, glitch art can increase their awareness of the issue. To overcome these challenges, we introduce a social media platform for marine protection, designed with four visual arts depicting the primary types of marine debris, including radioactive waste, heavy metals, plastic, and red tide. In the creation process, the techniques of data manipulation and distortion were applied to create glitch arts. This paper contributes to current understanding of the potential of glitch art for marine protection. Moreover, it highlights the significance of new media in raising awareness and mobilizing efforts for marine protection. By leveraging glitch art and social media, we hope to engage a broader audience and encourage collective action to safeguard our oceans for future generations.

Keywords: Marine Conservation · Glitch Art · Social Media

1 Introduction

1.1 Marine Pollution

A wide range of human activities have a profound impact on marine ecosystems, including fisheries, mariculture, shipping, dredging, land reclamation, sewage and industrial chemical discharge, as well as more subtle, unintentional effects from diffuse sources. Atmospheric pollution and climate change also have indirect consequences (Bowen and Depledge 2006). The United Nations Convention on the Law of the Sea (1982) officially defines pollution of the marine environment as "the introduction by man, directly or indirectly, of substances or energy into the marine environment, including estuaries,

C. Stephanidis et al. (Eds.): HCII 2023, CCIS 1834, pp. 554–561, 2023.
https://doi.org/10.1007/978-3-031-35998-9_71

which results or is likely to result in harm to living resources and marine life, hazards to human health, hindrance to marine activities, impairment of quality for use of seawater and reduction of amenities" (p.21). However, our understanding of the biological, environmental, social, and economic effects of marine pollution is limited (Bowen and Depledge 2006). We currently lack the ability to accurately identify local marine pollution impacts on the global ecosystem over a long time period. While the general public tends to associate marine pollution with garbage, there is less awareness of other types of pollution such as oil pollution, red tide, heavy metals, and radioactive pollutants. Due to the lack of information, it is challenging to quantify marine protection efforts or make them visually apparent to the general public.

1.2 Glitch Art

The term "glitch" typically refers to a minor malfunction, a sudden and unexpected event, a surge of current, or a spurious and illegitimate signal that disrupts the flow of energy or information (Sundén 2015). The popular media first began using the term during the space age of the 1960s, describing it as "a spaceman's word for irritating disturbances" (Time 1956). Glitch art is a genre of digital art that intentionally creates glitches, errors, or other forms of digital distortion to produce aesthetic effects (Betancourt 2014). Glitches are ambiguous phenomena, holding both anxiety and beauty. They are slips of the tongue or momentary slip-ups, and while the machine may still be running, the performance is often poor, resulting in a shift in the experience of the performance. As unexpected breaks in the flow, glitches are often undesired and anxiety-inducing when they occur. They represent a momentary loss of control over technologies, systems, and devices (Sundén 2015). Glitch art can be created by capturing an image of a glitch as it occurs randomly or by manipulating programming errors, hardware malfunctions, or manually manipulating digital files (Betancourt 2014).

2 Connecting Glitch Art with Marine Pollution

Glitch art is often associated with the aesthetic of the "broken" or "ruined" digital image. Similarly, the marine ecosystem is also vulnerable and can be easily destroyed. Glitch art intends to express the frustration, annoyance, and anxiety that arises from technologies that become stuck, much like the emotional response we hope to evoke in viewers regarding the state of the marine ecosystem. The aim is to subvert the viewers' expectations and capture their attention regarding the health of the marine ecosystem. Glitch art often involves the manipulation and distortion of digital images, making it a powerful tool for creating visual representations of the effects of pollution on marine ecosystems. In this paper, we use glitch art to create distorted and fragmented images of marine life or simulate the visual effects of water pollution on underwater environments. The aim is to raise awareness about the issue of marine pollution and encourage viewers to take action to address it. Moreover, glitch art is used to repurpose and recycle digital waste, which is an important consideration in the context of marine pollution. We intend to transform what would otherwise be discarded into something new and meaningful by using digital artifacts and waste as source material for glitch art. This approach draws attention to the ways in which waste and pollution can be repurposed and recycled.

3   Visual Design with Glitch Art for Marine Conservation

Marine debris refers to waste of humans that has been intentionally or accidentally released into the sea or ocean. Four types of marine debris were selected for visual design, namely radioactive waste, heavy metal, plastic, and red tide. Blue is selected as main color to represent the ocean. To create a striking visual impact, the color palette also includes colors seen on malfunctioning or disrupted television screens, with highly saturated colors added to the mix. The process of creating glitch art involves using two techniques: data manipulation, hardware failure, misregistration, and distortion. Data manipulation involves modifying the digital file itself to intentionally create glitches (Betancourt 2014). Distortion is one of the earliest and most well-known forms of glitch art, in which the magnetic field of a television disrupts electronic signals, resulting in abstract visual distortions that can be manipulated by moving the magnet (den Heijer 2013).

3.1   Radioactive Waste of Pollution in Marine Environment

Between 1946 and 1993, thirteen countries utilized ocean dumping as a method of disposing of nuclear and radioactive waste, resulting in the disposal of an estimated 200,000 tons of waste primarily generated by the medical, research, and nuclear industries (Calmet 1989). This waste consisted of both liquids and solids contained in various vessels, including reactor vessels with or without damaged or spent nuclear. The potential consequences of nuclear waste are far-reaching and can include genetic mutations, developmental or reproductive changes, cancer, reduced lifespan, and mortality. To convey the severity of the impact caused by radioactive waste, this theme incorporates collage elements that reflect the disorder and chaos resulting from its presence (Fig. 1). This visual art represents the biological mutation of marine organisms in response to radioactive pollution, where fish have developed mutated legs and their feet have become a pair of hands. The design aims to evoke an eerie and terrifying experience. If the issue of radioactive waste in the marine ecosystem is not addressed, the future of humanity and all life remains unpredictable.

3.2   Heavy Metal Pollution in Marine Environment

Toxic heavy metals pose a significant threat to aquatic organisms, as well as to the health of humans who consume contaminated seafood. The accumulation of these metals in the tissues of aquatic life through the process of bioaccumulation can lead to severe health risks, including genetic mutations, developmental abnormalities, reproductive issues, and cancer. Naser (2013) reports that consumption of contaminated seafood can lead to acute and chronic health effects in humans, such as neurological damage, cardiovascular disease, and kidney damage.

To visualize the destructive effects of heavy metals on the ocean, we have incorporated a skull-shaped plastic bottle combined with various heavy metal elements in the design (Fig. 2). The emission of heavy metals into the atmosphere and rivers by human activities can have detrimental effects on the marine ecosystem. Eventually, these pollutants will enter the ocean through the water cycle and become a part of the ocean pollution, causing harm to aquatic organisms and impacting human health.

Fig. 1. Radioactive waste in marine environment (designed by the authors)

Fig. 2. Heavy metal pollution in marine environment (designed by the authors)

3.3 Plastic Pollution in Marine Environment

Plastic pollution refers to the pollution caused by plastic materials of different sizes, ranging from large objects such as bottles and bags to smaller fragments such as microplastics

(Weisman 2008). The consequences of plastic pollution in marine environments are significant and varied. Marine organisms can mistake plastic debris for food, which can lead to ingestion and subsequent harm or death. Plastic waste can also entangle and suffocate marine animals, such as sea turtles, seals, and whales. Additionally, plastic pollution can disrupt natural ecosystems and contribute to the spread of invasive species. The chemicals used in plastic production and found in plastic waste can also harm marine life and enter the food chain, ultimately affecting human health. Microplastics, which are small plastic particles that result from the fragmentation of larger plastic materials, are particularly concerning as they are widespread throughout the surface ocean and can be ingested by marine life, causing harm at the cellular level. In this design, we intend to present that the impact of plastic pollution on marine life is severe. Marine organisms, such as seaweeds, fish, and other plants that would typically thrive in the ocean, perishing and becoming skeletons (Fig. 3). The ocean becomes a giant graveyard of remains, and plastic debris. We select an aerial view to creates a devastating effect on the marine ecosystem, highlighting the severity of the situation. To further intensify the visuals and create a powerful impact on viewers, we have employed the use of the glitch art technique with its flashing and stuttering effects. This technique serves to amplify the visual representation of the catastrophic consequences of the widespread disposal of plastic waste into the ocean, drawing attention to the urgent need to address this pressing environmental issue.

Fig. 3. Plastic Pollution in marine environment (designed by the authors)

3.4   Red Tide of Marine Debris in Marine Environment

A harmful algal bloom (HAB), also known as red tide in marine environments, refers to the excessive growth of algae that can harm other organisms by producing natural toxins, causing mechanical damage or other negative impacts. HABs can be defined as algal blooms that produce toxins or any excessive growth of algae that results in the depletion of oxygen levels in natural waters, leading to the death of organisms in marine or fresh waters (Heisler et al. 2008). The visual representation of "red tide" illustrates the devastating consequences of this phenomenon (Fig. 4). The combination of undistinguishable marine organisms, fish tanks, and fish bones with a swirling background of water that can engulf everything serves as a stark reminder of the impact of HABs. The tide brings ocean debris and marine corpses to the shore while also posing a threat to humans who generate garbage and pollution. The dynamic effects of the animation, particularly the changes in color, create a striking visual impact that draws attention to the severity of the situation.

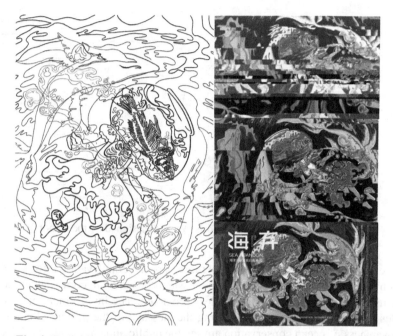

Fig. 4. Red tide pollution in marine environment (designed by the authors)

4 Visual Design with Glitch Art for Marine Conservation

The design of social media platforms can also play a critical role in promoting marine protection. By implementing features that facilitate the sharing of glitch art and other marine-related content, social media platforms can create a space for dialogue and community-building around marine conservation.

Additionally, by partnering with conservation organizations and promoting their initiatives, social media platforms can leverage their massive user bases to amplify the impact of conservation efforts. Based on the poster content, a website is designed for promoting ocean conservation (Fig. 5). The website is divided into several sections. The About section provides information on the current state of ocean pollution and conservation, the dangers of ocean pollution, the display of poster content, and the relationship between the poster theme and ocean conservation. The Shop section includes peripheral products designed around the poster theme, which extend the poster's design and increase its promotional value, leaving a lasting impression on viewers. The Contact Us

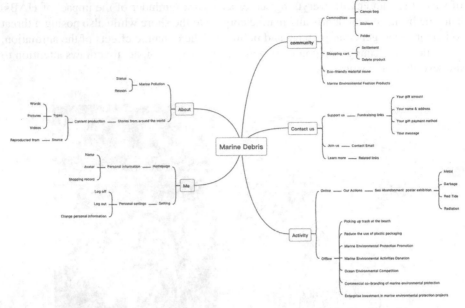

Fig. 5. Structure of Marine Debris Website (designed by the authors)

section encourages viewers to participate more in ocean conservation efforts and hopes to gain more support and promotion. The website is designed to complement the poster design itself, allowing it to be more widely promoted. The involvement of new media provides additional channels for spreading the message of the poster, which will help raise awareness of ocean conservation among the public and encourage participation.

Fig. 6. User Interface Design of Marine Debris Website (designed by the authors)

5   Conclusion

Marine conservation has become an increasingly pressing issue in recent years, as our oceans face numerous threats such as pollution, overfishing, and climate change. In this context, the use of visual art and social media platforms as tools for marine protection has emerged as a possible strategy. In this paper, glitch art - an art form that involves the intentional creation of digital errors and distortions - has been suggested as a means of raising awareness about the fragility and importance of marine ecosystems. Glitch art has the potential to capture the viewer's attention through its unique aesthetic and challenge their preconceived notions of what constitutes "proper" art. By using this form of art to depict marine environments, we can draw attention to the vulnerability of these ecosystems and the urgent need for action to protect them. Furthermore, by leveraging social media platforms to share glitch art, we can reach a wider audience and encourage public engagement with marine conservation efforts. In summary, the combination of glitch art and social media platform design holds great potential as a tool for marine protection. By harnessing the power of visual art and digital platforms, we can engage a broader audience and encourage collective action to safeguard our oceans for future generations.

This work was supported by the Faculty Research Grants (FRG) of Macau University of Science and Technology [grant number FRG-21–025-FA].

References

Sundén, J. (2015). On trans-, glitch, and gender as machinery of failure. *First Monday*

Bowen, R.E., Depledge, M.H.: Rapid assessment of marine pollution (RAMP). Mar. Pollut. Bull. **53**(10–12), 631–639 (2006)

United Nations: United Nations Convention on the Law of the Sea (1982). https://www.imo.org/en/OurWork/Legal/Pages/UnitedNationsConventionOnTheLawOfTheSea.aspx. Accessed 1 Feb 2023

Time: Space: the Glitch & the Gemini (1956). https://content.time.com/time/subscriber/article/0,33009,901786,00.html. Accessed 7 Feb 2023

Betancourt, M.: An Easy 7-Step Protocol for Databending. Tammy McGovern.(comp.) Signal Culture, Cook Book (2014)

denHeijer, E.: Evolving glitch art. In: Machado, P., McDermott, J., Carballal, A. (eds.) Evolutionary and Biologically Inspired Music, Sound, Art and Design. LNCS, vol. 7834, pp. 109–120. Springer, Heidelberg (2013). https://doi.org/10.1007/978-3-642-36955-1_10

Calmet, D.P.: Ocean disposal of radioactive waste. Status report. IAEA Bull. **31**(4), 47–50 (1989)

Naser, H.A.: Assessment and management of heavy metal pollution in the marine environment of the Arabian Gulf: a review. Mar. Pollut. Bull. **72**(1), 6–13 (2013)

Weisman, A.: The world without us, vol. 34. Macmillan (2008)

Heisler, J., et al.: Eutrophication and harmful algal blooms: a scientific consensus. Harmful Algae **8**(1), 3–13 (2008)

Research on the Design of Digital Experience of Sichuan Opera Face-Changing Based on Flow Theory

Xiuhui Zheng, Xudong Cai, and Fangfang Huang(✉)

Guangdong University of Technology, No.729 Dongfeng East Road, Yuexiu District, Guangzhou, China
840391201@qq.com

Abstract. Face-changing is a traditional performance form of Sichuan Opera in which the performer can switch between multiple faces in a short time. Special costumes and props are required for the performance, and the audience must enter the theater to watch it, making it impossible for this performance to be widely distributed. The digital products of Sichuan Opera face-changing in the market today only simulate the process of face-changing and do not allow users to have an immersive cultural experience. In this design study, we designed a Sichuan Opera digital face-changing interactive app based on the flow theory. According to the three principles of unambiguous objectives, accurate and timely feedback, and balancing skills and challenges, the app is divided into four modules: exploration, experience, interaction, and innovation. We recruited 23 users to experience the app, and the results showed that most users found the app interesting and were willing to accept them. This paper combine traditional cultural elements with modern digital technology allows traditional art performances to be widely disseminated and provides a reference point for other traditional cultures to be experienced in the digital society.

Keywords: Face-changing · Flow theory · Face filters · Digital experience

1 Introduction

Changing faces is a way of expressing the inner characteristics of a character in the art of Sichuan Opera [1] and is also one of China's important intangible cultural heritages. It expresses the changing emotions within the character as a constantly changing face, with different faces representing different emotions. This form of performance is designed to allow the audience to directly experience the character's changing psychological and emotional aspects in a limited performance space [2].

1.1 Face-Changing Cultural and Creative Products

The most crucial feature of Sichuan Opera is "face changing," so the key to preserving Sichuan Opera is to maintain this important form of "face changing." Research has shown that the digital development of Intangible Cultural Heritage (ICH) is not only a mechanism for protection but also plays a vital role in the display of content, the development of digital cultural industries, the protection of copyright in digital resources [3]. Digital heritage innovation refers to using digital technology in ICH projects to generate new values, and digital cultural creative products are one of the most critical research areas.

Many consumers recognize and love Sichuan Opera face-changing because of its unique cultural elements and crucial artistic value. Many tourist attractions and shopping malls continue to launch related products. The cultural and creative products of Sichuan Opera face-changing are still mainly mystery boxes and peripheral products, see Fig. 1. Although these products have some communication effect, the backward product form makes it difficult further to promote Sichuan Opera face-changing in the digital era.

Fig. 1. Current Sichuan Opera Face-changing Cultural Creative Products

1.2 Digital Cultural and Creative Products of Face-Changing

Digital cultural creation is a more popular form of artistic expression, with strong infectious and affinity power. There are mainly the following types, as shown in Fig. 2: A. Using mobile apps as a carrier, Sichuan Opera face-changing is made into a digital cultural creation app platform, where users perform face-covering actions to realize face-changing. B. Gamification based on game NPCs with Sichuan Opera and other related elements, such as the game character of the mobile game "Honor of Kings." C. Turning faces into digital collections to form virtual images.

A   B   C

Fig. 2. Current digital cultural and creative products of Sichuan Opera face-changing

Analyzing the current situation, we found some problems with the digital cultural creative products of Sichuan Opera face-changing. These products lack innovation because they simply present the process of face-changing. Moreover, these products lack interactivity, and the expressions could be relatively simple. As a result, users cannot get an excellent immersive cultural experience, and it cannot make them want to understand the culture of Sichuan Opera represented by these products.

1.3 Flow Theory

The flow theory was developed by the American psychologist Csikszentmihalyi. It refers to the emotions that arise when an individual devotes all of their energy to a particular activity and is best experienced when people are immersed.

Csikszentmihalyi believes that challenge and skill are critical factors influencing flow formation [4], see Fig. 3. Users develop unease and anxiety when they face difficulties greater than their skills. Only when challenge and skill have balanced, and a state of flow is generated for a higher user experience.

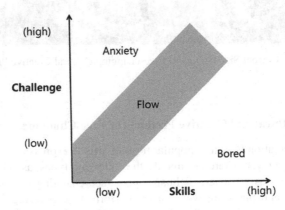

Fig. 3. Flow channel model

Csikszentmihalyi summarized nine features of flow [5, 6], which were later categorized by Novak [7] and others into three experience factors: condition, process, and outcome, while Chen [8] and others divided flow into three experience stages: pre-experience, experience, and effect. As shown in Table 1, the three stages are the characteristics before and after the generation of flow, and strengthening the connection between them can further enhance the user's experience.

Table 1. Characteristics of the different stages of the flow theory

Stage	Condition stage (prior stage)	Experience stage (experience stage)	Results stage (effect stage)
Characteristics	1. Unambiguous objectives	4. Combining action and awareness	7. Loss of self-awareness
	2. Accurate and timely feedback	5. Complete concentration	8. Difficult to feel time
	3. Balancing skills and challenges	6. Potential sense of control	9. Real engagement

This paper is based on the flow theory to guide the interaction strategy of the Sichuan Opera Face Changing digital experience to enhance interactivity. Firstly, clear goals need to be set so that the user clearly understands the task and purpose of the engagement before starting the interaction. Secondly, accurate and timely feedback should be provided during the interaction process to engage the user on an ongoing basis further. Finally, there is a need to balance skills and challenges, adjusting the difficulty of the experience to guide participants to higher levels of experience.

2   Design Principles

The preliminary stages of the flow theory profoundly impact the subsequent interaction experience [9]. Therefore, the digital experience app developed in this paper will be based on the three principles of the pre-stage of flow theory. These three principles include unambiguous objectives, accurate and timely feedback, and balancing skills and challenges, See Fig. 4.

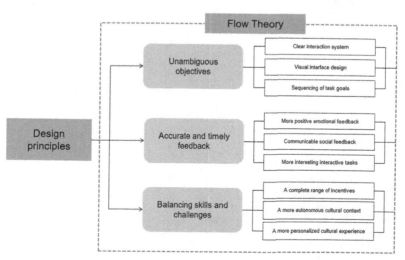

Fig. 4. The design principles of the Sichuan Opera face-changing digital experience app

2.1 Unambiguous Objectives

(1) Clear interaction system. Turn the goals of the interaction into staged tasks. Users experience the basic faces first and can subsequently create their faces. (2) Visual interface design. Make the status of the current task more apparent to the user in the interaction interface and get timely feedback. (3) Sequencing of task goals. Guide the user during the task and set different objectives at different stages.

2.2 Accurate and Timely Feedback

(1) More positive emotional feedback. The most meaningful user incentive is to adopt a 'user-centered' philosophy [10], where users are satisfied and respected during the interactive task. (2) Communicable social feedback. Building a socially enabled communication area can give users an excellent interactive scenario to stimulate their emotional experience [11]. Users can post their designed faces to communicate with other users in the communication area. (3) More interesting interactive tasks. Use fun rewards and set user levels to guide users to keep experiencing different parts of the app so they gradually become long-term users.

2.3 Balancing Skills and Challenges

(1) A complete range of incentives. Incentives mainly include emotional, benefit, and honor incentives [12]. The right incentives can make users participate in the task voluntarily and continuously. (2) A more autonomous cultural context. According to Maslow's hierarchy of needs, the highest level is the need for self-actualization. Constantly motivating users to create faces in the app's interactive tasks allows them to feel creative to increase their self-satisfaction. (3) A more personalized cultural experience. Digital faces need to be visually innovative and personalized so that users can be drawn in at the start of the experience.

3 Design Practice

The information architecture of the Sichuan Opera Digital Face-changing app can be divided into three parts under the guidance of the three elements of the pre-stage of flow theory. The first part is a clear and explicit goal, in which two modules are set: "Exploration" and "Experience." The second part is accurate and timely feedback, with an "Interaction" section in the app. Regarding balancing skills and challenges, the modules "Innovation" and "Profile" were set. The information architecture of the app is shown in Fig. 5. These three elements were applied to the app's design to enhance users' cultural experience.

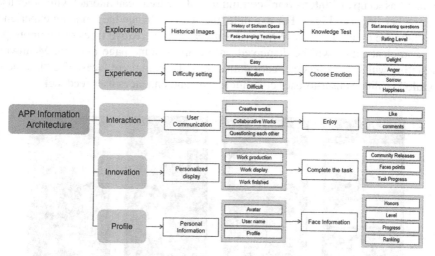

Fig. 5. The information architecture of the app

3.1 Exploration and Experience Module

The "Exploration" module introduces the culture and history of face-changing to the audience through pictures and videos, see Fig. 6. The app will also match the user with the appropriate difficulty of face interaction based on the user's knowledge test results. In addition, in the "Experience" module, users can adjust the interaction's difficulty by themselves so that users can find the direction and difficulty they are most interested in to interact.

Fig. 6. The exploration and experience module

3.2 Interaction Module

The app has set up an "Interaction" community where users can interact with other users in face-changing, see Fig. 7. For example, they can exchange face-making experiences or collaborate to create faces. When users upload more creative faces or get more positive comments, they will be displayed on the app's home page ranking. Meanwhile, interacting with other users can earn points for unlocking more faces. The "Interaction Module" facilitates user-to-user communication and enhances user feedback.

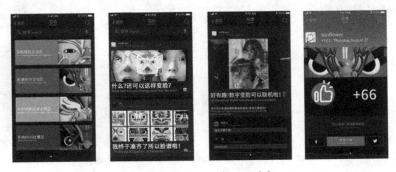

Fig. 7. The interaction module

3.3 Innovation Module

The "Innovation" module mainly encourages users to earn points and improve their rank by creating personalized face works, thus motivating them to use it for a long time, see Fig. 8. The app provides an example of making a digital creative face, see Fig. 9. During the experience, users can return to the "Profile" setting screen to adjust the task's difficulty or check the progress and ranking of the task.

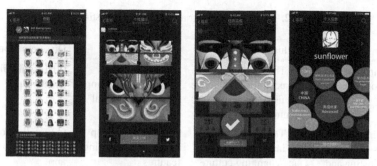

Fig. 8. The innovation module

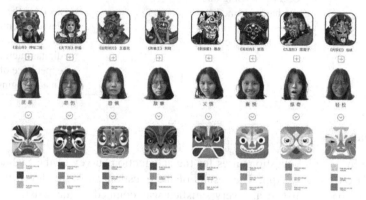

Fig. 9. Example of making Sichuan Opera digital creative faces

4 Questionnaire and Results

We recruited 23 users to experience the interactive app interface to verify the functionality and understand the user experience. After the users completed the incident, they were required to complete a questionnaire to learn their feedback.

4.1 Questionnaire

The survey questionnaire is set up to set relevant questions from four aspects: function, culture, creativity, and dissemination, as shown in Table 2. The satisfaction level is divided into strongly unsatisfied, unsatisfied, neutral, satisfied, and strongly satisfied.

Table 2. Questions on four aspects of the questionnaire

Function	Culture	Creativity	Dissemination
Q1: I think the app is easy to operate	Q1:This app satisfies my need for knowledge acquisition and communication	Q1:I think the elements of this app have unique visual characteristics	Q1:I would like to use this app
Q2: I think the contents of the app are interesting and reasonable	Q2:This app stimulates my interest in face-changing culture	Q2:I think this app has some interesting features	Q2:I will recommend my friends to use this app
	Q3:I think using this app has deepened my understanding of face-changing culture		Q3:I think there is a need for the development and existence of the digital interactive experience of face-changing

4.2 Results

We received 23 valid questionnaires for the satisfaction survey of the Sichuan Opera Digital Face Changing App. The results of the questionnaires are shown in Table 3. The proportion of satisfied and very satisfied was counted as the satisfaction rate to understand the participants' feedback on the app.

Table 3. Results of the questionnaire

	Question	Strongly disagree	Disagree	Neutral	Agree	Strongly agree	Agreement rate
Function	Q1	0	3	6	10	4	60.9%
	Q2	0	0	2	14	7	91.3%
Culture	Q1	0	0	3	13	7	87.0%
	Q2	0	1	2	16	4	87.0%
	Q3	0	1	2	13	7	87.0%
Creativity	Q1	0	0	2	13	8	91.3%
	Q2	0	0	2	14	7	91.3%
Dissemination	Q1	0	1	2	15	5	87.0%
	Q2	1	0	7	10	5	65.2%
	Q3	0	0	1	14	8	95.7%

The satisfaction rate of 80% of the questions in this questionnaire exceeded 87%, indicating that users are satisfied with the Sichuan Opera Digital Face-changing Experience App. Most of the users think that after using this APP, they deepen their understanding of Sichuan Opera face-changing culture and stimulate their interest in learning, which shows that this APP has achieved the promotion and dissemination of Sichuan Opera face-changing culture to a certain extent. However, only 60.9% of the users think that the operation of this app is simple, and this part will be optimized and improved subsequently.

5   Conclusion

This paper applies the flow theory to the digital experience of Sichuan Opera face-changing, proposes a specific application strategy, and develops an experienced app. The app provides users with novel immersive cultural experiences regarding cultural perception and visual innovation and continuously enhances their sense of participation. The complete digital experience of Sichuan Opera face-changing proposed in this study can provide a practical reference for the research of digital interaction of other cultural or art. Users are overall satisfied with the app, and the ease of use and dissemination of the app will be further improved subsequently.

References

1. Pu, H., Luo, X.: The current market situation and diversified perspective of the preservation and inheritance of Sichuan Opera face -hanging culture. China J. Commer. **792**(17), 76–77 (2019)
2. Xu, J.: Exploring the artistic heritage and basic status of Sichuan Opera face-changing. Home Drama **263**(23), 15 (2017)
3. Wang, J., Li, S.: Current status of domestic research on digital preservation of intangible cultural heritage. Hunan Packag. **36**(05), 1–6+37 (2021)
4. Deng, P.: Flow: experiencing the potential and joy of life. J. Distance Educ. (03), 74–78 (2006)
5. Csikszentmihalyi, M.: Flow: The Psychology of Optimal Experience. Harper & Row, New York (1990)
6. Nakamura, J., Csikszentmihalyi, M.: Flow theory and research. Handb. Positive Psychol. **195**, 206 (2009)
7. Chang, C.C.: Examining users' intention to continue using social network games: a flow experience perspective. Telematics Inform. **30**(4), 311–321 (2013)
8. Peng, Q.: Research on interactive online advertising design under the guidance of flow theory. Packag. Eng. **35**(02), 122–125+130 (2014)
9. Li, J., Tan, Q., Qiu, P., et al.: Research on interaction design of cultural and creative products based on flow theory. Packag. Eng. **41**(18), 287–293 (2020)
10. Wang, B., Zhou, B.: Multidimensional induction, improving user innovation performance——research on user innovation induction mechanism in manufacturing industry. Chin. Foreign Entrepreneurs **662**(36), 50–52 (2019)
11. Zhao, S., Shen, L.: Research on the interaction interface design of children's smart watches based on flow theory. Packag. Eng. (2023)
12. Jiang, J., Sun, T., Zheng, Z.: Research on refined intelligent service design for people aging at home. ZhuangShi **349**(05), 40–45 (2022)

Research on the Phygital Innovation Path of the Art Museums Based on Public Participation

Li Zhuang[✉] and Muzi Zheng

Central China Normal University, No. 152, Luoyu Road, Hongshan, Wuhan, China
zhuangli@ccnu.edu.cn

Abstract. As an important place for public art aesthetics and art education, art museums increasingly emphasize the importance of public participation. Phygital in the paper is a compound word, which is composed of Physical and Digital, and it means to blend offline and online environments to deliver an enhanced customer experience. The essential characteristics of Phygital are immediacy, immersion and interactivity. The research on the Phygital innovation path of art museums aims to explore how to expand and innovate the art presentation form, service function and service mechanism in the physical space of museums through the appropriate application of digital technology, which is based on the in-depth investigation of public participation needs and habitual behaviours, so as to better stimulate the public's awareness of independent participation and cultivate active participation behaviour. In essence, it is also exploring how to use digital technology as a link to establish a good interactive relationship between artworks, space and people. On the one hand, it enables the public to obtain a better user experience and visiting feeling in the whole process including before, during and after the exhibition; on the other hand, it brings the public the possibility to participate in artwork creating directly as a creator role, it encourages them to directly enter into the semantic construction and conceptual expression of the artworks, and projects the individual consciousness into the final presentation of the works.

Keywords: Public Participation · Art Museum · Phygital

1 Introduction

In recent years, many art museums are trying to explore new digital service methods to optimize and improve their own public service functions. While providing the public with a better art experience, they can also effectively improve the quality and efficiency of public services. On the one hand, promote the construction of virtual digitization, including: deepen the construction of online cultural resource platforms to enhance the accessibility and sharing of cultural and art resources; develop various mobile apps to enhance public interactive and experiential about some themes such as online art education, online cultural entertainment, online cultural popularization and so on; promote and disseminate new services and new products about art creation to increase public attention and participation through various social media platforms. On the other hand, an increasing number of art museums are also actively exploring "Phygital", gradually expanding the powerful effect of digitization to offline physical spaces.

"Phygital" is a new term composed of "Physical + Digital", which refers to the methods of an internal communication system establishment for the physical architectural space environment by using new media technologies such as the Internet and digitalization, and at the same time enhances its connection with the outside world, and then effectively expand and strengthen the service function and interactive experience in physical space. "Phygital" brings us not only the interactivity and convenience of online experience, but also the embodiment and reality of offline experience, so it has become an important means for art museums to realize functional innovation and experience upgrading.

2 Phygital—A Necessary Transformation to Enhance Public Participation

"Phygital" is not a new concept out of thin air. Its emergence just reflects human's philosophical review and reflection based on personal experience and practical problems in conforming to and chasing the digital trend. The advent of the new media era has changed people's cognitive methods and behaviour habits to a large extent, and built a new cultural form with its unique expression and interaction modes, and bring out people's diverse cultural demands. These appeals are finally projected in the participation behaviour based on digitalization. Digitalization does have incomparable advantages in improving service efficiency, innovating service methods, and expanding service space. At the same time, it can also provide various conveniences for the public to visit the exhibition. It not only breaks the spatial boundaries of physical spaces, enhances the exhibition experience, but also gives individuals more voice and a sense of participation. It is easier for audiences to connect cross-age, cross-region, and cross-type exhibits, and to recreate and express concepts based on their thinking, which makes exhibit resources have more room for improvement in terms of openness and re-creation. The industry and academia, including art museums, have explored and practiced actively the transformation and upgrading of product development and service innovation in the past 30 years. The emergence of online-based services and products such as Digital Museum, Online Museum, Electronic Museum, Hypermedia Museum, Web Museum, and Virtual Museum is a typical example.

A new problem gradually emerged in the process of exploration, that is, although viewing the exhibition purely online is convenient, it lacks the sense of the physical experience of directly facing the works. As Feng Nai'en, the curator of the Prince Kung's Palace Museum of the Ministry of Culture and Tourism mentioned in a speech titled "Addition and Subtraction in Digital Museums": "No matter what advantages the future Museum Metaverse has in terms of experience and interaction, it cannot replace the physical museum. The entity, and the history and culture contained in it are the foundation of our foothold." [1] Whether it is cultural relics or modern and contemporary artworks, the ideology and culture displayed in a specific field are what the audience wants to feel most. And so, a focus on Phygital began to take shape.

In 2010, Nina Simon put forward the idea of museum services in her book "The Participatory Museum", which encouraging audiences to participate in art creation and establish mutual connections relying on new media. [2] In 2014, research conducted by the AMT Laboratory of Carnegie Mellon University showed that more and more public cultural institutions have begun to use digital technology to quantitatively measure user engagement and guide user behaviour. The Metropolitan Museum of Art in New York has formulated a comprehensive strategy around social media to meet the diverse experience and expression needs of users before, during and after the exhibition, it has also created international social media accounts to establish connections with global users. The art museum can be regarded as an information flow system about "Person-Content-Object-Field". The fundamental purpose of Phygital is to establish a natural, expandable, and content-generating relationship among the public, themes, works, and museum space through the combination of virtual and real.

3   Research on Public Participation Needs Basing on Physical Exhibitions

When the public visits in art museums, what are their actual needs for digital functions? On this issue, the project organized an online and offline survey and analysis. The total sample size of participants in the online questionnaire survey was 1020 people, and the sample size for offline interviews was 120 people. The samples are divided into professionals, amateurs and general audiences.

First of all, 86.41% of the respondents had different degrees of digital experience during physical exhibition viewing. Among them, 56.27% of the respondents believed that the guidance of digital means improved their initiative in the exhibition process; 48.04% of the respondents believed that digital means could increase their immersion in the exhibition process; 47.45% of the respondents said that digital means inspired their thinking. It can be seen that the general public has a high degree of recognition of digitization in physical exhibitions visiting, and most visitors have tried to obtain the information they want through digital means and have achieved success (Fig. 1).

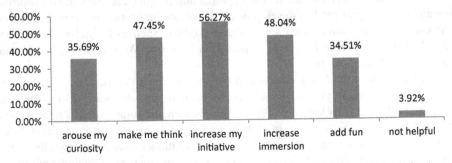

Fig. 1. How can digital means help you in your exhibition visiting (multiple choices)

Secondly, in terms of acceptance of digital devices, 37.45% of the respondents expressed a great interest in interacting with unfamiliar interactive devices; 46.27%

of the respondents indicated that they might, but it depends on the degree of complexity of the device operation; 16.27% of the respondents clearly expressed their reluctance to interact with unfamiliar digital devices because they believed that they might interfere with normal exhibition visiting or had unsatisfactory experiences (Fig. 2).

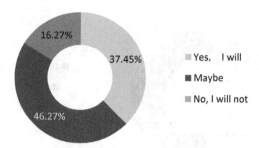

Fig. 2. Will you take the initiative to experience unfamiliar interactive equipment in art museums?

Regarding the question about directly participating in artistic creation using digital means, 60.39% of the respondents indicated that they wanted to try to create their art through digital means, among which the three options with the highest votes were: create by touch screen (54.22%); create by equipment carried by yourself or renting equipment from the venue (47.08%); create through virtual reality technology (46.1%). Among the respondents who showed a positive attitude towards participating in artistic creation, 85.71% of the respondents expressed their desire to show their creations to others and communicate with them. In fact, guiding the public to actively participate in the creation is a necessary link set by some artists for artistic expression, and public participation has become an important part of the semantic construction of artworks; in addition, it is an effective means to expand the influence of exhibitions and increase the attention of exhibits (Fig. 3).

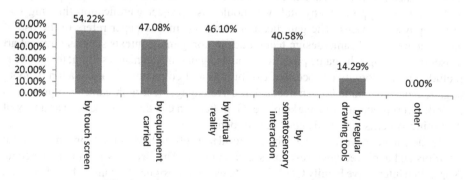

Fig. 3. What means do you expect in your creation?

There is also a fact worth paying attention to. 52.75% and 15.88% of online respondents said that they went to art museums for entertainment and relaxation respectively. Furthermore, 90% of the offline respondents said they are open to using digital means to enhance the fun and gameplay of exhibition visiting. This means that around the theme of the exhibition and the content of the exhibits, it is possible to construct the game situation and design the game mechanism through Phygital way, and insert plot-like and story-like participation links during the public visiting process to enhance public participation (Fig. 4).

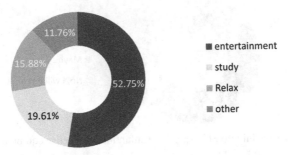

Fig. 4. What you want in art museum?

4　Phygital Innovation Path

4.1　Enhancing Public Participation by Gamification Thinking

With the deep implantation of Internet thinking, many public cultural institutions have already engaged in online games development and event planning around exhibitions and collections. For example, The British Museum has an adventure game called "Time Explorer", which is to guide the public to rescue a precious cultural relic in ancient China, ancient Rome, and Mexico. If the mission is successful, the visitors will be able to obtain more detailed information about the cultural relic as a reward. Based on the perspective and technical support of Phygital, we should also project gamification thinking into offline physical spaces, The gamification discussed in this paper refers to the use of game elements and game-design techniques in non-game contexts such as physical art museums. Through the game plot deduction and game mechanisms setting, the public is included in the cognitive process of exhibitions and collections. Gamification is about engagement. The same human needs that drive engagement with games are present in both the workplace and the marketplace. Gamification can therefore be seen as a way of designing systems that motivate people to behave [3].

In fact, in recent years, some public cultural institutions have started some meaningful attempts and achieved good responses. For example, The British Museum launched an App called Interactive Family Guide in 2016, which is designed for family-based visitors. Install the App on your smartphone, and you can connect and use it with a family interactive guide device provided by the museum. To realize the collective participation of family members and meet the different needs of different ages, the family interaction guide sets up a variety of game situations, including Imagine, Find, Pose, Count, Quiz and Recollect, etc. Game participants need to find specified objects in the museum, pose like a Greek statue, roar like an Assyrian lion, guess the answer, and more. The game helps up to 6.9 million annual visitors explore the British Museum in a fun way, connect and share knowledge. After the exhibition, family members can also access the interactive guide via email, get a visit summary and player rewards.

4.2 Enhancing Public Participation by Low Tech Thinking

Digitalization has inherent technological attributes, and the continuous iteration and update of technology will bring a new look to the Phygital process of art museums. The rational application of technology can greatly enhance the rendering power and interest of artworks, enrich the level of cultural perception, enhance the public's sense of experience, and break the boring stereotypes brought to the public by traditional exhibition visiting. However, we also need to be vigilant to avoid falling into the misunderstanding of excessive technology. The colourful light and shadow special effects, dynamic and interactive plots and the huge shocking scene experience are indeed easier to attract our attention, but if only have homogeneous technology stacks, the result is that the work only pays attention to the sense of form and ignores the expression of content.

In recent years, "immersive" seems to have become a versatile prefix applicable to any exhibition. People are accustomed to equate "immersion" with certain technological implementations, it's a superficial interpretation of "immersion", and it will make the artwork's original intention disappear, and the relationship between technology and art is misunderstood. The word "immersion" refers to the "contemplation and edification" of culture, and it needs to filter out all irrelevant external stimuli that may cause interference so that people can fully immerse themselves in certain emotions and situations. Excessive technical application will only increase unnecessary noise and impurities, dispelling the sense of substitution and destroying the immersion. Under the influence of technology, artistic connotation should be amplified, rather than covered and dispelled. Once the relationship between the two cannot be balanced or reversed, the works and even the exhibition will face the embarrassing situation of losing their spiritual height, cultural connotation, and artistic value.

Bloomberg Connects is a funding project initiated by Bloomberg Philanthropies, which aims to promote museums, art galleries and other public cultural institutions to enhance their interactive exhibition viewing experience. The project initially funded six museums in New York and achieved good results, and then gradually expanded to some influential and well-known public cultural institutions around the world, including the Tate Modern Art Museum in London, UK. In Tate Modern, interactive touch screens displaying the words "Bloomberg Connects" can be seen everywhere, and some short questions are set on the touch screens for visitors to make short answers, such as: "Have you seen an Artwork today that matches your mood? What, and why?" "Do you think it's ideas or skill that counts most in art?" "How can art change society?" and so on. Of course, if you don't feel like typing, you can just take your photo. Regardless of which interaction method you choose, your opinions and your photos will be pooled in the system and then displayed on monitors set up on walls throughout the museum. Furthermore, Bloomberg Connects also demonstrated the creative analysis and creative process of some artists through these electronic screen terminals. In addition, a "Drawing Bar" was set up for child visitors, a row of electronic drawing screens is placed under a huge wall, on which children can paint and communicate with each other. Their works will be displayed on the huge wall immediately after the submission is completed, and will also enter the display screens around the museum. These have greatly increased the sense of public participation and interest in the process of visiting, and brought them into the exhibition system in most simple and efficient way. A relationship of communication and sharing has been established among the authors and audiences with "creation" as the link, and the personal visiting process has been evolved as a group consensus and resonance activity.

In Tate Modern, all functional settings based on interaction experience exist quietly and play the good roles in art guidance. What we perceive from it is not the existence of technology, but a functional system with high applicability, behind which is the mechanism design around the potential needs of users in the whole process of visiting. Some of these links are even completely non-technical and non-new media, but they also appear to be highly adaptable in the entire system. These are also highly consistent with the service concept of Tate Modern, that is, to bring art in close contact with citizens, and to encourage audiences of different groups and ages to visit exhibitions and participate in art activities together.

5   Conclusion

Guiding the physical visiting process of the public in a low-tech and moderate digital way will help to amplify the tension of the artworks and enhance the space for public discourse, which makes it better to find a balance between the visual performance, semantic construction and user experience of the artworks. Science and technology are only means and forms, it cannot independently constitute cultural content. The forms of sound and light, somatosensory interaction and other forms of science and technology can bring audiences stronger sensory stimulation, however, if it is not used excessively or even abused according to actual needs, it will weaken the theme, form audio-visual interference, increase cognitive difficulty, and bring bad experience.

It will effectively activate the enthusiasm of the public to participate and make the physical exhibition more experiential and interesting by designing the game mechanism, building the game situation, and giving the public a sense of mission and role in Phygital way according to the exhibition and exhibits, further triggering behavioural interaction and information exchange which between person and person, person and objects, person and fields, and then establish a multi-dimensional dialogue relationship of "Person-Content-Object-Field", which is to enhance the depth of public cognition.

Enhance the public's embodied cognition experience by using Phygital in the exhibition visiting process is not only an advocacy of diversified presentation forms and expressions of artworks, but also an active exploration to make artworks have more human meaning and humanistic care. Embodied cognition advocates using the intuitive experience from the body as the source material of the brain's cognitive activities to replace the usual cognitive methods based on indirect experience, which significantly enhances the sense of situation and interest of artistic activities, and it also helps to encourage the public to perform personalized interpretation and re-creation of artworks, thus bringing the public into the semantic construction and dialogue relationship of "thinking-creation-cognition" with artworks as a link, and the "publicity" of art will be truly enhanced.

References

1. BJNEWS. https://www.bjnews.com.cn/detail/165951748014646.html. Accessed 10 Mar 2023
2. Simon, N.: The Participatory Museums. Museum 2.0 (2010)
3. Kevin, W., Dan, H.: For the Win: How Game Thinking Can Revolutionize Your Business. Wharton Digital Press, The Wharton School University of Pennsylvania, pp.31 (2012)

Author Index

A

Aguirre Baique, Nazario 311
Alvarez-Tello, Jorge 303
Amaluisa Rendón, Paulina Magally 187, 238, 318
Ang, Richie 3
Aoki, Yukino 10
Arévalo Reátegui, Julio 311
Attard, Andrew Emanuel 194
Azócar, Isidora 83

B

Babaian, Tamara 18
Baird, Harriet M. 103
Ball, Robert 24
Basir, Muhammad 103
Becking, Dominic 60
Becks, Daniela 97
Boecker, Martin 40
Bukauskas, Linas 273

C

Cai, Shasha 202
Cai, Xudong 367, 562
Cai, Yihui 367
Chen, Wei-Ting 210, 216
Chen, Yingting 118
Cheng, Chia Wen 325
Cheng, Hui 376
Chiu, Shu-Ling 453
Cho, Dong Min 358
Cho, Yongyeon 343
Chou, Wen-Huei 32
Choudhury, Niki 225
Cui, Yue 385, 426

D

Darmois, Emmanuel 40
de Boer, Jelle 231
Deng, Yifan 46
Dingli, Alexiei 194

Dong, Jeyoun 54
Duan, Lingjing 393
Dung, Trinh Tuan 325

E

Eller, Dennis 60
Espinosa-Pinos, Carlos Alberto 187, 238, 318

F

Faltakas, Orestis 408
Fan, Yixin 399
Fatahi, Somayeh 334
Fernando, Owen Noel Newton 3, 156, 325
Field, Hannah 68
Foukarakis, Michalis 408
Frantzeskakis, Giannis 408
Fu, Jiaxin 518
Fukata, Mayo 76

G

Gao, Songhua 461
Gao, Tanhao 415
Gao, Xian 518
Gao, Zhanying 279
Godoy, María Paz 83
Goto, Mitsuhiro 168

H

Hasnine, Mohammad Nehal 246
Hayakawa, Eiichi 76
He, Chenglin 385, 426
Hosobe, Hiroshi 110
Hou, Jiayi 351
Hu, Xiaoping 399
Hua, Guanqing 415
Huaman Monteza, Alexander 311
Huang, Fangfang 562
Huang, Yan 478
Huang, Yao-Fei 32

Huddy, Vyv   103
Hung, Chung-Wen   32
Hurtado Villanueva, Abelardo   311
Hwang, Jaejin   251

I

Ichikawa, Masanari   176
Inoue, Satoru   118

J

Jensen, Joshua   24
Ji, Yi   367

K

Kajita, Kaisei   90
Kanei, Akari   259
Kang, Dongyeop   54
Kanno, Taro   118
Kapnas, George   499
Karikawa, Daisuke   118
Kashihara, Akihiro   168
Kim, Hyunsu   296
Kim, Nayoung   267
Kim, Yanghee   251
Kojić, Tanja   440
Kontaki, Eirini   408, 499
Krinickij, Virgilijus   273
Kruse, Christian   97
Kumar, Jyoti   225
Kusumadewi, Aromah Udaningrum   446
Kuttal, Sandeep Kaur   149

L

Laak, Matti   60
Lanfranchi, Vitaveska   103
Lee, Jui-Hsiang   453
Lee, Sungchul   251
Li, Chenlu   461
Li, Jinzhu   279
Li, Maoning   358
Li, Zhenni   367
Lim, Huiwon   343
Liu, Bingjian   376
Liu, Dashuai   385, 426
Liu, Jia-Yi   486
Liu, Lian   470
Liu, Yu   478
Lu, Li-Shu   486
Luo, Shijian   376

M

Maikore, Fatima   103
Manabe, Hiroyuki   259
Mangina, Eleni   288
Manoli, Constantina   408
Matin, Farzin   288
Matsumura, Kinji   90
Mazumdar, Suvodeep   103
Mckinney, Brett   149
Methimakis, Michalis   499
Mihalik, Brian J.   296
Mihalik, Linda   296
Minakawa, Yoshino   110
Mohammed, Phaedra S.   133
Molina-Izurieta, Rosa   303
Möller, Sebastian   440
Mondragon Regalado, Jose Ricardo   311
Montenegro Juárez, Jannier Alberto   311
Montenegro Juárez, Julio César   311

N

Nakamura, Satoshi   10
Nam, Seung-Woo   54
Namura, Saki   118
Neroutsou, Vassiliki   499
Ng Yong Xin, Jabez   325
Nonose, Kohei   118
Norman, Paul   103
Ntafotis, Emmanouil   408
Ntoa, Stavroula   408, 499
Núñez-Torres, María Giovanna   187, 238, 318

O

Ohtake, Go   90
Orji, Fidelia A.   334

P

Padilla Suárez, Norma Judit   311
Park, Hye Jeong   343
Partarakis, Nikolaos   408, 499
Peng, Xueyan   124
Petraki, Argiro   499
Pi, Lingli   351

Q

Qiao, Yue   415
Qiu, Xiao   376
Quinatoa-Casicana, Juan   238

R

Ramai, Divindra   133
Rauterberg, Matthias   510
Robledo, Pedro   303
Romine, Samuel   24
Rowe, Richard   103
Roychowdhury, Sneha   103
Rusu, Cristian   83

S

Saariluoma, Pertti   510
Sahoo, Lipsarani   141
Salah Ali Mohamed, Ihab   554
Schmitz, Anne-Kathrin   60
Scott, Alexander J.   103
Sedhain, Abim   149
Seelmeyer, Udo   60
Shehab, Mohamed   141
Shen, Yu   554
Shih, Jia-Yin   32
Shyam Sundar, Palaniselvam   156
Spierling, Ulrike   478
Srnec Hamer, Iva   440
Stephanidis, Constantine   408, 499
Sukmono, Filosa Gita   446
Sykianaki, Eirini   499

T

Tada, Sunichi   118
Takeuchi, Yugo   176
Tan, Jessica   163
Thomas, Lisa   68
Tolboom, Jos   231
Tsekleves, Emmanuel   68
Tsuei, Mengping   210, 216

U

Ueda, Hiroshi   246
Umetsu, Hiroka   168

V

Vassileva, Julita   334
Vergari, Maurizio   440

W

Waag, Philipp   60
Wang, Binyu   176
Wang, Fei   351
Wang, Tianxiong   518
Wang, Yao   149
Webb, Thomas L.   103
Webber, Richard   103
Weinhardt, Marc   60
Wu, Junji   246
Wu, Yue   535

X

Xia, Liang   376
Xiang, Weiqing   176
Xiao, Yinghe   367
Xie, Jing   376
Xu, Mengli   527

Y

Yang, Liu   518
Yaser, Noor   83
Ye, Junnan   527, 535
Yiming, Zhao   543
Yokoyama, Kouta   10
Yoshida, Haruka   118

Z

Zaman, Mobasshira   251
Zapata, Mireya   303
Zhang, Boyuan   470
Zhang, Dingwei   415
Zhang, Jie   385, 426
Zhang, Jingyu   351
Zhang, Mickey Mengting   554
Zhang, Ying   385, 426
Zhang, Yuan   124
Zhao, Qiuyue   358
Zheng, Muzi   572
Zheng, Shaolong   367
Zheng, Xiuhui   562
Zheng, Yangshuo   393
Zhou, Hongtao   415
Zhuang, Li   572
Zidianakis, Emmanouil   408, 499

Printed in the United States
by Baker & Taylor Publisher Services